Applications Strategies for Risk Analysis

Robert N. Charette
ITABHI Corporation

Intertext Publications
McGraw-Hill Book Company

New York St. Louis San Francisco Auckland Bogotá
Hamburg London Madrid Mexico Milan Montreal
New Delhi Panama Paris São Paolo
Singapore Sydney Tokyo Toronto

Library of Congress catalog card number 90-81569

10 9 8 7 6 5 4 3 2 1

ISBN 0-07-010888-9

Intertext Publications / Multiscience Press, Inc.
One Lincoln Plaza
New York, NY 10023

McGraw-Hill Book Company
1221 Avenue of the Americas
New York, NY 10020

Composed and typeset by Christopher Chabris,
Castle Productions Limited.

*To Dr. Charles McKay and Dr. John Spackman,
who instilled in me the rules of survival necessary
if one wishes to go pioneering in the building
of large-scale computer systems*

Table of Contents

Foreword

As the author correctly explained in his excellent companion book, *Software Engineering Risk Analysis and Management*, most (if not all) organizations with a future must have a growing, critical dependency upon software intensive information systems and other forms of supporting automation. Appropriate systems of automation and appropriate applications of such systems are a necessary—but not sufficient—commitment if an organization is to have any chance of surviving and prospering in an increasingly competitive and complex world marketplace.

The spiraling growth of world competition and complexity in the marketplace is both a stimulus for and a response to the spiraling growth of world competition and complexity in automated systems and their applications. The good news is that there has never been such a plethora of opportunities for proactive organizations with viable approaches to dealing with risks. The bad news is that these opportunities are being lost by an increasing number of declining, reactive organizations which will not or cannot cope with the risks associated with these opportunities. More specifically, the losing organizations fail to be proactive in identifying feasible, promising opportunities and in identifying, analyzing, and managing the risks associated with capitalizing upon the opportunities. Exclusively reactive behavior burdens the organization with the highest risk of all—failure to retain a sufficiently competitive or otherwise viable market position while striving to fulfill the missions of the organization.

This groundbreaking book and its companion present a pragmatic approach for technical and management personnel to identifying, analyzing, and managing those risks and opportunities. Such personnel may have responsibilities for either or both of these "appropriate systems of automation" and "appropriate applications of such systems." The books also remind the reader that such automated systems and their applications are necessary but not sufficient components of an organization's success. Therefore, the software engineering risks and opportunities addressed by these books are a necessary but not sufficient subset of the total risks and opportunities to be managed by an organization. The point is that computer systems and software engineers are typically constrained by risks and challenged by opportunities where both may originate externally to the automated systems and their applications. Thus automated systems and applications which meet their specifications could still fail to support the management of important risks and opportunities of an organization within its environment. These books provide extremely valuable insights that should help the members of the organization recognize and control such management gaps.

Within the above limitations, computer systems and software engineers are further challenged by the fact that computing-related risks and opportunities can be encountered, created, and/or exacerbated at any point in the life cycle of the automated systems and their applications. The longer these risks and opportunities remain unmanaged, the more they diminish the chances of the computing project's success and, therefore, the chances of that portion of the organization's success which depends upon the project. As before, these risks and opportunities should be identified, assessed, and explicit actions and controls should be applied which are appropriate for each risk and opportunity. The author's practical guidelines to the evaluation of alternative responses help the professional to reach well-considered, explicit decisions regarding these risks and opportunities and to identify appropriate actions and controls to effect these decisions.

Ultimately, opportunity and risk management in computer systems and software engineering can only be based upon:

- Contexts for decisions and decision processes—both external and internal to the life cycle of the automated support systems and their applications.
- Decisions—those technical and management decisions that have been baselined and the rules for their utilization, evaluation, and modification.
- Decision processes—those technical and management processes currently in effect and the rules for their utilization, evaluation, and modification.
- Interfaces among the above.

In summary, this superb book presents pragmatic, proactive, decision-making guidelines for identifying, analyzing, and managing opportunities and risks in the computer systems and software engineering of automated systems and their applications. The underlying concepts, principles, and models are essential to good engineering practices and to good management strategies such as Total Quality Management (TQM).

Charles W. McKay, Director
Software Engineering Research Center
  National Aeronautics and Space Administration
High Technologies Laboratory
  University of Houston Clear Lake
May 1990

Preface

This book and its earlier companion, *Software Engineering Risk Analysis and Management*,[1] together describe the field of risk analysis and management, how they are performed, when and where to apply them, and provide an identification of the origins of risk in the building of software information systems. A primary motivation behind these two books is to provide a framework from which software engineering risk analysis and management can be conducted in a realistic and pragmatic fashion by practicing software professionals.

In the first book, our concentration was primarily centered on the mechanics of risk analysis and management; i.e., the investigation of the general processes, methods and techniques that can be applied when called upon to perform a risk analysis. This provided us with the basic tools required to successfully conduct risk analysis and management, but tools alone do not make a competent software engineering risk analyst. One requires both a general understanding of the greater context in which software engineering resides, as well as the limitations contained within the software engineering process itself that keep our industry from building software information systems that are reliable on time and within budget. Thus, *Applications Strategies for Risk Analysis* focuses on a broader perspective than just the mechanics of risk analysis and management, by examining the totality of the software engineering enterprise, with all of its associated risks.

The concentration and perspective taken in this book are those of the hard-headed world of business. Organizations use software information systems for one of three reasons: for automating office functions, as aids to decision-making, and/or for the automatic control of operations. Thus, information systems in all forms are created for one primary reason: to avert an organization's exposure to business risk. This risk may be in the form of increased competition, increased cost, decreasing raw material availability, etc. A business's information systems try to mitigate these risks by increasing the efficiency and/or effectiveness of its operations.

However, these information systems, which are intended to avert risk, are themselves becoming a business liability. These systems are tending to increase a business's cost both from the perspective of the high monetary cost of the systems themselves, as well as often making the business only operate marginally more effectively or efficiently, if not in fact worse.

The primary reasons for this unfortunate turn of events are that the risks in planning for, the development of, and the use of these software information systems in a business are not well understood by the two major groups responsible for their existence: the software engineers responsible for their creation, and the business persons responsible for defining what the systems will be used for and how much time and money will be spent to create them. Lamentably, both groups' goals and objectives too often are in variance, which means both contribute to the risks that already threaten the successful building of an information system, which in turn exposes the business to more risk, rather than less. Unless the business and technical decisions on how best to avert risk in the planning for, development of, and operation of these software systems are commensurate, with both the software engineer and business person understanding how he or she each, respectively, contributes to the increase in the other's risk, then we will continue to see the high cost, poor quality, and late systems that are inflicted upon us today.

Both the software engineer and business person have a difficult time, however, in understanding his or her own, and his or her counterpart's, underlying problems. The simplest way of explaining this is by analogy: a cow looks much different to a butcher than to a zoologist. Thus, when building software information systems, the risks with which one is confronted appear much different in a business context than in a systems engineering context or in a software engineering context. What may be perceived as a minor risk from a business perspective may in fact be a huge risk when viewed from a software engineering perspective, and vice versa. Without understanding how each group perceives a risk, or even articulates the risk, one can be guaranteed problems will arise.

For instance, a finance person thinks that a good investment is one with a positive net present value (NPV), while marketeers often think about a project's NPV as merely the result of some financial arithmetic.[2] In reality, NPV is an outcome of the overall business risks, including financial and marketing, that are taken. In other words, does the product or service have enough value to enough customers to support the prices and costs of supplying them, including the opportunity cost of capital? And does the company have enough sustainable competitive advantage to exploit, develop, and defend the opportunity? The risks are complementary, and directly link the objectives of the financial person with those of the marketeer. We will use the concept of risk to serve as the common currency which links the various perspectives held by the different stakeholders in an information technology enterprise.

We have chosen to divide this book into two distinct parts. The first encompasses Chapters 1, 2, 3, and 4. Chapter 1 quickly reviews the fundamentals of risk encountered in *Software Engineering Risk Analysis and Management* and presents the motivation for this book. Those who have read my first book may want to skim over this chapter, although there is some added material. Chapter 2 provides a systemic examination of risk analysis and management as it applies to the systems engineering and business environments. This will aid us in identifying the sources of risk which originate outside of, and are carried into, the software engineering enterprise. Chapter 3 next examines the software engineering risks that exist in the software engineering process itself; i.e., the process models, methods, and automation applied throughout the software enterprise. Chapter 4 investigates the risks involved in the product, i.e., the software engineering risks associated with the development of computer applications.

The second part contains Chapters 5, 6, and 7, and focuses on specialized aspects of risk analysis and management. Chapter 5 investigates the risks associated with software information system safety, security, and computer operations, the latter specifically concerning disaster recovery issues. Chapter 6 examines the important issues of the subjective perception vs. the objective reality of risk as it applies to risk taking, as well as describing how a risk management organization may be set up in a business. Chapter 7 provides a look at some future risk issues, postulates a new paradigm of software development based upon a nonlinear risk model, and provides a step-by-step review of the major issues of the book. The reader may wish to begin at the review section to get a flavor of the book, and to skip to sections of individual interest.

For those who have not yet read *Software Engineering Risk Analysis and Management* and wish to know what was covered, Chapter 1 provided the motivation for the software engineering risk analysis and management. Chapter 2 provided a definition of risk, its history, and an overview of the elemental components of risk analysis and management. Chapters 3, 4, and 5 investigated the specific topic of the mechanics of risk analysis in depth. The issues of risk identification, estimation, and evaluation were examined, with practical advice given as to their proper application. Chapter 6 examined risk management, covering risk control, aversion, and monitoring. How to make decisions about risk were also discussed. Chapter 7 provided a summary, which showed a step-by-step "guide to performing software engineering risk analysis and management," cross-referenced back to the appropriate section in the book where more detail could be found. A slightly abridged guide is contained in Appendix A of this book.

Together, *Software Engineering Risk Analysis and Management* and *Applications Strategies for Risk Analysis* provide the necessary perspectives and robust foundations needed from which to apply risk analysis and management to your own situation, whether you acquire, develop, market, or apply information technology. Although I tried to write these two books in a way that one did not have to read them both to gain a complete set of benefits, doing so may help in gaining a deeper understanding of the field.

It is appropriate to mention at this time the great debate swirling around risk analysis and management. There are two major philosophical schools of thought on risk analysis, qualitative and quantitative, which are often at odds with one another.[3,4] The qualitative school holds, as one strong proponent explained, that "statistics don't count for anything ... they have no place in the engineering field anywhere," and that risk is minimized and contained not by statistical test programs, but by paying a great deal of attention to the detail involved in a system's design. The philosophy of the quantitative school, on the other hand, holds that "the real value of probabilistic risk analysis is in understanding the system and its vulnerabilities," and that given proper data, risk analysis can indicate when a project should be not implemented or stopped.

My personal view leans more toward quantitative analysis, recognizing the limitations that the quality of the input data imposes on the quality of the analysis, and the limitations of probability theory itself. I have tried wherever possible to explicitly point out the limitations of risk analysis and management as they exist. I do not believe, for example, that there is "an answer" that can be unequivocally relied upon when using quantitative techniques.

As in the first book, however, we have accepted the view that subjective perception of risk or safety is the basis of their acceptance, regardless of their objective or quantified evaluation. As you will see, both approaches to risk analysis are discussed, and in many cases, only qualitative risk analysis can be conducted. By its nature, this book is more qualitative than quantitative, whereas the first was quantitatively slanted. Quantitative models are of limited value in softer applications such as encountered in this book; i.e., when they are applied to evaluate new business markets, new computing technologies, or new computer applications, especially large-scale ones. This is not to say that the postulated models are necessarily wrong, but instead, just that data is scarce and more irregular to come by. One should not necessarily throw out modeling, but conduct more forensic software engineering instead to attain the missing data. We must leave it to the reader to determine which risk analysis approach is most applicable to their own situation, but in either case, risk analysis and management should be applied.

Throughout this book we will view quality and reliability engineering as mandatory means to managing and containing risk, and they are a significant element of the repertoire of what should be applied as normal engineering discipline during a system's development. But note, we believe quality and reliability engineering are necessary, but not sufficient, conditions in building software systems. It is the same with software engineering and risk analysis and management—they are necessary, but not sufficient, to make the computing field a true profession. However, we believe that *risk engineering*, i.e., the analysis and management of risk, is of such importance today, on a par with the efforts of Total Quality Management (TQM) or Integrated Resource Management (IRM), that it should also have its own organization reporting directly to senior management. By the end of this book, I do not think that I will need to convince the reader as to why. In fact, TQM and IRM are prime risk management approaches which should be integrated into an overall risk engineering process. Unfortunately, both are often mistaken for risk analysis and management, much to the detriment of both. We will explore their differences a bit later.

In keeping with our initial book on the subject, this book was written with an intent to have it serve as a kind of guidebook, with the software engineer and management information science professional on the firing line in mind, and not necessarily as a scholarly tome for a person in the computer science academic community. My approach is to provide breadth-first coverage and, where appropriate, the necessary exploration of a concept in depth, but the reader should otherwise consult the many references for the necessary detail. Therefore, this book may not, at times, seem serious enough, or have the proper academic writing flavor, for my friends teaching at universities. I again make no apologies. The book is not meant to be a traditional textbook, written in a language and style that is inaccessible to most practitioners, with quickly forgotten theoretical foundations followed by boring exercises. Nor was it written to only be enjoyed by a small cadre of risk analysts. I prefer another style to convey the requisite information, but in a more enjoyable style. I believe that professionals and academics have different goals and approaches to the situations they live with each day, and a traditional textbook approach on these subjects is not useful to most professionals in the computer field. William Rouse articulates the reasons better than I in his article, "On Better Mousetraps and Basic Research: Getting the Applied World to the Laboratory Door."[5]

For people like me, software engineering is a business, not an academic problem to be neatly solved. It is our living, and we must make use of sometimes imperfect theories and hypotheses on how to proceed, especially if more academically sound ones are not offered. Too often, the models or theories on how computing should be used are shown to be lacking in the academic literature, which is useful to know, but in few instances are constructive criticisms on how to improve them proffered. The professionals in industry need help now, in quantities both large and small. Pragmatically, they really do not have the time to translate from the theoretical into the practical, nor the time (nor in many cases, the experience) to tell the difference between the two. They just need some practical advice using the "best available knowledge" on how to get the job done more easily, or to get out of a jam without making the situation worse for themselves or for others. If these books help them accomplish that, I have achieved a good number of my objectives.

Thus, I have tried to base these two books upon a few "tenets of book writing for computer professionals" that I happen to believe in. These are: a book, for it to be used, must be simple, but not too simple, enjoyable to read, and not take itself or the subject too seriously; most of the ideas must have been used in practice at least once, so people can have some faith that they work; a book must save time by synthesizing the ideas from the various references and texts about a subject; and a book must be easily borrowed from and used by those who are working, but who may not have advanced degrees in computer science or engineering. The last criterion is important, because it is this group which forms the majority of the professionals in our field.

I hope others outside the software field, such as those in engineering management, industrial engineering, and business management, will find these two books useful as well. I have tried to write them in such a way that they can be read from many different levels of experience. The techniques described in both books can be easily translated into their own specialities. Given that their business decisions are becoming increasingly dependent on software systems, it would be an advantage to have a bit of knowledge about where an important ingredient of their businesses's risk lie. Toward this end, I have included some tutorial-like material in Chapter 1 and later chapters for those not really familiar with the concepts, or buzzwords, associated with software and software engineering. Those wanting a more complete explanation can turn to another one of my books, *Software Engineering Environments: Concepts and Technology*,[6] or any other of the McGraw-Hill series on software engineering, for which these books are companions.

I haven't totally neglected the academic community, though. Graduate students or seniors in computer science, management information science, or computer systems engineering programs or seminars may also benefit from these books by examining what goes wrong with software engineering theory, once it is put into practice in the real world. As one NASA official put it, "Software development is never as the textbooks have told it should be. Let's chase fact, not fiction."[7] The single most important lesson my working experience has taught me, after managing to get a couple of degrees in computer systems engineering, was that I was faced with dilemmas to manage, not compact technical problems with solutions to resolve. A few professors made this abundantly clear in their classes, but the problems of the outside world of real engineering are not often encountered in university computer science or engineering settings.

To help instill a truer perspective about working in the computing field, I have added a series of questions at the end of each chapter which explore some supplementary information, as well as comments about various aspects of the subjects covered in the notes. These questions, I hope, will make students think a bit more about what really happens out there, beyond their present horizon, and reinforce some of the major themes of the text. And just as a warning, some of the questions do not have standard textbook solutions.

Instructors might also find the text useful in seminar situations, applying the Socratic method to challenge the "truths" their students have about the concepts they have been taught in other classes. One technique I have found to be useful is to ask a student to take a research or general journal article home for a week and act as if he or she were the author. This forces them to review a technical paper very critically. Then I ask the remainder of the class, who have also been given the paper to read, to act as very skeptical and quarrelsome "reviewers," forcing the "author" to defend the work. The results can be rather interesting, as the student realizes that there aren't nice, tidy answers out there, and that the "solutions" offered are often a little thin and sometimes wrong. It also helps Ph.D. and M.S. students writing theses to learn to look for errors in their own work, and gain confidence defending an idea in front of a hostile group. Similarly, selecting current subjects from computer science literature and the general press, and examining them from a risk perspective would help fill out the text. Chapter 2 includes a business scenario which the instructor can use as a core of a full risk analysis case study, or which can be used to make specific instructional points.

Some final thoughts—risk engineering exists for only one reason: to increase your business's success. Keep in mind that management's primary responsibility is to manage risk, and do it in a systematized fashion, rather than intuitively or by ad hoc procedures. The hardest problem management faces in the 1990s is how to manage risks that have never before been encountered. Every product or service that is sold contains many more different domains of technology than its predecessor, which means trying to contain business and technological risks that are coupled in an ever-more complex fashion. Those who do manage these types of risk the best will win in the 1990s, as it is they who will gain the true competitive edge.

Risk engineering is not, however, a silver bullet or a magical cure. It is, at best, quantitative common sense. However, viewing the world through a risk perspective can radically change how successful one can become when trying to acquire, use, or build information systems. It helps one focus on the diseases that affect our industry, not merely the symptoms that many claim are the real problems: high cost, lateness, poor quality, low productivity, etc. Increased productivity won't make a poorly specified system work any better, for example. Looking at a software tool from a perspective of whether it increases my risk of building a poor system, rather than increasing my productivity, is a better viewpoint to take when approaching the problems we face in this business. It is much easier to avoid mistakes than to quantify promises.

Too much in our industry is hype and of little real value in making systems that respond to both business and user needs. Too much is poor value for the money spent. Too often we try to fool ourselves, and the public, that our systems are safe, that we really understand all the risks involved. Too often we are too lazy to change our ways of thinking, using inappropriate models and techniques that others profess as being correct, but only shackle our minds. Too often we look for solutions only where the light is good.

The late Nobel Prize winner, Dr. Richard Feynman, wrote: "For a successful technology to take place, reality must take place over public relations. Nature will not be fooled."[8] Until we learn this lesson, until we start to face reality, we will continue to reap the current harvest of inferior systems.

In summing up, I would like to point out that these books are a collaboration of effort and ideas from the many individuals I worked with here in the United States, the United Kingdom, and Belgium, and those authors who preceded me in this area. It is very hard to describe accurately where one idea came from or to give that person the proper credit, but I have tried hard to give credit where credit is due, and if I have missed someone, it's purely unintentional. All the credit for the good ideas in these books should go to those who are listed in the chapters' lists of references—I merely synthesized their ideas together. Special thanks, however, do go to Ron House of the U.S. Naval Underwater Systems Center in Newport, Rhode Island, Mac Murray of General Dynamics Corporation, McLean, Virginia, and Dr. Charles McKay of the University of Houston Clear Lake, all of whom helped review the initial drafts of this document. Greatest thanks go out to Maureen Albrecht, my Vice-President at ITABHI Corporation, and Alan Rose, my publisher, who afforded me the time and opportunity to finish this book.

Bob Charette
Fairfax, Virginia
January 1990

References

1. Robert N. Charette, *Software Engineering Risk Analysis and Management*, McGraw-Hill, Inc., New York, 1989.

2. Patrick Barwise et al., "Must Finance and Strategy Clash?" *Harvard Business Review*, Vol. 89, No. 5, September-October 1989.

3. "Special Report: Designing and Operating a Minimum-Risk System," *IEEE Spectrum*, Volume 26, No. 6, June 1989.

4. William D. Rowe, *An Anatomy of Risk*, Robert E. Krieger Publishing Co., Malabar, FL, 1988.

5. William B. Rouse, "On Better Mousetraps and Basic Research: Getting the Applied World to the Laboratory Door," *IEEE Transactions on Systems, Man, And Cybernetics*, Vol. SMC-15, No.1, January/February 1985.

6. Robert N. Charette, *Software Engineering Environments: Concepts and Technology*, McGraw-Hill, Inc., New York, 1986.

7. James Raney, "Concepts and Expected Use of the Software Support Environment," *NSIA Conference on "Software Initiatives and Their Impact on the Competitive Edge,"* 10 May 1988.

8. Richard P. Feynman, *"What Do You Care What Other People Think?"* Bantam Books, New York, 1988.

Ockham's Razor

"It is of the utmost importance that all those responsible for large projects involving computers should take care to avoid making demands on software that go far beyond the present state of the technology, unless the very considerable risks can be tolerated."

S. GILL *in "Software Engineering," report on a conference sponsored by the NATO Science Committee, Garmisch, West Germany, Oct. 7–11, 1968*

1.0 Introduction

William of Ockham should hold a cherished place among risk analysts, as he was one of the first to formally attempt to define, contain, and balance risk in his particular profession. Ockham, you may recall, was a preeminent fourteenth-century English *theologicus-logicus*, or theologian-logician, who believed in the medieval rule of economy; i.e., that "plurality should not be assumed without necessity."[1,2] However, Ockham took this belief beyond its then-normal bounds when he insisted that it should be applied also to evaluations of theology. These evaluations, he wrote, should be extremely rational, with distinctions formulated between the necessary and the incidental, and differentiations made between evidence and their degrees of probability. Ockham further wrote that God's saving action consisted of giving without obligation, with nature serving as an "existence" proof of this belief.

Ockham went on to argue that no one creature was intrinsically better than another in God's eyes, and therefore man was not intrinsically better than the other creatures that inhabited the earth. This was pretty radical thinking for the fourteenth century, a time in which most people believed in man's natural superiority over unreasoning animals, as well as the inherent God-given superiority of certain individuals over others. Ockham argued strongly that God did not stack the deck in anyone's favor, as it were. Come to think of it, this particular concept *still* is pretty heady thinking to many people. Anyway, the foundation of Ockham's thesis swirls around the separation of truth from its perception and, in very simplified terms, states that if two competing explanations could establish the same "truth," the simpler, more elegant theory should be the one to triumph.

The importance of Ockham's theory, or Ockham's Razor, as it is often called, for the software engineering risk analyst (and business person) is that it offers a guiding principle to help one understand why software development is in the mess it currently seems to be in. As we described in some detail in Chapter 1 of our previous text, *Software Engineering Risk Analysis and Management*, the historical record of software developments can be generally characterized as over budget, behind schedule, and of questionable quality or effectiveness.[3]

Many activities over the past 20 or so years conducted under the label of software engineering have been applied to remedy these problems, yet for the most part the results seem rather dismal for the overall effort expended. Consider the words of Air Force General Bernard P. Randolph, recently retired, commander of the U.S. Air Force's Systems Command, who said, "We have a perfect record on software schedules—we have never made one on time yet and we are always making excuses." [4] Or if you like, take Dr. Howard Yudkin, who as a prominent industry observer and spokesman, as well as the director of the Software Productivity Consortium, said,

> My impression after thirty years with the [computer] business is that we are failing over and over again. We are compounding our failures with self-delusion. We are making matters worse by refusing to honestly admit our failures in ways to allow us to change.[5]

Or even better, contemplate for a moment this simple thought problem: consider an old specification for a financial accounting system; e.g., a specification defined ten years ago, say, of 70,000 lines of code. Now, think about trying to implement the system using today's technology, but using the originally defined resources; i.e., the numbers of people, amount of time, expenditures (accounting for inflation), and so forth. Given this problem, do you think that it can be implemented on time, within budget, to user acclaim, and with a quality and reliability that make one proud of using today's new and improved development technology?

I would answer emphatically, *no*, even with the "improvements" in productivity tools and software engineering techniques we have supposedly gained in the intervening period. One *might* get closer to meeting the development targets than ten years ago, but probability of overall failure would be as certain today as it was then. What we have achieved today, however, is a proud promise of even more costly systems which will be developed behind schedule and consist of even more dubious usefulness or quality.

Viewed in this light, after the thousands of papers, hundreds of books, and decades of discussion, software engineering must truthfully be seen as not performing adequately to the tasks at hand, if not as an abject failure. If the effectiveness of software engineering were evaluated in the same light as a therapeutic remedy is in medicine, its application wouldn't be sanctioned by any responsible body any longer. One is moved to ask the obvious question: "Why?" Are the problems in software engineering itself, or do they really lie somewhere else? Although software engineering does deserve a great share of the blame, not everything can be laid at its feet.

To find the true cause, I argue as Ockham once did that it is essential we throw away our current preconceived notions and initiate a search for cures other than new technology alone. There is likely some other, simpler, and more elegant solution than the ones we have now, if we could only understand the root causes of our problems. In trying to answer this perplexity, we need only turn back to Ockham's idea of parsimony; i.e., "What can be done with fewer is done in vain with more."

Let us try to explain further what we mean by examining some of the currently fashionable proffered causes of the "software crisis." One sees that these causes concentrate almost exclusively upon a singular rationale or, better yet, can be overcome by a unique solution. The "crisis", we are told, is precipitated either by: (a) the improper definition of software requirements; (b) poorly written and documented designs; (c) the nonutilization of computer-aided software engineering (CASE) tools; (d) the improperly applied theory of management to the software development; or (e) the lack of skilled personnel. Take your pick. Of course, these "unique" causes of the software crisis aren't the only ones by any means, and some go back over twenty years!! In fact, the marketplace teems with various disciples of the unique problem/unique solution proposition. If industry would only do this or that, all the difficulty with software development would disappear! Just apply *their* unique solutions to any one of the aforementioned difficulties, these individual apostles will tell you, and all will be made right in your software development! Hallelujah!! Just send money!!! And, you know, what is really amusing (or distressing) is that some people actually do!

In this book, we propose that the reader take a more skeptical view, while we attempt to separate the hype, hucksterism, and miracle cures from the truth. We contend that, while each of the above explanations has some truth to it (poor requirements and poor management certainly do not contribute to the success of a software project, for example), at best they formulate only part of the underlying causes of failure. The fundamental difficulties of software development in reality originate elsewhere. *The over-cost, late schedules, lack of effectiveness and quality of software developments encountered today are merely symptoms of a deeper malady, rather than being the malady itself.* Trying to cure software engineering cost overruns solely with the application of CASE, for instance, is like trying to cure lung cancer by the medieval practice of arterial bleeding.

Our assertion in this book is that the causes of software development failure are manifested in risks which can be found, created, and exacerbated at any point in the development life cycle, starting from the initial business decision made to acquire, use, or develop a software system, through its systems engineering, down to the software engineering process model, methodology, and automation that are used in the system's implementation. There are no simple solutions available to eliminate these software risks, and you won't find any in this book. Software risks are *dilemmas* which are inherent within, and fundamental elements of, the process of any system's development. Remember, dilemmas, by their very nature, *can only be managed, not solved.* Also, software risks in one form or another existed yesterday, they exist today, and they will exist tomorrow. At best, then, one can manage the risks so that their potential impacts are minimized.

The longer these risks remain ignored, unnoticed, or unmanaged, the greater they diminish the chances of a project's success. We contend that it is the mismanagement of these risks which most often causes software development failure. As we will see, not all the risks can be or should be avoided, but they should all be assessed, and explicit controls should be applied in proportion to each risk identified. Ultimately, as we will soon see, risk analysis and management can only be based upon context, decisions, decision processes, and their interfaces to other decision processes, for any project existing within a model of a *business enterprise*;

i.e., *an undertaking that is difficult, complicated, and has a strong element of* **risk**.

1.1 Ever Try Dismissing a Computer?

"It's Late, It's Costly, Incompetent—But Try Firing A Computer System." So ran the catchy title to a recent article in *Business Week* magazine.[6] The feature concerned the problems that companies were running into when trying to develop automated information systems.[7] For instance, it described an insurance company's computer system, initially predicted to cost $8 million, that because of foul-ups on the part of the company contracted to develop it is now estimated to cost $100 million to complete, as well as to be delivered 6 *years* later than originally scheduled. In another instance, a project was described as being delivered on time and within budget, the only trouble being that the system didn't work. And in a third case, after consuming $1 million, a company canceled a projected $1.2 million system because nothing was delivered at all. These examples in the commercial sector, however, pale in comparison to various government software projects where anywhere from $50 million to $2.5 billion in cost overruns have occurred. One department in the British Ministry of Defense, for example, currently spends one third of its budget of £9 billion to cover cost overruns, much of it caused by computer system problems.[8] Another British project to computerize their social security system is costing at least $2 billion more than the original estimate of $1 billion (it isn't completed yet, either).

The typical rule of thumb on software projects is to think like a baseball player and be satisfied with a .333 batting average. In other words, you can have your software project on time, within budget, or working, but never expect to achieve all three simultaneously. If you're real lucky, and have a hot bat, maybe you will go two for three. The reasons for these disasters are many and have been documented in detail previously,[9] but in general they can be traced to three fundamental factors: the lack of information, the lack of control, and the lack of time.[10] These are manifested in three primary determinants for software failure: the underperformance and undercapitalization of resources, and the lack of understanding of risk.

Underperformance of resources concerns the inefficiency and ineffectiveness in resource application. In software development, the most commonly used term is the "lack of productivity," but this is misleading and often compels one to focus entirely too much on the software development process itself.[11] True productivity really comprises two elements: efficiency and effectiveness. Therefore, when describing the adequate performance of resources, one must examine first the effectiveness of the total business enterprise in which a software project is a part; e.g., are the business objectives correct? If the objectives are incorrect, regardless of how productive the resources are, the result will still be ineffectual. Second, one must be concerned about the efficiency of the total business operation; e.g., the corporate and divisional overheads, the decision-making process, the complex coordination mechanisms, and the like.[12] If these operations are overly complex, the resources cannot be effectively applied across the entire business enterprise or efficiently used when they are applied to a specific enterprise.

When underperformance occurs, the parts making up the whole of a business operation are worth more separately than when packaged together. Thus a business's operations are not generating sufficient profits to meet the requirements of the competition and its own competitive strategies. Underperformance is a "bottom-up effect;" in other words, the inefficiencies generated percolate upwards to constrain business decisions and business profit. Other times the cause of software failure originates at a top-level source instead, such as the undercapitalization of resources.

Undercapitalization of resources concerns the lack of sufficient or proper resources being made available for a software acquisition, development or a software system's application. These resources are typically time, financing, and/or (experienced) people that can be applied against the software project. We also include as a resource *ideas*, thereby leading to the subproblem of the *undercapitalization of ideas*; i.e., not knowing why, for what explicit purpose, a particular information system is needed to support the business. It can be to lower cost, increase revenue, meet governmental regulations, protect market share, or diversify the business, but a *raison d'être* for supporting the business is mandatory to have before trying to buy, acquire, or use an information system. This doesn't matter if you are in the publishing business, financial sector, in telecommunications, or slinging hamburgers.

All too often, an information system's purpose is vague and is typically related to gaining some "competitive edge," some "increase in productivity," or some "increase in quality." These are byproducts, and sometimes even side effects, of using information technology. All too often, while a system is being developed, its requirements are constantly being changed by its sponsors to reflect some new understanding of its purpose. This then causes a deviation between what was originally resourced and what actually is required to be resourced. All too often the developers overcommit to what can actually be done, because they want to be "team players." The results frequently are a waste of large amounts of time and money, as well as ending up with a nonusable system.

While the nature of the project highly influences its initial resource capitalization, unfortunately, a project's undercapitalization is very often not recognized until it is too late, by which time the project is compelled to be reduced in scope, extended, or canceled. Sometimes the undercapitalization is seen, but deliberately not recognized, such as when a proposed project's budget is "too high," and arbitrary reductions are made to the budget, but not to the information system's functionality. Once again, the project continues for awhile but, after some decent interval of trying to defy the laws of physics and economics, is compelled to be reduced in scope, extended, or canceled. Not surprisingly, the cost to develop this descoped system frequently is many more times the cost that would have been incurred if that course of action had been planned for in the first place.

The lack of understanding of when undercapitalization is occurring is one of the greatest problems faced in the software engineering field today, more so than underperformance. One can handle the effects of underperformance if adequate capital is available, but the opposite situation is harder to manage.[13] Undercapitalization is also blamed for 90% of new business failures, and since a large development project can be viewed as a new business, it isn't surprising that the figures are remarkably similar.[14] However, many software projects are over budget, behind schedule, and of poor quality in perception only; i.e., the original price and time were underestimated, either on purpose or through ignorance, and the time and money that it is now taking to complete the project is most likely the true one.[15] As Jefferson said, "Every country gets the government it deserves," and the same maxim holds true for organizations which undercapitalize software developments or overestimate the performance attainable by the resources that are provided. The organizations have no one to blame for their failure except themselves.

To see what we mean, let's take an example constructed by Myers using some de facto industry standard software development estimation models.[16] Let's assume we are developing a software system consisting of 2,000,000 source lines of code system (source lines of code are usually the primary input parameter to software estimation models and also the origin of greatest uncertainty of their usefulness). Using these models, one can derive estimates for the length of time and cost (and, implicitly,

TABLE 1.1 Comparison of Productivity Level for 2,000,000-Line System

Factor	Organizational Productivity Level		
	Average	Optimistic	Highly Optimistic
Min. Develop. Time (yrs)	8	5	4
Effort (man-yrs)	10,833	4,167	2,250
Cost (constant $)	$1,600 m	$600 m	$300 m
Peak Staffing	2,100	1,300	860
LOC per man-month	15	40	74

quality) of the resulting software system under: (a) average; (b) optimistic; and (c) highly optimistic organizational productivity conditions, as shown in Table 1.1. The cost difference from the average to the highly optimistic is $1.3 billion dollars, and the time difference, 4 years. To say the least, those are rather large variations. If one were to relax one of the constraints, say allow for a 5% increase in development time, the cost differential is now "only" $1 billion, and in time, 4.2 years, as illustrated in Table 1.2. However, the time increase allows productivity to increase by over 20%, and, implicitly, the quality of the system produced is improved.

There are a number of points that can be derived from this simple example. First, a little bit of extra time added to software development reduces the underperformance of the organization by reducing the undercapitalization in the resource which money can't buy; i.e., time. An inadequate amount of time is generally thought to be the single most important reason why software projects fail, which again supports the argument that many software failures are self-induced.[17] One should remember this maxim: System "requirements" which do not have the proper amount of resources are not requirements, they are fantasies.

TABLE 1.2 Comparison of Productivity Level for 2,000,000-Line System with 5% Addition of Time

Factor	Organizational Productivity Level		
	Average	Optimistic	Highly Optimistic
Min. Develop. Time (yrs)	8.4	5.2	4.2
Effort (man-yrs)	8,582	3,368	1,792
Cost (constant $)	$1,300 m	$500 m	$300 m
Peak Staffing	1,571	1,004	655
LOC per man-month	15	40	74

Second, the range of costs and schedules for a software development is very uncertain, and depends highly on how trusting one is of all the underlying parameters used in the estimation, such as the accuracy of the prediction concerning the source lines of code estimate. Software development estimation models use human, and therefore subjective, judgment in determining whether a highly optimistic, optimistic or average productivity scenario should be used. Even disregarding the human biases which come into play, there is still a 30% to 70% chance that the estimates will be wrong because of the inherent probabilistic imprecision of estimates.[18]

Third, since most developments are trailblazing in spirit, they have few if any precedents from which to draw any knowledge or experience. When one really starts to think about it, it is truly amazing that any new software system works at all. Look at the situation in this way: Usually one is trying to create an unfamiliar application, using untried hardware, applying new development techniques, and using personnel who have never built a system like it ever before. Trying to accomplish all four tasks simultaneously is like trying to solve an equation having four unknowns, but without possessing any of the knowns to start with. There may be an exact solution, but only through trial and error will one discover it. It is little wonder one finds a mess in software engineering today.

The final point, and one implicitly made by the *Business Week* article, is that the failure of these developments can severely and ruinously impact a company's future business prospects. Failure can be computed in many ways, but in general, if the information system costs you more than anticipated, isn't delivered on time, and/or doesn't do what was promised, it has to be considered a failure to some degree. The number of failures, or to what level a business can tolerate these failures, will determine how long the business survives. The Lockheed Corporation is finding this out, as the failure of several software developments forced the company to write off over $450,000,000 in earnings in a single year.[19] In fact, one development failure alone was responsible for a $300 million loss. These failures drove down the value of Lockheed's stock, and it has had to fight off a hostile takeover.

Information systems are increasingly becoming the cornerstone of a majority of companies' current and future competitive edge, as well as representing a larger part of their budget and potential for affecting the bottom line. Their lack of timeliness in becoming operational and their increased cost are now matters of business survival. Trying to avoid these failures, or at least contain the damage they may cause, carries us to our final determinant and source of risk for software development disasters: *the lack of recognition, consideration or appreciation of the very factor of risk.*

It has been a strong contention of mine that developing software is *much too easy* to initiate and perform on a professional level. One does not require physical strength (such as in athletics or construction work), one does not have to be of a certain age (such as for driving a car, drinking, or voting), one does not need to possess special training (such as for practicing medicine or electrically wiring a house) or even any understanding of basic engineering principles (such as in building a cantilevered staircase). The ease with which a computer can be programmed masks the difficulty involved in creating usable and reliable software systems. It is not unusual to encounter a person who should know better (usually a senior manager or program sponsor), who assumes that since he or she can develop a 100-line Cobol program in an afternoon on their personal computer, then a 100,000-line program should be just as easy to create with 10 people in less than 3 months' time. They cannot understand why the time and budget estimates call instead for 18 months and 50 people. The differences between a 100-line *program* and a 100,000-line *system* are not perceived or appreciated, nor is the fact that one cannot simply "scale everything up." Just as the ability to drive a car doesn't make one a professional race car driver, and bandaging a deep wound doesn't make one a doctor, writing small programs does not make one able to build software systems. There are limits to what can be done because of the inherently increasing scale of complexities involved, regardless of the amount of resources available or efficient methods applied, as is illustrated in Figure 1.1. Like being pregnant, some things take a minimum amount of time to successfully complete.

The eventual harvest of failure that is fertilized by the lack of understanding of software development risks can be found daily in the industry. The most common risk manifested by this lack of understanding is the undercapitalization of resources. One can, with regularity, encounter some software project sponsor who doesn't know all the potential risks involved in a software development, and who therefore, is so afraid to lose all of his or her investment that sufficient resources will not be committed to the project. As a result, the project will be starved of the minimum resources required, therefore, in turn, forcing its management into taking high-risk decisions, such as estimating exaggerated coding production from each of the project's personnel to compensate. Not surprisingly, the project will most likely begin to "fail" when those estimates are not met. By failing to mitigate the risk of not

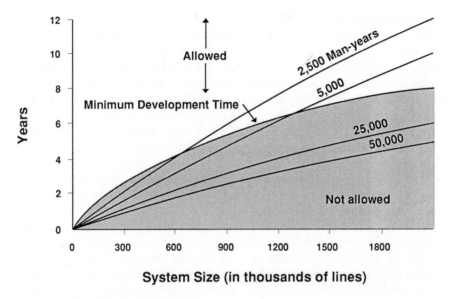

Figure 1.1 Allowable Development Time

knowing the risks, the sponsor starts the project off, and keeps it behind the power curve—a self-fulfilling prophesy situation if there ever was one.

The effects of the lack of the recognition of risks manifest themselves in other ways as well. The massive concentration on competitive opportunities through the application of information technology, without the simultaneous mention of risk, is mind-boggling. Large opportunity, consequently high risk, does not seem to be in our collective vocabulary. The attitude is supremely expressed by the eternal and unbounded optimism of those trying to build complex systems on tight budgets and schedules when the whole previous history of such attempts has shown failure outweighing success by a factor of at least 5, if not 10. Nevertheless, every day in the computing press, one reads of yet another high-risk venture, with its sponsors saying with arrogant pride that theirs will work where everyone else's failed, while on the opposite page, a humble tale of failure will be told by somebody else who tried the identical thing two years before! It is amazing, but we seem to think in this industry that if what we have done in the past doesn't work, well then, more of the same in the future will fix it. Are we in computing really this feeble-minded, just lazy, or masochistic?

Some friends of mine will argue with me, and say that there are many successful software projects. I will concede that some successful projects do exist, but I still argue that these constitute the vast minority of projects undertaken. I am not arguing that all software development is a failure because it isn't risk-free. That's missing the point. Failure also happens in other industries. Bridges still occasionally fall down, dams burst, engines fall off planes, and cars are designed with oil filters that require the engine to be removed when the oil needs changing. However, the trouble is with our dismal record at succeeding at what should be considered as medium or low-risk software projects. Compared with other industries, information technology projects have a 3–5 times higher failure rate.[20] That is why I personally consider *all* current software projects as high-risk endeavors today. As the old saying goes, if it walks like a duck, quacks like a duck, swims like a duck, and looks like a duck, it probably *is* a duck.

As we said earlier, there are no unique causes of the problem of software failure. The individual parameters that create the situations of undercapitalization and underperformance are multifaceted, requiring a combination of solutions, hard work, and common sense. At best, one can only hope to manage the risks that each of these separate parameters bring to a development. Until this is understood and recognized, people will continue to look for easy solutions that do not exist. We would do well to take heed of the Down-easterner's advice, "You can't get there from here."

The risks involved in software developments do not only manifest themselves in the guises of underperformance or undercapitalization, either. Even when sufficient resources are available, the risks to a successful development are often misunderstood or are out of the total control of the project's management whose job it is to effectively limit their impact. A typical example is the unforeseen resignation of a key person on the project who alone has the full understanding of a crucial element of the system. Others include: rapid or unexpected changes in government regulation affecting the business; natural disasters; negotiation failures for new business; corporate politics; personality conflicts; or major market changes. Thus, even in the best resourced development project, uncontrollable events can occur which will increase the probability of project failure. One must not only be aware of these types of risks, but one must be able to plan for and contain their possible impacts. No software development is perfectly planned or executed, and there is a need to control the associated risks to an even greater degree as businesses become more dependent on software systems.

In summary, we will state that information technology development risk can be defined as *the difference between the amount of capital and performance required to successfully develop a system and the amount actually provided, and the recognition that a difference exists.* The limitations imposed by both resource performance and capitalization, as well as its perceptions on developing systems, restrict the effectiveness of a business to deal adequately with this risk. Before we go much further in our discussion about the individual parameters that make up software risk, it might be instructive to review the basic concepts of risk.[21]

1.2 Risky Business

What exactly do we mean when we speak of risk? Risk can be viewed from a number of perspectives. First, a risk is an aspect of future happenings and events. The concerns of today and yesterday are beyond immediate anxiety, as we are already reaping what was previously sowed by our past actions. The question, therefore, is, can we create an opportunity for a different and, one hopes, better situation for ourselves tomorrow by changing our actions today? If the answer to this question is yes, it implies, second, that risk involves change, such as in changes of the mind, opinion, actions, or places. In a static world, there would not exist a concept of risk, for permanency implies certainty. This brings us to the third aspect of risk, that of choice. Risk involves choice, and with it, all the uncertainty that choosing alternatives itself entails. Paradoxically, then, risk, like death and taxes, is one of the few certainties in life.

1.2.1 Risk

The derivation of the word "risk" dates back to at least the seventeenth century and is thought to be Italian in origin.[22] Before that time, the word used generally in everyday writing and conversation was "hazard." "Risk" came to England from France in the mid–seventeenth century as the word *risqué* and quickly followed a path to the United States.[23] The anglicized spelling appeared in 1830, appropriately enough appearing in the records of insurance transactions in London's financial brokerage houses. The two spellings for risk were used interchangeably for about 100 years, until the twentieth century, when *risqué* became the word for a joke that risks offending. Notice that the word "risk" can be used both as a noun (i.e., a risk as in a gamble, peril, or menace) and as a verb (i.e., to risk as in to wager, speculate or dare), thus allowing the expression of two ideas: a danger itself, as well as a way of acting that involves taking a chance.

The dictionary definition of risk is "to expose to the chance of injury or loss." Thus, for risk to exist, the chance involved must have some loss associated with it. Some writers have tried to divide risk into two distinct types: *speculative* (or dynamic) risks and *static* risks.[24] Speculative risks are those having both profit and loss attached to them, while static risks are considered to only have losses associated with them. Gambling, for instance, is considered a speculative risk, whereas for an individual about to go into battle, the risks are primarily static in nature (getting healthier is not usually planned as an expected result). For this book, we will consider risks to be of a dynamic nature, since software risks, as we shall see, have aspects of both gain and loss associated with them.

Let's spend a little time clarifying this idea about "potential loss." A potential loss can either (a) make things worse off than the *status quo* or, (b) produce an outcome not as desirable as some other outcome that might have been achieved. A second type of loss, an *opportunity loss* or an *opportunity cost*, occurs whenever a resource is sacrificed to a specific objective.[25] This resource cannot be spent on some other objective and is therefore lost for future use. Opportunity losses may be very difficult to measure because they may not be obvious until after some time has passed, while the type of loss in (a) is easily understood as constituting a real loss. A prime example of an opportunity loss often encountered is when a project is over budget, since any resources spent that were not budgeted for are resources not able to be spent on some other opportunity. Likewise, when a project is late, it means that sales within the marketplace are also lost. Opportunities gained can change a risky situation into a nonrisky one, as well as vice versa.

There are a couple of other points to ponder. One should observe that a risk in general, and a loss in particular, is very dependent upon one's point of view. Obviously, people are concerned most with the consequences of a risk. However, one individual may view a situation in one way, and another may view the exact situation in another. In other words, risk is not an objective beast. For example, John D. Rockefeller built Standard Oil to minimize his risk and ensure company profitability. Rockefeller did so by systematically destroying the predictability of his competitors' business conditions by the creation of a monopoly. His loss was a competitor's gain, and vice versa. Figure 1.2 summarizes this point of

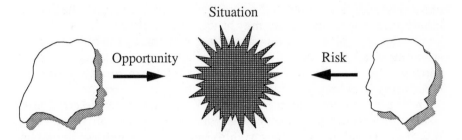

Figure 1.2 Risk Perspectives

view. One should not be misled, however, into thinking that losses are only determined in the form of zero-sum games. Sometimes there are no winners, as all choices bring about some level of loss for all participants. How people react to risk (i.e., whether they are risk-favoring or risk-averse) will be studied in Chapter 6.

Another item to observe is that complex systems contain sets of risks, each of which is comprised of many contributory risks. It is impossible to find a software project that is not confronted with many different types and kinds of risks. Some of them are important, some are not. As we will see later, our concern will be with the risks created by the processes encountered in the creation of software intensive systems and the risks inherent in the type of software application being built.

1.2.2 Chance

The definition of the word "risk" also makes a very clear statement that there will be a chance of loss associated with it. For instance, a sure loss is not a risk, because it has a certainty of occurrence. In "certainty situations," the gains or benefits are able to be objectively traded straightforwardly against the losses or costs that exist. Thus, decisions are not influenced by a lack of information about the situation. Standing in front of a locomotive traveling at a high rate of speed will do you no little amount of harm. The requisite information to make a decision about the situation is known beforehand.

Uncertainty, on the other hand, exists in the absence of information about past, present, or future events, values, or conditions.[26] This means there is a lack of confidence in the correctness of the estimated probability distribution. Uncertainty also exists when each possible outcome can be identified, but the probability of the occurrence can neither be determined nor assessed.[27] There are degrees of uncertainty, meaning that some information about the system may be known, but there is not sufficient knowledge about it to provide certainty. For example, the probability of standing in an open field during a thunderstorm in Kansas in June, getting struck by lightning, and surviving is not known exactly, although it certainly is not recommended.

There are three types of uncertainty.[28-30] The first, called *descriptive* or *structural uncertainty*, is concerned with the absence of information relating to the identity of the variables that explicitly define the system under study. This is the information necessary to describe the system in a taxonomic sense, representing the "degrees of freedom" of the system. It consists of a set of variables that, when totally determined, fully describe the system being considered. The variables may include physical as well as nonphysical attributes such as political, legal, or economic. What is included and excluded from consideration of "the system," we will soon see, is vital for the later valuation of the risk consequences.

The second type of uncertainty is *measurement uncertainty*. This is the absence of information relating to the assignment of a value to the variables used to describe the system. This comes from the fact that there exist limits to the observations and/or data available for either their calibration or validation. In situations which involve political issues, for instance, it is often difficult to determine what is a proper measurement scale for evaluating a decision. What does a decision that is "good for the people" really mean? How good? And for which "people?" If it is good for the people of one county or state, but bad for the populace of the nation as a whole, is it a really sound choice?

The third type of uncertainty is more theoretical in nature and is called *event outcome uncertainty*. It occurs when the predicted outcomes, and therefore their probabilities, cannot be identified. Thus, a person does not know what possible outcomes can occur, given a particular course of action. Some call it belonging to the realm of "chance" or "luck," but in truth it is just a manifestation of random processes.[31] This is called *ignorance* and exists when neither the variables nor the measurement of their values for a system exist. Event outcome uncertainty becomes important in risk analysis when predictions about future outcomes, say of using a new technology or taking a new course of action, have no prior basis to draw from.

If we were to take an entropic viewpoint, where zero entropy represents total order, then complete knowledge or certainty would represent zero entropy, while total entropy would represent zero knowledge or total ignorance, as shown in Figure 1.3. The knowledge one often possesses

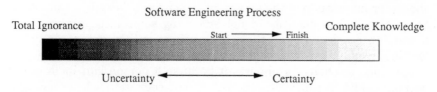

Figure 1.3 Spectrum of Uncertainty

when beginning a software system's development lies somewhere to the left of center, and (ideally) proceeds to the right as more knowledge of the system under construction is gained. We will deal with the state of ignorance only implicitly, although on many software developments, this state seems to be more the reality than of only theoretical importance. It should be noted that some authors try to distinguish between certainty (the absence of risk), risk (the probabilities of alternative, possible outcomes are known), and uncertainty (the frequency distribution of the possible outcomes are unknown), as shown in Figure 1.4.[32] In this book, we will not make a distinction between decision making under uncertainty and risk, believing that uncertainty is but a fundamental characteristic of a risk.

1.2.3 Choice

The third aspect in the definition of risk, which has been already alluded to, is the fact that a choice among alternatives is involved. For our purposes, we will say that being "exposed to the chance" means that a person making a decision can take actions to increase or decrease the

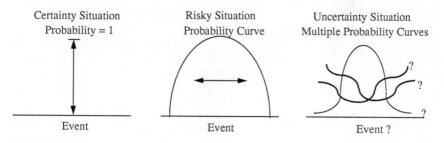

Figure 1.4 Certainty vs. Risk vs. Uncertainty

chance or magnitude of the loss or gain incurred. Thus, by implication, there also is a probability of not achieving something. Again do not forget, if there is no choice, there is no risk, even though there may be a loss incurred.

This idea of choice is important because a person can incur a risk without explicitly taking it, such as being placed into risk by others than oneself.[33] This is illustrated in Figure 1.5, which shows the different ways an individual can be placed into risk. The idea of running a risk without explicitly taking it also means that: (1) a person can run a risk without recognizing that it exists, and (2) perceived risks are as important as real risks. In the first case, we will assume that a person involved in a decision is both rational and has some control over their actions.[34] In other words, the person, if unsure of the situation, will strive to obtain the information required to make a decision, resulting in their benefit. Ideally, this person, if given the greatest flexibility in choices and perfect information, will opt for the one with the greatest benefit or least loss. It also means that risks that are wholly circumstantial in nature; i.e., "acts of God," as in case 3 of Figure 1.5, are not considered acts of risk taking on the part of an individual who finds himself in that situation.

In case (2) above, people have no option but to react the same way to real risks or perceived risks, if there is no way to tell the difference. This

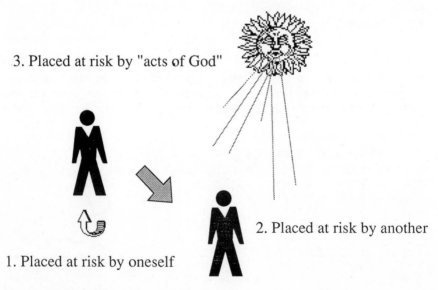

3. Placed at risk by "acts of God"

2. Placed at risk by another

1. Placed at risk by oneself

Figure 1.5 Ways of Being Placed into Risk

implies there exist perceived choices, as well as perceived risks. Although we will strive to deal only with real risks and real choices, the subjective element must always be recognized as being present. Again, we defer the examination of the psychology of risk and risk taking until Chapter 6.

1.2.4 Risk definition

Summing up, for an event, action, thing, etc., to be considered a risk, there must be:

1. A loss associated with it
2. An element of uncertainty or chance
3. Some choice among alternatives

Appreciate, also, that not choosing is considered a choice. In MacCrimmon and Wehrung, the three aspects above are called *the magnitude of the loss, the chance of loss,* and *the exposure to loss.*[35] Each is a necessary, but not a sufficient, condition to define risk. One can reduce a risk by reducing the loss, reducing the uncertainty or chance involved, or increasing the choices available which present less risk.

Based upon the discussion above, the general definition of risk we will use in this text is the same, with caveats, as stated in Rowe's book, *An Anatomy of Risk*: "Risk is the potential for realization of unwanted, negative consequences of an event."[36] Three things are important to notice about this definition. The first is that magnitude of the loss and the chance can both be measured, but may not necessarily be independent. Dependance can rest very heavily on time, for instance. Coastal hurricane warnings are a prime example of this dependance. A tropical storm on a particular storm track outside the Gulf of Mexico may have a very low probability of reaching the Gulf coast, and thus residents along the coast may only receive minimal warning from the U.S. Center for Weather Forecasting about possible wind and flooding damage. But if the storm later gains strength and develops into a hurricane, the damage may be very great, the Gulf may have a higher probability of being directly hit, and, thus, the risks (and the subsequent warning) are increased.

Second, risk is caused by the lack of information, the lack of control, and/or the lack of time. To reduce or avert a risk, one or more of these causes must be changed. Often the trade-off in software development will be to reduce risk by exerting more control, but this may mean an increase in the risk if time is also not increased. For example, applying a software requirements methodology to the planning phase where one was not used previously will lower the risk of producing bad specifications (more information will be gained, as will more control), but the risk reduction might be offset if more time is not provided as well. Similarly, in large-scale software developments, the very fact that there is a long time period involved means that there is more chance for risks due to the lack of control to occur. As we will see later, it is difficult to reduce risk by reducing only one of its root causes.

Finally, for simplicity's sake, we do not distinguish among single events, multiple events, and continuous events, or between single types of loss and multiple types of loss. Risk is associated with the ultimate loss to the risk taker. It should be obvious that outcomes that depend on only one type of event (e.g., actions of one competitor) are less risky than those that depend on multiple events (e.g., actions of many competitors), or an event that has multiple losses (e.g., political, social, and economic) is more risky than one that has only one (e.g., economic).

1.3 Risk Engineering: Risk Analysis and Management

If there is risk involved in a decision, it is prudent that the risk be identified, assessed, and controlled in some way, unless, of course, you like adventures. Questions such as the following must be addressed:

- What are the risks?
- What is the probability of loss from them?
- How much are the losses likely to cost?
- What might the losses be if the worst happened?
- What alternatives are there?
- How can the losses be reduced, contained, or eliminated?
- Will the alternatives produce other risks?

The process of identification, estimation, and evaluation of risk we will call *risk analysis*. The planned controlling of risk and monitoring the success of the control mechanisms we will term *risk management*. Both together we term risk engineering.[37] The basic goals of risk engineering are to attempt to find out what may go wrong, and to do something positive to prevent it.

1.3.1 Risk analysis

Risk analysis identifies potential problem areas, quantifies risks associated with these problems, assesses the effects of these risks, and generates alternative courses of actions to reduce risk. Although the exact form that risk analysis will take depends highly on the specific program requirements and organizational concerns, we choose to divide risk analysis into three discrete steps:

- First, comprehensively identify potential risk items using a structured and consistent method; i.e., what can go wrong?
- Second, estimate the magnitude of each risk, their consequences, and the creation of options; i.e., what is the likelihood of that happening under the current plan?
- Third, evaluate the consequences of risk, including their prioritization; i.e., if the risk occurs, what is the damage?

The answers to the above questions are illustrated in Figure 1.6 and constitute our software engineering risk analysis.

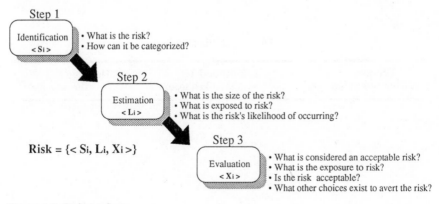

Figure 1.6 Risk Analysis

The answers to the questions above can be arranged as shown in Table 1.3. The first column contains the scenarios of what can go wrong, and can be labeled s_i. The second column contains the generic likelihood, l_i, of the scenarios in column one happening. The third column, x_i, represents a measure of the consequences of the "ith" scenario. This sometimes is called the "damage index." The triplet $< s_i, l_i, x_i >$ constitutes a particular risk, whereas the set of all such triplets forms the totality of risk to the software development being performed. Therefore,

$$\text{Risk} = \{< s_i, l_i, x_i >\}$$

becomes our formal definition of software engineering risk.[38]

Thus, risk analysis is used to identify potential problem areas, quantify risks associated with these problems, and generate alternative choices of actions which can be taken to reduce risk. The first action, *risk identification*, is undertaken so that there can be a reduction in descriptive uncertainty.[39] In other words, the variables that will be used to describe the degrees of freedom of the system are identified. This is done by surveying the range of potential threats to the system, as well as the threats to required system resources. Threats are defined as the broad range of forces which could produce an adverse result, while the resources are considered assets which might be affected.[40] A *Risk Estimate of the Situation* (RES), as shown in Figure 1.7, is often used to aid in the identification of the risks that are assumed at the beginning of the development.[41] The RES is also meant to identify the objectives of the enterprise and its critical factors for success. This is especially important,

TABLE 1.3 Risk Table

Scenario (s_i) (What can go wrong?)	Likelihood (l_i) (What is the likelihood?)	Damage (x_i) (What is the damage?)
s_1	l_1	x_1
s_2	l_2	x_2
s_3	l_3	x_3
s_4	l_4	x_4
.	.	.
.	.	.
.	.	.
.	.	.
s_n	l_n	x_n

RISK ESTIMATE OF THE SITUATION

References: (Project plans, budgets, schedules, etc.)

1. **PROJECT AND ITS ANALYSIS**

    a. Indicate the source of incentive of the project

    b. State project's mission

    c. Study project's mission in relation to overall organizational goals

    d. Study project's mission

        (1) Identify the objective(s)
            (a) Economic
            (b) Non-Economic
        (2) Note contribution to organizational objective(s)
        (3) Note significant elements of the project
            (a) Obvious planning constraints and opportunities
            (b) Assumptions

    e. Note the relationship with other projects or other parties involved in the project

    f. Note general competitive situation

    g. Summarize key points of the analysis

2. **CONSIDERATIONS AFFECTING POSSIBLE COURSES OF ACTION**

    (For each factor considered, the analyst should draw conclusions as to how it may affect project operations)

    a. The general situation

    b. Characteristics of the project's operations

        (1) General factors
            (a) Political
            (b) Economic
            (c) Organizational
        (2) Fixed factors
            (a) Facilities
            (b) Personnnel
            (c) Other resources

    c. Examine project's requirements

        (1) Compare resources available vs. needs
        (2) Compare quality requirements to project's complexity

Figure 1.7 Risk Estimate of the Situation Outline (*Continued on next page*)

    (3) Compare organizational capabilities
    (4) Compare time and budget factors

  d. Assess external forces

    (1) Identify deficiencies in information
    (2) Tabulate strength and weakness factors
    (3) Make initial determination of adequacy of own resources

3. ANALYSIS OF OPPOSING COURSES OF ACTION

  a. Factors Opposing Project Success (FOPS)

    (1) List and weigh factors which may keep project from achieving its objectives
    (2) Weigh relative probability of factors occurring
    (3) Estimate severity of factors if they were to occur

  b. Project's Courses of Action (PCA)

    (1) List tentative project's courses of action
    (2) Consider concept for each course of action
    (3) Test for suitability and make preliminary test for feasibility and acceptability
    (4) List retained project's courses of action

  c. Analysis of Opposing Courses of Action (OCA)

  Commencing with the first OCA and FOPS, each analysis consists of the following four parts:

    (1) Actions which can occur to increase the stated FOPS occurring
    (2) Actions which the project must take to implement each stated course of action in the face of these occurrences
    (3) The interactions resulting from (1) and (2) above
    (4) Conclusions as to the probable outcome of the above interactions, which lead to a basis for judging the feasibility and acceptability of the stated course of action, and comparing its merits with other courses of action being tested

4. COMPARISON OF PROJECT'S COURSES OF ACTION

  a. List and consider advantages and disadvantages

  b. Make final test for suitability, feasibility, and acceptability

  c. Weigh relative merits and select the course of action for the project

  d. List project's final objectives, strategies, tactics, and means

Figure 1.7 *(Continued)* Risk Estimate of the Situation Outline

as risks will be directly linked to each objective and its critical success criteria. These success criteria often change in time, or will not be known for a long period of time, but they are measurable and controllable.[42] Once the risks have been identified, they typically are broken down into different categories for ease of understanding and completeness.

Risk estimation is the reduction of measurement uncertainty.[43] During this phase, three things are accomplished. First, the values of the variables describing the system are determined. This requires some acceptance of a measurement scale on how these values will be weighed. Second, the various consequences of an event occurring are identified. Actions cause reactions, and these must be made known. Third, the magnitude of the risk is determined using the previously selected measurement scale. Also, any modifying factors which tend to increase or reduce the probability of a threat becoming a reality, or the severity of a consequence if it does occur, are considered.[44] The uncertainty of the estimates is expressed in many ways, such as probability distributions, confidence intervals, or point estimates.

Risk estimation can be categorized as either subjective or objective. Objective risk estimation is linked to situations where a history of precisely the same situation exists; i.e., two people can assemble the facts at hand and reach the same conclusion, whereas subjective estimation assumes the nonexistence of a base history. Usually both types of estimation are required, because a situation in real life is usually not black and white or one of *déjà vu*. In software risk analysis in particular, subjective estimation is the rule, as published project histories upon which project planners can draw from are extremely rare. Very little forensic software engineering (i.e., the systematic examination of projects to find the causes of their failure or their success) has been performed, nor have systematized post-mortems been published.[45]

One reason given is that new technology is often used in a project, which makes previous project histories of little value. Another is that published "lessons-learned" reports on what went wrong on projects are not seen as adding value to a company's self-interest quotient—especially if it is participating in competitive bid work, where it has to have been great and wonderful yesterday in order to get tomorrow's job. However, if you don't know where you have been, you sure don't know where you are going, or how to improve the comfort involved in the journey to get there. Having this data available, even if it is just lessons learned on internal company projects, can be very valuable in keeping a company from making the same types of errors over and over again.

Risk evaluation is the process whereby the responses to the risks are anticipated. Insight is sought into the consequences of the various possible decisions confronting the decision maker, with the general acceptability of individually projected outcomes to a decision postulated. Since some risks are more acceptable or more detrimental than others, there may be a prioritization required of the risks involved for later aversion. For example, during the Vietnam War, Lyndon Johnson wanted to fight the war but did not believe the country would be willing to pay for it with new taxes. The chairman of the economic advisors, Gardner Ackley, went to the president, and said, "Mr. President, you're making a mistake," to which Johnson basically replied, "Well, you're probably right. I'm making an economic mistake, but politically, I'm not making a mistake." As one economist later put it, "Fouling up the economy wasn't done by accident. It was done deliberately, with everybody's eyes wide open."[46] The United States is still performing risk aversion for the prioritization of risk decisions made 25 years ago.

Evaluation methods may be quantitative or qualitative in nature, such as generating scenarios of possible outcomes. Usually, only after the type, quality, and uncertainty of the data gathered during the estimation process has been evaluated will it be determined whether a quantitative or qualitative evaluation will be performed. Sensitivity analysis to determine the impact of changing a risk's magnitude is often conducted to help identify the various consequences that might be encountered. Initial approaches to risk aversion by reduction, transfer, containment, or elimination (if possible) are identified and are added to the options to be considered during risk management.

Risk identification, estimation, and evaluation are not precisely separable in practice. Each overlaps the other in some areas, and the same types of techniques may be used in obtaining information. Figure 1.8 illustrates the overlap. The process is very iterative and can be very complicated. Often the number of risks are reduced to a "top-10 list" or something similar. For instance, the Department of Defense (DoD) primarily groups risks into two groups: acquisition risks and decision risks.[47] Acquisition risks are made up of three interrelated risk elements: technical risk (the degree of uncertainty in the engineering process), schedule risk (the degree of uncertainty in meeting desired milestones), and cost risk (the degree of uncertainty in acquisition and/or life cycle budgets). Decision risk has to do with the operational risk (the degree of uncertainty in fielding a system which meets its intended functions) and support risk (the degree of uncertainty in maintaining or enhancing a system within planned resources). Events that can occur to increase

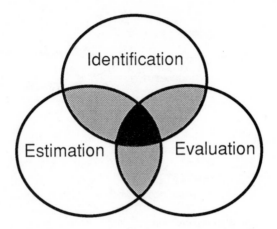

Figure 1.8 Risk Analysis

risks in each of these areas are identified as threats, and these are then subject to risk management.

1.3.2 Risk management

Risk management is the second phase of risk engineering and is involved with the decision-making process involving the risk(s) after it has been analyzed. It usually consists of a *planning,* a *controlling,* and a *monitoring phase.*

There are two aspects to the planning stage. In the first, the decision makers select a final course of action concerning the situation under study. Based upon the evaluation results, as shown in Figure 1.9, one can either accept the risks, decide to abandon the project, or revise the goals and objectives of the project, such as scoping the system requirements down or increasing the resources available, and update the risk analysis. The key is to reduce one of the three basic causes of risk; i.e., the lack of information, the lack of control, or the lack of time, by either increasing the number of choices available, changing the probability of a risk's occurrence, or changing (reducing) the size of the magnitude of the risk's consequence.

Once a course of action is designated, a plan for carrying out the decision is formulated. Often, this means a second analysis phase is conducted to ensure the plan's feasibility, especially checking that it

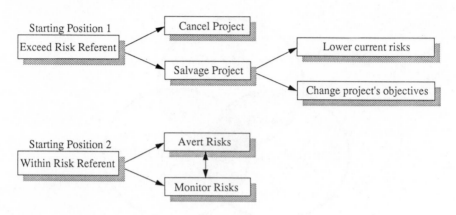

Figure 1.9 Monitoring Starting Positions

does not interfere with other decisions made or about to be made. This may seem a bit redundant, or somewhat late, but the *principle of late binding* applies (wait until the last possible moment before making a decision to ensure maximum flexibility). The selected course of action is "signed for;" i.e., the risks are acknowledged explicitly and publicly, to ensure that there are no doubts about what (or whom) is involved. With a decision being made, it now becomes a "certainty," and so brings with it more information about future potential risks, as well as the aversion of others. Because of dependency relationships, a decision which was previously acceptable may no longer be feasible to implement.

The second aspect of planning concentrates on the selection of the appropriate risk aversion strategies to be employed along with the selected course of action to achieve the "optimal risk level" (or at least one which is acceptable), as illustrated in Figure 1.10. This is documented in the risk management and aversion plans. What should be covered in a typical risk aversion plan is shown in Figure 1.11. As time goes on, tighter and tighter boundaries will be placed around what is considered an acceptable risk; therefore, during this period, selection of the measures against which the monitoring of the risk aversion strategy has to be accomplished. Furthermore, any contingency resources that might be required for future risk aversion situations are identified. Finally, replanning is involved with getting a risk aversion strategy back on track if a problem shows up during monitoring.

Risk control involves implementing the plan's control mechanism for the risk aversion strategies. The plan is realized by providing the

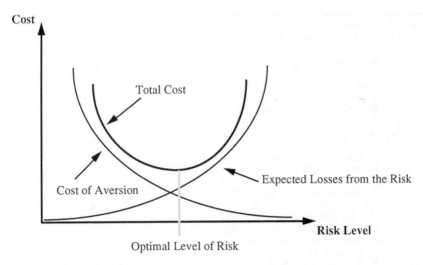

Figure 1.10 Optimal Risk

required resources to the project. Project plans are changed as necessary, and new estimates of cost and schedule become the operational imperatives. Contingencies are created in case the aversion approaches fail to contain the risk. The Apollo space program, for instance, came in at $21 billion, only $1 billion over its initial estimates. However, also included in that amount was $8 billion, or 75% of the original budget in contingency.[48] The key aspect of control is the fact that definitive action is taken to contain a risk's possible adverse effects.

Monitoring occurs after the decisions have been implemented, in order (a) to see if the consequences of the decision were the same as envisioned, (b) to identify opportunities for refinement of the action plans, and (c) to help communicate and provide feedback to those making future decisions. To put it a bit more succinctly, monitoring deals with the aftermaths of current decisions and predicts where risks in the future may lie. Monitoring is also meant to help calibrate the precision of the estimations and evaluations of risk made previously to enhance the accuracy of future decisions. It is also meant to identify *why* the variances in the predicted estimations and evaluations and actuals occurred. Additionally, monitoring identifies risks that were not observable, known, or were overlooked when the project started, but which appear later. Diseases that kill today were not observed before because people did not live that long. In other words, "The seeds of tomorrow are buried in today. But

---

I. Introduction
   1. Scope and Purpose of Document
   2. Overview
      a. Objectives
      b. Risk Area Summary
      c. Organization
      a. Management
      d. Aversion Program Description

II. Risk Aversion Summary
   1. Identification of Project Risk Areas
      a. Survey of Risk Factors
      b. Project Vulnerabilities
   2. Risk Assessment and Prioritization
      a. Description of Major Project Risks
         i.   Probability of Occurrence
         ii. Cost of Occurrence
      b. Overall Risk Impacts on Project's Objectives
   3. Risk Management Alternatives
      a. Feasibility and Costs
      b. Impacts on Projects
      c. Recommendations

III. Aversion Action Plan
   1. Implementation Plan
      a. Integration with Other Risk Plans
         i.   Risk Coupling/Compounding Threats
      b. Organization Resource Assignment
         i.   Responsibilities and Duties
      c. Schedule/Milestones
   2. Aversion Plan Monitoring Procedures
      a. Feedback Points
      b. Red Flag Criteria
   3. Contingencies

IV. Corporate Approval
   1. Authorizing Officials
      a. Corporate
      b. Division
      c. Section

V. Appendices
   1. Risk Estimate of the Situation
   2. Risk Management Plan

Figure 1.11 Risk Aversion Plan Outline

they lie much too deep, and germinate much too subtly, for ordinary eyes ... to detect all of their fruit."[49]

Risk monitoring is vital and must occur whether or not a risk has been deemed acceptable. Further, because of our imperfect foresight, actions concerning a particular risk may have unintended deleterious consequences of large magnitude. If a wrong decision has been made, it must be recognized early enough so that corrective action can be taken. But it is just as important to recognize when a prior decision is correct, and not to change it prematurely, or else one risks snatching defeat out of the jaws of victory. Premature decision making is a deadly vice to be avoided, if possible. Constant changing of direction will waste valuable project resources and increases risk tremendously. This we term *decision management whiplash*. It is similar to a system controller constantly receiving feedback and never stabilizing.

The process of risk management should not be viewed as necessarily a sequential or a compartmentalized one. Different aspects proceed in parallel, and there is constant iteration and feedback among the various activities. New options are always being created, and adjustment to decisions are being made. Risk management, especially monitoring, operates continuously throughout a software project's life, from initiation until retirement. This is especially important in long-lived projects where success criteria change with time, or inflation effects might take hold, or diversification of risk control mechanisms might be needed to avert the project's risks. At all times, however, risk management must be balanced against the resources available, or one may find that the management process becomes so expensive that there will exist a temptation to do it improperly, or not at all, thus defeating its whole purpose.

Finally, risk management should not be viewed as a negative process, but instead as a positive one. Risk management is a proactive, not reactive, management approach. Risk management provides an orderly approach to making decisions about the threats to the assets and earnings of a business, and making plans to combat the risks that are associated with those decisions. Risk management looks for possible problems early on, finding alternative approaches which have been thought through, rather than the more typical management approach to go into a reactive crisis mode every time a problem appears.

In summary, risk engineering is a powerful tool for increasing business stability in its efforts to cope with business uncertainty. Increasing stability greatly increases the power to act, as well as the probability of making correct and successful decisions. Until the government stepped in, John D. Rockefeller's oil monopoly was a direct result of taking positive, risk management actions, for he knew that a monopolistic environment is the least risky way to run a business that exists.

Risk engineering is especially important in successful businesses, as they must confront unknown risks and respond quickly to competitive threats they themselves have created to continue to expand their business. It is especially useful in validating budgets in an age of diminishing resources. Risk engineering is solution, not problem-oriented, and thus exists to reduce a business's risk.

1.4 Sources of Risk

Earlier in this chapter, we mentioned three determinants which influence the poor record of software developments: underperformance, undercapitalization, and the inadequacy in the understanding of risk as it affects software acquisitions, use, or developments. Underperformance and undercapitalization are obviously risks in themselves, but as we have mentioned, even with sufficient amounts of resources and their efficient use, there is no guarantee of project success. For example, in software developments there currently is too much uncertainty with which one must deal. Let's illustrate this by examining three examples.

In Figure 1.12, we have drawn a simple chart depicting the various stages of a representative software development life cycle, and the possible positions one can arrive at given specific decisions. The nodes represent a decision point, given a set of previous decisions as inputs. For example, at the requirements phase of the software development, one can start with either a correctly or an incorrectly derived conceptual design (we will assume for simplicity's sake that correctness or incorrectness is binary, and each life cycle stage is statistically

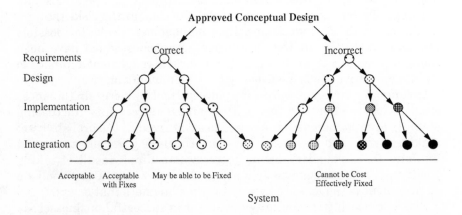

Figure 1.12 Flow of Errors

independent of the one above). After the requirements stage, one can pass on to the software designers a requirement's specification that is: (1) a correct specification based upon a correct conceptual design; (2) an incorrect specification based upon a correct conceptual design; (3) a correct specification based upon an incorrect conceptual design; or (4) an incorrect specification based upon an incorrect conceptual design. The process, and the flow of errors, is repeated throughout the life cycle stages which follow.

Examining the figure, we can see how easy it is to build an unacceptable software system. One can be skillful and build an acceptable system, or one that is acceptable with some degree of fixes, or one which might be able to be fixed (although there is some doubt about whether this can in fact be achieved), or one can end up with a system that is not worth fixing and should be abandoned. One can think of these outcomes as abstract representations of the different rings in Dante's *Inferno*: the choices are to serve in heaven, spend long spells in purgatory, or lunch with Lucifer. Or as Conrad's Law states, "The sins of the designer will manifest themselves in the products of the developers and in the budgets of the maintenance team."[50]

Cost and schedule overruns are created in many places, usually after it is realized that one is proceeding down the right half of the tree, thereby forcing one to retrace the path up the tree again. The trick, of course, is to realize when you are proceeding down the wrong path, and whether there is a way to get back up and to the other side. After arriving in some nodes, it is better just to start over.

An interesting exercise is to place probability estimates on the nodes and compute the probability of ending up at the acceptable node at the lower left-hand corner. For example, the probability of ending up with a correct requirement rather than an incorrect one may be 90%. Even assuming there is a 90% chance of moving left rather than right, in a four-stage development, the probability of success (i.e., ending up with everything correct) is only 66%. Given that many software life cycle developments have 8 to 10 steps, the probability is reduced even further.[51]

It should be noted, though, that many of the issues identified as problems seen in an information system project development, such as poorly specified requirements, are in fact not issues about poor requirements methods, but issues about poor business or systems engineering practice. Businesses often create their own information system development risks by asking the least knowledgeable group; i.e., the software engineering specialists, to define what their business problems and information system solutions are. The software engineer may know something about creating information systems, but he or she knows very little about running a business, determining the net present value, or the cost of money and its impact on the business's bottom line. However, software engineers often get stuck by default with "hot potato" problems, which the business managers and/or systems engineers can't or won't solve. If the software engineers could toss the problem to someone else, they would. Unfortunately, they are at the bottom of the pond, and that's where all the dirt settles. So do not immediately blame the software engineer or software engineering itself for all the problems. However, there are certain times when software engineering should shoulder some of the blame for the current lack of success of information technology application, as we will see.

Another example which may help explain where some of the sources of risk reside in software developments is the concept of the technology pyramid by Alan Stoddart shown in Figure 1.13.[52] This pyramid depicts the four requirements for developing and measuring a technology's maturity. At the lowest level are standards, or metrics. These are the basic building blocks or atomic elements with which everyone wanting to use or describe the technology can communicate. Above that are the theories about the technology, its fundamental laws, how it reacts under certain events and conditions, and so forth. On top of that are the

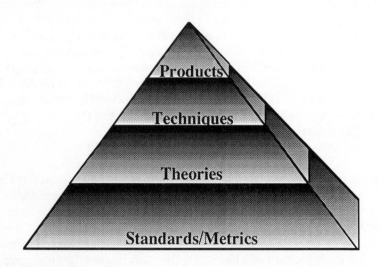

Figure 1.13 Technology Pyramid

techniques used to build a product from that technology. These are the operations, methodologies, practices, processes, or expressions that translate the theory into practicable use. Finally, at the apex of the pyramid is the product itself borne from the technology. Figure 1.14 illustrates the pyramid for a radar technology. Notice that there is nothing implied about timing or precedence of one stage in relationship to another. In other words, one may develop a product using a certain technology without necessarily having defined the techniques used or developed well-understood theories about it either. The ability to articulate each level and encompass it within a (large) body of recognized and agreed-upon knowledge simply shows the maturation level of the technology.

The same can be done for computing technology as well, as shown in Figures 1.15 and 1.16. Notice that for the hardware/firmware technology pyramid, there are gaps or weaknesses that appear toward its base. The reason is that the underlying theory of computing is not fully articulated, nor are there common, accepted standards available which all hardware/firmware designers can use to communicate. The latter is coming, with the push for open systems, albeit slowly. On the software side, things are even worse. There are some generally accepted theories of software development, but they are few in number, and the last real theoretical additions were made in the early 1970s. There are even fewer agreed-upon standards. In other words, the base of the pyramid, at the present time, is very weak. The software pyramid can easily collapse and is basically supported by a craft technology, not an engineering discipline.

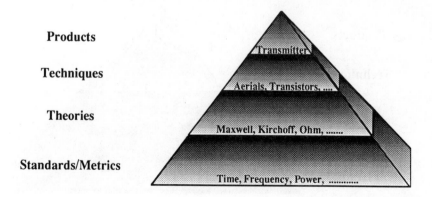

Products

Techniques

Theories

Standards/Metrics

Figure 1.14 Technology Pyramid for Radar

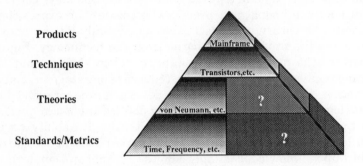

Figure 1.15 Hardware/Firmware Technology Pyramid

As one can see, these two examples show why there is some uncertainty, and therefore risk, in software development. The lack of good theoretical and standard foundations exacerbate the flow of errors exhibited in Figure 1.12. This in turn leads to underestimations in the development time and expenditure required for a software project, the pressures of which lead one to look for solutions to the perceived resultant high costs and delays. Unfortunately, if one is not careful, one will search for solutions that are not there. This brings us to our third example of the poor state of current software development.

According to Fernand Braudel in his fascinating book, *Les Structures du Quotidien: Le Possible et L'impossible,* a vital ingredient for any

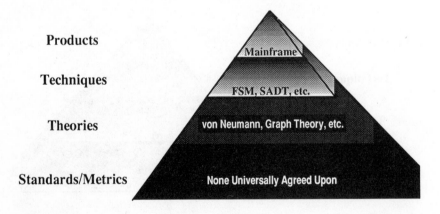

Figure 1.16 Current Software Technology Pyramid

technology is a societal need for it.[53] This, he says, was summed up succinctly by Henri Pirenne when he wrote, "America [when the Vikings reached it] was lost as soon as it was discovered, because Europe did not need it yet." Technology, Braudel writes, can represent the possible, which for a variety of reasons—economic, social, or psychological—society is not yet capable of fully utilizing, and at other times, it represents the ceiling which materially and technically obstructs its efforts. There is a time, however, when the ceiling can no longer hold back the pressure, and a technological breakthrough occurs. The seeming simultaneous invention of a new technology, called *Zeitgeist*, is often a visible effect of this pressure. But the force which overcomes the obstruction is never the simple internal development of technology. In other words, the existence of a technology by itself does not ensure a market. This has been shown many times, as illustrated by the predictions of flying cars, videophones, and 1000-seat airplanes.[54] Each of these items are technologically possible, but there is no current market for them. Only in the area of computers were the predictions of growth tremendously understated. For example, RCA in 1966 forecasted that only 150,000 computers of all types would be in use worldwide by 1985, whereas in reality the figure was somewhere closer to 30 million.

In society, and within business, computing technology has been embraced in a very important way. Businesses are literally dependant on computer systems running their information systems. In a survey by the *Wall Street Journal*, 65% of the firms interviewed reported that they are heavily dependant on their computers to conduct their business, while 20% reported they are *completely* dependant.[55] Many businesses would fold without them, and some fold because of them. Consider, for instance, an interesting study by the Chubb Insurance Group, which calculated that many organizations' operations would be halved within 5 days of a major computer disaster. Furthermore, 90% of companies hit by such a disaster go out of business within 18 months.[56]

Cost overruns, schedule delays, and poor quality information systems are important today because information technology has been embraced by business. Fifteen years ago these problems were not of such major concern because the dependance was not as great. Today these issues are a major headache, and tomorrow they will become deadly. Furthermore, it is important to understand that because business has embraced computing, the risks in their development are being impacted more and more by business decisions, not technical or fiscal ones.

Again, 15 years ago computing departments were in a cloistered environment within large corporations. Users were separated from the developers, and only provided requests for the types of reports that were desired. They did not operate the computers in any way, shape, or fashion. Users were for the most part computer illiterate. In fact, there was a special term for it that one doesn't hear too often anymore: *the closed shop*.[57] Now users, because of the explosion in personal computers and local area networks, have the skill and understanding to create the reports themselves and control the operation of the machine producing the reports.

As computing and information systems have become more of an integral part of the business environment, there has been a shift away from thinking of computing as something divorced from business. The business perception of computing has changed dramatically. Companies see the information system part of their budget as the fastest growing aspect of their business expenditures, which means it gets into senior managers' meeting agendas. There is a better understanding of what information systems can do to help meet the company's objectives (although there is less understanding of what they can do to obstruct them). There is also a growing realization that managing the use of information technology is a mandatory business activity, not just a technical support one. It is often the case that the technical management is divorced from the company and third parties manage it.[58] This new-found understanding has been termed *IT Perestroika*.[59]

The implications for information systems development are profound. One must be concerned not only with how technically sound the engineering of the system is, but also take into account its business aspects. This is the way it always has been in reality, but both the computing technologist and the business person have conveniently left the other out in their thinking. This means that to do software engineering risk analysis and management properly, one must begin with the risks found in the business environment. These are reflected in the undercapitalization aspects of risk we encountered earlier. Further, to apply information systems effectively, the business person must understand the risks and limitations of its underlying technology. These are likewise reflected in the underperformance aspects of risk we encountered earlier. Comprehending how risks from these two levels of problem abstraction inexorably merge and affect one another, from a top-down and a bottom-up perspective, as shown in Figure 1.17, is vital. Moreover, these principles do not change whether one is trying to acquire, use, develop, or sell information technology. Risks are generated not only in the development cycle itself, but originate in the business use of the information. Solving one, without consideration for the other, will

Business Problems & Needs

Market Sector Risks

Competition Risks

Organizational Structure Risks

Impacts
&
Constraints

:
:
:

Impacts
&
Constraints

Programming Language Risks

Database Risks

Decentralized Computing Risks

Information Technology Solutions

Figure 1.17 Flow of Risks

only continue to lead to cost overruns, delays, and poor quality systems. Identifying these risks, and how to balance and contain them, is what the remainder of this book is all about.

1.5 We Have Identified the Enemy, and He Is Us

Pogo's saying is rather apropos to those of us in the computing industry. We are faced with a number of challenges in developing software systems today, some not of our own making, but many which indeed are. For example, we have this peculiar difficulty in dealing with the rapidly evolving computing technologies in which we are immersed. The new technology, if you believe the marketing specialists, seems to make deployed systems almost obsolete upon delivery. This disregards the fact that most of the systems developed are not effective, nor do they meet the original requirements or allow us to build systems even defined 20 years ago any faster, cheaper, or better.

Then there is the susceptibility of those requesting software systems to the *technology imperative*. We are easily seduced by new technology in this business. It's like getting a digital watch, and becoming enamored with the fact that it has the latest electronic chip, is accurate to .001 seconds, can tell time for 100 cities around the world, etc., and forgetting that all you want it for is to tell you when it's lunchtime. Because new technology is always just "over the horizon," the demand for the technology to be included in the system development is often that which is the latest, the most untried, and therefore the most expensive. This also forces a system's architecture to change from the bottom-up, as we try simultaneously to build it from the top-down.[60] The unevenness of the industry, where new hardware is introduced and applied, but where the software impact is unknown, exacerbates the problem. And we wonder why a system costs so much!?!

Next, there is our inability to deal effectively with the essence of software, especially with its complexity. Because software is easy to create and alter, it is seen as a simple, and easy, way to accommodate change. Frequently, too much is asked from our software systems. Systems are continually pushing the edges of the envelope. In 1968, the software crisis could be characterized by the fact that computer hardware changes were occurring so quickly that the software could not keep up. In the 1990s, especially with open systems becoming more of a reality, the demand for computer software to possess new capabilities is occurring so quickly that the hardware cannot keep up. To paraphrase Einstein, software may be simple to change, but it is not necessarily easy to make the resulting system work.

And then there is our unwillingness to recognize the fact that software is, and ought to be, much more expensive than hardware, and one ought to be willing to pay that increased price. As long as software systems continue to be custom built, they will continue to be labor intensive. This unwillingness to recognize the true cost of software leads to undercapitalization of the resources required, which in turn leads to a high probability of failure.

Finally, there is the complication that our previous experience does not always help in coping with the rapidity of change seen in the information technology arena. Russ Ackoff writes,

> Increases in the rate of change of technology have decreased the effectiveness of experience as a teacher. It is too slow. Trial and error require more time than is currently available between changes that require a response. The lag between stimulus and response brought about by reliance on experience permits crises to develop to a point where we are forced to respond to them with very little relevant knowledge. An increasing portion of society's responses are made out of desperation, not out of deliberation.[61]

It is not only society in general that is making responses out of desperation, but businesses as well, especially those acting as providers or users of information technology. As we will see in Chapter 7, we will need to change our view of information technology use and its development to better cope with this rapidity of change. Processes which we developed in the 1960s and 1970s to deal with software developments are obsolete, as the situations faced then are no longer applicable.

All these come together to form a rather tightly coupled problem, resembling a fishing reel that has its line all knotted and tangled together. And, of course, when one is close to straightening things out, there is always something else around the corner to make life just a bit more difficult. As an example, people come up with plenty of reasons for not doing software engineering risk analysis and management. These include that they are impractical, too expensive, inefficient, unworkable, disruptive of current procedures, prejudiced against one side of a dispute, too radical, or unappealing to others. Another reason for disregarding a risk analysis is that it is also unappealing to the one conducting it, especially if it results in bad news. The Air Force, for instance, disregarded its own risk analysis to award a $260 million contract to a company with a technically inferior bid when three other offerers bid, some with technically superior submissions, over $400 million. This occurred even though its own risk analysis showed a 90% probability that it would cost at least $415 million, and the internal Air Force estimate was scoped out at $498 million![62] This cavalier attitude extends across international boundaries as well. The British Royal Navy spent £30 million on a computer system for a new Navy frigate, then scrapped it because it didn't work, and then announced that it would be placing a contract worth £2.5 million with the company responsible to work on a replacement system.[63] Pogo was right: We are sometimes our own worst enemies.

Developing software systems is difficult enough without these added burdens. The outcome of not being able to adequately govern these challenges often means that decision management whiplash occurs. Decision management whiplash, as you may recall, results when a software project is proceeding poorly and management attempts to "correct" it. Since the initial project was behind the power curve from the beginning, decisions to fix things exacerbate the problems even more. Like a microphone getting negative feedback, management makes more and more decisions until the project grinds to a halt. This forces one into the position of dealing with the effects of *budget whiplash*; since more resources and effort are being spent on this project, it takes away resources available for others. This causes them to be undercapitalized, and the whiplash process begins anew.

The implications of this are clear from an expenditure point of view, but not from a cost point of view. The expenditures, or out of pocket expenses, can be calculated when a software project fails. However, the true cost of the failure is harder to calculate. Cost includes the value of the opportunities lost because the system was not operational in time, was of such poor quality that your customers left, cost so much that it robbed you of the resources and capital required to expand or just hold onto your market. These lost opportunities are not recoverable, because they are time sensitive. Although most things can be replaced, time is not one of them. As business becomes dependant on software-driven information systems, and the market place becomes truly global with greater numbers of competitors competing for the same slice of the market, the cost of a failed system may not be affordable. Figure 1.18 depicts the deadly effects a poorly constructed information system can have on a business because of software failures. These range from mere annoyances to life-threatening situations.

One recent example of the disruption a software error can cause was the partial paralyzation of AT&T's telephone network.[64] Some faulty software in a 4ESS switching device in lower Manhattan started a chain reaction which blocked long distance, international, and 1-800 calls for

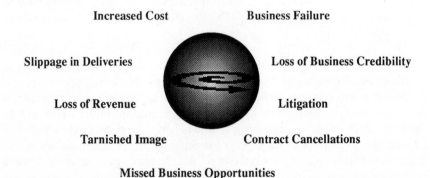

Increased Cost		Business Failure
Slippage in Deliveries		Loss of Business Credibility
Loss of Revenue		Litigation
Tarnished Image		Contract Cancellations
	Missed Business Opportunities	

Figure 1.18 Potential Effects of Not Performing Risk Engineering

nine hours, preventing millions of calls from getting through. Volume of the network was reduced to half of normal. The cost to AT&T's clients ranged to the tens of millions of dollars. However, AT&T's costs are much more than monetary: Its reputation has been damaged as a reliable carrier of information. Now it must worry about and spend a tremendous amount of time and resources in damage control to stem a wave of possibly new defections of customers. AT&T had recently been able to slow the loss of market share to competitors MCI and Sprint through massive ad campaigns and lowering the price of telephone calls, but this single event may waste much of that effort. As one can see from the AT&T example, an individual company is culpable for each direct software failure, and at the end of the day, they will pay, either through regulation or market pressure—customers will spend their money elsewhere.

1.6 Summary

Anyone who has ever been mountain climbing during the winter season knows about risk. It is a subject that is always present in your mind, especially as you are about two thirds of the way up the mountain and the weather starts to turn bad. It is then, as you dig out your heavy weather gear, pull your crampon straps tighter, and readjust your grip on the ice ax, that you ask yourself what the devil made you decide to climb *that* peak *that* day. You also give thanks to the climbing team leader for being insistent about carrying all the heavy, extra gear you have been cursing about lugging around all day. In climbing, one stays away from foolhardy risks, especially if there is no need to undertake them. The penalties for taking such risks are usually swift and severe. Acceptable risks are taken, such as climbing the bloody mountain in the first place, but one tries to be as prepared as possible under the circumstances of the weather, difficulty of the climb, and experience of the climbing team. It is a well-known fact that more people are killed in England during hill walking than while climbing the rugged peaks in Scotland. As the saying goes, there are old climbers, and there are bold climbers, but there are very few old, bold climbers.

In business, as in climbing, there is nothing wrong with taking risks. Taking unwise risks, or ignoring them, is foolish. If one cannot afford what the possible acceptance of the risk may bring, then one better think about doing something else. Corporate raiders, for example, are real optimists in this regard. Their underlying faith is based upon the foundation that underperformance and undercapitalization of a business they are buying can be corrected.

Everything in life involves risk, and one must be careful not to create risk by worrying overly about risk. Otherwise, one could live in constant fear of doing something wrong. As we will see in Chapter 6, the psychology of risk taking is as important to understanding risk as are the formal methods for evaluating it. Risk analysis and management will not guarantee success, but *not* performing them will go a long way towards guaranteeing failure. It is best to remember that one cannot control risk, but one can certainly control one's response to it, like insisting upon satisfying specific requirements but providing no additional resources.

For the remainder of this book, we will be exploring how one controls one's response to the risks that are anticipated or encountered in developing and using software systems. But to do so, one must understand that software risks can be found, created, and exacerbated at any point in the development life cycle, starting from the initial business decision made to acquire or develop a software system, through the systems engineering of it, down to the software engineering methodology that is used in its design. The process also acts in reverse.

All too often, we in the software engineering field have ignored the impacts of our technical decisions on the health of businesses for which we work or the customers who use our systems. Computing cannot be, and should not be, done for the sake of computing, nor should it be technology, rather than market, driven.[65] One cannot ever forget it is the customer's needs that are supreme, as they pay the salary. Thus, to be truly effective, software engineering risk analysis and management must go beyond merely the technically oriented aspects of developing systems. It must encompass the totality of the business-oriented aspects as well. One cannot possibly answer questions such as "What are the risks of making changes today vice the benefits of change, i.e. what are my future risks?" without enlarging one's field of vision to encompass this greater vista.

For instance, cost per se is not a risk, especially if it has been budgeted for. Meet the budget, then no risk exists.[66] Being *over* the expected cost is a risk, however, as resources that were not in the budget now have to be spent in an unplanned way. As a result, opportunities are likely to be missed by not having resources to pursue them. Opportunity losses steal the future away, not only from the system development, which may not be able to add new functionality, but more importantly from the business the system was meant to serve. Moreover, if the loss was not felt by the business, then the system was not truly needed.

Viewing information technology or software engineering as part of the business environment and using risk as a common vocabulary to link them allows for the benefits of a different perspective to be gained. Instead of debating the technical merits of a new programming language like Ada, or a new CASE tool, one can ask more relevant questions such as, does this tool help reduce my business risk? Does it reduce the exposure to risk of my near-term or far-term capital investments? Will it increase the quality or reliability of my information systems? Will it lower my capital expenditures for evolving systems? As it has been put, information technology is now too important to a business's competitive position to be left in the hands of the computer specialists alone, as they do not have a deep enough understanding of where the business is going.[67,68] To continue to do so will guarantee that a business's future is in trouble.

For the most part, risks confronted in developing and applying information technology are business problems, rather than technical problems. They are seen as poor management, planning, and financial administration, or not knowing what type or why one wanted to have an information system in the first place. The lack of comprehension of this fundamental idea used to amaze me, but there has been so much effort spent, deliberate and not, to make computing incomprehensible that it probably is understandable. This is why I am amused when companies spend a tremendous amount of money on acquiring computer-aided software engineering (CASE) products to try to improve their underperformance problem, when the real issue and risk is the lack of sufficient initial project capitalization. One needs to balance capitalization and performance before a project or program starts, and this requires the balancing of a company's objectives, strategies, tactics and means. This calls for refocusing on how decisions are made within an organization, and gaining a true perspective on its capabilities.

To avoid mismatches and to get that balance right means that the top corporate leadership has to understand all the risks and opportunities affecting their companies. The first thing that must be accomplished is to get a business to realize that it needs to manage via information, not manage information. Information technology is the servant, not the master. It isn't necessary to have information systems try to do everything in a company. This often means that the balance struck is not *aurea mediocritas* (the golden mean or happy medium), but instead is a *modus vivendi* (a working arrangement in a situation where the two parties are at odds with one another). I believe that a proper balance can be achieved, but I am not so sure that many companies are even aware they should try to accomplish it. For example, the London *Times* in 1987 reported that more than 43% of all British chief executives either did not have a corporate strategy or were not involved with the development if there was one.[69] I am sure that U.S. corporations are not much better.

The longer the risks remain unrecognized, uncontrolled and unconstrained, the more the chances will diminish of developing a successful software system. Even if all the risks are recognized, and by fortuitous planning we have a match between our business strategy and information technology requirements, we will still need to do risk engineering to ensure that the risks that are present (and there will be *some*) are contained and do not overwhelm the implementation. As we will see, not all risks can or should be avoided, but they all should be assessed, and explicit controls should be applied in proportion to each risk identified. Ultimately, risk engineering can only be based upon context, decisions, decision processes, and their interfaces to other decision processes for any project existing within a model of a business enterprise.

Where are we going to journey to from here? Chapter 2 provides a systemic examination of risk engineering as it applies to the systems engineering and business domains. This will help us identify the sources of risk which originate outside of, and are carried into, the software engineering enterprise. Chapter 3 then examines the software engineering risks that may exist in the software engineering process itself; i.e., the process models, methods and automation applied throughout the software enterprise. Chapter 4 investigates the product risks; i.e., the software engineering risks associated with the development of different types of computer applications. Chapter 5 investigates the risks associated with software safety, security, and operational/disaster recovery issues. Chapter 6 examines risk taking as it applies to individuals and describes a risk management organization. And finally, Chapter 7 provides a step-by-step review of the major issues of the book and a forecast of future risk issues.

At the beginning of this chapter we started out with the story of William of Ockham, and it is probably the best place to end as well. We know for certain that the current paradigms for software development are not working well, and that the current fads in software engineering are not providing the solutions either. It is time that software engineers and developers heed the words of Francis Bacon: "He that will not apply new remedies must expect new evils; for time is the great innovator." We ignore this advice at our own peril.

By merging the business view with the software engineering view we can cultivate an atmosphere of business-tolerant software engineering; i.e., the reduction in the amount of distortion between what is wanted (or required) by the business and what one has to do in software engineering to achieve it. What is really required is a Grand Unification Theory of computing in the spirit of Ockham, which can fuse the different competing perspectives and technologies together into a simple, yet elegant approach so we can finally build successful software systems. As Saint-Exupéry wrote, "Perfection (will be) reached, not when there is no longer anything to add, but when there is no longer anything to take away." By the end of this book, I hope the reader will better understatnd how we can start on the long journey necessary to achieve this goal.

Questions

1 Explain William of Ockham's idea of parsimony. What are its implications concerning current software engineering theory and practice? Is it compatible or in conflict with them?

2 Define the term "underperformance of resources." How is it similar to low productivity? How is it different?

3 Define the term "undercapitalization of resources." List at least five ways one can avoid undercapitalization of resources in a software engineering development, and indicate who is responsible for: (a) granting, (b) obtaining, and (c) using the resources. Where do the responsible parties reside in the organization?

4 Benjamin Franklin identified the problems of undercapitalization and underperformance in verse 200 hundred years ago. He penned,

> For want of a nail the shoe was lost-
> For want of a shoe the horse was lost-
> For want of a horse the rider was lost-
> For want of a rider the battle was lost.

Explain the implications of Franklin's verse to software development.

5 Examine Tables 1.1 and 1.2. How does one decide which type of estimate, i.e., average, optimistic, and highly optimistic, to use? Figure 1.1 illustrates estimation "dead zones," i.e., areas where given past experience, a software project of those sizes has never been completed with the indicated resources. How else can one avoid underestimating the time and budget required? What are the risks if one does underestimate? What are some of the causes of underestimation?

6 What is the definition of risk? What are its constituent parts? How does the statement "the probability of project failure is 60%" relate to the concept of risk?

7 Why is risk subjective? To what degree can risk ever be measured in an objective fashion? Justify your answer.

8 What is risk analysis? How does it differ from risk management? What are the benefits of risk analysis and management? What are the limits of risk analysis? How does one evaluate the biases of the persons, or techniques, involved in making a risk estimation? What are the steps involved in risk control? Risk monitoring? (*Hint*: Review the Appendix.)

9 What are some of the sources of software development risk? Categorize the risks you described in some fashion. Which are directly controllable, which are not? Which risks are known at the start of the project, and which are not?

10 Review Figure 1.12. What are the implications to the software engineering process, especially its automation? Will applying automation, such as CASE technology, reduce the errors inherent in the process? Which errors and/or risks will it not help reduce?

11 Examine the technology pyramid in Figure 1.13. Using CASE technology as a basis, fill in the pyramid to your best knowledge.

12 Why should one use risk analysis? When should it be applied? When is it not useful? Whose responsibility is it to conduct it?

13 Where do the majority of software development risks originate? In the software development itself? Or in the systems engineering process? Or in the business decision making process? How can you be sure?

14 Reduction of uncertainty alone does not reduce a risk. Only if the increase in certainty can be used for direct action, such as gaining control, is it useful. Explain.

15 Thomas Edison laid down six rules for invention: define the need for the innovation; set yourself a clear goal and stick to it; analyze the major stages through which the invention must pass before it is complete, and follow them; make available at all times data on the progress of work; ensure that each member of the team has a clearly defined area of responsibility; record everything for later examination. Compare these six rules to the process of risk engineering.

16 British Rail recently postponed plans to introduce a network of 90-mph Class 158 express trains because the new trains cannot be built in time. They are already 42 weeks late, and it is costing BR £20 million in lost fares and extra costs to maintain the existing trains. The existing trains are currently 10 years past their intended operational life. Explain some of the possible opportunity losses caused by this delay, and by the original decision not to replace the trains 10 years earlier.

17 A government decision maker once was quoted in the late 1970s as saying, "You software guys are too much like the weavers in the story about the Emperor and his clothiers. When I go out to check on a software development, the answers I get sound like, 'We're fantastically busy weaving this magic cloth. Just wait awhile and it'll look terrific.' But there is nothing I can see or touch, no numbers I can relate to, no way to pick up signals that things aren't really that great. And there are too many people I know who have come out at the end wearing a bunch of expensive rags or nothing at all." Do you think this is still a fair assessment of the software industry as it stands today?

References

1. Robert Wright, *Three Scientists and Their Gods*, Times Books, New York, 1988.

2. "William of Ockham," *Macropaedia*, Encyclopaedia Britannica, Inc., Vol. 13, Chicago, IL, 1980.

3. One may sometimes feel that problems in the software field are exaggerated. However, the historical record is filled with examples of horrendously poor software developments, and very few good ones. One would not lose very much money betting against a new project ever being able to meet its initial requirements. The record can

be reviewed in Robert N. Charette, *Software Engineering Risk Analysis and Management*, McGraw-Hill, Inc., New York, 1989, and Robert N. Charette, *Software Engineering Environments: Concepts and Technology*, McGraw-Hill, Inc., New York, 1986.

4. "Washington Roundup," *Aviation Week and Space Technology*, McGraw-Hill, Inc., 6 February, 1989.

5. Howard Yudkin, speech given to National Security Industrial Association Conference on "Software Initiatives and Their Impact on the Competitive Edge," 10 May, 1988. Dr. Yudkin recently passed away, and his insightful commentary on the computing industry will be sorely missed.

6. Jeffrey Rothfeder, "It's Late, It's Costly, Incompetent—But Try Firing a Computer System," *Business Week*, 7 November, 1988.

7. Although technically, computing is defined as mechanized symbol manipulation, I will use the terms information system, computing, software system, software project, and so forth, interchangeably. Further, I no longer feel any necessity to distinguish between computing and telecommunications, which are technically different kinds of information processing technologies, but which have merged in practice. In its truest sense, a company's information system includes both automated and nonautomated systems, such as simple Rolodexes. Understanding this will become important later in Chapter 2, where we will see that a company's information in total is considered an asset, and how well it is utilized impacts whether a competitive edge can be attained. How this can be achieved by programming computers (i.e., human symbol manipulation) we will see in Chapter 3.

8. Niall Ferguson, "The Arms Race Against Rocketing Costs," *The Sunday Times*, 24 April, 1988.

9. See Chapter One in Robert N. Charette, *Software Engineering Risk Analysis and Management*, McGraw-Hill, Inc., New York, 1989.

10. Kenneth R. MacCrimmon and Donald A. Wehrung, *Taking Risks*, Free Press, New York, 1986. The lack of time is considered the primary reason for software failure. Going back to our thought problem, ten years ago it is likely that the amount of time to produce a 70,000 line of code section would have been estimated as only 25–45% of what was truly required. With software engineering productivity increasing at only 4% compounded per year over the past decade, one can see why I am confident that even today one couldn't build a software system of ten years ago.

11. Consider this parable: You wish to make a tunnel through a mountain. So, you hire two teams to begin working from opposite sides. When they meet the tunnel is done. If they don't, you have two tunnels. Either way you double your productivity.
    Real productivity must include cost considerations as well. As Edsger Dijkstra has said, one should not regard lines of code used in a system as "lines produced," but as "lines spent." Further, true productivity in software developments comes when you can reduce the rate of your hiring, or increase your "tooth-to-tail" ratio. Overhead will then go down, and profit likewise will go up. However, one must be also aware, as Byran Kocher, president of the ACM has stated, of a hidden cost. Although computer systems may be able to replicate the tasks of the people they replace, they infrequently have any of the "common sense" of the people replaced.

12. Michael Farmer, "Pumping Profit," *Management Today*, June 1989. Not all definitions of software productivity focus only on the software development process. For instance, Tarek Abel-Hamid and Stuart Madnick in their paper, "Lessons Learned from Modeling the Dynamics of Software Development," in the *Communications of the ACM*, Vol. 32, No. 12, December 1989, define actual software productivity as potential productivity minus the losses due to faulty processes. Potential productivity is defined as the maximum productivity that can occur when an individual or group makes the best possible use of resources, and is a function of two sets of factors: the nature of the task and the group resources. Losses are due to low morale or high communication/coordination overheads. This definition relates underperformance with productivity in a more meaningful way with the general business environment than those typically used in the computing industry which concentrate on items such as lines of code developed.

13. It is similar to an individual facing the effects of inflation and recession. One can deal with the effects of inflation if one has a job, but it is very difficult if one is out of work.

14. In an October 23, 1989, news item in *U.S. News and World Report*, across all businesses, regardless of their maturity, the reasons for failure in 1988 were as followed: insufficient profits (22.2%), poor growth (19.8%), too much debt (14.7%), inexperience (12.0%), heavy operating expenses (11.7%), industry weakness (10.5%), other economic factors, such as high interest rates, poor location, competition (5.3%), neglect (2.0%), fraud (0.9%), and poor planning (0.9%).

15. Often the development schedules are sheer nonsenses. On more than one occasion I have encountered "drop-dead dates," dates which the organization wanting the system had to have it or else their project would come to a stop. After many crises, the development was redefined and delivered on time. When the system appeared on time (or sometimes late), nothing happened. The requesting organization hadn't said they were also late and could not make use of the system anyway. In general, one should regard schedules and costs only as guidelines, not rules. This makes their inherent uncertainty explicit.

    Also, beware of the people controlling the purse strings of a project who act like the farmer who, in order to save money, stopped feeding his horse. The strategy worked fine, until the day the horse died.

16. The software estimation models used are called, respectively, the Putnam and COCOMO models. This example is based upon the article by Ware Myers, "Allow Plenty of Time for Large-Scale Software," in *IEEE Software*, July 1989. One needs to treat cost and schedule estimation models with skepticism. They are frequently based upon incomplete, obsolescent, or inaccurate data, and do not consider certain items such as the cost of adding safety features to a program or the amount of scaffolding software that is required. As an example, the most common metric used in cost estimation is lines of code developed per programmer at some cost. It is not extraordinary to read reports of code costing only $15 per line to develop, and that the programmers produced 5000 lines of code per month (industry averages are two to three times the cost, and one-half to one-third the productivity). What often is not revealed is that the programmers worked an average of 60 hours per week, 20 of which was uncompensated overtime. Using the $15 per line and a 40-hour work week as cost bases will blow the budget big time. Further, what also is not usually reported is whether the system developed actually worked.

The databases used to develop cost estimate models usually are not large enough to be considered statistically complete, nor are the biases taken out, to be of much use other than gross estimations. As an indication, most models are skewed to underestimate costs, rather than overestimate them. To be fair, most models do have warnings stating their level of (in)accuracy, but most people chose to ignore them.

For further information on the two software estimation models, refer to Robert N. Charette, *Software Engineering Risk Analysis and Management*, McGraw-Hill, Inc., New York, 1989; Barry Boehm, *Tutorial: Software Risk Management*, IEEE Computer Society Press, Washington, D.C., 1989; Barry Boehm and Philip Papaccio, "Understanding and Controlling Software Costs," *IEEE Transactions on Software Engineering*, Vol. SE-14, No. 10, October 1988; Barry Boehm, *Software Engineering Economics*, Prentice-Hall, Inc., Englewood Cliffs, NJ, 1981, and; L. Putnam, "A General Empirical Solutions to the Macro Software Sizing and Estimating Problem," *IEEE Transactions on Software Engineering*, Vol. SE-4, No. 4, July 1978. It might also be useful to review L. A. Laranjeira, "Software Size Estimation of Object-Oriented Systems," *IEEE Transactions on Software Engineering*, Vol. SE-16, No. 5, May 1990, which attempts to reduce one of the uncertainty parameters involved in cost estimation.

17. Fred Brooks, *The Mythical Man-Month*, Addison-Wesley Publishing Co., Reading, MA, 1975. Fred Brooks noted the undercapitalization of time in software developments 15 years ago, and still no one pays any heed!!!

18. Ware Myers, "Allow Plenty of Time for Large-Scale Software," *IEEE Software*, July 1989. As we will see in Chapter 6, expectations of the development's sponsors, managers, system engineers, software engineers, etc., however, tend to override this fact. These expectations make it natural for one to be optimistic rather than pessimistic at the start of a project. This occurs because: (a) people want to succeed, (b) people have too much invested in a project to opt for its cancellation, regardless of how hopeless it appears, and (c) one does not often get promoted by possessing an "attitude problem," i.e., "negative." These, of course, increase the probability that the estimates will be on the "aggressive" side.

19. "Harold Simmons Is Playing a Crafty War Game," *Business Week*, 12 March, 1990. Lockheed saw its earnings drop *99%* from $624 million in 1988 to $2 million in 1989, even though it had revenues of $9.9 billion.

20. Peter Morris and George Hough, *The Anatomy of Major Projects*, John Wiley & Sons, Chichester, England, 1987. We acknowledge that the quoted figure can be argued against. The comparison failure rate is an estimate made from data contained in various reports on all types of projects' success and failure rates surveyed by the Major Projects Association (MPA) located at Templeton College, Oxford, England. The MPA specifically examines why major projects, such as tunnels, bridges, etc., succeed or fail.

Overall, across all industries, success rates for different projects are reported to range usually between 40% and 60%. Software and information technology projects, on the other hand, typically show a 12% to 20% success rate. In both software- and non–software-related projects in specific domains, much higher and much lower success patterns have also been reported.

Regardless of whether the estimate is accurate, few would argue that software projects tend to succeed at rates equal to, or higher than, nonsoftware projects. What would be useful to the computing industry is a very accurate accounting of project success and failure.

21. The following two sections are derived from Chapter 2 of Robert N. Charette, *Software Engineering Risk Analysis and Management*, McGraw-Hill, Inc., New York, 1989.

22. Kenneth R. MacCrimmon and Donald A. Wehrung, *Taking Risks*, Free Press, New York, 1986.

23. Peter G. Moore, *The Business of Risk*, University Press, Cambridge, England, 1983.

24. Neil Crockford, *An Introduction to Risk Management*, Woodhead-Faulkner Ltd., Cambridge, England, 1980.

25. Kenneth R. MacCrimmon and Donald A. Wehrung, *Taking Risks*, Free Press, New York, 1986.

26. William D. Rowe, *An Anatomy of Risk*, Robert E. Krieger Publishing Co., Malabar, FL, 1988.

27. Walter B. Wentz and Gerald I. Eyrich, *Marketing, Theory and Application*, Harcourt, Brace & World, Inc., New York, 1970.

28. William D. Rowe, *An Anatomy of Risk*, Robert E. Krieger Publishing Co., Malabar, FL, 1988. Uncertainty is really a measure of the limits of information of a particular knowledge area. One must be concerned with a number of elements of uncertainty in risk analysis, such as tolerance (a measure of the relevance of the information available), statistical confidence (a measure of the accuracy of the sampling), incompleteness/inaccuracy of the information, and ambiguity of the problem domain.

29. Andrew P. Sage, "Systems Engineering: Fundamental Limits and Future Prospects," *Proceedings of the IEEE*, Vol. 69, No.2, February 1981.

30. Walter B. Wentz and Gerald I. Eyrich, *Marketing, Theory and Application*, Harcourt, Brace & World, Inc., New York, 1970.

31. For the moment ignore the work being done in catastrophe and chaotic theories which might contest this view. These will be revisited in later chapters.

32. John Canada, *Intermediate Economic Analysis for Management and Engineering*, Prentice-Hall, Inc., Englewood Cliffs, NJ, 1971.

33. Nicholas Rescher, *Risk*, University Press of America, Lanham, MD, 1983.

34. Rational decision makers are related to the idea of the "Economic Man" of W. Edwards as described in the *Psychological Bulletin* article, "The Theory of Decision Making," Vol. 51, July 1954. Economic man is an idealized person who knows no uncertainty. An economic man has the following attributes:

    1. Economic man is completely informed. In other words, he knows all courses of action open to him, and also knows which state will occur and what the outcome of each will be.
    2. Economic man is infinitely sensitive. In other words, he is capable of distinguishing among alternatives which may have only infinitesimally small differences between them.
    3. Economic man is rational. In other words, he possesses consistent preferences for the outcomes of selected courses of action, and he chooses the best alternatives available to him.

35. Kenneth R. MacCrimmon and Donald A. Wehrung, *Taking Risks*, Free Press, New York, 1986.

36. William D. Rowe, *An Anatomy of Risk*, Robert E. Krieger Publishing Co., Malabar, FL, 1988. This will form our basic operational definition. We also accept with this definition the ideas, as stated by Rowe, that "the assessment of risk is as important as the quantification of risk; and second, that the subjective perception of risk is the basis for risk acceptance regardless of the objective or quantified evaluation."
   Furthermore, we distinguish a risk from what is sometimes called a hazard, which is an intrinsic property or condition that has the potential to cause an accident. Hazards will be studied more in detail in the chapter on software safety. It is useful to remember too that consequences are the immediate results of an occurrence, while losses define the results of the consequence. Cost places a value on these losses.

37. It should be noted that different authors use different terms or invert risk analysis with risk estimation (some call that risk assessment), although in all texts the basic concepts of identifying, analyzing, evaluation and controlling risks are used throughout. Ours follows generally those stated in Rowe for risk analysis and Boehm for risk control, although we have made some necessary modifications. The important point is that risk engineering has *two* specific and interrelated phases.

38. "Post-Challenger Evaluation of Space Shuttle Risk Assessment and Management," National Academy Press, January 1988.

39. William D. Rowe, *An Anatomy of Risk*, Robert E. Krieger Publishing Co., Malabar, FL, 1988.

40. Neil Crockford, *An Introduction to Risk Management*, Woodhead-Faulkner Ltd., Cambridge, England, 1980.

41. Robert N. Charette, *Software Engineering Risk Analysis and Management*, McGraw-Hill, Inc., New York, 1989.

42. For instance, in an oil development project, there are three distinct phases with different measures of success. The first is the exploration stage, which has as a success criteria finding enough oil to justify development. The next phase is development, which has as its success criteria developing the field in the most economic manner. And finally, there is the production phase, which must maximize daily production and optimize total oil field recovery. A related topic is when a project is rated as a failure at the beginning, because it did not meet its original objectives, but it turned out to produce unexpected beneficial side effects. Airline computer reservation systems are prime examples of these. The airlines never would have been able to cost justify them if they knew what the final costs were to end up being, given their *original* objectives. All of them were over cost and late. However, they now are being used in different ways then originally envisioned, and are the most profitable parts of many airlines. Other examples of projects whose success criteria was not known for a long time were the Maginot line, the Apollo program, and the Aswan Dam. For more information on success criteria for projects, see Peter Morris and George Hough, *The Anatomy of Major Projects*, John Wiley & Sons, Chichester, England, 1987.

43. William D. Rowe, *An Anatomy of Risk*, Robert E. Krieger Publishing Co., Malabar, FL, 1988.

44. Neil Crockford, *An Introduction to Risk Management*, Woodhead-Faulkner Ltd., Cambridge, England, 1980.

45. Some preliminary work in forensic software engineering is being conducted at a few places, such as in the United States, such as at the U.S. Air Force Rome Air Development Center and NASA's Goddard Space Flight Center. See, for instance, the articles by Joseph Cavano and Frank Lamonica, "Quality Assurance in Future Development Methods," *IEEE Software*, September 1987; by David Card et al., "Evaluating Software Engineering Technologies," *IEEE Transactions on Software Engineering*, Vol. SW-13, No. 7, July 1987, and Victor Basili et al., "Experimentation in Software Engineering," *IEEE Transactions on Software Engineering*, Vol. SW-12, No. 7, July 1986. Also review the special issue of *IEEE Software*, March 1990, which is devoted to software metrics.

    The Japanese, however, have been much more in the forefront of this discipline. Companies such as Hitachi and Toshiba have been gathering forensic information on their software projects since 1966, and have complete databases from which to conduct post-mortem analyses. The result is that they can identify what goes wrong in a project by analytical means, rather than by guesswork. In some Japanese companies, target rates of time, schedule, and budgets are set for different software application types, and data on how well these are met are also tracked.

    Unfortunately, most current forensic software engineering studies in the United States provide information that is gathered over short intervals, and cannot be related to whether the system under development was effective or not. So you cannot tell the value of the data presented in these studies. It does little good to be told that typical error rates are 1 per 1000 lines of code on large systems, if all the systems from which the data was gathered were complete flops. Further, without historical data, one cannot tell whether 1 error in 1000 lines of code is good, bad, or indifferent.

    At best, and if you are lucky, one encounters case studies which include information about what things went wrong, but usually the information is not put together in a systematized manner, thus one cannot compare different projects. What is needed are post-mortem analyses which identify *demonstrable and repeatable* processes that can be used to make a project succeed, or are the sources of why projects fail. We in the computing field, it seems, do like to fail repeatedly for the same reasons, and it would be useful to have available concrete data postulating why projects fail or succeed, rather than just project error rates. We also need to have the engineering concept of probable cause applied to this data, especially since there is no way to know when future information may change our conclusions about why projects indeed fail or succeed. The best source of this type of information today is from the Major Projects Association at Templeton College, Oxford, England. Unfortunately, although information technology projects are investigated, their prime concentration is not on these types of projects.

46. Charles C. Mann, "The Man With All The Answers," *The Atlantic*, January 1990.

47. "Software Risk Management," Air Force System Command, AFSCP 800–45.

48. Peter Morris and George Hough, *The Anatomy of Major Projects*, John Wiley & Sons, Chichester, England, 1987.

49. Frank Trippett, "Why Forecasters Flubbed in the '70s," *Time*, January 21, 1980.

50. Thomas Conrad, private note. Conrad is one of the Navy Department's leading computer scientists.

51. Note that one can get into trouble by trying to extend this line of reasoning too far, such as by trying to overcome the lower probability of success by reducing the development steps to 1. As we shall see, software process models are meant to reduce risk, and having many stages in a process model is a way of reducing the risk of

generating incorrect requirements, designs, etc. by placing in appropriate risk monitoring and containment mechanisms. It is when these mechanisms fail that one has a problem, thus making the probability of an incorrect stage blossom upward.

52. Alan Stoddart, "The Case for Research and Development into System and Software Engineering," British TELECOM Internal Research Report HD 113, 20 June, 1986.

53. Fernand Braudel, *Les Structures du Quotidien: Le Possible et L'impossible,* Librairie Armand Colin, Paris, 1979. This book is published in English under the title *Structures of Everyday Life,* Harper & Row, New York, 1980.

54. Steven Schnaars, *Megamistakes: Forecasting and the Myth of Rapid Technological Change,* The Free Press/Collier Macmillan, New York, 1989. Successful technological innovation is very rarely related to technological push, instead being much more dependant on demand pull. In one study, 80% of technological innovation started from there being a market need, and only 20% arose from someone saying that we can find a use for this great technical idea. Half of R&D failures rather were also shown as being due to marketing failures than technical difficulties. For further information, see Arthur Gerstenfeld, "A Study of Successful Projects, Unsuccessful Projects, and Projects in Progress in West Germany," *IEEE Transactions on Engineering Management,* Vol. EM-23, No. 3, August 1976.

55. *Wall Street Journal,* editorial, 24 July 1989.

56. Stephen Mead, "Soft Landings for DP Disasters," *Software Management,* February 1989.

57. Antony Ralston et al. (eds.), *Encyclopedia of Computer Science and Engineering,* 2nd ed., Van Nostrand Reinhold Company, Inc., New York, 1976.

58. Jeffrey Rothfedder, "More Companies Are Chucking Their Computers," *Business Week,* 19 June, 1989.

59. Ian Meiklejohn, "A New Hybrid Breed for It," *Management Today,* June 1989.

60. Herb Krasner, "Requirements Dynamics in Large Software Engineering Projects," *11th World Computer Congress (IFIP89),* Elsevier Science Publishers B.V., Amsterdam, August 1989.

61. Russ Ackoff, *Redesigning the Future,* John Wiley & Sons, New York, 1984.

62. "Air Force to Rethink C2 System Software Award to GTE," *Federal Computer Week,* July 24, 1989. See the Comptroller General of the United States, Decision B-234558, TRW, Inc, dated June 21, 1989 for the full details. The Air Force, at the Comptroller's direction, reviewed the award, but insisted that it was proper and correct. For details, read "AF Puts $400M GTE Award Back in Motion," *Federal Computer Week,* August 7, 1989.

63. Niall Ferguson, "The Arms Race Against Rocketing Costs," *The Sunday Times,* 24 April, 1988.

64. See Evelyn Richards and John Burgess, "AT&T, Back to Normal, Plans Day of Discount Calling," *The Washington Post,* 17 January, 1990, and "Vulnerability Exposed in AT&T's 9-Hour Glitch," *The Institute,* IEEE, Vol. 14, No. 3, March 1990.

This situation is very embarrassing for AT&T since it has been running aggressive ads attacking the slowness and unreliability of its competitors' networks, as well as touting itself as "Old Reliable." Quips at AT&T's expense are making the rounds, such as "It's 2:30 pm, do you know where your network is?" At the very least, many businesses will think very hard about getting a second network as backup, just in case.

AT&T is telling customers that another failure will not recur, but this is impossible for them to guarantee. The 4ESS switch software, for example, consists of over 2,000,000 instructions. As we will see later, it is more likely that some new, and different, failure will occur that brings the network down, than that it won't. Consider also that one of AT&T's competitors, Sprint, in June of 1989, had a totally different type of software bug in *its* network software which caused service impairment to its 1-800 and travel card customers.

And one final, but sobering, note. Many who questioned the reliability of an SDI system were told that they were wrong. Many doing the telling were top AT&T Bell Lab executives. One, in fact, told a congressional subcommittee that the phone system was a model for the type of reliability achievable for SDI. One may want to draw some slightly different conclusions now.

65. Robert N. Charette, "Software Engineering and the Competitive Edge," presentation given to IBM T. J. Watson Research Center, 11 September, 1989.

66. At least in the software engineering context. It may still be considered a risk in the business context, as the resource spent still represents an opportunity cost since it could not be spent on other things.

67. Thomas Davenport et al., "How Executives Can Shape Their Company's Information Systems," *Harvard Business Review*, Vol. 89, No. 2, March–April 1989.

68. Carl Newton, "IT: Too Important for Specialists," *Director*, June 1989.

69. Mike Freedman, "How Important Is Manufacturing?" letter in *Director*, September 1989.

The Business and Systems Engineering Dominions and the Risks to the Business

"The business community, which, having been sold the idea that computers would make life easier, is mentally unprepared to accept that they only solve the easier problems at the price of making much harder ones."

EDSGER DIJKSTRA

2.0 Introduction

This chapter and the two that follow commence our apprenticeship in the application of the mechanics of risk analysis and management, which were sketched out in the previous chapter and detailed in *Software Engineering Risk Analysis and Management.* Our objectives in this chapter are twofold. The first objective is to establish an association between software engineering risk analysis and management and a wider, more applicable, universe of discourse. As we have stated, software development risks can be found, created, and exacerbated at any point in the development life cycle, starting from the initial business decision made to acquire or develop a software system, through the systems engineering of it, and continuing through to the software engineering methodology that is used in its design. However, software engineering risks are too often discussed in the literature as if they occurred solely within, and *were confined to,* the classical software development domain and the context defined by it. However, software engineering is not something that can be separated from basic business objectives, in a cocoon of its own, removed from worldly influences or constraints. Software engineering, or the more generic term information technology (IT), is as much a part of the business equation as capital fund raising or marketing, and requires the direct involvement of every business person. Information technology development and application are, in many ways, too important to a business' success to be left solely as the responsibility of the software specialist.

The view fostered by the literature and by many practitioners, with its "electric fence of jargon, unjustifiable complexity, and sheer dogma,"[1] has caused, not without some justification, senior corporate management to view software developers as playing in sandboxes, contributing little in the way of helping the company except by consuming its hard-earned profits. It must also be said, however, that senior business managers are also not usually competent to stand and judge the true business contributions of software developers, nor are they completely without culpability either, as their own actions contribute to, cause, or exacerbate many of the problems they bitterly complain about. These diametrically opposed mindsets pose a difficult conundrum to resolve. We plan to challenge the closed minds of both parties to recognize their mutually linked dilemma over the next few chapters. Thus, as one of our primary goals, we have set out to make both parties aware of their imperfect thinking. To do so, it will be necessary to examine the mutual contributions and interrelationships of business environment risks to software engineering risks, especially if one wishes to really make information technology pay off.

Along these lines of confronting one's biases and beliefs, our second objective is to try to stimulate one's thinking about truth and beauty, and their relationship to software engineering risk and its management:[2,3] truth, because one must be able to separate the real (risks) from the perceived, and beauty, because it often is used heuristically, via one's own experience, to judge truth using the ideas of parsimony and aesthetics. Without comprehending both, one may know all the mechanics of software engineering risk analysis and management, but not possess any affinity for their application. This can be better understood in the light of an analogy found in the petroleum business.

The oil and gas drilling industry can be said to be a business primarily of failure, intersprinkled with brilliant flashes of success.[4] An extreme example can be found in western Wyoming. Oil was always thought to exist in Wyoming, but it took over 100 years, 130 dry holes, and some new ideas about oil deposits before oil was finally discovered. The primary reason for the lack of success was the fact that the standard seismic models used to predict oil deposits were wrong. The models had worked well in predicting oil deposits since 1921, and they were doggedly used in Wyoming, but to no avail. But we are a little ahead of ourselves. We need a bit more background first.

Oil exploration is predominantly performed by what is called seismic prospecting. Seismic prospecting involves recording the seismic wave generated by small explosive charges, which are strung out in a line over a suspected petroleum field. These waves are then picked up on geographically dispersed seismographs. As the waves move through the different underground strata, they become bent, therefore delaying their return to the surface. The subsurface structure can be reconstructed from the returning wave patterns by analyzing the time-distance curve of the generated patterns as they pass through the subsurface rock formations. Both direct waves and those reflected or refracted at the boundaries of the underground layers are used. The depths of the rock formations (to over 20 km), their angle of inclination, and speed of seismic waves in each underground layer can be determined from the time-distance analysis. Suspected regions of oil, called oil domes, appear as "humps" in the reconstructions of the underground strata. Ordinarily, the analysis process is a straightforward, if time-consuming, process. Most of the time, that is.

The seismic models that were used in the Wyoming explorations to reconstruct the subsurface structure assumed that the local geology followed a simple stratification pattern. This pattern was assumed because it was prevalent in other oil depositing regions, and therefore was the standard model of choice in the industry. Further, geologists had been trained for decades in this simple model, and it had served them very well throughout the world. The model assumes that layers of rock align fairly uniformly on top of one another, like a stack of dishes. There is nothing inherently wrong in the model, except that in the particular areas of exploration in Wyoming, the exposed surface rock formations exhibited a great amount of overthrusting and severe bending, which would be evidence that the subsurface pattern may not be so regular. However, these outward signs that the model might be in error were discounted. In fact, reconstructions from new and very extensive seismographic surveys seem to indicate the typical stratification that geologists were always taught to believe in, and the faith in the standard models became even stronger, even though no oil was found using them.

As any one who has dealt with sound wave propagation knows, a key element used in any subsurface reconstruction algorithm is the speed of sound moving through the medium of study, in this case rock. If this parameter is incorrect, then unless there are compensating factors, the reconstruction will also end up being incorrect. As serendipity would have it, because of the way the rock formations bend and fold over in Wyoming, it *appeared* that simple stratification of the local rock formations had in fact occurred. The assumptions concerning how sound travels through rock, and especially about its speed, in the mathematical models to reconstruct the subsurface formations combined in such a way to give results which were exactly what the geologists were *expecting* to see. They were looking for oil dome formations, and indeed, there they were! The analysis said so. The only problem was, the results they were examining were wrong. Thus, every time an oil company drilled in an area which indicated by the analysis that an oil dome was present, it came up dry. It wasn't until some geologists threw out conventional wisdom, realized that the analysis was only a *representation* of the subsurface strata, and started asking what would happen if the rock formations were indeed folded over in the underground strata exactly as they appeared on the surface, that the error was found. Once the analyses were corrected for this different strata layering model, the oil discovery rate reached almost 100%.

The moral of the story is that in the development of software systems, one must strive to avoid the unwitting adoption of piecemeal and/or optimistic thinking which confuses representations with reality, and only sees parts of both the situation and its generative mechanisms.[5] This situation, which one often encounters, is described by Barbara McClintock, the Noble Prize geneticist, in the following way, "I feel that much work is done [in genetics] because someone wants to impose an answer on it. They have the answer ready, and they know what they want the material to tell them."[6]

There are a number of implications resulting from this way of thinking. One prime result of piecemeal thinking is nonrational thinking, where only the extremes (i.e., "simple") in any range of problem solutions are seen as feasible. Thus, situations (and their risks) will appear to exhibit counterintuitive behavior, or possess consequences which are rarely as expected, concluding in unpleasant surprises for user, sponsor, and developer alike. These are not intrinsic properties of the situation, either, but rather are the results of the lack of respect paid to, or neglect of, the nature and complexity of the situation and the processes under analysis.[7]

Furthermore, the potential for conflict between fact and theory is strong in all sciences, but it is especially troublesome for sciences in which the empirical base is weak.[8] This seems to be the case in computing as a whole, which is only 45 or so years young, and software engineering in particular, which is half that. Because of the low maturation level of the software engineering field, the balance between the coherence theory of truth (the representation of phenomena mathematically) and the correspondence theory of truth (generalizations made from empirical evidence) will weigh naturally more towards the coherence side.[9] The result is a tendency to focus on small aspects of the problem, rather than on the larger ones, e.g., on the risks involved in coding programs, rather than on the risks involved in building systems.

Returning again to Barbara McClintock, at one time corn was the premier model for conducting genetic studies. But in the 1940s, this changed to simpler models, such as bacterial and viral ones, because of both practical and theoretical reasons. There was a cost, however. As another Nobel Prize winner said, this change required geneticists to believe that what was true for *E. coli* would be true for an elephant.[10] McClintock was one of the very few who continued to study higher organisms, which placed her further and further out of the mainstream. This allowed her to see things that others did not, because she was not locked into preconceived notions. This led her to her breakthroughs in genetics. Two recurring questions should be constantly resurfacing in one's mind: Are the models we are trying to apply in the development of our software systems representing the way software systems of this size and complexity *are* developed, or are they instead how we *perceive* them to be based upon tradition?

The lessons to be learned from these concerns as will be shown later in this chapter and others, are that in applying software engineering risk analysis and management, one must continually question the "conventional wisdom." In other words, one must challenge all the assumptions made, all the models used, all the methodologies applied, and all the automation required in developing a software system, as well as the tendency to apply risk analysis only within the development context, while ignoring the business environment in which the development resides. One must overcome the habit of dealing only with the comfortable. As in the case of *E. coli*, many assume that what is good for a small project is just as good for a large one, only on a larger scale. And as we will see, this more often than not is untrue. If we cannot overcome our preconceived notions about software engineering, then the true sources of risk will lay undiscovered, and on whatever project we are working, we will be placing its successful conclusion in jeopardy. As Sage states, there is a plethora of data, but a dearth of information, to really do risk analysis and management satisfactorily.[11] This chapter and the two that follow attempt to provide some of that missing information.

2.1 Software Engineering Risk Analysis—A Hypothetical Situation

To allow the ideas presented above, as well as those that follow, to become more meaningful, we are going to start by constructing a hypothetical situation to provide a proper context for the ideas to be explored in this and later chapters.[12] The reader should occasionally refer back to this situation and think how you might, acting in the capacity of a risk analyst, deal with it. We have purposely based this situation upon an amalgamation of the different types of risks typically encountered when one acts as a (software engineering) risk analyst. It is unlikely—and pray that it doesn't occur—that one would encounter all of them at once, but over the course of a few years, each type will most assuredly be found lying in wait for you.

Assume that you have just been hired as a consultant to the chairman of a medium-sized firm. The firm has been in business for 23 years, operates in 17 states and 3 foreign countries, is earning $54 million in pretax profit on $375 million in annual revenue, and has a cash reserve of approximately $96 million. Approximately 25% of the company's revenues are derived from defense, while the remainder is based upon commercial sales.

The company is privately owned, with the chairman holding 65% of the stock, but the corporate board has recommended introducing a public share offering within the next 2 years to finance a major expansion effort. The company conducts both government and commercial business, building specialized software systems for the government for two military services, as well as selling a number of moderately successful software products and small/medium sized information systems in the process control field.

The company chairman has hired you because he has a couple of challenges that require independent, expert advice on how to resolve them. He is contemplating: (a) undertaking a bid for a major defense contract, that will double his government business; (b) revamping the current range of products and services for the commercial market to gain entry into the systems integration market, and (c) making corporate-wide investments in new information technology, such as computer-aided software engineering (CASE) products, to increase his productivity of the software development staff, including a new network system to link all of his office locations together. The chairman wants to ensure that his risk/return-on-investment ratio is above average on each of these efforts. Even though the company has a healthy cash reserve, spending money on too many speculative ventures is not in the Chairman's character. He likes to invest for the future for reasons such as increasing bidding capability, enhancing the corporate image, and expanding market-share, rather than solely increasing short-term profit. However, the chairman used to work at 3M and typically uses the same criteria 3M does to judge ventures. That is, each enterprise undertaken, big or small, must meet three financial criteria: a 20% to 25% pretax return on sales, a 20% to 25% return on stockholder investment, and an earnings growth of 10% to 15% per year.

The chairman also suspects, however, that a number of his corporation's projects, both commercial and government, are having problems meeting their current software development contracts. If they get out of hand, the situation might impede the company's ability to bid for the new defense contract. His expansion efforts might also suffer from the bad publicity. Making a wrong decision now, in any one of these areas, might send the company's earnings down, and could affect the price it could obtain on the shares offered to the public.

The chairman understands that you are knowledgeable about information technology risks and how to control them in his type of business from your work as an independent corporate troubleshooter. He wants to understand four things: (1) what risks may be confronting him on the government bid; (2) what he can or should do about the problems in the software developments; (3) how his product line should develop; and (4) your recommendations on the corporate investment in new information technology. He believes that his job is to make decisions, and that the most critical decision any effective manager can make on a project or venture is whether one can afford the risk. The chairman, therefore, would like a report on how he can effectively achieve all these objectives, and recommendations on specific strategies and tactics he requires.

Oh, by the way, the chairman's full-time planning staff does not have any relevant information technology development or acquisition experience, they are suspicious of you, and you must win them over to succeed. The chairman also likes seeing the rationale behind specific recommendations, and you can be sure that his staff will be examining them in great detail. The information should be contained in the appendices of the report, because, like most chairmen, he wants the recommendations on one page, in the front piece of the report. You are given free rein to go investigate whatever you want and to speak to whomever you please. So get with it, he says to you, as you leave his office to the icy stares of his staff.

Hmm, you say to yourself, a bit wider in scope than some other tasks you've taken. So, the chairman *just* wants to know what risks *he* is facing, what *he* needs to know about them, and what *he* can do about it? You say to yourself, damn, what do *I* need to know to do this job? So, you decide the best place to begin, as Aristotle said, is at the beginning, and this means understanding the business environment in which the firm operates.

You muse for a moment, and smile, because the verb "environ" typically means "to surround or enfold with a condition, atmosphere, or other intangible things: to surround permeatingly." The term "environment," you know is defined as "something that environs" or "the surrounding conditions, influences or forces that influence or modify." That is exactly what you are searching for. You silently thank your sixth-grade English teacher for making you do all those seemingly ridiculous word drills.

Over the next several sections, you should mentally review the chairman's tasks, and try to perform some preliminary analysis and derive a few recommendations. Occasionally, we will provide some extra information to help this process along. But first, a good analysis requires a firm foundation and a proper context from which to begin, therefore one should conduct a rapid review of some of the basics.

2.2   Software Systems Development—What Is a System?

First principles are always a good place to start, since by reasoning first and acting second, one can avoid the "usual, half-baked, conflation of intuitive and heuristic thought that emerges as a body of ideological material,"[13] analyses of this kind breed. Reflecting for a moment, you see that what you have is a situation involving decisions concerning part of the real world beyond that which are thought about in most software projects. This situation is made up of a group of elements, both human and nonhuman, that are organized and arranged in such a way, that the elements need to act as a whole towards the common objectives, as set out by the chairman. You recall this is the description of a *system*.[14] More formally, the system consists of: (1) a description of the situational world that is the direct subject of the decision, called the system of interest, and (2) the environment(s) with which the decisionable part interacts.[15] This is illustrated in Figure 2.1.

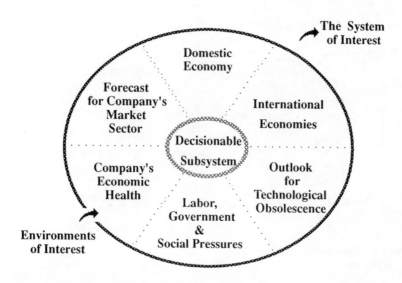

The System
of Interest

Domestic
Economy

Forecast
for Company's
Market
Sector

International
Economies

Decisionable

Subsystem

Company's
Economic
Health

Outlook
for
Technological
Obsolescence

Labor,
Government
&
Social Pressures

Environments
of Interest

Figure 2.1 The "System" Equals a Decisionable Subsystem of Interest and Its Environments of Interest

Usually, when beginning a new risk analysis assignment, the definition of the system under study will be the most important aspect as well as most difficult, to define. In fact, all later analysis flows from what assumptions are made about "the system," and if these are not defined properly, then there can be problems later. Therefore, the analyst should begin any analysis by first reviewing the principles found in formal systems theory.[16]

2.2.1 A short introduction to systems theory

The description of a system starts with it being an assembly of elements related in some organized whole. By an *element*, we mean anything that is discernible by a noun or noun phrase, and is agreed to exist by all informed observers of the *situation*. Elements must normally have properties that can change with differences in behavior. Relationships, then, are said to exist between elements, if either element is influenced by the other in any way. An attribute of an element or process is said to exist if a characteristic quality or property can be ascribed to either one.

Environment of Interest

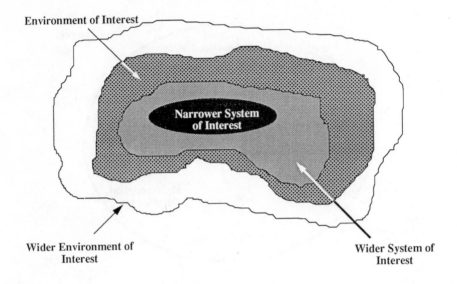

Wider Environment of
Interest

Wider System of
Interest

Figure 2.2 Systems and Environments of Interest

It is the concentration of relationships between elements that helps distinguish a system from its environments. A system has sets of concentrated feedback relationships among elements, whereas an environment has input-output relationships with the system. There may be more than one environment (i.e., set of distinct input-output relationships) which can significantly influence the situation under study, albeit these may be less influential than the primary environment. These environments are often said to be contained within the *Wider Environment of Interest* (WEOI), where the WEOI is considered a meta-environment to the others. Similarly, there may exist a number of individual sets of concentrated relationships contained within a system, and these are called *subsystems*. Subsystems form the *Narrower System of Interest* (NSOI). These concepts are illustrated in Figure 2.2.

A system is separated from its environment(s) by a demarcation called a *boundary* (subsystems may have boundaries as well). How absolute this boundary is determines whether a *closed system* or an *open system* exists. In a closed system, relationships do not exist between elements of the system and the environment, whereas in an open system, exchanges of energy (information, etc.) take place between the system's elements and the environment.

A system can be defined by elemental attributes called *state variables*. These state variables define the set of possible values of the system (at some time, **t**). The system, therefore, can be described by a *state vector*,

$$
\mathbf{x} \quad = \quad
\begin{vmatrix}
x_1 \\
x_2 \\
x_3 \\
... \\
... \\
... \\
x_n
\end{vmatrix}
\tag{2.1}
$$

such that, for each x_i ($i = 1..n$) of the state vector, **x** represents one of the system states. The changes to the states over time form what is called the *state trajectory*. The totality of the space in which the trajectory may move is called the *state space of the system*. If $x_1(t)$ is the value of that state in the present time, and $x_1(t + s)$ the value of the variable at some future time, one can write a mapping of present state trajectory into the future state trajectory as follows:

$$
\begin{vmatrix}
x_1(t) \\
x_2(t) \\
x_3(t) \\
... \\
... \\
... \\
x_n(t)
\end{vmatrix}
\quad
\begin{matrix}
\rightarrow \\
\rightarrow \\
\rightarrow \\
\cdot \\
\cdot \\
\cdot \\
\rightarrow
\end{matrix}
\quad
\begin{vmatrix}
x_1(t + s) \\
x_2(t + s) \\
x_3(t + s) \\
... \\
... \\
... \\
x_n(t + s)
\end{vmatrix}
\tag{2.2}
$$

When this mapping is as above, where a one-to-one mapping exists, one says the system is *deterministic*. However, when the state variables can map to a many-to-one or a one-to-many basis, then the system is said to be *indeterminate* or *probabilistic*.[17] In systems where there are many different types of state variables, or they are not well defined, or the state trajectory has many complex mappings, one says the system is poorly structured, or messy, resulting in boundaries that may be unclear or difficult to identify.

The activities of a system are thought of as processes which have structure. The structure defines how the elements relate to each other, providing a conceptual framework in which the processes occur, such as in a software life cycle. By observing the system in sequential times t_1, t_2, ..., t_s, one can begin to characterize the situational behavior of the system. The behavior may reflect the process of goal seeking, such as the firm's desire for increasing market share as a percentage of increased investment. By then combining the structure with the situational behavior, one can represent the specific process involved in the situation and its possible next state at t_{s+1}. If the processes occur in a step-like fashion, then one says it is *systematic*.

A risk can be defined in the context above as the likelihood of making a particular state transition, say from $x_n(t)$ to $x_n(t+s)$. By evaluating the other x_n's of the vector x, one can describe a consequence (that may not be desirable) of the transition. By listing all such possible situation state transitions, we end up formulating the risk set, $\{< s_i, l_i, x_i >\}$, which was introduced in Chapter 1, and is explained in greater detail in Appendix A.

Situations often form levels of structures called *hierarchies*. Reduction of the situation (downward) increases the resolution of the situation structure. Determination of the correct level of resolution is important to being able to properly understand the situational behavior of the system. To do so effectively requires holding simultaneously a holistic view (viewing the system as a whole) as well as a reductionist view (converting the system into simpler forms). This is often termed possessing a *systemic view of the situation*.

If the structures of the hierarchy ascend, instead of reduce, then this is called *emergence*. Emergence means that the whole is greater than the sum of its parts. Synergy is a term used to describe the emergence of unexpected and interesting properties of the situation. The installation of information systems which provide new ways of allowing a type of business to be conducted for a company is an example of emergence. Similarly, how well software engineering affects a business's profitability is connected to emergence.

If the situation deteriorates from a structured one into a nonstructured one, it is due to *entropic action* of some kind. Entropy relates to the tendency of situations to move to a greater degree of disorder or disorganization. To keep entropy from occurring, negentropic activities must occur, which themselves require energy. The release and use of energy, however, itself involves entropic action. Holding back entropy, or increasing the level of order in a situation, is the underlying objective of all software development efforts.

The structures of systems may be very complex. Complexity relates to the degree of difficulty to which: (a) the parts of the system interrelate or interact, or (b) the parts relate to, or interact with, the environment. Attributes of complexity include: significant numbers of system interactions; a high number of system elements, or degrees of freedom; nonlinearity of the system's behavior; asymmetry of system processes, and nonholonomic behavioral constraints (i.e., parts of the system are not operating continuously under the regime of a central control mechanism).

Complex situations have a number of other aspects. Complex situations are often partly or wholly unobservable, with measurements being noisy or unachievable. Laws to establish behavior are difficult to formulate, as there isn't enough data available, and/or the data is so unreliable that only probabilistic laws of behavior are achievable. Complex situations also are often messy, incorporating value systems that are abundant, different, and extremely difficult to observe. Finally, complex situations are open, and evolve with time.

A system's definition is a subjective one, and rests entirely with the definer, whether it be a group or an individual. For example, a car may be seen as a system of transportation by highway engineers, a threatening system of destruction by environmentalists, or a system to generate income by automotive manufacturers. Each group has its own definitions for the state variables, state trajectory, and boundary conditions to separate the system from its environment. The *Weltanschauung*, or, what makes this view of the system important, is dependent on the context or environment in which each group resides.

Systems that are well-structured lend themselves to quantitative analysis, while messy situations normally are attacked using qualitative methods. Well-structured situations are also called *hard situations*, or ones which are easy to measure and quantify, often have their behavior performing according to known laws, and thus have a high degree of predictability. Physical situations typify this type of situation. Messy situations are also called *soft situations*, being typified by possessing poor structure, having difficulty in measuring, having no general laws about (or instead having conflicting theories about) their behavior, thus having little predictability about them. Situations which involve human activity are normally considered messy.

2.2.2 Implications and ramifications of system theory on software engineering risk analysis and management

The section above provides only a taste of what system theory is all about, and consultation of the references is required to ensure nothing of importance is overlooked. However, even from this small sample, a number of ramifications to our situation are apparent.

One of the first is that one must be careful in the definition of the "system" of interest. Where does one draw the demarcation line? To do a risk analysis well, one must use a *systemic* point of view. This requires three things of the risk analyst:[18]

1. An understanding of where the systems belong; i.e., looking at the system as a single unit within the greater context of the systems and environments with which it interacts or interfaces.
2. An understanding of what the system does; i.e., an enumeration of the system elements, their functions and relationships.
3. An understanding of how the system acts; i.e., the flow of energy patterns via data and control flows, the emergence and synergy of the system as elements form subsystems and cooperate to form a system, and the entropic nature of the system.

As Lifson and Shaifer note, the success of the activities of a project's life cycle and performance of the developed product are profoundly affected

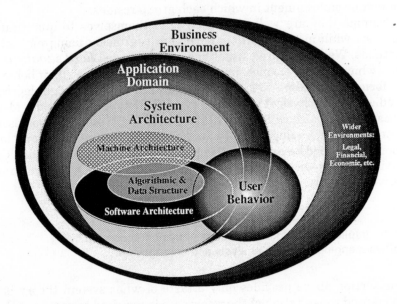

Figure 2.3 Environments of Interest

by the environments in which the project exists.[19] Furthermore, the design of the specific system of interest, in turn, profoundly affects the environments. The analysis and evaluation of decision alternatives are, in fact, only meaningful in terms of the total system, illustrated in Figure 2.1. The boundaries of the specific system of interest and its associated wider system of interest depend upon the *decisions* to be made concerning a risk. Therefore, *decision criteria are attributes, not of the system of interest, but instead, of the environments of interest.*

Throughout this book, one will encounter the terms "technical risk," "cost risk," and "schedule risk," to name only a few. If these fall into the system of interest, which they do, then the wider system of interest must be extended to include the relevant business aspects pertaining to, and which can exert influence on, the software developments, the new product line, and so forth., as described in the scenario—i.e., anything which is meant to improve or make revenue for the company. In other words, *software engineering* risk analysis and management in this situation *must* include consideration of an open system, spanning a very wide environment of interest, as illustrated in Figure 2.3.

Identifying the system of interest, the environments in which it interacts, and defining their pertinent relationships are essential for performing proper risk identification, estimation, evaluation, and management. Too often, the software engineering system of interest, and its related environment of interest, are too narrowly defined to include only the inner circles. Other times, the system of interest only includes the software product itself, with the process of software engineering being considered as the only environment of interest. Sometimes the systems engineering process, and the product itself, are included in the system of interest, but the environment of interest is then usually poorly defined.

To see what we mean, take, for instance, the following two statements made in different papers, one concerning programming and one concerning safety:[20]

One problem which does not have much to do with software engineering is whether there is sufficient application-oriented knowledge to start an implementation.

What risk is acceptable or unacceptable must be defined for each system, and often involves political, economic, and moral decisions outside the decision-making realm of the software engineer.

The first is not only false, it is in fact the way large-scale systems are being built all the time. Engineers have always plunged into activities they do not understand.[21] How many designers of automatic flight control systems know how to fly? How many submarine combat systems designers have ever been aboard a submarine? Large-scale system developments are constantly pushing at the edges of knowledge of the application domain. The continual evolution of an application, and its requirements, are daily proof of this. Even in programming-in-the-small projects, let alone in building large software systems, this statement does not hold true. If this situation were not the case, many of the concerns about fuzzy, unstable, or missing requirements would disappear, along with their associated risks. The attitude expressed is one which consistently dogs the field of software engineering; i.e., equating it with programming, and not the building of systems, where programming is at most a minor aspect.

The first half of the second statement above is definitely true, and should be a maxim for anyone involved in risk estimation and evaluation. However, the second half, starting with the word "outside," is not totally accurate. Every decision one makes affects decisions made outside his or her own environment, either directly or indirectly. All too often this thinking is used as an excuse to alleviate the software engineer from considering the potentially negative impacts of his or her decisions on the political, economic, legal or moral domains. A closer reflection of the truth in the computing industry today, and one which is short-sighted and dangerous, of the way software engineers and computer scientists view their own domain is to leave out the word "often" in the second statement.

Now, we should give the benefit of the doubt to the authors of the statements above, and conclude that I probably have misinterpreted the intent of the sentences in question. However, even if that were true, the statements are illustrative of the wider body of opinion and practice in today's software engineering field. This opinion sees software development as a closed system, and its risks, such as not having sufficient application knowledge to proceed, or not having any impact on higher level decisions, are considered issues *necessarily* and *rightly* outside the software engineering domain. The insularity, and purposeful isolation, of the field from outside influences is well known, and is seen even among the subdisciplines making up computing as a whole.[22] Unfortunately, the software system developers and users have to live with the risks anyway, and you, as software risk analyst, had better be prepared to deal with the consequences they present.

The holding of these narrow viewpoints has proven to be a weakness in the successful development of software intensive systems, especially ones of larger size and complexity. It has been pointed out on numerous occasions that the origination of the risks identified in software development lie more in the direction of the systems engineering process. They do not reside exclusively in the software engineering domain.[23] The reason is that many of the so-called "software engineering risks" are funnelled into its environment from the meta-environment, but are overlooked by the current models used to develop software systems. Recall the issue of undercapitalization. Or consider, for example, a common software engineering risk cited: software's complexity.[24] The complexity of the software originates in the user's requirements, which are in response to short- and long-term market requirements, internal company requirements, and/or policy decisions on how the system will be built. These aspects of risk exist well in advance of the time one has to deal with it at a software project level. Unfortunately, by the time one typically confronts them at this lower level, it is already too late to control, contain, or avert the risks they represent in any meaningful way.

Furthermore, software development standards, such as the Department of Defense's DOD-STD-2167A, institutionalize this situation. They focus almost exclusively on a very systematic (not systemic) software development process and definition of the artifacts of the process, but not on the relationships to the environment in which the development operates. Other standards, such as MIL-STD-499A, are intended to

---

The contractor shall establish and implement risk management procedures specified in the SDP for controlling risk. The procedures shall include:

(a) Identifying the risk areas of the project and the constituent risk factors in each area.
(b) Assessing the risk factors identified, including the probability of occurrence and potential damage.
(c) Assigning appropriate resources to reduce the risk factors.
(d) Identifying and analyzing the alternatives available for reducing the risk factors.
(e) Selecting the most promising alternative for each risk factor.
(f) Planning implementation of the selected alternative for each risk factor.
(g) Obtaining feedback to determine the success of the risk-reducing action for each risk factor.

Figure 2.4 Software Development Plan Risk Requirement

describe the systems engineering processes and relationships within the wider environment of interest, and identify the risks carried into the software engineering process, as defined within DOD-STD-2167A. But, unfortunately, they fail to adequately accomplish this in any useable fashion. Within the Software Development Plan (SDP) required in DOD-STD-2167A, there exists a section to explicitly define the software development risks involved, as shown in Figure 2.4, but there is nothing comparable in the system engineering documents from whence the SDP follows. Software standards too often confuse the map with the territory.[25]

2.2.2.1 Product-oriented versus process-oriented paradigms. As we will see in Chapter 3, this same confusion holds true for most of the common and dominant software development paradigms.[26,27] This confusion is owed to the actuality that the prevalent paradigms in use today, such as DOD-STD-2167A, are *product-oriented* in nature; i.e., they consider the system of interest to be the software product itself and the information it contains. Product-oriented processes are a result of viewing the world using a coherence perspective on truth. Thus, software is regarded as standing on its own, consisting of programs (which are themselves considered as formal mathematical objects) and related definitional text. Programs are derived by formal procedures starting with an abstract specification, and their ultimate correctness is established by mathematical proofs with respect to the specification. The environmental context; i.e., the EOI, is considered fixed and well understood. This leads to an assumption that requirements can be determined and made stable in advance. This implies the system is closed, with predefined interactions between the software and the environment in which it will be used. Furthermore, quality is associated with the characteristics of the product (reliability, efficiency, etc.), which can be influenced by changes in the program. In addition, quality is determined by testing and "proofs" using attributes "measuring" user friendliness or acceptability. Finally, software development is considered, and viewed, as being on its own, separated from the business mainstream.

The other paradigm, which is not so commonly used, being based upon a correspondence theory of truth, is termed *process-oriented*, and concentrates on behavior. Here, software is viewed as intimately connected with wider environments of interest. Thus, the process of the software development and the system developed from that process are interweaved with themselves and the various environments of interest. Programs are seen as tools for people to accomplish goals in the environments, and not as goals in themselves. System adequacy, rather than correctness, is established by its controlled use and evolution. The environmental context; i.e., the EOI, is considered open and only partially understood, thus there is an assumption that requirements cannot be fully determined in advance. This implies the system itself is open, where the interaction between the software and the environment in which it will be used is tailored by the users in response to the actual work that arises. Furthermore, quality is associated with the characteristics of the processes (reliability, efficiency, etc., of program use). Quality is thus influenced by changes in the environments, not by the quality of the product itself. Moreover, quality is determined by user evaluations applying attributes such as relevance, suitability, or adequacy. And finally, software development is considered, and viewed, as being part of the *total* system development (i.e., the meta-system made of the software engineering situation of interest and all of its relevant environments).

The product-oriented paradigm is a subset of the process-oriented view, once again showing the shift from a coherence to a correspondence perspective of truth. Think back to the state vector **x** in Equation (2.1). Using this as an example, the elements of interest included in the process-oriented paradigm are described by the set of variables x_1 through x_n, while the number of elements in the product-oriented paradigm includes only the variables x_1 through x_k, where k < n. The variables {n, n-1, n-2, ..., n-k} are not described in the paradigm, but still influence the development. Similarly, a risk using a process-oriented perspective might be able to be described by a set of variables, say x_1 through x_n, but the number of elements observed (or averted) at the software project using a product-oriented paradigm may only be x_1 through x_k, where k < n.

The differences between the product- and process-oriented views are born in history. Early software development was very much an art, with very little in the way of disciplined development or management imposed. The product-oriented view grew out of the original software engineering efforts in the mid-1960s, which were aimed at trying to contain the software crisis caused by the introduction of third-generation machines. This generation of machine provided the capability to routinely build software systems of size and functional complexity only seen previously in large, costly, and mostly governmental sponsored projects. Instead of coding small programs, people now possessed the capability to construct many large programs which communicated and passed data between themselves. These communicating programs were the foundations of software *systems*, which forced a fundamental change in the way one thought about applying computing. Thinking about developing systems instead of programs meant that one had to turn away from contemplation about designing and building specific applications, to that of implementing, out of generic processes and data which modeled the various system aspects, a range of applications, one which might have been specifically crafted previously.

This was a radical change in perspective that was not (and is still not) fully understood, nor accounted for, nor kept pace with, in software development models. One could say the old development model state vector was not expanded to take into account these new variables of interest. The paradigm of building software, for the most part, was rooted in building programs, which were less than 25,000 lines of code, and required on the whole a (currently considered) smallish-sized development staff, and could be completed using a self-contained organizational unit. The user of the programs, in many cases, were the developers, and the introduction of information systems to the rest of the organization was still to come.[28]

Over the intervening years, hardware and software technology introductions have provided even more potential capability to those

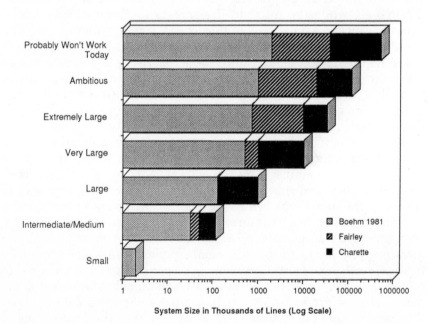

Figure 2.5a Redefinition of System Sizes

TABLE 2.1 Software Engineering Milestones

First Era of Evolving Capability
"Programming-in-the-Small"
- 1832—Ada Byron and Charles Babbage
- 1943—Aiken et al.
- 1949—von Neumann
- 1957—High Level Languages

Second Era of Evolving Capability
"Programming-in-the-Large"
- 1966—Bohm and Jacoppini
- 1968—Dijkstra
- 1969—Codd

Third Era of Evolving Capability
"Computer Systems and Software Engineering-in-the-Large"
- 1972—Parnas
- 1976—Chen
- 1979—Ichbiah

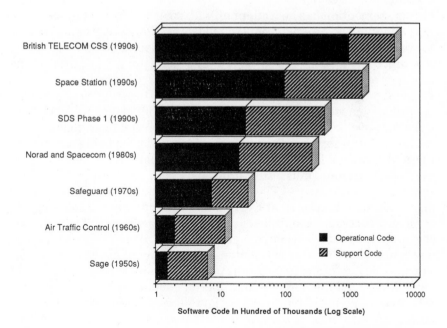

Figure 2.5b Selected Software System Sizes and Growth Trends

wishing to build larger-sized systems. One needs only to review Figures 2.5a and 2.5b, depicting the change in perceived measures of system size, to see this. An unfortunate result of the size increases is that a single programmer is now assigned to build part of a system considered only suitable for a small programming team 10 years ago, thus contributing to the underperformance problem.

Information systems which are used by "computer illiterates" (not to be taken in a derogatory way) is the norm, not the exception. Charles McKay, as illustrated in Table 2.1, has depicted the software engineering technology milestones which marked the shift between programming in the small, to programming in the large, and the last shift towards software systems and software engineering of the large. The effects of this last shift are only now being fully recognized and understood.[29]

Thus, what was started as an approach to better control the fundamental process in which software was being built has ended up placing a fundamental schism between the way software systems are perceived to be built and the way they actually are built, the effects of which continue today. The paradigm of building software today, for the most part, is still rooted in building programs of less than 25,000 lines of code. Much like a small child tries to place a square peg into a round hole by pounding harder, perception has not caught up with reality.[30] As we will see in the next chapter, the product-oriented models are constantly being revised to try to account for the change in system development characteristics, but are continuously falling short. The persistent ignorance of the inherent error that exists today in the models used to build large-scale systems, only leads to frustrated attempts to fix the wrong problem. This is a primary cause of the cost overruns, schedule slippages, and technical risks that one is confronted with in software development today.

This is not to say that the product-oriented view is being completely rejected, however. Recollect that to perform proper software engineering risk analysis, one must simultaneously employ both holistic and reductionist approaches. The control offered by the product-oriented approach, with its systematic division of the software engineering life cycle, is a necessary condition of the process paradigm. In fact, without the original product-oriented approach with all its limitations, the development of the process-oriented approach would not be understood. Thus, we do not intend to throw the product-oriented perspective totally away, but intend to embrace it more like one would a sister than a lover.[31] What we are saying is, however, that for the construction of medium- and large-scale systems, one must reach beyond the closed perspective offered by a strict reductionist product-oriented view. Otherwise, the pressures and influences that originate in the environments are not taken into consideration, and neither are their risks.[32]

A few organizations have recognized the limitations of the product-oriented paradigm, and have shifted toward applying a process-oriented paradigm instead. This may account for the better than average success shown in building very large-scale, integrated systems. Not surprisingly, the organizations that seem to be moving most in this direction are telecommunication companies, such as AT&T, with their SPIS/ISPP methodologies, and British TELECOM with their TELSTAR paradigm.[33,34] Creation of telecommunication systems have to explicitly cut across the boundaries of business, systems engineering, and software engineering. British TELECOM's TELSTAR development standard, for example, begins by mapping the elements of a software engineering system (i.e., the process and product elements), along with their interrelationships to, and through, the various environments of interest until the meta-environment, which defines the company's fundamental business objectives, is reached. These business objectives, the environments, and the software engineering system are interweaved with a corporate Total Quality Management (TQM) approach, which helps equate quality with the user's view of relevance, suitability, and adequacy. The ideas of TQM will be discussed in more detail later.

The delineation and interweaving of a tapestry consisting of the business, systems engineering, and software engineering processes and products, the identification of the relationships and interactions among them, and the risks inherent and related within each (and to each other), are of paramount importance to a risk analyst's complete understanding of the problem that he or she is faced with. In regard to the scenario in Section 2.1, it means the *Weltanschauung* spans the business and systems engineering environments, down to the subsystems like the operating system, with its relationship to the application.

2.2.3 Other systems theory implications and ramifications

Developments of large software systems can be said to form complex situations. By implication, this means they are inherently soft and open, which again is a reason for utilizing a process-oriented development paradigm instead of a product-oriented one. Interactions, be they human-to-human, human-to-machine, or machine-to-machine, in these complex systems will be unexpected and incomprehensible for some periods of time. If the elements of the state trajectory form certain combinations, then accidents, such as those that occurred at Three Mile Island, Chernobyl, and Port William Sound, or any one of hundreds of others of lesser magnitude must be expected to occur.[35] Although the accidents listed are not software system–related, there are many others which are.[36]

Systems created in response to situations which possess characteristics of complexity (i.e., interactive complexity and tight coupling, or interactive complexity and very loose coupling) will likely be brittle. That these types of systems will go out of control in unexpected ways must be viewed as the norm, as is the inevitability of multiple and unexpected interactions of failures.[37] It is important to realize that these are an expression of integral characteristics of the system, and are not statements of their frequency. For example, we all die, but only once.

This is not only true within software systems, but within any large system, such as dams. For many years, the relationship between dams and earthquakes was unknown, because the environment of interest did

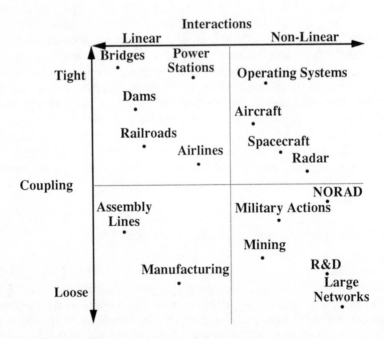

Figure 2.6 Types of Systems Interactions and Coupling

not include the dams themselves as being sources of risk in causing earth tremors. This was due to the fact that in many areas where dams were built, geologists dismissed the idea that the geologic stresses caused by dams could affect local changes in plate tectonics. Again, preconceived notions were a main cause of this thinking. Later, when investigations were made into the causes of dams inexplicably collapsing, this long-held belief was discovered to be wrong. Figure 2.6 illustrates a measure of different types of systems and where they can be measured in respect to complexity and coupling. One must understand the wider coupling between environments and the systems of interest to fully comprehend the risks involved. Chapter 5 will look at this issue again, but in the context of software engineering and safety.

Andrew Sage points out other implications which are related to Goedel's "Incompleteness Theorem."[38] This theorem indicates that certain classes of propositions can, in principle, be neither proved nor refuted within the limits of their own language. In complex systems, performance and utility measures are given in a manner similar to the following:

- *System Performance Measure* is a specific measure of a system's capability to perform its own internal activities or processes, without regard for the consequences of those activities,
- *System Utility Measure* is a specific measure of the impact of a system upon some portion of the external environment with which it relates.

Using these operational definitions, Sage has extended Goedel's Incompleteness Theorem as follows:

Any system is, in an ultimate sense, deficient with respect to external utility measures. The deficiencies may be reduced or eliminated, by modifying the system design in such a manner as to directly reflect, in a dynamic sense, these utility measures. These utility measures cannot, by definition, be expressed exclusively in terms of system performance measures, since they are external to the system.

The consequences of this statement are threefold. First, a system is often designed to fulfill one set of utility or value criteria, but is ultimately evaluated in terms of another. This is a natural consequence of the change resulting from a system entering into an environment in which it has never been before. A system influences the environment, and vice versa, and the manner in which both are perceived. Advertisers attempt to exploit this fact by trying to sell, not hamburgers or transportation, but a way of life.

Second, there is always a larger set of social utility measures for a system than the set presently under consideration. Whichever set is identified, then a new, larger, external set will eventually be identified, and the system will be evaluated under this new set. We will see an instance of this in a few moments, when we examine the issue of *Grand Designs*.

Third, many engineering performance variables used in a system's design tend to be relatively well defined, with simple and stable relationships among them. However, the opposite seems to hold true for societal system utility variables. Fundamentally, how does one balance the protection of the rights for one group against infringements on another? Or the acceptability of one risk over that posed by another?

A danger exists in attempts to simplify complex issues to the point where the models used become increasingly divergent from reality itself. The ability to understand seems to be a function of the ability to model, and the ability to model seems to be a function of the ability to understand. Sage asks the question, are we doomed, as a consequence, to be perpetual intellectual cripples, who continually strive to understand but, instead, only become confused at some higher state?

2.2.3.1 Chaos. The answer to Sage's question may be starting to become visible, and it does not look attractive. The time when information systems cannot be built with any degree of confidence in their reliability, or be built at all, especially with the use of the product-oriented paradigm, or even utilizing the process-oriented one, may be still over the horizon, but definitely seems to be drawing closer. Consider, for instance, the case of a large global network recently installed by TRW which started to exhibit strange, unpredictable behavior.[39] Nothing could be found wrong with the system design, or with any of its component parts. As it turns out, the system's behavior matches the signposts indicating the presence of the mathematical concept termed *chaos*.[40,41]

Chaos is a natural phenomenon that describes the nonlinear behavior of systems, which exists when the same input into a system does not necessarily result in the same output. Basically, chaos is a form of steady-state response which is bounded, but not periodic. In nonlinear systems, playing the game, as it were, changes the rules. Systems that exhibit chaotic behavior, although able to be mathematically modeled, are not inherently predictable experimentally. Weather is subject to chaotic behavior, which makes its long-term accurate predictability impossible, regardless of computational power applied against it. If a chaotic condition so exists in the TRW network, and this turns out to be an inherent problem in large-scale networks in general, the ramification is that there may exist software systems that can elude the control of their designers. In fact, experiments seem to indicate that the more one attempts to control, dampen, or eliminate the chaotic conditions, the worse the chaos actually becomes.[42] The use of new types of computation, such as provided by advanced architectures (e.g., non–von Neumann machines and neural networks), in which errors are occasionally *expected*, as well as the continued use of current system software which can set up chaotic conditions, may only exacerbate the problem.[43]

Alan Perlis, a Yale computer scientist who unfortunately recently passed away, suggested that the chaos problem lies in the inevitable disparity between the real world and the models used to simulate it.[44] All models, even at the finest level of fidelity, are only approximations of reality, as depicted in Figure 2.7. At some point in time, the discrepancy between reality and the computer system's simplified view of the world will lead to chaotic breakdown. The only way to improve our systems, Perlis believed, is to be prepared to continually redesign them when they fail—which they will almost certainly do. The implications for attempts

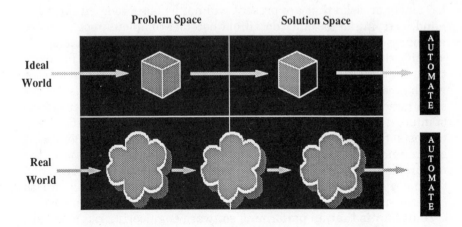

Figure 2.7 Ideal vs. Real World

to build systems, such as SDI, are immense. The AT&T communications network problem mentioned in Chapter 1 shows what can happen, even in systems that are thought reliable. The real problem may be not that we cannot test systems like SDI, but that even if we can, and a system passes all tests successfully, the system still may not work as desired. We will return to the subject of chaos in the last chapter.

2.2.4 Where does this leave us?

From a software engineering risk perspective, system theory seems to indicate that the job of a risk analyst is both larger and harder than first envisioned. It is, on both counts.

The second point is that it is vital to select the proper system of interest and environment of interest. The aspects of what the system is, what the system does, and how it acts must be made explicit. The boundaries of the "system of interest," if not carefully drawn, may increase the firm's risk potential greatly. In most cases, the wider environment of interest will include, as a minimum, the business and systems engineering environments. It will also possibly include the political, legal, technological, development, and operational ones as well. The latter environments may be contained within aspects of the minimum set.

The third point is that risk analysis operates under fundamental limitations. One cannot simplify the models used to describe the system too much, or risks that are present will not be observed. On the other hand, by trying for too much detail, one becomes completely bogged down in nonessential trivia. Where it is necessary, one must attempt to identify risk-couplings in the narrow system of interest; for instance, those that exist in computer systems with very tight dependencies, which account for the high costs of changing operating systems. On the other hand, the identification of risk-couplings within the wider system of interest needs also to be considered. These account for the 16–24% of the costs of system evolution which are directly due to software engineering environmental changes.[45] Another source of limitation may be the requirement to use the currently installed and paid-for information technology. This constrains the avenues available for planning for risk aversion and may increase the risk to the new project tremendously.

Point four is that, in performing software engineering risk analysis, there may be times when everything is done properly, but the system still exhibits behavior deviant from the expected. Built-in risks that exist in system support software or unobservable risks such as those created by chaos may be at work. Risks, do not forget, usually cannot be eliminated. At best they can be controlled or contained.

Point five is that a process-oriented paradigm of software engineering will help a great deal in performing software engineering risk analysis and management. Whereas in the product-oriented approach, the end of the journey is all-important, in the process view, it is the journey itself that is important.

And the last point is that software development risks can be found, created, and exacerbated at any point in the development life cycle, starting from the initial business decision made to acquire or develop a software system, through the systems engineering of it, down to the software engineering methodology that is used in its design. Remember, the longer the risks remain unmanaged, the more they diminish the chances of project success. Consider also, not all risks can be or should be avoided, but they all should be assessed, and explicit controls should be applied in proportion to each risk identified. Ultimately, risk engineering can only be based upon context, decisions, decision processes, and their interfaces to other decision processes for any project existing within a model of a business enterprise.

There is much more to systems theory than has been shown in the brief introductory material above. But we have enough background material, and it is time to examine the two environments of interest to the chairman in regard to the scenario: those of the business environment and those in systems engineering. In this way, we can start identifying the risks that originate in these environments that will affect software engineering risks, which we will ultimately have to deal with.

2.3 A Wider Environment of Interest: The Business Environment

It is by now obvious that many of the software engineering risks really originate at a business's formation.[46] What a business does, what products it makes, or services it provides, ultimately influence how software engineering risk analysis and management are conducted. Furthermore, the type of firm, commercial or government oriented, the culture of the firm, the basic beliefs of the owners of the firm, the organizational structure, and so forth, determine how a business perceives risk, and software risk specifically. To some, software is magic and a necessary evil, and anything that has to do with it is a risk. Others produce software and use the profits from its sale to sustain their livelihood. Often, today, because of its dependence on information technology, a company will have both perspectives about software expressed by internal groups simultaneously, which often leads to a bit of schizophrenia in its business planning, as well as its effective use of the technology. A prime example are software companies which sell information technology consultancy/support services, but are usually behind their clients in their own internal use of the technology.

Recall from the section on systems theory that the software risks encountered in a project are composed of the possible trajectories (i.e., consequences) state transitions may take, as defined in the risk set $\{< s_i, l_i, x_i >\}$. One needs to understand exactly what influences may cause a particular transition or set of states to initially exist, and to accomplish this, we need to investigate the software engineering risks that originate in the business meta-environment.

2.3.1 First principles: Objectives of the firm

There are two primary objectives of a firm.[47,48] The first is economic, which is the creation of long-term profit, given some initial level of investment. Profit is the difference between revenue and cost, and will always be the primary goal of a business.[49] It is also the primary measure of how well a company is achieving its purpose; i.e., the business that it is in.

Profit is an incentive for the owner(s), whether they be stockholders or a small group of individuals. Profit is required for gaining time; i.e., survival into the future. Without profit, there is no lasting power, no survival, no seed to plant for the next year in the form of technological innovation; i.e., no R&D.

Along with the economic objective of profit, exist many (and just as important) noneconomic or social objectives to the firm. These include organizational longevity, acquisition of a positive public and self-image, achievement of employee security, availability of employee advancement, acquisition of market share, obtainment of competitive edges, and the avoidance of unacceptable risk.

These two objectives, the economic and noneconomic, together form the basic and only valid purpose of a business, which, according to Peter Drucker, is to create a satisfied customer.

The totality of objectives influences the goal-searching behavior of the firm. This is seen in the continuous stream of products and/or services produced by the firm to be sold to gain revenue. The creativity, innovation, and discipline created the year(s) before are inputs into the current creation of the product or services offered. This totality of objectives, when combined with the business environment, also helps differentiate competitors in the market by varying their individual product or service purchase price, function, time utility, place utility, or customer perception of the product or service.

The art of management within the firm is contained in the knowledge required for balancing of the firm's objectives—making rational trade-offs between the objectives presented above which might be in conflict. Business management, therefore, is the management of scarcity. The trick is to exercise the economic criteria defined within the context of the noneconomic objectives. For example, there is strong association between R&D spending and growth in sales, but there is no established link to profitability.[50] Each deployment of capital is exposed to varying degrees of risk. If the balance is not correct, competitive frictions build, such as overhead inefficiencies, poor quality of goods or services, misdirected innovation, etc., all of which contribute to an increased cost and lowered profit. Thus, the overall risk to the firm's survival grows as a result of each increase in the individual competitive friction points. How a

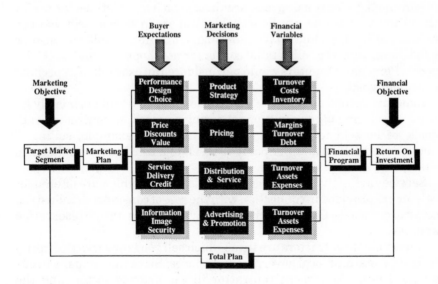

Figure 2.8 Balancing Marketing and Financial Objectives

balance can be achieved between two different types of objectives, such as those found in finance and marketing, is illustrated in Figure 2.8.[51] We said that the primary objective of the firm was the creation of long-term profit, given some initial level of investment. The balance between profit and investment is the one we are most interested in, as it is this basic business equation, the balancing of risk and return, that this book is really all about. From an economic perspective, as risk increases, the potential return must also increase. Supply and demand are the parameters used to determine the inputs to the equation. Business decisions are driven by this equation, and the application, or not, of software engineering or information technology are part and parcel of the set of business decisions that have to be made. The marketing, organizational, liability, competitive edge, technical, political, regulatory, and social risks are just some of the additional kinds of risks a company must consider in its risk/return equation.

2.3.2 Industry sectors

The firm will usually produce goods or services for one or more of four industry sectors: (1) consumer, (2) industrial, (3) service, or (4) government.[52] Consumer goods are those which are destined for use by the ultimate consumers or households, and are in such a form that can be used without commercial processing. Consumer goods can also be subdivided into the subsets of convenience, shopping, and specialty goods. Personal computers would be considered an example of a specialty consumer good.

Industrial goods are those which are destined to be sold primarily for use in producing other goods or rendering services, as contrasted with goods to be sold to the ultimate consumer. For example, selling of network services to another party to resell to a third party would be an example of an industrial good.

Services are activities, benefits, or satisfactions which are offered for sale, or are provided in connection with the sale of consumer or industrial commercial goods. One such service is provided by the airline reservation systems.

Government contractors are firms which sell goods or services directly to federal, state, or local government agencies. Since the company in our scenario is a government contractor in the defense sector, and the changes in Eastern Europe and the Soviet Union have radical implications for defense, it would be instructive to take a look at the risks that exist in this environment.[53] This is especially relevant as the massive uncertainty and changes affecting the defense industry are not only high, and one can learn much from these types of situations, but also because it likely is to be a speeded-up microcosm of what happened to other industries in the commercial sector, such as automotive, shipping, steel, and consumer electronics.

2.3.2.1 Government market—Defense sector. There are a number of basic differences between the government and the commercial sectors of business. The most important difference is the concept of the market and its characteristics of supply and demand. In the commercial business, price is regulated by the market, based upon the balance between the number of suppliers offering products or services and the demand by a multitude of customers for that particular good or service. If there are fewer suppliers than customers, the price goes up. If there are more suppliers than customers, the price goes down. At least in theory. This is typically called a *free market* situation. In contrast, in the governmental sector, there is only one customer, but many suppliers. Price, instead of fluctuating according to what the market will bear, is tied directly to the cost of the goods or services sold. This situation is called a *monopsony*.

Other factors that distinguish a free market from that of a monopsony are that a commercial firm selling in the free market has direct control over the technical specification of the product, data rights, patents, and delivery schedule of the product or service to be sold in that market. Changes to the product are accomplished when, and if, it's economically feasible, and often these changes are planned only after careful consideration of the risk/return involved has occurred. If the product, delivery schedule, quality, and so forth, do not meet the market demand or expectation, then the firm will suffer by a resulting loss in revenue and profit. However, the amount of profit made is determined by the market forces of supply and demand, as well as the producer's ability to lower cost for some fixed revenue. The exact opposite is true when selling to a monopsony. Here, the customer controls the specification, controls changes to the requirements, controls the amount to be purchased, and controls the amount of profit to be made.

In monopsonies the demands of the market do not hold, as the demands of, and upon, government are often at odds with the commercial market. In the defense arena, this is especially true. It becomes even more complicated in that while the defense market is tightly controlled

TABLE 2.2 DoD Operational Pressures

- Global changes resulting in changing nature of the threat
- National policy changes
- Budget constraints
- Unpopularity of many programs
- Sole buyer of military/specialized systems
- System costs, especially in software arena, keep increasing
- Large bureaucracy
- At mercy of congressional pork-barrel whiplash
- Internal procurement and oversight inefficiencies

---

by the government, it is highly influenced by decisions of other governments who are not purchasers of the goods or services. The "threat," perceived or otherwise, will always be a force swaying the amount of goods or services procured. The results of *glasnost* and *perestroika* are making that abundantly clear.

To help illustrate the differences in the commercial and government market, the pressures under which the DoD operates are outlined in Table 2.2. These are the risks with which the government must contend in accomplishing its objectives. The "market demand" is primarily caused by the first risk driver listed, a changing, sophisticated threat, and second, the technological push accelerated by a U.S. military policy of quality over quantity of armaments. Ignoring the reasons for, and morality of, the arms race,[54] the rapidity of "market demand" variation will influence the extent to which pressure is created within the other items of Table 2.2. The greater the threat, the more the defense appropriations have to be spread across even greater numbers of defense programs, thus fewer become available for any one program in particular.

In times of transition, such as currently being experienced, the pressures are even greater, as the other influencing agents; i.e., the public's (and Congress's) perception of how much should be spent on defense, how well DoD contract firms are performing, and how to increase the "peace dividend" come into greater play. The popularity of defense (spending) is cyclic in nature, where a cycle of popular perception typically lasts 4–6 years, and unpopular 6–8 years.[55] Individual programs have their own popularity contests, and may have cycles different from those above, although they are at least indirectly coupled.

At times like this, when all the cycles are negative; i.e., a perceived decreasing threat, a tight national budget, and a poor public perception of defense contracting firms' performance, the Defense Department responds in a natural way—politically. In other words, DoD uses the

TABLE 2.3 DoD Acquisition Policies

- Progress payment rates for large contractors have been reduced from 90% to 75%.
- Defense contractors are being asked to share development costs of new programs through the use of high risk, fixed-price contracts and/or cost sharing arrangements.
- Payments to contractors have been delayed.
- The weighted guideline method of computing target earnings has been revised to result in lower precontract markups.
- Ceilings on recoverable independent research and development costs have not kept up with spending requirements.
- Profit is no longer allowed on general and administrative expenses including independent research and development.
- Tax reform has eliminated the completed contract method of accounting and totally eliminated the investment tax credit.
- Contractors now fund a significant share of special tooling and special test equipment.
- The list of unreimbursable costs has been expanded.
- Contractors are being asked to provide fixed-price options for future production contracts at early stages of a program's life.
- Contractors are being required to provide warranties in a wider range of situations, often without adequate study of their cost-effectiveness or appropriateness.
- Second sourcing has become the standard way of doing business, sometimes without adequate consideration of production qualities, startup costs, and other factors which determine cost-effectiveness.

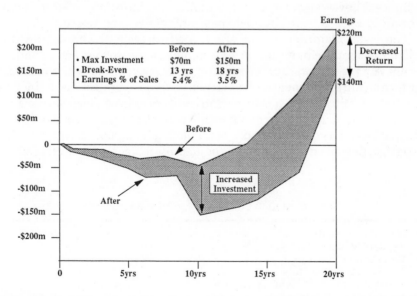

Figure 2.9 Cash Flow of a Defense Contract, Before and After New Acquisition Legislation

power of its regulated government market (i.e., the fact that it is the sole purchaser of military goods) to try to lower the risks to itself shown previously by instead increasing the risks in its suppliers' domain. This action also results in increasing DoD's return on investment, by lowering it for the suppliers. This is, from the DoD's and probably most taxpayers' perspectives, just good "business" practice. When in trouble, shift the responsibility to someone else. After all, this is nothing more than applying the risk aversion strategies of risk transference and pooling.

However, if you switch to the contracting firms' side (and do not forget, that is the perspective of the company in the scenario), the results of the policy are not all that wonderful. The aspects of DoD's policy are shown in Table 2.3, which shows new government regulations, and the results of these regulations on a company's cash flow for a selected program,[56] as shown in Figure 2.9. These regulations, coupled with the way the defense market is operated, creates a number of pressures and/or risks of their own, for firms selling to DoD, as shown in Table 2.4. Obviously, these are in response to the pressures created by the government side, which controls the size, demand, and profit within the defense market, since it is a very regulated market. As a result, the continual distortion of the market demands have recently increased the burden on government contract firms to a point where the risk/return ratios are moving out of balance. They were always out of balance with the commercial sector, as shown in Figure 2.10, but now are seemingly getting worse.[57]

The risks identified above are passed directly as inputs into the software engineering situation. For example, because the defense market is heavily regulated, the *cost* requirements, as opposed to the schedule or technical requirements, of a defense (software) project (as defined by the type of contract) are the primary driving forces in defense contracts.[58,59] Contrary to popular belief, being within cost, above all else, is the criteria for success for a government project. The contract type, such as cost plus fixed fee, firm fixed price, cost plus adjustable fee, cost plus/level of effort,

TABLE 2.4 DoD Contractor Operational Pressures

- Budget constraints
- Tighter bidding requirements
- Cost sharing
- Tight and costly auditing
- Lowered return on research investment
- Lower real profit margins
- Extreme adversarial relationship with government

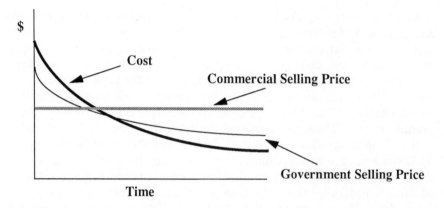

Figure 2.10 Commercial vs. Government Price Curves

or time and material (or some other special combination), determine how costs are to be recovered and the amount of profit to be made. These contracts, especially the fixed price type contract, where theoretically unlimited profit can be made, are meant to mirror the commercial market supply and demand environment, but also to take into account the special nature of the regulated and risky government business environment.[60] Many defense projects, for example, use untested technology, where the probability of failure in trying to make it work in a practical manner is especially high.

However, when this type of economic environment is coupled with the technical environment DoD is required to operate in, then one has a very risky situation indeed, for both sides.[61] It in fact influences the way one views risk all the way down to the software engineering level. For example, review Table 2.2 and reconsider the list in Chapter 1 of DoD software engineering risks. Look familiar? The sophisticated threat requires highly technical systems (technical risk source) to be fielded quickly (schedule risk source), within budget constraints (cost risk source), with a high degree of reliability (operational risk source) and enhanceability (support risk source, also caused by uncertainty in future budget limitations). Software engineering risks are transformed almost directly from this meta-environment to the software engineering situation within defense contracting firms. But as we noted earlier, DoD software engineering standards do not consider these meta-environment risks as part of the system of interest at the software engineering level. Interesting, isn't it?

As stated earlier, most of the pressures seen by contractors are attempts by the government to lower its own economic and noneconomic risks in each of the areas above. However, in so doing, these compound the risks on the DoD contracting firms' side trying to meet DoD's objectives. Since the contract firms have almost the opposite set of risk drivers, there will be constant conflict between the two. Contractors must make a profit, which is price sensitive, while the government must reduce its cost. Thus, contract type becomes the most important risk.

It is exactly the same bind faced when using advanced technology in DoD systems. The application of new technology by the threat is driving mission requirements, but the limiting factor to achieving new mission requirements is also the technology to create the new technology.[62] DoD often "shoots itself in the foot" by evaluating technically advanced projects on their cost, rather than on their ability to be successful. The Air Force program in Chapter 1 which ignored its own risk assessment is a prime, yet by no means unique, example.

Overall, the government defense market is so thoroughly filled with business risks that are only increasing, that many firms are leaving it.[63] Deputy Secretary of Defense Donald Atwood acknowledged as much when he stated that between 1982 and 1987, despite a sharp growth in defense spending, the number of defense contractors decreased by 71%.[64] Others are not taking so precipitous an action, but there is a stronger inclination to balk at bidding projects because they are seen as too risky.[65] They remember the rule often quoted by the Pentagon to contractors: "Live within your resources or join the wounded. Second, we shoot the wounded." And in times of tight budgets, the Pentagon shoots even the only slightly wounded. The reasons stated above only scratch the surface as to why. With "peace breaking out all over," the pressures and risks will only mount. There will be too many contractors chasing too few programs, with the result being that Congress will turn many defense programs into job-saving exercises as the defense budget shrinks.[66] Thus, to perform effective software engineering risk analysis in the future defense market, one has to understand the risks at the "sharp end;" i.e., the business sector in which it belongs.

Later in this chapter, we will encounter other government initiatives that directly impact the business risks of those wishing to supply the DoD with the goods or services, such as the contractor's capability/capacity review, which will show even more strongly the linkage between the meta-environment risks and software engineering risks. The chain of risks, from the business environment to the software engineering situation shown above in the defense sector, are also prevalent in the commercial sector. However, they are not so convoluted, or at least not perceived by many in the defense industry to be. Those wishing more background on the current experience of doing business with the Department of Defense should consult the references.[67-70] Although the rest of government has not followed DoD's heavy-handed method of acquiring goods and services, the general results are the same. In summary, a risk analyst must be acutely aware of what the industry sector influences will be on software engineering situation.

2.3.3 Business culture/Business approaches

Another element of the business environment, which will ultimately influence the types and likelihood of the risks encountered in the software engineering situation, can be found in the culture of the firm. Culture comprises the values, rules, philosophy, heros, rites, and ceremonies of the firm.[71,72] There are four basic types of organizational cultures: *tough guy / machismo; work hard / play hard; bet-your-company;* and *process type*.

The tough guy/machismo organization is made up of individualists. The environment they perceive is one of big stakes, big risks, quick feedback, and make-or-break decisions. The organization focuses on speed, not endurance, and success is an all or nothing affair. Firms in construction, cosmetics, venture capital, investment banking and brokerage, advertising, and entertainment possess this type of culture.

The work hard/play hard culture is similar to the tough guy/machismo type, but instead of a few high-risk ventures, the firm is faced with many low-risk ones instead. Sales operations are examples of this type of culture. Firms in computer and office automation, automotive dealerships, door-to-door distributors, fast food franchises, and manufacturing production companies fit this type.

In contrast to the short-term operating styles above are companies which exhibit long-term cultures. The first type is the bet-your-company type. Firms with this culture are engaged in work that has extremely high risks, extremely high return, but very slow feedback on the success of the efforts. Survival takes stamina. Organizations in aerospace, mining, nuclear power, petroleum, space, and the military exhibit this culture.

The last type of culture is called the process type. This culture operates in a low-risk environment, where feedback is basically nonexistent.

Employees concentrate on how things are done, rather than on what things are done. Governmental organizations are a prime example. Others include banks, insurance companies, utilities, and pharmaceutical companies.

The culture of the firm plays a significant part in how it perceives its environment and what its expectations are from the environment in the way of risks. In tough guy/machismo type firms, the management of a software system under development might not be too bothered or concerned with software engineering-type risks at all. Risks are to be taken, not avoided, and if the system works, fine, and if not, well, there is always a new project to work on. Large-scale developments would probably not be undertaken by these types of firms, because the feedback is not immediate, and the payoff is too far in the future. Thus, the size of the systems to be developed would be smaller, as would be the likelihood and magnitude of the risks involved. If the company tried to take on a job larger than its inherent culture, it would most likely fail. A recent study by Banker and Kemerer seems to bear this out.[73]

Companies have what are called *Most Productive Scale Sizes* (MPSS), which highly influence the success of managing a software development of different sizes. The MPSS is a measure of the productivity of an organization, based upon its internal overhead, which is greatly swayed by its own internal culture. Each company appears to have its own MPSS. At the average MPSS, a company's marginal productivity equals average productivity, whereas beyond that point, average productivity being beyond marginal productivity, the productivity of the company declines. Thus, software developments undertaken which go beyond the company's MPSS are more likely to be underestimated both in capital terms and performance terms, and are therefore more likely to fail.

Local business cultures are themselves affected by national cultures. These add yet another ingredient to the perception of software engineering risk. For instance, we have already mentioned that in Japan, the availability of reusable software parts influences the amount of system requirements changes that are acceptable. United States and Western European companies proceed from the opposite direction, where requirement changes are based first upon need, then upon feasibility. This difference in attitude can be seen in two other examples.

The world market for robots shrank by 15% between 1985 and 1987 (30% in the United States and Europe) and only stabilized in 1988.[74] However, in Japan, robots are still being used in ever-increasing numbers. One of the reasons can be found in the way robots are used. There are basically two ways to make use of robots: to make the robots adaptable to the task on hand, or to adjust the task and adapt it to the skills of the robot. The first approach is tricky and expensive, although if you are able to accomplish it, it has tremendous payoffs. This is the primary way Western firms have tried to apply robotics. The second approach is the way the Japanese apply robots. They change the organization of the task to fit the use of simpler robots. This may mean using more robots, and a bit more time to accomplish the task, but the overall benefits outweigh the additional cost. The judicious use of technology is a hallmark of the Japanese way of thinking.

This can be seen once more in one last example. The Japanese are often reported as being sluggish to introduce new technology into their corporations, as opposed to U.S. or European companies. The reason is that they concentrate first on changing the organizational structure to meet the changes demanded by the technology. A belief is held that optimum results are often gained from maximum business restructuring and the minimum use of information technology. This approach is again opposed to the thrust of U.S. and European firms, which is to buy technology first, and then try to figure out how to use it.[75,76] Corporate reorganizations also most often occur in U.S. and European firms as a reaction to internal budgetary problems caused by shortfalls in revenue.

Knowing which type of business culture the firm exhibits will help you, as a software risk analyst, understand the type of risks likely to be encountered and the type of risk aversion likely to be accepted. Oil well speculators are different from government program managers. The former can afford to be wrong, because his risk is spread over a number of ventures, while government managers work on one program at a time. They don't get a second chance. Also, by understanding how other cultures view risk, one can discover new ways of averting it. In each of the three examples above, there is the recognition of one crucial fact: Risks whose consequences, if realized, might adversely impact the software engineering situation should be reduced a priori wherever possible. The only way to avert a risk is not to let it exist at all by eliminating its source. Total Quality Management (TQM) is an outgrowth of this recognition.[77]

2.3.3.1 Total quality management. In the TQM approach, pioneered by Edward Demming, Joseph Juran, and Genichi Taguchi, the economic and noneconomic objectives are brought together under a management unification approach. The principle is, higher quality results in lower cost and shorter lead times, which increases the ability to produce goods

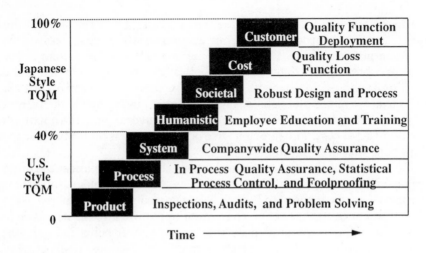

Figure 2.11 TQM Process

in a timely fashion, achieving a competitive edge by increasing customer satisfaction and thus market share. Since each deployment of capital is a risk, by lowering the amount and time required to be exposed, risks to the firm can be significantly reduced. Savings up to 50% in cost and time, or equivalent increases in effectiveness for the same cost, are possible.

Figure 2.11 illustrates the buildup of quality over seven stages in time. Each of the efforts conducted in a particular stage are to reduce the likelihood and/or magnitude of a known or predictable risk from occurring later on. A key element of TQM is the reliance on statistical process control, which sets strict, quantitative levels against which the product under development is measured. When products do not meet these criteria, then the development process is changed in order to achieve the improvements. Quality improvements are the result of tiny improvements in a thousand places. It should be noted that deviations from acceptable limits are directly linked to the financial loss to the customer. This is called a quality loss function, as shown in Figure 2.12. By taking this approach, quality is built in, rather than inspected in.

A practical example of the result of a TQM-like approach can be seen in the 1989 Baltimore Orioles baseball team.[78] In 1988, they set a baseball record by starting off the season with 21 losses in a row, and eventually lost 107 games for the season (fortunately, not a record). In 1989, they were leading the American League's Eastern Division well past the All-Star break, and had a chance to set a record for being the only

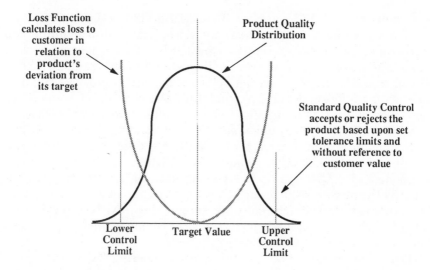

Figure 2.12 Quality Loss Function

team ever to go from the worst in the game to being the best. They failed to accomplish this, coming in second in the division, but they in fact did set a record by remaining in first place past August 24, and ended up having the fourth best recorded improvement ever from one season to the next. The reasons for this tremendous improvement the previous year's record? They can be measured on the input side by the team committing fewer errors on the defense, making many more catches by the outfield, allowing fewer walks by the pitching staff, which, when all added up, meant about one less run allowed per game. On the output side, the team had more walks, a higher team average (achieved at the expense of power), many more steals and extra bases (due to faster players), which resulted in about one more run scored per game. These changes are almost invisible in any one game, but over a period of time, they add up.

TQM is very akin to holistic health or preventive medicine programs. It often requires a change in company philosophy and organizational structure, which means a change in its culture.[79] To be effective, TQM requires a company's *whole* operation to be responsive to the various information and control flows and processes involved. Another way to say it is that all of a company's senses must be involved, or to use a Japanese word, the company's *kansei* must be highly attuned. Ford, for example, has been working on achieving TQM for the last five years, and estimates it is only 15% complete. The U.S. Air Force is doing something similar with its R&M 2000 Initiative effort, which is to reduce maintenance down time, manpower, and support costs by half for the next generation of Air Force systems.[80] However, quality is a *relative* parameter, and it changes with time and perception. What was once thought of as a quality product is easily superseded by something else which is of even higher perceived quality. Thus, quality improvement is a continuous job.

As an analyst, TQM should be seen as a powerful means to avert risks in the business environment that can affect the software engineering environment. On the other hand, even if TQM is not being currently implemented, TQM approaches can be used as an effective tool to identify the quality risks in the business environment carried into, and outwards from within, the software engineering environment. In this mode, a software project is a customer of the company, and the business is a customer of the software project.

Do not, however, mistake TQM for risk engineering. TQM is basically a bottom-up approach which has a fundamental assumption that the product or service being provided is intrinsically the correct one for the market being served. TQM is only indirectly tied to developing a company's business or marketing strategy, and should never be mistaken for "the" marketing strategy, as many companies seem to do.

Risk engineering, in comparison, is both a top-down and bottom-up approach which is used in part to try to determine whether one should be in the business or not, and what strategies should be used to remain in business. Risk management parallels the work of the corporate planner. The planner charts where a business aims to be in the future, while the risk manager tries to avert the hindrances which may prevent it from reaching those goals.

To risk managers, the quality and reliability of the product or service potentially being offered (and which are to be improved by the TQM process) are viewed as risks which are *inputs* to the risk analysis process. For instance, take the quality loss function (QLF), or the loss that comes after a product is shipped, shown in Figure 2.12. When companies deviate from quality targets, they run an increasingly costly risk of loss. In fact, losses tend to increase at a geometric rate, and can be modeled by the square of the deviation from the target value, or $L = D^2C$, where the constant is determined by the cost of the countermeasure that might be used to get on target. As an example, assume that a software product manufacturer decided not to spend an extra $50 per software package in increased testing to get the product exactly right. The QLF suggests that the manufacturer would end up spending (when the customers got angry) $200 for two standard deviations from the quality target ($50 times the square of two), $450 for three, $800 for four, etc. One well-known computer company has been experiencing exactly this type of increased cost and lost market share because it had bugs in one of its premier products.

In other words, quality is not an end product in itself, but an inherent attribute of a product. Whether a product will or won't sell is based upon many factors, of which *one* is quality. It does not matter how high the quality is if the product is not initially desired by the customer. Another way of stating it is that one can degrade customer preference for a product by poor quality control, but one can't increase customer preference by good quality control if the product is not wanted in the first place.

The big three U.S. automotive companies, for instance, have been able, through increased attention to quality, to reduce customer complaints 20-fold over the last 10 years, yet they have lost 9.2% to the market to the Japanese during the same period.[81] Automotive industry analysts are saying that the reason for the market share decline isn't only a matter of quality, but more a matter of new functionality and styling that Japanese cars possess which more closely match the taste of the U.S. customer. The *efficiency* in retooling, as well as the quality of the product, allows Japanese car manufacturers to bring out two brand-new models to every one by an American manufacturer, and at a price that is less than one-third the average American manufacturer's cost. In the 1990s, automotive analysts say, quality will be a nonissue between Japanese cars and American cars. Meeting customer preference, however, will, as before, remain.

Therefore, the proper context in which to view TQM is as a part of the risk management procedures or strategies to help keep a business viable. TQM is a necessary, but not sufficient, condition to compete. A more reliable, higher quality system, if attained, reduces those specific risks, as well as secondary, knock-on effects caused by maintenance costs, system redesign costs, and so forth. The application of software engineering techniques are in fact TQM approaches. Getting it right the first time, and making sure one provides what the customer wants, are equally important. Unfortunately, many companies are trying to stretch these basic tenets of the TQM *philosophy* into an all encompassing umbrella doctrine. They are using TQM as a substitute for proper risk engineering, and in so doing, are becoming disappointed at the perceived lack of results when their expectations are not met.

One must be careful to understand that although the underlying TQM philosophy is a good one to have in business, it is not some magical cure.

It takes a long and steady application to make it work. Take caution in applying TQM where it is not meant to be used. It has led more than one naive company to make incorrect management decisions. Extending TQM into domains beyond its original intentions will only dilute its effectiveness. However, TQM can enhance the value of risk management, as well as vice versa.

2.3.4 Organizational influences

Another aspect of the business environment from which software risks will originate is to be found within the organization itself, regardless of culture. It is, after all, the individuals in the firm's organization that ultimately produce the goods and services, and the competitive edges, to the market. A key point to keep in the forefront of one's thinking is that the value of any information system is only as good as the managerial and organizational *practices* it supports.

2.3.4.1 Organizational skills.

Due to demographic, economic, and social factors, shortages of skilled personnel are becoming a major problem in developing software systems worldwide.[82] And the situation is likely to get only worse over the next decade. Even though software development is considered the primary obstacle to U.S. industrial growth, undergraduate enrollments in computer technology and engineering are beginning to drop. The situations in Europe and the United Kingdom are much the same. There, the effects of the skill shortage are compounded by a labor shortage. The Western European governments, with their economies currently booming, are very worried that the economic growth will not be able to be sustained. Their populations are getting older, and future demographics show a continued decline in the available work force for at least the next 20 years.

This skill(s) shortage, which has always been a problem, is starting to cause major concerns for U.S. industry and government. It is especially acute within the DoD. The lack of capability and capacity of certain government contracting firms to develop software, has negatively impacted several major military programs. Thus, a number of efforts have been initiated to try and reduce the risk of using unskilled personnel on a project. One such program, meant to determine how good a company can be in developing software systems, is the U.S. Air Force's

TABLE 2.5 Capability/Capacity Review: Areas of Review Concerning a Project's Management Approach

- Organizational structure
- Software management system
- Software configuration management
- Software system structure
- Development process
- Product assurance
- Software contracting
- Make or buy

Software Development Capability/Capacity Review.[83] It is applicable to both commercial and government companies.

The Capability/Capacity Review (CCR) solicits software development capability and capacity information as part of the request for proposal (RFP).[84] The information to be provided includes internal standards, procedures and tools used within the company, and examples or evidence of their application. An in-plant review of the information provided during source selection is part of the process. There are five development review areas:

- Management Approach
- Management Tools
- Development Tools

TABLE 2.6 Capability/Capacity Review: Sample Review Questions Concerning a Project's Management Approach

- Where does the program management responsibility reside?
- Who does the program manager report to?
- Is the program dependent on any development activity outside the control of the program manager?
- Where does the overall technical responsibility reside?
- Do all technical activities report through the lead technical manager?
- How does software engineering interface with systems engineering?
- Does the lead software engineer depend on matrix resources?
- How are resources managed?
- Who controls the access and funding for resources?
- How are the development staff organized?
- How does software management interface and integrate with other internal disciplines such as engineering, configuration and data management, cost performance reporting, test and quality assurance?

- Personnel Resources
- Ada Technology

Table 2.5 provides an example of what is sought in the management approach review area, while Table 2.6 shows an example of the type of questions asked. The CCR is used as an evaluation factor in the project's source selection process by the U.S. Air Force. This illustrates again the concept of how the business environment impacts the software engineering situation and vice versa.

Another, slightly different, approach is provided by the Software Engineering Institute's Software Engineering Capability Assessment Method.[85] This assessment of software engineering capability is meant to be used not to select contractors, but to provide information to defense contracting firms upon the state of software engineering in their organization, indicating strengths and weaknesses therein. By showing where weaknesses lie, the firm can undertake graduated steps recommended by the SEI to remove them. Whereas the CCR is a stick, the SEI assessment is meant to be a carrot.[86]

The premises of the SEI assessment are illustrated in Table 2.7. The key factor is that the software engineering process is seen as a major contributor to product quality.[87] The quality of a software system is governed by the quality of the process to create and sustain it. Immature processes, characterized by ad hoc, high-risk applications of technology usually end up with unpredictable results in the cost, schedule, and quality domains. Mature processes usually achieve higher levels of success and reasonably consistent results. Therefore, the two major

TABLE 2.7 Premises of SEI Software Engineering Capability Assessment

- The quality of a software product stems from the quality of the process used to create it.
- Software engineering is a process that can be managed, measured, and progressively improved.
- The control and improvement of this process is itself a software engineering technology.
- The quality of a software product is impacted by the technology used to create it.
- The level of technology used in software engineering should be appropriate to the maturity of the process.
- The process provides the framework or infrastructure for software development and support, acting as a "glue" which holds together disparate software activities.
- The process increases the likelihood that the efficiency and effectiveness of software activities improve with experience.

TABLE 2.8 Sample Questions in the SEI Software Engineering
Capability Assessment

- Is there a software engineering process group function?
- Does the software developer have a private computer-supported workstation/terminal?
- Is there a required software engineering training program for software developers?
- Is there a mechanism used for assessing existing designs and code for reuse in new applications?
- Are design errors projected and compared to actuals?
- Has a managed and controlled process database been established for process metrics data across all projects?
- Is there a mechanism used for ensuring traceability between software requirements and top-level design?
- Are interactive source-level debuggers used?

parameters examined and rated in the SEI assessment are the process maturity level and the level of technology used in conjunction with the application of the process. The approach is to conduct an inquiry that probes the firm's standard software engineering practice in three areas: (1) organization and resource management, (2) software engineering process and its management, and (3) tools and technology. Table 2.8 illustrates some of the typical questions asked.

The answers to the questions are weighted and scored. Depending on the score achieved, a firm can be rated anywhere from 1 to 5 in process maturity, and A, B, or C in technology usage. Process maturity rating Level 1 indicates a chaotic, unpredictable, or poorly controlled software engineering process. Luck is the primary criterion for a project's success of failure. Level 2 means a firm can repeat previously mastered tasks.

TABLE 2.9 SEI Software Engineering Capability Assessment Scoring Matrix

		Process				
		1	2	3	4	5
	A	Region 1 (Risky)			Region 3 (Inefficient)	
Technology	B					
	C	Region 2 (Higher risk)			Region 4 (Target)	

Level 3 indicates a general understanding of the software engineering process; i.e., individual groups have a good understanding of what needs to be done. Level 4 means that the process is well-measured and controlled. Level 5 is an optimized, or institutionalized, software engineering process. Technology usage rating A shows little or no technology used to support the process, whereas a rating of C means technology fully supports the process. The B rating is deemed partial technology support of the process.

A matrix, as shown in Table 2.9, depicts the scoring possibilities. Firms that appear in Region 1 are considered to contain significant risks for the efficient, at cost, and on schedule development of quality software. The reasons for this are the low level of process maturity and the low level of technology employed as standard practice. Region 2 is considered to be of even greater risk than Region 1. The advanced use of technology, with low levels of understanding of how they should be used, can lead to even more technical, cost, or schedule problems. Power without the wisdom to wield it is a dangerous mix. Basically, it is like giving a Porsche to a newly licensed driver. Region 3 is characterized by the inefficient use of technology resources. The low level of technology constrains the capability and/or understanding of what has to be accomplished during a development. Region 4 is the region one wants to achieve, as this shows process maturity and technology to fully support it. Based upon these results, the SEI also indicates how one should strive to improve from one level to the next.

Application of the SEI assessment to 178 contractors by the U.S. Air Force has indicated that 84% were ranked at Level 1 of the process maturity, 14% were ranked at Level 2, and 2% at Level 3.[88] No contractor reached Level 4 or 5. Technology rating measures were not available.

There are a number of other assessments which exist in the Air Force.[89] To name only a few, there are: the *Grey Beard Teams*, the *Red Teams*, and *Software Audit Teams*. The objectives of the Grey Beards are to obtain insight into the ability of contracting firms to execute the management and technical aspects of the program. A small team of highly experienced personnel conduct a face-to-face fact-finding mission at the contracting firm's site. Their major objectives are to understand the risks facing the bidder and the government and to determine what the bidder believes the government is asking for, or what has been done that is "dumb" or adds unnecessary risk to the project. The results are added into the overall source selection information, and newly discovered risks are assessed.

Red Teams are similar to the Grey Beards, but are called into existence after a program is in trouble. Basically, a Red Team is a risk assessment team whose mission is focused on providing a quick response to current problems. It is used to identify problems and recommend solutions and options.

Software Audit Teams are similar to Red Teams, but are part of the normal program management control procedures. These are conducted during the Software Specification Review on all major programs with significant software development content. The idea is to try to surface the risks to successful accomplishment of the software development, including specifically system performance.

Both the SEI assessment and CCR are useful to the software engineering risk analyst in identifying risks early in the meta-environment that will carry into the specific software situation. The SEI approach is also very useful for monitoring and controlling risks associated with the process aspect of a software development. Again, all of the procedures above are applicable to both DoD and commercial environments. Like TQM, the SEI and CCR procedures should be part of the risk analysis and management arsenal available for use.

2.3.4.2 Organizational structure. The analyst must not only be concerned with sources of risk that the lack of skills might bring to a software development, but also needs to consider the risks that might originate in the organizational structure itself. Organizational structure is related to how a firm perceives it can best achieve the process of communicating and accomplishing its primary business objectives. Therefore, structure is related closely to a firm's culture.

There are three common ways to organize and manage a firm's structure: *matrix, participatory,* and *directive.* Matrix management is a bottom-up approach, where each manager reports to several superiors, each of whom has specific responsibilities within the firm and fixed resources to accomplish the task. Competition for resources is the normal state of affairs. Participatory management, sometimes called parallel management, is when employees at all levels are involved in deciding the firm's direction. Sometimes direction is determined by consensus, sometimes by a benevolent dictator. Japanese firms are characterized by this type of management. In the directive, or top-down, organizational style of management, decisions are passed down through a chain of command with minimum involvement by the managers ultimately responsible for the work.

Even though it is difficult to judge the relationship between organizational structures and the limits of organizational performance, each way of organizing does appear to influence software engineering risk. In matrix organizations, the responsibility for who owns the software project and, therefore, who owns the risks, may be confusing. Participatory management may mean that risks are identified, but extensive time may be required to show how they should be estimated, evaluated, and averted because all stakeholder's value and utility functions must be accounted for. Directive management may mean risks which are not seen by upper management and may not be observed by lower management either; decisions are not to be questioned, but carried out. Even when risks are identified, there may not be an effective mechanism to communicate these upwards.[90]

The organizational structure also impacts on how well organizations embrace information technology[91-93] and to what level software engineering elements of the firm play in distributing decision-making power within the firm.[94,95] These aspects, along with other intangibles, such as the overall morale of the firm, the fact that no organization is more effective than its key employees, that an organization form does not remain fixed for long periods of time, etc., also should be considered by the software engineering risk analyst.

2.3.4.3 Organizational survival—Bidding. The issue of bidding for a contract, whether for a commercial job or government contract, will be the most common way the software risk analyst will encounter the influences of the risks that originate in the business environment. Putting together and winning bids constitute the front lines of business activity. Bidding is the specific time when the risks from the business environment are accepted and *passed down* into the systems engineering domain, as well as the time when certain risks are accepted and *passed up* from the software engineering domain. If both of these sources of risks are not contemplated seriously, the results can be severe.[96]

As was mentioned briefly earlier, different contract types have different risks associated with them. In many software engineering situations, the type of contract will be *the* prime driver in influencing what kind of risks will exist, the priority of the risks, and the way that risks will be averted and monitored. In bidding, cost verses price is everything, and one must avoid getting into situations which are nothing more than pyrrhic victories. Therefore, cost recovery and contract deliverables will be the key items of importance, because they go to the heart of the basic

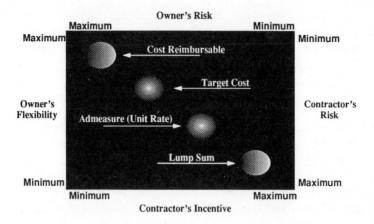

Figure 2.13 Risk vs. Loss for Different Contract Types

business objective of making a profit. Figure 2.13 illustrates the allocation of risk and incentives between bidders and sponsors for different contract types. Whether the risk/return equation is within acceptable limits (as defined by company culture, objectives, needs, wants, probability of win, investment required, etc.) will determine if a bid is pursued or not. The lowest risk are build-to-cost approaches, where functionality is based upon funding. Otherwise, the price is not related to cost, and many more risks occur.

Sometimes, as a risk analyst, one sits on the other side of the fence, and instead of bidding for a software project, one is advising how to lower the risks for a sponsor of a software project. In requesting a bid for a software product, one needs to understand not only how the contract type affects a prospective bidder, but how issues such as a closed or open tender offer change the risks assumed by both purchaser and bidder.

2.3.5 Information technology and the business environment

It should be clear by now how situations in a meta-environment originate, compound, couple to, or at the very least influence the risks encountered in a software engineering situation. However, this process also works in reverse. In other words, the "application" of software engineering presents a risk to a firm's revenue and cost, and ultimately its profit. By the application of software engineering, we mean it in the sense of the process-oriented paradigm. The manifestation of its application is typically found in the utilization of information technology or information systems.

2.3.5.1 Information technology theory. Information technology is a difficult term to describe. It is one of those clever public relations/marketing terms that sounds good but is a bit woolly under closer scrutiny. In general, it is defined as the technology involved in the processing and utilization of information by people and/or information systems. Information systems then are a mechanism for the capturing and processing of data and producing information. Information is an organized assemblage of facts in a meaningful context, or data given relevance and purpose. A little circular, perhaps, but the definition will do.

The three ways information systems are typically used in an organization are for office automation, decision support, and/or automatic control of operations. One approach to understanding how an organization uses these types of information technology is to examine their importance to an organization's business objectives. Michael Porter of Harvard, in his research of corporate competitive strategies and competitive advantage, uses the concept of the "value chain" to represent where

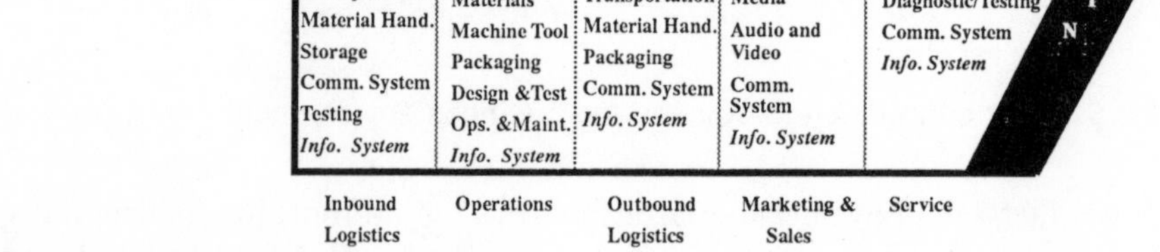

Firm Infrastructure	*Information System Technology* *Planning, Budget, Office System Technology*				
Human Resources Management	Training Technology	Motivation Research	*Information System Technology*		
Technology Development	Product Technology *Computer Aided Design*	Pilot Plant Technology *Software Development Tools*	*Information* *System Technology*		
Procurement	Communication Syst. Tech.	Transportation Syst. Tech	*Information Syst. Tech.*		
	Transportation Material Hand. Storage Comm. System Testing *Info. System*	Basic Process Materials Machine Tool Packaging Design &Test Ops. &Maint. *Info. System*	Transportation Material Hand. Packaging Comm. System *Info. System*	Media Audio and Video Comm. System *Info. System*	Diagnostic/Testing Comm. System *Info. System*
	Inbound Logistics	Operations	Outbound Logistics	Marketing & Sales	Service

Figure 2.14 Porter's Value Chain Depicting Representative Technologies Used in a Firm

information technology is involved in a typical firm's business activities.[97-99] Porter's value chain is shown in Figure 2.14.

The lower part of the figure depicts the major activities involved in any competing industry, while to the left are shown the company's supporting activities. The value of the activities increase as raw material moves through to production. For instance, inbound logistics are where raw materials (including data or information) required for the organization's finished goods or services are procured, delivered and inspected. Operations are where the raw materials are shaped, assembled, and turned into a finished good or service. Outbound logistics are where the finished goods or services are processed for warehousing or delivery to customers. Marketing and sales are where the products and services are defined, shaped, and promoted, and then sold to the customers. Service is where the installation, maintenance, and support of the product or service occurs. How well a company adds value will determine its eventual competitive position and margin. The italicized areas indicate where information technology comes into play in the support activities of procurement, technology development, and human resource management, as well as each of the firm's business activities. Information technology also supports a firm's infrastructure, which is the generic collection of corporate culture, philosophy, structure, and so forth.

Software engineering is especially important for adding value within the technology development area (mainly in application of the process of software engineering) and within the firm's infrastructure (mainly in the outputs of the process of software engineering; i.e., software products). However, it must be applied effectively, both in the sense of being able

TABLE 2.10 Implications of Information Technology for a Business

- The explicit information content of employees' work increases.
- The work performed by employees becomes more demanding and complex.
- The majority of employees must be retrained to be effective.
- The business's organizational structure must become flatter.
- The business's investments must be made on faith.
- The core business processes (i.e. production, marketing, and administration) must become transparent.
- The business must take higher risks.
- The business's traditional markets become more volatile as competitors use information technology to respond quicker, more efficiently, and at a cheaper price than previously.
- The business must participate in a global market with no place to hide from its competitors.
- There exist instantaneous international judgments on the business's performance.

to build information systems that can help the firm accomplish its business activities, and in the application of these systems by its users. Some of the implications of the introduction of information technology into business are shown in Table 2.10.[100-103]

The market expectation and demand are for: (a) even more information systems that integrate information via telecoms and data processing in an open systems fashion, and (b) the totality of means to define, create, and manage the integration of these systems. The larger the firm, the more critical these two issues become. Both of these are additional reasons for changing to a process-oriented paradigm. The paradigm for businesses using information technology is for data to be transformed into information, which is then transformed into knowledge. This can be seen in corporate investment trends. Currently, U.S. businesses are spending 40% of their investment dollars on information technology, double the 1978 share, with even a higher percentage forecast.[104]

2.3.5.2 Information technology and the competitive edge. Competition makes life turbulent and uncertain. Competition almost always eats into profits. Worse, you can lose at competition. The competitive world makes it necessary that we take risks, however. One of the ways to use information technology is as a competitive weapon to increase the competitive edge; i.e., greasing the business friction points identified earlier.[105]

The competitive edge is the tangible and nontangible items a firm has to offer to a customer, in order to influence that customer to show a preference to buy from that firm, rather than another. In other words, the competitive edge is the ultimate (perceived) value of the product or service as seen by the customer. Value is the relationship of cost to worth as seen by the customer in light of his or her needs and available resources in a given situation. The ratio of cost to worth, or likewise, utility to cost, will be the measure of value placed by the customer. Thus, the competitive edge can be gained by price advantage, higher quality, more functionality, better service, sounder image, etc., or any combination of these. These are, of course, related directly to the economic and noneconomic objectives of the firm. How well the balance is maintained between the objectives, and how many objectives can be achieved, will help determine the eventual competitive edge a firm achieves. Of course, the actions of the market environment in which the firm resides impacts the actual competitive edge attained.

For instance, on-line reservation systems were not considered critical to the airline industry before deregulation, and before the aviation fuel prices exploded and cost containment was a must. Reservation systems were created to help in the productive and efficient handling of what was a time-consuming and costly business function. The changing market conditions, however, made reservation systems a crucial part of the competitive edge. This continues today, with the American Airlines–Delta Airlines agreement first to merge, and subsequent "agreement" not to merge (under threat of antitrust litigation), their reservation systems into a new system, at a total cost of $2 billion.[106] Because of the change in market conditions and the benefits accrued by using airline reservation systems, today they not only book airline tickets, but hotels, car rentals, and other travel services. Some 80% of all ticketing and marketing of these types of services go through airline reservation systems, meaning whichever company controls the most access, controls the biggest market share. The proposed American-Delta system would have controlled some 48% of the U.S. market, which the Justice Department thought was too much.

So important are these reservation systems to profitability and gaining a competitive edge that Texas Air bought Eastern Airlines, not for the potential passengers, planes, or air routes, but specifically to obtain its reservation system. Similarly, Northwest bought into half of TWA's reservation system, and U.S. Air shares in United's. In these industries and others, such as financial services, information *is* the product. It is not unusual in these industries to see between 15% to 20% of their total company expenditures, not just investment capital, going towards information technology.[107]

The risk to the firm's competitive edge, if a system like the one above is not available, can be significant. For example, a few months before the merger, American lost an estimated $50 million in revenue due to a flaw in a new software enhancement added into their reservation system.[108] The enhancement, meant to improve the yield management capability of American (i.e., make as many otherwise empty, full-fare seats into available, discounted seats to attract new customers), instead restricted the number of discount fares available on American flights, even though some were available, which sent customers seeking low fares from American's competitors. An interesting aspect of this episode was that American is considered the industry leader in performing yield management, so the problem could not be related to a lack of understanding of the problem domain. It was more than 60 days before the error was discovered.

2.3.5.3   Do computer systems pay off?   Whereas airlines like American have been able to reap competitive edges through information technology via their reservation systems, the unthinking application of information technology can also be fraught with risks of which a software risk analyst must be aware. Blind acceptance of information technology is not always the proper business risk aversion strategy to increasing revenue and/or decreasing cost. Not accepting the risk of the technology is also a consideration. Peter Strassman has stated that "Most companies have been lucky in reaping the competitive edge in the application of information technology ... Money spent on computers is largely spent on faith."[109] Strassman has suggested that 40% of British companies are actually suffering a loss on their information technology activities through the failure to gear themselves into applying it in a commercially effective manner.[110]

In two studies, one by IBM, "Do Computer Systems Really Pay-off?," and one by the Imperial College, London, "Does Information Technology Slow You Down?," indications are that computer systems are in general good investment risks, making around 40% return on investment (ROI) on the average. However, the two studies also warn that to make a good ROI, information technology is best applied when the following three principles are followed: (a) improving the quality of the finished product, (b) offering better customer service, or (c) enabling management to do things that were not possible previously.[111,112] Much too frequently, the reports state, problems for which information technology is seen as a cure are presented in terms of solutions; i.e., more processing power, more software tools, and so forth. It is important to realize that the reason why information technology alone *cannot* result in greater advances is that many of the problems faced in organizations are unstructured.

Thus, when potential applications of information technology are not analyzed correctly, fiascoes result. One example was the mothballing of a $20 million cargo computer system right after its final acceptance test because it could not meet a new international classification system (i.e., it violated the principles of offering the customer better service and improved management).[113] Another example is the splintering of the International Stock Exchange (i.e., the old London Stock Exchange), where cheaper, ad hoc market networks are now stealing away trading, because the information technology used by ISE traders is "theoretically perfect, and unbearable"[114] The ISE system designers, in their rush to "computerize," violated all three of the above principles of getting the best ROI from information technology.

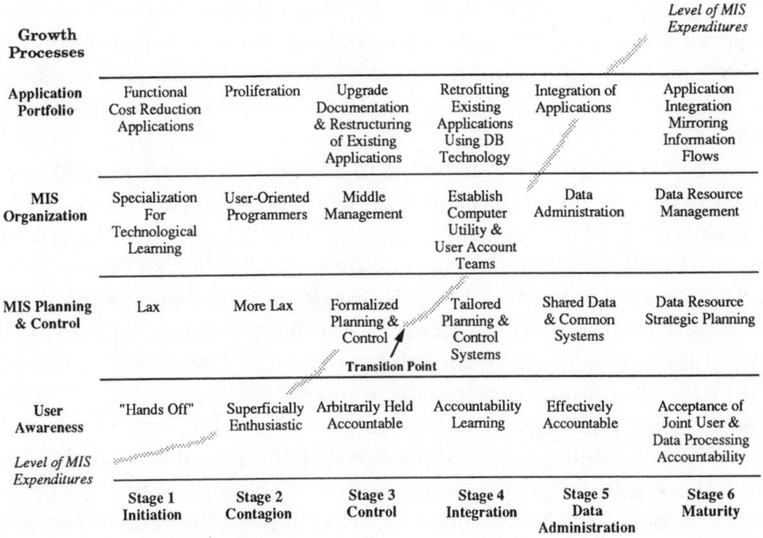

Growth Processes	Stage 1 Initiation	Stage 2 Contagion	Stage 3 Control	Stage 4 Integration	Stage 5 Data Administration	Stage 6 Maturity
Application Portfolio	Functional Cost Reduction Applications	Proliferation	Upgrade Documentation & Restructuring of Existing Applications	Retrofitting Existing Applications Using DB Technology	Integration of Applications	Application Integration Mirroring Information Flows
MIS Organization	Specialization For Technological Learning	User-Oriented Programmers	Middle Management	Establish Computer Utility & User Account Teams	Data Administration	Data Resource Management
MIS Planning & Control	Lax	More Lax	Formalized Planning & Control (Transition Point)	Tailored Planning & Control Systems	Shared Data & Common Systems	Data Resource Strategic Planning
User Awareness	"Hands Off"	Superficially Enthusiastic	Arbitrarily Held Accountable	Accountability Learning	Effectively Accountable	Acceptance of Joint User & Data Processing Accountability

Level of MIS Expenditures

Figure 2.15 Nolan Stage Model

Richard Nolan has postulated that there are six stages through which companies progress in their maturation process of applying information technology, as depicted in Figure 2.15.[115,116] Stage 1 sees computers being introduced into the organization, usually in several low level operational units having to do with finance and accounting. In Stage 2, seeing some success with the use of automation (or believing that there will be), the organization encourages more innovated, and extensive, use of computing. Unfortunately, the increased growth in applying information technology overextends the organizational ability to develop these internal systems, absorb, or control them. The systems which are produced, typically in an ad hoc manner, become maintenance nightmares, consuming 60–80% of the organization's computing resource. The forecasts for future budgets for computing support increase exponentially, as well, frightening senior management into action. Stage 3 begins when the organization tries to bring some order and control to the process. It is marked by two major aspects: the rebuilding and professionalizing of the computing organization, and the fact that the users of the computing resources are directly charged for them. Common tools and techniques replace ad hoc methods, data management begins to occur, and the computing resources become centrally managed. Also, a manager who is part of the senior management team is usually appointed to give the computing organization direction and to bring it more in line with business objectives. Elements of the company's business plan start to reflect information technology concerns.

A result of an organization being in Stage 3 is that the users, who before were able to get any type of computing support they required, will see a tightening of budget and less visible support. The users may express rather loudly that the computing organization is not supporting them adequately. However, Stage 3 marks a transition point for the organization, one where the shift of the perspective is one of entering the computer age to one entering the information age. Nolan calls it the shift from managing computers to one of managing data.

Stage 4 begins with the end of the retrenchment that took place during Stage 3. With reliable computing resources available, data management accomplished, and a better understanding of how computing can help the organization, another explosive period of growth occurs. Users will demand more and more of the computing organization, but unlike Stage 2, where the supply of computing outstripped the internal demand, the computing organization will now have to manage the demand for its support. This demand will, unless planned for early, cause another wave of problems like those seen at the end of Stage 2. Calls for more and better control and efficiency will be the result. Thus, in Stage 5, corporatewide data administration is introduced. When the demand and supply become balanced at a equilibrium point, the organization moves into Stage 6.

There are critiques concerning the validity of Nolan's model and other stage models in general, but it seems apparent that the stage of computing maturity in which the organization exists will influence the ultimate answer one obtains when trying to answer whether computing is paying off.[117,118] For example, when an organization has been able to obtain control of its computing resource and streamline its delivery to its users, it is very clear that investments in computing will pay dividends. If, on the other hand, ad hoc developments are occurring throughout the organization, as in Nolan's Stage 2, the payoff may be much less because the decentralized approach incurs higher overheads. In the first three stages effectiveness of the computing resources is important and is the measure, while in the last three the concern shifts to their efficiency.

Another method of measuring the value of information technology within a company is the system used by the magazine *Computerworld* to rank the most effective users of information systems.[119] Information system effectiveness in this approach is measured by how well an organization executes its technology plans against competitors; to what extent it trains and manages the information system staff; and to what extent the employees have access to information technology.

The *Computerworld* ranking procedure uses as its first criterion the annual information technology budget as a percentage of revenue. This is compared with industry averages from the Fortune 1000 companies, with the difference between the company and industry ratios ranked and the resulting score weighted by a factor of 30. The second parameter used is the market value of the systems as a percentage of total revenue. This illustrates the currentness of the equipment. This parameter is weighted by a factor of 15. The third parameter is company five-year profitability, which shows the relationship of using information technology and business performance. This is also weighted by a factor of 15. The fourth parameter is the amount spent on staff costs, with lower amounts given more value. This factor is then weighted by a factor of 10. The fifth parameter to be taken into account is the amount of the information technology expenditure spent on training. This is weighted by a factor of 15. The final parameter measures the access of employees to information technology. This parameter is defined as the ratio of personal computers and terminals to the total number of employees and is weighted by a factor of 15.

Computerworld's metrics are very useful in gaining a general perspective on the effectiveness of information technology, and can be used to examine an organization for where it has weaknesses in effectively applying information technology. It also, along with Porter's value chain, can be used to highlight the potential risks caused by the dependency on information technology. Information technology cuts both ways: Although information systems can provide competitive edges, the more one is dependant upon IT to achieve the competitive edge, the more important the ability to develop and apply effective information systems (correctly) becomes. Effective application of IT may be the most difficult aspect for companies to accomplish, since it more often than not requires them to reorganize, which is difficult and expensive to do, especially if you aren't sure *how* to reorganize to make effective use of the information technology at hand. Thus, companies, because information systems are complex and therefore brittle, become hostages to the very systems they require to achieve the basic objective of profit. The latter choice of avoiding the use of information technology (or software engineering principles to develop them) to contain their business risk no longer seems to be a viable choice any more, either.

The competitive world also routinely requires that information systems be built quickly, which often means taking quick and dirty approaches which are not well thought out or are in direct conflict with the company's internal doctrine. One must account for and adjust, in the here and now, a business's future requirements, and hope that one is not increasing future risks to a degree where they cannot be managed. Even in the best of times, balancing the value, performance, and cost of information services to minimize risks that occur in the meta-environment from influencing risks encountered at the software engineering level is difficult.[120,121]

In summary, information systems have changed from being *cost-driven* to *competitiveness-derived*. This means the future will see an increased level of acceptable business risk, larger systems being built with even less justification then they have now. Those companies that can build and use their information systems effectively and, most importantly, *manage their risks*, are in positions of dominating their market segment. If they are aggressive, they will be able to dictate the competitive terrain to fight on. They will also be able to impale their competitors on the horns of a dilemma: Not to use information technology will not mean that they cannot compete as effectively, because the market expects it, but to employ it would be so expensive that they may not be able to survive to compete either. Winning companies of tomorrow must be able to tolerate uncertainty, cope with it, and use it to their advantage.

Basically, the effective application of software engineering and information technology:

- Helps set the rules and pace for the race
- Provides creative breakthroughs to new levels of operations that transcends competition
- Creates value monopolies

If it is done effectively, instead of the risks of software engineering flowing up to the business environment, the benefits rise instead. This is a primary example of the concept of emergence at work, and is the ultimate objective of using information technology. Reservation systems are a prime example of this concept of emergence or synergy, where a business cost function was changed into a business revenue and profit-generation function. American Airlines, for example, makes more profit as a result of its Sabre system than as an air carrier.

On the other hand, the misapplication of software engineering confuses information processing with creativity and innovation, thus exposing poor company practices. This results in the codification and internalization of past inefficient practices, turning them into patterns of failure for the future. But again, be aware that technology by itself is not a competitive advantage. Technology can be rapidly duplicated. It must deliver something to the market that is needed and unique, lower the risk of doing business, or be used to enter into a new market where others cannot.

2.3.6   Future environmental changes

We wish to end this section by commenting on how potential future modifications to the business environment might influence software engineering risks further. In other words, where are new potential risks arising, and what can be done to manage them? We will mainly comment on the business technology aspects, rather than on the business economic aspects, such as the impact on the U.S. economy due to cuts in the defense budget caused by the changes in Eastern Europe, or whether there will be a recession caused by the budget deficit, or whether trade wars will

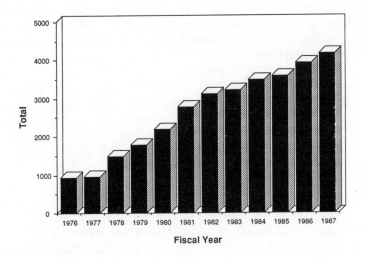

Figure 2.16 Growth in Nongovernment Standards

occur, or whether terrorism will increase, etc. Better prognosticators on those subjects exist than I, and sources such as economist William Shepard's paper on causes of increased competition in the United States and how it is changing,[122] Malone et al.'s paper on the forthcoming explosion of electronic marketing,[123] or the Office of Technology Assessment's book on technology and the American economic transition[124] should be consulted. However, the risk analyst must be aware that national and international economic issues will sharply affect what one concludes from a risk analysis study. Recall what happened in the oil industry in 1986. The massive downturn in oil prices not only affected the building of oil refineries, but also oil company information technology projects.[125]

A full accounting of all the trends in information technology is beyond the our limited scope,[126] but a few major trends should be of concern to the risk analyst. The first is the accelerating drive toward standards, as shown in Figure 2.16, especially those supporting the OSI protocols to support the so-called *open systems model*. In this model, there is some agreed-upon set of standards which will allow the user to connect any set of hardware and/or software in any configuration the user requires. Proprietary hardware/software as it currently exists , which locks in a user to a single supplier, will be the users' choice, not the suppliers'. Third-party black-box solutions will be the key, thus resulting in lower costs and more flexibility.

Now, whether one believes open systems will ever truly come to pass— and there are many doubters—the trend in the computing industry is definitely moving towards achieving some part of its objective. Consider, for example, IBM's System Network Architecture (SNA), the Government Open Systems Interface Profile (GOSIP), AT&T's UNIX operating system, IEEE's version of UNIX called the Portable Operating System for Computer Environments (POSIX), AIX (IBM's version of UNIX), and the outgrowths of various industry groups such as X/OPEN (20 major vendors supporting POSIX), OSF (supporting a rewritten version of AIX), or UNIX International (supporting UNIX). Each effort is lending a tremendous amount of corporate prestige and money to the open systems concept.

How the concept of open systems resolves its clash with certain aspects of TQM, which is also gaining momentum in the computing industry (such as nurturing sole suppliers), will be an interesting battle to watch. Further, there are a couple of risks waiting for companies wishing to embrace open systems. The first is in trying to decide whose vision of the open system concept (and there are at least two competing visions in the

U.S.) will ultimately win out. Making a poor choice could put a firm at an economical disadvantage, and ultimately out of business. The second is that if open systems indeed come to pass, then there will exist a *level playing field of competition*. This means that a company will have to compete even more than it does now, since competitive edges previously found by possessing proprietary computing technology will be greatly reduced since everyone will have access to the same technology. It may be, in fact, that companies will desire to stay with one supplier because that may be the only way to keep what is left of any *technological* competitive edge.

On the opportunity side, as a result of this confusion about standards, a number of firms are working hard on developing alternative methods of communicating data among different standards, not only between systems using different communication and operating system protocols, but also between heterogeneous software development tools. This work may eventually eliminate the requirement for having common standards at all and allow technological competitive advantages to reappear. At least two companies, one in the United States and one in the United Kingdom, using semantic modeling techniques have already developed commercial products that can achieve this objective.

This move toward open systems also means a stronger push for systems integration at all levels.[127] Systems integration is the attempt to build a completely harmonious system from dissimilar units, with minimal risk. One can either integrate at the systems level or at the application level. In either case, it implies larger and more complex systems (following *Parkinson's Law*). The risks involved with complex, integrated systems will be discussed in a short while, although we have already encountered one in the form of chaos.

Systems integration will help increase the acceleration in the merging of general computing and telecommunication. The capability to integrate voice and data via integrated-services data network (ISDN) services, and the tremendous potential of electronic data interchange (EDI), the latter of which is already being felt across all of industry, will force this systems integration to occur even faster, and will change every industry's underlying enterprise model. Already there is a perceptible shift in attitude toward the realization that it is telecommunications technology that is becoming a limit to the successful achievement of large-scale software systems, as much as software engineering. In other words, telecom knowledge and experience concerning network creation, integration, and management are becoming the new bottleneck, and thus, the highest risk item, to software systems development. In many

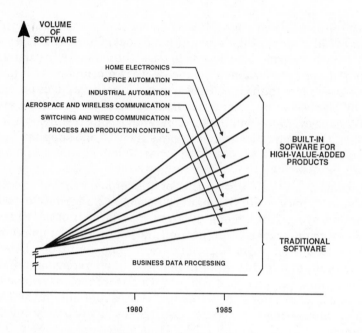

Figure 2.17 Software Value-Added Trends

cases, large-scale systems are *C&C* systems (i.e., computer & communications), since most telecommunication systems' components use embedded computers. Growth in telecommunications are expected to increase by 600% in the next 5 years.[128]

Obviously, new computer hardware such as reduced instruction set computers (RISC) will continue to change the price/performance curves, and new software in the area of computer aided software engineering (CASE) will change the software productivity equations. So will the greater availability of commercial off the shelf software, which is shifting the build vs. buy business equation. Databases, such as object management systems or IBM's repository, in conjunction with object-oriented development approaches (which fit closer to the process-oriented models), will likely be the jet engines the industry has been waiting for to increase productivity, reliability, evolvability, and system safety. Value-added products across the board will increase the volume of software produced and required,[129] as illustrated in Figure 2.17. The shift from mainframe computing to distributed networks of mini- and micro-computers will only accelerate. Whether mainframes will have a real market in the future, as IBM believes, will be another interesting battlefield to watch. What is certain is that computers at all levels, are becoming commodities in a buyer's market, instead of the seller's market of the past 30 years, which has many significant implications for the future of the computing industry.

In summary, a number of trends stand out.[130] These include worldwide expansion of scientific knowledge, with a huge growth in global competitors. This will lead to an increase in the fragmentation of markets and rapid shifting of customer preferences. Process technologies will continue to allow for greater responsiveness and flexibility, and for any given system, product, or service, the number of technologies directly involved in its manufacture or use will continue to proliferate at an unprecedented rate. General knowledge is doubling every 10–12 years, and the knowledge required to produce any given product will likely follow the same trend.

These are only a whiff of what is in the competitive winds. Take heed to remind yourself always that technology, especially information technology, is not a competitive advantage in itself. A technology can always be duplicated. Thus, the paradox: When technology drives competition, you cannot compete on technology alone. Technology must be used to deliver something to the market which is necessary and unique, such as lowering your customers' business risks, or allowing them to enter markets that others cannot without using that specific technology. Those companies that become too enamored with technology and forget that the customer pays the bills will quickly find themselves out of business.

Tomorrow may not be better than today, but it certainly will be different. The software analyst needs to be cognizant of these trends to look not only for new risks, for each technology change presents many new ones, but also for opportunities to avert current ones.

2.3.7 Summary

By now, it should be clear how the business meta-environment contains risks which will affect, influence, or be directly carried into the software engineering situation that we, as software engineering risk analysts, will be asked to identify, estimate and evaluate. One cannot ever avoid or ignore the fact that a software project is an integral part of a firm's overall business. Thus, we need to look at software risk analysis as starting not only from a software development plan, but from the moment someone: (1) entertained the idea of bidding or not bidding on a contract, (2) began conceptualizing a new software product to be marketed, or (3) contemplated how an organization might utilize an information technology product.

Your job as a software engineering risk analyst is to search for the sources of risk that exist in the meta-environment before they reach your current software engineering situation. Once these risks are known, one must try to alert the firm's business managers of their existence, work with them to avert them, or at least make them understand what impact they will have on the software situation you face.

It is important to remember, however, that although new technology often presents opportunities to reduce business risk, automation is not the answer in every case, and as we pointed out in Chapter 1, it is not computing technology per se that conjures improved competitiveness. Often automation may create many more problems than it solves. Automation, for example, will not automatically reduce the number of people in an organization. It can only place a cap on the number needed in the future. Nor can automation compensate for sloppy business practices. It is the responsibility of the risk analyst to point out these common fallacies as well.

Finally, *the ultimate competitive edge is profit*. Without it, a business does not survive to compete the next day. It has never been my experience that one doesn't have enough opportunity. What one almost always encounters is the lack of resources to pursue those opportunities.

2.4 The Systems Engineering Environment

Many of the influences of the business environment only indirectly affect the software engineering situation. The risks, before they reach the software engineering project, permeate down through many "layers" of environments, each changing or impacting the original risk. By the time a business influence reaches the software engineering project, it is hard to tell what the initial set of conditions were that are now causing the problem. Reconsider again the state vector x in Equation (2.1). Although a risk might be able to be described by a set of variables, say x_1 through x_n, the number of elements observed at the software project level may only be x_1 through x_k, where $k \ll n$. It is not so easy, until things go wrong, and with hindsight as it is being 20-20, to (potentially) pinpoint the causes of the risks (i.e., path of state trajectories) that have placed the project into trouble at this point in time. One of the environmental layers that business risks are typically filtered through first, before they reach the software engineering system of interest, is the systems engineering environment, as illustrated in Figure 2.18. We will not try in our discussion to provide a comprehensive examination of systems engineering, but will instead describe the major sources of risk one encounters.

2.4.1 Systems engineering

Systems engineering has been defined as:

> The process of selecting and synthesizing the application of the appropriate scientific and technological knowledge in order to translate system requirements into a system design, and, subsequently, to produce the

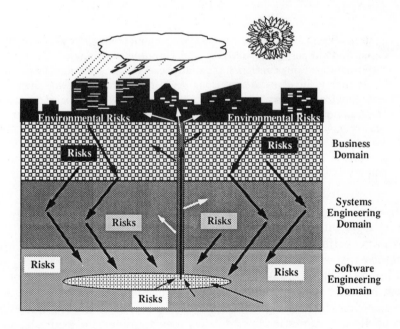

Figure 2.18 Risk Environment

composite equipment, skills, and techniques and to demonstrate that they can be effectively employed as a coherent whole to achieve some stated goal or purpose.[131]

Compare this to the definition of software engineering:

Software engineering is the definition, creation and application of:

1. A well-defined methodology that addresses a software life-cycle of planning, development, and evolution;
2. An established set of software artifacts that documents each step of the life cycle and demonstrates traceability from step to step, and,
3. A set of predictable milestones that can be reviewed at regular intervals throughout the software life-cycle. [132]

The two definitions are very close, as one might expect where parentage is involved. One should not mistake the two, however. There is a broader view of systems engineering that we should be aware of, which has been defined by Andrew Sage. This is paraphrased below:[133]

Systems engineering is a branch of management technology whose aim is to assist and support policy making and planning decisions which result in resource allocation or action. It is usually reserved for systems of large-scale; i.e., when it involves interactions with many *environments* including *technological, economic, legal, managerial, political, social, cultural, professional trade and intellectual, ethical and religious, military, and/or environmental.* Systems engineering accomplishes its objectives by a structured approach to qualitative and quantitative formulation, analysis, and interpretation of the impact of policy and action alternatives upon the perspectives of the various parties affected by the system.

Systems engineering, then, addresses two areas: the broader issues of policy alternatives, and the actual engineering issues themselves. The primary difference between systems engineering and software engineering is that systems engineering is primarily concerned with building the right product, whereas software engineering is concerned with building it right. Or another way of approaching it is, systems engineering is primarily a systemic view, while software engineering is primarily a systematic view.[134] A systems engineer, for example, often assesses the market place, determines product needs, recommends ways

TABLE 2.11 Objectives of Systems Engineering

- To assist in developing clear rational thought processes.
- To encourage full identification and consideration of all impacts of proposed action alternatives or policies.
- To encourage consideration of different value perspectives, needs perspectives, and technology perspectives, in order to provide rational, holistic solution potential for complex problems.
- To solicit the identification of the value of information for use in planning and decision-making.
- To provide explicit identification and consideration of all normally implicit trade-offs, assumptions, constraints, and intentions, and recognition of what is, and is not, important for planning and decision making purposes.
- To improve the understanding of how current systems and the evolution of future products are impacted by present day decisions.
- To improve the accuracy, performance, and efficiency of the overall product under development.
- To apply well-defined methodologies for the resolution of software/system issues.
- To provide rational resolution of conflicts and documentation of differences when resolution is not possible.
- To encourage the recognition of risk and uncertainty considerations into planning and decision making.
- To provide for system changes in response to new or modified requirements.
- To provide an understanding of the role of all stakeholders in the resolution of complex issues and the differing sets of constraints under which they operate.
- To provide clear communication among management and the members of the system/software engineering teams.
- To provide anticipation of contingencies and identification of the impacts of proposed situations.
- To document decisions, the rationale behind decisions, and the actions taken; create and maintain a corporate memory.
- To provide explicit descriptions of schedules and milestones, and an understanding of the effects of time upon issues under consideration.
- To encourage sound action plans for system operational deployment.

of satisfying those needs and developing a market approach.[135] The various roles of the systems engineer are shown in Table 2.11.[136] As a software risk analyst, you must examine closely the outcomes of this systems engineering process, as it will include all the trade-offs resulting from negotiations among all the stakeholders (or money-purse holders) concerning the enterprise's requirements.

This is not simply a search for the risks originating in the system engineering environment, either, which affect your software engineering situation more directly than those of the business environment. The identification of these risks is extremely important. The real reason is that systems engineering is where the risks that come down from the business environment and up from the software engineering environment will be balanced. Many times, you will be the one providing input to the systems engineer in his or her task of the definition, analysis, and evaluation of both policy and engineering risks, and you can have some control over the fate of your situation, which was not so directly available with business risks. The systems engineer should also have the best idea of what is truly required in the application area and should be able to tell you what is feasible and what is not if the identified risks turn into reality.

Let's examine the first aspect of the systems engineering environment—policy.

2.4.1.1 Policy objectives. Policy can be defined as a definitive course of action(s), method of action(s), or doctrinal approach(es) selected from alternatives in the light of present conditions, to guide and usually determine present and future decisions. If the method to select a policy sounds very much like the outcome of a risk analysis, it should. The differences lie only in the scope policy selection addresses. However, this difference in scope is nontrivial, as it very profoundly effects the identity, probability, and magnitude of the risks that will be faced in the software engineering domain that follows.

Let's take an example found in the U.S. government. There exists a general policy toward building large-scale software systems called the "Grand Design." The term was coined in a report by Francis McDonough, the Deputy Commissioner of Information Resources Management Services, U.S. General Services Administration.[137] As he relates it, the Grand Design, based upon the systems approach of the mid-1960s, is used to provide a way to identify and coordinate all related system-level requirements and to wrap them up in a single bundle for planning, oversight, design, and implementation.

The key words are "all related requirements wrapped up in a single bundle." The problem is, at some level, everything in the government is related. For example, suppose an agency requires a new payroll system. The requirements analysis will uncover requirements related to personnel inventory, position inventory, and the skills inventory systems. Soon, the agency is led into considering not just a new payroll system, but a combined and broadly defined payroll and human resources system. Often, some "important" title is assigned to the effort, such as "Human Resources Management for the Year 2000." So, what was a challenging, but doable system's development turns into a very high risk, complex, costly, and probably not doable Grand Design, of what could have been four separate systems. As is usual in government, desire seems to outreach its grasp.

Central policy agencies such as the Office of Management and Budget, the General Services Administration, Congress, including the General Accounting Office, and specific agency oversight officials endorse this approach (which by implication, so do the American people). All requirements are described in a single proposal, in order that there will be no surprises next year or in later years.

The Grand Design has led to few successes, but many failures. One reason has been the inordinate amount of attention from Congress, and from oversight officials at all levels of the executive branch. As a result, Grand Designs have been hard to sell in the executive branch and/or to Congress, if it is not "their" system. Grand Designs are also hard to award, because the huge sums of money involved makes a big difference to winning or losing contractors, to the point of staying in or going out of business. Grand Designs, when they do sell, are usually compromised decisions among all the stakeholders involved, which means suboptimal decisions and difficult to implement systems. Finally, Grand Designs require 10 years or more to implement, after a 2–3 year analysis and bid phase have taken place. During this time, agency managers, vendor managers, political administrations, and congressional members (and the resulting political environment) have changed so often that no one remembers what was originally being sought. The Grand Design approach is being questioned by McDonough as a policy approach, and he is looking for other ways, such as an incremental approach, to get the government out of the box they have placed themselves in.

The Grand Design is seen not only in the federal government, but also in the commercial sector as well. Part of the reason for the Grand Design philosophy has been that proponents of systems engineering often espouse the "big is better" mindset as a point of departure for their analysis. This implicitly (and, in government, explicitly) means global system element relationships, interconnectivity and structure. Also, there is the fact that systems engineering has been taught and accepted as a feasible approach to building systems for many years. Since the design of a system is tightly intertwined with the process used in building it, if this is the basis of knowledge of the system engineers, one could not reasonably expect them to use some other approach. This is certainly true in the federal government, where the political arena does not tolerate problems or failures. Using a nonstandard approach, even if it worked, would get one into trouble, and if it did not work, it would cost one one's career. Of course, trying to use something nonstandard in government is like trying to push water uphill, so most people don't try anyway. Government is amazingly self-correcting when confronted with deviant behavior.

Of course, misunderstanding that there is nothing inherent in systems engineering per se that specifies the Grand Design approach as it currently exists as the only true approach doesn't help matters either. The Grand Design of today is an outgrowth out of the McNamara Defense Department era in the Kennedy administration. McNamara and company tried to reduce what they saw as the unnecessary duplication of effort in the Defense Department, such as the Navy and Air Force each designing and building airplanes that seemed to have identical missions. A single air frame, with minor modifications, it was reasoned, could do the job just as well. They saw the decisions to purchase different airplanes, radars, etc., as being guided by individual service policy and rivalry and sought a way to stop it. It was not, they claimed, good engineering practice.

Sometimes the Grand Design worked, most times it did not.[138] The problem is, if *all* duplication is viewed as unnecessary, and the "minor" (but significant) differences ignored, then one will find oneself rapidly in trouble. The cure has become worse than the disease, at least in government. Again, the Grand Design is a prime example of how environmental influences; i.e., those contained in the political arena, will cause software engineering risks. The SDI is another instance of where political objectives; i.e., the political desire to make the United States impregnable to nuclear attack, gets wrapped up in the technical objective. When it was found that technical solutions were not possible, the political objectives had to change. It should be noted, however, that systems engineering policy objectives exist in all companies, whether they be explicitly defined or implicitly defined. And many are as confused as the U.S. government's.

Thus, the origins of the Grand Design were politically inspired, or *ideologically-based,* and not engineering-based. Not recognizing that simple fact continues to cause trouble. The masquerading of engineering objectives by political ideology is now so entrenched that for many programs, the cost of a program is a function of what dollars are available, as opposed to being based upon a set of achievable and testable requirements driven by an organizational or operational need. It is rare to find a program which can specify its bottom-line, break-even point. It has even been suggested that this state of affairs should be made explicit and called *political systems engineering.*

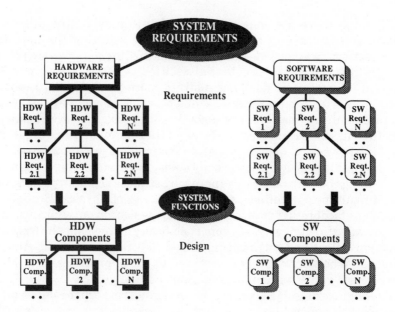

Figure 2.19 Hardware First Approach

2.4.1.2 Engineering objectives. One can understand how the setting of policy influences software engineering risks even more clearly, if one considers the debates in the Defense Department, which involve not only the Grand Design, but a specialized version of it. This is called the "Software First" policy of systems engineering. In this policy, the premise is basically the same as the Grand Design. However, the policy is for the engineering objectives to be geared not around the hardware purchased, but instead around the software to be developed. Many of the purveyors of this policy believe that there is nothing inherently wrong with the Grand Design approach, but that the problems lie instead with the translation of the system level requirements into the software design. This view holds that the problem is when the computer hardware or system architecture is specified too early, it unnecessarily and fatally constrains the software design, as shown in Figure 2.19.[139] If only this were reversed, in other words, if the system design was software-driven instead, with the hardware selected later to meet the requirements of the software design, then all our problems with software development would go away. Or so we are told.

Although there are some merits in this argument (the degrees of design freedom are in fact reduced because selecting the hardware architecture first places some sometimes difficult software design constraints, and therefore potential risks to the software design can't be averted as easily), it does not address more fundamental problems associated with complex systems, one of which is whether the system requirements are feasible. The Software First idea begs the question of whether it, the Grand Design, or any other approach, serves as good engineering *policy*, or if it is just an example of yet another political ideology taking hold. One can easily envision a system that could not be built using the Software First approach because the requirements were too difficult, poorly defined, or defied the laws of physics. Moreover, it flies in the face of other government policies, which forces the procurement of hardware first anyway. Without specifically delineating the boundary between policy and engineering, ideas like Software First, America First, or Who's on First, will continue to cause problems for systems developers. Policy without common sense is dangerous.

The engineering objectives of system engineering are to relate a public (or private) policy, in the form of the stakeholders' value or utility functions, such as the policies on the right to confidentiality of taxpayer records, into an engineering approach and design. System designs cannot maximize every stakeholder's value or utility function, and it is a grave mistake and unfair to ask those that perform systems engineering to decide who will lose, or who will win. It is the policy side of systems engineering which deals with social issues, and politicians, who must make that decision. Furthermore, politicians substituting engineering objectives for policy objectives (or vice versa) is in itself dangerous. The threat of nuclear war, for example, is a *political* problem, and solutions in the human realm must be sought, rather than trying to solve it with *technology*. As Einstein once said, nothing is harder than politics, but one needs to avoid mixing and confusing its objective with that of technology.

Unfortunately, one encounters the substitution of policy for engineering, or vice versa, all the time, albeit in different disguises.[140] Sometimes the guise is obvious, as when the selection of equipment, subcontractor, schedule, budget or allocation of responsibilities are blatantly considered on a political basis, rather than a technical one. Other times, the substitution of policy for engineering isn't so obvious, such as when the system functionality slowly expands, or the choice of equipment seems a bit strange, or the schedule or cost creeps upward or downward (in this case, one might suspect that marketing (i.e., internal politics) rather than technical objectives are being met). Then there are the times when new technology or proprietary equipment is used, but where current technology or third-party equipment is more than adequate. This case often indicates that a technical solution is looking for a political problem to be solved. Then, of course, there is the selection of short-term political solutions, instead of, and at the expense of, more practical, technically longer-term ones. Each of the above can be considered a source of risk for the software engineering situation.

Systems engineering is meant to promote a stable, and repeatable, process to building systems by synthesizing the various requirements into a single tapestry. The part of systems engineering which deals most directly with software is software engineering, and it is upon the crossing of this boundary that we will concentrate our attention next. But the risk analyst must be aware of the two aspects of systems engineering, and must strive to keep policy decisions from unduly placing risks on the engineering side. Furthermore, the software engineering risk analyst must be sensitive to the risks that do originate in policy and systems engineering, as that is what will be carried into the software project.

2.4.2 System/Software engineering boundary

Recall from the beginning of the book that the application of software engineering risks analysis and management is most effective as the system developments increase in size and complexity. It is in these type of system developments where the systems engineering environment and the software engineering situation (i.e., system) boundaries meet, and where the two tend to merge into one. For smaller systems, the boundary demarcation is fairly clear, but as the scale of the system grows, both in size and complexity, this boundary becomes more and more fuzzy.

The fact that merging of the two boundaries occurs is an indication of the complexity of the system being developed, and also an indication of the greater risks involved: The greater the reward (e.g., the more capability provided), the greater the risk (e.g., over budget). Furthermore, this merging of boundaries implies that the energy which passes between the environment and the system (refer back to the section on systems theory) will not be severely impeded or filtered. Thus, policies like those of the Grand Design or Software First, which dictate engineering objectives, and the risks associated with them will rapidly permeate the software engineering situation of interest, making their aversion all the more difficult. The boundary issue between the systems engineering environment and software engineering situation of interest also have some other significant implications.

We presented earlier the idea of the product-oriented and process-oriented paradigms. It is clear that policies like the Grand Design are product-oriented, which accounts for much of the differences, frustrations, and hardships encountered when trying to match (or force fit) the reality of developing large-scale systems with the perceived view of how they are built. This can be explained by the scaling direction problem, as described by Charles McKay.[141] It is, McKay states, easier to scale down, from an intellectual foundation of depth and breath in the life-cycle issues and goals, to a less demanding set of requirements for implementation at a specific time than to scale up from the latter to the former.

What this says, in effect, is that trying to build large-scale systems without the proper tools or understanding to do so increases risk exponentially. The primary areas of risk within the software engineering system of interest one must watch out for are attempts to apply current software engineering models, methodologies, and automation to large-scale systems without resorting to, or taking into account, a proper paradigm of large-scale software systems engineering. This also holds true, but not to such a great extent, in medium system developments. Most of the current models and methods are only applicable for software systems of less than 200,000 lines of operational source code, which have little or no parallelism, fault tolerance, or nonstop operations requirements for them to fulfill. McKay has developed a model to attack the large system issues that possesses a definite process orientation, and which is the basis for development of the Space Station software engineering environment.[142]

Furthermore, for large-scale systems, the support code required to develop, control, and evolve the operational code is often 10 to 20 times larger than the operational code itself, as was shown in Figure 2.5. Large-scale systems are like bridges, where most of the material and time is spent putting up the scaffolding and piers, and very little in order to hold up the roadbed. This is the principle of "increasingly unfavorable internal structure," which states that as an organized system grows larger, the accompanying demands on its structure and infrastructure may grow disproportionally.[143] A gnat, for instance, if its dimensions were enlarged by a freak genetic experiment to the size of a horse, would not be able to stand because its legs would break under the weight. The same would occur if a horse were enlarged to the size of an elephant. The problem is that an animal's volume, and thus its weight, grows cubically as the thickness of its supporting limbs grows linearly. The same holds true of most systems. Thus, attention must be focused not only on the risks that lie buried in the software applications, but also on those that exist in the software support.

The point is, large-scale system acquisitions, developments, or applications will prove to be the most difficult problem for the software risk analyst to handle, because they combine in one place all the elements; i.e., social, business, engineering, political, etc., of a very complex ecosystem. If the proper understanding of where the risks originate are related, and/or change, influence, or are influenced by other risks is not gained, then the project will have a very low probability of success.

2.4.3 Summary

The systems engineering environment is made up of two parts, one that concerns *policy*, and the other that concerns *engineering objectives*. Systems engineering serves to filter both the risks originating in the business environment, as well as those originating in the software engineering environment which are passed upwards. Unfortunately, it also can create some new risks of its own. For instance, risks that should be resolved at the systems engineering level are instead having to be dealt with at an inappropriate software engineering level, or risks that are created by the software engineering level are never, but should be, debated at the appropriate business level, or risks that could be resolved by software engineering methods are preempted by system engineering decisions.

Systems engineering serves as the fulcrum which can reduce risk from one side, and increase benefit to the other. Where one places that fulcrum will determine the benefit and risks to be incurred. The software engineering risk analyst must take into account these risks, and understand their origins, to be able to develop a cogent risk assessment and aversion strategy. This brings us at last to the situation, or system, of interest we will examine: software engineering.

2.5 Software Engineering

The inherent difficulties or risks within software relate to what is called their *essence*.[144] Risks, such as those related to the domain specific knowledge, or to those difficulties that currently attend its production, are termed *accidents*. The essence of software is the permanent, unchanging elements, in contrast to the variable nature of the domain software is applied to or the process involved in developing it. The essence of a software element, then, is defined to be the abstract, conceptual construct formed by the interlocking concepts of data sets, relationships among data, algorithms, and invocation of functions.

Similarly, the essence of software engineering risk analysis and management are the identification, estimation, evaluation, and control of software risks which are formed by the *product* and *process* of software engineering. The risks involved in the product are inherent, and are described by an irreducible set of attributes. The risks associated with these can *never* be eliminated, but only controlled within ever-changing limits. On the other hand, the risks involved in the process are variable, and change with the application of technology and/or appearance of new knowledge.[145] These risks, then, can practically be contained or averted.[146]

The inherent risks in software are due to the irreducible attributes of its *complexity, changeability, conformity,* and *invisibility.* Complexity is an attribute directly related to the capability of a human being's understanding of both the nonbehavioral and behavioral aspects of a system.[147,148] Nonbehavioral complexity in software is measured in terms of its computational, structural, and form/functional complexity. Computational complexity deals with the time and space (memory) requirements necessary of the software, while structural complexity concerns the size and connectivity (or redundancy) among software components. In contrast, form/functional complexity is linked to the range and domain of the software's ultimate application. Software can support a wide range of application domains, not being limited in any way by its material form. In other words, a piece of wooden plank can be used to build a house, but not a dam. The inherent form of the material (e.g., strength, density, malleability, etc.) is a limiting factor of the functions (i.e., structures) for which wood is a suitable medium. Software has neither inherent form nor function limitations.

This inherent complexity of software can also be seen when one attempts to scale up the size of a software element. The computational and structural interactions are not merely repetitions of the smaller elements in bigger sizes, but change in a *nonlinear fashion*. The span of conceptual hierarchies faced by a system designer or programmer is greater than in almost any profession. The result is that granularity increase changes the overall complexity in a nonlinearly way as well, as was shown earlier by the scaling direction problem. Small changes do not have necessarily small effects.

The behavioral complexity concerns the aspects of perceptual complexity (the human's ability to recognize, rotate, reverse, etc., displayed patterns as a function of various attributes of pattern; e.g., segments or line patterns) and problem-solving complexity (the ability of humans to reason about and problem-solve certain types of problems, such as syntactic or arithmetic problems). In software systems, especially large ones, no one has the full understanding of the system. Pieces of knowledge are strewn across all the developers involved. Further, what is being manipulated are symbols, both by the computer and the human, which makes perceptual complexity extremely difficult.

The attribute of changeability is the constant pressure for the software entity to keep changing. These pressures are caused by the existing environmental pressures (i.e., the business environment and systems engineering environment). New computer technology, new domains for information technology application, new social policy demands, etc., all add to the pressure. Because software is the element which can change most easily in a system, it will also be the element which will feel the impact of the pressure to change the most. A single program may undergo thousands of modifications until it reaches a point that none of the original code exists, but it is the "same" program. No physical system undergoes as many rapid changes as software can. System sizes will increase, the understanding of the system will decrease, leading the complexity of the system to increase to a point beyond anyone's understanding.

Another essence of software is its conformity, both in form and function. As opposed to the building of houses or bridges or star systems, which are complex systems in themselves and conform to basic physical laws, software does not. Software does not conform to the laws of God, but instead to the laws of man. The software in a system is designed to conform to all the capriciousness and arbitrariness that can be found in the human condition, in which it must interact. Although houses or bridges must also conform to societal laws, their conformity is regulated by much more than software, and by their inherent function (i.e., to provide housing or a path across an obstacle).

The last essence of software is its invisibility and, thus, un-visualizability. Software has no physical elements associated with it to map it into three-dimensional space. Its structure is abstract, having no smell, weight, or feel. It is almost the stuff of dreams. And like dreams, because one cannot let another experience it for themselves, we are limited by our language ability to communicate it only inexactly to another.

2.5.1 Sources of software engineering risk

The risks involved in software engineering come from many quarters. There exist the risks that originate in the *business* and *systems engineering environments*, and which cross the boundary into the software engineering domain. Then there are risks that exist within the *process* and *product* of software engineering itself, which combine with the business and systems engineering risks to compound or influence the overall risks to the enterprise. The union of all these sources of risk forms the totality of risks one must contend with in software engineering risk analysis and management. For the remainder of the book, we will examine the aspects

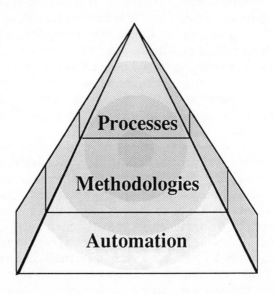

Figure 2.20 Software Engineering Model

of risk that exist within the process and product of software engineering, trying to identify where, and what risks, might arise (remember, a risk is not a certainty—just a possibility).

We will start in Chapter 3 by examining the process of software engineering, pointing out some of the risks therein. For this book, we will claim that the process part of software engineering consists of a hierarchy of three interconnected layers, as illustrated in Figure 2.20, which forms an emergence model. At the bottom is the logical, systematic process, used to define how the software product will be developed. Above that are the software engineering methods and techniques which implement those models. At the top of the structure is the automation of the methods and techniques.[149]

The definitional *process* of developing a software system is the foundation of the software engineering. It is the most important aspect of software engineering and acts as the framework for software development. The basic function of the process is to describe the chain of events required to create a particular software product. It is also meant to avert the category of risk associated with the lack of control. The

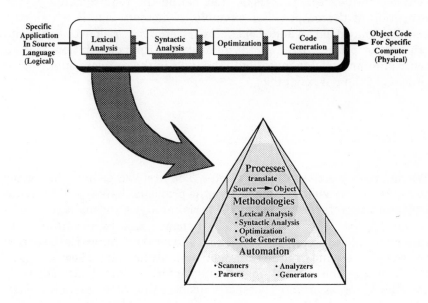

Figure 2.21 Software Engineering Model

methods in a software engineering environment include all the techniques which are required to define, describe, abstract, modify, refine, and document the software entity. The methods used are defined by the development process shown below it in the illustration. Methods are meant to avert the types of risk associated with the lack of information. The use of the computer to implement the methods necessary to develop the software product we term *automation*. Automation is meant to avert the kinds of risk associated with the lack of time.

We will conclude by stating that the software engineering process and the application of risk analysis and control are directly analogous to the operations of a compiler, as illustrated in Figure 2.21. Roughly speaking, a compiler translates a set of desires (logical input) into a reality (physical output). This translation is defined by a series of well-defined steps (lexical analysis, syntactic analysis, code generation, etc.), each performing a "subtranslation" with its own input and output descriptions; i.e., a process. The output descriptions of one step are reused as inputs to the next. Certain methods are used to implement each of these steps, and each step is in turn automated. The specific steps and methods used are dependent on both the original input description (the language used) and ultimate output description (the target computer), as well as the "outside influences;" i.e., risks, that define the requirements on the execution of the output. For example, if memory size is a risk, the compiler may need an added optimization step (i.e., risk aversion) in its translation process to reduce the quantity of output description. We will use a similar model to investigate the risks in the software engineering process in the next chapter.

2.6 Summary

We had two objectives in this chapter. The first was to help the reader to expand upon what was learned in the previous chapter and to create the connection of software engineering risk analysis and management to a wider universe of discourse. We managed this by examining the fundamentals of system theory, which showed that many risks seen in the software engineering environment actually have their beginnings in the business and system engineering environments. This led us to consider a process-oriented perspective concerning software engineering. This in turn forced a reevaluation of what should be included into the domain of traditional software engineering risk analysis.

Our second objective, also along the lines of confronting one's biases and beliefs, was to try to stimulate one's thinking about truth and beauty, and their relationship to software engineering risk and its management. We accomplished this by trying to show that one must look past all the mechanics of software engineering risk analysis and management to the essence of what it is we are trying to accomplish by creating and using software intensive systems. Our risk analysis must not only be inward looking, but outward looking as well.

We do not want to leave the impression that all the risks faced in software engineering can be blamed on something, or someone, else. It is all too easy to blame outside forces. Software engineering, as we will see in the next chapter, provides plenty of fertile soil in which to grow risks. The software engineering risk analyst must take into account all sources of risk, and resist staying in the comfortable software environment cocoon. Ultimately, risk analysis and management can only be based upon context, decisions, decision processes, and their interfaces for any project existing within a model of a *business enterprise*.

In summary, to fully employ software engineering risk analysis and management in an effective manner, an analyst must:

1. Identify, estimate, evaluate, and control the risks that originate in the business and system engineering environments as a minimum.
2. Identify, estimate, evaluate, and control the risks that originate in the software engineering situation of interest (i.e., the process and the product of software engineering).

The risks that originate in the business and system engineering environments may directly impact the software engineering situation (e.g., you are working on a defense contract, and Congress cuts your specific defense project's budget) or indirectly influence it (e.g., Congress cuts defense budgets across the board). To determine whether a risk is a direct risk or indirect risk requires a systemic approach, where the risks in the software engineering environment flow upwards, and the risks from the environments can be tracked and dealt with. The union of the two sets provides the complete set of risks that will be encountered and must be contained or averted.

Do not forget, however, the fact that whatever decision to avert a risk is taken, it will likely be suboptimal.[150] Funding is both finite and rationed, and only a few of the variables are controlled. This reflects the inability to manipulate all the factors that may affect the final outcome, and of this you *must* be aware. Organizational inertia and distribution of authority will also increase suboptimization of your recommendations concerning the reduction of risk. Given this situation, it will be up to you, as software risk analyst, to apply the appropriate techniques and methods of risk analysis and control, as well as their manner of communication.

Questions

1 Return to the scenario presented in the beginning of the chapter and assume you are the risk analyst. What would you consider its *Weltanschauung* to be?

2 Explain what is meant by emergence. Is the concept a violation of the laws of entropy? Reservation systems are a prime example of the concept of emergence or synergy. Name some others.

3 It has been written that software has no physical properties, and is not subject to the laws of gravity or to the laws of electrodynamics. How about to the laws of thermodynamics and entropy?

4 Information technology is forcing the restructuring of company organizations, making them less hierarchical. Core business practices (production, marketing and administration) are becoming more transparent. The marketplace is no longer geographic, but global, where firms cannot hide from potential competition, or from others' judgments on their performance. Judgments on governmental actions are made instantaneously, with the results shown in the stock markets and currency exchanges, which some feel are leading to a major loss of national sovereignty. Given Nolan's model, what are the above implications for businesses who find themselves in Stage 2? Stage 4? Stage 6?

5 Other implications of information technology are these: Information technology does not make work simpler, but instead more complex. The explicit information content of work actually increases. As a result of information technology spreading across all industry sectors, according to the Office of Technology Assessment, 75% of the U.S. working population will have to be retrained by the year 2000. What impact will this have on U.S. businesses' ability to compete? What actions would you advise an individual business take to reduce its business risk in the light of these projections?

6 Both mainframe and personal computer sales are slowing down, as it appears that the market is becoming saturated at both ends of the spectrum. Many observers are saying that this marks the changing of the computer industry into a commodity business, with all the risks associated with cyclic industries. Given that commodity businesses typically make industrial components with a high obsolescence factor, how will this change affect the risks seen by a business using, developing, or selling information technology systems?

7 Explain the differences between the product-oriented perspective and the process-oriented perspective. Why is the product-oriented perspective dominant? Show how the addition of TQM-like product and process metrics, say using the IEEE Standard Dictionary of Measures to Produce Reliable Software, Std 982.1-1988, could be used to help change a product-oriented process like DOD-STD-2167A into a process-oriented one.

8 Reread Andrew Sage's extension of Goedel's Incompleteness Theorem. How does it affect the perception of a software project's success criteria in the developer's eyes? The customer's? What about the risks involved, both from a development perspective and operational perspective?

9 In the *Star Trek* television series and movies, there is something called the Prime Directive, which basically states that when visiting a planet, nothing must be done to interfere with the normal evolution of the planet's life forms. What is the Prime Directive's relevance to Goedel's Incompleteness Theorem, risk analysis, and risk management?

10 What is chaos? What are its implications to building software systems? Do you think it is or will become a major problem? Explain.

11 Return to the scenario presented in the beginning of the chapter, and assume you are the risk analyst. What are the basic objectives of the firm depicted? What are its risks in doing business with the government? In the commercial sector, especially as a diversified company? What type of culture does it exhibit? Will the culture be the same for all business units in all geographic areas? What are the risks that originate in its business approach that might find their way into the software engineering projects? Postulate some reasons as to why the current software projects might be in trouble.

12 *Glasnost* and *perestroika* are radically changing the defense industry. One major problem will be the return on investment that defense companies can expect from much smaller programs. Describe some of the other new risks faced by companies who wish to stay in defense. Trace some of the impacts of these new business risks through the systems engineering environment down to the software engineering environment. What advice would you give firms doing business in defense?

13 Using again the company described in the scenario, let's turn to risks faced by a corporation when it does commercial business. Investigate and describe the risks it faces in the systems integration market. Detail the near-term and long-term competitive risks and the technological risks, both as a product and service supplier and user. What other types of risks does the company face? Summarize your findings in a concise one-page note to the chairman.

14 Many companies use the slogan, "We sell what we use, and we use what we sell." The company in the scenario is one of these. What risks are there to a company with this approach? How does the firm in the scenario reduce its business risks caused by its dependency on different computing technologies, both for its internal and external use?

15 In developing commercial products, the market is the final arbitrator of success or failure. Often, when a product fails, it can be traced to the fact that the product developers' view did not match the market view. From what you know, discuss some of the risks involved to a business in undertaking commercial product developments. What are some steps that a company can take to mitigate these risks?

16 Small companies tend to avoid many of the business risks of information technology by buying systems off the shelf, rather than developing them themselves. When their businesses must integrate data, then usually a company is moved into creating its own custom-tailored systems. Describe the general risks of information technology to a business as it moves from being a small business, to a medium-sized business, to a large business.

17 What are TQM and the Software Engineering Capability Assessment? Describe the objectives of both. Where do they fit in risk analysis and/or control? Define some metrics that can be used for improving the software engineering process. What are their strengths? What are their weaknesses?

18 TQM can be a great help in collecting software forensic engineering data, since a fundamental element of TQM is the incremental improvement of a stabilized and repeatable process. Explain how you would use TQM to support forensic software engineering.

19 What is systems engineering? What is the difference between policy and engineering objectives? When are they different? When are they the same? When should they be the same? Different?

20 Revisit the technical literature concerning the SDI debate. Detail how the political objectives drive the technical solutions sought, and later, how did the technical solutions force a change in the political objectives? Trace the technical objections, counterobjections, and the change of minds among key participants over time. Could a more realistic balance of the two result in a system that could have been built, given the world and domestic political situation at the time?

21 Name at least three risks that are formed in the systems engineering environment that directly affect the software engineering process. Name three that indirectly affect it. How are the risks that originate in the business environment changed by the systems engineering process?

22 Why is the boundary between systems engineering and software engineering blurred? How can one separate the two? Should they be separated?

23 Why isn't domain-specific knowledge considered part of the essence of software? Should it be? How are the two related?

24 What is the most important element of software engineering? The process model, the methods used, or the automation? Where do most of the risks originate? Justify your answer with examples or counterexamples.

References

1. Carl Newton, "IT: Too Important for Specialists" *Director*, June 1989.

2. K. R. Hammond, "Generalization in Operational Contexts: What Does It Mean? Can It Be Done?" *IEEE Transactions on Systems, Man, and Cybernetics*, Vol. SMC-16, No.3, May/June 1986.

3. Lola L. Lopes, "Aesthetics and the Decision Sciences," *IEEE Transactions on Systems, Man, and Cybernetics*, Vol. SMC-16, No.3, May/June 1986.

4. On average, about 30% of all oil and gas explorations end in the total failure of a dry hole. The rate is closer to 80% or higher in a new oil exploration area. In 1982, the drilling of over 24,000 dry holes (out of 78,000) cost the industry $4–6 billion.

5. Robert L. Flood and Ewart R. Carson, *Dealing with Complexity: An Introduction to the Theory and Application of Systems Science*, Plenum Press, London, 1988.

6. Lola L. Lopes, "Aesthetics and the Decision Sciences," *IEEE Transactions on Systems, Man, and Cybernetics*, Vol. SMC-16, No.3, May/June 1986.

7. Robert L. Flood and Ewart R. Carson, *Dealing with Complexity: An Introduction to the Theory and Application of Systems Science*, Plenum Press, London, 1988.

8. K. R. Hammond, "Generalization in Operational Contexts: What Does It Mean? Can It Be Done?" *IEEE Transactions on Systems, Man, and Cybernetics*, Vol. SMC-16, No.3, May/June 1986.

9. Ibid.

10. Lola L. Lopes, "Aesthetics and the Decision Sciences," *IEEE Transactions on Systems, Man, and Cybernetics*, Vol. SMC-16, No.3, May/June 1986.

11. Andrew P. Sage, "Systems Engineering: Fundamental Limits and Future Prospects," *Proceedings of the IEEE*, Vol. 69, No.2, February 1981. This article is an excellent overview of the limitations a risk analyst will face when doing software engineering risk analysis and management.

12. We will also use the scenario as a source of questions at the end of the next three chapters.

13. Theodore C. Taylor, "Perspectives on Some Problems of Concept Selection, Management and Complexity in Military System Development," *Naval War College Review*, Vol. XXXIV, No. 5/Sequence 287, September-October 1981.

14. George J. Chambers, "What is a Systems Engineer?" *IEEE Transactions on Systems, Man, and Cybernetics*, Vol. SMC-15, No.4, July/August 1985.

15. Melvin W. Lifson, and Edward F. Shaifer, Jr., *Decision and Risk Management for Construction Management*, John Wiley & Sons, New York, 1982.

16. The information from this section was derived from Robert Flood's and Ewart Carson's book, *Dealing With Complexity: An Introduction to the Theory and Applica-*

tion of Systems Science, Plenum Press, London, 1988. This book is an outstanding book on systems science and its relation to understanding complex systems. It is a must read by anyone involved in risk analysis.

17. Chapter 3 of Charette's *Software Engineering Risk Analysis and Management* contains a discussion on the concepts of discrete and random variables.

18. John A. Mills, "A Pragmatic View of the System Architect," *Communications of the ACM*, Vol. 28, No.7, July 1985.

19. Melvin W. Lifson, and Edward F. Shaifer, Jr., *Decision and Risk Management for Construction Management*, John Wiley & Sons, New York, 1982.

20. Because the authors do not have an opportunity to respond, to be fair, we have chosen that they remain anonymous.

21. Richard DeMillo et al., "Social Processes and Proofs of Theorems and Proofs," *Communications of the ACM*, Vol. 22, No. 5, May 1989.

22. Domenico Ferrari, "Considerations on the Insularity of Performance Evaluation," *IEEE Transactions on Software Engineering*, Vol. SE-12, No. 6, June 1986. This insularity is sometimes so strong even within the field of computing itself that some techniques, such as computer performance analysis, which can be helpful in reducing the risks found in operating systems design, computer architecture, software engineering, or systems organization, are virtually ignored because it requires one to take a systems, and therefore, a wider, perspective than that of the individual subdiscipline.

   The real problem is that most software developers do not, or don't want to, take any moral responsibility for their code, even if it can cause harm. The software profession likes to keep itself shielded when faced with this question. In a situation like the one faced by the Aegis cruiser crew when it shot down an Iranian Airbus A300, who is at fault? The operator, or the system designer who didn't understand that the display could be misinterpreted during high stress situations? How many designers of systems ever operate them in anger? Damn few, from what I have seen. It would be much better to have designers of systems who had to "pack their own parachutes."

23. A recent national EIA Workshop was held on the theme: "The National Software Crisis—A Re-Assessment." The conclusion at the workshop was that there was not a software crisis, but a systems engineering crisis. For more information about why this conclusion was reached, refer to the reports: "Software Development Methodology," by Robert Charette, Hank Stuebing, and Tom Conrad, and "Software Management and Organization," by Morton Lenske and Jerry Raveling, *Report of the 22nd Annual EIA Computer Resources and Data and Configuration Management Workshop*, September 1988.

24. Bill Curtis et al., "A Field Study of the Software Design Process for Large Scale Systems," *Communications of The ACM*, Vol. 31, No. 11, November 1988.

25. Claude Banville and Maurice Landry, "Can the Field of MIS be Disciplined?" *Communications of the ACM*, Vol. 32, No. 1, January 1989.

26. Robert N. Charette, *Software Engineering Environments: Concepts and Technology*, McGraw-Hill, Inc. New York, 1986.

27. Christiane Floyd, *Computers and Democracy: A Scandinavian Challenge*, Dower Publishing Company Ltd., Aldershot, England, 1987, Chapter 9.

28. The bottom-up concentration (i.e., concentrating on code efficiency, then worrying about whether the requirements make any sense) was another important historical reason for today's dominance of the product-oriented view.

29. This can also be seen in the fact that it takes 15–18 years, on average, for a software engineering method to become accepted after its inception. Thus, one can safely assume the models used by many businesses today for large-scale systems are nearly 15 years out of date. For more information, see William Riddle, "The Magic Number Eighteen Plus or Minus Three: A Study of Software Technology Maturation," *DoD Related Software Technology Requirements, Practices, and Prospects for the Future*, IDA Paper P1788, 1984.

30. A large problem today in computer science research, especially at universities and colleges, is that the product-oriented view is taught, and the resulting experience is gained by students on this model only. Thus, when they get into the industry, they join three generations of previously trained students who are trying to apply models that do not work to their current jobs. There are some good reasons for this; the primary ones are that: (a) there isn't enough time for students to be part of the building of large- and small-scale systems that would demonstrate to them the problems and differences in each, although some universities, like the University of Houston, Clear Lake City; University of Massachusetts, Amherst; Carnegie-Mellon University, Pittsburgh; and University of Southern California, Los Angeles, are concerned about the issue and have initiated ongoing large-scale projects to try to help students gain some experience; (b) there are no specific textbooks on the process-oriented approach and the deficiencies of the product-oriented one; and (c) most of the experience in the subject resides in the industry, not academia. Very few university professors have ever been a party of (not consultant to) a very large scale project, and fewer still, two. What you do not know is difficult to teach.

31. They said I had to write in some sex and violence bits into the book to make it more interesting. So there is the sex part, in case you hadn't noticed.

32. Reducing the impact of the reductionist view is the primary role of the Risk Estimate of the Situation, with its emphasis on objectives, strategies, tactics, and means, mentioned in Appendix A.

33. "Business Success Through Market-Wise Systems," AT&T Consumer Communications Services, AT&T, 1989.

34. *TELSTAR II Techniques and Procedures*, TELSTAR Control Office, British TELECOM, London, 1989. TELSTAR II consists of 12 interrelated elements: strategic planning; planning and resource management; architecture management; instruments management; systems development; computer installation management; data management; project management; quality management; office automation; verification, validation, and testing; and security.

35. For those ready to dismiss these as "unlucky" accidents, or not caused by computer failures, but human failure, please think again. The system includes the human operator. Furthermore, without computer technology many of these systems would not be cost-efficient or technologically feasible.

36. "SEN Risk Index, 1976 to Present," *ACM Software Engineering Notes*, Vol. 14, No. 1, January 1989.

37. Charles Perrow, *Normal Accidents: Living with High-Risk Technologies*, Basic Books, New York, 1984.

38. Andrew P. Sage, "Systems Engineering: Fundamental Limits and Future Prospects," *Proceedings of the IEEE*, Vol. 69, No.2, February 1981.

39. John Markoff, "In Computer Behavior, Elements of Chaos," *New York Times*, 11 September, 1988.

40. The underlying principles of chaotic attractors have been known about since 1892, when written about by Jules Henri Poincaré. For more extensive coverage, please see James Gleick, *Chaos: Making a New Science*, Penguin Books, New York, 1988, as well as the *IEEE Proceedings* "Special Issue on Chaotic Systems," Vol. 75, No. 8, 1987.

41. For graphic representations of chaotic systems, see to John Briggs and F. David Peat, *Turbulent Mirror, An Illustrated Guide to Chaos Theory and the Science of Wholeness*, Harper & Row, New York, 1989, as well as Ralph H. Abraham and Christopher Shaw, *Dynamics: The Geometry of Behavior; Part 2: Chaotic Behavior*, Aerial Press, Inc., Santa Cruz, CA, 1984.

42. The importance of the cardinal rules of risk management listed in Appendix A, especially the one "do no harm," becomes more obvious.

43. Certain non–von Neumann architectures, such as data-flow machines, are not sequentially controlled. Thus, any specific output cannot be correlated with certainty to any specific input. An error of computation may occur, but not be able to be detected. In applications such as signal processing, this does not matter very much, since it is the aggregation of data that is important, rather than any single piece of data. Similarly, in neural networks, since it is a learning system, there will be things outside the domain of experience of the computational system, which means that errors are part and parcel of the system. Without errors, the system cannot learn.

Furthermore, system software is a leading suspect in creating chaotic states. Review Figure 2.5, which shows the tremendous increase in the support software required for applications. This software not only cannot cope with the unexpected states that the application systems finds itself in, but may actually promote these states of chaotic behavior itself, because of the complex and mosaic pattern of alternatively tight and loose couplings in the support software. These were caused by the support software almost exclusively being created with the product-oriented paradigm. The disparity between this model and reality are thought to be prime motivators for chaos to exist.

44. Which again lends weight to the argument of moving away from a product-oriented paradigm for systems development. For more detail, see the article by John Markoff, "In Computer Behavior, Elements of Chaos," *The New York Times*, 11 September, 1988.

45. Robert N. Charette, *Software Engineering Environments: Concepts and Technology*, McGraw-Hill, Inc. New York,1986.

46. It is similar, I suppose in reflection, to the concept of original sin.

47. F. T. Haner and James C. Ford, *Contemporary Management*, Charles E. Merrill Publishing Company, Columbus, OH, 1973.

48. Walter B. Wentz and Gerald I. Eyrich, *Marketing, Theory and Application*, Harcourt, Brace & World, Inc., New York, 1970.

49. A couple of things should be kept in mind. First, profit is not "predictable," but is a result of actions to obtain revenue and lower cost, both of which are continuous random variables. Second, one may also substitute "price" for "revenue" in determining profit. And third, profit is not the mission of the company. It is only a measure.

50. "Managing Technology," *IEEE Spectrum*, Vol. 26, No. 3, March 1989.

51. "What Happened to Britain's Economic Miracle," *Director*, April 1988.

52. Walter B. Wentz and Gerald I. Eyrich, *Marketing, Theory and Application*, Harcourt, Brace & World, Inc., New York, 1970. One should note that products and services have also been grouped along different lines. For example, E. S. Savas has categorized them along four axes: private goods, toll services, common pool services, and collective goods. Further, services can be provided by: government service; intergovernmental agreement; contract; franchise; grant; voucher; free market; voluntary service; and self-service. For more information, see E. S. Savas, *Privatizing the Public Sector*, Chatham House, Chatham, NJ, 1982.

53. We will draw heavily from James J. Cunnane's article, "The Business Equation: Is it Out of Balance? The Impact of Government Policies on Defense Contractors," *National Defense Magazine*, Vol. LXXIII, No. 439, July/August 1988. Although the changes in Europe have only happened in the past 6 months, the risks facing contractors in the defense industry were already increasing almost 2 years previously. It will be very interesting how the defense industry reacts to the increased uncertainty. Some contractors seem to be whining, some seem to be reacting well. After all, the attainment and preservation of peace is the reason for their existence.

54. The reasons for the arms race are very complex and are a subject for a different book. But they include defense issues such as how much is enough, whether the quality or the quantity of weapon systems provide the best defense for the money, and so forth. Hopefully, *glasnost* and *perestroika* will last and make these pressures a thing of the past.

55. For example, in 1984, the DoD was planning to spend $478 billion in fiscal 1990, but in actuality, it is getting $295.6 billion. Part of the reason is that there is a growing mismatch between public perceptions of the defense problem and its realities. A recent poll indicated that the public believes that 50% of the defense budget is lost to waste and fraud, and more than 25% to straight fraud. In reality, study after study shows that the money spent on defense is better than many projects of similar size in the private sector, and is better than twice as good as any other part of the federal government. See Jacques S. Gansler, *Affording Defense*, The MIT Press, Cambridge, MA, 1989.

56. James J. Cunnane, "The Business Equation: Is it Out of Balance? The Impact of Government Policies on Defense Contractors," *National Defense Magazine*, Vol. LXXIII, No. 439, July/August 1988.

57. Ibid.

58. Howard Yudkin, in a speech given to *National Security Industrial Association Conference* on "Software Initiatives and Their Impact on the Competitive Edge," 10 May, 1988.

59. Norman R. Augustine, *Augustine's Laws,* American Institute of Aeronautics and Astronautics, New York, 1983.

60. This is not true in reality. Above a certain profit limit, the DoD terms profits excessive and tries to recover it. Thus, above a certain level, which is always changing, there is no incentive to lower cost. Also, when using a fixed price contract on research and development projects, the incentive becomes even less because of the inherent risky nature of overspending on R&D efforts. The U.S. government has an underlying assumption that all technical problems can be solved as long as money (but not too much) can be thrown at them.

61. To get an idea of the risky nature of doing DoD business, consider its basic characteristics: The market size is "voted" in every year, thus providing little continuity or stability to a firm; small groups of individuals can severely constrain the market size by canceling major programs; payment of bills takes 6 months or more; vying for market share does not really exist, as the DoD will second source if the contact is considered too big; cost sharing on large programs is becoming the norm; technical qualifications are important, but will be sacrificed for low cost; and so forth. The result is one where the DoD pretends to act like a commercial market, when this suits it, and then like a closed and regulated one, when it can get a better deal for itself. Instead of buyer beware, the environment is more like seller beware.

62. This type of arbitrary market pressure tempts government contract firms to either try to "beat the system," or leave it. The periodic defense scandals are results of the former. The scandals are exacerbated by stories of air crash–survivable coffee pots that cost $10,000, even though this cost is legally justifiable by the mandated requirements placed on the coffee pot by the government and, often, Congress.
    Legal ways often used to beat the system are for defense firms to bid on systems that they do not believe will really work as specified by the government and thus will require massive maintenance efforts, or to offer more than they can deliver at no cost to the government, which will result in the same thing. By winning the contract, the system might be able to be made to work, and if it doesn't, then at least some revenue to keep the company alive is coming in, even if the profits are capped. This is in preference to saying, "Hey, this specification is idiotic, will not work after 25 years of implementation effort, and you ought to start again." Taking that attitude will not win many contracts or many friends. And the whole situation is exacerbated when the government decides to award a contract on cost alone, even when the evaluation criteria priorities are supposed to be technical ones.

63. "Contractors Adapt To Survive Under New U.S. Acquisition Policies," *Aviation Week & Space Technology*, March 20, 1989.

64. Richard Lapolice, "Government Oversight—How Much?" *Improving Defense Industrial Competitiveness*, NSIA LOMC-REC-QRAC-SWC Joint Conference Proceedings, 19 July, 1989. In 1982, 138,000 companies sold goods to DoD. In 1987, only 38,000 decided it was worth the effort. Additionally, the pressure on defense firms has been so high, and the future outlook so bleak, that Wall Street has given a thumbs down to defense stocks. This increases the risk to anyone wanting to stay in the industry, as their primary means of obtaining capital has been removed. The situation, as described by Atwood: "The extent of the mistrust that exists in the Pentagon, in

industry, and in Congress, is shocking. I have never seen anything like it. I will be candid and tell you that if a major corporation—whether it be a General Motors or a Ford or a General Electric or an AT&T—ever had the relationship with its suppliers that DoD has with its contractors, that company would be out of business. The existing confrontational atmosphere is completely, unnecessarily and, more importantly, it wastes scarce resources that could be used in other, more productive endeavors." From "Once More, With Feeling: Atwood Takes the Baton," by David Bond, *Aviation Week & Space Technology*, December 18, 1989.

65. Kymberly Taylor and Scott Palmer, "Vendors Balk at FAA RFP And Call Pricing Too Risky," *Federal Computer Week*, May 1, 1989.

66. Congress loves to micro-manage defense projects. It went from taking personal interest in 650 DoD programs in 1970 to 1900 in 1985, with over a 15-fold increase in the number of studies and reports requested by Congress, many of which dealt with social impacts of the defense dollars spent in certain districts. Those 1900 programs mean jobs, and therefore reelection, in a lot of congressional districts.
   The downsizing of the budget also causes other strange reactions such as: when faced with bad times, a business will react by cutting its losses quickly, while a government program will react by reducing program scope in order to stretch it out in hopes of more money becoming available in the next budget cycle.

67. "How Are Complex Military Systems Procured, And Can It Be Done Better?" *IEEE Spectrum* (special issue), Vol. 25, No. 12, November 1988.

68. Norman R. Augustine, *Augustine's Laws*, American Institute of Aeronautics and Astronautics, New York, 1983.

69. Amos A. Jordan and William J. Taylor Jr., *American National Security: Policy and Process*, John Hopkins University Press, Baltimore, MD, 1981.

70. Robert F. Coulam, *The Illusions of Choice*, Princeton University Press, Princeton, NJ, 1977.

71. Joseph Campbell, *The Power of Myth*, Doubleday, New York, 1988.

72. Howard Frank, "The Influence of Corporate Culture," *TPT Network Management Magazine*, February 1988.

73. R. D. Banker and C. F. Kemerer, "Scale Economies in New Software Development," *IEEE Transactions on Software Engineering*, Vol. 15, No. 10, October 1989.

74. "Ecce Robo," The *Economist*, October 15, 1988.

75. "Face-to-Face with Paul Strassman," *Inc. Magazine*, March 1988.

76. A reader may be tempted to say that the Japanese approach is the result of using a process-oriented paradigm, and the U.S. approach is a result of using a product-oriented one. This would be a mistake. The differences in approach are grounded in beliefs that existed within the separate culture centuries before computing came into being. It is true that process-oriented paradigm *resembles* Eastern-type philosophy, but to extend it into an argument that Japanese computing may be better because they use a process-oriented approach would not hold. Japanese computing, like American computing, is still based very much on product-oriented approaches. A

better line of study would be to see if Japanese or Asian philosophies might be useful in helping make the process-oriented approach more robust.

77. Thomas R. Stuelpnagel, "Total Quality Management," *National Defense Magazine*, Vol. LXXIII, No. 442, November 1988.

78. Thomas Boswell, "There's Joy in Birdland," *The Washington Post Magazine*, 9 July, 1989. The Orioles rapid change was due in large part to paying renewed attention to the basics of the game, and not deviating from them. Unfortunately, the Orioles did not manage to keep their first-half pace, and the number of games in the lead, which was six at the All-Star break, shrank until on the next to last day in the season, they were eliminated, and had to settle for second place in their division. The cause can be traced to the fact that their pitchers' earned run average increased, hitters' batting averages fell, and errors increased. This illustrates important points about TQM: you have to keep at it, and the measurement criteria must be *both* measurable and *controllable*.

79. The Japanese are constantly amused by U.S. commercials promising high-quality products, as if this is supposed to be something one should be grateful for. The Japanese expect, and assume, high quality in their products, and to claim a stereo possesses high quality makes about as much sense to them as claiming credit for water being wet. Also, do not confuse quality with reliability. Quality is a static descriptor of the system, while reliability is dynamic. A battery on the shelf, for example, may be of high quality, but over time, its reliability goes down. Quality is intrinsic, whereas reliability is a measure of performance. Further, the concept of reliability *excludes* the consequences of failure and their causes, which happen to be external to the system or component. This means reliability analysis is not the same as *risk* analysis either.

80. "Special Issue on USAF R&M 2000 Initiative," *IEEE Transactions on Reliability*, Vol. R-36, No. 3, August 1987. TQM is a good idea for government projects, since one has, in effect, decided what the goods or services are to be provided.

There are some special problems of applying TQM in the government, however. Despite calls for increased quality, the government still emphasizes low cost. Improving quality increases costs, thus placing more pressure on profit. Second, the government is advising contractors more and more on how to develop a system, as well as what to develop. This can impede TQM as the flexibility for making improvements is reduced. Third, the government does not like long-term contracts, which again impedes TQM, which depends on small improvements occurring over a long period of time. Fourth, the Competition in Contracting Act requires all procurements to be open and fully competitive, whereas TQM emphasizes close long-term relationships with suppliers. If the relationship is too close, a company can find itself under investigation for collusion, price fixing, unfair trade, and so forth. Fifth, in applying TQM to improve a product, one must engage in an adversarial role. The product must be torn down, and the problems identified. To improve the process, however, the developer and customer must work together. Unfortunately, the current adversarial relationship between the government and its suppliers will only be exacerbated by the first requirement, and not be implemented in the second. Finally, as Figure 2.10 illustrates, any improvements gained by TQM by contractors only reduces the government's cost, and does not increase the profit to the contractor. Thus, there isn't any incentive to apply TQM. For more information on the problems of TQM in government, refer to Bruce Smith, "Total Quality Management Will Require Procurement Changes, Perseverance," *Aviation Week & Space Technology*, December 18, 1989.

81. "Detroit's Drive for the Fast Lane," U.S. News & World Report, 22 January, 1990.

82. *Technology and the American Economic Transition: Choices for the Future*, Office of Technology Assessment, USGPO, May 1988.

83. "Software Development Capability/Capacity Review," *ASD Pamphlet 800-5*, 10 September, 1987.

84. Notice that the lack of skill in software engineering is now a business risk in the DoD environment. Too few skilled workers are available for the proposed contract, and the company will not be allowed to bid.

85. Watts S. Humphrey et al., *A Method for Assessing the Software Engineering Capability of Contractors*, Software Engineering Institute, February 1987.

86. Although use in acquisition and source selection is not too far behind. The use of the assessment for source selection is already starting to appear in some DoD projects. The SEI assessment technique has also been used in some military programs in the Production Readiness Review to assess the feasibility of proceeding with the program. Also, its use in helping provide information for a Risk Aversion Plan is also considered a prime objective, which is a good idea.

87. In the SEI context, a process is a systematic series of steps directed towards some end.

88. "News Briefs," *Aviation & Space Technology*, McGraw-Hill, Inc., November 14, 1988.

89. Robert B. Doane, "Acquisition Process Initiatives at Air Force Electronics Systems Division," in the National Security Industrial Association Conference on *Software Initiatives and Their Impact on the Competitive Edge*, 10 May, 1988.

90. Organizations which have moved to flatter, directive management schemes seem to be more effective. See "The Roaring Mouse," by Yale Lubkin, *National Defense Magazine*, Vol. LXXIII, No. 12, December 1988.

91. John L. King and Kenneth L. Kraemer, "Evolution and Organizational Information Systems: An Assessment of Nolan's Stage Model," *Communications of the ACM*, Vol. 27, No. 5, May 1984.

92. Izak Benbast et al., "A Critique of the Stage Hypothesis: Theory and Empirical Evidence," *Communications of the ACM*, Vol. 27, No. 5, May 1984.

93. Peter G. W. Keen, "Information Systems and Organizational Change," *Communications of the ACM*, Vol. 24, No. 1, January 1981.

94. Robert N. Charette, *Software Engineering Environments: Concepts and Technology*, McGraw-Hill, Inc. New York, 1986.

95. M. Lynne Markus and Niels Bjorn-Anderson, "Power Over Users: Its Exercise by System Professionals" in *Communications of the ACM*, Vol. 27, No. 5, May 1984.

96. Walter R. Beam, James D. Palmer, and Andrew P. Sage, "Systems Engineering for Software Productivity," *IEEE Transactions on Systems, Man, and Cybernetics*, Vol. SMC-17, No. 2, March/April 1987. Risk management is especially important in bidding situations where there are multiple teams involved. The worst feeling is not knowing what risks your subcontractors or team members are bringing to the

contract. Too often this is forgotten in the rush of a bid as companies look at potential teammates for what they can add to the team, not how they can detract from it. The emphasis is on courtship, and in its frenzy, as the old saying goes, love is blind.

97. Michael Porter, *Competitive Strategy,* The Free Press, New York, 1980.

98. Michael Porter, *Competitive Advantage,* The Free Press, New York, 1985.

99. Bruce D. Henderson, "The Origins of Strategy," *Harvard Business Review,* Vol. 89, No. 6, November-December 1989. Henderson points out that competitors that make their living in the same way cannot coexist, that something must differentiate them in order to survive. In biology, this is called *Gause's Principle of Competitive Exclusion.* The application of information technology to provide a differentiator is one of the means available to a business.

   Henderson goes on to list five basic elements of strategic competition which are important for the analyst to recall when evaluating information technology risks, especially whether a company is getting any value for money. The elements are: (1) an ability to understand competitive behavior as a system in which competitors, customers, and resources continually interact; (2) an ability to use this understanding to predict how a given strategic move will rebalance the competitive equilibrium; (3) resources that can be permanently committed to new uses even though the benefits will be deferred; (4) an ability to predict risk and return with enough accuracy to justify commitment; and (5) a willingness to act.

100. "Smart Machines, Smart People," *Inc. Magazine,* January 1989.

101. "Dinosaurs in the Modern Age?" *Director,* December 1988.

102. "Face-to-Face with Paul Strassman," *Inc. Magazine,* March 1988.

103. *Technology and the American Economic Transition: Choices for the Future,* Office of Technology Assessment, USGPO, May 1988.

104. Ibid.

105. Blake Ives and Gerald P. Learmonth, "The Information System as a Competitive Weapon," *Communications of the ACM,* Vol. 27, No. 12, December 1984.

106. The proposed merger was viewed as a possible antitrust violation by the U.S. Justice Department, which threatened to block the merger. It was called off a few months later. See "American, Delta Computer Reservations Deal May Intensify Global Competition," *Aviation & Space Technology,* McGraw-Hill, Inc., 13 February, 1989, and "Delta and American Cancel Their Deal," *Business Week,* 10 July, 1989. However, this has not kept Delta from trying a merger with someone else. On 29 September, 1989, Delta, TWA, and Northwest Airlines announced they intended to merge their reservation systems into one to provide global operations. To avoid Justice Department objections, a separate operating company will own the newly created reservation system. See "3 Airlines to Join Reservations," *The Washington Times,* 29 September 1989.

107. Ian Meiklejohn, "Slowly, Slowly into the Open," *Management Today,* August 1989.

108. "Computer Glitch Costs American $50 Million in Lost Ticket Sales" *Dallas Morning News,* 11 September, 1988.

109. "Face-to-Face with Paul Strassman," *Inc. Magazine*, March 1988.

110. Carl Newton, "IT: Too Important for Specialists" *Director*, June 1989.

111. T. Lincoln, "Do Computer Systems Really Pay-Off?" *Information Management*, Vol. 11, No. 1, August 1986.

112. *Does Information Technology Slow You Down?*, Kobler Unit, Imperial College, London, 1988.

113. "Agency Will Mothball Cargo Computer System Unless New Operator Is Found," *Aviation & Space Technology*, McGraw-Hill, Inc., 12 December, 1988.

114. "The Splintering Stock Exchange," *The Economist*, 11 February, 1989.

115. Richard Nolan, "Managing the Crisis in Data Processing," *Harvard Business Review*, March-April 1979.

116. Richard Nolan, "Managing the Computer Resource," *Communications of the ACM*, Vol. 16, No. 7, July 1973.

117. John L. King and Kenneth L. Kraemer; "Evolution and Organizational Information Systems: An Assessment of Nolan's Stage Model," *Communications of the ACM*, Vol. 27, No. 5, May 1984.

118. Izak Benbast et al., "A Critique of the Stage Hypothesis: Theory and Empirical Evidence," *Communications of the ACM*, Vol. 27, No. 5, May 1984.

119. Michael L. Sullivan-Trainor, "Leaders Go Beyond Basics, Link IS to Business Strategy," *Computerworld*, September 11, 1989. The ranking according to Computerworld of the top 10 U.S. companies using their method are, in order: MCI Communications Corp.; GTE Corp.; AMR Corp.; Bankers Trust; Banc One Corp.; General Dynamics Corp.; Security Pacific Corp.; Baxter Healthcare Corp.; Contel Corp.; and the Gillette Company.

120. Vijay Gurbaxani and Haim Mendelson, "Software and Hardware in Data Processing Budgets," *IEEE Transactions on Software Engineering*, Vol. SE-13, No. 9, September 1987.

121. Giacomo Bucci and Dario Maio, "Merging Performance and Cost-Benefit Analysis in Computer Systems Evaluation," *IEEE Computer*, Vol. 15, No. 9, September 1982.

122. William G. Shepard, "Causes of Increased Competition in the U.S. Economy, 1939–1980," *The Review of Economics and Statistics*, November 1982.

123. Thomas Malone et al., "The Logic of Electronic Markets," *Harvard Business Review*, May-June 1989.

124. *Technology and the American Economic Transition: Choices for the Future*, Office of Technology Assessment, USGPO, May 1988.

125. Review Chapter 4 of Robert N. Charette, *Software Engineering Risk Analysis and Management*, McGraw-Hill, Inc., New York, 1989.

126. Consult Tom Forestor's books, *High-Tech Society*, and *The Information Technology Revolution*, published by The MIT Press in 1989 and 1985, respectively, for current information technology trends.

127. William Hoover, "Are We Ready for the Systems Integration Boom?" *Management Conference of the ADAPSO*, March 1988.

128. John Gantz, "The Network of 1998," *TPT Network Management*, January 1988.

129. Yulio Mizuno, "Software Quality Improvement," *IEEE Computer,* Vol. 16, No. 3, March 1983.

130. Kim B. Clark, "What Strategy Can Do for Technology," *Harvard Business Review*, Vol. 89, No. 6, November-December 1989.

131. W. P. Chase, *Management of Systems Engineering*, John Wiley & Sons, New York, 1982.

132. Robert N. Charette, *Software Engineering Environments: Concepts & Technology*, McGraw-Hill, Inc. New York, 1986.

133. Andrew P. Sage, "Systems Engineering: Fundamental Limits and Future Prospects," *Proceedings of the IEEE*, Vol. 69, No. 2, February 1981.

134. Recall that systemic views of software engineering also include reductionist, i.e., structured, approaches.

135. George J. Chambers, "What Is a Systems Engineer?" *IEEE Transactions on Systems, Man, and Cybernetics*, Vol. SMC-15, No. 4, July/August 1985.

136. Andrew P. Sage, "Systems Engineering: Fundamental Limits and Future Prospects," *Proceedings of the IEEE*, Vol. 69, No. 2, February 1981.

137. Francis A. McDonough, *An Evaluation of the Grand Design Approach to Developing Computer Based Application Systems*, Washington, DC, Information Resources Management Services, U.S. General Services Administration, September 1988. There has been much fallout from many in government over this term, and the charge that GAO leveled against organizations using the Grand Design approach. Not unexpectedly, few of the targeted organization have said they are doing Grand Designs, but if they were, the real problem anyway was not the Grand Design, but instead the Grand Implementation (I am still trying to figure out the difference). Others have taken another tack and have proudly proclaimed that they have been able to implement Grand Designs successfully. Listening to all the rebuttals could make one believe that there isn't a problem, or that the Grand Design was a problem that has been solved!! Take these rebuttals *cum grano salis.*

138. A graphic example of what can happen because of Grand Design occurred in the 1960s during the joint U.S. Air Force/Navy effort to build a common aircraft. It was meant to save money by providing a common airframe that could be tailored to meet each service's individual mission requirements. The TFX's (Tactical Fighter, Experimental) airframe was required to support the minimum aerodynamic properties necessary for it to be tailored for use in a ground attack tactical fighter, interdiction strike aircraft, low-altitude supersonic penetrating nuclear bomber, or fleet air-defense

role. As it turned out, the requirements were incompatible. The first time the aircraft landed aboard a carrier, it buckled the deck. The requirements to support all the other missions increased the weight to such an amount that the plane was too heavy to land on aircraft carriers. Needless to say, the Navy never got its plane and had to start over. This is described, as well as the background to the politicalization of systems engineering by the Department of Defense, in Robert F. Coulam's excellent book, *The Illusions of Choice*, Princeton University Press, Princeton, NJ, 1977.

139. Edward H. Schlosser, "The Role of Requirements in the System Development Process," presentation given at Requirements and Engineering and Rapid Prototyping Workshop, TTCP XTP-2, Ft. Monmouth, NJ, November 1989. We should note that Schlosser presented what was wrong with the current procurement strategy, and that he postulated a more reasonable approach where neither hardware nor software was selected until much later in the development cycle.

140. Barry Boehm, *Software Risk Management Tutorial*, TRW, April 1988.

141. Charles McKay, *Ada and the Intel iAPX432 Support of Networks*, AIAA-83-2417-CP, 1983.

142. Charles McKay, Robert Charette, and David Auty, "A Study to Identify Tools Needed To Extend The MAPSE to Support the Life Cycle of Large, Complex, Distributed Systems Such as the Space Station Program," University of Houston, NASA Contract NAS9-17010, May 1986. It is also being used in one of the environments under development for the Software Technology for Adaptable and Reliable Systems (STARS) project.

143. Robert Wright, *Three Scientists and Their Gods*, Times Books, New York, 1988.

144. Frederick P. Brooks, Jr., "No Silver Bullet," *IEEE Computer*, Vol. 20, No. 4, April 1987.

145. R. L. Henneman and W. B. Rouse, "On Measuring the Complexity of Monitoring and Controlling Large-Scale Systems," *IEEE Transactions on Systems, Man, and Cybernetics*, Vol. SMC-16, No. 2, March/April 1986.

146. In the future, it is easy to envision that technology will increase productivity to a point where the time or efforts required to develop software code is practically eliminated, and that type of risk will no longer be one of concern. Off-the-shelf software is an example. The key word is "practically," however, as there will always be a limit as to what can be effectively accomplished.

147. Robert L. Flood and Ewart R. Carson, *Dealing with Complexity: An Introduction to the Theory and Application of Systems Science*, Plenum Press, London, 1988.

148. W. B. Rouse and S. H. Rouse, "Measures of Complexity of Fault Diagnosis Tasks," *IEEE Transactions on Systems, Man, and Cybernetics*, Vol. SMC-9, No. 11, November 1979.

149. The automated combination of these three elements form a software engineering environment. The model of the process of developing a software system is the key to its automation. See Robert N. Charette, *Software Engineering Environments: Concepts and Technology*, McGraw-Hill, Inc. New York, 1986.

150. Walter B. Wentz and Gerald I. Eyrich, *Marketing, Theory and Application*, Harcourt, Brace & World, Inc., New York, 1970.

Chapter

3

Software Engineering and the Risks to the Business

"Every decision you make is a mistake."

EDWARD DAHLBERG

3.0 Introduction

Every now and then a person of genius appears, and the world is changed by their unique insight. One such man was Mr. Francis Webb. At the end of the last century, Mr. Webb was a locomotive engineer working for the London and North Western Railway, and was a man of no little importance. You see, the railway engines he designed were exalted everywhere because of the sheer inspiration they imparted to others who came into contact with them. He achieved, in their design, that state of parsimony expressed by Ockham that so often eludes others in their pursuit of greatness. You must understand, not only were Webb's engines no faster or more powerful than the others of the day, they fired everyone's wildest imaginations with their staggering costs and inefficiency.

As Webb's locomotive designs grew in style and maturity, the costs and inefficiencies steadily grew, while simultaneously avoiding unnecessary increases in performance. In fact, his engines were able to increase the price/performance ratio by simple but elegant solutions, such as not starting. But even here, he was able to improve. After much intensive work, Webb amazed even his most ardent admirers, when pure genius was expressed in his crowning achievement: the Teutonic class locomotive. This machine, whose description matches the wonderment one must surely feel if one could travel beyond the stellar void, where words have only emotion and no meaning, had, among other novel design features, two pairs of driving wheels which were not connected, thus enabling them to turn in opposite directions at the same time. Thus built, the Teutonic locomotive could, at full power, remain absolutely motionless, while each gear and flywheel met its functional requirement and design specifications perfectly, thereby achieving a level of brilliance few others could ever hope to obtain, although many try to emulate it today.[1]

In the previous chapter, we showed that an information system and the development practices used to create it must be linked intimately with the business and systems engineering contexts in which it resides. Every information system is created for use in a business situation, and in order to be effective, it must be developed with that understanding in mind. This is analogous to a physician needing to know the environment in which a patient lives in order to fully understand what may be the cause of an illness.

We also examined in the last chapter a myriad of risks typically associated with software engineering, but demonstrated that many in reality originated outside the software engineering situation of interest. Now we wish to refocus our attention on the risks that are born of the process of software development itself. For even if all the risks generated by the business and system engineering environments were within acceptable limits, there still remains a multitude of risks associated with the software engineering process and application being developed which could affect the business environment of interest. Again, using a medical analogy, this is the same as understanding the risks of a cure to the patient's well-being. We will defer the examination of the application-specific risks until Chapter 4.

From what we have encountered previously, the characteristic elements of the process of software engineering can be said to be: (a) avoiding unmanageable, unmasterable complexity,[2] and (b) improving software's effective efficiency and quality.[3] All software process models, software methodologies, methods, and techniques, as well as their automation, have these two elements as their common purpose. Underperformance of resources is a primary risk encountered in the software engineering domain whose consequences are encountered under the guises of cost overruns, schedule delays, technical problems, evolution problems, and so forth. The application of the discipline of software engineering is meant to avert these risks, and avert the consequences these risks have on the business environment. Therefore, one can say the process of software engineering is primarily targeted at averting the risks associated with the accidents and essence of software, as defined previously, and, second, at averting business risk.

In general, the degree of aversion or containment of the accidental and essential risks of software is proportional to the efforts undertaken to manage them. By applying the discipline of software engineering, the risks encountered will be averted to a greater degree than by not applying it. However, to achieve this end, there are a number of caveats attached. First, one must know how specifically to apply the aversion techniques associated with requirements, specification, design, etc., methods. Otherwise, risks will likely be increased instead. This was illustrated by the SEI Contractor Capability study reviewed in the previous chapter. The application of automated methods without a process model will increase the risks to a software project, in comparison to only using a good process model with minimal automation support. Thus, there exists an explicit ordering in the application of these efforts which can either avert, or increase, the likelihood and magnitude of risks encountered, as well as create new ones of their own. This may also seem obvious, but many software developments today focus on the provision of the automation first, and the enterprise model last. The reasons for this can be traced to: (a) ignorance of the risks incurred by automating first, and (b) purchasing automation, such as CASE tools, seems like a cheap way to demonstrate progress. This in turn makes continued development "by fumbling around" easier (i.e., less costly) than starting with, and applying, a disciplined approach.

Second, the application of the discipline of software engineering requires strong management backing. Although some might take offense and see the following comment as disparaging to the computer field, given the general results of the software engineering, it is very close to the mark: "I would describe software engineering as heavy-handed management based on modest common-sense principles....To enforce such standards across the board is a management breakthrough, but not a technical one." [4] The application of software engineering is similar to risk control and monitoring: You only get out what you put in. We will devote some time to the implicit and explicit risks involved in software engineering management during the remainder of this chapter.

Our third and final point is that even if we possess good management, and proceed to apply software engineering principles in the proper order, a specific software engineering technique itself may have risks associated with them. These risks may be caused by specific circumstances, such as the size and complexity of the software system trying to be built. Some techniques do not work as well as others in large software developments versus small, just as certain programming languages do not seem to fit as well for implementing one type of design versus another. We do not pretend to have all the answers to where risks lie. It would be ludicrous to try, as each situation is distinct. Therefore, it is ultimately up to the individual risk analyst to take into consideration the particular nature of the software project and how the risks associated with software engineering methods exhibit themselves in those circumstances. However, to effectively do so, the risk analyst requires a firm understanding of how to build software systems and what is considered the "correct" practice to applying sound software engineering principles. Thus we will spend a great deal of time in this chapter explaining the basic objectives of software engineering and how it is applied.

We will, where we can, point out possible risks and the circumstances in which they appear.[5] We will also point out sources to consult concerning these possible risks. However, the analyst should look critically at the processes described and think about where inherent risks might also be lurking. To do so successfully, it is critical not to lose sight of the three essential elements of risk analysis and management: (1) risks are only possibilities, they are not certainties; (2) the basic causes of a risk originate from the lack of information, the lack of time, and/or the lack of control over events, so concentrate on identifying the circumstance when these occur; and (3) risks are subjective, so the perception of risk in the dimensions of identity, likelihood, and consequence are necessarily unique in time and space.

We will start with an examination of the representative risks associated with software process models. Next, we will turn our attention to the characteristic risks involved with software engineering methods/techniques. And finally, we will investigate the typical risks involved with the automation associated with both of them. The primary source material for this chapter is my previous book, *Software Engineering Environments: Concepts and Technology* (McGraw-Hill, 1986). The material has been updated to reflect new research and practitioner findings about the software engineering process.

3.1 Software Engineering Enterprise

The software engineering process model is the most important element of the process of software engineering. Putting it in another light, the capability to achieve software quality, productivity, and the management of complexity *all* stem from this foundation, as do the risks involved and opportunities available for exploitation in the creation of a software system. The quality of a software system is limited by the quality and applicability of the process used to develop and evolve it.[6,7] Without a defined process, software engineering isn't a discipline, but an ad hoc assemblage of disparate parts which are not very effective when applied.

When one speaks of the process of software engineering, one is simply describing a *model of expectations*; i.e., what is expected to occur during the development of a software product. A specific process model contains, therefore, the policies and doctrines of a particular software development. The model embodies a certain perspective on the development process and the mechanisms that are able to influence it and, as such, is a hypothesis. The model also provides the common vocabulary by which all the participants involved can communicate. The process model of software development describes what will be done, how it will be accomplished, how long it will take, when it will be finished and by whom, using what to implement it. It introduces stability into the the development process and provides avenues for improvement. A poor model of the process can lead to confusion as to what the goals of the project are, as well as a misapplication of the resources to accomplish them. We will see later that undercapitalization of resources, as well as their inefficient use, are linked closely to the software process model used.

A process model also describes the connections and relevance to the business and system engineering environments of interest discussed in Chapter 2. Thus, it is used to describe, either implicitly or explicitly (depending on the fidelity of the model) the *enterprise* the business or organization is ultimately going to use the software system in. If these connections are minimal, then the software development process will operate very much in a vacuum and therefore will not, or cannot, serve a business's necessities very well. Thus, process models attempt primarily to overcome the causes of risk associated with the kinds of lack of control found in a software enterprise.

One point before we go on to characterizing a process model: We have used the word "enterprise" many times already in this book, but we should remind ourselves that it means *an undertaking that is difficult, complicated, and has a strong element of risk*. One would agree that any software project but the most trivial-sized one meets this definition. However, most process models only cover a minimal part of what should be included in a business enterprise involving information technology. This can be seen by examining Figure 3.1, which illustrates that the software engineering domain is only a subset of the large set of systems engineering and business domains.

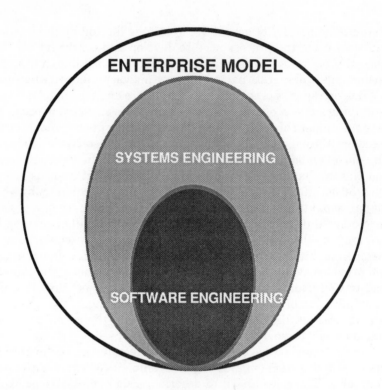

Figure 3.1 Organization of Risks

The process models we will shortly examine, to be totally effective, should be part and parcel of a total business enterprise model, such as British TELECOM's TELSTAR, mentioned in the previous chapter. Recall that it covers the total life of an information system, from the initial business strategic plan where a business need has been determined, to its external acquisition, internal development or use, all the way to the system's eventual retirement. Current process models have concentrated mainly on the software engineering dominion, and have not integrated themselves into the overall business enterprise. Business enterprise modeling, and how software engineering process models can be expanded to include the business process model, is one of the weakest elements in effective utilization of information technology today. We will necessarily spotlight only the software engineering aspects of the process models in the following sections, but the above caveat should be recalled every now and then to place them in their proper context.

3.1.1 Process model characterization

Given infinite time and infinite resources, for any currently contemplated software enterprise, all three basic causes of risk (i.e., lack of information, lack of time, and/or lack of control) could eventually be overcome, and we could enjoy a software system that met all of our critical success criteria. Unfortunately, we are not usually afforded this luxury. Thus, when time and money are constrained, the causes of risk appear.

A process model tries to avert these fundamental causes of risks, especially risks caused by the lack of control, by introducing predictability into the process, thereby providing some degree of regulation of the risks encountered.[8] This predictability (and its resulting stability) is also crucial to the attainment of quality, by providing the metrics needed to compare the enterprise against certain specified tolerance levels. Additionally, a process model provides a framework for achieving effective efficiency, or productivity, by making the process repeatable, since it is limited by the equation:[9]

$$\text{Time of the task} = \sum_i \text{frequency}_i \bullet \text{time}_i$$

We said *effective* efficiency, because productivity can be increased by *any* increase in the output in relationship to input. Simply increasing the output in relationship to input can be deceptive, as one can increase programming productivity by simply adding NOPs into the code. Effective productivity increases include many intangible items that are not easily measured, such as increased quality of a development process, reduced personnel or inventories, and so forth. The point is, if development efforts and resources are aimed at the wrong target, it does not matter how quickly one gets there. Thus, when we speak of effective productivity, we are talking about *efficiency* of resources.

Process models are also important in averting the other causes of risk, the lack of information and lack of time. The process model reduces the lack of information by providing prescriptive information about what is expected to be accomplished. This provides a uniform framework in which to undertake problem solving, thereby reducing the risks associated with descriptive uncertainty. In other words, they help one think. A process model further articulates when something is required to be performed and when. This reduces wasted time by diminishing the friction incurred by development personnel thrashing about. As a side benefit, by prescribing the steps that must be accomplished in the enterprise, one is capable of producing better estimations of the time and resource requirements. This reduces the risks encountered with the undercapitalization of resources.

There are a number of other characteristics of process models of which one should also be aware.[10,11] A good process model, as well as possessing the attributes already presented, should fulfill three main requirements. It should possess *good descriptive power, generality,* and *suitability to computerization.* Descriptive power means possessing the capability to describe the essential aspects of the enterprise in a realistic manner. Therefore, it must support the description of the development process itself, as well as its management. This means providing the ability to describe the concurrent and distributed activities that take place (across the width of the enterprise) and provide it across the life cycle (i.e., its length). In addition, the model must be able to accommodate the inevitable and continuous change that always occurs in software developments, and be flexible enough to handle "special cases" where the model does not fit especially well. Finally, it must provide for a sufficient definition of detail (i.e., depth).

Generality means that the model should have the capability to describe a wide variety of software systems and the components and actions that compose a particular system. This also means accommodating the issues related to uncertainty of requirements caused by delaying commitment or specifying too early. Thus, the model should be able to support many different submodels that occur within any single development.

Suitability to computerization means that the model must be amenable to computerization. The last point is important, if we are to fully exploit the power that automation provides in the attainment of lower productivity risks.

Like all models, process models are limited by their fidelity in regards to reality. Some models are more "robust" and "complete" than others. By robust and complete, we mean the system of interest and environments of interests associated with the information system itself match closely to the business enterprise that it is required to support. This is of consequential significance to the type, likelihood, and magnitude of the risks likely to be encountered during the development itself. If the wrong model is selected, then there will be a mismatch between what is happening and what is "supposed" to happen. If the mismatch is great enough, at best, it will only frustrate the developers by increasing friction in the development, thereby lowering productivity, quality, and the manageability of the software complexity (i.e., increasing the risks in each). At worst, it may mean that the project collapses because "you can't get there from here." The right side of Figure 1.12 depicts what happens when traveling down this path. As we will see shortly, the complexity of the software, which can be characterized generally by its size, will be a prime driver in which a model is required, and whether there exists a mismatch.[12]

3.1.2 Some software engineering process models

There exist a number of models describing the software development process, commonly called *life-cycle models* in use and in the literature. Currently, there appear to be five major types of software development life-cycle models: *Waterfall / Design-driven, Rapid-prototype / Strategy-driven, Operational, Spiral,* and *Knowledge-based.* Others are described elsewhere by different names, but they also fall into one of these five categories. Since most models do not describe the many risks that are involved in their application, especially their assumptions about the software enterprise, we will examine each in turn and try to point out where some of their sources of risk exist.

3.1.2.1 The waterfall model. The waterfall or design-driven life-cycle model is perhaps the oldest and most well-known of all process models. It was developed during the 1960s as an outgrowth of earlier stage-wise models of the late 1950s,[13] and has as its major characteristic the view of software development as proceeding through successive stages called "phases," as illustrated in Figure 3.2. Each phase is culminated in essence by a validation and verification activity whose objective is to eliminate as many problems as possible in the products or "artifacts" of that particular phase before it it used in the next phase. The waterfall model was one of the first formal attempts to impose a discipline and philosophy on the development of software. This discipline was meant to try to reduce the major cause of risk related to the lack of control experienced in early software developments, thus the model reflects primarily an economic view as seen through an engineering project manager's eyes of a software enterprise.

The phases generally are categorized in the following fashion:

- *Requirements Analysis* is the definition and analysis of the users' or stakeholders' criterion. Often a feasibility phase precedes this

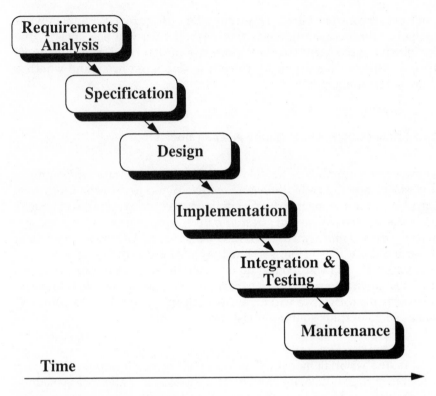

Figure 3.2 Waterfall Process Model

phase to determine the software enterprise's economic or technical viability, and superiority of alternative concepts.

- *Specification* is the translation of requirements into a precise description of the externals of the software system, including functions, interfaces, and performance aspects.
- *Design* is the creation of an abstraction of a software system (including the hardware and software architecture) that is consistent with the specification, and provides a reasonable description for implementation including its control structures, data structures, interface relations, sizing, key algorithms, and assumptions concerning each program component.
- *Implementation* is the creation of a verified and properly functioning set of software components which implements the design.
- *Integration and Testing* are the creation of a fully functioning software system from the software components implemented, and the

determination of whether the system satisfies the requirements.
* *Maintenance* is the updating of the software system necessary to fix problems, modify the system architecture, or enhance the software. The process model is repeated during this phase.

The names and precise description of each phase differs from company to company or author to author. Requirements, for example, have alternatively been called "Needs Analysis," "System/Software Requirements," and "Concepts Definition," among others. In all cases, however, the phases are thought to be discrete, and one does not move into the next phase without completing its successor. Therefore, a large amount of specification and design detail is required before coding can be started. More importantly, since the system under development is seen as a monolithic entity, a single delivery date for the system is also assumed.

Notice that each phase moves from a higher level of abstraction to some lower one.[14] Each phase is one of a series of abstractions that proceeds from a high level of abstraction (less detail) to a lower level of abstraction (more detail). In some sense, each phase is an implementation of the previous phase's "design."

A derivative of the waterfall model is called the design driven model. This approach modifies the waterfall model somewhat by loosening the constraints that a predecessor phase must be completed before moving into its successor phase. This change was made necessary because, after applying the waterfall model to larger type system developments, it was quickly realized that trying to define everything before moving on to the next step was unreasonable in practice, especially since in reality little is known, can be described, or can be adequately changed. This modification allows a software enterprise to be in two or more development phases simultaneously, with iteration occurring between stages. Notice, however, this modification does not imply that any steps of the process can be omitted.

3.1.2.1.1 Opportunities and risks. There are a number of opportunities, or advantages, to using the waterfall/design-driven model. Conceptually, it describes intuitively at a high level of granularity how most practitioners feel the software development process ought to take place. *Ideally*, one ought to define everything that is required before moving on to the next step, to ensure nothing is lost or forgotten. After all, each of the tasks described in the model must be done at some point, and, on the surface, any different ordering would seem to produce a less successful outcome. Boehm has shown that, overall, the model does indeed match fairly well to how software is actually developed in practice, at least in small systems.[15] Additionally, trying to improve efficiency by reordering the steps has proven to be suboptimal. Furthermore, one always should be cognizant of what is being produced at any particular time; i.e., where one is in the development process. Since, as Thomas Mann once wrote, "time has no divisions to mark its passing," some artificial demarcation of time (and space) is required. Phase definitions, reviews, and software products (or artifacts, in the current vernacular) accomplish this task fairly well. They also serve as important development reset or resynchronization points, where if the development is proceeding poorly, control can be regained. Finally, there exists a large body of experience, tradition, and success in applying the model, which makes it very attractive to use.

However, there are a number of risks associated with the waterfall/ design-driven model as well. First, the model doesn't possess a high degree of descriptive power. It fails to realistically integrate "activities" that span life-cycle phases, such as resource management, quality assurance, configuration management, or verification and validation. These activities tend to sit "outside" this model and are not fully integrated into it. This makes the management and control of the enterprise very difficult.

The model also lacks generality in three key areas. First, the model assumes a near-perfect process will take place. Thus, when problems (i.e., risks) inevitably occur, the model has a difficult time making the necessary adjustments to avert or contain them. For instance, it is the nature of the software business to change requirements throughout development, based upon schedule, cost, or some other influence. Since making an error in a requirement or specification may not be found until design time or later, iterating back to the requirement phase is necessary to correct the problem. It is also necessary to correct anything that followed in subsequent phases that depended on that particular requirement. Because this is not easily accomplished, great pressure is then placed on defining the requirements only once, which then often results in poorly defined requirements and poorly implemented systems. It also leads to poorly documented software, because new changes are not "rippled back" into all the appropriate places. "Fix it in maintenance" or, worse, "We need to build it over again" are the often-heard cries when using a waterfall/design-driven process model, often renamed, the "build it twice" process model.

Second, this model was developed when the problem of small systems with a monolithic nature was the dominant influence on software engineering. The model does not scale up very well to large or complex enterprises, where constantly changing requirements and integration of system components are the key operational parameters. In these developments, the unknowns in the front end of the development cycle are much greater than in small- or medium-sized systems. The system needs to be partitioned and pieced together, rather than constructed all at once. Likewise, evolution of a system using a waterfall approach is difficult because one does not really evolve a system, but starts over again from scratch.

Third, the model does not reflect the fact that the process is part of a larger process of developing a system, or of the even larger process of supporting a business. The waterfall model exemplifies the closed system and reductionist view presented in Chapter 2, and represents a very insular, systematic perspective of developing software.

Finally, the model lacks suitability to computerization. It was developed during the period of time when computer-aided engineering was not well understood. Thus, the model is geared towards and is processable primarily by humans, not computers.

Overall, the waterfall/design-driven model is the archetype of the *product-driven model* examined in Chapter 2. As one can see, there is little protection provided against the basic causes of risk for anything but small software development projects. Moreover, when scaling up to larger projects, the creation of a monolithic system becomes inappropriate, with the risks of using the model outweighing any advantages gained.

3.1.2.2 Rapid-prototyping model. The rapid-prototype model was created to overcome the perceived deficiencies of the waterfall/design-driven model.[16-21] As we noted above, the deficiencies really center more around the fact that the waterfall model does not cope well with the challenges of uncertainty and changes which confront software developments, especially larger ones which take place over the course of many years. The major deficiency was the assumption that requirements could be specified and made stable, when in fact they cannot be, especially when these requirements are meant to satisfy *predicted* user needs 5 or more years in the future. During the time interval created by the system development, significant changes to the user requirements and organizational operating procedures are likely, thus making the requirements volatile. Applying the waterfall model in a situation with unstable or erratic requirements would mean that one would never get out of the requirements phase. The incremental model was meant to correct this deficiency.

Incremental development is the creation of a software system in small, manageable functional components of the system called increments, where each successive increment is made up of the currently existing system with additional functionality, as illustrated in Figure 3.3. The software system is not viewed as a monolithic entity with a single delivery date, but as an integration of the outputs of successive steps of each iteration. Only at the end is the "complete system" available, although each increment is a working system in and of itself.

The incremental development approach is meant to accommodate uncertainty by the elimination of the necessity to possess an exhaustive set of requirements, specifications and designs for the complete system before the start of the software system implementation. Because refinement and elaboration of these increments, called "builds" (baselined intermediate software products), are formally specified at the beginning of each new increment, a natural evolutionary framework, which can

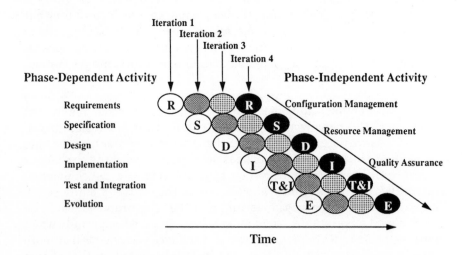

Figure 3.3 Incremental Process Model

flexibly reconcile change, can be provided. Incremental development also helps avert and contain the potential damage of a risk's occurrence, since smaller system builds imply less complexity, which implies a reduced chance and risk magnitude.

The incremental approach was an advancement over the waterfall model, but there were still problems. Though the incremental approach allows for continually changing requirements (new ones are simply added into the next increment), there still existed the problem of determining if the requirements proposed were valid. Errors in requirements were still being made and were found to be almost as costly to fix as when using the waterfall-type models. What was needed was an approach to obtain insight early into the development process, so the concept of prototyping was added. Prototyping allows for errors to be found before the design and implementation phases, rather than after, as in the waterfall model.

A prototype is one of two types: analytical or operational. Thus, a prototype can take the form of a mathematical model, a simulation of parts of the actual or proposed system (hardware and/or software or both), a hardware mock-up, pseudo-code, etc.; i.e., whatever is needed to get early feedback on the feasibility of the system being built, from both the developers and eventual *users*. The primary purpose is to buy information in order to provide early warning to the developers and management of possible risks before too much money, and time, is spent on possibly building the wrong system.[22] Many prototypes might be constructed, each individually directed toward determining if the requirements are reasonable, or if the specifications are complete, or if the design is even possible. The prototype may or may not form the basis of the final system, although the general approach is to plan to throw it away.[23]

The addition of prototyping was useful, but there still existed two issues that needed to be addressed. One issue was the problem of trying to define the requirements quickly enough. The longer it took for requirements to be defined, the higher the probability that the software as defined would not match current user needs because of changing operational conditions. The second aim was not to spend enormous sums on the prototype itself, which would take resources away from the development itself. Thus, the concept of rapid-prototyping, and its current refinement, *software storming*, came into being.[24] Software storming uses brainstorming problem-solving techniques along with knowledge engineering to reduce the time and cost of a conventional prototype by up to a factor of six in some cases. Further refinements are seeing the use of rapid-prototyping in the area of software maintenance and evolution.[25]

The rapid-prototyping model has been elaborated to include the integration of the *resource management, configuration management, verification,* and *validation activities.* As previously noted, these activities span across all the life-cycle phases. Resource management is concerned with making decisions about the enterprise from both a day-to-day viewpoint (i.e., have we met this week's milestones, is everybody available for a meeting, etc.) and from a more global perspective (i.e., will the project be on time, within budget, etc.).

Configuration management is the ability to provide a controlled and baselined version of the software system currently under development. This is necessary to ensure that each incremental version is built as a successor to the current version, and not as an "unauthorized," and therefore suspect, modified version. Only those changes which do not detrimentally affect the development of a current, or future, system are approved.

Verification, from the Latin word *veritas,* or "truth," is the establishment of the correspondence between what is being built and what was specified. Validation, from the Latin word *valere,* or "to be worth," is the establishment of whether the system built meets the operational goals. We will review each of these subjects a bit more extensively later in the chapter.

3.1.2.2.1 Opportunities and risks. The major advantages of the rapid-prototyping model are the enhancements it brings to the descriptive power of the process model. It more closely resembles the reality of the development process, and allows for the usual iteration of a system to take place more naturally, than in the waterfall model. Experience gained from the previous increment can be incorporated into the successive increment to provide a more refined system. Combining the elements of incremental development with rapid-prototyping thus provides the capability to implement the concept of *build a little, test a little,* which makes finding and repairing errors much more easy that in a monolithic process. This is a necessary condition to building large systems successfully.

Additionally, the rapid-prototyping model allows for better control of the process by incorporating the aspects of resource management, configuration management, verification, and validation. The control is accentuated by being able to build larger systems with smaller development teams, thus allowing parallel development. This results in increasing overall developer communications and productivity skills.[26] The model also promotes the obtainment of the user's inputs early in the system development process, thereby reducing the scarcity of information that often occurs.

There are some risks to using the rapid-prototyping model, however. First, the coupling between the management aspects and the development aspects of the life-cycle process is not clear. This coupling is usually made through the configuration management activity,[27] which mixes the two unnecessarily. The management and development aspects are distinct (but related) processes, as is shown in Charette,[28] and requires separate treatment.

Furthermore, incremental development acts as a double-edged sword. While allowing for smaller parts of the total system to be created, if a risk is encountered in one build, everything following it must wait for its resolution. The problem is the same as that found on an automotive assembly line, if the winch to hold transmissions were to break. Everything from that step onwards would be delayed. Practically speaking, if an error goes undiscovered in one of the first increments to be delivered, then that error is in the system "forever." The cost to change it is extremely high, as can be seen by reexamining Figure 3.3. A requirements error found in increment 1 at integration time could affect not only its four previous phases, but at least nine additional phases the other increments are presently in or have already completed. Every previous increment containing the error has to either be fixed or used in knowledge that an error exists, or the error has to be resolved in the next increment to be started. Either way, the baseline is destroyed, and at least one incremental build must be changed.

Additionally, allowing many "systems" to be built simultaneously, each in different stages of the life cycle, significantly increases the management overhead. Management coordination and control of tasks can become a nightmare, especially if problems start to arise in the development. It becomes hard for management to estimate the resources needed to perform the development at any particular moment, since many systems are in a partially completed state. Resource juggling taxes management's abilities, and becomes an unwanted added "influence" on the development. Finally, the model is not very suitable for complete computerization because of these coordination and control issues.

One other risk associated with the application of rapid-prototyping models, but not inherent in the model itself, is that they are often *document or code driven*. Recall that software artifacts produced and reviewed are ways of measuring time and progress. Carried to the extreme, developers will tend to concentrate on developing artifacts of the development to the detriment of creating an effective system. This is sometimes encouraged by the organization sponsoring the development, since the artifacts often are the only signs of anything being accomplished. One should remember that the documents reflect what has been accomplished and are not objectives in themselves. Getting this order reversed is a major risk.

Finally, prototyping is not cost-free, nor is there a guarantee that the prototype build can scale up. In many circumstances, especially where a novel design approach is to be taken, *rapid*-prototyping is just not possible.[29] The reason is that one usually needs to build complex rapid-prototyping tools (often more complex than the application being built), which cost a lot of money and are themselves filled with errors. When this occurs, the locus of cost is shifted from the application to the the prototyping tools, which defeats the whole purpose.

Further, even if a "successful" prototype can be built, this may not mean a full-scale system can be constructed. For example, the Beech Aircraft Corporation built an 85%-scale prototype of a new line of aircraft called the Starships. However, the data gathered from the prototype led to an overly optimistic and unrealistic development and delivery schedule.[30] The data gathered from the prototype was virtually worthless, according to the president of Beech. The prototype effort ended up causing the development effort to last somewhere between 45% and 60% longer than it should have, in retrospect.

Overall, the rapid-prototyping model, if it is intelligently applied, can help reduce risks caused by the lack of information, lack of control, and lack of time, and thus many of the risks that are present in the waterfall model. However, the improvements may also provide sources of new risks with which to contend.

3.1.2.3 Operational/enactable model.

A somewhat different approach from that of the rapid-prototype model, which was suggested to alleviate the risks of the waterfall-design driven model, is the operational or enactable process model.[31,32] Enactable models are sometimes referred to as *process programs* in the literature. The enactable model varies from the previous two by concentrating on operational, rather than behavioral abstractions, of the system being developed. The implementation mechanisms used during the development are not hidden, but are instead used as a basis to specify system behavior. In other words, the

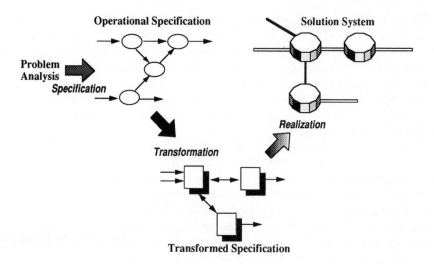

Figure 3.4 Operational Process Model

operational model creates executable specifications (called operational specifications) that are successively transformed into efficient implementations as depicted in Figure 3.4. Thus, the *external* behavior of the system is implicit in the specification, while the *internal* structure is not.

Paraphrasing Zave, the operational model description of a system makes the operational specification appear to be very close to a design seen in previous models. However, designs refer to specific run-time environments, whereas the structures provided by the executable specification language are independent of resource allocation strategies or configurations. Furthermore, unlike the previous models discussed, which place great emphasis on separating requirements (i.e, their external behavior) from the internal structure of the system, the operational model interleaves the two. This interleaving is necessary to achieve an executable form, but also expresses inseparably what the system is doing as opposed to how it is to be accomplished. This makes the operational specification structure, then, more process-oriented, rather than product-oriented.

3.1.2.3.1 Opportunities and risks. There are a number of advantages to the operational/enactable model. First, it has great descriptive power directed at solving software system risks. The descriptions are formal, rigorous, and can be analyzed. The user and developer have an executable model (i.e., a rapid-prototype) from which to evaluate possible system solutions very early in the system development. These rapid-prototypes come for "free" upon specification definition. The greatest benefit is that the model is very suitable to computerization, and most research efforts in this area are aimed at automating the transformations of the operational specifications.

The risks associated with the operational/enactable model also lie mostly in its powerful descriptive nature. Since one needs to transform the external behavior into internal structures before specifying them, the result may be overconstrained, and prematurely produced, designs. Additionally, the complete set of transformations, from an operational specification to efficient implementations, haven't been completely determined yet, and may never be able to be determined. Then there is the problem that enactable models are heavily context dependent, thus applying general sets of transformations that may not be useful in many developments.[33] Finally, there hasn't been widespread use of the operational model, which makes it difficult to evaluate, especially for use in large system developments. It is unclear how a full software enterprise can be modeled using this approach. Thus, the model seems more aimed at the process of developing small to possibly medium software systems. How it supports the management process, or provides full life-cycle coverage, also isn't clear. Overall, the model seems to help avert the risks associated with lack of control, information, and time, but only in a very limited domain.

3.1.2.4 Spiral model. The spiral model is a relatively recent addition to the process models available.[34,35] It is an evolutionary approach drawing from the rapid-prototyping model, as well as from the operational model. The spiral model is specifically aimed at large, government-type software enterprises that fall into the Grand Design category. Boehm considers the other process models as being subsets of the spiral model, and in certain circumstances, more suitable for use. These occur when the project under development is: (a) a low-risk project, where the system requirements are stable, or (b) a project where the resources such as money, time, and people are plentiful, and/or (c) a project where a highly automated development environment is in use.

A modified spiral model is shown in Figure 3.5. The model is said to be "risk driven;" i.e., one moves from stage to stage only when the risks have

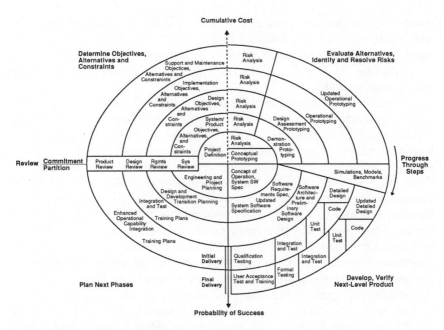

Figure 3.5 Modified Spiral Model

been analyzed, aversion strategies have been formed, and a decision has been made to either accept the risks as being feasible to avert or not. Thus, risk analysis and control are undertaken at each stage of the life cycle. Prototypes or other approaches to buy information to reduce uncertainty are advocated as central to each stage's risk analysis. The objectives of each installment of the software system being developed are elaborated, alternative means of implementing and achieving these goals are examined, the constraints on each alternative are evaluated, and selection of an alternative approach is made. In projects using the spiral model at TRW (using good automation support), first indications are of a 50% increase in productivity and, in some cases, up to 100% has been gained over that which was previously forecast in the same situation using a rapid-prototyping model alone. TRW claims the quality of the systems produced also seem to be noticeably improved.

3.1.2.4.1 Opportunities and risks. The spiral model represents a definite improvement over any of the models presented so far. By using risk analysis and management as its foundation, the model provides the means to understand, avert, and/or contain software development risks which might not otherwise have been possible if the other approaches had been applied. Applying a model which makes risk explicit provides an important "political" benefit in undertaking government software enterprises as well.

The spiral model allows for the early and continuous evaluation of the means to avert risk, such as software reuse. The model is well suited for accommodating uncertainty in the requirements and helps avoid too hasty a commitment to a specific specification or design. Importantly, it also allows for initial consideration of system evolution risks, such as those having to do with operational and support issues. The model focuses on the elimination of error and unattractive design alternatives. Finally, the spiral model allows information to cross back and forth between the systems engineering environment boundary in a fashion more feasible than any of the earlier models. Whereas the first two models we examined were representative of product-oriented paradigms, the spiral model is is a step towards a process-oriented paradigm.

There are a number of risks with the spiral model, however. The greatest risk is that it relies on knowing how to perform risk engineering. As we have already seen, risk engineering are not quite mainstream occupations yet. To move from phase to phase, knowing how to set the appropriate risk referent level, is the crucial parameter for successfully making effective use of this model. Set the level too low, and the risk analysis becomes a farce. In fact, the use of the spiral model by untrained individuals is more hazardous than starting off originally with a rapid-prototyping model. One may be lulled into thinking that the risks have been identified and evaluated properly, when in fact they have not. This can lead to overconfidence, where none is deserved.

Second, the spiral model is still immature. It hasn't yet been used in any programs outside of TRW, and thus it will take a few more years to get sufficient data on its applicability. Further, the programs it has been used on are not yet of significant size, thus making its true value for dealing with issues involving large-scale systems development still speculative. This is especially true when it comes to being able to handle changes to the system requirements. The ability to identify, estimate, and evaluate the risk of a system's requirements' instability may in fact encourage them, rather than discourage them.

Third, the model, not being fully process-oriented, is still too narrowly focused. The merging of the spiral model into a systemic view of a system interacting with business and system engineering environments has not yet been accomplished. The perspective the model takes is still very closed, with it being too much software product-oriented only, and not enough software enterprise-oriented. For example, risks that originate or are funnelled from outside the project are not explicitly investigated, and the risks that continue from phase to phase are handled only through a listing mechanism instead of through a continuous, proactive risk monitoring and management approach. The model requires expansion to account for more of the influences from outside the software domain, especially those from the user domain, and requires the strengthening of its TQM aspects.

Additionally, the spiral model views the process as a risk-driven process, which is an inaccurate perspective. Risk-driven process implies that the risks approach certainty; i.e., the risks faced are higher than the levels of acceptability. This insinuates that a particular risk is inevitable, which therefore drives the process in directions that are not under one's control. This is exactly the state one doesn't want to be in. One may be risk-coerced or constrained; i.e., the risks approach the level of acceptability, but even these circumstances are not desirable. The desired situation is one which is risk-influenced, where one recognizes the risks, but finds either alternatives to them or ways to reduce their impact.

The risk-driven attitude in the spiral model can be seen also in its overemphasis on risk reduction techniques, instead of on examining all the choices provided by the range of risk aversion techniques of which risk reduction is but one. Further, by being risk-driven instead of, say, being risk influenced, the spiral model may overlook opportunities for making use of synergy in using the system for some new purpose.

Again, a better choice of words would be that the process is risk influenced, which implies it is risk management driven. One wants to manage the causes associated with risk; i.e., lack of control, lack of information, or lack of time. Management choices for averting risk, for instance, include changing a risk's acceptability by applying risk protection, risk transference, or pecuniary aversion strategies as well as risk reduction. Acceptance of a risk, even as it currently exists, is also a perfectly good risk aversion strategy, which seems neglected in the spiral model.[36]

Finally, the spiral model may be difficult to contract for, especially in government situations. Current costing models and budgetary procedures do not readily lend themselves to this type of process model. Contingency funding is explicitly needed, for the costs and value of doing the risk evaluations (although recognized as necessary) may not be able to be quantified to a degree required by many organizations. The contracting issue may end up being a major impediment to the spiral model's eventual use, which would be unfortunate.

Overall, the opportunities and advantages of using the spiral model far outweigh the risks involved in not using it. Properly applied, it helps overcome each of the basic causes of risk much more than anything yet developed, and is a major step towards a process-oriented paradigm. Probably the most important aspect of the spiral model is its political nature, in that it does make risks and their management a priority and very visible requirement of the development.

3.1.2.5 Knowledge-based model. The last model we wish to examine is the knowledge-based model. This model is based upon a combination of the previously discussed models, and the work done with artificial intelligence in the expert system realm. The computer acts as a partner in the system development, guiding the developer throughout the process. The key is the separation of the software engineering knowledge domain from the application knowledge domain and the capturing of this information along with the process paradigm into a database. Rules are formed based upon accepted software engineering techniques, encoded into expert systems, which then are used in conjunction with expert systems containing application knowledge rules, to form a specific instance of a software system.[37,38]

The above description is part speculation, since complete knowledge systems do not exist today, and may take as long as 10–12 years to create for building small systems, and probably closer to 20 years for larger-scaled system enterprises.[39,40] Scaling up from small prototypes to practical-sized expert systems has proven to be far more difficult than first thought. The main advantages of using such a model would be the tremendous potential for increasing productivity and quality by a factor of three or more. It also could support the process-oriented paradigm more easily than any of the previous models.

The knowledge-based model's descriptive power, generality, and suitability for automation would theoretically be integrated into a single unit, generating a capability which would allow the construction of systems orders of magnitude larger than those being conceived today. This model may be the only way these systems will be able to be built, because the complexity of the current models are being overstretched by today's enterprise modeling requirements.

The potential risks related to the knowledge-based model are that the expert systems needed may be beyond our present technological capability to build them. Experts are still needed to create both the software engineering and application domain rules, and there are few, if any experts, available. Some specialized research into prototyping systems to explore the feasibility of certain aspects of a knowledge-based model, (e.g., in the areas of requirements analysis, specification, design, and implementation) is being conducted, but the results are still tentative.[41]

3.1.3 Model comparison

Note that each process model described has some measure of advantages, and risks, associated with it. The waterfall/design-driven model represents a model that is intuitively attractive, and has an experienced user base behind it. The rapid-prototype model improves upon that model, by including life-cycle activities like management, develops the system incrementally, and provides rapid feedback to the developers and users. The operational model produces specifications that are executable, increasing the role of automation, and tightens the link between what is specified and what is implemented. The spiral model uses risk as its main parameter to drive the model forward. The knowledge-based model helps separate the software engineering knowledge from the application

TABLE 3.1 Process Model Comparison: Operation

| | CATEGORY | | |
Process Model	Descriptive Power	Generality	Automation Suitability
Waterfall	Low	Low	Low
Rapid-Prototype	Medium	Medium	Medium-High
Operational	Medium-High	Medium	High
Spiral	Medium	High	Medium-High
Knowledge-Based*	High	High	High

* Speculation—no reliable data exists.

knowledge, and has the potential of building very large systems. Table 3.1 provides a relative rating of each process model in the categories of descriptive power, generality, and suitability to automation, while Table 3.2 illustrates the models' relative effectiveness in averting the three basic causes of risk for different-sized system developments.

Each of the process models described have some deficiency that makes it difficult to use as is, however. The waterfall/design-driven model is very restrictive in its monolithic approach to building software. It fails to specifically include activities that occur across the life cycle, such as project or configuration management, nor does it provide for feedback to the users or developers concerning the quality of the system being built. It also fails to account for the changes that inevitably occur in system development. The rapid-prototype model overcomes most of these deficiencies, but includes some of its own. The primary deficiencies are that it interweaves the process of management and development, and that incremental development makes management coordination difficult. This is exacerbated because there is no clear separation of the two.

TABLE 3.2 Process Model Comparison: Averting Risk

Process Model	Project Size	RISK CAUSE		
		Lack of Time	Lack of Information	Lack of Control
Waterfall	Small	Medium	Medium	High
	Medium	Low	Low	Medium
	Large	Very Low	Very Low	Low
Rapid-Prototype	Small	Medium	Medium	Medium
	Medium	Medium	High	Medium
	Large	Medium-High	Very High	Medium-High
Operational	Small	High	High	Medium
	Medium	Medium-High	Medium	Medium-Low
	Large	Medium	Low	Low
Spiral	Small	Medium	Medium	Medium
	Medium	Medium	Medium	Medium
	Large	Medium-High	Medium-High	Medium-High
Knowledge-Based*	Small	Medium-High	High	High
	Medium	High	High	Medium
	Large	Medium	Medium-High	Low

* Speculation—no reliable data exists.

Further, like the waterfall model, it wasn't designed specifically for automation. On the other hand, the operational and knowledge-based models are specifically geared for automation, but focus primarily on the process of developing a software system. The management aspect is implicit, rather than explicit, just as in the waterfall model. The spiral model requires a thorough understanding of risk engineering to work effectively. Without it, it becomes just one of the others, but with a potentially hidden and dangerous risk attached.

3.1.3.1 Ramifications. The risks associated with each of the process models above leads one to a very difficult question of whether the origins of enterprise processes are observed or imposed. In other words, is a process model a reflection of what happens, or should it be crafted as to reflect what should happen? The early process models were imposed to help avert the risks associated with the *management* of software development, not the risks associated with *techniques* used in the actual development of software. Many practitioners confuse the two, and believe the management and the process of development are identical. Each process model so far described, including the spiral model, is based upon the fundamental software development generalities that existed in the 1960s and early 1970s. But, as Robin Hogarth has written, "Generalizations decay. At one time a conclusion describes the existing situation well, at a later time it accounts for rather little variance, and ultimately it is only valid as history."[42]

But software process model decay has not been explicitly acknowledged or accounted for in software engineering papers or books. The continuous revision of the current genre of process models is an implicit admission of the occurrence of this decay, and also marks the increasing loss of validity of the coherence perspective on truth these product-oriented models hold. The past legacy of applying old models to inappropriate situations is currently seen in the high maintenance costs, whereas the push to automate these inappropriate models means that we will be faced with providing the same wrong answers, but in a less messy, more nicely packaged way.

Further, there are too many external risks within a software enterprise for closed models such as those previously described to encompass and deal with them as internally generated. For instance, the project may start with a customer having some very vague concept of what the system will be and, when it is partially completed, deciding that it isn't what was wanted after all. The "I don't know what I want, but I know what I don't want" syndrome, which is very prevalent in real software enterprises, is hard to duplicate in any of the process models, except perhaps the spiral model, and it is difficult to contain the risks this attitude generates. In fact, current process models tend to exacerbate this type of problem, instead of trying to resolve these issues before they get to the software engineering domain, which is the goal of process-oriented models.

Another problem in all current process models is that, although iteration exists, only the negative feedback mechanism is recognized as occurring over these channels. Negative feedback, such as management review, phase definitions, etc., is meant to keep a process from going out of control, in other words, it provides adaptive control. The fact that positive feedback also occurs over these same feedback loops is ignored. Yet positive feedback, such as unauthorized requirements being added to the software by programmers, or a key person quitting, can quickly cause the development process to become unstable. By not recognizing the limitations in process models, enterprises will inevitably be put at risk by their use.

What should one do? How does one choose between the risks presented in each of the models, especially if there isn't a fully developed process-oriented model handy? Perhaps the best advice, initially, is to "fake it."[43] What probably is important is not that a process model isn't perfect, but that one is being used at all. It is still less risky to use an incomplete model than none at all.[44,45] The SEI Contractor Capability study described in Chapter 2 illustrated this. By at least having some process model, project participants can think and communicate, while management can have some measurement of success against which to compare the enterprise. And using a model of some type does work.[46]

Also, the very act of using a model and finding its weaknesses moves one closer to the ideal. This is amply illustrated in the history of each of the process models above. New attempts to overcome past deficiencies have resulted in models which are more robust than their predecessors (even if the model itself has outlived its usefulness in many, if not most, instances).

A second alternative is to attempt, as Alan Davis et al. have, to compare alternative process models to find the one which is most applicable, or, better, causes the least amount of harm.[47] Their research postulates an approach which can help compare and contrast alternative software development process models in terms of their ability to satisfy user needs and life cycle costs. An example is shown in Figure 3.6, where a system's functionality across time is hypothesized, and the

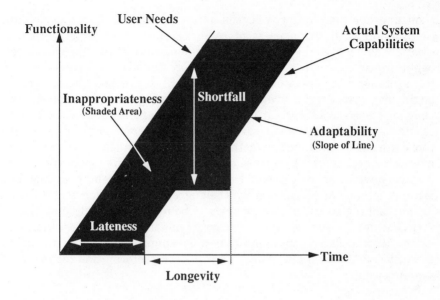

Figure 3.6 Davis et al. Process Model Comparison Technique

inappropriateness of different paradigms to meet users' needs are compared. Inappropriateness is defined as the difference between the user's needs and the capability of the process models to fulfill them. It is measured by metrics, including shortfall (how far the operational system is, at any time **t**, from meeting the actual requirements at time **t**), lateness (the time elapsed between the appearance of a new requirement and its satisfaction), adaptability (the rate at which the software can adapt to new requirements), and longevity (the rate at which software is adaptable to change and remains viable).

The work is very interesting, but by no means complete. More work is required to develop improved metrics and to determine how to construct actual paradigm curves that are project specific. The users' needs also must be modeled in a less linear fashion, especially taking into account the wider environments of interest's influences. However, the paradigm comparison is potentially a means to select the proper model for an application area and/or enterprise that is being considered. More importantly, the research shows where potential sources of risk exist and how they are linked to the process model selected. It underlines the importance of matching the correct paradigm to the application.

As another alternative, one could try to use the spiral model in conjunction with the aspects of the process-oriented procedures in Chapter 2. One could add a time element and draw the spiral as beginning at the environment of wider interest, and then spiral through the systems engineering environment until it reached the software engineering process situation, as illustrated in Figures 3.7a and 3.7b. By showing the risks as originating at these outer environments and being continuously fed into the software situation of interest, one is able to join the external environments to the system in a much more realistic manner. Another way to depict it would be to show the model spiraling inwardly over time, which would indicate that the probability of success is approaching one, or conversely, the degree of risk and/or uncertainty is approaching zero. This would seem to be more intuitively pleasing.

In Chapter 7 we will return to this very crucial issue of process models, as we will propose a theory behind a new paradigm of development which more closely matches the reality of developing information technology systems today.

3.2   Methods

The second element constituting the process of software engineering is the software engineering methods to be applied in the creation of the

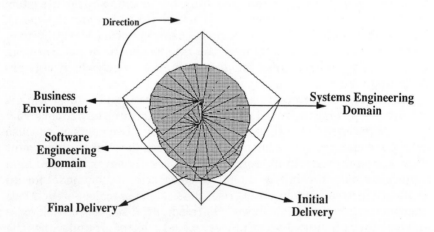

Figure 3.7a Spiral Model in Three Dimensions (top view)

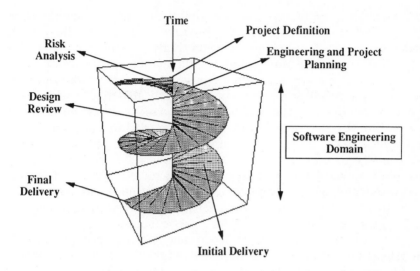

Figure 3.7b Spiral Model in Three Dimensions (side view)

software product. The purpose of software engineering methods is to reduce the types of risks associated with the lack of information.

The term "method" has many definitions, ranging from "principles of practice" to "tricks of the trade."[48,49] For the purposes of this book, we define methods as: "Explicit prescriptions for achieving an activity or set of activities required by the software engineering process model used to develop a software application." Note the dual nature of software engineering methods: to help create an application, as well as to implement part of the process model.

A particular process model defines the range and domain of methods to be used within it. As a process model is decomposed into finer levels of granularity, the lower levels are represented by specific methods that are used to define, refine, and implement the software system. The methods are used for the creation of something "physical" (e.g., code) from something logical (e.g., descriptions of ideas about a software system). Thus, a method is used to: (a) reduce the sources of risk related to the lack of information, (b) provide control of the process model in more detail, and (c) aid in the reduction of time required, by making the overall process more efficient. The closer a method is related to and supports the process model, the more effective (i.e., the less risk due to mismatches) they *both* become.[50]

One must be keen to note, however, that the methods applied must be suitable to the specific application being developed, as must the process model itself. No aircraft engineer would think of trying to persuade his or her customer that a plane could be built out of glass or ceramics, and neither should the software engineer believe that all methods or process models or, as we will see, automation are applicable in all situations. A major risk will arise from not using the correct models, methods, or automation for the situation at hand as much from not using any. Different situations require different approaches, just as different materials need different techniques to work them. A major portion of the risk analyst's job will be to identify where mismatches occur between the application and the process models, methods, and automation, *as well as* the business requirement identified for the system initially. Remember, the business requirement may be for a particular system, but the driver may be to get a system out quickly, with maybe a little less quality than could have been achieved if more time was taken. *The trade-off between quality and timeliness is a business decision, not a software engineering decision.* We will return to this issue in the section on requirements.

One should not confuse the term *methodology* with *method*. A methodology, in software engineering terminology, is a combination, and ideally, integration of some number of methods (i.e., more than one) into a comprehensive whole, for some particular purpose. A good way to think of methodologies is that they coerce a person to use a group of methods in a systemic fashion. Ideally, one would like to possess a complete set of methods integrated in some way to fully support the process model. An individual method which cannot be integrated with another is not only of little practical use, but can increase quality, productivity, and complexity risks. The automation of the integrated methods would be the ideal risk aversion strategy, but it is not a requirement. For instance, formal review of documents is a method that may never be automated, but the information provided within the document should come from the integrated methods themselves. This issue will be discussed in more detail in the section on automation.

3.2.1 Method selection

Trying to create or select the proper methods to build a software system or the determination of which ones work well, and when, is a matter of intense research. A risk inherent within most methods is that they have both implicit and explicit rules for their application. The explicit rules are usually well documented, whereas the implicit rules are not. When a software system is created, and a subsequent problem with it arises, it is difficult to repeat the original process used to create the system, especially if there are many implicit rules implied. Methods should not only prescribe which steps to take, but stipulate how to make the decisions involved in those steps. Another helpful addition would be the risk implications and ramifications of each decision. It is important that when a software system is delivered, the methods used for developing it be delivered also. To aid in the identification of the risks involved when a particular method is applied, one needs to be able to characterize it in some manner.

3.2.2 Method Characterization

In a seminal paper by Doug Ross et al., an attempt to characterize methods was made so that the issues above could eventually be addressed.[51] To begin with, they listed four fundamental goals of all methods: to increase the reliability, efficiency, modifiability, or understandability of the software system being built. Notice that these goals relate to Brooks's accidents of software in the previous chapter. Ross and company also described seven basic principles or techniques used by all methods as well. These were: (1) modularity (the appropriate structuring of the system), (2) abstraction (the identification of common properties), (3) hiding (make inessential information inaccessible), (4) localization (group like things together), (5) uniformity (information format descriptions are identical), (6) completeness (all information is present), and (7) confirmability (a description of what information is needed to describe the problem). These relate to Brooks's essence of software. By combining the seven principles with the four goals defined above and then mapping the result against the individual phase(s) a method was used in (as defined by a specific software engineering process model), a method could be fully categorized and understood. Its weaknesses and strengths could then be evaluated for a particular class of applications, thereby pointing out potential risks in its usage.

A particular method may only apply one or a few of the principles above. For instance, a specific method, say one that is based upon divide and conquer, may use the principles of modularity, abstraction, localization, and uniformity, while a different one adds information hiding. Each method, however, might have a different overall goal it is trying to ultimately achieve. Charette extended the basic work of Ross.[52] In this approach, a method consists of five parts: *viewpoint, domain, principles, media,* and *guidance.*

3.2.2.1 Viewpoint. The viewpoint of a method is basically the coordinate system from which it views the problem. There are a number of viewpoints, but three are basic: *informational, functional,* and *behavioral.* Informational views relationships between data. Functional means viewing data flow and transformations of data. Behavioral views concern the sequencing and concurrency of the data transformations.

As with the mathematics of linear algebra, the above viewpoints can be transformed into one another to provide a different perspective on risk. Each application domain problem has a viewpoint that is more useful than another, and if the view is not supported by the method, it will not work well.

3.2.2.2 Domain. The next aspect is that of the method's domain. The domain consists of two elements, one being defined by the software system itself,[53] and one defined by the phase of the process model the enterprise currently resides in. By the first element, we mean that a system being created contains certain attributes associated with it, such as possesses time critical interfaces, requires numeric computations, has human interface interactions, and so forth. By associating values with each attribute, an application can also be placed into certain classes. It can be shown that there exist orthogonol software application classes, where all methods may not be appropriate.[54] A method, to be useful, must be able to be applied to a suitable class of problems.

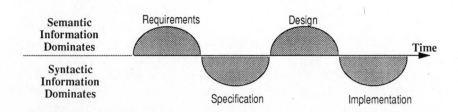

Figure 3.8 Dominant Types of Information Manipulated Throughout the Life Cycle

The other element that makes up a method's domain is the phase of the process model in which the system currently resides. The information required to be transformed in one phase is different from that found in another. Figure 3.8 illustrates that, in general, the types of information found and manipulated in each phase form a type of sinusoid alternating between "semantic-information" and "syntactic-information" transformations. The use of these terms may be a little misleading, so we diverge here for a bit to clarify them.[55]

What we mean by semantic information is the "mental activity or knowledge" that is necessary to be captured and manipulated by the methods used in a phase. The syntactic-information transformations define how this information can be captured and communicated. For example, in requirements analysis, we are faced with an "unbounded," or at best fuzzy idea of what the software system will be like in the end. We try to contain the context of our ideas, giving them meaning that others can understand by using methods that can shape, define, and document them. A common way to do this is by drawing a box, circle, or a cloud on a piece of paper and labeling it as representing something, like a processing algorithm. The methods used in this phase generally are applicable to almost any application problem domain.

In contrast, during specification, we have a fairly well-defined and bounded problem with which to work (i.e., the requirements). However, by applying actions described within specification methods, we change the requirement's representation, using a standardized box (i.e., one with a predefined meaning) that represents the algorithm, or by listing inputs and outputs in a predefined table or matrix, such as a decision table. Thus, the knowledge or meaning necessary to describe the software system (e.g., "processors," "module," "interface," etc.) are often embedded in the specification syntactic representations themselves.

In design, we shift focus again to how the specifications will be implemented, and once more the problem space becomes "unbounded." An infinite number of possible (but not necessarily correct) design choices are available to choose from, and again, the methods used do not embed very much knowledge of the application within them. In other words, we represent the design using boxes or circles which *we* label. (In specification methods, the labels are usually given.)

Once a design is fixed, it is transformed once more, but this time into a physical realization by way of a syntactic description (i.e., a programming language) of its execution. This syntactic representation is what is required to be transformed by a compiler into the form used to eventually control the pattern of a computer's execution.

Notice that as the level of abstraction becomes more detailed, the quantity of each transformation category increases. Interestingly, the majority of automated methods that exist occur within the phases with a majority of syntactic information transformations, and that the hardest methods to automate are those that attempt semantic information transformations. Again, a method that is not appropriate for the transformation required will not be very useful, and may pose a risk to attaining system quality or reliability.

3.2.2.3 Principles. The third aspect that characterizes a method are the software engineering principles it uses. The principles of a method are the fundamental "laws" or concepts that are used to define its actions. Software engineering principles are immutable, in the sense that they are *technology independent* by definition. For example, similar in nature to software engineering principles are the three basic structures—*sequencing, selection,* and *repetition*—that are the minimum number required to perform program implementation. These are used in different combinations to form other, more powerful, control structures to make programming easier. In contrast to the creation of control structures, software engineering principles are used to form methods that either synthesize information, analyze information, or, more commonly, do both. Synthesis creates new ideas to decompose, and analysis creates new ideas to synthesize. The seven principles listed by Ross et al., although not provable, are most likely the minimum required to define most methods.

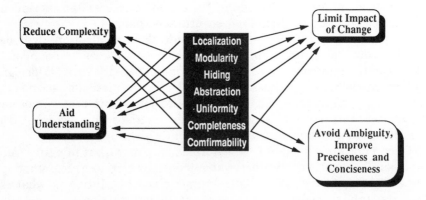

Figure 3.9 Properties of Software Principles

Software engineering principles, in addition to providing for synthesis or analysis of information, have other properties such as limiting the impacts of change, reducing complexity, and so forth. These are illustrated in Figure 3.9. Selecting the types and kinds of principles used by a method either restricts or enhances its usefulness.

3.2.2.4 Medium. Another aspect that a method is characterized by is the graphical medium used to implement the principles above. A method wants a media representation level which is appropriate, but it should be at the very least concise, correct, and readable. Figure 3.10, illustrates the spectrum of different media representations that can be used to describe a method, each differing in the level of interpretation required and information conveyed. Less formal representations are to the left, more formal to the right. Which representation is selected is important to the ability of the method to capture and convey information to the person and/or computer (if it is automated) applying it. The medium also defines how usable the method is for a particular application. For example, an electrical engineering circuit diagram is useful for conveying information in a precise and concise way to a specific audience. In contrast, text is not as formal or precise, but is usable by a wider audience. New representations, like those found in iconic languages,[56,57] may challenge conventional thinking about using traditional method representations in particular phases of the life cycle. A method wants an appropriate media representation level which is concise, correct, and readable.

3.2.2.5 Guidance. The final aspect of a method is the guidance provided to its users for its application. This is somewhat intangible, but goes back to the risks inherent in implicit and explicit rules for its use. Methods

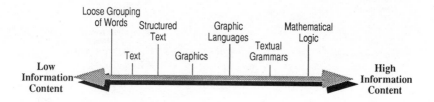

Figure 3.10 Spectrum of Media Types

should provide guidance in what decisions are to be made, how to make them, and in what order they should be made.[56] In other words, the guidance provided should describe how to bet started initially, how to stop (i.e., when has a method accomplished its goal), and what happens in between (i.e., what comes next). If these three ingredients are not specified, a method cannot be fully automated, nor when it is applied to a single problem repeatably will the same solution likely appear. Its *objectivity function* is said to be deficient.

This should not be interpreted as advocating that a method should restrict an individual's creativity in its use. Methods don't replace the thought processes required to create a software system. However, they do provide help in guiding them to a solution in an effective and efficient manner. For example, guidance can be in the form of directions equivalent to that found on a road map. How two individuals get from Point A to Point B is (somewhat) irrelevant, as long as by following the directions they both can arrive at approximately the same time, expending the same amount of effort. If they don't, the path can be retraced to find out why not.

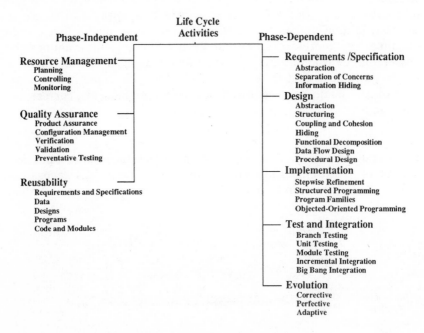

Figure 3.11 Phase-Independent and Phase-Dependent Activities

3.2.3 Phase-independent versus phase-dependent activities

Methods can be divided into either supporting phase-dependent or phase-independent activities of a process model,[59,60] as shown in Figure 3.11. Phase-dependent activities are applicable to only one, or at most a few, individual phases of the process model. An example is the application of the method Structured Analysis and Design Technique (SADT™), which supports activities typically defined in the requirement and specification phases. Phase-independent activities are used across all phases defined within the process model. An example of a phase-independent activity is configuration management. We will examine both types in the following sections.

3.2.3.1 Phase-independent activities. In this section, we will examine some of the activities that we link together as management activities; i.e., those components that management is ultimately responsible for in making the enterprise successful. For convenience, we have chosen to break enterprise management into three broad categories: *resource management*, *quality assurance* (product assurance; configuration management; verification, validation and preventative testing), and *reusability*.

Project management is an activity that should concern itself with averting or containing the risks within the process of developing a software system or product and the risks associated with the system or product itself.[61] This is accomplished initially by inward facing supervision (i.e., controlling and monitoring how scarce resources are being applied to the development of the system).[62] Project management is then directed outward, where concern is focused on the product integrity and how the user and customer perceive it.[63] This must match the overall enterprise management, which reflects the overall business requirements.

The personnel managing a software enterprise have the most important and difficult job of all. The larger the project, the more important good management becomes. Since management can have the greatest impact on the success or failure of the software system,[64] every decision made has the potential for making bad things better or good things worse. Thus, once again we see the requirement for effective risk management. Unfortunately, management starts off work every day with a definite disadvantage. It is the nature of things that the probability of doing something incorrect is higher than the probability of getting something correct. For example, a manager can adversely impact the risk to the software enterprise in all sorts of ways, such as:

- Assigning too much work to one group, and not enough to another.
- Assigning the wrong people to the wrong job.
- Failing to listen to technical personnel on technical issues.
- Choosing the incorrect organizational structure for the task at hand.
- Neglecting to obtain adequate resources to create and support the enterprise.
- Failing to fully comprehend what needs to be produced.

Each of the above are but a small sample of the risks with which a manager must contend. To many, management looks simple, as all one has to do is pull together the various functional disciplines required to achieve the enterprise's budgetary, schedule, and technical constraints. As stated earlier, this is far from true. However, the ideal manager is one who can understand and balance the technological, economic, and social bases, including their risks, through which software is developed.[65] Moreover, he or she must be a pragmatist, knowing what can and can't be realistically accomplished given the resources at hand.[66] Management may indeed be perceived as being simple, but it isn't easy.

The best way we can describe project management is that it is very much like being a coach of a sports team.[67] Your function is to select the team, then get everyone ready to play; i.e., obtain facilities and equipment, get them into shape, train them, select the proper positions for them based on their abilities, and so forth. On larger projects, you have in essence assistant coaches to whom you may delegate some authority (but not responsibility) for specific aspects of the project. When the game begins, you, as coach, can influence the game by deciding the general tactical strategy. How well the players implement it on the playing field is beyond your direct control, since, after all, you cannot play for them as well. If they do poorly, there aren't many options open to you. If you chose a poor strategy, then you compound your problems.

Thus, upon reflection, situations have many more ways of going wrong, then right. And in the end, the players get the cheers for a good play, and the coaches are blamed for their poor performance. Which brings us to the points of motivation, responsibility, and accountability.

As any good coach knows, to be successful the team has to act as a unit, and not as a rabble. For a manager, instilling the idea of teamwork and *esprit de corp* into the developers is important to the eventual success of the system. This requires specifically defining people's roles, functions, and responsibilities. Furthermore, the manager must make it clear that the responsibilities and risks, such as reliability, quality, correctness, etc., don't exist in any one role or person, but are the responsibility of all the project's personnel. What must also be avoided is the current trend in software enterprise management to totally shift accountability and the risks from the producers (i.e., developers) to the nonproducers (i.e., management and users).[68]

Every person involved in the development must take responsibility for the enterprise, and when one member is caught out of position, someone else must attempt to cover the gap. The key factor, and this has always been true, is that a manager's success or failure is most dependent upon the quality, skill, and motivation of the personnel. As Napoleon said, "Morale is to material as three is to one." Given highly skilled personnel who are motivated, a potentially marginal project can quickly be turned into a success. The quality of the personnel will make the greatest impact, both positive and negative, in any enterprise and, therefore, is the biggest risk. The analyst should spend an abundance of time investigating this issue in any project under evaluation.[69]

3.2.3.1.1 Resource management activities.

As we mentioned above, management has the greatest potential for making a mess of things. The primary reason is that management is really concerned with decision making under uncertainty.[70] These uncertainties are generated by circumstances such as incomplete requirements, changes in the scope of work, incorrect initial assumptions, and (negative) deviations in productivity.[71] Notice that each of these items is considered a software engineering risk. They are caused by lack of information (e.g., incomplete requirements), lack of control (e.g., changes in the scope of work), or lack of time (e.g., deviations in productivity or effective efficiency), or some combination of the three (e.g., incorrect initial assumptions). Risk aversion is management's highest priority, since it is the only organizational unit possessing the authority and sanctioned to do so.

Management risks are also caused by the trade-offs between reliability vs. efficiency, maintainability vs. efficiency, etc., which affect system effectiveness, development time and schedule, and system evolution. The resources or time to put out the "optimal" system are scarce, and therefore, it is management's responsibility to make these trade-off decisions with as little inherent risk as possible. Resource management

Develop Schedules
Define Milestones
Generate Budgets

Assess Quality
Perform Trade-offs
Act as Liaison

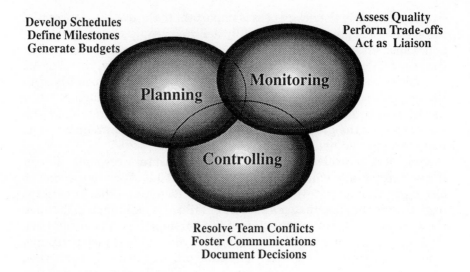

Resolve Team Conflicts
Foster Communications
Document Decisions

Figure 3.12 Management Methods

attempts to avert the risks caused by uncertainty are achieved by three general methods: *planning, monitoring,* and *controlling,* as shown in Figure 3.12.[72]

3.2.3.1.1.1 Planning. Planning is the activity which involves estimating what resources are needed to meet the objectives of the enterprise, and then organizing and allocating the resources to perform the work. This effort includes conducting risk analysis and management. Estimation must consider the size and complexity of the software being developed, the skill mix and productivity of the development professionals, the funding allocated to the development, the time allocated to the schedule, the potential risk areas, and the power and sophistication of the support resources, including development methods.[73] Estimating resources accurately and determining a realistic schedule to avoid undercapitalization are still the major steps in successfully planning software enterprises.[74]

Plans must be made to develop an integrated approach toward the overall enterprise and to develop cohesive working relationships among all the various support groups. Three very important issues that must be resolved in this activity are: (1) What *is* the product (i.e., what are its requirements)?, (2) What constitutes a successful enterprise *and* product?, and (3) What are the risks involved in the enterprise? For example, if a product under development is of both high risk and crucial for the future success of the company, two independent teams of developers might be called for. IBM often uses this strategy. Once the estimation process is completed, it is documented in the software development plan and risk aversion plan. The resources will then be organized and allocated to perform the work.

A number of tools and techniques have been developed to aid in the planning aspects of management, as well as the monitoring and controlling of a project. These include: contract administration, invented circa 2000 B.C., which negotiates prices and any changes to a project; formal cost control techniques, implemented about 1999 B.C., which keeps track of budgeted resources, committed resources, incurred costs, and forecasted costs; bar charts, which were invented by Gantt around 1900, which show the projected time required by project activities; work breakdown structures, a 1940s invention, which defines a project as a tree of functional activities which create individual products; and network schedulers, such as PERT charts, invented in the 1950s, which show the precedence relationships of tasks in a project. New refinements of the above techniques are constantly being added to the armory, mostly in ways of doing planning, especially strategic planning, and managing and motivating people.

3.2.3.1.1.2 Monitoring. Monitoring is the activity used to gauge the progress of the work to date, the quality of the products to date, the quality of the development process, the status of risks to the enterprise, and the adherence to standards. Management must be constantly aware of the expenditures of effort required to meet the project goals and the progress made towards the scheduled completion dates for each product.

Additionally, management must take corrective action on any expenditure which is not proceeding according to the plan, which may mean conducting policy impact assessments and updated risk analyses of the administrative and technical areas. The reason for the continuous monitoring is that there are so many software engineering risks present in a software enterprise. Wolverton lists just some of the typical risks one has to face during the development itself:[75]

- Simultaneous unattainable requirements
- Defective specifications
- Overinspection and testing
- Unsure customers

- New technology/designs
- Disputed interpretations of requirements

By using quality assurance techniques, the risks listed above can be contained. But it should be noted that many of the risks listed above by Wolverton are prime examples of risks that originate in the business environment and are not resolved before they reach the software engineering domain. Product assurance personnel are often left stuck with trying to resolve conflicts that rightly should never reach them.

During the application of quality assurance techniques, the quality of each product developed during a process phase is compared to a preestablished definition of quality. Products which do not meet the standards require rework. Progress is periodically evaluated and accomplishments are compared against the plan. Technical progress and resources expended are matched against the budgets and schedules of the development plan, and any deviations discovered are marked for correction. This is true of risks as well.

Quality assurance techniques are also used to evaluate the quality of the development process and monitoring the adherence to standards. The techniques such as inspections, audits, and walkthroughs are used to show that each product developed during a phase is complete, consistent, and up-to-date. Compliance with standards is important as standards are useful in preventing errors, finding errors early, directing reworking efforts, and making the developers more productive.[76]

3.2.3.1.1.3 Controlling. The management activity of controlling is concerned with maintaining control over both the development process and the products of the process. The control of the process focuses on meeting the goals and objectives (established in the development and risk plans) through the application of the available resources. Authority is *delegated* and responsibility *assigned* through the organizational structure to various groups in order that they clearly understand and execute their duties in a timely manner. Conflicts among the various organizational structures are resolved, and communication channels are forced to remain open.

Control of the process includes setting standards which the development will follow. These standards define the process model to be used, the methods to be applied, and so forth. Standards are useful for averting risks by providing a framework of control. However, the standards themselves are also a possible source of risk. It has been pointed out by Charles McKay, Director of NASA's Software Engineering Research

Laboratory, that many of the standards used or proposed today are based upon 20-year-old technology and/or ideas about systems development.[77] Standards are true generalizations which decay with time, and the software engineering analyst must be aware of the risks they pose. Too often, "good ideas" become de facto standards, which then become dicta and soon become institutionalized into policies, regulations, and procedures, while simultaneously becoming obsolete. This can impede technological improvements along the way. For a complete list of the type of software standards available for use, refer to the *IEEE Taxonomy of Software Standards*.[78]

The control of products focuses on the output or artifacts created by each activity in the software development process. Configuration management protects products by creating a master copy ("baseline") against which controlled changes are made. This ensures the consistency of the evolving product as requirements are defined, specifications are documented, the design is developed and implemented, and changes are made to it. We will examine configuration management in more detail later in this chapter.

3.2.3.1.2 Quality assurance activities.   Quality assurance (QA) is defined by the IEEE Standard for Software Quality as a planned and systematic pattern of actions, necessary to provide adequate confidence that the items or project conforms to established technical requirements.[79] It includes the specification of the methods, automation, training, quality measures, and statistical collection procedures that are to be used.[80] Additionally, QA personnel provide counseling to the project team on the application of quality approaches and monitors the adherence to project standards.

In other words, quality assurance ensures that the software system and the software engineering process adhere to preestablished standards. This is meant to avert the underlying causes of risk to the enterprise. Whereas the process model provides the framework in which the methods and automation play together, it is QA that is the glue among them all. Software QA is a subset of Total Quality Management (TQM), in that TQM spans a business enterprise, whereas SQA is concentrated on one element of the enterprise.

The quality of a product is defined as the totality of features and characteristics that bears on its ability to meet user needs.[81] The control of quality are the actions necessary to measure the characteristics of the product and compare them to the specification.

Quality can't be tested into a product, but must be built into it from the beginning. The process must start at the initialization of the process model and continue until the product is retired. The reason is simple. Each phase of a process provides a new opportunity for error. Even if one produces quality requirements, this does not guarantee quality specifications. And if we allow a poor specification to be produced and propagated, a poor design will result, as will an even worse implementation.

However, quality does have a price, regardless of claims of "quality is free." Not all quality factors can be attained simultaneously. Certain trade-offs have to occur since some factors are synergistic in nature, while others are in conflict. Some are also mutually exclusive. Table 3.3 illustrates how some of these factors interact, whereas Table 3.4 depicts some of the trade-off considerations.[82]

The responsibility of assuring quality rests with all development personnel, but a number of groups are tasked with the specific responsibility and authority to ensure that it happens. These are the *product assurance (PA), configuration management (CM),* and *verification, validation, and preventative testing (V, V, & PT)* groups. Realize, however, that the terminology used in product assurance is used in a widely varying manner. One person's QA is another's Test and Evaluation (T&E).[83] With these cautionary notes, we will start with product assurance.

TABLE 3.3 Quality Factor Interaction

IF A HIGH DEGREE OF QUALITY IS PRESENT FOR A FACTOR, WHAT DEGREE OF QUALITY IS EXPECTED FOR THE OTHER:

O = HIGH

● = LOW

BLANK = NO RELATIONSHIP OR APPLICATION DEPENDANT

Factors	Correctness	Reliability	Efficiency	Integrity	Usability	Maintainability	Testability	Flexibility	Portability	Reusability	Interoperability
Correctness											
Reliability	O										
Efficiency											
Integrity			●								
Usability	O	O	●	O							
Maintainability	O	O	●		O						
Testability	O	O	●		O	O					
Flexibility	O	O	●	●	O	O	O				
Portability			●			O	O				
Reusability		●	●	●		O	O	O	O		
Interoperability			●	●					O		

3.2.3.1.2.1 Product assurance. Product assurance is the activity concerned with product integrity; i.e., the construction of a software system which closely matches the user/customer's real needs.[84] The risks to be averted by product assurance are those in which the system:

- Cannot fulfill users' functional needs
- Cannot be traced throughout the development process

TABLE 3.4 Typical Quality Factor Trade-offs

Integrity vs. Efficiency	The additional code and processing required to control the access of the software or data usually lengthens run-time and requires additional code.
Usability vs. Efficiency	The additional code and processing required to ease an operator's tasks or provide more usable output usually lengthens run-time and increases storage.
Maintainability vs. Efficiency	Optimized code increases maintainer's efforts. Using components, modules, instrumentation, etc., however, will increase overhead.
Portability vs. Efficiency	The use of direct code, optimized code, or system utilities decreases the portability of the system.
Flexibility vs. Efficiency	Generally, a flexible system will increase overhead.
Interoperability vs. Efficiency	The added overhead for data conversion and interface routines decreases operating efficiency.
Flexibility vs. Integrity	Flexibility requires very general structures. Security may be harder to ensure.
Reusability vs. Integrity	As above, reusable software provides potential security problems.
Interoperability vs. Integrity	Coupled systems allow for more paths that can allow either accidental or purposeful access to data.
Reusability vs. Reliability	The generality required by reusable software makes providing for error tolerance and accuracy difficult.

- Cannot meet the specification for performance
- Cannot meet the agreed upon price as expected
- Cannot meet the agreed upon scheduled delivery date

3.2.3.1.2.2 Configuration management. CM, or configuration management, is the aspect of product assurance concerned with identifying the configuration of a system at discrete points in time. This is done for the systematic management and control of changes, for monitoring product integrity, and for ensuring method traceability throughout the enterprise process. This helps the developers understand what it is that they are supposed to build, what it is they in fact are building, and what has been built so far. Like other aspects of product assurance, there are many specific ways to conduct CM. The following discussion is based on Bersoff.[85]

Configuration management has four components:

- Identification
- Control
- Auditing
- Status accounting

Identification. Identification is the definition and recording of the product baseline. A baseline is a snapshot in time of the existing aggregate of information which defines the product. When this information is updated and another snapshot made (called "freezing the baseline"), the next (and newest) baseline is formed. Software identification is concerned with giving names to these baselines and tracing their parentage. This reduces the risk of losing control of the development process.

Identification is important because one baseline might be used as a basis of (i.e., is a parent of) a number of different modifications, each having its own baseline (i.e., are unique children of the original baseline). In large product developments, where many enhanced versions of the original are being worked on simultaneously, ensuring the integrity and availability of each version is vital.

Control. Software configuration control is an administrative mechanism for initializing, preparing, evaluating, and approving or disapproving all proposals for changing the baseline throughout the product's life. The administration of change proposals includes: (1) documentation, called an *engineering change proposal* (ECP) that is for the initiation of requests for change, as well as the definition of the proposed change; (2) an organization for formal evaluation and disposition of change proposal, called a *software configuration control board* (SCCB), and (3) the procedures for the control of changes to the baseline.

Requests for change might come from a change in the requirements or from a documentation defect. However, not every proposal for change is accepted. An assessment is made of the technical feasibility of the change, its impact on schedule and budget, and its risk to the product's integrity. Considerations of the effects on future baselines, product maintainability, flexibility, etc. are also investigated. The change is approved or disapproved based on its value and cost. If accepted, the baseline is modified once a fully verified change is created. The system is very autocratic, with the leader of the SCCB having final authority to disapprove or approve a change.

Auditing. Software configuration auditing is the mechanism for determining how well the current state of the software product maps to the requirement and specification documents. It also serves as the mechanism for formally establishing the baseline. A document is not sanctioned to be baselined until after it has been audited. The same is true for updates to the baseline.

Auditing has two functions: configuration verification and configuration validation. Configuration verification is meant to ensure that what is intended for each configured item specified in one baseline is achieved in the next. Configuration validation is meant to ensure that the configured item meets the customer/user's needs. These together help ensure a quality product, and quickly point out any externally based risks to management in a very visible fashion.

Status accounting. Configuration status accounting is a record of the baseline and any changes made or approved. Since approved changes aren't instantaneously incorporated, it is important for baseline integrity, and for future change proposal deliberations, that the baseline be tracked carefully. Configuration status accounting provides a history of the three other configuration components as well.

There are many versions of the basic principles of CM outlined above and many ways it can be applied. One need only consult the references to see how CM can be applied to large system developments, to managing multimaintenance projects, or to maintaining the various tools used to develop a system.[86]

However, when it is used, the benefits of configuration management are many. CM helps avert errors in the product, helps ensure its integrity, and ensures changes are made only to the areas that require it. Additionally, a history of the project's development is maintained. Although configuration management is a prime management risk aversion strategy, its implementation also presents a risk to the enterprise. Configuration management is not inexpensive. It is a difficult trade-off to decide how much current funding should be spent on configuration management versus the amount of funding that will be eventually saved by averting risks. Another risk to the enterprise exists if configuration management is only partially implemented, as is sometimes the case. One area that is usually not performed with as much rigor is the auditing portion of CM. Sometimes management will decide arbitrarily that next Friday whatever exists will become the new baseline. This does provide some level of traceability and does reduce the expenses, *if* nothing goes wrong later. If something does occur, it may be impossible to trace back between baselines, thus making CM a total waste of effort.

The final activity of product assurance we will examine is verification, validation, and preventative testing. These are very similar to configuration auditing in intent.

3.2.3.1.2.3 Verification, validation, and preventive testing. While both product assurance and configuration management can trace their beginnings to the hardware side of engineering, verification and validation (V&V) came into being expressly for coping with software and its development.[87] The preventive testing element has been an outgrowth of the realization that testing was not limited to a process model phase, but was part of management's tools for risk management that began at the beginning of the software development.[88]

Verification and validation are concerned with how well the software product fulfills functional and performance requirements, while product assurance is concerned more with the fact that specified requirements, are, first stated, second, stated correctly, and third, interpreted correctly. Preventive testing (PT) is concerned with minimizing the expected cost of software failure; i.e., how much damage a software failure can cause and the likelihood of that failure. By applying properly designed statistical testing, one can receive information about the probability of an error remaining in the code or the probability of a failure occurring in its use. The focal point of all three types of product assurance is the *customer* and making sure that what is delivered is that which is desired.

The *IEEE Glossary of Software Engineering Terminology* defines verification as the process of determining whether or not the products of a given phase of the software development cycle fulfill the requirements established during the previous phase.[89] This implies that the products must meet prescribed goals, as defined through the baselined data. In other words, are we building the system right? Validation is defined as the process of evaluating software at the end of the development process, to ensure compliance with software requirements. In other words, does the product meet its objectives and do the right job, or are we building the right system?

The evaluation criteria used in the performance of verification and validation are *completeness, ambiguity, feasibility,* and *testability.*[90,91] Completeness indicates that all product components are present, and all are developed. This implies there are no TBDs, no nonexistent references, no missing functions, or missing products. It also implies no extraneous information (i.e., gold-plating) exists either. Ambiguity means that each phase component does not have conflicting interpretations with the previous phase's output and that they are consistent. This implies that the products of each phase are traceable to the one previously produced. Feasibility means that the product will save more in terms of accomplishing some task than it costs to build, regardless of what is used as the "cost" criteria. Testability means the ability to find an economical way to test the product that will show whether or not they meet the specifications. Figure 3.13 illustrates some defect types for a requirements-inspection checklist.

Preventive testing is founded upon a three-pronged approach.[92] Tests of the product are developed after the requirements, design, and implementation phases. These tests are meant to stress the system's capability to withstand different types of software failure. The tests are based upon scenarios depicting the possible operational consequences if a software failure should occur. A particular failure is tested based upon errors that are, from past experience, likely to be infesting the system at the current time. By identifying the risks of a possible software failure early in the development, preventive measures (i.e., risk aversion) can be taken in each of the following phases to minimize or eliminate the possible consequences of the risk. After final acceptance testing and

---

Correctness
• Are all sources of input identified?
• What is the total input space?
• Are there any "don't cares" in the input space?
• Are there any timing constraints on the inputs or outputs?
• Are all outputs identified?
• What are all of the types of runs?
• Are all necessary performance requirements described?
• Should reliability requirements be specified?

Ambiguity
• Are all special terms defined?
• Does each description term and explanation have only one interpretation?
• Is the input to output mapping clearly defined?

Consistency
• Do any of the designated requirements conflict with other information?
• Are there any input states which map to multiple output states?
• Is a consistent set of quantitative states applied?
• Are all numeric quantities consistent?

Figure 3.13 Requirements Checklist

system delivery, further suggestions for safely operating the system to minimize the possibility of software risks and their consequences of failure are listed.

V&V and PT process model coverage. As with the other aspects of product assurance, the processes of verification and validation must span a typical process model as depicted in Figure 3.14.[93,94] The arrows reflect the paths taken, and numbers indicate the activities described below:

1. Review the requirements for completeness, consistency, feasibility, and testability. Since requirements aren't usually defined rigorously enough, the arrow is dotted. Evaluate the risks of software failure due to errors. Suggest risk aversion strategies for the specification stage.
2. If the criteria of completeness, consistency, feasibility, and testability can't be established at the requirements level, they should be established using the specification as the base.

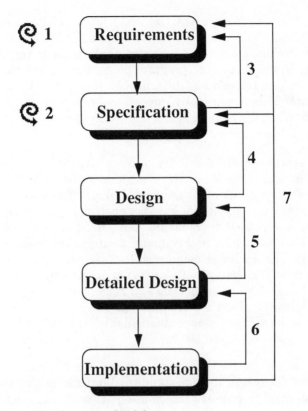

Figure 3.14 Span of Verification and Validation

3. Determine if the specifications correctly implement the requirements.
4. Determine if the design correctly implements the specification. Evaluate the risks of software failure due to errors. Suggest risk aversion strategies for the implementation stage.
5. Determine that the design decomposition does not violate the product design.
6–7. Determine if each component of the product implementation reflects the detailed design and that the product correctly represents the implemented requirements and specifications. Evaluate the risks of software failure due to errors. Suggest risk aversion strategies for the software during use.

Overall, the application of QA, CM, and V&V can ensure a much higher quality product, which management has an obligation to deliver to the customer. It should be noted, however, that software verification and validation do not guarantee program performance, and the customer, management, and developers must not be under a mistaken impression that it can.[95] This is especially important to realize, as we will see in Chapter 5, when developing safety critical systems.

3.2.3.1.3 Reusability activities. Reusability activities comprise the final independent activities we wish to explore. Reusability is simply the ability of a software element to be used again. There are a number of software elements at different levels of abstraction that are candidates for reuse, which include reusable data, designs, requirements and specifications, programs and common systems, and code/modules.[96,97] Reusability also includes commercial off-the-shelf software (COTS). Note, however, that reused software is not exactly the same as reusable software.[98] Using an existing code and reusing it after modification in some unplanned fashion is more commonly termed *salvaging*. Itemized below are some of the components available for reuse:

- *Reusable data* are the basic elements of information that can be reused. They may include standard database information, optical, voice, graphic, or music information. A standard data interchange format is necessary for this to fully work.
- *Reusable designs* are designs such as those found to describe compilers or sorting algorithms, which can be used in a variety of ways, but may be implemented uniquely; e.g., multiple target compiler backends.
- *Reusable requirements and specifications* are like designs, but represent their upper level descriptions. For many product developments of the same type of application, say, for instance in a radar system, the general requirements are going to be the same.
- *Reusable programs and common systems* include reusing complete, "shrink-wrapped" products like operating systems, spreadsheets, or word processor systems.
- *Reusable code, modules, or subsystems* are components of a specific implementation that can be used in other software systems or as a basis for a new one. Subroutines or math functions are examples of small reusable parts, while working prototypes illustrate reusable components of a larger scale.

These reusable elements have also been categorized in another fashion to help clarify what reusable software consists of: (1) those elements that can reused in a number of applications (e.g., a math function); (2) those that are used in successive versions (e.g., a new version of a product based on a previous one); (3) those that are reused whenever the program containing the element is executed (e.g., a compiler); and (4) those that are reused in a program (e.g., a subroutine).[99]

3.2.3.1.3.1 Why a management activity? The reader may be asking him or herself why reusability is considered a phase-independent management activity and not a developer's phase-dependent responsibility. Also, what does it have to do with risk aversion?

First, as one can see from the above list, there are many opportunities for software reuse that span the entire process model. The potential benefits accrued by reusing software whenever possible include increased productivity, better reliability, and so forth.[100] Furthermore, software reuse can potentially reduce the risks in both the process and product dimensions of the development enterprise. By reusing software, risks can be averted by not having to undertake the construction of certain parts of the software system in the first place. This can in turn reduce the sources of risk created by the lack of information, control, and/or time. Notice, however, that we qualify what we state above by using the adjective "potential." If one reviews the literature on reuse, it is easy to find that the 1970s, the 1980s, and now the 1990s were each proclaimed as the forthcoming "Decade of Reuse." Why this has happened is due in large part to the second reason for considering reuse as a management activity.

The decision authority to build, buy, or reuse software rests with the managers, and not with the developers, where it has resided for the last 25 years or so. Too often, reuse has been seen as a technical issue alone, but in fact, it is *management's* responsibility to avert risk, both for the project at hand as well as across the business enterprise. It is the only group that is effectively capable of doing so across the totality of the enterprise. This turns out to be a nontrivial exercise, not only because to reuse software, one must be able to find it, know what it does, and know how to reuse it,[101] but because of the intracompany and intercompany legal, contractual, and political conflicts associated with software reuse. Management must become involved, early and often, taking a proactive stance that reuse is important to the company's future, to successfully resolve these conflicts.[102]

Reusing software impacts how a project's organization does business and wins contracts, for example. This domain concerns management, not developers. The Defense Science Board made this point when it encouraged the use of off-the-shelf software components as a means to increase productivity and to reduce risk.[103] Below are some of the management considerations they noted as being required to be taken into account in undertaking reuse:

1. The extent of the adaptation of company operating procedures and practices that may be required to conform to the specifications of the outside system.
2. The amount of modification or custom tailoring that may be required to adapt the package to the prospective user's data processing environment.
3. The relative cost of acquiring and perhaps modifying a packaged system vs. the cost of an in-house development of an equivalent system.
4. The difference in lead time between acquiring an operational system and developing one from the beginning.

It is also management's responsibility to encourage, cajole, threaten or beg the technical members of the staff to apply reuse whenever possible. This approach may not be particularly efficient, but that's the current state of affairs. It is also one of the risk factors that must be taken into account when considering reuse.

Reuse does not happen by itself, it must be planned for. Management must be seen as supporting it, not only in words, but with deeds (especially with the added resources required). A more palatable approach may be to view reuse as an extension of verification and validation, where reuse becomes just another evaluation criteria of V&V. At each life cycle phase, it could be asked whether the product, or parts of the product are candidates for reuse. In this way, reuse has the same visibility as each of the other items in V&V and becomes an element of the overall quality assurance of the project. The spiral process model adopts this view.

3.2.3.1.3.2 Risks with reuse. Given the fact that a tremendous amount of money is being wasted on redundant code, why hasn't reuse been overwhelmingly embraced by the software community? After all, it seems like a perfect risk aversion strategy. For example, in selected projects at NASA, 70–95% of the systems were created using reused software.[104] This range for potential reuse has been supported by other studies, along with potential productivity increases of a factor of 10.[105] The reasons for resistance are difficult to pinpoint exactly, but one suspects the trouble lies equally in the technical and personal-attitude domains.

Despite cases like NASA, for software to be truly reusable, information on its cost of development, performance, characteristics, application domain, abstraction level, and context of development have to be available and easy to obtain.[106,107] Application applicability and the cost of reuse are the key pieces of information missing at present, and as we will see in the next chapter, they are likely to be unavailable for some time to come. It appears that in Japanese companies any component requiring over 20% of rework to make it reusable makes developing it from scratch more economically feasible, for instance. In most cases, the other information listed above isn't readily available either, which proves to be an additional impediment to any sort of reuse.[108] Without such information, the risks of using it cannot be judged accurately. Questions such as:

1. What is the probability that reusable software won't require rework, if it can be found in the first place?
2. What is the probability that the hardware or off-the-shelf software component will be delivered on schedule, or work as advertised?
3. What is the probability that the prototype, which will be reused, will scale up (vs. scale down), or that undocumented prototype code will be accepted by the customer as a means to save cost and meet the schedule?
4. What is the probability that the software size and computer resources are not underestimated, so the expected gains by using reuse are not as large as were estimated?

have to be answered to understand the risks involved.[109]

When studying the answers they get to the questions above, managers do not become particularly enthusiastic about reuse. For example, consider a software component developed in 1979 that may have potential for being reused. If it was a DoD project that the component was originally developed for, it was probably implemented and documented probably using MIL-STD-1679, which was a minimum set of documentation requirements. Reusing the component in 1989 means having it match DOD-STD-2167A, which reflects three later iterations of thinking about how DoD software components should be developed and documented (MIL-STD-1679A and DOD-STD-2167 preceded DOD-STD-2167A). Thus, a component reflects the assumptions of the day about what were good software engineering techniques to use, which may not be the same as today. This means one has to consider the *shelf life* of the reused code when determining if it is feasible to use. Even when good practice is used, a software component is not always suited for reuse. Top-down development is the current preferred method of development, but reuse is much easier when using a bottom-up approach.[110]

Unless managers are applying the spiral process model or some other risk-directed approach to their planning, they will typically opt to take the currently "approved" standard risk aversion technique. This technique assumes that doing anything different from what you are currently doing and familiar with, even if ineffective, is more risk intensive. Therefore, avoiding the application of reuse altogether is the best risk aversion course of action to take.

Even if management is enthusiastic about reuse, the other major difficulty in reusing software involves the developer's attitudes. Everyone wants to design or program the software system in their own, unique way. That is where the enjoyment and sense of accomplishment spring from in software enterprises. Take that away, and naturally there will be resistance. Only if it is a really hard problem, or a really easy one, or one where you don't know how to start, or you are stuck on a problem and can't find a solution, will you then begin to look around for something to steal from or use as a template. But unless it really is a problem, reusable components are just like program libraries. Things are always checked in, but never checked out. Then there are other management issues, such as who owns the intellectual property represented in a reused software component, the legal liability to the user and developer of reused software components, the warranties involved, and so forth.

Developers also are not trained nor given incentives to think about reuse. What incentive is there to put themselves out of work? Also, the cost of crafting components today for reuse is not cost-effective if the component is not going to be reused in a high-production system. Furthermore, the tools, methods, programming constructs, etc., that can encourage and make reuse a reality are not explicitly taught or applied with reuse in mind. A few significant strides are being made in this area,[111] but it will require major cultural changes on the part of developers and managers alike.

The three primary factors for software failure, underperformance and undercapitalization of resources, and the lack of understanding of risk are frequently indistinguishably lashed together under the umbrella term "management problems." It is often said that all the problems associated with software development can be solved, not by better technology, but "just" by better management. However, succumbing only to this belief, which has enough truth to it to be seductive, too often provides a tempting excuse to eliminate the more probable causes of software failure, which are harder to identify and control than just blaming a project's failure on mismanagement. Below we will show why one needs to look further than just to management for sources of software engineering risk.

3.2.3.2 Phase-dependent activities.

In the section above, we examined in some depth the activities that were considered phase independent. Not performing these activities is a major source of risk, since if the management does not possess correct information, it will make poor and often startlingly incorrect decisions. The same is true if the control of the software engineering process is slack.

Methods that support phase-dependent activities are those that are used in one or more (but not all) of the specific phases of a software development, as defined by a specific process model.[112] Phase-independent activities attempt to avert the causes of risk that relate more to the application than to the process itself. The latter, however, is more the domain of the phase-independent activities.

Risks and opportunities are associated with every method that one uses in a software enterprise, as well as where and when that method is used. For example, the use of a design method in the requirements phase for analysis purposes may prove to increase the basic causes of risks, because either missing information (exacerbating the lack of control), wrong information (exacerbating the lack of information), or extraneous information (exacerbating the lack of time) is created. Mismatches between what is desired to be accomplished in a phase and what the methods can and cannot provide are a major source of risk that a risk analyst must be sensitive to.

Rather than attempt to trek into detail about the activities occurring in each process phase; e.g., what it does, what risks are trying to be overcome, how particular methods avert those risks, etc., we will instead point out a few of the major representative risks factors in each phase a software engineering risk analyst must consider. We would like to be truly comprehensive and point out all the risks that occur in each life cycle phase, but this is impossible to accomplish in one chapter. However, we have provided references to the literature where further details of individual risks and their aversion can be sought. Those interested in the detail of each process phase should consult either Charette, Fairley or Pressman.[113-115] As a final caveat, the use of the following characterizing of life cycle phases is not meant as an endorsement, but only that it provides a convenient way of examining the potential risks involved.

3.2.3.2.1 Requirements/specification phase(s). As Plato said in *The Republic*, "The beginning is the most important part of the work," and so it is with a software development. The software requirements and specification stage(s) are the most important part of the software development. Software requirements are a description of what functionality was accorded to the software in a system and the reasons why. They bind or obligate the software to meet certain objectives of the system requirements, or as Alan Davis writes, they bind only the solution space.[116] Requirements are stated as "what needs to be accomplished," and thus are (ideally) unconcerned with where, or how, they are to be accomplished. The latter will be later described in the actual implementation. It should be noted that "what" and "how" are relative, in that one phase's "how" is another's "what," and there may be a need to understand, via preliminary design, prototyping partial implementations, etc., some of the "how" in order to specify the proper "what."

A working definition of a requirement is that it is a binding condition which states a mandatory characteristic of an abstract or physical object. Requirements may appear in many different forms, such as a description or a constraint, or as an evaluation criteria for judging quality. They also may be implicitly defined, being inferred by the context in which they occur. The basic notion is that a requirement is a condition that must be met for a software product to be termed *acceptable*.[117]

Specifications, on the other hand, focus explicitly on defining and describing the tasks the software itself must meet. Specifications are used to prescribe the binding or contractual agreements between the software requirements and the final implementation. In other words, a specification binds the software requirements to a particular implementation. This means the specifications are going to be used as the standard for gauging the correctness of the implementation and constitute the primary input needed for the design phase. Thus, the requirements and the resulting software specifications together must be as *complete* and *correct* as possible at the completion of the specification phase. Therefore, specifications *must,* as a minimum, be:

- correct and complete (as far as possible)
- consistent
- unambiguous
- verifiable
- traceable
- minimal
- modifiable

If the specifications do not meet the above criteria, or the process used to define the specification cannot meet these criteria, then both the process and the specification must be considered primary sources of risk to the enterprise.

Requirements are normally divided into two types: *functional* and *nonfunctional*. Functional requirements are those that are absolutely necessary to the functioning of the system, describe the input/output behavior of the system,[118] and are the "shall be's" of the software that can (and must) be tested. Nonfunctional requirements are the desirable but optional requirements that are subjective in nature, such as

Correctness	Usability	Flexibility	Interoperability
Acceptability	Operability	Adaptability	Noncomplexity
Completeness	User Friendliness	Extensibility	Modularity
Consistency	Accessibility	Structuredness	Communicativeness
Expressability	Convertibility	Expandability	Uniformity
Validity	Documentable	Augmentability	Timeliness
Performance	Understandability	Modifiability	Reliability
Clarity	Testability	Availability	Accountability
Accuracy	Inexpensiveness	Robustness	Self-descriptiveness
Maintainability	Portability	Preciseness	Stability
Manageability	Compatibility	Reusability	Integrity
Repairability	Generality	Security	Serviceability

Figure 3.15 Some Typical Nonfunctional Requirements

maintainability or ease of use, and therefore not conclusively testable.[119] Figure 3.15 illustrates some of the more common nonfunctional requirements.

Requirements and specification are closely aligned, and in some process models, they are seen as two aspects of the single phase of requirements analysis. Because of the close tie, there are a number of methods that are used both for requirements analysis and specification.[120,121] Table 3.5 lists some of the methods currently advertised as useful in requirements definition. Each takes a slightly different approach to the problem. Some are very formal, using grammatical-based approaches, while some others are more informal, such as structured textual descriptions that are later analyzed. Graphical methods seem to handle both the communication and domain issues very well. Logic or mathematical-based techniques, in comparison, are more formal and precise, but are not understood by as wide of an audience. No one method seems capable of supporting all the various viewpoints and media required to fully define requirements, however.

3.2.3.2.1.1 Requirement and specification risks. Requirements and specifications express the system's connection with the outside world, and therefore must anticipate all of the circumstances in which the

TABLE 3.5 Some Methods Claimed to Be Useful for Requirements Specification

Mnemonic	Full Name
ACM/PCM	Active and Passive Component Modeling
DSSAD	Data Structured Systems Analysis and Design
DSSD	Data Structured Systems Development
EDM	Evolutionary Design Method
GEIS	Gradual Evolution of Information Systems
IE	Information Engineering
ISAC	Information Systems Work and Analysis of Changes
JSD	Jackson System Development
PRADOS	Projektabwicklungs und Dokumentationssystem
PSL	Problem Statement Language
SADT	Structured Analysis and Design Technique
SARA	Systems Architect Apprentice
SA-SD	Structured Analysis – Structured Design
SDM	System Development Method
SEPN	Software Engineering Procedures Notebook
SREM	Software Requirements Engineering Methodology
STRADIS	Structured Analysis, Design, and Implementation of Information Systems

system might be used. These must be described, as well as what actions must be taken under those circumstances. Errors that arise during these activities cause the most fatal wounds, and therefore are the greatest risks.

A considerable source of risk revolves around the issue of functional and nonfunctional requirements. Up to 35% of all functional requirements are not defined on the first formal attempt to define them.[122] Even if one is successful in defining and meeting the functional requirements properly, it is difficult to measure the success with which nonfunctional requirements are met until after the system has been developed and delivered. The subjective nature of nonfunctional requirements precludes this from occurring. Take user-friendliness, for example. How "friendly" is friendly? To many people, if the system's access terminals do not have pull-down windows, is highly graphical in nature, and does not respond to a command in less than 2 seconds, it doesn't begin to be perceived as friendly. To others, these are unimportant and make the system very unfriendly, especially if you want to be able to quickly access and change some of the system's internal operations.

Functional and nonfunctional requirements are tied up with the success criteria of the enterprise, which, naturally, change in time. Refer back to note 42 of Chapter 1, for instance. Whereas functional requirements tend to dominate the development process and are used as this part of the enterprise's measures of success, nonfunctional requirements tend to dominate the evolutionary timeframe of an enterprise, where the criteria of success are much different and often are diametrically opposed.

In real systems, meeting the nonfunctional requirements often is more important than meeting the functional requirements in the determination of a system's perceived success or failure. Nonfunctional requirements also are responsible for a large proportion of the later efforts and related costs of evolving the system. For example, in two large development efforts, an average of 80% of the software had to be rewritten after delivery because of user/requirement mismatches.[123] More importantly, however, there do not yet exist heuristics on even how to deal with functional requirements for system software, let alone the nonfunctional ones. Figure 3.16 illustrates the rather scanty current state of knowledge in functional and nonfunctional requirements.[124]

The conflicts between functional and nonfunctional requirements can be such that the system can never meet them. This can easily be seen by drawing simple Venn diagrams, as depicted in Figure 3.17. Diagram (a) illustrates a system which has some nonfunctional requirements specified

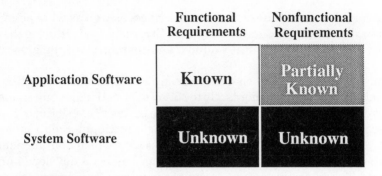

	Functional Requirements	Nonfunctional Requirements
Application Software	Known	Partially Known
System Software	Unknown	Unknown

Figure 3.16 Current State of Knowledge Concerning Functional/Nonfunctional Requirements

in such a manner that they all can be satisfied to some degree, whereas diagram (b) depicts a situation which is "impossible;" i.e., meeting one functional requirement may mean one or more are not met. Similarly, diagram (c) shows the same problem when carried to a higher level of requirement. While functional and nonfunctional requirements interactions are difficult to cope with, nonfunctional requirements

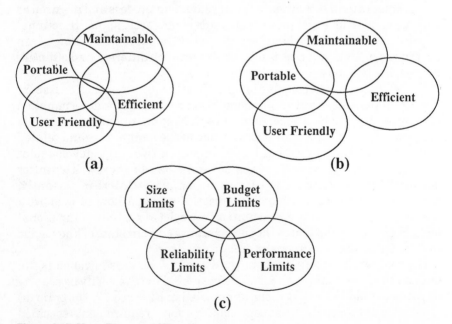

Figure 3.17 Venn Diagram of Requirements

interacting with other nonfunctional requirements are the most difficult to deal with, since these interactions are invisible, yet the effects are very visible.

The root motivation of the functional/nonfunctional problem is, as one harried requirements analyst put it, "Understanding the problem is the problem."[125] Requirements are usually characterized by one of four states: chaotic, informal, precise, or formal. For an example of the latter, imagine you are a cook and are trying to understand the DoD's 18-page recipe for fruitcake, which has requirements stating that it should be "organoleptically pleasing" and when "bisected vertically," it should not crumble, smear, and so forth. Does that mean when the fruitcake is bisected horizontally, it can?

In software developments that are the first of its kind—and most are, since the personnel working on it have never worked on a system like it before—there usually is a lack of relevant domain experience. In some firms, a person may be working on a banking application one day, and then find himself working on a fire control system for a nuclear submarine the next. Thus, when decisions have to be made about what is important or correct and what is not, there is a lack of information about what to do, since there are no previously implemented alternatives with which to compare possible solutions.[126] Then there is the issue of trying to satisfy what everyone thinks are "the requirements."

In software developments, as in development tasks in other disciplines, there are many stakeholders involved, many with conflicting needs. These include the customer, the user, and the developer, to name just three major groups. There also may be government regulators, other computer systems with which the system may need to interface, as well as "the market," which need to be included into the equation. In large system enterprises, it is not uncommon for 50 or 60 individuals from 20 separate organizations to have a part in determining "the requirements." It is often difficult to determine who has the legitimate authority to make or change requirements, and there are frequently turf fights over this authority. Then there is the necessary separation between what is wanted and what is needed. A customer may want an information system that is similar to the Grand Designs encountered in the previous chapter, but may in fact need something far less sophisticated and costly.

Real software developments are, in fact, nothing more than continuous negotiations over what constitutes "the system," which encompasses in actuality three systems of interest: the information system itself, the belief systems of the participants, and the political systems to which each stakeholder belongs.[127] Davis has graphically portrayed this general situation in Figure 3.18, which depicts different stakeholder's perspectives

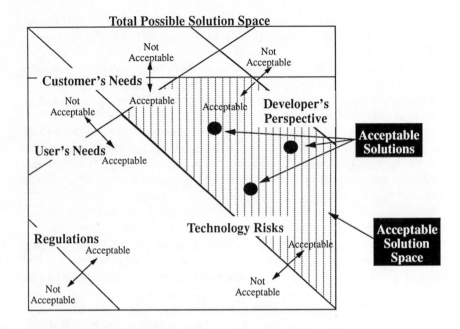

Figure 3.18 Differing Stakeholder Perspectives and Development of Acceptable Requirements

and the resulting solution space which can have multiple solutions.[128] The requirements analyst must then make the trade-offs to determine which of the solutions is optimal for the situation at hand.

This presents a major risk, since the original resources and performance estimates were made on a "mythical" set of requirements. Even with continuous changing system requirements, there usually is not a subsequent increase or change in resource or performance objectives. Sometimes the reason is deliberate. For example, one customer representative in discussing an ongoing software project said, "we try to talk the contractor into enhancements we didn't pay for.... We try to get a Cadillac for the price of a Chevy."[129]

Sometimes the reason for not increasing resources in the face of continuous requirements changes is ignorance. Customers and requirements analysts alike usually don't perform a comprehensive risk analysis before suggesting and accepting changes to requirements. Thus, they do not fully understand the ramifications to existing functions, the capability of existing technology to handle the changes, etc., they have created. Sometimes it is the fault of developers, who just aim to please, cannot say no, and do not understand the new risks to the enterprise (and business) they have just accepted. The risk caused by the lack of control of change is high. In Barry Boehm's COCOMO model, requirements volatility is in the top third of cost drivers for a software development. [130]

Another risk related to the lack of control is the development policy chosen. Recall from Chapter 2 the Software First vs. Hardware First approaches to building systems. This argument, when the ideological red herrings are stripped away, is about constraining the requirements and the subsequent design of the system. In most developments, the hardware system is fixed. This sometimes is caused by the simple fact that an organization already owns the hardware and does not want to throw it away. Sometimes it occurs because the hardware manufacturer has a discount sale and convinces the customer that an upgrade is "cheap." Sometimes it occurs because choosing hardware is the easiest problem to solve and shows that progress is being made. It is this last point that brings out the ideologues. In *ideal* software engineering practice, if there are no compelling reasons to do so (and the fanatics of the Software First argument do not believe there ever are), the requirements should not be partitioned into hardware or software until design trade-offs can be made. This makes sense, since one does not want to constrain the software or hardware unduly. Defining the hardware suite before the trade-offs can be determined is a risk, and in fact, often carries with it unobservable risks into the development which are not discovered until much later, by which time it is costly to change direction.

However, the Software First policy also has a risk in that one can easily partition requirements needing a hardware suite that is so expensive, or so technologically immature, that the system cannot be built. The risk posed by the development policy can be minimized by the proper selection of the requirements method. The point is, the risk analyst needs to investigate how and why requirements are partitioned into hardware and software. In general, the later that binding can occur, the better.

Another major source of risk in requirements that the analyst should investigate can be traced to the medium used. Requirement documents most often use textual descriptions which are prone to misinterpretation, may encourage the absence of certain necessary data, are difficult to check for consistency or adequacy, and are imprecise. Consider the following from the public laws of the State of Kansas: "In the case of two trains meeting at a crossing, both shall come to a full stop and neither shall proceed until the other is gone." Thus, before any representation medium is chosen for performing requirement phase activities, issues such as what kinds of questions are trying to be answered, who is going to be using it, how it will be used, and what the background of the practitioners is all need to be addressed.[131] Finally, any method used must be able to define, document, and manipulate the tremendous amount of conceptual knowledge (or information) involved, which is a hallmark of the domain of requirements definition.

Larger-scale software enterprises pose unique risks which must receive careful consideration during requirements analysis. One is the lack of control that often exists in the day-to-day development. For example, the larger the project, the greater the need for effective communication among the participants. Each new person added to a software team increases the number of communication channels by:

$$\frac{N\,(N-1)}{2} \tag{3.2}$$

In larger systems, 20 or more specialized requirements analysts (not including the other stakeholders) might be involved in creating the software requirements for the system. This means miscommunication is a definite possibility, although noncommunication is more the rule than the exception.[132] The selection of the requirements method can definitely either lower this source of risk or enhance it. Thus, the communication medium used by the method takes on added importance as the system size increases.

There are a number of other requirements risks that also need to be considered in large-scale developments. Some may be caused by *derived requirements* risks; e.g., a requirement that cannot be totally specified until some other phase such as design has been performed.[133] Another is *capacity planning requirements risks*; e.g., because of the projected longevity of the information system, new hardware technology will be introduced later and have to be dealt with. The risks caused by the process of *risk aversion* itself are yet a third type which need to be considered. For example, it is not uncommon that during the development process some new technology or new development approach which can reduce the overall enterprise risk is discovered, and but it also negatively impacts the system requirements.

Let's now turn our attention for a moment to the risks inherent in the specification of requirements. The most effective requirement specification methods are based upon the principle of formalism.[134,135] Formalism comes in many flavors. To some, it means a strict mathematical approach, while to others, a less rigorous approach consisting of tables and templates with rules specifying their organization, allowable operations, symbology, and extensions are used. Other methods use formal languages, similar to programming languages, to express specifications. Either way, formalism allows for detailed, precise, and concise specifications to be developed that can be reviewed for completeness, consistency, and correctness. This leads to easier automation of the specification for consistency and completeness, but not for correctness. Formal specifications also provide a means for reusing specifications, which can increase productivity.

There are risks, though, to the use of formal specifications. These risks lie in two directions. The first risk is in their application. Formal techniques are difficult to learn and apply, which can interfere with the process of developing, communicating, and gaining approval for the created specifications. The developers don't usually have the necessary background to apply formal methods, nor do the end-users, and they can be expensive in time and money to use. Formal methods are also susceptible to typographical errors. The second risk lies inherently within the principles used by many of the specifications methods and is called the *specifier's dilemma*.

Specifications are supposed to describe the externally visible behavior of the software system without describing how it is implemented. However, many methods use functional decomposition as the primary principle for specifying this behavior. In this case (as Heitmeyer explains it), a system is viewed as some collection of functions that generates output from input.[136] This function is then qualified into subordinate functions whose composition performs the total system function. The resulting specification reflects the system via these compositions.

The risk in applying this approach is that it may later exclude many acceptable, and less risky, software implementations. For example, neither the function nor the functional decomposition documented may be unique. If the system has input-output relations which are not functions (i.e., more than one acceptable response to a single input), any particular decomposition will exclude some acceptable responses. Furthermore, the decomposition is only one of many that can represent the required functions. Acceptable decompositions can differ with respect to the level of decomposition, the order of invocation for subfunctions, and even the basic units of decomposition.

These differences in decomposition become important because they imply a modularization of the way the software must perform its tasks; i.e., a decomposition may prematurely prejudice a designer. The way that the software is eventually decomposed into modules has serious ramifications. For instance, one decomposition can make certain parts of it easier to change, as well as ease the reusing of product components. The converse is also true where a decomposition can make it harder to change or reuse software components. It has been shown, for instance, that using functional decomposition to achieve modularization is not the best method in all cases.[137]

One approach to avert the dilemma is to acknowledge that functional decomposition has these *possible* risks, and that one ought to vigilantly monitor possible untoward consequences. This is an acceptable response to the risk, except it places a great deal of stress and responsibility on the software designer rather than the requirements analyst. The designer must be aware of the fact that the decomposition he or she gets at the end of the specification process doesn't portray a design. If this isn't recognized, the risk of producing an incorrect design increases manyfold. Thus, the designer has to evaluate the risks in deciding how far to stray from the specification. The risk might appear in exactly the opposite guise, as well. For example, if the specification is seen as representing an acceptable first cut at a design, then it may discourage the designer from looking for designs that might be much easier to implement and later evolve. The risks associated with increased system evolutionary costs might then be the result.

3.2.3.2.1.2 Risk aversion in requirements and specification. The risks in the requirements and specification phase(s) can easily be traced to the lack of information, lack of control, and the lack of time. The two primary causes are the lack of information and the lack of control, which manifest themselves in the constant and often unnecessary changing of requirements. The termination of the often unnecessary continuous negotiation process needs to be seen as a high priority, especially if a minimum set of requirements has been agreed upon. Any other industry, such as car manufacturers, would go broke trying to continually negotiate a labor agreement with their workers. To avert this particular risk, the requirements should be seen forming a "contract" between stakeholders in the system and its developers. As a contract, requirements form the standard against which the system will be judged by all the stakeholders, and must be explicitly linked to the business need of the organization. This can be done using something simple, such as a polar chart depicting required (and attained) functional and nonfunctional requirements, as shown in Figure 3.19.

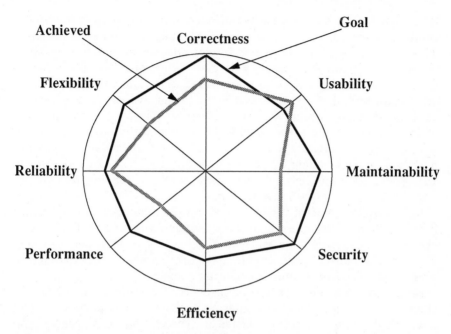

Figure 3.19 Desired vs. Achieved Stakeholder Requirements

Remember, a requirement is an expression of need, an imposed demand, or something someone will pay for, thus it should take on a form similar to a legal document. If a contract cannot be drawn up, then the analyst should question the development organization's capability to develop the system to the point of possibly recommending that the development not continue. This may seem severe, but if the output of requirements definition were taken with the same serious scrutiny as legal contracts are, much more care would go into their creation, and much less changing of them would occur later on, especially if the risks and monetary penalties for doing so were spelled out. Requirements changes, where necessary, could be negotiated in a similar fashion to the software change control board found in configuration management.

At the very least, it should be recognized that requirements are likely to change, and that modifications to most current acquisition processes or method of capitalization are required. One change in acquisition policy which a company might consider, for instance, would be not to build large systems that evolve at all, but to build systems that are "throwaways." It is a system's evolution, and the difficulty of predicting the future 5 to 10 years out, which forces many requirements changes. The situation is so bad today that, in many organizations, there is more software than can ever possibly be maintained or evolved. Instead of trying to do so, why not build many small, individual systems quickly which can be interfaced to another, but never evolve? These systems could be built more cheaply, and could be thrown away when not needed. This approach is the same as what happened in the hardware arena, where personal computers do today what mainframes use to do. When a better one comes along, you throw out your old PC and buy a new one. Using a similar approach, software systems would then be commodities, not major unique capital investments.

Adherence to some of the basic software engineering principles can help avert the risks present in the specifier's dilemma and should be strongly supported in the methods used to create the specifications. Three of the more important principles are the use of *abstraction, the separation of concerns,* and *information hiding.*

An abstraction represents some aspects of a system, but not all of them.[138] For example, a road map is an abstraction of a particular road network showing directions, relative lengths, and possibly speed limits, but probably will not illustrate whether the roads are sanded or plowed in the winter. By using abstraction, it is easier to investigate and study a system because irrelevant details are left out. Abstract interfaces are another example. An abstract interface represents more than one specific interface. In other words, it contains all the common assumptions of all of the interfaces it represents. An abstract interface omits the details that would distinguish one specific interface from another. Keep in mind, though, an appropriate level of abstraction is necessary, if relevant details aren't going to be omitted.

Another way to manage the dilemma is to use the concept of the separation of concerns.[139] Separation of concerns is the division of information about a system into clearly distinct, and relatively independent, parts. Separation of concerns has as its primary goal the minimization of the risks due to the impact of change. For example, functionality is separated from behavior, representation is separated from logical meaning, input-output mapping is separated from functionality, and expected changes in the product are separated from those elements that won't change. The latter are especially useful in systems undergoing incremental development. As a byproduct of using this approach, one always knows where to find an answer to a particular question.

Information hiding captures information that is likely to change into defined groupings or modules.[140] This grouping limits the amount of software that must be modified when a change is introduced. Notice information hiding and the separation of concerns describe the same principle, only from different risk perspectives.

By using abstraction, separation of concerns, and hiding in the specification process, designers are not constrained in any way. They are free to create whatever design can meet the specifications. For example, in a large project, one is likely to be creating a software product that will evolve over time. One can use a modularity decomposition strategy based upon the changes expected to occur as a guide to decomposing the requirements and specifications. The modules created will be separated into those that will likely change and those which will not, thus minimizing the effects (and risks) of changes that do occur.

Furthermore, the decomposition is such that it does not *imply* any particular design. This encourages the designer to explore many possible implementations. The information contained in the trial designs is captured, so these are available for later use, but not the designs themselves. Of course, it would be useful if the specification information captured by a method in this way provided the developer with hints on how to obtain feasible designs. Total freedom has its risks, too.

Selection and application of the particular requirements and/or specification methods are very important to the success of the software project. The consequences of producing incorrect requirements and/or specifications include system rejection, system reengineering or retrofit, the installation of a dangerous system, the total failure of the enterprise, and/or the loss of future business. In fact, errors in the requirement and specification phases account for most of the rework costs, seen in both development and evolution. This is not difficult to understand. Just reexamine Figure 1.12.

3.2.3.2.1.3 Requirements and specification risk summary. In most software enterprises today, formal requirements and specification methods have not been used, although the trend is beginning to change. A primary reason has been the lack of available and inexpensive automation of the methods themselves. Most enterprise managers feel the risks created by not applying requirement and specification methods are more acceptable than the risks entailed by applying them in a nonautomated fashion. This is because they see greater risk created by the losses in control and time than the gains achieved by overcoming the lack of information.

A number of studies have been conducted to compare different methods and evaluate their usefulness for different types of applications and system sizes.[141-145] So far, the studies to date concerning the effectiveness of the application of specific requirements and specification methods, unfortunately, have proven to be inconclusive. No single method seems to be intrinsically better than another, and the only conclusion these reports have reached is that there is still much more research to be done.

However, a number of findings important to the risk analyst have been reported by Alan Davis.[146-148] First, the quality of the requirements and specification which have been produced using formal methods has been demonstrated to be vastly improved when compared to those which do not use formal methods. Second, it is important that the multiple perspectives of the system under development be specified. Many requirements methods specify just the static dynamics, not the operational dynamics. One needs to specify the functional view, the nonfunctional view, the external behavior, and the data interactions.[149,150] And third, one may need to apply many different techniques to specify the requirements.[151] As Davis says, he is amazed when people ask whether they should use one requirements method or another. It is similar to asking if one should wear a sweater or boots today. One needs to ask each question separately, and answer depending on the specific situation. Davis has compiled the most recent survey of requirements methods, and has listed their strengths, weaknesses, and applicability in his excellent book, *Software Requirements: Analysis and Specification,* which can be used as a primer on the general sources of risk found in the requirements phase.

In summary, from a risk analyst's perspective, given the results to date of the studies, one needs to primarily: (a) consider the costs of using a requirements method versus not; (b) consider which methods are the most effectively applied, given the application domain and the skills of the personnel who are going to apply it; and (c) consider the total numbers and the rate of change in the requirements being added or modified. This last item will be a key indicator of whether the development will have a chance of succeeding or not. The greater the number of requirements or more rapid increase in the number of requirement changes over time, the higher the probability of a system's development not being successful. This goes double if the capitalization or performance needs are also not changed to reflect the deviations from the original plan. This information can be gleaned from carefully watching the changes to the system development plan and progress charts.

3.2.3.2.2 Design phase. During the design phase, an abstraction, commonly called a *design representation*, is created that will be later closely mapped into the physical implementation of the system. This transformation occurs in the implementation phase. When implemented according to this architectural design, the software should meet the software requirement specifications, as well as satisfy the evaluation criteria defined from the functional and nonfunctional requirements. This is a necessity for the design to be considered successful in meeting its own objectives.

The intellectual boundary is a bit fuzzy, but the focus is shifted from the activities of requirements and specifications which were to detail *what* the system will do, to *how* it will do it. Much of the fuzziness stems from the inability of process models to describe what occurs in each phase of the development. Regardless, the process of design is predicated on the designer's ability to make this transition occur successfully. Design phase activities also differ from implementation activities, in that its output should express a formal, coherent, and well-organized representation of how a computer program is supposed to accomplish the tasks allocated to software by the requirements specification, while the output of the implementation phase turns the design representation into an executable program(s) written in a particular programming language.

There are two primary activities occurring during the design process: *external* and *internal design*.[152] External design is the definition of the externally observable characteristics of the software system. Much of this externally defined behavior has been captured in the specifications that were created in the previous requirements phase, which is one of the reasons why these two phases so often become intertwined. In practice it is nearly impossible to completely separate the two phases at this level of abstraction.

Internal design, on the other hand, defines the internal processing details and the structure of the software partitioned aspects of the system. Internal design is itself made up of two subactivities: *architectural* and *detailed design*. Architectural design's focus is the refinement of the conceptual view of the software system being developed. Therefore, architectural design is primarily concerned with recognizing the overall system structure and precisely defining the interfaces and interconnections among program segments. This means performing a number of tasks, such as: decomposing the specification into software modules; identifying internal processing functions; decomposing of these functions into subfunctions; identifying the interfaces and interconnections among the functions and subfunctions; identifying the data used and passed among the functions; and, finally, identifying where the data is to be stored. An overall physical system structure can then be identified. This structure is the highest level physical mapping of what will be eventually executed, as opposed to the structure identified in the specification, which was the virtual system structuring.

Detailed design is more concerned with the definition and/or selection of the algorithms and data structures that are necessary to fulfill the requirements of specific software functions defined during the architectural design activity. Thus, the motivation of detailed design is the further refinement of the architectural design. During the detailed design process, along with algorithm specification, the protocols for handling the interfaces are described, and the packaging of the software system for execution will be identified. The ultimate objective of detailed design is to produce a design of a sufficient level of granularity from which the implementors can eventually code. The level of coarse or fine granularity one must reach depends upon many factors, including the complexity of the system, how much testing is to occur, what language is going to be used, and so forth.

3.2.3.2.2.1 Design risks. During the design phase, a number of different kinds of design errors can occur with which the risk analyst should be familiar. Parnas has classified them into four general categories.[153] The first is *design inconsistencies*. This occurs when the design with high probability will not work correctly in all cases during its operational use. An example of this kind of error is when two design statements make different assumptions concerning an angle used for navigation. One may assume that the angle represents true bearing, while the other assumes that it represents relative bearing. Another kind of design error is called *design inefficiencies*. These are points where the design imposes barriers to efficient implementation or use of the system. An example might be where requests for shared data will result in capturing not only the specified data requested, but unnecessary information as well. The consequence is a waste of time and space. A third kind of error is called *design ambiguities*. Here the design may have to be interpreted several different ways by the implementors. The last kind of error is termed *design inflexibilities*. These are situations where the design does not accommodate changes very well. These may happen when the specification is vague about what will or will not change during the evolution of the system.

From the tree diagram in Figure 1.12, one can easily see that the risk consequences of an incorrect design are high, although not as high as for incorrect requirements or specifications. Whereas it costs 30–50 times more to correct a design error found during the evolution phase than in the design phase, the ratio approaches 100:1 or more for a requirements error that is not found until the evolution phase.

The major reason that the design phase can be troublesome is that the process of design is extremely difficult to describe precisely. Many research efforts have tried to formulate a scientific foundation for it, but to date no single philosophy of design exists.[154] Thus, to understand the source of design risks, one must step back and try to comprehend the general processes involved.

Design is an information-creating process.[155] It is characterized by an intensive creative aspect, which is the primary reason it is difficult to analyze or categorize. The designer of a software system does not create this information at random, but instead tries to apply previously obtained knowledge and experience gained from other projects. What can be gleaned from the products of the previous phases is important in developing a line of thought based upon logical reasoning.[156] Occasionally, the results are unexpected, which restarts the process.

In most other branches of engineering, there is a tremendous amount of well-documented previous experience from which a person can draw in estimating what is needed to attack and solve a particular problem. In software engineering, and design in particular, this experience is almost always lacking.[157,158] The quality, then, of the ensuing system depends substantially on the capability of the individual designer.

It is a maxim in architectural design that one needs to build a system to know what design decisions and trade-offs are necessary.[159] Brooks has made some similarly interesting observations about the relationship of designs to designer's experience.[160] He indicates that using a completely inexperienced designer is not entirely bad, for it is a software designer's *second* design which causes the problem. The first is clean and sparse since the designer doesn't know what he's doing, so he's careful. New "bells and whistles" occur to him during this period to be saved and used on the next design project he participates in. The second system, then, as Brooks notes, becomes the most dangerous system a person ever designs. It is only after the third attempt that the designer realizes that he or she doesn't know everything and can begin to generalize about the problem.

Designers have a large degree of freedom with which to work during the creation of the software system. The problem with this is that, while it is easier for the designer to do an outstanding job, is is just as easy to do a terrible one. Software design is mostly a human and, therefore, manual job.[161] This only reinforces the idea of design as an intensely creative process.

The ultimate goal in software design is to produce something that the implementors can use to code the software system. Thus, given a set of specifications, the designer must formulate an efficient search through the design space in order to select an appropriate set of components.[162] To accomplish this successfully, the designer must solve two basic problems: identify the issues critical to the success of the design effort, and identify the design elements necessary to adequately meet these critical issues.[163] This means selecting a design approach, and then applying it to the specifications to obtain a design.

Selecting a design approach is a simple, but not necessarily easy, thing to do. It requires an in-depth understanding of the problem domain, which hopefully the requirements and specifications provide, and also of some things these documents may not provide. This includes information such as:

- What dominates, data or functions?
- What hardware is required to be supported?
- Is the hardware appropriate when the software is partitioned into executable modules?[164]

To better understand the challenge, and thus risks, a designer is faced with, it is helpful to understand the nature of the problem to be faced. Peters, in his excellent text on software design, describes design problems as "wicked."[165] A wicked problem is one that is particularly elusive, and the solving of one aspect of it may uncover others that present even more difficult solutions. Some of the various properties of wicked problems are:

- Wicked problems cannot be definitively stated. Every formulation causes more information to be required and necessitates a new formulation.
- There are no rules or guidelines for determining when a wicked problem is solved. Every "solution" provokes a proposal for a more refined solution, *ad infinitum*. The end is never apparent. Only when time runs out on the project schedule or the designer tires out does the design effort end.

- Wicked problems have only good or bad solutions, not right or wrong ones. These problems don't have closed form solutions like mathematical formulas, but instead depend on the feedback received after the design is implemented and in use to determine if the design was successful. The satisfaction of the nonfunctional requirements, such as reliability, modifiability, user friendliness, etc., come into play here.
- Wicked problems can't be definitively tested, and the solutions are too significant to be experimented with. It probably is too dangerous (as well as politically unfeasible, not to say disturbing to the local residents) to live-test the capability of a short-range missile's nuclear warhead to stop an armor attack in the West German plain. A designer normally gets one lick at solving a wicked problem.
- Neither the number of solutions to a wicked problem nor means to obtaining them are limited. Any approach that solves the problem is acceptable. As important, any solution is also potentially acceptable.
- Every wicked problem is unique, as is every solution. The process of design is meant to eliminate all but one eventual solution. This solution never existed before, meaning that it was nonexistent prior to this time. No knowledge existed from which to gather previously detailed information or past history about the solution. This solution may thus change or affect the requirements in unexpected ways.
- Wicked problems may be symptoms of higher-level problems. If the requirements, or the schedule, or budget are unreasonable, or the technology is unavailable, the problem may be unable to be solved in any way, shape, or form.

The above properties have likely been encountered many times by anyone who has had to deal with design, no matter what particular field of endeavor. One shouldn't despair about these risks though. It is natural that the search for a design approach take on the iterative (and creative) nature of the process itself. Many different approaches are going to be tried, each attempting to control the ebb and flow between creating more detail and structuring or abstracting it into less detail.[166]

3.2.3.2.2 Design risk aversion strategies. Design methods in general are meant to define the structure and construction of the software system.[167] Design methods are very similar to requirements and specification methods in their emphasis on disciplining the creativity of the designer as a means of averting risk by increasing control. The designer has great freedom in creating a design, but only a disciplined approach will keep this freedom from turning into chaos. Moreover, most methods can be used in both architectural and detailed design, thus presenting the designer with the paradoxical challenge of keeping extraneous detail out of the early design, but simultaneously being as specific as possible.

As in requirements specification practice, delaying commitment in regard to the design details is a prime risk aversion strategy. Some of the other techniques used to accomplish this in design methods are *abstraction, structuring, coupling and cohesion,* and *information hiding.* Each is used to help define the structure of a software system design, which presents the greatest source of risk to the enterprise at this point in time.

We've seen how abstraction was used in both the requirements and specification methods we examined, and it is applied in design in much the same way, except with a different domain and viewpoint. Abstraction is used in two ways. First, it is used as a means to concentrate on one set of risks at a time to reduce the amount of complexity required to be understood at once. This is yet another example of Ockham's idea of "parsimony" of never doing more than you have to.[168] Second, abstraction is used as a means to separate similarities from differences in the software design. These are expressed through some type of abstract interface.[169]

Another technique used in software design is that of structuring. Structuring is the linking of a system that has been decomposed into smaller units through the use of well-defined relationships with other units. These units may or may not be packages, depending on whether abstraction was used or not. The number of ways the units may be linked is generally infinite, with the designer trying to establish the minimal number of links necessary to perform the specified tasks. Some aspects of structuring are connectivity and modularity.

The principle of modularity can be seen as another aspect of structuring. Modularity is the construction of interconnections using some standard pattern or plan, thus reducing the number of linkages that a designer needs to consider. Modularity can be viewed as the dual of connectivity. In other words, one may instead attempt the definition of the connections required between system units, which then implicitly defines the possible units. Defining units first implicitly defines the possible interconnections between them. Neither truly exists without the other. The use of a standard pattern of linkages causes a reduction in the number of connections possible.

Other principles used in design of the software system are *coupling* and *cohesion*.[170] Coupling is aimed at reducing the number and types of interconnections that exist between modules. For example, as the number of interconnections increase, the more difficult it is to control data access and message passing. These interconnections are defined by the type of information communicated in the interconnection, whether it be data, control, or modification of internal module information. Content coupling is when one module modifies data or instructions in another module. Control coupling occurs when one module passes information to another that can control its processing sequence. Data coupling occurs when data items are passed as parameters between modules.

Some type of coupling has to occur between modules, since all attempts to eliminate them would seem to be counter to the principles of abstraction and structuring. However, coupling based on content is the least desirable, whereas data coupling is most desirable. Data coupling also seems to lower the later cost of the implementation, and should be high on the list of risk aversion strategies to use.[171] Low coupling and minimal interconnections are a desirable property of a design.

Cohesion is aimed at increasing the relationship among elements within a single module. The stronger the binding, the better the module can be viewed as a single entity. Coincidental cohesion is when elements within a module have no obvious relationship to one another. Logical cohesion is when some relationship occurs, but the relationship is complex and/or superficial. Temporal cohesion occurs when the elements are bound by time; i.e., all elements execute simultaneously. Communicational cohesion means that the elements within a module use the same set of input or output data. Sequential cohesion is when the output of an element is the input to another. Finally, functional cohesion occurs when all the elements are related to the performance of a single function. The goals that should be aspired to reduce risks are low coupling (i.e., data coupling) and high cohesion (i.e., functional cohesion).

The last general principle we want to review is information hiding. We discussed information hiding in the previous section in relation to specifications, and it is used in a similar way in design. Each module that is defined hides information about its internal processing from other modules, and only presents well-defined interfaces through which to communicate to other modules. This enhances the effectiveness of the principle of low-coupling. Moreover, information that is likely to change is also grouped together, enhancing cohesion within an element.

Design risk aversion techniques. Next we will discuss some of the generic approaches that use the above principles of risk aversion in various forms, based upon a particular design viewpoint. There are basically four basic design methods: *functional decomposition, data-flow design, data-structure design,* and *procedural design.*

Functional decomposition is simply the old divide-and-conquer technique or "step-wise refinement."[172] It usually involves the step-by-step division of functions into subfunctions, in a top-down manner. One can decompose the software with respect to data flow, control flow, time, or any other criterion. The strategy is to:[173]

1. State the intended function of the software as clearly and concisely as possible. The specifications should aid this process.
2. Divide the function into subfunctions according to the decomposition criteria, and connect them keeping in mind some of the previous principles and techniques, ensuring that the resulting structure still solves the problem.
3. Redo the second step with each individual subfunction that was defined until one feels that the level of detail is sufficient.

The generality of the functional decomposition approach is both an opportunity and a risk. The opportunity is that it promotes general applicability to numerous problems, and by doing so, it is probably the most commonly used approach. The risk involved is that there can be innumerable decompositions of the same problem. No two designers will decompose the system in precisely the same way, and in large systems, this often leads to confusion as one group will use one set of decomposition criteria, while another will use something else again. Functional decomposition also has a risk, in that it usually works best with specifications that are well understood and stable. If this isn't the situation, the decomposition may need constant and "infinite" reiteration.

Another general method is the data-flow design approach. In its simplest form, it is the same as functional decomposition, but with the decomposition limited to data-flow.[174] The specification is decomposed into input modules, transformation modules, and output modules.[175] A series of "black boxes" (i.e., functions) are created that transform an input data stream into an output data stream. Each black box is refined successively, and then integrated together to form a complete system. The principles of coupling and cohesion are extensively used. An advantage of this approach is that it works well in data-driven systems, such as signal processing systems, where most of the modules created exhibit very high cohesion. A risk is that not all systems are data driven, thus leading to artificial partitioning because the transformations on the data may be difficult to identify.

The data-structure design approach is based upon the hierarchical decomposition of data structures that perform input and output functions. The relationship between different levels tends to resemble an "is composed of" relation. A basic premise of this approach is that the data structures created closely map to the problem space (i.e., the actual implementation), thus ensuring that whatever decomposition is attempted, it will be consistent between designers. A risk with this approach is that it is too difficult to apply to processes that are highly concurrent.[176]

The last approach is procedural. Here, the focus is on specifying the set of algorithms and their control flow. The design is described as a set of procedures using some type of language. The language may range from an informal, textual description, such as a pseudo-programming language called Programming Design Languages (PDL), to something very precise, like axiomatic mathematics using predicate calculus. The idea is to be able to precisely describe the software implementation, yet still be expressive enough to design with it. A major push has been, as in the data structure approach, to closely map the design to the problem space. An advantage is that in the case of using axiomatic mathematics, the implementation can be proven to be correct as it is designed, or in the case of PDLs, the design inherently and closely matches the actual implementation. The risks are that it is hard to build large systems using this approach, designers will tend to concentrate on the implementation rather than the design, and the expressive power of the language used may severely limit design capability.

3.2.3.2.2.3 Design risk summary. No single design method is right for all the different types of problems that a designer may encounter, thus increasing the importance of matching the right method to the particular application problem. Further, these design techniques need to be matched against design strategies and requirement criteria. An example is in trying to achieve system responsiveness (the lack of which may be considered a risk to the project's perceived success) in a large-scale application by means of applying the design synthesis strategies of fixing, locality design, process vs. frequency trade-off, shared resources, parallel processing, and centering.[177] The software engineering risk analyst must be aware of the trade-offs involved which might cause risks to be hidden.

As in the requirements analysis and specification phase, a large set of design methods are available. Similarly, there have been a number of studies that have evaluated these methods,[178] but unlike the others, some quantitative results applicable to risk analysis have appeared.[179] The study by Dallas Webster is the most recent,[180] and evaluates over 40 different design representations in respect to such issues as conceptual complexity, processable expressiveness, application ranges, scale of application, the degree of formality and procedurality, and automation support. Figure 3.20 illustrates, for example, the scale of usefulness of some particular design representations against the size of the software application being developed (portions of the study are also applicable to the requirements and specification phase, as some of the methods evaluated are used in those phases as well). From information such as this, one can avoid the mismatch of method to application and understand the difficulty in their actual application to a project.

By coupling Webster's study with work by Lampson and others,[181,182] which provide hints on where the risks lie in system design, the risk analyst can identify, estimate, and evaluate the risks present in the design process fairly accurately.

3.2.3.2.3 Implementation, detection and demonstration testing, and integration phases. Implementation, test, and integration form the last development

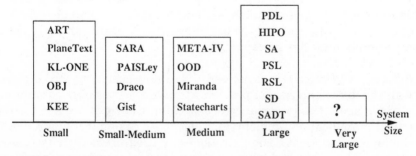

Figure 3.20 Design Methods and Applicability to System Size

phases of a typical process model. They are also the ones that have received the most attention over the years. The implementation phase involves the efforts required in the production of a physical realization of the design abstraction that was created in the previous phase. The code produced in this phase should implement the design correctly and meet the resource, accuracy, and performance constraints defined in the specifications.

Detection and demonstration testing are the activities of: (a) executing the physical realization created to identify differences between expected and actual results (i.e., finding errors), and (b) exercising the system to validate that it satisfies the specified requirements. Testing is often considered as an aspect of the implementation phase alone, but it is also part of the verification and validation efforts applied across the process model, as was described previously.[183]

Integration is used when the design approach divides the software system into components that are individually created and tested, which are then melded together to form a complete system. Detection and demonstration testing are both applied to the full system and the partial builds. Typically, integration occurs when incremental approaches to development of some kind are required.

3.2.3.2.3.1 Implementation risks. As was mentioned, the implementation phase is primarily concerned with translation of the design abstraction into another abstraction (the program), which represents the system. The techniques used in this translation process are meant to first, control the process, and second, to create the software. As anyone who has ever programmed knows, the translation process is neither trivial nor straightforward. It is a phase which is usually in a confused state, where management is having difficulty keeping track of everything that is going on, and where it seems there is always one more thing that has to be coded or fixed before the program will run. Its a phase, especially for large system developments, that can easily be termed chaotic or unstable. Most research and practical efforts today are aimed at making it less so.

One major problem that causes the instability lies in the difficulty of translating a design into an implementation. First, a design is never going to be an exact one-to-one mapping to the implementation, unless the design *is* the implementation. Thus, even with good designs, some effort has to be made to translate the design into an implementation, and that means a possibility of introducing error and risk. Careful thought is a necessity on the part of the designer to balance his or her needs in creating the design, against those of the implementor, who has to make it work.

Second, the translation process is made more difficult when a design isn't complete, consistent, or somehow does not communicate what was required in such a way that it can be understood. Design errors of omission or commission cause many implementors to spend their time solving the wrong problem.[18]

Third, some aspects necessary for the implementation are just outside the designer's domain, and therefore are not defined. The exact impacts and ramifications of using a particular operating system or programming language are usually beyond the scope of the designer, but definitely are a concern to the implementor.

Fourth, the implementation itself is prone to be error-filled, since creating a system implementation is an intensely human affair. A major reason for the automation of software support tools, starting with assemblers, then compilers, etc., had as much to do with the elimination of error as gains in efficiency.

Finally, there is the implementation risk created by the implementors themselves, with no outside help. Often called *creeping elegance*, it is the addition of features not called for by the original requirements. These "new requirements" are not planned for, not budgeted for, can cause major expenditures of effort, and can add to the system's instability and poor operating performance. These bottom-up, implementor-driven requirements are a source of performance risk that flows up, just as new unplanned-for customer-driven requirements and their risks flow down.

A few examples will help illustrate some of the risks typically encountered during the implementation phase.

Translation risks. As we stated, a risk which is inherent in the implementation phase concerns the translation process from a design into an implementation. Any translation process is prone to error, and the higher the level of abstraction that exists between the design and implementation, the more potential for error.

For example, consider the common use of abstract data structures in designs. From a designer's point of view, a particular data structure type may be seen as an ideal selection. The data structure provides all the things required and is a perfect way with which to manipulate the data to be produced. Most designers, however, don't concern themselves with how much actual space is going to be required to store all the variables, once the physical structure itself is programmed. This is not their job, and thus is left up to the implementor. Depending on the programming language used, however, and the physical size and partitioning of the real hardware's memory, it could pose serious implementation difficulties (data structures, especially ones with dynamic ranges, can eat up memory faster than a swarm of hungry locusts).

A problem similar to the data structure example is how the implementation will synchronize its various components. A designer may say that module 1 will communicate with module 2, and pass information "x" between them, but implementing this may not be so easy. For instance, consider an individual process module that in the design is designated to share information with a number of other modules.

First, this module, a logical abstraction in the design, must be programmed into a physical entity, which resides in some physical space in a particular machine. The same is true of the other modules, too. The implementor must then use the specifications to determine how many times, and for how long, this module needs to communicate with the others. The choices available to the implementor for communication may be via shared memory, I/O channels, networks, etc. If these modules are time-critical (i.e., they must pass information that is needed in real time) then the physical location where any one of them ultimately resides in the system may decide whether the system can meet the specifications.

Additionally, it matters not only where an individual module is located in the system, but whether the communication timing is so critical that it must occupy physical memory at all times. Even if it can be made nonresident, the issue of swapping a module in from secondary storage to primary memory, and the increase in overhead that this may cause, then becomes a new risk issue to be resolved. The impacts of these issues may not be discovered until an actual implementation is completed and fully exercised, regardless of how many prototypes were built previously.

The physical distribution of modules may not be a small feat either. If a module is about 200–500 programming lines long (a typically recommended "standard" size), in a system like NASA's Space Station with a 100,000,000 lines of code, we are discussing possibly up to 50,000 modules. Now, if these are spread across a network of computers, and if the majority of modules are time-critical, the poor implementor has a job that will keep him or herself occupied for awhile, just keeping track of what the names are, let alone where they are located. In addition, the requirement of creating the system in increments might necessitate the rearrangement of the modules for each new increment. Thus, new locations for the modules must be selected, which means a great deal more work. We can readily see why the implementation phase takes a long time and is marked by errors and high risk.

Logic risks. Another risk issue which is a form of translation error is called an error of logic. In this case, an implementor interprets what the design is supposed to do differently from what the designer had in mind. This is a very frequent occurrence, and is one of the major sources of errors found in a system.[185] Overcoming this problem is not particularly facile, unless humans are completely removed from the process. That is why using methods which can express designs (and requirements and specification) in a rigorous but understandable manner is so important.

Domain risks. Implementors also have to worry about information which is not explicitly defined in the design (it being outside its domain), but which must be taken care of by the implementation. Such an example is in trying to recover from execution-time errors. Since the implementor who can write perfect programs the first time, and every time, hasn't yet appeared, errors will likely exist in the system. One doesn't want the system to stop working because of these errors, so some way must be found to keep the program executing even in the case of errors. The SDI system is an example. It is estimated that it will have over 100,000 undiscovered errors in the (if ever) deployed software, yet it is required to be built in such a way to continuously execute and still accomplish its mission.[186] A design can help in making recovery possible by adding in redundant components, modules, etc., but it is up to the implementor to discover the details of all the possibilities the designer didn't think of.

Another issue a designer usually isn't concerned with, but which almost always impacts the implementation of the design, is how the system software (i.e., operating system, run-time executives, etc.) is used. A program doesn't exist in a vacuum, and when executing, is dependent on these supporting programs to manage resources such as memory, the processor, and the I/O hardware. The system software can, as much as the language being used to implement the design, impact throughput, timing, or efficient memory utilization. Again, it is usually left up to the implementor to figure out how to reduce the risks and still make the design work within these constraints.

Language risks. Even with all the above problems resolved, the implementor may still not use the language correctly. This means that time and effort have to be spent correcting the errors, which then delays other work that must be completed. Unfortunately, error correction has never proved to be an easy task. An implementor only has a 50% chance of successfully correcting an error if it can be narrowed to only 5–10 lines of code, and only a 20% chance if 40–50 lines are involved.[187]

Furthermore, the language used might not be suitable for the particular application, or may make the implementation of the design less efficient than some other. Procedural (von Neumann), functional, object-oriented, logic, and rule-based programming languages are only some of those available and can be selected to apply to a programming problem. The problem of understanding the implications of selecting only one to solve a problem, when applying many different ones to specific aspects of the system may be more appropriate, is called the *multiparadigm programming problem*. It is only now beginning to receive serious attention.[188] Also, an analyst should not forget that, in many cases, assembly language programming is still a less risky choice than using a high level language of any type, especially where the application demands high performance, high reliability, has memory space limitations, and so forth. These issues often override concerns about productivity and/or cost.

In confronting each of the problems above, an implementor is continually making a number of important trade-offs, such as the maintainability of the system, its reliability, availability, or efficiency. It is advisable to keep in mind what Dijkstra said, that an efficient program is an exercise in logical brinksmanship. Although many of these trade-offs have been determined, or at least constrained, by decisions made during the previous phases, it is the implementor's ultimate responsibility to choose the correct degree of trade-off. Most of the factors being traded off are nonfunctional in nature, thus it is difficult to tell what the end result will be, until the total system is completely built, tested, and delivered to the user or customer. As has been stated, it is the trade-offs among the plurality of goals that is an implementor's hardest task.[189]

3.2.3.2.3.2 Implementation risk aversion. There have been many methods touted as means to control the programming process and avert risk. Four of the methods more commonly used in the past have been *step-wise refinement,*[190] *structured programming,*[191] *program families,*[192] and *object-oriented programming.*[193]

Stepwise refinement is the decomposition of programs into levels, with each upper level calling one or more subprograms in the next lower level. Structured programming, on the other hand, is the orderly and disciplined construction of programs as hierarchical, nested programming structures, sometimes called the non-GOTO approach. Program families instead view a program as consisting of a set of modules that will evolve over time. As a module changes, or a new one is added, a new program is created. Objected-oriented programming looks on the application as being made up of abstract objects, and the program applies operations to those objects. The actual definition of objects begins in the design or specification stage, and a body of literature has grown on how to best go about defining, designing, and implementing systems using object-oriented approaches.[194]

An interesting thing that has occurred is that these implementation techniques have moved up a level of abstraction into the design phase, in order to avert one or more of the causes of risk that originated there. This is similar to what occurred with design techniques. One should not be too surprised, for if the design has been done properly: (a) the software should have been decomposed into modules using some stepwise refinement method; (b) possible program families should have been already identified; and (c) the basic algorithms, data and control structures should have been derived. But what has also happened is that these techniques have been embedded within programming languages, too.

This has helped avert some common implementation risks in a variety of ways. First, it makes the control of the translation process more apparent to the implementor. The implementor knows where to begin, what to do next, and when to end. Second, the design can be captured more closely by the implementation. The mapping between the design and implementation is closer because the languages to describe the two use the same "vocabulary." Finally, the software system has a better chance to be reliable and maintainable, because the controlling process is inseparable from the creation process. The Ada programming language is a prime example of this merging of implementation technique and language.

The number of studies concerning implementation, the risks therein, the "best" language to apply, etc., are legion, and date back to the 1950s. We will not bother to try to list them all, as the reader can easily find at least two contradictory papers on any subject within the subject area of implementation.[195] However, an analyst can find in the references a general language comparison guide and evaluation of a number of popular languages which can be used to compare their various strengths and weaknesses.[196,197] The risk trade-offs that an implementor must make usually end up revolving around: a) how effectively the design can be translated using the implementation language; and b) how proficiently the language can be translated onto the target architecture and its operating system; and c) how efficiently it can be executed by the target architecture. By keeping these in mind, as well as how the implementation principles above can be used to avert the basic causes of risk, one can perform some level of intelligent risk analysis.

3.2.3.2.3.2 Testing risks and their aversion. Surprisingly, testing wasn't considered a discipline of software engineering for a very long time.[198] Testing is concerned with executing a program with the intent of finding errors, either by physical or logical means. It is used to try to avert the causes of risk associated with the lack of information, as is seen by the type of errors discovered by testing depicted in Figure 3.21.

Two types of testing exist: *informal* and *formal.* Informal testing is usually conducted by the implementor to discover errors in a particular software component still under development. The standard approach taken is to make the software perform the specified actions for that part of the system. Once a reasonable level of certainty that only a few errors exist has been ascertained by the programmer, then formal testing is usually initiated. One to two errors per thousand lines of new and changed source code is often the target aimed at, but any target set must take into account the application domain. For example, in many safety critical applications, one error in a thousand lines of code is unacceptably high.

In formal testing, detection and demonstration testing are concerned with showing precisely what the system will actually do using unpredictable inputs, rather than in making the system respond to a predetermined input, as is the case in informal testing.[199] Implied in formal testing is the testing at the level of the unit (or module), as well as at the system level (either partially or fully complete). System level

Types of Errors   Occurrences

Logic ⟶	When data structures are filed to capacity
Overload ⟶	Mistakes when coding from the design
Timing ⟶	Coordination among parallel processes cause deadlock
Throughput ⟶	When response is slow
Capacity ⟶	When memory limits are hit
Recovery ⟶	What happens when the system fails
System Software ⟶	Assumptions about the software are not true

Figure 3.21 Types of Errors Found in Testing

testing also is related to the integration approach required to tie the system parts together into the final comprehensive whole.

A *tested program* is one in which the conditions that make it fail have not been found yet. This means that if the test result is consistent with the expected result, the component tested is deemed "correct" within the limited context of the test. However, it would be a grave mistake to equate correctness with successful completion of a test. Further, passing a test only demonstrates that no errors have been detected, not that errors do not exist. It is virtually impossible to test all possible paths of a program. Even moderately complex programs can have up to 10^{20} paths, which, means that given a computer which could check out one path per nanosecond (10^{-9} sec) and having started the check at the start of the Christian era (A.D. 1), the job would still have 1200 years to go. Even having a computer operating checking a trillion paths per second (10^{-12} sec) would take over 3 years, assuming no errors were found. The best one can hope to accomplish is to apply properly designed statistical testing which can be used to provide information about the probability of an error remaining in the code, or the probability of a failure occurring in its use.

It is up to management to determine how much effort should be expended in testing. Testing, like anything else, can be over- or underdone. The criticality of the system is an important determinant in the amount of testing to be required. The greater the reliability requirements, the higher the necessity to thoroughly test, although totally error free software, for whatever that is really worth, is economically unfeasible.[200] In high reliability situations, testing costs can run as high as 45% of of the initial system development cost, and in some cases of commercial software products, 200%.[201] In other cases, it may be cheaper to wait for the users to eventually find the errors than it is for money to be spent on testing. (This may not seem good customer relations policy, but it often is good testing policy.) Management must decide the acceptable range of risks that exists in selection of testing extensively, against that of foregoing it. However, it also should be kept in mind that not all errors are created equal, and that even one error can have catastrophic effects.

Quite a bit of work has been done to attempt to address the risks and benefits involved in different kinds of testing strategies, such as isolated unit testing, random selection of test data, branch testing, modified module coverage, etc., although the results are very mixed and often contradictory.[202] Some researchers have reported, for instance, that random selection of test data is a good testing strategy, while others have reported just the opposite. Some work is being done on defining the theoretical limitations of different testing methods, but the results are only preliminary.[203] For example, a test's effectiveness is said to equal the number of defects avoided divided by the sum of the defects avoided plus the defects missed.

Because of the dearth of information comparing accurate testing methods, the risk analyst will need to exercise care in estimating and evaluating the risks inherent in a test method. Performing no testing should be considered the highest risk, and the use of several methods should be seen as posing lower risks.

3.2.3.2.3.3 Integration risks and their aversion. Assuming incremental development, once the testing is completed on the modules, they are integrated together. This integration usually requires that the *scaffolding* components which were being used as either stubs for, or drivers of, the modules be replaced by the real things. There are two basic types of integration: (1) the "big bang" approach, where all tested modules are brought together at once and integrated together, or (2) the incremental integration approach, where modules are brought in one at a time, and a new module isn't integrated in until the last set works as expected.

The big bang approach is easier to control from a management perspective, but presents a number of risks. Errors are difficult to isolate, as it is hard to determine where an error originated, since all the modules are acting as one. Both hard and easy errors to fix appear the same. Fixing one error can spawn many more, *à la side effects*, which cannot be tracked to the original one. And there is no success criteria for ending a test, since one never knows when one is done.

Incremental integration, in contrast, eliminates all of the risks found in the big bang approach, but substitutes a number of other risks in their stead. One of these risks is the possibility of spending more time (and thus more money) than one would by using the big bang approach. Module-by-module integration to form partial systems, and their subsequent testing, requires great amounts of time and coordination. Configuration management efficiency is extremely important. There is no real aversion strategy for this risk, other than optimal ordering of module integration, as we will see below. The trade-off which needs to be made is whether the time spent now will reduce time spent later fixing errors.

The second risk is related and concerns the frequent necessity of increasing resource expenditures at the end of the implementation and testing phases to attempt to complete modules on time to meet a revised schedule. This new schedule reflects the complete times required to optimally order the modules to spend the minimum time in integration testing. This risk can often be averted during the initial project planning to ensure the system modules are completed in a priority order for integration testing.

One other risk that is found in integration testing, but not really a part of it, is that caused by system requirements which many system modules must meet, but not all may do so in the same manner. This is frequently found in large system developments with many modules being designed and implemented by different groups. Each group will interpret the requirements in a slightly different manner, and thus when the modules are integrated together, their interfaces do not match.

This is a very common occurrence. In Figure 3.22, for instance, are depicted the various locations of software groups developing modules for a system the author worked on. The communication and coordination problems alone were tremendous, and exacerbated the problem of misinterpretation of requirements, designs, test requirements, etc. The scattering of development groups also contributed to various types of requirements volatility, especially requirements creep. Additionally, the scattering of development groups made incremental integration a must, rather than an option. This issue is really a design phase risk and

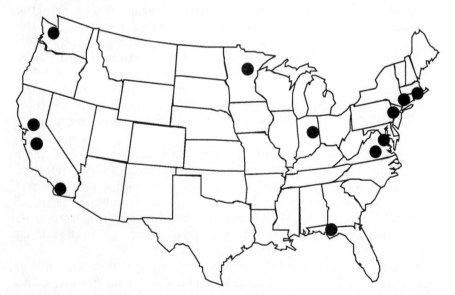

Figure 3.22 Example Locations of Organizations Involved in a Systems Integration

can be averted only by tight coordination and coupling of the interface definitions of all defined modules.

A related risk, also not found until integration testing, is system operational underperformance. Frequently, it is only during integration testing that the true performance of the system can be accurately assessed. Then the problems with the system architecture become "obvious." Sometimes the risk starts with the requirements, and the lack of understanding that they ask more of the hardware than can possibly be provided, or sometimes it starts with the design. Sometimes it is caused by the scaffolding components, because up to integration time, they were being used to provide "real" data inputs, which may in fact not be very closely matched to what actually occurs. It can even start with the procurement practice of specifying the use of a specific hardware/ system architecture before all the ramifications are known. Whatever the case, the analyst must be aware early on of performance risks and search for them before integration testing, where any fundamental changes are very costly as one must perform *distortion engineering*, i.e., engineering the differences between what is desired and what one has to do to make the system work.

One final point needs to be made. The phase-independent techniques, such as configuration management, quality assurance, etc., also exist to help avert many of the risks identified. Only through their combined action can the risks in the phase dependent processes be adequately managed to acceptable levels.

3.2.3.2.4 Evolution phase and its risks. The evolution, or renewal, phase is the last phase we wish to examine.

> Those who regularly code for fast electronic computers will have learned from bitter experience that a large fraction of the time spent in preparing calculations for the machine is taken up in removing blunders that have been made in drawing up the programs. With the aid of common sense and checking subroutines, the majority of mistakes are quickly found and rectified. Some errors, however, are sufficiently obscure to escape detection for a surprisingly long time.[204]

So wrote three British mathematicians in 1952. So the problems inherent in fixing a program are not new.

Although we consider the evolution phase to be the last dependent phase, in reality, it is phase independent since all the phases of a development are potentially affected. The evolution phase begins once the software has been officially accepted by the customer. Evolution can be divided into three basic types: *perfective maintenance, adaptive maintenance,* and *corrective maintenance.* Perfective maintenance is the modification of the system in response to customer requests to make the system more usable, or implementor requests to make it more efficient. Adaptive maintenance is the incorporation of enhancements into the system that were previously planned, such as a change in the operating system or hardware used. Corrective maintenance is the fixing of errors in the system found after the product's release, or which were known at release, but not yet corrected.

Each of the risks confronted in the earlier process model phases will be encountered once more in the evolution phase, but the magnitude of consequences may be more difficult to estimate. Intuitively, one may feel that the magnitudes and consequences or the risks faced will be lower than those encountered in the original development, but this is not necessarily the case. It is often the situation that in fixing a primary error, new ones will be introduced. In fact, experience has demonstrated that there is usually a 20–50% chance that correcting one error will introduce a new error.[205]

Further, the probability of fixing the error correctly decreases rapidly as the time increases from when it was first created; i.e., the phase in which it was originally introduced. These are termed *ripple effect errors.* Ripple effect errors appear in locations away from the original source of error and are very hard to track down, often causing major perturbations in system reliability. Also, by continually enhancing the system, the system's performance and utility inevitably degrades. Further, enhancements that increase the structural complexity of the software will negatively impact the ease and ability to find or fix errors compared to the original system.[206]

Whenever a system undergoes renewal, the stability of the system is being tampered with, thereby changing its current state. There is a high probability of increasing the entropy of the system; i.e., making it less stable and more brittle, instead of decreasing it. The more the structural change, the higher the probability of introducing uncontrollable entropic changes. Therefore, the risk of introducing new errors must be weighed against the benefits of removing old ones.[207] Unless careful consideration is given to this risk, one can easily increase the entropy of the system to a point that the energy required to regain stability is no longer a cost-effective expenditure. The system then must be "thrown out," or be given a major overhaul.

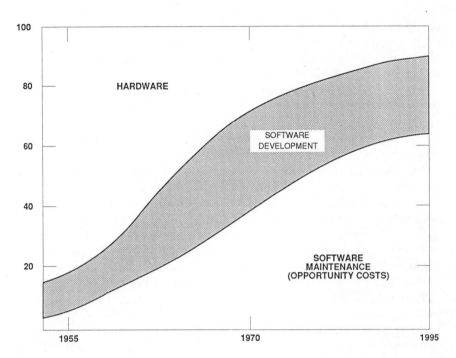

Figure 3.23 Hardware-Software Cost Trends

To lower the sources of risk associated with system evolution, the process of renewal has to be considered very early in the planning and requirements stages. It has been estimated by the GAO that anywhere from 40 to 60% of federal software expenditures go into system evolution, with 50% of these expenditures going for perfective maintenance, 26% for adaptive maintenance, and 24% for corrective maintenance, as shown in Figure 3.23.[208] Taking the GAO numbers on an (optimistic) dollar basis, for every $4.00 spent on a software development, $3.00 more can be expected to be spent on perfective maintenance, $1.56 on adaptive maintenance, and $1.44 on corrective maintenance. Notice that this means that even if one is able to increase system quality and reliability to a level where corrective maintenance is reduced by 50%, one will still need to spend $5.28, as opposed to $6.00, on other evolutionary costs.

To make real savings, one needs to attack the evolutionary process across the board. This means placing a premium on having solid requirements and designs early in the development process. One can easily envision the evolutionary risk consequences of poorly executed early phases of a development. Effective early risk avoidance of all of these cost risks will not only avert risks in evolution, but also in future developments, by allowing more money to be spent on the next project. Not to do so must be counted as a business opportunity cost. Projects such as the FAA's new Air Traffic Control Advanced Automation System (AAS) program provide case studies on how evolution phase criteria can be considered early in the development process to lower subsequent risks.[209]

Another way to increase the visibility of the importance of system evolution is to consider currently built and operated software as an asset, much like furniture. There have been suggestions to even consider software as a capital asset, instead of an expense, as it is usually funded today.[210] The argument is that expenses are resources to be consumed, whereas assets are resources invested for the future. Assets are also managed, while expenses are not. Third, assets have a planned-for capital budget for maintenance and improvements, expenses do not.

These three things would help change the attitude of working on evolving software systems from where it is often shunned as menial, unimportant, dirty work, to something that is crucial to the survival of the company. In many cases today, the word is, "If it's broke, don't fix it," because the cost of fixing it or improving it is just too high. The additional positive effects include that documentation might be up to date, renovation of systems might take place on time, and changes might be put in more rapidly. The argument of software as a capital asset has some merit to it, if only it reduces the risks caused by the current self-defeating practices of applying junior people to system evolutions, or turning the evolution effort to a group different from that which originally developed it. Throwing the least experienced on the most complex job is a risky mixture.

Finally, one should consider that the real risks of evolution costs are not incurred today, but some time in the future. They are in reality opportunity costs. System evolution, especially for corrective maintenance, takes resources that could productively be spent on new projects. This can be seen in Figure 3.23 by the way in which the relative amount of expenditures for new software systems has remained fairly constant for the last decade. If one reduces evolutionary costs by just 8%, one could effectively increase by 25% the amount of new development started.[211]

3.2.4 Summary

Figures 3.24 and 3.25 depict some average Air Force software development problem types and their time of closure.[212] It is readily apparent that the greatest risks are in the requirements and design phases, and it is vital to concentrate on aversion strategies in these areas. The software engineering risk analyst must be sensitive to how the process model, in combination with the methods used to support the process, can increase or decrease these risks. Furthermore, the figures again point out the importance of looking for how risks, especially requirement risks, can be averted or contained even before the software engineering enterprise gets started. Many of the requirement translation problems shown earlier exist because there was little comprehension of what the system was supposed to end up doing. Requirement changes then continually poured in, as both the developer and user tried to figure out what was satisfactory. Even in the best managed enterprises, there will be some level of requirements manipulation throughout the process. The question is how many can be made before the development reaches chaos.

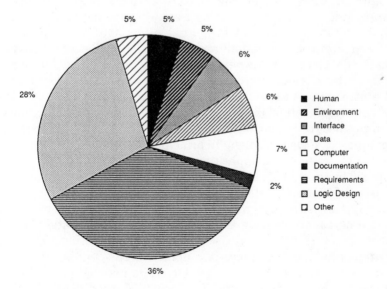

Figure 3.24 Software Problem Types

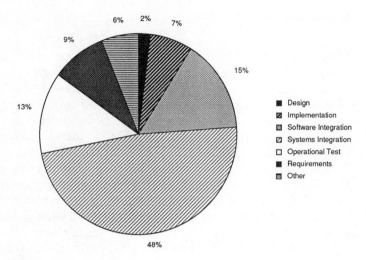

Figure 3.25 Error Closure by Phase

In each phase, the risk analyst should be asking, "How good is good enough?" In other words, (1) how much risk exists in the enterprise, both from a business perspective and from a software engineering perspective, at that point in time, (2) what is required to avert it (in terms of methods, etc.), and after these questions are answered, (3) what are the types of risks the developers in the next phase of the process model most likely will face? It is obvious, more than ever, how important risk monitoring and control are, as the risks faced in each phase are different and the techniques and methods required to avert them also differ. Care must be taken to select only that which is needed to do the job. Just because a technique can solve a problem "in principle" does not mean that it is the best, is applicable to all applications, is the least risky. Risks must be tempered by the specific application the development is engaged in and the users of that application.

Finally, the risk analyst must continue to keep management informed of the progress in averting the risks confronting the enterprise. One cannot spend all the enterprise's resources in averting risks in the requirements phase, as there is a point where spending more effort doesn't cost-effectively reduce risk. Or, there may be a need to spend more resources to reduce a risk, if it is particularly difficult. Whatever the case, it will be up to management to make the decision on how best to deploy the resources of the enterprise. And this is true whether management is properly informed or not. For your (and the enterprise's) best interests, since management (at all levels) usually understands the least about software, you must make them aware of the ramifications of their decisions before they make them.

3.3 Automation

The final aspect of the process of software engineering we wish to investigate is the automation of the methods. Automation focuses on averting the types of risks associated with the lack of time.

The term "automation" is preferred to the other, more commonly used "software tool." The term software tool implies a focus on a singularity of purpose; i.e., the automation only of a single method without the context of which it is a part. Automation, on the other hand, means to support a method which is an integral piece of the total process of a software enterprise through computer-aided mechanisms. Recall that methods are most effective in reducing risk if they form an integrated partnership with the underlying process model. Similarly, the automation of a single method that cannot interact with the other methods used in the process model is not only not very useful, but poses a risk in itself. The exacerbation of the risks in software engineering have typically been the result of applying software tools which tend to fail to support any standard development process, are too narrowly focused, or do not fit well with other methods, thus leaving information gaps between process phases.[213,214]

But remember, the aversion of risk lies *primarily* in the integration of the methods into a comprehensive methodology, and *not* in their automation. Automation is the final step, not the first. Too often the focus has been on providing tools, tools, and more tools without purpose. As has been noted, "Tools alone, do not products build."[215]

Automation has a number of obvious benefits in averting risk, especially in respect to the lack of time. Automation has the potential to reduce the labor needed to use the methods, and in many instances is the only realistic manner for applying many software engineering methods. The clerical aspect of most methods requires the keeping track of large amounts of information, and it is mentally and physically impossible to do so by hand on any enterprise of size. Because the clerical aspect of using methods is reduced through automation, there is a corresponding rise in productivity and a decrease in development cost and schedule— sometimes.

Recall from Chapter 2 that the automation of a process in fact increases the amount of work required to be performed. This means that although one may be doing the original work faster, one usually has more work to do in the same time frame. For example, often work, such as checking for completeness or correctness, or even creating documentation, was left undone because the clerical aspects were too hard or too expensive to accomplish. The net gain after adding in all these new tasks, therefore, may be zero. One must examine the effective productivity, or the improvement in quality, that is gained for the same expenditure. The whole issue of productivity, and the risks involved in trying to improve productivity, are discussed in detail in Capers Jones's book *Programming Productivity*.[216] Within it are covered approximately 40 risk factors that impact productivity, ranging from program size to moving a project from one location to another. The reader is encouraged to use this text as a source of evidence for identifying risks in this area.

3.3.1 Types of automation

There are a number of different types of automation available. The industry is overflowing with commercially available products that will help automate the development process. Figure 3.26 takes our model of

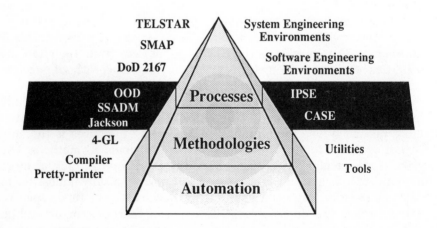

Figure 3.26 Examples of Processes, Methods, and Automation

the software engineering process and lists a number of different examples of techniques and methods that are automated and commercially available down the left side, while down the right side of the pyramid are generic automation categorizations. The level of complexity increases from top to bottom; i.e., a systems engineering environment is more complex than a simple utility.

From an automation viewpoint, the right side of the illustration is the more interesting one. Starting with the lowest two levels of automation are the utilities and tools. This is automation aimed at the programmer. Utilities are very simple tools, such as pretty printers and map-file checkers. One specific transformation of data is usually provided. Utilities are sometimes called *tool fragments* because of this characteristic. Tools are combinations of two or more tool fragments used to achieve some set of transformations. Compilers, debuggers, or UNIX pipes are prime examples of automated tools.

Whereas tools are typically aimed at the programmer to use during the implementation phase, CASE (computer-aided software engineering) automation is primarily aimed at the requirements specifier/analyst or designer of the software system. CASE systems tend to automate a single method, such as Structured Analysis or Jackson Structured Design, providing assistance to the drawing of graphs, ensuring consistency, correctness in the application of the methodology, and so forth. CASE automation may cover one or more phases of a process model, although they tend to be process model independent.

It should be noted that CASE automation also exists for the programmer and maintainer, where a set of tools is linked to cover say the implementation and test phases or the system evolution phase. The tools for system evolution are typically divided into two basic types. Those which are said to form *CASE restructuring tools,* which focus on perfective maintenance and corrective maintenance, and *CASE reengineering tools* (also called renovation, reclamation, or renewal tools) which focus primarily on adaptive maintenance.[217] In other engineering disciplines with less hype, this is termed *value engineering.* Also sometimes included in this group are *CASE reverse engineering tools*, which focus on system design recovery or system redocumentation, but do not necessarily involve the changing of the base system or creation of a new system. Reverse engineering is an examination process, not a change process, although it is often used in conjunction with restructuring or reengineering. Figure 3.27 illustrates the coverage areas of three types of tools. All three types of tools are attempts to bring order by injecting the discipline of software engineering, in the form of a refined process

Requirements   Implementation   Design

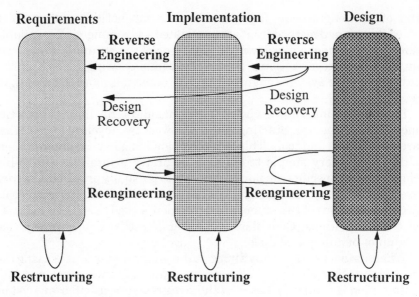

Figure 3.27 Differences Between Reverse Engineering, Reengineering, and Restructuring

model, a set of methods, and automation, into an enterprise that has never previously utilized software engineering in any disciplined manner.

CASE is usually aimed at an individual or small team working on a project, and represents an outgrowth of the application of a single method by a single analyst on a project. In other words, CASE encapsulates the single interviewing approach. If we start requiring different teams of developers to work together, say from different organizations within a company or from different companies themselves, we move to a level above CASE, at which rests the Integrated Project or Programming Support Environments (IPSE). What differentiates CASE automation from IPSE automation are: (a) an integration of two or more methods *or* set of tools which cover more than one phase of a process model; (b) a fundamentally stronger linkage to a recognized process model (e.g., an incremental development process model in the form of DOD-2167A); (c) information is linked into a central repository of some type. Examples are the Martin methodology-based information engineering IEF and IEW products, or the Softlab Maestro products.[218,219]

IPSEs are strange beasts, because they do not fully cover a process model from start to finish, and typically cover either the requirements and design, or design and implementation, or implementation and test phases. Furthermore, the methods that are tied together are often interfaced, instead of integrated, which reduces the efficiency and effectiveness of their use together. IPSEs form an intermediate level of evolution on way to the next level of complexity.

Above the IPSE in automation complexity is the Software Engineering Environment (SEE). A SEE provides automation support across an entire process model, integrating a number of methods into a methodology.[220] To qualify as a SEE: (a) there must exist at least one method in each phase of the process model; (b) the method must be automated and integrated together with a central repository; (c) information generated by one method can be passed to, and used by, at least one other method on either "side" of it in the process model; (d) a set of basic management activities, with CM as a minimum, must also be supported across the process model; and (e) the methods support a recognized process model. The software engineering environment described above is considered a minimal SEE, since it has only one complete path from start to finish. Where multiple paths exist, all methods are integrated (rather than interfaced), and the full set of management activities are supported, then we have a fully populated software engineering environment. Figure 3.28 illustrates the types of generic automation support across a generic process model that should be supported in a populated SEE.[221]

As was mentioned at the end of Chapter 2, in most respects, the concept of a software engineering environment is directly analogous to a compiler (see Figure 2.21). Roughly speaking, a compiler's job is the translation of one type of input (logical) into output of another type (physical). This translation is defined by a series of well-defined steps (lexical analysis, syntactic analysis, code generation, etc.), each performing a "subtranslation" with its own input and output descriptions. The output descriptions of one step are reused as inputs to the next. Certain methods are used to implement each of these steps, and each step is in turn fully automated. The specific steps and methods used are dependent on both the original input description (the language used) and ultimate output description (the target computer), as well as the "outside influences" that define the requirements on the execution of the output. For example, if there are tight memory constraints, the compiler may need an added optimization step in its translation process to reduce the quantity of output description. The matching of these interdependencies is crucial to the efficiency, effectiveness, and correctiveness of the process.

An "ideal" software engineering environment is analogous to the compiler model, where everything is automated except the initial input

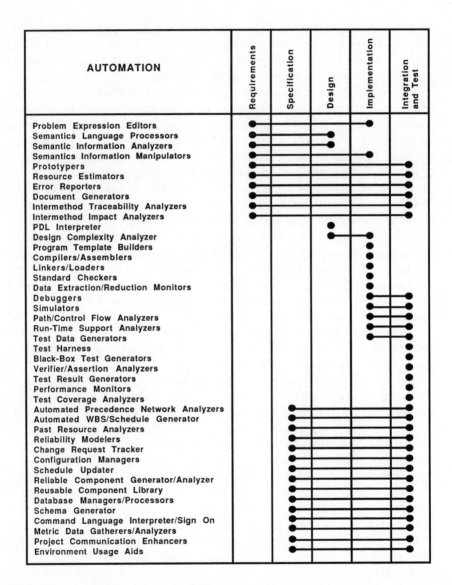

Figure 3.28 Automation Across the Development Life Cycle

description.[222] However, as with automatic programming, an ideal SEE is many years, if not a decade, away.[223] Worldwide governmental efforts are being undertaken to create IPSEs and SEEs because of their potential to avert, to a significant degree, all three basic causes of risk.[224] The commercial sector hasn't been quiet either, as minimal SEEs are being built today, with several minimal SEEs, such as Softlab's Maestro II, being available for purchase in today, and at least one commercially populated SEE being available by late 1990, early 1991.

Finally, at the highest level of complexity, if one were to start with a software engineering environment, extended it to include higher levels of abstraction as input, support numerous process models and methods, and extend the system of interest boundary to include the system engineering and business environments of interest, one would end up with a Systems and Software Engineering Environment (S^2EE).

S^2EEs are SEEs with increased capability, along with one important addition. Instead of being logically and physically separate from the application, the application, the application architecture, and the development environment can be either loosely coupled or tightly merged together. Thus, the integration of the methodologies and the application will together form one base component, which, when interfaced with the run-time system and hardware, will form a complete system. The push for S^2EEs comes from the continuing fusion of telecommunications and computing, where network management systems, applications, development environments, etc., together form an operational system. One cannot take one part out without adversely affecting the system's operation.

S^2EEs reflect the evolutionary process in much the same way as that which happened in compiler technology, when more front-end capabilities were added to the first assemblers to transform them into compilers. There is at least one large-scale effort to construct a minimal S^2EE in Europe with limited merging of methodologies and application, which should be available in the commercial domain in the 1992–93 time-frame.

3.3.2 Automation risk aversion

As one would envision, there are risks associated with automation, as well as with process models and methods. Again, they exist whenever the basic sources of risk are present. Rather than trying to put together a compendium of software automation risks, it is simpler and more informative to point out a few ways of averting them, before you start. These pointers also might be useful when evaluating the use of automation in an enterprise. For this, then, we will assume that you, as a risk analyst, have been tasked to explain to management the ways to lower the risk associated in acquiring automation in the form of either a CASE, IPSE, or minimal SEE system to support the software enterprise under consideration. Thus, you must explain the basic characteristics that the automation should possess, to ensure that it does not violate the first cardinal rule of risk control: Do no harm.

The first way to lower automation risk is to ensure that the product being acquired is open. By this, we mean that we do not desire to be locked into any manufacturer's individual tool set, method, or hardware suite, if possible. The product should be able to be extended; i.e., other automation products and/or methods should be able to be interfaced with it as a minimum, or better yet, integrated into its repository. The risk of being tied to one manufacturer does not allow one flexibility of growth, and the need to support the integration and (unlimited) expansion of various data management components are essential.

Any automation project should allow us to recapture our previous investments in software automation and the expertise of the current personnel using it. Personnel expertise is the single most important factor in quality and productivity, and if this expertise cannot be recaptured, then the risks to the project will likely increase to an extent greater than the new automation can avert.

The automation should support the labor-intensive efforts within the process model. This can be done using specialized automation, such as fourth-generation languages (4GLs), which have helped increase development productivity and quality in many *specific* areas.[225] Another area that should be carefully examined is the automation available in the design area,[226] which is especially important in reducing the essential risks of software.[227] But do not forget that productivity is effective efficiency. Without building the right system in the first place, building it quickly is meaningless.

The automation acquired should support both the production of the software system and the product itself. In other words, it should provide both phase-dependent and phase-independent support. Management support is crucial, especially in the CM area. This support is fundamental to controlling and monitoring the risks to the enterprise.

The automation should support not only yesterday's investment, but also be able to support tomorrow's. It is important that whatever automation is acquired, it must be able to make use of the newer technologies waiting in the wings, such as object-oriented databases. It also means that it can support different and sometimes divergent process models.

Finally, the automation must be able to truly support multiple business software programs, or a range of business enterprises, and not just individual software projects. To increase the return on investment, and lower economic risk to the organization or business, it makes sense to be able to support as many projects at once as are feasible. But just as important, if a single project is dispersed, as is typical in large development efforts, then some common framework is required. Thus, the final criteria is that the automation support distributed and decentralized development.

3.3.3 Summary

Automation is a primary element to averting the accidental risks associated with a software enterprise. It is also a crucial key in allowing the approaches (i.e., the process models and methods) to reduce the essential risks to be applied in a cost-effective manner. Without automation, it would not be possible to apply many of the software engineering risk aversion strategies currently available. Further, automation of the process and methods provides a synergistic effect, which is substantial. The problem for the risk analyst is in trying to measure what these effects are and to not decrease them. Figure 3.29 depicts software technology and productivity trends, giving you, as the risk analyst, some idea as to how productivity risks, for example, can be reduced by the use of automation, methods, and process models, singly as well as in combination.[228]

A *warning*, though, on applying or acquiring automation: Do not be seduced by the fact that automation may increase productivity, and therefore into thinking that one can automatically reduce the amount of money being spent on software developments. More likely, the amount of monetary expenditure will need to remain the same, whereas the probability of successfully meeting the deadlines, budget, and quality requirements will increase dramatically. The cost savings, and lowered business risk, will accrue over time from achieving successful projects and the eventual reduction in evolution costs.

To understand why this is true, just recall from Chapter 1 the consequences of undercapitalization, and the reasons why

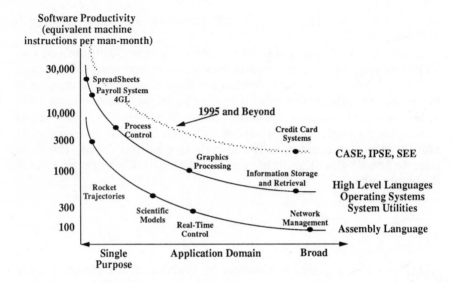

Figure 3.29 Computing Technology and Productivity

undercapitalization usually occurs. Underestimating the resource requirements has always plagued software developments, and it will be even easier to fall into this trap by embracing automation unthinkingly. One could easily envision a scenario where one invests in automation because one is constantly failing, reduce the information technology budget because one thinks the increase in productivity will more than make up for it, and have failure occur on an even grander scale. It is important to determine what are the root causes of the organization's failure in software development and attack those, not some will-o'-the-wisp. Keep in mind that the basic causes of risk are caused by lack of information, lack of control, or lack of time. If one is not careful, investments in automation may only mask the true problems.

For instance, consider Tables 3.6 and 3.7. Table 3.6 depicts some of the costs of developing different projects.[229] One can see the vast differences in the productivity of the personnel, as well as their cost. In Table 3.7, we have depicted some estimated costs for introducing CASE into a development organization of approximately 75 people using some of the average costs from Table 3.7.

Assuming a five-year period, one can see that an investment of over $3 million is needed to introduce CASE into the organization. Or looking at it in a different light, to make up for that $3 million investment, one

TABLE 3.6 Some Project Costs

Project Name	1989 Lincoln Continental	Space Shuttle	Citibank Teller Machine	Lotus 1-2-3 Ver.3	IBM Checkout Scanner
LOC	83,517	25,600,000	780,000	400,000	90,000
Cost	$1.8 m	$1,200 m	$13.2 m	$22 m	$3 m
Effort (Myrs)	35	22,096	150	263	58
$/Myr	$51,429	$54,299	$88,000	$83,650	$51,72
$/LOC	$22	$47	$17	$55	$33
LOC/Myr	2,386	1,159	5,200	1,520	1,552
LOC/Month	199	97	434	127	29
LOC/Week	46	22	100	29	30
LOC/Day	10	5	20	6	6

TABLE 3.7 Cost of Case Automation

Investments
Workstation hardware (50 @ $7,500)	$375,000
Central Server	$200,000
CASE software	$500,000
Training	
Trainers (10 days @ $1,500/day)	$15,000
Staff (250 staff-days @ $200/day)	$50,000

Total: $1,140,000

Yearly costs
CASE staff (5 people @ $55,000)	$275,000
CASE maintenance	$50,000
Upgrades	$75,000
Training (100 staff-days @ $200/day)	$20,000
Miscelaneous related costs	$15,000

Total: $435,000

Five-year costs
Investment	$1,140,000
Five-year annual costs	$2,175,000

Total: $3,315,000

would have to save approximately 18% of currently forecasted project costs on average per year, starting in year one. This assumes, in addition, zero inflation, no salary increases, and a zero cost of money. Realistically, however, productivity increases will probably be zero, or even negative, the first year, as the introduction of the system will create some significant amount of turmoil. Therefore, to justify the initial investment, one would probably need to see productivity increases more in the range of 30% by the end of 5 years. This level of productivity gain is not impossible, as one can see from Table 3.6. Examining the chart, one sees there is a greater than 430% difference in productivity between the best case and worse case project. Thus we can assume, in many organizations, there is room for similar amounts of improvement. However, whether productivity can be improved by this magnitude by applying CASE technology alone is still an open question.

For instance, there is little doubt that CASE does increase productivity, or at least is perceived to do so.[230] In a recent study, Norman and Nunamaker concluded that software engineers perceive that their productivity was improved with CASE technology. However, the perceived improvements were attributed primarily to how well the CASE product could be related to an organization's standard enterprise/process model. Even when this was the situation, productivity increases seen by such organizations applying CASE have only amounted to about 6% per year on average, not the 18% or 30% required by the analysis above.[231]

It should also be pointed out that the jury is still undecided on the usefulness of CASE-assisted reengineering or reverse engineering, although CASE restructuring seems to have some valid applicability. The assumption is that these approaches are best applied when the original development has resulted in a system possessing high evolutionary costs, especially in adaptive and perfective maintenance. Thus the original development was probably poorly documented, didn't use standard programming techniques, contains a large amount of spaghetti code, and so forth.

A major problem in trying to apply reengineering, restructuring, or reverse engineering to these poorly designed systems is that they currently are primarily aimed at the program code, not the totality of the system. Even the best constructed program code reflects only a portion of the system's functional requirements, and even less of the nonfunctional ones. The latter are very important to recapture, as they often are considered the success criteria for the system. This poses a real problem since even in the original development, explicit capturing of the functional requirements was probably done sparsely, and the nonfunctional not at all. Trying to recapture all relevant design information once it is gone has theoretical, let alone practical, limitations.

Then there is the problem that code in systems that are targets for restructuring is often locally optimized because of an initial poor design or poor performance. Attempting to restructure the optimization can actually make the newly developed code perform worse. It is like an equation, $x + y + z = 2x + y + z - 6$. When solved, one gets $x = 6$, but one doesn't know what y and z were, and one forgets that they even existed. Reverse engineering is supposed to recover the fact that y and z existed in the original design, but other than in simple situations, this is extremely difficult to accomplish. Things get even trickier when the optimized code in the original is nonreentrant, and contains portions of the program's thread of control. Then one can completely shut down the system by changing one programming instruction, without even knowing why. It may be better to stick to pinpointing the 20% of the code causing 80% of the problem, and spend the effort trying to improve that by minimal restructuring instead.

Further, maintaining and evolving the newly engineered code may not make the overall situation all that much better. Recall that there is a high probability of introducing errors into a system when trying to adapt it or correct errors within it. These same issues do not magically disappear when applying reengineering, restructuring, or reverse engineering. A related problem is how not to make a mistake when applying any of these three approaches. Since a single error can cause massive problems, one has to be extremely careful when making any type of change. The best way to make changes and isolate errors is to have well-defined interfaces between program components. Unfortunately, in systems which are candidates for reengineering, restructuring, or reverse engineering, interfaces are not usually defined, let alone well defined. So one has a major effort on one's hand, in any case.

Since reengineering, reverse engineering, and restructuring are meant to increase stability in the evolutionary phase of a system, it should be noted that these attempts will go for naught without first applying good configuration management techniques to the system to be reengineered or reverse engineered. If CM is not applied, then one will have a new system that will quickly turn into a state much like the original, where changes are not controlled in a disciplined manner. It is amazing to see these types of tools, in fact, any CASE tool, marketed without one word of mention of this fundamental need.

The thing to recollect, at the end of the day, is that the system being reengineered, restructured, or reverse engineered will *not* be the same system, it will be different, and have its own new set of problems. There is a significant risk that the new system will not be any major improvement over the old, and that there is a good possibility of making things worse. A careful cost analysis is needed to justify the reengineering, restructuring, or reverse engineering of a system even which has high evolutionary costs. In one case study, for example, it required *two-thirds* the cost of the original development effort to reengineer the system.[232]

The point is to cast a skeptical eye on all of the claims of automation, especially those proclaiming that CASE equates to software engineering or automation. Automation is never as easy or cost-free as its advocates would like to make us believe. Most automation improvements today are aimed at making the software developer more efficient. Few are aimed at making him or her more *effective*.

Finally, recognize the problem and risk of competitive automation; i.e., CASE, IPSE, SEE, etc. manufacturers have a vested interest in selling their tools and/or methodologies, which makes automation the primary focus, rather than process, which it should be. This is not to say that they are unscrupulous, but instead, these manufacturers are motivated by different goals than you are, thus, what may be good for them may not necessarily be good for you. Think before you spend a lot on automation.

3.4 Summary

Software engineering has been described as heavy-handed management based upon modest common-sense principles, where the enforcement of standards across the board is a management breakthrough, not a technical one. If we are honest, this is in most part true, and for software engineering to get even better at putting out software systems, it will need even more "heavy-handed" approaches. One aspect will be the need for software engineering to become market driven, rather than technology driven. The risks it creates for business, not only in the application of the development processes themselves, but in the failures that can result, must be taken into account. If software systems are ever to become what we desire of them, we must change our way of thinking. Mass production of automobiles was also the result of heavy-handed management on the part of Henry Ford, who was a master at applying technology to the market.

In this chapter, we have tried to point out just some of the principal risks, either in the form of limitations or difficulties, that are inherent within of the process of software engineering. These risks, which have as their causes the lack of information, the lack of control, or the lack of time, reside within the process models used, the methods and techniques applied, and their automation. *The failure of the software enterprise is not only a failure of the product, but the failure of the total business enterprise process of which it is a part.* If you truly desire to avert software engineering risks, then you must begin with this idea as the central one to guide you in your work.

In the next chapter we will explore the risks that reside in the application domain.

Questions

1 Why is Equation 3.1 considered a limit on risk aversion for the accidental risks?

2 Compare and contrast the five major software process models named in this chapter. In what circumstances is a waterfall model less of a risk to use than a rapid-prototyping model? How does one go about relating the risks referents in Chapter 5 of *Software Engineering Risk Analysis and Management* to each process model?

3 Review the Davis et al. paper, "A Strategy for Comparing Alternative Software Development Life Cycle Models," cited in Reference 47. Use this methodology to evaluate the five major software process models named in this chapter.

4 What are phase-independent methods? How do they differ from phase-dependent methods?

5 Why is management hard? In the Department of Defense manual DoD 4245.7-M entitled, "Transition From Development To Production," it states that the causes of acquisition risk are not managerial, but technical. Do you agree? If so, why, and if not, why not?

6 A problem with off-the-shelf (OTS) software is that it doesn't reflect the implicit requirements a built-from-scratch (BFS) software component meets. How does this impede OTS software from being reused?

7   Take a requirements analysis or design method that you are familiar with. Analyze it in detail using the criteria listed in the section on methods; i.e., viewpoint, domain, principles, and so forth. What are the method's strengths and weaknesses? In what situations would using the method incur a risk? Avert a risk? Consider a mission or safety critical application, as one of the examples.

8   Repeat the question above, but instead, use examples of a second-, third-, fourth-, and fifth-generation programming language.

9   Name four design phase risks. Which methods, or principles in those methods, will avert them? To what degree?

10   Why is module size a particular risk? To help answer this question, examine the paper, "Error Density and Size in Ada Software," by Carol Withrow in *IEEE Software*, January 1990, in which Withrow demonstrates that below or above certain sizes (around 250 lines of code), error densities increase.

11   How do the techniques stepwise refinement, information hiding, separation of concerns, and program families, avert risks? What are their strengths and weaknesses?

12   What risks are inherent in testing? What are the differences between preventative testing and what is generally thought of as phase-dependent testing?

13   What is *systems integration*? When does it occur? What risks arise out of performing integration? How can they be averted?

14   What is an IPSE? How is it different from CASE or a S²EE? How does automation avert risk? How does it increase it? Where is the crossover point? Describe and draw a process model for reengineering and reverse engineering. How are they alike, and how are they different? What type of automation support are required?

15   In a SEE, how does the concept of emergence work? Give some examples.

16 What is an application? How can software engineering environments be tailored to particular application domains?

17 Describe how you would explain to the chairman of the company in Chapter 2's scenario that the lack of a standard enterprise model, or the use of standard methods, might be causing his company's software engineering trouble. How would you advise him to change?

18 Each deployment of capital by the chairman is a risk. How does one quantify the risks in the software engineering processes, especially in monetary terms, so that steps can be taken to avert them?

19 The chairman wants to invest in new information technology, like CASE. Do you think this investment is sufficient, given the size of the company? Are IPSEs or SEEs more appropriate?

20 The *semantic gap* is a measure of the difference between the concepts in high-level programming languages and the computer architecture supporting the machine-level instructions. A wide gap was thought to contribute to several software-related risks: software unreliability, performance problems, large program size, compiler complexity, etc., all of which add to a system's cost of development. Given hardware technology advancements such as RISC, is the semantic gap one risk which no longer exists? Does it exist in any other forms, say between CASE tool output and program execution, requirements input and CASE tool output, or the developer and program execution when a CASE tool or IPSE is used? If not, why not? If so, what are the implications?

21 Describe how you would conduct a cost/benefit analysis on the use of computer standards. What is some of the information you require?

22 As explained in my previous books on software engineering, the process of building a system must be dominant, with methods and their automation following. The United States tends, however, to focus on automation first, while Europe focuses on processes. Does this difference in perception increase or decrease the risks likely to be perceived in a software system's development?

References

1. Stephen Pile, *The Book of Heroic Failures*, Routledge & Kegan Paul Ltd., London, Great Britain, 1979.

2. Harold Thimbleby, "Delaying Commitment," *IEEE Software*, May 1988.

3. Barry Boehm, "Improving Software Productivity," *IEEE Computer*, Vol. 20, No. 9, September 1987.

4. Richard Hamlet, "Special Section on Software Testing," *Communications of the ACM*, Vol. 31, No. 6, June 1988. I would also go further and argue that since Parnas' work in 1972, and possibly Chen's model of databases in 1976, there has been no significant breakthroughs technically in software engineering. Edsger Dijkstra, a world class computer scientist, has gone further and written that software engineering "should be known as the 'Doomed Discipline', doomed because it cannot even approach its goal since its goal is selfcontradictory. Software engineering, of course, presents itself as another worthy cause, but that is eyewash. If you carefully read its literature and analyze what its devotees actually do, you will discover that software engineering has accepted as its charter, 'How to program if you cannot.'" For more on Dijksta's comments, refer to "On the Cruelty of Really Teaching Computing Science," *Communications of the ACM*, Vol. 32, No. 12, December 1989.

   Although the industry hasn't really invented or discovered anything profoundly new in the past 10 years, rather than leave on a hopeless note, it should be pointed out that a major rethinking is occurring about the management and control of information technology developments. The most novel ideas, and the ones that I predict will radically change systems development for the better, are coming from Tarek Abel-Hamid and Stewart Madnick, who express, as do others, such as this author, a nonlinear view of systems development and management. We will explore some of these ideas later in Chapter 7. See also Tarek Abel-Hamid and Stuart E. Madnick, *Dynamics of Software Project Management*, Prentice-Hall, Englewood Cliffs, NJ, 1990.

5. But the reader must not take what is said as the final word. Skepticism is a healthy attitude to have in the risk business.

6. Robert N. Charette, *Software Engineering Environments: Concepts and Technology*, McGraw-Hill, Inc., New York, 1986.

7. Watts S. Humphrey, et al., *A Method for Assessing the Software Engineering Capability of Contractors*, Software Engineering Institute, February 1987.

8. Recall from Chapter 2 that this is what Rockefeller did with Standard Oil.

9. Frederick P. Brooks, Jr., "No Silver Bullet," *IEEE Computer*, Vol. 20, No. 4, April 1987. Note that this equation is also the fundamental limit on the effectiveness of averting risks that have to do with accidental risks involved in the software enterprise.

10. W. Linwood Sutton, "Advanced Models of the Software Process," *Representing and Enacting the Software Process*, Proceedings of the 4th International Process Workshop, IEEE 88THO211-3, 11–13 May, 1988.

11. R. Lauber, "Development Support Systems," *IEEE Computer*, Vol. 15, No. 5, May 1982.

12. In Chapter 7 we will revisit this very real and very important problem, which is caused today by using linear models of development where the situation is very nonlinear.

13. Stagewise models stipulated that software be developed in successive stages. The waterfall model was a refinement of these early attempts, which were outgrowths of the original code and fix approaches of the very early software development endeavors. See H. D. Benington, "Production of Large Computer Programs," *Proceedings of ONR Symposium on Advanced Programming Methods for Digital Computers*, June 1956; and W. Royce, "Managing the Development of Large Software Systems: Concepts," *WESCON Proceedings*, August 1970.

14. Note, as was also stated in Chapter 2, that this condition is true of all process models, including the fundamentally systemic ones. However, attacking the systemic aspects of a software enterprise are not a part of waterfall process models.

15. Barry Boehm, *Software Engineering Economics*, Prentice-Hall, Inc., Englewood Cliffs, NJ, 1981. However, there is some debate whether the model accurately reflects practice, or practice reflects the model.

16. J. Garman, "Data Systems for the Space Station and Beyond," *AIAA Conference on Computers in Aerospace*, 1985.

17. *A Software Engineering Environment for the Navy*, a Report of the Naval Material Command's Software Engineering Environment Working Group, 31 March, 1982.

18. Barry Boehm, *Software Engineering Economics*, Prentice-Hall, Inc., Englewood Cliffs, NJ, 1981.

19. Harlan Mills, "Software Development," *IEEE Transactions on Software Engineering*, December 1976.

20. David Parnas, "On the Design and Development of Program Families," *IEEE Transactions on Software Engineering*, Vol. SE-2, No. 1, March 1976.

21. V. Bassilli. and A. Turner, "Iterative Enhancement: A Practical Technique for Software Engineering," *IEEE Transactions on Software Engineering*, Vol. SE-1, No. 1, March 1975.

22. Buying of information, and what value can be placed upon it, is discussed in some detail in Chapters 3 and 4 of Robert N. Charette, *Software Engineering Risk Analysis and Management*, McGraw-Hill, Inc., New York, 1989.

23. Frederick P. Brooks, Jr., *The Mythical Man-Month*, Addison-Wesley Publishing Co., Reading, MA, 1975. Do not take this throw-away attitude as dogma. Prototypes are not *required* to be built. Sometimes a prototype will not reveal anything worthwhile.

24. Pamela Jordan et al., "Software Storming: Combining Rapid Prototyping and Knowledge Engineering," *IEEE Computer*, Vol. 22, No. 5, May 1989.

25. Luqui, "Software Evolution Through Rapid Prototyping," *IEEE Computer*, Vol. 22, No. 5, May 1989.

26. Barry Boehm, "Verifying and Validating Software Requirements and Design Specifications," *IEEE Computer*, Vol. 17, No. 1, January 1984.

27. Barry Boehm, *Software Engineering Economics*, Prentice-Hall, Inc., Englewood Cliffs, NJ, 1981.

28. Robert N. Charette, *Software Engineering Environments: Concepts and Technology*, McGraw-Hill, Inc., New York 1986.

29. Harold Thimberly, "Delaying Commitment," *IEEE Software*, May 1988.

30. Edward Phillips, "Optimistic Data, Schedule Balmed For Starship Certification Delays," *Aviation Week & Space Technology*, 4 December, 1989.

31. G. E. Kaiser, "Constructing Enactable Models," *Representing and Enacting the Software Process*, Proceedings of the 4th International Process Workshop, IEEE 88THO211-3, 11–13 May, 1988.

32. Pamela Zave, "The Operational Versus the Conventional Approach to Software Development," *Communications of the ACM*, Vol. 27, No. 2, February 1984.

33. M. M. Lehman, "Some Reservations on Software Process Programming," *Representing and Enacting the Software Process*, Proceedings of the 4th International Process Workshop, IEEE 88THO211-3, 11–13 May, 1988.

34. Barry Boehm and Philip Papaccio, "Understanding and Controlling Software Costs," *IEEE Transactions on Software Engineering*, Vol. SE-14, No. 10, October 1988.

35. Barry Boehm, "A Spiral Model of Software Development and Enhancement," *IEEE Computer*, Vol. 21, No. 5, May 1988; and Hebert P. Woodward, "Ada—A Better Mousetrap?" *Defense Science*, Vol. 8, No. 10, November 1989.

36. One would prefer some changes in terminology to make the ideas a little more useful.

37. One is not restricted to just expert systems. Applying heuristic search techniques, formal inference systems, or knowledge representation systems are also applicable. See, for instance, P. Paolo Puncello et al., "ASPIS: A Knowledge-Based CASE Environment," *IEEE Software*, March 1988.

38. K. Frenkel, "Toward Automating the Software Development Cycle," *Communications of the ACM*, Vol. 28, No. 6, June 1985.

39. Richard Waters, "Automatic Programming: Myths and Prospects," *IEEE Computer*, Vol. 21, No. 8 August 1988.

40. R. Balzer et al., "Software Technology in the 1990's: Using a New Paradigm," *IEEE Computer*, Vol. 16, No. 11, November 1983.

41. "AI/Software Engineering," *IEEE Expert* (special issue), Vol. 3, No. 4, Winter 1988.

42. Robin M. Hogarth, "Generalization in Decision Research," *IEEE Transactions on Systems, Man, and Cybernetics*, Vol SMC-16, No. 3, May/June 1986.

43. David Parnas and Paul Clements, "A Rational Design Process: How and Why to Fake It," *IEEE Transactions on Software Engineering*, Vol. SE-12, No. 2, February 1986.

44. N. Howes, "Managing Software Development Projects for Maximum Productivity," *IEEE Transactions on Software Engineering*, Vol. SE-10, No. 1, January 1984.

45. Tom Demarco, *Structured Analysis and System Specifications*, Yourdon, Inc., New York, 1978.

46. Barry Boehm, *Software Engineering Economics*, Prentice-Hall, Inc., Englewood Cliffs, NJ, 1981.

47. Alan M. Davis et al., "A Strategy for Comparing Alternative Software Development Life Cycle Models," *IEEE Transactions on Software Engineering*, Vol. 14, No. 10, October 1988.

48. Sam Redwine et al., "DoD Related Software Technology Requirements, Practices, and Prospects for the Future," IDA Paper P-1788, 1984.

49. William Riddle, "Software Development Environments: Present and Future," *Proceedings of the International Computer Technology Conference*, San Francisco, August 1980.

50. However, there is a difficulty in separating the individual processes defined by the process model from the methods used to implement them. This makes for slow progress on developing new software paradigms which are process-oriented. Paradigms like the operational model blur the distinction even further.

51. Doug Ross et al. "Software Engineering: Process, Principles, and Goals," *IEEE Computer*, Vol. 8, No. 5, May 1975. There has been some discussion that software engineering methods may have been developed backwards. In other words, instead of trying to enunciate general principles as discussed by Ross, and then proceeding to develop methods which follow these principles, it is suggested that we should study how real systems are designed, systematize the thought processes involved, and then proceed backwards towards general principles. Using the current deductive approach, one can apply correctly methods such as the Jackson Method, and get nonsensical results, which is not an insignificant risk. Inductive approaches to methodology development may be more useful. For further insight, see David Lefkovitz and Helen Hill, "The Applicability of Software Development Methodologies to Naval Embedded Computer Systems," Naval Air Development Center, Contract No. N62269-81-R-0455, November 9, 1982.

52. Robert N. Charette, *Software Engineering Environments: Concepts and Technology*, McGraw-Hill, Inc., New York 1986.

53. B. Blum, "Understanding the Software Paradox," *ACM Software Engineering Notes*, Vol. 10, No. 1, January 1985.

54. Ibid.

55. All syntactic representations have some meaning. The meaning of language exists at three levels: the semantic, which relates words to things, giving them meaning; the syntactic, relating words to other words, expressing connected meanings such as the action of one thing upon another; and the pragmatic, which relates these words to the context that encompassed their creation. For a full explanation, see Arno Penzias, *Ideas and Information*, W. W. Norton, New York, 1989.

56. R. J. Buhr et al., "Software CAD: A Revolutionary Approach," *IEEE Transactions on Software Engineering*, Vol. 15, No. 3, March 1989.

57. R. J. Buhr, *System Design with Ada*, Prentice-Hall, Inc., Englewood Cliffs, NJ, 1984.

58. P. Freeman and T. Wasserman, *The Context of Design: IEEE Tutorial On Software Design Techniques*, 2nd ed., IEEE Catalog No. 76CH1145-2C, 1977.

59. C. V. Ramamoorthy et al., "Programming in the Large," *IEEE Transactions on Software Engineering*, Vol. SE-12, No. 7, July 1986.

60. Robert N. Charette, *Software Engineering Environments: Concepts and Technology*, McGraw-Hill, Inc., New York 1986.

61. Program management is the activity that concerns averting or containing the risks within the process of developing multiple software systems or products. We will freely interchange the terms system and product, as they both logically represent the same idea.

62. Edward Bersoff, "Elements of Software Configuration Management," *IEEE Transactions on Software Engineering*, Vol. SE-10, No. 1, January 1984.

63. Note that, in a strict process-oriented development paradigm, the user and customer are part of the "inward view," whereas the outward view is directed to the impacts on the business and/or social environments (e.g., on company profit or image).

64. Barry Boehm, "Software Engineering Economics," *IEEE Transactions on Software Engineering*, Vol. SE-10, No. 1, January 1984.

65. Walt Scacchi, "Managing Software Engineering Projects: A Social Analysis," *IEEE Transactions on Software Engineering*, Vol. SE-10, No. 1, January 1984.

66. Joseph Fox, *Executive Qualities*, Addison-Wesley Publishing Co., Inc., Reading, MA, 1976.

67. The use of the coaching analogy is a personal bias. This supposedly represents a Theory Y approach to software management, as opposed to a Theory X (autocrat), Theory W (politician), or Theory Z (facilitator). Each has their own strengths and weaknesses, and which should be used depends on the company culture, company organizational structure, company understanding of the benefits, opportunities, and risks involved in applying automation to its business, and how dependent the company is on automation for acquiring or sustaining the competitive edge. For a description of one of these types of management, refer to "Theory-W Software Project Management: Principles and Examples," by Barry W. Boehm and Rony Ross, *IEEE Transactions on Software Engineering*, Vol. 15, No. 7, July 1989.

68. Robert N. Charette, *Software Engineering Environments: Concepts and Technology*, McGraw-Hill, Inc., New York, 1986.

69. Determining the quality of the personnel is not always easy. The factors which, as a minimum, need to be taken into account are: the experience in the application domain; any direct previous project experience in the application domain; the amount of training in the application or software engineering to be applied; the amount of formal education; the number of years of direct experience in the industry sector; the number of previous projects worked on; the degree to which the person's experience matches the job occupied; and the time in the project.

70. Barry Boehm, "Software Engineering Economics," *IEEE Transactions on Software Engineering*, Vol. SE-10, No. 1, January 1984.

71. N. Howes, "Managing Software Development Projects for Maximum Productivity," *IEEE Transactions on Software Engineering*, Vol. SE-10, No. 1, January 1984.

72. *A Software Engineering Environment for the Navy*, A Report of the Naval Material Command's Software Engineering Environment Working Group, 31 March 1982.

73. A. Wolf et al. "Ada-Based Support for Programming-in-the-Large," *IEEE Software*, Vol. 2, No. 2, March 1985.

74. T. Abel-Hamid and S. Madnick, "The Dynamics of Software Project Scheduling," *Communications of the ACM*, Vol. 26, No. 5, May 1983.

75. R. Wolverton, "Software Costing," *Handbook of Software Engineering*, C. Vick and C. Ramamoorthy (eds.), Van Nostrand Reinhold Co., Inc., New York, 1984.

76. R. Poston, "Determining a Complete Set of Software Development Standards: Is the Cube the Answer?" *IEEE Software*, Vol. 1, No. 3, July 1984.

77. Charles McKay, in a speech given to National Security Industrial Association Conference on "Software Initiatives and Their Impact on the Competitive Edge," *NSIA Proceedings*, 10 May, 1988.

78. *IEEE Taxonomy for Software Engineering Standards*, ANSI/IEEE Standard 1002-1987, IEEE, New York, 1987.

79. *IEEE Standard for Software Quality Assurance Plans*; ANSI/IEEE Standard 730-1981, IEEE, New York, 1981.

80. "SQA: In Pursuit of Perfection," *IEEE Software* (special issue), September 1987.

81. F. Buckley and R. Poston, "Software Quality Assurance," *IEEE Transactions on Software Engineering*, Vol. SE-10, No. 1, January 1984.

82. "Software Quality Measurement Manual, Vol. II," *RADC Report TR-80-109*, June 1979.

83. Dolores R. Wallace and Roger U. Fujii, "Verification and Validation: Techniques to Assure Reliability," *IEEE Software*, May 1989.

84. Edward Bersoff, "Elements of Software Configuration Management," *IEEE Transactions on Software Engineering*, Vol. SE-10, No. 1, January 1984.

85. Ibid.

86. For a current listing of the current research and application of configuration management, refer to the *ACM Proceedings of the 2nd International Workshop on Software Configuration Management*, October, 1989.

87. Edward Bersoff, "Elements of Software Configuration Management," *IEEE Transactions on Software Engineering*, Vol. SE-10, No. 1, January 1984.

88. David Gelperin and Bill Hetzel, "The Growth of Software Testing," *Communications of the ACM*, Vol. 31, No. 6, 1988.

89. *IEEE Glossary of Software Engineering Terminology*, ANSI/IEEE Standard 729-1983; IEEE, New York, 1983.

90. Dolores R. Wallace and Roger U. Fujii, "Software Verification and Validation: An Overview," *IEEE Software*, May 1989.

91. Barry Boehm, "Verifying and Validating Software Requirements and Design Specifications," *IEEE Software*, Vol. 1, No. 1, January 1984.

92. David Gelperin and Bill Hetzel, "The Growth of Software Testing," *Communications of the ACM*, Vol. 31, No. 6, 1988.

93. *A Software Engineering Environment for the Navy*, A Report of the Naval Material Command's Software Engineering Environment Working Group, 31 March, 1982.

94. Andrew Ferrentino and Harlan Mills, "State Machines and Their Semantics in Software Engineering," *COMPSAC 77*, Congress on Computer Software Application, 1977.

95. James H. Fetzer, "Program Verification: The Very Idea," *Communications of the ACM*, Vol. 31, No. 9, September 1988.

96. T. Jones, "Reusability in Programming: A Survey of the State-of-the Art," *IEEE Transactions on Software Engineering*, Vol. SE-10, No. 5, September 1984.

97. E. Horowitz and J. Munson, "An Expansive View of Reusable Software," *IEEE Transactions on Software Engineering*, Vol. SE-10, No. 5, September 1984.

98. W. Trasz, "Software Reuse Myths," *ACM Software Engineering Notes*, Vol. 13, No. 1, January 1988.

99. Peter Wegner, "Capital-Intensive Software Technology," *IEEE Software*, Vol. 1, No. 3, July 1984.

100. David Card et al., "An Empirical Study of Software Design Practices," *IEEE Transactions on Software Engineering*, Vol. SE-12, No. 2, February 1986.

101. W. Tracz, "Software Reuse Maxims," *ACM Software Engineering Notes*, Vol. 13, No. 4, October 1988.

102. W. Tracz, "Software Reuse Myths," *ACM Software Engineering Notes*, Vol. 13, No. 1, January 1988.

103. "Report of the Defense Science Board Task Force on Military Software," Office of the Under Secretary of Defense for Acquisition, Washington, D.C., September 1987.

104. B. Silverman, "Software Cost and Productivity Improvements: An Analogical View," *IEEE Computer*, Vol. 18, No. 5, May 1985.

105. T. Jones, "Reusability in Programming: A Survey of the State-of-the Art," *IEEE Transactions on Software Engineering*, Vol. SE-10, No. 5, September 1984.

106. Y. Matsumato, "Some Experiences in Promoting Reusable Software: Presentation in Higher Abstract Levels," *IEEE Transactions on Software Engineering*, Vol. SE-10, No. 5, September 1984.

107. Thomas Cheatham, "PDS, Overview of the Harvard Program Development System," *Software Engineering Environments*, H. Hunke (ed)., Proceedings of a Symposium, June 1980, Lahnstein, Germany, 1981.

108. B. Silverman, "Software Cost and Productivity Improvements: An Analogical View," *IEEE Computer*, Vol. 18, No. 5, May 1985.

109. "Report of the Defense Science Board Task Force on Military Software," Office of the Under Secretary of Defense for Acquisition, Washington, D.C., September 1987.

110. Refer to note 23 of Chapter 6 as to why this is true.

111. See, for example, the *IEEE Software* Special issue on "Making Reuse a Reality," July 1987. Also, as more products such as general semantic translators are developed that let heterogeneous products communicate, many of the problems preventing reuse will disappear.

112. Note, database activities usually will span the entire process model, and therefore, so will the methods associated with it. However, this is a special case that fits into a grey area of phase independence/dependency. Refer to Chapter 8 of Robert N. Charette, *Software Engineering Environments: Concepts and Technology*, McGraw-Hill, Inc., New York, 1986, for more detail of the activities and methods used.

113. Robert N. Charette, *Software Engineering Environments: Concepts and Technology*, McGraw-Hill, Inc., New York, 1986.

114. Richard Fairley, *Software Engineering Concepts,* McGraw-Hill, Inc. New York, 1984.

115. R. Pressman, *Software Engineering: A Practitioner's Approach*, McGraw-Hill, Inc. New York, 1982.

116. Alan Davis, *Software Requirements: Analysis and Specification*, Prentice Hall, Englewood Cliffs, NJ, 1990.

117. Acceptability in this case is the not the same as whether a risk is "acceptable." It is an objective acceptability, rather than a subjective acceptability.

118. C. Ramamoorthy et al., "Software Engineering," *IEEE Computer*, Vol. 17, No. 10, October 1984.

119. A. Ralston and E. Reilly, eds., *Encyclopedia of Computer Science and Engineering,* 2nd ed., Von Nostrand Reinhold Co., New York, 1983.

120. Robert N. Charette, *Software Engineering Environments: Concepts and Technology*, McGraw-Hill, Inc., New York, 1986.

121. Richard Fairley, *Software Engineering Concepts*, McGraw-Hill, Inc., New York, 1984.

122. Robert C. Fink, "Using JAD Techniques to Accelerate the Requirements Definition Process," presentation at the *Requirements and Engineering and Rapid Prototyping Workshop*, TTCP XTP-2, November 1989.

123. Barry Boehm, "Software and Its Impact: A Quantitative Assessment," *Datamation*, May 1973.

124. Charles McKay, "Some Thoughts on DRLI58 and Subsequent Increments of Evolution," SERC Position Paper, August 24, 1989.

125. Herb Krasner, "Requirements Dynamics in Large Software Engineering Projects," *11th World Computer Congress (IFIP89)*, Elsevier Science Publishers B.V., Amsterdam, The Netherlands, August 1989.

126. David Parnas, "Software Aspects of Strategic Defense Systems," *Communications of the ACM*, Vol. 28, No. 12, December 1989.

127. Jim Toher, "The Nature of Requirements," presentation at the Requirements Engineering & Rapid Prototyping Workshop, Ft. Monmouth, NJ, November 1989.

128. Alan M. Davis, "A Taxonomy for the Early Stages of the Software Development Life Cycle," *The Journal of Systems and Software*, Elsevier Science Publishing Company, Vol. 8, 1988. Davis makes a critical point when he shows multiple solutions. We will encounter this again in the next chapter on application risks. It is important to remember that there is no one solution to a particular set of system requirements. There exist many trade-offs in the solution space which can affect, both positively and negatively, the final cost and schedule.

129. Herb Krasner, "Requirements Dynamics in Large Software Engineering Projects," *11th World Computer Congress (IFIP89)*, Elsevier Science Publishers B.V., Amsterdam, The Netherlands, August 1989.

130. Barry Boehm, "Improving Software Productivity," *IEEE Computer*, Vol. 20, No. 9, September 1987.

131. Alan Boring, "Computer System Reliability and Nuclear War," *Communications of the ACM*, Vol. 30, No. 2, February 1987.

132. Frederick P. Brooks, Jr., *The Mythical Man-Month*, Addison-Wesley Publishing Co., Reading, MA, 1975.

133. Alan Davis, *Software Requirements: Analysis and Specification*, Prentice Hall, Englewood Cliffs, NJ, 1990.

134. Alan Davis, "The Design of a Family of Application-Oriented Requirements Languages," *IEEE Computer*, Vol. 8, No. 5, May 1982.

135. Katherine Heninger, "Specifying Software Requirements for Complex Systems: New Techniques and Their Application," *IEEE Transactions on Software Engineering*, Vol. SE-6, No. 1, January 1980.

136. C. Heitmeyer and J. McLean, "Abstract Requirements Specification: A New Approach and Its Application," *IEEE Transactions on Software Engineering*, Vol. SE-9, No. 5, September 1982.

137. David Parnas, "On The Criteria to Be Used in Decomposing Systems Into Modules," *Communications of the ACM*, Vol. 15, No. 12, December 1972.

138. David Parnas, "Use of Abstract Interfaces in the Development of Software For Embedded Computer Systems," NRL Report 8047, 3 June, 1977.

139. David Parnas, "On The Criteria To Be Used In Decomposing Systems Into Modules," *Communications of the ACM*, Vol. 15, No. 12, December 1972.

140. Ibid.

141. Surya B. Yadav et al., "Comparison of Analysis Techniques for Information Requirements Determination," *Communications of the ACM*, Vol. 31, No. 9, September 1988.

142. Robert N. Charette, *Software Engineering Environments: Concepts and Technology*, McGraw-Hill, Inc., New York, 1986.

143. "Requirements Engineering Environments; Software Tools for Modeling User Needs," *IEEE Computer* (special issue), Vol. 18, No. 4, April 1985.

144. Robert G. Babb II et al., "Workshop on Models and Languages for Software Specification and Design," *IEEE Computer*, Vol. 18, No. 3, March 1985.

145. David Lefkovitz and Helen Hill, "The Applicability of Software Development Methodologies to Naval Embedded Computer Systems," Naval Air Development Center, Contract No. N62269-81-R-0455, 9 November, 1982.

146. Alan M. Davis, *Software Requirements: Analysis and Specification*, Prentice-Hall, Englewood Cliffs, NJ, 1990.

147. Alan M. Davis, "A Comparison of Techniques for the Specification Of External Behavior," *Communications of the ACM*, Vol. 31, No. 9, September 1989.

148. Alan M. Davis, "A Taxonomy for the Early Stages of the Software Development Life Cycle," *The Journal of Systems and Software*, Elsevier Science Publishing Company, Vol. 8, 1988.

149. Robert N. Charette, "SOEM: Putting Theories into Practice," *Third International Workshop on Specification and Design*, London, August 1985.

150. Robert N. Charette, "A Methodology for Addressing System Operability Issues," NAECON 1985, Dayton, May 1985.

151. For example, see Robert Wallace, John Stockenberg, and Robert Charette, *A Unified Methodology for Developing Systems*, McGraw-Hill, Inc., New York, 1987.

152. Richard Fairley, *Software Engineering Concepts*, McGraw-Hill, Inc. New York, 1984.

153. David Parnas and David Weiss, *Active Design Reviews*, NRL Report 8927, 18 November,1985.

154. P. Freeman, P. and T. Wasserman, *The Context of Design: IEEE Tutorial On Software Design Techniques*, 2nd ed., IEEE Catalog No. 76CH1145-2C, 1977.

155. L. Peters, *Software Design: Methods and Techniques*, Yourdan Press, New York, 1981.

156. C. Kooman, "The Entropy of Design: A Study on the Meaning of Creativity," *IEEE Transactions on Systems, Man, and Cybernetics*, Vol. SMC-15, No. 1, January/February 1985.

157. A. Ralston and E. Reilly, eds., *Encyclopedia of Computer Science,* 2nd ed., Von Nostrand Reinhold Co., New York, 1983.

158. P. Freeman and T. Wasserman, *The Context of Design: IEEE Tutorial on Software Design Techniques,* 2nd ed., IEEE Catalog No. 76CH1145-2C, 1977.

159. Henry Petroski, *To Engineer Is Human,* St. Martin's Press, New York, 1982.

160. Frederick P. Brooks, Jr., *The Mythical Man-Month,* Addison-Wesley Publishing Co., Reading, MA, 1975.

161. A. Ralston and E. Reilly, eds., *Encyclopedia of Computer Science,* 2nd ed., Von Nostrand Reinhold Co., New York, 1983

162. S. Dasgupta, *The Design and Description of Computer Architectures,* John Wiley & Sons, New York, 1984.

163. L. Peters, *Software Design: Methods and Techniques,* Yourdan Press, New York, 1981.

164. We have, for the most part, avoided the issue of hardware selection in our previous discussions. We believe that, theoretically, hardware should not be selected until after the specifications are complete, but this is almost never true in practice. In fact, in many large scale projects, the hardware suite has been selected years in advance of the first software requirements specification, let alone design (because it is the easiest thing to do, and makes a project appear to be making progress). This should be considered during the requirements and specification phases, with the designer providing key data on suitability for meeting the performance criteria requirements.

165. L. Peters, *Software Design: Methods and Techniques,* Yourdan Press, New York, 1981.

166. C. Kooman, "The Entropy of Design: A Study on the Meaning of Creativity," *IEEE Transactions on Systems, Man, and Cybernetics,* Vol. SMC-15, No. 1, January/February 1985.

167. G. Bergland, "A Guided Tour of Program Design Methodologies," *IEEE Computer,* Vol. 14, No. 10, October 1981.

168. J. Enos and R. Van Tilburg, "Software Design," *IEEE Computer,* Vol. 14, No. 2, February 1981.

169. David Parnas, "Use of Abstract Interfaces in the Development of Software for Embedded Computer Systems," *NRL Report 8047,* 3 June, 1977.

170. W. Stevens et al., "Structured Design," *IBM Systems Journal,* Vol. 13, No. 2, 1974.

171. David Card et al., "An Empirical Study of Software Design Practices," *IEEE Transactions on Software Engineering,* Vol. SE-12, No. 2, February 1986.

172. N. Wirth, *Algorithms + Data Structures = Programs,* Prentice-Hall, Inc., Englewood Cliffs, NJ, 1976.

173. G. Bergland, "A Guided Tour of Program Design Methodologies," *IEEE Computer,* Vol. 14, No. 10, October 1981.

174. Ibid.

175. C. Ramamoorthy et al., "Software Engineering," *IEEE Computer*, Vol. 17, No. 10, October 1984.

176. Ibid.

177. Connie U. Smith, "Applying Synthesis Principles to Create Responsive Software Systems," *IEEE Transactions on Software Engineering*, Vol. 14, No. 10, October 1988.

178. Leonard L. Tripp, "A Survey of Notations for Program Design—An Update," *ACM Software Engineering Notes*, Vol. 13, No. 4, October 1988.

179. Richard A. Zahniser, "The Perils of Top-Down Design," *ACM Software Engineering Notes*, Vol. 13, No. 2, April 1988.

180. Dallas E. Webster, "Mapping Design Information Representation Terrain," *IEEE Computer*, Vol. 21, No. 12, December 1988.

181. Butler W. Lampson, "Hints for Computer System Design," *IEEE Software*, Vol. 1, No. 1, January 1984.

182. Barry W. Boehm, "Verifying and Validating Software Requirements and Design Specifications," *IEEE Software*, Vol. 1, No. 1, January 1984.

183. Testing and debugging are similarly confused. When debugging, a program is tested for correct execution by the programmer as it is being built. However, this is a localized affair, concerned with fixing faults and making sure a segment of code runs. Testing is concerned with the detection of faults in the overall software, and making sure it solves the problem that it was originally built for, before it is released.

184. R. Jenson, "Structured Programming," *IEEE Computer*, Vol. 14, No. 3, March 1981.

185. R. Wolverton, "Software Costing," *Handbook of Software Engineering*, C. Vick and C. Ramamoorthy (eds.), Van Nostrand Reinhold Co., Inc., New York, 1984.

186. J. Adam and P. Wallich, "Star Wars—SDI: The Grand Experiment, Part 1," *IEEE Spectrum*, Vol 22, No. 9, September 1985.

187. Barry Boehm, "Software and Its Impact: A Quantitative Assessment," *Datamation*, May 1973.

188. Pamela Zave, "A Compositional Approach to Multiparadigm Programming," *IEEE Software*, September 1989.

189. Barry Boehm, *Software Engineering Economics*, Prentice-Hall, Inc., Englewood Cliffs, NJ, 1981.

190. N. Wirth, *Algorithms + Data Structures = Programs*, Prentice-Hall, Inc., Englewood Cliffs, NJ, 1976.

191. E. Dijkstra, "Notes on Structured Programming," *Structured Programming*, Academic Press, New York, 1972.

192. David Parnas, "On the Design and Development of Program Families," *IEEE Transactions on Software Engineering*, Vol. SE-2, No. 1, March 1976.

193. G. Booch, "Object-Oriented Design," *ACM Ada Letters*, Vol. 1, No. 3, March/April 1982.

194. See G. Booch, *Software Engineering with Ada*, The Benjamin/Cummings Publishing Company, Inc., California, 1983; or articles in the *Journal of Object-Oriented Programming*, SIGS Publications, Inc., Vol. 1, No. 1, April/May 1988.

195. The reader should consult any of the specialized journals on programming languages, such as the *ACM Transactions on Programming Languages and Systems*, for in-depth reviews on their relative advantages/disadvantages.

196. R. Wallace, *Practitioner's Guide to Ada*, Intertext Publications, Inc., New York, 1986.

197. J. V. Cugini, "Selection and Use of General Purpose Programming Languages," NBS Special Publication 500-117, Vol. 1, October 1984.

198. E. Miller, "Software Testing Technology: An Overview," *Handbook of Software Engineering*, C. Vick and C. Ramamoorthy (eds.), Van Nostrand Reinhold Co., Inc., New York, 1984.

199. Ibid.

200. J. Munson, "Software Maintainability: A Practical Concern for Life-Cycle Costs," *IEEE Computer*, Vol. 14, No. 11, November 1981.

201. Lotus 1-2-3 version 3 required $7 million to develop and $15 million to test. For more information on the costs of testing, see Brenton Schlender, "How To Break The Software Logjam," *Fortune*, 25 September, 1989; and E. Miller, "Software Testing Technology: An Overview," *Handbook of Software Engineering*, C. Vick and C. Ramamoorthy (eds.), Van Nostrand Reinhold Co., Inc., New York, 1984.

202. John Rowland and Yu Zuyuan, "Experimental Comparison of Three System Test Strategies: Preliminary Report," *Proceedings of the ACM SIGSOFT '89 Third Symposium on Software Testing, Analysis, and Verification (TAV3)*, December 1989.

203. Richard Hamlet, "Theoretical Comparisons of Testing Methods," *Proceedings of the ACM SIGSOFT '89 Third Symposium on Software Testing, Analysis, and Verification (TAV3)*, December 1989.

204. R. A. Brooker et al., "The Adventures of a Blunder," *Mathematical Tables and Other Aids to Computation*, Vol. 6, No. 38, 1952.

205. G. J. Meyers, *Software Reliability: Principles and Practices*, Wiley, New York, 1976.

206. Virginia R. Gibson and James A. Senn, "System Structure and Software Maintenance Performance," *Communications of the ACM*, Vol. 32, No. 3, March 1989.

207. Nathan H. Petschenik, "Practical Priorities in System Testing," *IEEE Software*, September 1985.

208. "Software Maintenance: Tweaking Programs to Boost Performance," *Federal Computer Week*, December 5, 1988.

209. Jean-Marc Garot, "Evaluating Proposed Architectures for the FAA's Advanced Automation System," *IEEE Computer*, Vol. 20, No. 2, February 1987.

210. William Perry, "Software Is as Solid an Asset as Office Furniture," *Government Computer News*, 4 September, 1989. Company liquidators warn, however, that they do not, nor ever will look at software as a capital asset. It is too difficult to set a value on it, especially with licenses, third-party software, homegrown software, and so forth. The internal revenue service, however, would like to consider it a capital asset. Then it could levy a tax.

211. This isn't exactly right, since new developments themselves would have to be started. More likely, for every percentage saved on evolution, an additional 2% increase (rather than 3%) on new development could be started.

212. Phil S. Babel, "Software Integrity Program," Aeronautical Systems Division, U.S. Air Force, April 1987.

213. Watts S. Humphrey et al., *A Method for Assessing the Software Engineering Capability of Contractors*, Software Engineering Institute, February 1987.

214. A. Wasserman, "The Future of Programming," *Communications of the ACM*, Vol. 25, No. 3, March 1982.

215. J. Garman, "Data Systems for the Space Station and Beyond," *AIAA Conference on Computers in Aerospace*, 1985.

216. Capers Jones, *Programming Productivity*; McGraw-Hill, Inc., New York, 1986.

217. Elliot J. Chikosfsky and James H. Cross II, "Reverse Engineering and Design Recovery: A Taxonomy," *IEEE Software*, January 1990. Note that this issue of *IEEE Software* contains many articles on maintenance, reverse engineering, and design recovery. One of the claims of the reverse engineering/reengineering/restructuring advocates is that one can do reverse engineering at any point in time, that one does not need to have a completed system to apply them.

218. For information concerning the Information Engineering Facility, contact either Texas Instruments, 6550 Chases Oaks Blvd., Austin, TX, or James Martin Associates Plc., James Martin House, Little Road Ashford, Middlesex, Great Britain.

219. For information concerning Maestro, contact Softlab Inc., Bayside Plaza, 188 Embarcadero, San Francisco, CA.

220. Robert N. Charette, *Software Engineering Environments: Concepts and Technology*, McGraw-Hill, Inc., New York 1986. For an update on automation progress, refer to the special issue on software tools of *IEEE Software*, May 1990.

221. Ibid.

222. Ibid.

223. Charles Rich and Richard Waters, "Automatic Programming: Myths and Prospects," *IEEE Computer*, Vol. 21, No. 8, August 1988. Many claim that it is only a matter of time before automatic programming is here. However, being realistic, the level of difficulty of trying to automatically generate systems increases nonlinearly as one moves up in levels of abstraction. Generating machine code from higher level languages is many time less difficult than generating machine code from requirements.

224. Robert N. Charette, "Software Engineering and The Competitive Edge," speech given to *Europe 1992 Conference*, January 1989, Birmingham, England.

225. "Shedding Light on 4GL's," *IEEE Software* (special issue), July 1988. It has to be noted, however, that the currently available 4GLs will tend to decrease overall system performance, because the code produced is not very efficient.

226. Karen Norby et al., "The Design Generator," *RADC F30602-85-C-0245*; 31 December, 1986.

227. Frederick P. Brooks, Jr., "No Silver Bullet," *IEEE Computer*, Vol. 20, No. 4, April 1987.

228. Barry Boehm, "Improving Software Productivity," *IEEE Computer*, Vol. 20, No. 9, September 1987.

229. Brenton Schlender, "How To Break The Software Logjam," *Fortune*, 25 September, 1989. One may want to compare these numbers against the estimates derived in Chapter 1, shown in Figure 1.1 and Table 1.1.

230. Ronald J. Norman and Jay F. Nunamaker, Jr., "CASE Productivity Perceptions of Software Engineering Professionals," *Communications of the ACM*, Vol. 32, No. 9, September 1989.

231. In a presentation to the EIA Annual G-33/34 Workshop on 26 September, 1988, by Hank Stuebing of the Naval Air Development Center. Stuebing showed that the increases in productivity reported by Barry Boehm and others using the COCOMO model from 1977 to 1985 could be traced primarily to the use of CASE technology, and that the increases in productivity reported only amounted to 6% per year, compounded.

232. Harry M. Sneed, "Software Renewal: A Case Study," *IEEE Software,* July 1984.

Chapter

4

Application Systems and the Risks to the Business

"Our business in life is not to succeed, but to continue to fail in good spirits."

ROBERT LOUIS STEVENSON

4.0 Introduction

The previous two chapters were concerned with an examination of the processes involved in developing software-driven information systems and the risks contained therein. We found ourselves having to expand our universe of discourse beyond that which is traditionally viewed as encompassing software engineering. This course has allowed us, however, to build the conceptual framework with which to be able to understand why some of the risks commonly considered as having their origins within the application of software engineering actually originate outside the software engineering project domain. It was only by comprehending and separating these other domains that we could hope to make software engineering risk analysis and management truly effective. These actions, in turn, forced us to reconsider the scope of what was also included in software engineering risk analysis and management.

In this chapter, we will continue our examination of software engineering risks by studying the risks associated with software applications; i.e., the product that results from the process of software engineering. We will define the risks stemming from the application environs as arising from three areas: (1) the application knowledge, which is domain specific; (2) the logical application architecture; and (3) the physical realization of the application architecture. Certain application types provide different sources of risk, and by studying their attributes, one can find promising ways to avert these risks when they are encountered.

4.1   What is an Application?

The term "application" is another one of *those* words that the members of the marketing community within the computer field love to overuse, and thus any semblance to its original meaning has disappeared. About 15 years ago, the meaning of an application was that of a program which is created to solve a specific problem and produces specific reports or updates specific files.[1] The current meaning of application, because of the shift to the creation of systems, rather than programs, is now so confused, or better yet, so subtle, that it's to a point of almost being sublime. This of course allows the term to be defined by the marketeer to fit into whatever customer sales circumstance is encountered, usually in order to discourage everyone outside (and sometimes inside) the industry from asking too many hard questions. Let's illustrate what we mean by way of an example.

Let us consider military Command and Control applications (C^2), for a starter. Literally thousands of people across the United States are involved in C^2 application developments, making it, naturally enough, one of the most talked about subjects in the industry.[2] So much has been written on Command and Control that after all this communication, no one really knows what it actually entails.[3] In the political field, this is called a "popularization effect." Anyway, this is just grand, of course, because it allows the marketing people for companies bidding on C^2 systems to claim they have the necessary relevant experience. Try proving otherwise!

After all, there is no unifying theory of C^2 applications, let alone a definition. Each military service formulates the theory differently, and there is frequently not even an agreement within a single military service as to what constitutes C^2 application characteristics above a very rudimentary level. The only consensus opinions that have been reached and seem semi-noncontroversial are: (a) the military is involved, somewhere in the process; (b) there is some degree of decentralization of the information processing occurring somewhere within the application, which implies connectivity of a kind exists; (c) there is a time-critical requirement involved, implying that certain information has more value than others; and (d) the information produced or gathered is related to a set of decision-making processes for one purpose or another, which may or may not include weapon systems. Beyond those rather equivocal attributes, one gets into very heated discussions. And to some, even those are too unequivocal. A case in point are some of the new London taxi companies' radio control systems which, when you examine the new computer consoles appearing in taxis which provide next-fare information, time to destination, optimal routing to the fare, and fare journey and price, look suspiciously like command and control systems to me. Throw in a few extraneous letters to get C^3, C^2I, or C^4, and the arguments get even more vociferous.[4] It makes rational conversation inquiring about, for instance, "What are the unique risks involved in Navy C^2 applications, as opposed to say, Air Force C^2 applications?" unlikely, if not impossible.

The confusion prevalent in C^2 applications is not unique, by any stretch of the imagination. Endeavor to distinguish among the software applications which are marketed "specifically" for banking, finance, and business applications, for example. Unfortunately, this confusion is a major impediment to the risk analyst. If you cannot talk about applications in some logical manner, risk engineering is going to be difficult to apply very effectively in a systematic manner. To understand why there is this seeming difficulty in defining the term application, let's examine some prior attempts at application classification.

4.1.1 Application classification

In the early years of computing, there existed basically two classes of applications: business and scientific. The essential differences between the two were that scientific applications involved substantial arithmetic operations on rather small volumes of data, whereas business applications involved modest amounts of arithmetic operations on substantial amounts of data.[5] Another difference was the speed and type of the transactions required by both. For the scientific applications, the internal processing speed of the Central Processing Unit (CPU) was crucial, while in business applications, it was the Input and Output (I/O) speed and versatility that were critical. With the spread of computing, the categorizations of scientific and business applications became blurred as: (a) applications became increasingly categorized by the type of business-sector organization using it (e.g., banking, manufacturing, etc.); (b) generic functions were developed to be used across sectors (i.e., "application packages" for budgeting, payroll, etc.); and (c) changing business requirements necessitated more and more CPU speed, while changing scientific requirements necessitated more and more I/O speed. Using one or more of these three factors as a key definitional parameter seems to be the current fashion in the attempts to categorization of applications.

Take, for example, the Defense Science Board's (DSB) classification approach. The DSB "solved" the problem of specific application classification very neatly. They ignored it. Instead, the DSB changed the problem into one of classifying software systems instead. From their perspective, they saw the commercial market developing generic, functional packages, which could be used across different knowledge domains. This appeared to indicate that most functions in a specific application domain were non-unique. Thus, instead of trying to specify the unique attributes, it was easier to define the non-unique ones. The DSB postulated that software systems, regardless of their knowledge domain, therefore fit into one of four classes, depending on their "uniqueness and novelty."[6] Using the DSB's scheme, software systems are defined as being one of the following:

- *Standard*: Off-the-shelf (OTS), commercially available.
- *Extended*: Extensions of current systems, DoD and commercial.
- *Embedded*: Functionally unique and embedded in larger systems.
- *Advanced*: Advanced and exploratory systems.

Table 4.1 provides some attributes of each of these classes. As one can see, the characteristics of a system class are a bit intermixed. "Date and place of birth" of the software seems to be the most important distinguishing "unique and novel" attribute one needs to be concerned about.

To try to make the classes a bit more distinctive, the DSB suggested that the size of the software system be another discriminator. The size criteria against which a software system can be measured are defined as being:

- *Modest*: Under 2K lines of source code.
- *Small*: 2–10K lines of source code.
- *Medium*: 10–100K lines of source code.
- *Large*: 100K+ lines of source code.

TABLE 4.1 Defense Science Board Classification Scheme

Standard
Commercial Hardware
Commercially Available Operating System
Commercially Available Application System
Fully Reusable
 - Specification
 - Documentation
 - Code

Extended
Commercial Hardware
Commercial Available Operating System
Commercially Available Software and Custom Extensions
Reusable
 - Specifications
 - Algorithms
 - Source Code
 - Object Code
Some Use of a Prototyping Facility

Embedded
Commercial and Special-Purpose Hardware
Commercial and Special-Purpose Operating System
Special-Purpose Application Software
Reusable
 - Specifications
 - Designs
 - Algorithms
 - Code
Use of a Prototyping Facility
Risk Management Discipline
Heavy User Involvement in Evolutionary Acquisition

Advanced
State-of-the-Art and Uniquely Designed Hardware
Uniquely Designed Software

The definition of "large," in contrast to the others, is very interesting to note. There is a recognition that there are differences in complexity between 10,000 and 100,000 lines of source code, but not between 100,000 and 500,000 lines of source code, or between 100,000 and 2,000,000 lines of source code. Complexity doesn't seem to be a "unique and novel" factor after a certain size of application.

These 16 permutations were recommended as guidance to acquisition policy in the Department of Defense. Each program manager would classify their system, its subsystems, major components, major increments, and phases into one of these 16 classes, with the manager shouldering the *burden of proof* to illustrate why the element should be in a higher class, instead of a lower one.[7] The DSB's aim was to try to "incentivize" DoD programs to adopt more OTS and reusable components, rather than trying to build their own, unique components all the time. Of course, without having a clearinghouse of information to help determine which OTS or reusable components are available or a cross-reference to an application domain of interest (which requires an application knowledge domain classification scheme), it is likely that program managers will have a little trouble following through with the intended purpose of the recommendation. Although a clearinghouse of information was also recommended by the DSB, its focus was to be on an application's individual module's (25–50 lines of code) level, which is of no real use for a risk analyst in trying to determine application area risks. Although this classification approach may solve the DSB's concerns, unfortunately, it doesn't help us very much.

Luckily, the Association for Computer Machinery (ACM) has tackled the application classification scheme problem head-on, but for a different purpose than the DSB's. The ACM, in 1982, developed an application classification scheme for its reviewers to use in writing critiques on articles and books appearing in the computing literature.[8] These critiques appear monthly in the journal *Computing Reviews*. The ACM classification scheme is depicted in Table 4.2.

As one can see when reviewing Table 4.2, there are seven general, and two catch-all, application areas of interest, as well as numerous specific topics under each. Each topic is defined according to a subject area, such as government, law, medical, and so forth. The ACM classification scheme reflects a definition of applications according to their organizational use, as opposed to their implicit architecture or size, as was present in the DSB scheme. One quickly notices, however, that a specific application can be mapped into several topics, such as a military real-time command and control application. This again points out the blurring of the twofold taxonomy present in early computing.

Unfortunately, neither the ACM scheme nor the DSB approach aids the risk analyst that much as they currently stand. Merging the two gives a picture of the application, but not a very clear one. We need general attributes, like those presented in the C^2 example earlier, where an attribute such as decentralization implied distribution. One can at least then look for risks that are inherent in distribution of elements or functions, and say something about how to avert the risks involved.

TABLE 4.2 ACM Application Classification Scheme

---

1. General

2. Administrative Data Processing

Business	Education
Financial	Government
Law	Manufacturing
Marketing	Military

3. Physical Sciences and Engineering

Aerospace	Astronomy
Chemistry	Earth and Atmospheric Sciences
Electronics	Engineering
Physics	Mathematics and Statistics

4. Life and Medical Sciences

Biology	Medical Information Systems
Health	

5. Social and Behavioral Sciences

Economics	Psychology
Sociology	

6. Arts and Humanities

Music	Language Translation
Literature	Linguistics
Fine Arts	Performing Arts

7. Computer-aided Engineering

Computer-aided Design
Computer-aided Manufacturing

8. Computers in Other Systems

Military	Command and Control
Publishing	Consumer Products
Real Time	Industrial Control
Process Control	

9. Miscellaneous

However, the two classification schemes above, although representing extremes of one another, do indicate a possible path that may help us out of our dilemma. What seems clear, from reviewing both of them, is that there exists a differentiation among applications, based upon the domain of knowledge, the logical architecture of operations, and the physical architecture executing the application. Therefore, it is possible to list some general attributes of an application which can help us from a risk perspective.

4.1.2 Application attributes

What is it that one can say about an application, given what we know so far? First, one can state that an application has a specific "use" associated with it. In other words, there is some *purpose* in its creation. This is good, as all applications should meet some need. Thus, there is some intent in its use. Second, one can state that there is a *domain of knowledge*, and a *process* used to manipulate that knowledge, which is also part of an application. This follows, if there is some purpose to the application. This process is a logical, or abstract, description of how the specific domain knowledge is manipulated to achieve some purpose. If there were not a process associated with an application domain, or a purpose, then one could never automate it. Third, this process, however it is defined, must have some inherent elements that can be captured in a *structure or organization*, based upon a sequencing of internally and externally driven events. (This is similar to the definition of a system provided in Chapter 2.) Therefore, a process implies that an abstract architecture exists. Given that there is an architecture, one can assume that one can compare it to some other architecture defined by another application process. But even more than that, if an application has an abstract architecture, it *may* also have a physical instantiation of that architecture.

For this book, then, we will state that an application has a process part, an architecture part, and a physical instantiation called an *application realization* (i.e., a system). We will further define an application architecture as being its conceptual structure and functional behavior, which is distinct from its physical instantiation. The physical instantiation of an application architecture is technology dependent; i.e., an application architecture may be physically implemented in many different ways, just as a unique computer architecture can be physically implemented using CMOS or NMOS. An architecture, then, is the bridge used between the process defined within, and by, the application knowledge domain and its physical realization.[9] Do not mistake either the process or the physical realization with what we are describing as the application architecture. They are each separate and distinct in their own right. Furthermore, an application architecture can be considered as the union of a logical software architecture and a logical hardware architecture, but *not* by the union of their physical realizations. The physical realization of an application architecture, which implements a knowledge domain's process, we will hereby define as constituting *the application*.

Moreover, in this chapter, we wish to make a distinction among programs, applications, and application systems. *Programs*, following Wirth,[10] are made up of data structures and algorithms. Programs by themselves, therefore, are not considered applications. It is true that there is a domain of knowledge involved, and there exists a specific process involved, but a physical instantiation does not exist.[11] The risks involved in program construction, and their aversion, are part of the implementation process discussed in Chapter 3.

Programs, bound with their execution environments (i.e., execution/ run-time support), together with the hardware in which they execute, we will also consider as defining *the application*. The importance of the run-time support programs should not be overlooked, because they provide the glue between the program and the physical computing hardware. Hardware is useless without software, software is useless without hardware, and the execution environment controls the emergence or synergistic process between the two. Although run-time programs are arguably applications in themselves, since they do not serve any "purpose" without another program existing, we consider them as becoming "part and parcel" of the application process itself during execution.[12]

Multiple applications, together with the hardware they execute on, we will state as defining an *application system*. C[2] systems are thus considered application systems under this classification schema. Application systems may share physical resources (e.g., use of embedded computers or multiprocessors), but each has its own unique abstract architecture. The type of application system will be defined by the genre of applications that execute as part of it, and the genre of applications are those that meet, as a minimum, the categories as defined in Table 4.2.

4.1.3 Classification importance to risk analysis

As can be readily observed, application classification is like mud-wrestling. At the beginning, everyone starts off clean, but by the time one is through, it is hard to distinguish yourself from the other contestants. This can be seen by reexamining Figure 2.3, which illustrates the overlapping generic knowledge domains required in the construction of an application system.

We know instinctively that certain types of applications are harder to develop than others. But why is this true? Do the risks reside in the application domain knowledge alone, or is there something else? How much is the application architecture constrained by the application domain process? How does one determine the risks in an application system, where many specific application domains and application architectures overlap? What are the risks associated with the intersection of different application domains and architectures? And how does one take into account the risks presented by the physical realization of an application architecture?

We do not pretend to have any definitive answers to the questions above. But by using the assumptions and definitions of applications made previously, we can look for sources of risk in either the application process, its architecture, and/or its physical instantiation. Again, the basic approach we will use is to look for the basic causes of risk in each that are associated with the lack of information, the lack of time, or the lack of control (i.e., the three root causes of risk). However, to attempt to accomplish this for all three possible sources of risk for any application is beyond our present scope of knowledge.

First, the number of different types of applications is limited only by the limitations of human creativity. Therefore, there exists an unlimited number of application processes. Even trying to limit it to the seven general ACM categories would be difficult to accomplish. For a particular application, however, the analyst can look for fundamental limitations of knowledge, and see where the risks may accrue.[13] For whatever application process is being automated, the risk analyst should not only be well versed in the knowledge domain of interest, but also in the limitations of knowledge about the domain. These limitations, and thus risks, are often viewed only indirectly, in the form of a lack of skill among the developers, but often it exists in the knowledge domain itself. These limitations are of major concern in trying to determine a system's risk referent. For example, trying to automate an application process where the basic knowledge domain is weak implies a high level of risk. No matter how flawless the hardware is, or the software engineering process, if the application knowledge is missing, then the ultimate system delivered will likely be a failure.

Second, the variations in physical instantiations of an application architecture are also too great to analyze effectively—the different ways that a Digital VAX or an IBM AS400 can be configured number in the dozens, if not hundreds. For an application system, the number of physical realizations are almost limitless. But again, the risk analyst can examine risks of a specific realization when it is proposed.[14]

In general, the risks associated with either the most general source of risk (i.e., the application process) or the most specific (i.e., the physical realization) are peculiar to the specific circumstances of a software enterprise. However, before one despairs about being able to say anything about application risks, the risks associated with the application architectures can be identified, estimated, and analyzed. And this is what we will begin to do in the next section.

4.2 Application Architectures

The virtually limitless physical instantiations of application architectures normally lead to the selection of one, which may not be the optimal or near-optimal one that is possible to select. To try to reduce this possibility, we intend in this section to explore the sources of risks that lie within application architectures. To achieve this goal, we are going to concentrate on the topology of the application architectures. This is admittedly more of a qualitative approach than quantitative, but a topological approach at least allows one to say, "If we do not know all the measurements (of an application architecture), at least we can say something about its overall structure."[15]

The topological model, which will be used to explore the risks in application architectures, is based upon the results of the distributed processing research work of Philip Enslow, published in 1978.[16] Enslow was interested in trying to characterize the range and domain of distributed architecture systems, to show what was, and was not, included in distributed data processing systems. Then, as now, the term distributed data processing system was being overused, and there was a need to bring some order to the chaos surrounding the subject. By so doing, however, Enslow also was able (perhaps without realizing it) to characterize the range and domain of application architectures in a manner that is very suitable for risk analysis.

Enslow based his topological map of distributed data processing systems on a cube, which is illustrated in Figure 4.1. The axes of the cube indicate decentralization among three key attributes of distributed architectures: the hardware architecture, the execution control, and the database (i.e., files and directories) organization. The degree of

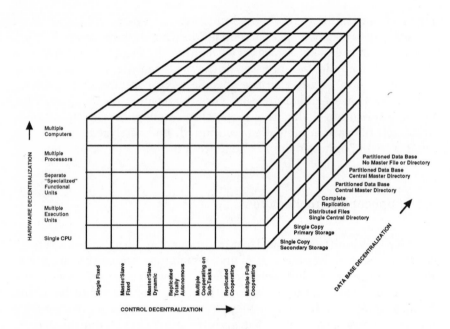

Figure 4.1 Enslow's Application Architectures

decentralization is shown by an axis that embarks from a position of fully centralized and increasingly ranges to fully decentralized. For example, the cube which can be formed on the far left of the diagram depicts a single computer, having a single CPU, with a single copy of the program or task in secondary storage, executing under a single, fixed control architecture. Similarly, one can formulate a cube which defines an architecture that uses multiple heterogeneous processors fully cooperating on the execution of the task, has multiple control points, and utilizes a partitioned database, with no master file or directory (i.e., no single source of information as to the location of a specific file).

It should be obvious that the partitions shown are examples of the decentralization. One can easily expand the degree of decentralized granularity shown, if one so desires. The important point to be taken away is that the risks in the application architecture domain can begin to be qualified. In general, one can state that the greater the decentralization, the greater the risk due to the complexity of the distribution of the architecture's resources. The risks are linked to the complexity of each distribution selected, as well as the totality of the

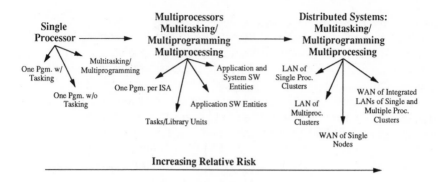

Figure 4.2 Relative Risks of Different Application Architectures

complexity in each dimension. One should hasten to add that these are relative risks, and there is no definitive way of determining (yet) the relative severity of the decentralized risks in an axis in relation to the other two. But, based upon experience, it is less risky to build an application that demands only a single CPU than one that demands a multiple computer architecture utilizing multi-processing. Figure 4.2 illustrates a few other examples.[17]

The word "demands" used at the end of the previous paragraph is one that the risk analyst must continually bear in mind. The greatest problems in evaluating the risks in the application arena will be: (a) whether the application process requires the architecture as specified, or instead demands another; and (b) at what point, based upon changes in application requirements, does one cross from one "cube's domain" into another.[18] Much of the information required to determine the trigger points for changing, will be based upon the original granularity of the decentralization parameters used to characterize the application architectures. Above a certain level of granularity, one may not be able to tell that a change is necessary. Thus, the degree of resolution about a risk may not be fine enough. Again, the analyst will be required to make a decision based upon his or her experience, analysis, and gut reaction.

Each cube, in a sense, represents a system risk referent level, as well as a single-point risk referent, for an application architecture. At a system level, the application process must be evaluated against this referent to determine if it can be satisfied by the specific architecture. But also notice, there may be many architectures that satisfy the particular process requirement. For example, the grey area shown on Figure 4.3 is the region allowable for distributed data processing, as defined by Enslow.[19] Therefore, each cube representing a particular application architecture must be evaluated against each of the feasible others for the risks that they each inherently possess.

One may ask the question, "Why use these dimensions, and not some others, and just what are some of the risks inherent in and along these axes?" To answer the second part first, we will examine some of the risks in each of the dimensions in the next three subsections. The answer to the first part is twofold. One, this taxonomy is easy to use, the identification and evaluation of the risks in each of the dimensions have over 10 years of detailed study behind them, and most importantly, each dimension corresponds nicely to the three basic causes of risk. The lack of time is related to the hardware architecture axis, the lack of control to the control axis, and the lack of information to the database axis.

Notice something else: The increase in decentralization along each axis was made in response to existing shortfalls in an application architecture to meet the demand of the application process. These responses were, in fact, risk aversion responses. But the net effect was

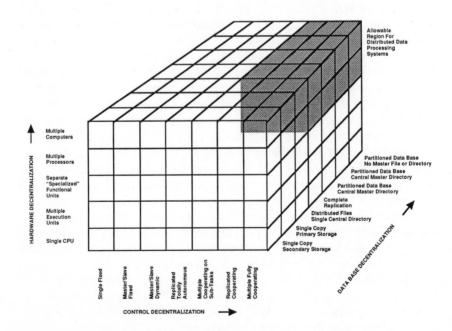

Figure 4.3 Application Architectures with Distributed Processing Possibilities Illustrated

also an increasing of risk in some other dimensions as well. The combination of shifting along multiple dimensions simultaneously, in many circumstances, increased the overall risk several times more than the aversion strategy reduced the original risks. This is a prime example of: (a) how risk and opportunity are mirror-like images of one another; (b) the scaling issue (i.e., it is easier to scale down, than up) we encountered earlier in Chapter 2; and (c) the subjective nature of risk. Item (c) is important. As more experience has been gained, application architectures that were once considered very risky are not nearly considered that way any more. The new risks appearing in application architectures today are created by the expansion of the range in each of the axes, and from being able to define and create finer levels of granularity within the existing categories. Taking smaller steps along one axis limits the amount of risk having to be chewed on at once.

Refer again to the illustration in Figure 4.2. The granularity of the distribution (entities, relationships, temporal attributes, spatial attributes, etc.) is a pervasive concern shaping the perceptions of both the issues and approaches used to implement applications, and therefore the risks involved.[20] How effectively one can map from the application architecture granularity to a physical realization, and vice versa, is important to the actual risk possibilities present. The combination of expansion and increased granularity means there has been a major increase in the number of application architectures, as well as in the resulting risk of selecting the wrong one for the application process being automated.[21]

As we have mentioned, the types of risks involved in each dimension of our topological map have been researched extensively in the distributed processing research, database, and operating system communities, and to try to detail them in any depth is beyond the space available here. What we will provide over the next three sections are some major risk areas that the software engineering risk analyst should at least be aware of and can use as a bootstrap to identify the risks that may confront his or her software enterprise. However, the literature in these fields should be thoroughly investigated for up-to-date information.

4.2.1 Computing architecture decentralization

The first aspect we wish to examine is the axis concerning the decentralization available within hardware architectures. The level of granularity specified in Figure 4.3 basically depicts two degrees of granularity. First, there is a single computer, with various architectural aspects to it (i.e., fine granularity), and then a second general category identified as "multiple computers" (i.e., coarse granularity). For the risk analyst to conduct risk analysis in an effective manner, one needs to examine the effects and implications of these two degrees of architectural granularity in closer detail. Let's start with the finer granularity aspects first.

Computer architectures have traditionally been divided into four classes, based on work by Michael Flynn.[22,23] These four classes are based upon how the instruction streams and data streams can be replicated to perform useful work. The classes are termed SISD, SIMD, MISD, and MIMD, where the letters "SI" stand for single-instruction stream; "MI," multiple-instruction stream; "SD," single-data stream; and "MD," multiple-data stream. The SISD defines serial architectures, while the remainder are part of the family called parallel architectures. These four basic classes of architectures are shown in Figure 4.4.

SISD (single-instruction, single-data steam) architectures denote the family of serial computers; i.e., the classic von Neumann machine that

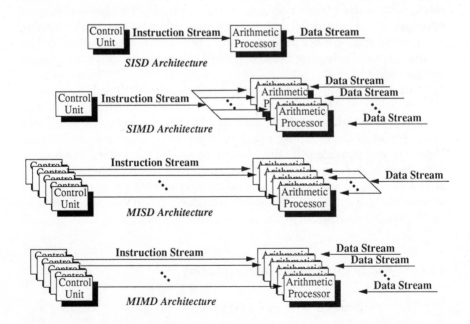

Figure 4.4 Computer Architectures

most people are familiar with. The SIMD (single-instruction, multiple-data) architectures represent a subset of the family of parallel computers termed vector-based architectures. SIMD architectures include array, pipelined, and data-flow (reduction) machines, too. In this architecture, there is a single instruction simultaneously operating on a vector of data, instead of on just a single operand. Each vector element is executed on a different arithmetic processor. MISD (multiple-instruction, single-data) architectures have, on the other hand, each operand operated on simultaneously by several instructions. This case is usually only of academic interest, since it has no real practical use that anyone has come up with. The final architecture is the MIMD (multiple-instruction, multiple-data). MIMD architectures are commonly called multiprocessors. In these architectures, there are N independent processors, N instruction and data streams, and one data stream per instruction stream. Each processor is a complete computer in its own right, as opposed to the arithmetic processors in the SIMD case. Arithmetic processors have individual memory, but not the control of their own instruction stream.

Each of the architectures are represented in Figure 4.3, although it may not be exactly clear how. For example, multiple "execution units" are related to the arithmetic processors of the type found in a SIMD, while "multiple processors" corresponds to the type found in MIMDs. By combining the appropriate control mechanism and data store available on the other two axes, one can depict each specific class of hardware architecture.

4.2.1.1 Granularity issues. As we mentioned earlier, there are two types of granularity depicted in Figure 4.3: fine granularity and coarse granularity. Granularity, of course, is a subjective term. Flynn's classification of the architectures above can, from one perspective, be considered coarse, because within each classification there are numerous subclasses that represent other types of specialized architectures. We have already mentioned array, vector, pipeline and data-flow as subsets of the SIMD type architecture. Even these in turn have subclassifications. For instance, there are at least three different architectures, which can all be considered as data-flow, but vary architecturally in their interconnections among instruction and data processors, memory hierarchy, and switches. Skillicorn has developed a refinement of the architectural classification scheme of Flynn, arguing that there are really 28 architectural subclasses of the four general classes defined.[24]

Expanding the hardware axis in Figure 4.3 to reflect the 28 possibilities is probably not practical (there are 245 architectures defined by Enslow; the 28 more would make at least 1372 architectures necessary to consider using Skillicorn's approach), but the risk analyst should be aware that these fine differences do exist, and that each subclass has its own particular set of associated risks.

From a coarse category of granularity, one can view each architecture as being "stand-alone." Thus, each can be tied together by some intercommunication medium called a network to form another set of architectures. These architectures have all been grouped under the "multiple computer" label in Figure 4.3. A few comments about network architectures. Networks are usually dependent upon the requirements of the distribution of functions, data, and control of the application (system). These architectures take many forms (e.g., meshes, rings, trees, cubes, etc.), and may have one class, or many classes, of specific computer architecture as members of it.[25] It is beyond this chapter to investigate these network architectures, the inherent risks involved in their construction, or the different risks created by different network topologies, such as stars, rings, meshes, and so forth. However, you as a software engineering risk analyst should be aware that these other sources of risk do exist and can turn to the references on distributed processing and networks for further, detailed, information.[26-29]

4.2.1.2 Architectural limitations/risks. Each architectural class and subclass is an attempt at balancing conflicting requirements concerning performance, flexibility, functionality and efficiency, among others. But because a myriad of trade-offs exists, each architecture presents some unique opportunity for gain, as well as a source of risk. These risks pose limitations not only on being able to successfully support the technical implementation of an application (system), but also places limits to its cost-effectiveness, timeliness, and/or ability to be evolved. A risk analyst must be aware of at least a few of the major architectural limitations. Granularity comes into play once more here, too.

In SISD architectures, for instance, the most severe problem is the ability to support a wide range of applications efficiently. SISD architectures generally accept sacrifices in their performance range, in order to gain flexibility to support numerous kinds of application processes. However, to adequately understand the flexibility and performance trade-offs, one must proceed to apply a finer level of detail and study the instruction set architectures (ISA) of the different SISDs.

There is a continuing argument over whether complex instruction set computers (CISC) or reduced instruction set computers (RISC) provide the best flexibility/performance trade-offs. There is no agreement on which is better, although for narrow application domains, the RISC architecture seems better than the CISC, but for application system support, CISC seems more appropriate. Thus, the risk analyst must take into account the application process, the number of different processes to be supported, and the realization of the architecture in its physical form to fully comprehend the possible limitations in SISDs.

Parallel architectures are meant to overcome the risks that the limitation of performance in SISD architectures present. However, this increase in performance is accomplished at the expense of the flexibility to support a wide variety of application processes. Additionally, the increased performance includes another price and risk of its own making. The risks, in this case, center more around the limitations imposed by the distribution of processors, control, and memory. The efficiency of the distribution and redistribution of information among the different architectural components is a key to the risks involved. What this means is that the application must be partitioned, in some way, to make effective use of the distribution of resources and control. For instance, in architectures with shared memory, updating of memory can present a major risk to data integrity. This occurs if more than one processor or arithmetic unit wishes to utilize and change the identical set of data residing in memory. Parallel architectures having their own private memory which cannot be read or written to by any other processor do not pose this risk. But for lowering the risk of data corruption, parallel architectures generally trade off opportunities for performance increases, thus possibly posing a different kind risk which the first architecture did not possess.

Other examples abound. SIMD architectures, for instance, have processors which are synchronized, so there do not exist scheduling risks or precedence constraints on task execution that must be considered. SIMD have, in fact, a single *thread of control*. MIMD processors, however, have both scheduling risks and precedence constraint risks but, nevertheless, provide more flexibility than SIMD architectures because they allow multiple threads of control. This added flexibility is gained at an increased cost of control and programming, however. To give you a feel of some of the trade-offs between risks and opportunities, Figure 4.5 illustrates when and where different types of parallel architectures might be useful. On vectorized loops, for example, directed

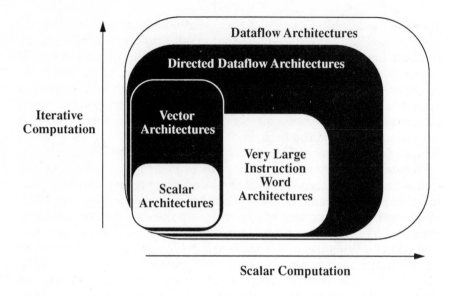

Figure 4.5 Relationship Between Various Single Processor Architectures

data-flow architectures are slightly better than the vector architectures, which are in turn better than Very Large Instruction Word (VLIW) architectures, which are better than scalar architectures. On sequentially coded programs, directed data-flow architectures are at least as good as VLIW architectures, which are better than both vector and scalar architectures. On nonvectorized loops in a program, directed data-flow is significantly better than any of these other architectures.

The risk analyst must be aware that the usefulness of any type of architecture will ultimately be determined by how well the fundamental processes of the application can be mapped onto it. Certain application processes can be partitioned and mapped better to SISD architectures than MIMDs, or to an SIMD better than a SISD. The efficiency, not only the effectiveness, of the mapping is also critical. An evaluation of the algorithms used to define the processes is often necessary to determine this. For example, it has been shown that a single processor executing an efficient application process algorithm can outperform 64,000 processors executing inefficiently in parallel.[30]

Parallel speed-ups are limited by Amdahl's Law, which states that parallelism is limited by the execution of the sequential part of an algorithm. Amdahl's law points out a few other problems with trying to apply parallelism as well, especially in the mapping of application to architecture. First, there are currently no software design paradigms that exist exclusively for parallel architectures. The design paradigms used today are the same as for sequential applications, which are being found to be of limited value. Second, development processes for parallel application systems also do not fit nicely into current life-cycle models. The processes discussed in Chapter 3, for example, all assumed an underlying sequential application was being built. However, certain phases, such as testing, require more thought and planning since there are so many more ways to fail. Third, because of the lack of support tools, the designer and application programmer must know much more about the detailed workings of the architecture itself. Current sequential processor architectural design is almost irrelevant, as the translation process of code to machine is transparent. This is not yet so in parallel systems. Finally, humans do not consciously think in parallel, and thus the mappings of application to architecture will be inherently more difficult to do. This is important, as very few individuals (only about one person out of three) have an instinctive ability for applying spatial visualization often required to program these types of architectures.

The risk analyst needs to consult the references for a small sample of information available on architectural risks.[31-37]

4.2.1.3 Architecture realization risks. Before we end this section on architectural risks, we would like to spend a short time on one other risk consideration, which concerns the physical realization of the architectures above. These risks are the technology dependent risks and involve the price per bit, the general performance such as millions of instructions per sec (MIPs), the amount of memory available, the number and speed of the I/O channels, and so forth. Therefore, one of the prime risk drivers in an application is that its execution performance is geared to the fundamental time/space trade-offs made in the architectural design and implemented in the design's realization. Additionally, the risk driver on performance in implementing the application in a software enterprise is linked to cost, (i.e., the bang for the buck). Since the 1940s, the price/performance ratio of a computer architecture's implementation has been a major factor in deciding which computer architecture realization is to be used. Currently, the definition of this ratio, more so than the inherent risks in an architecture, presents the analyst with possibly a major source of risk, especially when a dogmatic Hardware First approach to software system design is used. Let us try to explain.

In the 1950s, a hypothesis, called Grosch's Law, stated that the cost of computer systems increased at a rate equivalent to the square root of their power.[38] Another way of saying it is that the average cost of computing decreases as the square root of its power. This is an economy-of-scale argument, which says a computer with four times the power of that which you currently own should only cost twice as much. Power has been defined in many ways, but in general, it is the ability of a computer architectural realization to execute a given program within a given time.[39] Over the past 40 years, this hypothesis seems to have held true, and has been a predictor of what type of computer should be used to implement an application or application system. By type, we mean here the generally accepted market classification of computer realizations, rather than architectural classification presented earlier. These types are supercomputers, large mainframes, small mainframes, minicomputers, and microcomputers. Table 4.3 illustrates the current market definitions of these classes.[40]

However, with the increasing number of different realizations of the types and kinds of computers, the networking of computers, the continued price decline in computers, and the increased power across all classes of computers (as shown in Figure 4.6), etc., Grosch's Law, as defined, has become suspect. A risk analyst must be aware of this, because in most software enterprises, a dogmatic Hardware First syndrome is at work. In other words, the physical computer or network will have been chosen or designed first, before the software requirements have been fully defined or even generally understood. In a strict Hardware First approach, software usually will have to be shoehorned in later, being constrained a priori by the physical system constraints and limitations.[41] The fact of

TABLE 4.3 Computer Classification

Category	Price Range (in $1000)	MIPS
Super Computers	3000+	5 < MIPS
Large Mainframes	600–3000	1 < MIPS < 5
Small Mainframes	100–600	MIPS < 1
Minicomputers	20–100	MIPS < 1
Microcomputers	2–20	MIPS < 1

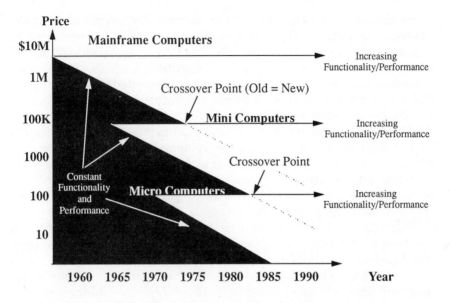

Figure 4.6 Comparison of Functionality, Performance, and Cost

the matter is, the selection of the hardware in these circumstances will most often be based upon Grosch's Law. Thus, any change in it will have significant risk implications to the analyst.

Luckily(?), it has been shown that Grosch's Law still holds true, but not across all classes of computers as it once did.[42] Instead, it holds within each class of computer, as defined in Table 4.3. Thus, a revised Grosch's Law now states, it is most effective to accomplish any task on the least powerful type of computer capable of performing it. The tendency to decentralize and distribute computing power is an indication of the practical application of Grosch's Law. But it also means the most powerful computer in that class is still the most advantageous, although between 1981 and 1985, there seemed not to be any economies of scale for mainframes and superminis.[43] Other implications are that one powerful microprocessor is better than two less powerful micros, but many micros are better than one minicomputer of equivalent power.

Implementation of Grosch's Law must be tempered by the fact that there are important factors working against decentralization, too. Communication costs increase, decentralization of control and data makes implementation more difficult and time-consuming, and the reliability of the total system may not be as high as intuitively envisioned.

Therefore, some combination of computers with varying power will most likely be the optimal physical realization for implementing a specific application process. For the risk analyst, then, the considerations of inherent architectural risks, relative architectural power, and actual realization power via Grosch's Law must be accounted for to accomplish effective risk analysis. This also means that future hardware possibilities should be considered very early in the requirements phase of the development. For example, it is much easier to meet certain application performance risks, and reduce other development risks, using a computer which has 10 MIPs vs. 2 MIPs, or that has 10 times the memory, I/O channels, and so forth. Differences such as these allow one to take a brute force approach, which is often easier than trying to finesse the application into a constrained physical realization.

What additionally must be taken into account are the nonfunctional and functional requirements involved and the criteria of success during development as well as during evolution. Again, if the project is long-lived, then the application will likely need to execute on new hardware, and the future risk impacts can be reduced if this possibility is treated early in the development process. As shown in Figure 4.7, all these

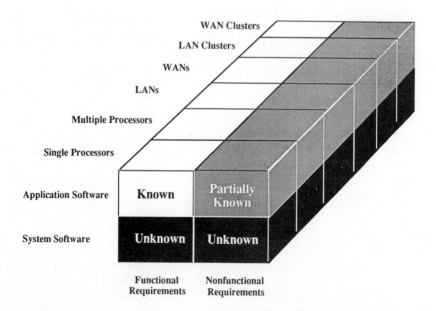

Figure 4.7 Functional and Nonfunctional Requirements Across Architectures

considerations span all the combinations of application and support software, as well as physical architectures.

4.2.2 Database decentralization

The second aspect of decentralization we wish to examine is database decentralization.[44-46] At the highest level of abstraction, a database is just a repository of information with mechanisms for data access and deposit. However, as we saw in the section concerning the decentralization of processing, the decentralization of information is a major opportunity as well as a major source of risk. Either, or both, information or the directories can be decentralized, although some combinations of the range of possibilities make less sense than others. In any case, for whatever degree of decentralization that exists, there must be support for data transparency (i.e., data may be geographically distributed, and move place to place, but it appears upon access that data is all at one location), replication transparency (i.e., data may be replicated in several locations, but it is treated as if only one copy exists), and access transparency (i.e., data may be geographically distributed and replicated, but access to it is treated as if it was located locally and only one copy existed).

For instance, the types of decentralization of directories that can exist include a centralized directory, where a single master directory is kept at one location, and all accesses for data are served by this directory. Included are also multiple master directories, where a master directory is located in a cluster of processor nodes and serves the cluster. There also may exist local file directories, where no master directory appears at all, or at the other extreme, fully replicated master directories, where a master directory resides at every processor node. As we have stated, each case presents opportunities, as well as risks, that the analyst should consider. For example, full replication of master directories presents an opportunity for achieving increased response time, but at the risk of increased communication cost.

Similarly, the decentralization of data provides opportunities to access information faster by retaining nearby local copies of data that are used the most often. On the risk downside, the multiplicity of copies of data incurs a risk when information is required by some other database. The time it takes to send the information may mean that it is out of date upon arrival, or if an error occurs in transmission, corrupted data can flood the system. Multiple copies of data also means that deadlock might occur, as simultaneous access to information may not be able to be honored.

4.2.2.1 Database limitations/risks. The information that resides in the database is normally contained in an abstraction termed a record or relation. A record is an entity of a certain type. Relationships are formed between records, which indicate how records can interact with one another. A collection of records, their relationships, and the rules to access and update records is considered as defining a database. The different ways records can interact and be accessed and updated form distinct database architectures. There are basically four database architectures that are recognized as existing.[47,48] These are, in increasing complexity, *hierarchical, network, relational,* and *object.*

In hierarchical database architectures, each record type may be involved in only one relationship as a subordinate. This forms a "tree"-like structure or hierarchy. In other words, each record in the hierarchy (except for the top) is associated to a single record in the next level of the hierarchy.

In network database architectures, the hierarchical structure is loosened to allow for unlimited relationships between records. A single record may be a subordinate to 4, 40, or 400 records. In both hierarchical and network architectures, a pointer is used to depict the direction (i.e., who is the subordinate) in the relationship between records. This is not true in relational database architectures.

In relational database architectures, the same relations defined within network databases are possible, but data is now viewed as an extension of a table. A relationship between two record types is expressed implicitly, by means of having a data item in each record type take its values from a common domain of values. This allows various associations between record types to be made. Furthermore, the items (or items) of one record type must serve as a unique primary key for the record type.[49] The lack of pointers in a relational architecture allows for dynamic creation of new data items and more flexibility in accessing information.

Object-based architectures combine aspects of relational architectures and network architectures. An object is an instantiation of a data abstraction which contains a collection of data and the set of operations that are defined upon them.[50] This means that objects are defined and characterized by a set of invariant properties that define an object and its behavior within the context of defined parameters.[51] Relationships are defined among objects as an intrinsic part of its identity. Object-based architectures allow for the inheritance of relationships and operations. New object types can be created from old types, allowing existing properties and operations to be redefined and reused.

The risk analyst must be careful how the distribution of data matches with the decentralization of processing and control. The various combinations provide a number of risks which are almost unique. Figure 4.8 illustrates where the different architectural types most closely match needs, not only in the type of data item support required, but also in the types of applications they are useful to support.[52] The differences in architectural applicability depend greatly upon whether there is a need for (1) dynamic access and updating of information, (2) high-volume prespecified access and updating of information,[53] and/or (3) decentralization of information.

Network and hierarchical database architectures are basically equivalent in capability, are good for high-volume prespecified access, but are poor for use in dynamic updating, and decentralized, situations. The major penalties are in performance and ability to recover from failure. Relational database architectures are good for dynamic updates and are better than hierarchical or network for decentralization, although penalties in the performance can be expected. Relational architectures are poor for high-volume prespecified access and updating of information.

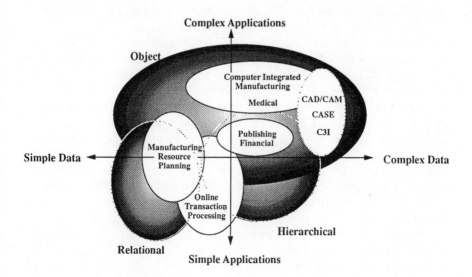

Figure 4.8 Different Types of Databases and Sample Applications

Object databases are good for all three cases, although this should be tempered with the knowledge that there are few commercial object databases currently available.[54]

4.2.3 Decentralized control

The final aspect of decentralization we wish to examine is that of decentralized control. Control revolves around the efficient management of the architectures' processors, data storage, devices, and information. This management involves the controlled sharing and enforced separation of resources.[55] Decentralized control is concerned with where, when, and how this control originates.

Obviously, the amount and type of decentralized control is directly tied into the degree of decentralization inherent in the processing architecture, combined with that present in the data store. For example, SISD architectures typically utilize centralized control procedures, whereas MIMD use partially decentralized control, while networks utilize fully decentralized control. Thus, a risk analyst will be required to examine the specific application architecture to ferret out the specific risks created by the control schema used. But, in general, the risks associated with increasing levels of decentralized control revolve around the issues of coordination and cooperation of the distributed control functions. That is, how can the processors, data store, devices, and information be coordinated effectively to efficiently and accurately perform the requirements demanded by the application (system) processes? The greater the distribution, the greater the requirement for unification and integration of control of all the distributed resources.

In systems utilizing centralized control, there is premise that all the execution processes (and data) share a coherent and deterministic view of the entire system state. There are also problems of virtual memory management, information update, resource deadlock, interrupt and context switching, etc., that plague any centralized or partially decentralized operating system which must be addressed. These increase if multitasking or multiprogramming is used. For a full description of the risk issues raised by the various trade-offs made in the utilization of centralized control, the risk analyst need only turn to any standard reference on operating systems.[56]

However, as control becomes distributed, the problems exhibited in the centralized situation multiply. The more decentralized the control becomes, the more the system view becomes increasingly less coherent, and less deterministic. There no longer exist globally shared variables, nor synchronous control. Asynchronous operations imply, among other things, that instructions have to be sequenced correctly, data has to be routed to different processors, data shared can change value at any time, arbitration among simultaneous requests must be sorted, error recovery must be possible, and livelock controlled. This is in conjunction with the normal functions of a centralized control operation. The risks which confront the risk analyst when decentralized control is present could fill a book.[57]

4.2.4 Summary

In this section, we have defined application risks in terms of the application architecture. This was done in order to allow the risk analyst the capability to evaluate risks within and across application domains, which prove too difficult to accomplish if the analysis concentrated on either the domain knowledge or application realization itself. The key aspects are that the architectural approach allows for a technologically independent perspective of risk and allows one to operate at different levels of granularity to investigate risks.

It should be clear that risk analysis evaluation techniques such as queueing models, simulations, etc., can also be used to evaluate and gain more insight to the risks inherent in application architectures, and should be made use of, if feasible.[58] Identifying, estimating, and evaluating application risks will prove to be the most difficult for the risk analyst, and much of the quality of the risk analyst's recommendations for risk aversion, will be based upon his or her experience, rather than qualitative analysis.

4.3 Application Risk Issues—Some Areas of Concern

So far, we have investigated the risks that are associated with application architectures, but we have deliberately strayed away, for the most part, from trying to examine the risks involved with the application processes or architectural realizations. But because of this, we have skipped over a number of issues associated with the characteristics that involve not only the application architectures, but the application processes. These characteristics do not fit neatly into the business or system engineering environments, the software engineering enterprise process, or even the product itself. (We will discuss why in a moment.) What we are talking about are the risks due to the complexity, size, time-criticality, dynamic execution environment, fault tolerance, human factors associated with an application, and/or application match to development process.

4.3.1 Complexity and size

Complexity and size risks were examined earlier, but the issue bears another short review. Review again Figure 2.6, which illustrates some different systems and their relative position on a chart depicting interaction complexity and the degree of coupling within the application architecture.[59] As we can see, a number of computerized systems are depicted on the chart, along with noncomputer-intensive systems, such as dams and bridges. Complexity and size in computer systems pose risks that are very difficult to ascertain, let alone evaluate, other than the fact that they exist. Size of a software system is very dependent on the application (systems) being constructed, as is the resulting complexity. But for a risk analyst, this leaves one a bit perplexed. For example, does complexity follow from size, or does size follow from complexity? For instance, an application may be complex but not large in size, but an application that is large in size may be complex. And how does one make trade-offs against complexity and size? And where? Is the trade-off made at the application architectural level, or does it happen before that, in the application process level instead? And how are trade-offs made among different application processes, some of which are in conflict? We don't have the answers, only a great many questions. However, you, as a risk analyst, will need to try to find answers if, for nothing else, size and complexity risks are to be monitored.

An area where there are more answers available to the risk analyst is in algorithmic size and complexity risks. By investigating the various core algorithms involved in an application system, we can at least get a better handle on whether there is a risk involving the type of hardware we have selected as our execution platform. In the algorithmic analysis domain, the size of the problem is represented by some measure of the quantity of the input data and is denoted by the term n. The time (space) complexity of an algorithm is the time (space) required as a function of

n. The limiting behavior as n approaches infinity is called the *asymptotic complexity*. When the time (space) required as a function of n depends on the actual data values as well, we will then be interested in the worst-case, expected (average), and best-case complexities of the algorithm.

To express the time (space) complexity, something called the big "**O**" notation is used. For example, a function $g(n)$ is said to be $O(f(n))$, which is read as **order $f(n)$** if there exists a constant **c** such that $g(n) \leq cf(n)$ for all but some finite (and possibly) empty set of nonnegative values for n. Thus, an algorithm's execution time, or storage requirements, are dominated by the order of the algorithm. For example, consider the following five algorithms having the specified time complexities:

Algorithm	Time Complexity
A_1	n
A_2	$n \log_2 n$
A_3	n^2
A_4	n^3
A_5	2^n

The time complexity is computed as the execution time $t(n)$ in milliseconds. For instance, $t_1(10)$ equals 10 milliseconds for algorithm A_1, whereas $t_2(10)$ equals $10\log_2 10$, or approximately 33 milliseconds, for algorithm A_2.

With the above information, one can illustrate the limits of problem size as determined by the growth rates, as shown in Table 4.4. As one can quickly see, the algorithms with high levels of complexity take much longer to execute. This should come as no surprise, but its implications are rather important. For example, consider Table 4.5, where we show the effects of a 10-fold increase in execution speed on the size of the problems that can be solved in a fixed amount of time. As is obvious, the

TABLE 4.4 Limits on Problem Size Determined by Growth Rate

Algorithm	Maximum Problem Size That Is Solvable		
	1 second	1 minute	1 hour
A_1	1000	6×10^4	3.6×10^6
A_2	40	4030	2.0×10^5
A_3	31	244	1897
A_4	10	39	153
A_5	9	15	21

TABLE 4.5 Effects of a 10-Fold Increase in Execution Speed

Algorithm	Growth Rate	Max Size Before	Max Size After
A_1	n	n_1	$10n_1$
A_2	$n \log_2 n$	n_2	@$10n_2$
A_3	n^2	n_3	$3.16n_3$
A_4	n^3	n_4	$2.15n_4$
A_5	2^n	n_5	$n_5 + 3.5$

higher the complexity, the more space intensive and computationally intensive the algorithm. It may, therefore, be more important to find efficient algorithms than to acquire a faster execution platform when there are performance problems found or suspected. Choosing something simple, such as the wrong sorting algorithm, can severely increase any space or timing problems that may be present in the application system. An analysis of the application system for high order algorithms, especially ones with order n^3 or 2^n, would prove very beneficial in increasing execution and space efficiency and reducing these sources of overall risk.[60] In Figure 4.9 we show some projected computational requirements

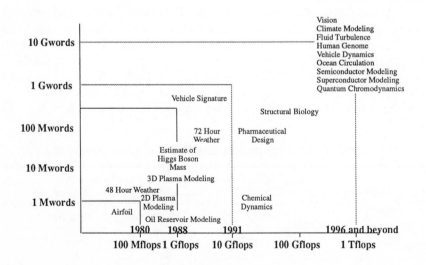

Figure 4.9 Computational Requirements for Different Applications

for a number of different applications which will challenge how algorithms are developed today.[61]

One other point also needs to be made. While examining the issue of algorithmic complexity is important, one must not overlook the straightforward performance factors. CPU cycles are important, especially if one is being forced to upgrade a machine due to CPU overload. Many programs are elegantly designed, with tremendous amounts of general purpose code, all nicely modularly constructed, which take up extraordinary amounts of CPU time. With some work and a few "programming tricks," these CPU hogs can be coded in such a fashion that they have significant performance speed-ups. Jon Bentley has specialized in this area, and his book on how to speed up performance is a classic.[62] It is useful to remember that 80% of most CPU cycles are used by 20% of the code, and to concentrate on improving the performance at these locations. There are plenty of instrumentation packages which can help locate these areas, and these occasions for performance improvements should not be overlooked.

4.3.2 Time-critical/Real-time

Time-critical, or what are called real-time risks, haven't been explored in this book much either. Real-time applications are those where information has a value, but which decays in time. Time-critical application processes are dependent on information that they gather from outside the application process domain to make decisions about what should be the next state transition within the process. If this information is not available, is delayed, or is untimely in any way, the probability that the state transition is correct will be reduced. For some systems, such as radar systems on a naval platform, receiving late information about an incoming hostile weapon can be fatal to the users who are dependent on the system.

The sources of risk for time-critical applications are the same as we encountered before: the lack of information, the lack of time, and the lack of control. But now, they take on greater, and more fundamental, importance. Whereas previously, an application could still be built and effectively used if one, or even two, of the risks in those categories were not completely averted, in time-critical systems, this is not possible. Even the avoidance of all information and control risks is not good enough, if there still exist risks associated with not having enough time.

One must avert all three basic causes of risk to a much greater degree than in most other application processes, regardless of application domain knowledge. Moreover, when many applications are time-critical, and form a time-critical application system, the overall risks increase almost exponentially. It should be obvious what consequences occur when time-critical applications are also large and/or complex.

To the risk analyst, large, complex, real-time applications pose the greatest set of risks. Unfortunately, the software engineering process, and the dynamic execution support paradigms which execute their realizations, to state just two crucial issues, are ill equipped to support the development of time-critical applications.[63-65] As an example, in time-critical systems, where data resides on the disk drive may be important. No current popular software engineering method looks for this type of problem.

Most software engineering paradigms do not handle the time dimension at all, let alone make it a central principle of the process. Time and system behavior are usually an afterthought, a result of the realization of the application, rather than a driving factor. Needless to say, this is a little late in the process. Most requirements, specification and design methods abstract out the time element on purpose, so as to not bring in implementation details too early.[66] Software engineering techniques which do not consider the application and system in which it runs as a whole, including the interactions between hardware, software, and human operators, have limited usefulness in real-time application development. Some work has been done to alleviate that omission, but it will take a radically new software engineering process to change it.[67]

4.3.3 Dynamic execution support

The idea of using time as the central parameter must also be applied to the design of time-critical execution environments. These, too, are woefully inadequate for most complex application system requirements. Application tasks today are seen as requesting resources from the control environment, as if the tasks were random processes. This view must be changed to be able to accept the fact that there are two types of time-critical processes: *cyclic* and *event-driven*. Without acknowledging this fact, the current state of resource deadlock and livelock that is prevalent will continue, with the effects being late information, the lack of real control of the application process state, and excess waste of the one resource that cannot be bought at any price, and that is time. The application of algorithmic analysis, as discussed earlier, can help immensely in reducing this risk as well.

4.3.4 Fault avoidance/Fault tolerance

Naturally, time-critical applications also bring up the issue of trying to avert and/or contain the risks they pose.[68] The two basic approaches are fault avoidance and fault tolerance, which are illustrated in Figure 4.10. The goal of fault avoidance is to reduce the probability of failure. This is done by averting the risks in the process of a software enterprise, which we explored in Chapters 2 and 3. Fault tolerance is used to try to avert the consequences of failure, in the event of a failure. This may be accomplished in numerous ways. One might try to confine the fault to a certain location, thereby preventing contamination of other areas. Or the fault may be searched for continuously, and if one is suspected or found, to reconfigure the application processes available for execution. This is sometimes called *graceful degradation*. One may also try to mask the fault; i.e., hide its effects by using redundancy. Or one may try to repair the fault, and correct the resulting effects.

Whether an application uses fault tolerance or not is of importance to the software engineering application (i.e., in hardware and software architectures and realizations) because it provides numerous

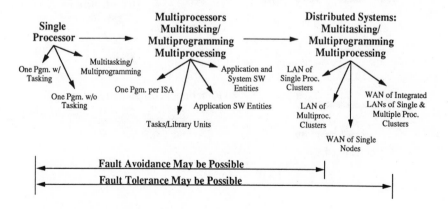

Figure 4.10 Risk of Different Application Architectures

opportunities for risk aversion. But it may also increase the risks involved by increasing the complexity and size of the processes to monitor the application, which not only may hurt performance, but be sources of errors in themselves. In other words, who watches the watchers?

There is a delicate trade-off in applying fault-tolerant techniques in applications and across different applications. Figure 4.11 illustrates a number of different application architectures and the applicability of fault avoidance and tolerance.[69] There are two axes which must be considered: controllability and coordinability. Controllability indicates the degree of resistance to faults that exist in an architectural subsystem. Hierarchical distributed and autonomous decentralized architectures have high levels of controllability, which means they can continue to function, even in the presence of errors. Centralized and functionally distributed architectures possess low controllability, and thus must use avoidance techniques that stress fault avoidance.

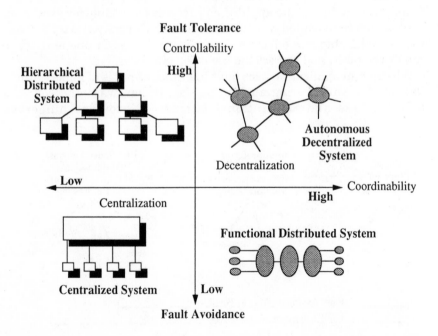

Figure 4.11 System Architectures and Applicability to Fault Tolerance and Fault Avoidance

Coordinability, preventing the failure of any architectural sub-system, is greatest for autonomous decentralized and functionally distributed architectures. In high coordinability architectures, functional reconfiguration efforts are able to ensure continued operation in the face of errors, as opposed to ensuring that no faults exist. On the other hand, since hierarchical distributed and centralized architectures have low coordinability, efforts must be made to ensure that a fault-free operating condition is the norm, before the system is turned on.

As one can see, certain application types are better able to use fault avoidance and tolerance schemes more effectively than others. Tightly coupled application architectures, with highly complex and nonlinear interactions, require efforts directed towards providing fault tolerance, rather than fault avoidance. However, very loosely coupled application architectures, also with highly complex and nonlinear interactions, require the use of fault avoidance and tolerance techniques because of the possibility of chaotic action, which was discussed in Chapter 2.

4.3.5 Human factors

The second to last area of application risk concerns human factors risk. We will not dwell too long on the subject here, as we will encounter it again in the next two chapters.

Human factor risks are primarily those which are created by human operators trying to interact with a system; i.e., use a system for a specific purpose, or gather information from a system. It entails the issues of perception, comprehension, viewing environment, psychological factors, and operator comfort, among others. Typically, these are thrown in all together to help define "user-friendly" systems, and are most often encountered by the analyst in terminal screen design. However, all the elements that go into making an "effective and friendly" design is a nontrivial concern.

The challenges of allowing a human to interface with a system, any system, and especially a computer-driven system, have proved to be not only very great, but very important to a system's effective and safe operation. Human operators are the most unreliable part of many systems, especially when the factor of fatigue is involved. Humans are especially poor at monitoring systems and in many uses of automation, this is exactly the role in which humans are placed. This has been shown dramatically by the problems human operators had at the nuclear power plants located at Three Mile Island and Chernobyl. It is also a major concern of airline pilots. Some 60% to 80% of all air crashes are caused by pilot error. Pilots are afraid that increased automation in the cockpit will reduce their flying skills to handle crises either caused by the automation failing to perform its proper function, or situations which the automation is not able to cope with adequately. It is in the latter situations, more so than the first, that automation becomes a major hazard.

We should also mention that human factors risk not only concerns human interaction with the computer, but also extends to how effectively a human can apply different software engineering techniques to build an application. For example, are requirements methods that use graphics more effective, and less error-prone, than using those which are more textually based, or are flowcharts effective or not effective as programming aids?

There is a whole body of literature on human factors, and the risks that they pose. The risk analyst should consult the references for more information.[70-73]

4.3.6 Application match to development process

We have already mentioned this issue throughout this chapter and the last, but not in any formal way. The type of application highly influences the success criteria of the development. For instance, if the application is a safety-critical one, then it will be judged along that axis. If it is meant to help noncomputer personnel do their job better, then it may be judged along the lines of user friendliness. However, much of the eventual success of the system will be determined by the way the development process, especially the methods used, matches the application's needs. We need to evaluate, then, the *kansei* of the development approach against the needs of the application. Alan Davis has developed a general taxonomy against which to help determine this match, and can be used to evaluate the risks of applying different types of development methods.[74] By using Davis's taxonomy with what we have learned so far, we can complete our analysis of application risks.

Basically, the taxonomy rates applications along five axes: (1) the difficulty of the problem; (2) the relationship in time between data and processing; (3) the number of simultaneous tasks to be performed; (4) the relative difficulty of data, control, and algorithmic aspects of the problem;

and (5) whether the application is deterministic or nondeterministic. The difficulty of the problem can be divided into hard or not hard. Hard problems are those which haven't been solved before, are new, unknown, and so forth. They are sometimes called *unprecedented systems*. Not hard problems are ones for which solutions are reasonably sure to exist, and are often called *precedented systems*.

If one looks at the relationship in time between the availability of input data and the processing on that input data, one can further classify an application. Using temporal relationships, applications can be either static or dynamic. Static applications have all their input data available before processing, whereas dynamic applications have new data received during processing. This is sometimes divided into the batch vs. interactive applications.

We have talked at some length about the decentralization of control already. Applications can be either sequential, concurrent, or parallel. Sequential applications are expected to do only one task, and to execute the task without interruption until completion. Concurrent applications can do multiple tasks, but the individual tasks required are executed sequentially for a while, but then are interrupted while another task is executed to perform some other task. Parallel applications can perform multiple tasks simultaneously.

An application can also be classified along the lines of the relative difficulty of data, control, and algorithmic aspects. Here, we are concerned with the application's external behavior. The data aspects involve the difficulty in defining, describing, organizing, and formatting the data that crosses the interface between the application system and its environment. The control aspects involve the difficulty in defining and describing how the external environment will control the system, or how the system will control the environment. Timing is usually crucial in these types of applications. The third aspect is the difficulty involved in defining and describing the transform function that depicts the interrelationships and interplay between an application's inputs and outputs.

The final way of classifying an application is based upon the predictability of the application's outputs given a set of inputs. If the application gives the same outputs given the same inputs, then it is deterministic. However, if the output varies with the same input, then it is nondeterministic. Deterministic applications can, at least theoretically, be well understood. Nondeterministic applications are less predictable, and therefore can be very risky to develop.

Certain applications will be dominated by one or more of these aspects. For example, real- time systems are often hard, dynamic, parallel, have difficulty in describing all the data, control, and algorithmic aspects of the application, and are frequently nondeterministic. Payroll systems, on the other hand, are not hard, static, are dominated by the data aspects of the application, and are deterministic. By evaluating an application in this way, one can better come to terms with the overall risks to the software enterprise.

4.4 Summary

Trying to identify, classify, and evaluate application risks may seem similar to attempting to solve a nonlinear equation: the act of playing the game changes the rules. However, we have tried to demonstrate how the risk analyst can use a standard framework in which to conduct such a risk analysis. This framework provides a context in which application architectures, as opposed to the application knowledge domain or application realization in hardware and software, can be evaluated for risk. Although the other two realms must also be investigated, the application architecture approach provides a more appropriate starting point. The major advantage is that an architectural approach is technology independent. The major limitation is that if the level of granularity is not correctly selected, then there may not be enough resolution to observe possible risks which may exist. The risk analyst's judgment will be critical in finding the proper trade-off required.

In the next chapter, we continue investigating some other risk issues of importance which do not rest easily in any previous categorization of software engineering process or product. These are the issues concerning safety, security, or catastrophic system error and recovery risks. Safety risks involve the possible risks to human life or property, security risks involve the possible compromise of the integrity and privacy of the application's execution, and catastrophic system error and recovery involve what risks exist when an application stops working.

4.5 Book Intermission: Time to Cement the Gaps

We started out in this book contending that software engineering risks can be found, created, and exacerbated at any point in the development life cycle, beginning with the initial business decision made to acquire or develop a software system, through the systems engineering of it, down to the software engineering process models, methodology, and automation that are used in the system's implementation. We demonstrated that the longer these risks remain unmanaged, the more they diminish the chances for project success. We have also shown that not all risks can or should be avoided, but that they all should be assessed, and explicit controls should be applied in proportion to each risk identified. Ultimately, how we conduct risk engineering can only be based upon context, decisions, decision processes, and their interfaces for any project existing within a model of a business enterprise.

Our approach has been deliberately top-down. The primary concern has been the risks, in the form of undercapitalization, underperformance, etc., which flow or are funnelled from the business enterprise down to the software engineering enterprise, as well as how the software industry, by ignoring these externally generated risks, negatively impacts their ability to attain software project success. This ignorance has been exacerbated by the deliberate compartmentalization of the industry, surrounded by its "electric fence of jargon, unjustifiable complexity, and sheer dogma." This impenetrable fence has kept businessmen from understanding the risks they have placed upon the development efforts, and the risks that they have been incurring arising from the development approach taken and system delivered. This fence has not served, and will continue not to serve, software developers' best interests either. Only by comprehending that many of the problems we are attacking in the software industry have their origins elsewhere will software engineering have a chance of succeeding in its objective.

But there is another side to consider, and this can only be seen from taking a bottom-up approach. It must be remembered that there exist risks in the systems engineering and software engineering environment processes which percolate upwards. The fairly constant occurrence of failure in developing successful software systems, with the associated losses of monies and market opportunities by the companies affected by the failures, have frequently demonstrated quite graphically the manner in which software engineering risks flow upwards. We need to understand better how the flows of risk and opportunity affect both the application and development of software systems, if we are to build successful information systems which meet the business need.

For example, in Chapter 3 of our previous book, *Software Engineering Risk Analysis and Management*, we discussed that any enterprise has an objective, strategies to meet that objective, and various tactics to implement the individual strategies which utilize various means or assets. The objective of an enterprise is constrained, however, by the means and tactics available. If the means or resources are not available for use, the best tactic or strategy in the world is futile. Therefore, a balance has to be struck between what is wished for and what is possible, or there will be a fundamental disconnect. Given the means availability, the objectives, strategies, and tactics are then adjusted accordingly. The military has been working the last 3000 years or so to perfect this balance of top-down/bottom-up planning, and still doesn't always get it right. We in the software field have been at the process less than 50 years, and haven't yet, in many cases, recognized that the problem even exists. Business objectives need to be balanced against software engineering means, as well as vice versa.

We see the effects of this lack of balance between our means and our objectives by the poor results that the software community continues to achieve. We see the effects also in issues which "don't fit in," like the development of real-time applications, where time has been extracted or ignored in the development of process models. Time (or behavior) is an asset; i.e., they act as constraints on the overall ability of the system to meet its objective. The influence of assets on current development approaches; i.e., process models, has been largely forgotten. Only in the debates over the adequacy of enactable/process programming models do these considerations ever make a reappearance. We also see the effects of the lack of balance in the never-ending arguments over the merits of Software First approaches to development vice Hardware First approaches, neither of which considers the influence of business risks, or assets, at all on the success of the development.

We can achieve a balance between business risk and software engineering risk by forming a gestalt structure, in other words, a structure which is so integrated as to form a single functional unit. This is sometimes called the "whole-part-whole" view.[75] To do so, we still need to consider a few more issues of risk, namely safety, security, disaster recovery, and the psychology of risk taking itself. When we have completed this examination, we will discuss an approach to how this balance can be finally attained.

However, we wish to review nine maxims concerning how one can avert some of the major risks in the processes and products of creating information systems.

The first maxim is to:

Look Before You Leap

There is nothing inherently wrong in taking on high-risk information technology developments or acquisitions, as long as you have calculated the risks in some intelligent fashion. The problem really lies in jumping off a 20-foot cliff into the ocean and not knowing if the bottom is 3 feet, or 30 feet, from the surface.

The second is to:

Check the Estimates

When a project starts to get behind, or exceed its budget, one needs to quickly determine if there is a technical problem, or if there was something wrong with the original estimates. Most projects underestimate the resources and performance required. Recall the discussion of undercapitalization and underperformance in Chapter 1. Do not make major changes to the project until one has figured out where the problem really lies.

The third is to:

Stabilize the Process

Without having a stable process, little can be done to make any lasting improvements in the development or acquisition approach. Whenever you wish to improve the quality, control, prediction of the cost, schedule, etc., the process must be stabilized first. In developing systems, this means the process involved in developing software across all three levels of abstraction; i.e., the process model used, the methods applied, and the automation exercised.

A corollary to the above maxim is to also:

Stabilize the Data

If one can define and capture the data in a system, then one can control and evolve the system in a low-risk fashion. Capturing functions is not enough. Stabilizing the data is also easier then stabilizing the process.

Fifth, you must be able to:

Trace the Consequences of Your Decisions

The disciplines and techniques involved in business enterprise modeling, systems engineering, and software engineering are meant to reduce risk, and risk involves decisions. If one cannot trace the potential effects of a decision, then one is just guessing. For example, in software engineering, tracing the effects of system requirements through design into implementation and throughout the evolution phase is a major way of averting the risks involved in the lack of information and the lack of time. Traceability also helps in maintaining stability within the various processes.

The sixth maxim is to:

Crush Unrealistic Expectations

Unrealistic expectations about how much a software development needs in resources, what can be created in a period of time, etc., all lead to overcommitment, which ultimately leads to undercapitalization and underperformance. Look constantly look for the risks caused by unrealistic expectations, and deflate them as soon as possible.

The seventh maxim is to make certain:

Forensic Engineering is Applied

Even stabilizing the process and tracing the effects of decisions is not good enough to make improvements for future developments. The only way to make these improvements is to keep track of historical data and conduct post-mortems to identify why a project failed or succeeded. Total quality management is superb for gaining this type of data.

Eighth,

Never Reinforce Failure

This is an old military maxim that we like to ignore. All too often, even with things going badly, the thinking is that maybe with a little more money, time, etc., success might still be achieved in the end. More times than not, a project will have defeat snatched away from the jaws of victory rather than the other way around. Projects which are failing must be given a hard look, and cutting losses and starting over is frequently the best route to take.

Finally, make sure every decision made during a software enterprise is made with the physician's credo in mind:

Do No Harm

The reasons should be self-evident.

Questions

1 What is your definition of an application? How is it similar to, or different from, the one given in the text? How would you use it to perform risk analysis?

2 Try and categorize different application knowledge domains. What is the source of your taxonomy? Do the same with computer realizations. Are these taxonomies technology dependent or independent?

3 How would you improve the Defense Science Board's classification scheme? The ACM's? Justify your answers by showing how they could be used for risk analysis.

4 Compare and contrast the differences among application process, application architecture, application, and application system? Draw a Venn diagram of an application system, showing its various logical and physical components.

5 The scheme used to classify different application architectures is technology independent, that is, a feature is not dependent on the technology required to implement it. What are the advantages and disadvantages of this approach in performing risk analysis? In performing risk control and monitoring?

6 What does decentralization mean? How is it similar to, or different from, distribution? What are some generic risks involved in decentralization and distribution?

7 Resolution of risks has to do with the ability to observe risks. If the resolution is not fine enough, a risk may not be observable. What, then, are the differences between resolution and granularity? How are these differences important?

8 Show where in Figure 4.3 SISD, MIMD, and MDMD architectures exist.

9 In Figure 4.3, show the relative risks of each partition shown. In other words, a single processor may have a relative risk of 1, whereas a multiple processor may have a relative risk of 5 in comparison. Try to justify your ratings.

10 Refine the granularity of the decentralized database axis shown in Figure 4.3. What are your criteria for doing so?

11 Why do you suspect an object-oriented database does not have the risks that are present in hierarchical or relational-type databases? What type of risks do they pose?

12 Why is Grosch's Law of concern to the software engineering risk analyst? Describe some of its implications on the risks associated with the software engineering process.

13 What are the risks involved in the Hardware First and Software First approaches? How are they alike? How are they different? Which poses less risk, and why? Provide an alternative approach which averts the risks you identified.

14 Define what a real-time application is. Give an example, showing how the value of information changes with respect to time. Is it possible to write a mathematical expression for this change? How would you use this equation to evaluate risks? For example, could you evaluate each data item in an application system, to see if it met the limits of the equation?

15 How might time be included in software engineering process models? How about in the methods used? Describe the possible risks in leaving time out of consideration when developing time-critical applications. How does the hardware realization come into play in considering these risks?

16 What are fault avoidance and fault tolerance? How are they different? In what circumstances would one use one over the other? Are the approaches used in software different from those used in hardware?

17 Refer back to Figure 2.6, which indicates the degree of coupling and complexity of interactions of different applications. Which of these systems require fault avoidance? Which require fault tolerance? Why?

18 Spreadsheets might be considered nonapplication programs. Although they were designed with financial applications in mind, they can be used for any application area that requires the general operations provided. What is your opinion? Give reasons for your position.

19 In the future, there will most likely be a merging of IPSEs and SEEs with applications processes. In other words, the software engineering process will be tightly bound to the application process. How does this trend affect the risks likely to be encountered? How can one change the application architecture taxonomy presented to account for this trend? What other future technology trends might affect the application risks confronted?

20 How does one perform risk monitoring for application risks? What should be monitored? What should be controlled? How?

21 In the scenario in Chapter 2, the chairman wished to make a major investment in new technology to increase the probability of success of his current and software enterprises. Given what you now know about the different types of risks inherent in the business environment, systems engineering environment, software engineering process, and application, what is a good strategy for him to take?

References

1. Antony Ralston et al. (eds.), *Encyclopedia of Computer Science and Engineering*, Van Nostrand Reinhold Company, Inc., New York, 1976.

2. See, for instance, the "Special Issue on Information Technology for Command and Control" *IEEE Transactions on Systems, Man, and Cybernetics*, Vol. SMC-16, No. 6, November/December 1986.

3. M. L. Metersky, "A C² Process and an Approach to Design and Evaluation," *IEEE Transactions on Systems, Man, and Cybernetics*, Vol. SMC-16, No. 6, November/December 1986.

4. These acronyms mean Command, Control and Communications; Command, Control, Communications, and Intelligence, and Command, Control, Communications, Computers, and Intelligence, respectively.

5. Antony Ralston et al. (eds.), *Encyclopedia of Computer Science and Engineering*, Van Nostrand Reinhold Company, Inc., New York, 1976.

6. "Report of the Defense Science Board Task Force on Military Software," Office of the Under Secretary of Defense for Acquisition, Washington, D.C., September 1987.

7. This recommendation says something about the state of government computing, doesn't it!

8. "The New CR Classification Scheme," *Communications of the ACM*, Vol. 25, No. 1, January 1982. The full classification scheme is very comprehensive and has 11 top-level classes, over 65 second-level classes, and a couple hundred further subclasses.

9. Often, an application architecture is referred to as its design, but more often than not, the term either specifies a particular physical implementation or the software design, instead.

10. N. Wirth, *Algorithms* + *Data Structures* = *Programs*, Prentice-Hall, Inc., Englewood Cliffs, NJ, 1976.

11. Commercial OTS "application packages" fall into this group, since they too lack a physical instantiation.

12. Execution environments will manage memory, the processor, devices, etc., whether an external program is or is not present, because it requires to do these tasks for itself anyway.

13. "Special Issues on Fundamental Limits in Electrical Engineering," *Proceedings of the IEEE*, Vol. 69, No. 2, February 1981.

14. Again, a software engineering risk analyst must have a working knowledge of the currently available computing hardware and their intercommunication (i.e., networking) equipment. Manufacturers are more than happy to supply certain information, and there are numerous books available on different hardware and networks. These must be scoured for problems, limitations, etc., to determine the risks inherent in their implementation. Without computer hardware knowledge, one is only covering part of the job of a risk analyst. This is especially true when heterogeneous computers are interconnected.

15. James Gleick, *Chaos: Making a New Science*, Penguin Books, New York, 1988.

16. Philip H. Enslow, Jr., "What Is a 'Distributed' Data Processing System?," *IEEE Computer*, Vol. 11, No. 1, January 1978.

17. Charles McKay, speech given to National Security Industrial Association Conference on "Software Initiatives and Their Impact on the Competitive Edge," *NSIA Proceedings*, 10 May, 1988.

18. The whole issue of changes to requirements is a very complicated one. Often, requirement changes are due to a desire to change the application architecture, because the physical realization of the architecture was deficient in some way. Before this is accomplished, the risk analyst must remember the first cardinal rule of risk control: *any decision taken should do no harm*. Thus, a determination must be made to see if a new realization is warranted, instead of a new architecture. Part of the answer can be found by conducting capacity planning studies (see for instance, "An Empirical Study of Computer Capacity Planning in Japan," by Shui F. Lam, *Communications of the ACM*, Vol. 31, No. 8, August 1988.). Valid requirement changes, more often than not, are the results of changes in the application domain process, which indicates that more of an understanding is being reached about the knowledge domain.

19. Philip H. Enslow, Jr., "What Is a 'Distributed' Data Processing System?," *IEEE Computer*, Vol. 11, No. 1, January 1978.

20. Charles McKay, "Ada and the Intel iAPX432 Support of Networks," AIAA-83-2417-CP, 1983.

21. The more technology advances to reduce risk, the more technology advances to increase it. Sometimes it is hard to tell who is winning at any point in time.

22. Harold S. Stone, *Introduction to Computer Architecture,* 2nd ed., Science Research Associates, Inc., Chicago, IL 1980.

23. Michael J. Flynn, "Very High-Speed Computing Systems," *Proceedings of the IEEE*, Vol. 54, 1966.

24. David B. Skillicorn, "A Taxonomy for Computer Architectures," *IEEE Computer*, Vol. 21, No. 11, November 1988.

25. Some authors, like Fathi and Krieger, argue that networks are a form of loosely coupled MIMD architectures. Distributed systems are moderately coupled, whereas multiprocessors are tightly coupled MIMD architectures, where coupling refers to the ability to share resources. We agree with the above definition of coupling, but do not restrict it to MIMD architectures alone. See the paper by Joshua Etkin and John A. Zinksy, "Development Life Cycle of Computer Networks: The Executable Model Approach," *IEEE Transactions on Software Engineering*, Vol. 15, No. 9, September 1989; also Eli Fathi and Moshe Krieger, "Multiple Microprocessor Systems: What, Why, and When," *IEEE Computer*, Vol. 16, No. 3, 1983, for other perspectives.

26. Nathan J. Muller, *Minimum Risk Strategy for Acquiring Communications Equipment and Service*, Artech House, Norwood MA, 1989.

27. William Stallings, *Tutorial: Computer Communications: Architectures, Protocols, and Standards,* 2nd ed., IEEE Computer Society Press, January 1988.

28. S. K. Tripathi et al., "Local Area Networks: Software and Related Issue," *IEEE Transactions on Software Engineering*, Vol. SE-13, No. 6, August 1987.

29. John Stankovic, "A Perspective on Distributed Computer Systems," *IEEE Transaction on Computers*, Vol. C-33, No. 12, December 1984.

30. Harold S. Stone, "Parallel Querying of Large Databases: A Case Study," *IEEE Computer*, Vol. 20, No. 10, October 1987.

31. "Real Machines: Design Choices/Engineering Trade-offs," *IEEE Computer* (special issue), Vol. 22, No. 1, January 1989.

32. Harold S. Stone, *High-Performance Computer Architecture*, Addison-Wesley, Reading, MA 1987.

33. Carl Howe and Bruce Moxon, "How to Program Parallel Processors," *IEEE Spectrum*, Vol. 24, No. 9, September 1987.

34. "Parallel and Distributed Processing," *IEEE Transactions on Computers* (special issue), Vol. 36, No. 4, April 1987.

35. "Design for Adaptability," *IEEE Computer* (special issue), Vol. 19, No. 2, February 1986.

36. Eli Fathi and Moshe Krieger, "Multiple Microprocessor Systems: What, Why, and When," *IEEE Computer*, Vol. 16, No. 3, 1983.

37. Harold S. Stone, *Introduction to Computer Architecture,* 2nd ed., Science Research Associates, Inc., Chicago, IL 1980.

38. H. A. Grosch, "High Speed Arithmetic: The Digital Computer as a Research Tool," *Journal of the Optical Society of America*, Vol. 43, No. 4, April 1953.

39. Philip Ein-Dor, "Grosch's Law Revisited: CPU Power and the Cost of Computation," *Communications of the ACM*, Vol. 28, No. 2, February 1985.

40. Ibid.

41. The trend is starting to change, with hardware/software trade-offs occurring at an architectural level instead of at a design level, but there is still a long way to go. The other extreme is to design the software first, and then fill in the hardware after, but this is as risky as the Hardware First syndrome.

42. Philip Ein-Dor, "Grosch's Law Revisited: CPU Power and the Cost of Computation," *Communications of the ACM*, Vol. 28, No. 2, February 1985.

43. Young Moo Kang, "Computer Hardware Performance: Production Cost Function Analyses," *Communications of the ACM*, Vol. 31, No. 5, May 1989.

44. Wesley Chu, "Distributed Database Systems," *Handbook of Software Engineering*, Van Nostrand Reinhold Company, New York, 1984.

45. Bharat Bhargava, "Concurrency Control and Reliability in Distributed Database Management Systems," *Handbook of Software Engineering*, Van Nostrand Reinhold Company, New York, 1984.

46. Philip H. Enslow, Jr., "What Is a 'Distributed' Data Processing System?" *IEEE Computer*, Vol. 11, No. 1, January 1978.

47. Robert N. Charette, *Software Engineering Environments: Concepts and Technology,* McGraw-Hill, Inc., New York, 1986.

48. J. Ullman, *Principles of Database Systems*, Computer Sciences Press, Rockville, MD, 1982.

49. A record type is also termed a relation, and a relationship is termed an interrelational dependency.

50. John Stankovic, "A Perspective on Distributed Computer Systems," *IEEE Transaction on Computers*, Vol. C-33, No. 12, December 1984.

51. Paul Fortier, *Design of Distributed Operating Systems*, McGraw-Hill, Inc., New York, 1986.

52. "Spotlight: Distributed Databases," *Government Computer News*, August 29, 1988.

53. James Martin, *Managing the Data-Base Environment,* Prentice-Hall, Inc., Englewood Cliffs, NJ, 1983.

54. Charles McKay et al., "Distributed, Object-Based Information Systems, Research Institute of Computing and Information Systems," University of Houston, 1988.

55. Richard Sites, "Operating Systems," *Introduction to Computer Architecture,* 2nd ed., Harold S. Stone, ed., Science Research Associates, Inc., Chicago, IL, 1980.

56. Still one of the best texts on the principles and risks of centralized and partial decentralized operating systems is *Operating Systems,* by S. E. Madnick and J. J. Donovan, McGraw-Hill, Inc., New York, New York, 1974.

57. See for instance, Paul Fortier, *Design of Distributed Operating Systems,* McGraw-Hill, Inc., New York, 1986.

58. Robert N. Charette, *Software Engineering Risk Analysis and Management,* McGraw-Hill, Inc., New York, 1989.

59. Charles Perrow, *Normal Accidents: Living With High-Risk Technologies,* Basic Books, New York, 1984.

60. One cannot just go to non–von Neumann machines, such as parallel architectures, to solve the problem either. Many algorithms are not amenable to parallelization, and many of the current algorithms have not been written for use on these machines, meaning that one has to recode them. If one is not careful, one can end up with algorithms which actually run slower in certain cases.
    The key issue is the granularity of the problem. Coarse-grained parallelism splits the problem into only a few subtasks, but the load at each processor is increased. Fine-grained parallelism distributes the tasks more evenly, but increases the communication load. See "How To Program Parallel Processors," *IEEE Spectrum,* Vol. 24, Number 9, September 1987, for a good introduction to the opportunities and risks found in parallel architectures.

61. "The Federal High-Performance Computing Program," Office of Science and Technology, September 1989.

62. Jon Bentley, *Programming Pearls,* ACM/Addison-Wesley, New York, 1986.

63. John A. Stankovic, "A Serious Problem for Next-Generation Systems," *IEEE Computer,* Vol. 21, No. 10, October 1988.

64. Ray Ford, "Concurrent Algorithms for Real-Time Memory Management," *IEEE Software,* September 1988.

65. Nancy Leveson, "Software Safety: What, Why, and How," *ACM Computing Surveys,* Vol. 18, No. 2, June 1986.

66. Reread the section on design methods in Chapter 3, for instance.

67. Robert N. Charette, "SOEM: Putting Theories into Practice," in *Proceedings of the Third International Workshop on Specification and Design,* London, August 1985.

68. See the "Special Issue on Fault Tolerance," *IEEE Computer,* Vol. 17, No. 8, August 1984. Note also that the risk aversion techniques are basically the same as the ones

we encountered in *Software Engineering Risk Analysis and Management*, by Robert N. Charette, McGraw-Hill, Inc., New York, 1989.

69. Hirokazu Ihara and Kinji Mori, "Autonomous Decentralized Computer Control Systems," *IEEE Computer*, Vol. 17, No. 8, August 1984. One should also consult Mengly Chean and Jose Fortes, who wrote an article entitled "A Taxonomy of Reconfiguration Techniques for Fault-Tolerant Processor Arrays," *IEEE Computer*, Vol. 23, No. 1, January 1990. This article details the various techniques available and compares the capability of each for different situations.

70. The analyst can consult articles in the *IEEE Transactions on Software Engineering*, the *IEEE Transactions on Systems, Man, and Cybernetics*, the *SIGCHI Bulletin* of the ACM dealing with computers and human interaction, or examine the *IEEE Guide to Evaluation of Man-Machine Performance in Nuclear Power Station Control Rooms and Other Peripheries*, IEEE 845-1988,

71. Bill Curtis, *Human Factors in Software Development*, 2nd ed., IEEE Computer Society Press, New York, 1986.

72. Nancy Leveson, "Software Safety: What, Why, and How," *ACM Computing Surveys*, Vol. 18, No. 2, June 1986.

73. H. Rex Hartson and Deborah Hix, "Human-Computer Interface Development: Concepts and Systems," *ACM Computing Surveys*, Vol. 21, No. 1, March 1989.

74. Alan Davis, *Software Requirements: Analysis and Specification*, Prentice Hall, Englewood Cliffs, NJ, 1990.

75. Charles McKay, "Some Thoughts on DRLI58 and Subsequent Increments of Evolution," SERC Position Paper, August 24, 1989.

Chapter

5

Software Safety, Security, and Operational/Disaster Recovery and the Risks to the Business

"Programs are conjectures, while executions are attempted—and all too frequently successful—refutations."

JAMES H. FETZER

5.0 Introduction

While I was attending graduate school, I ended up taking a course in advanced engineering mathematics which I found interesting, but sometimes a little discombobulating. The course made such a lasting impression that, even after more than a decade, I still occasionally wake up in the middle of the night finding myself trying to comprehend what is really ensuing when one applies the special case of Euler's equation to the Bachistochrone Problem. Strange, eh? The full understanding of this mathematical fragment, as well as many others of the same, seemingly opaque, origin, continues to elude me, as well as continuing to interrupt my night's sleep. I can still even feel exactly the same trepidation I experienced whenever I recall my graduate advisor telling me, after I had indicated to him that I was enrolling in this particular course, "Fine. A little pain is good for the soul."

Anyway, the professor teaching the course was a Chinese-born American, whom I'll call Dr. Lao. Dr. Lao was a wizened, very disciplined mathematician, with a wry sense of humor. His seeming single goal in life was to figure out ways to motivate a student to genuinely learn, which meant he had to coerce us to throw off any of our preconceived notions concerning the usefulness of higher mathematics, even if he had to use subtle means to accomplish it (it is well known that graduate engineering students are not at their best when it comes to the appreciation of higher mathematical theory). He believed, as Nietzsche did, that to achieve mental maturity meant reacquiring the seriousness one had as a child at play. To achieve his goal, Dr. Lao sometimes had to act as a part time philosopher and con artist.

For example, Dr. Lao would suddenly state, in the middle of a deep explanation on the intricacies of the Riemann and Lebesgue theorems and why we should esteem their practical application, "I just thought of something. A hunter sees five birds in tree. He shoots one of them. How many birds are left?" Well, the class, somewhat startled from our collective intensity on trying to determine what the Riemann and Lebesgue theorems were, let alone their practical applications, would naturally answer four. Dr. Lao, remarking disparagingly about the quality of graduate students today, would answer there were no birds left. The others had flown away at the sound of the shot. He would then continue on with his lecture as if nothing had happened, leaving the class in an outwardly indignant state at being "conned," but inwardly, we were all laughing. By the end of the semester we were getting pretty good at spotting his acts of subterfuge, which of course, meant we were almost getting back to the state of wide-eyed thinking that students have before they forget how to learn, and instead spend all their time trying to just get through the educational system.

Dr. Lao also felt that too much examination was not particularly conducive to learning, thus he only gave two exams, a midterm and a final examination, each consisting of two questions a piece. Therefore, one could pass, fail, or fail miserably. When questioned about this policy, Dr. Lao said that graduate students were expected to already know the subject, thus the exam was only a reflection of that belief, so why all the fuss? His confidence in our knowledge was flattering, but not all that reassuring. Upon taking the exam, the questions were worded in such a way that demonstrated the breadth and depth of one's understanding of the subject, so the examination, upon reflection, was pretty fair.

At the first exam, I was fairly nervous, and was glad when it was through. I felt that I had solved the two questions adequately, and was not overly worried about my grade. Well, when I got the exam back, I was surprised and dismayed to see a bright red "50" on my examination paper. Breathing rather hard, I turned to the offending question and soon realized that I had indeed calculated the correct answer, but had carelessly mistranscribed it to the box where the answer was suppose to appear (to Dr. Lao, neatness counted).

I didn't quite know what to make of this, since Dr. Lao had obviously read over my solution text carefully (there were red scrawls all over the paper, commenting on alternative ways to attain the solution). I squirmed through the lecture, not really paying any attention to it, as I was anxious to speak to Dr. Lao about my grade. Well, after a seeming eternity, class was over and I went over to his office. I showed him my paper, pointed out where my mistake had been, and asked for my grade to be changed to at least reflect some partial credit for getting the right solution, even if I hadn't managed to copy the answer three inches across the page. To my surprise, he said that he remembered my solution, thought it was very good, had also seen the transcription error, but, sadly, reiterated to me that my grade would stand as is. When I inquired why, Dr. Lao said, "You build a bridge. Bridge falls down because of unthinking and careless transcription error on plans. You get no partial credit."

As it turned out, I wasn't the only one with a poor grade. Dr. Lao had marked one of the questions incorrect, even if you got the "right" answer. The question required a differential equation to be solved, and Dr. Lao kept saying during the term that one should always take the Wronskian of a differential to see if there existed an exact solution. Otherwise, one could spend a lifetime trying to find something that didn't exist. We should have learned that fundamental notion as undergraduates, he kept reminding us. Thus, if you didn't take the Wronskian as part of your exam solution, no credit. Luckily, I didn't have to worry about that, too. These little lessons in "exactitude as a virtue" were not exactly well received at that moment, but I, and the rest of the class, made sure that we paid close attention for the remainder of the course (most of us had to "ace" the final to pass, and none of us wanted to ever have to repeat the course). Well, when the final exam eventually rolled around, it was really a bear, covering everything we had learned throughout the course. I made sure that I didn't make any stupid mistakes, while the whole class applied Wronskians to anything that moved. Needless to say, I was ecstatic when it was over, and went home for Christmas break wondering what other things might have gone wrong.

During the winter break, my semester grades came in, and I was dumbfounded to receive an "A" for the course, having previously calculated the best my grade could be was a "C." I had passed the final, and so did most of the class. As it turned out, Dr. Lao believed it was what you ultimately ended up learning that should determine your final grade. Thus, Dr. Lao went back and changed the exam grades of those individuals whom he had marked down in the first exam for not taking the Wronskian, if they did not repeat the mistake in the second. Unknown to us, he kept track of the various reasons for our first exam mistakes, and if we learned not to repeat them, then he felt he had taught us something. As Dr. Lao told us later, he was there to teach, not to keep score.

The point of the story is that Dr. Lao's lessons, "exactitude is a virtue," "one cannot expect partial credit for failure," and "one must learn from one's past mistakes," are three concepts for the risk analyst to bear in mind when dealing with the situations involving software safety, security, and disaster recovery. Although all of software engineering risk analysis and management techniques are meant to ensure that software will execute within a system context without resulting in an unacceptable risk, the consequences of the risks involved in safety, security, or disaster recovery situations differ from those normally encountered by their increased severity and magnitude. The consequences of risks in these situations are the potential for loss of life, damage to health or property, or utter business failure. These potentially profound effects have impact on the degree of accuracy required of the risk engineering far above that which is typically needed. This can be readily seen when the potential of these types of risks become realities.

Take, as an example, the first prototype of the Saab JAS-39 Gripen, a new multirole combat aircraft proposed for the Swedish Air Force. It had the misfortune to crash during landing on its sixth test flight in February 1989.[1] The pilot escaped serious injury, while the aircraft sustained very heavy damage. The cause of the crash was quickly discovered to be a flaw contained in the control algorithms used in the flight control system software. As it turned out, this flaw caused severe, uncontrollable oscillations in the aircraft's pitch while it flew at low altitude, which of course makes the prospect of landing a bit more exciting. The crash of the Gripen prototype resulted in a delay in delivery of the first production aircraft from early 1992 until at least mid-1993.

In November of 1988, a Cornell University graduate student wrote an experimental, self-replicating, self-propagating program affecting Sun Microsystems' Sun 3 systems and VAX computers running variants of 4 BSD UNIX, and injected it into the Internet computer network. Within hours, over 6000 computers all over the United States became infected with this computer worm, causing them to become overloaded, shutdown, or disconnected from the network. While no known damage to any files occurred, an estimated 8 million hours of lost access time, and over a million hours of direct labor costs were wasted in getting the worm out of the systems, and it exposed the vulnerability of networks to attack.[2] The cost of the attack has been estimated at $98 million.

In November of 1985, software corruption of its financial transactions forced the Bank of New York to shut down, which resulted in becoming accidentally overdrawn by nearly $32 billion within the New York Federal Reserve Bank. By the end of the 24 hours it took to clear the problem, the resulting cost to the bank was over $5 million in interest on the overdraft from the Federal Reserve. The mistake also caused a panic in the platinum market because rumors were floated that the bank was about to collapse.[3]

The instances above represent just some of the more interesting occurrences of software safety risks, security risks, and disaster recovery risks that have been reported. Many, especially those occurring where computer security linked to fraud is involved, are never reported. For those interested, a more complete list of software-associated incidents can be found in the "Risks to the Public in Computers and Related Systems" section of *ACM's Software Engineering Notes*.[4]

Each of these risk domains are very important for the risk analyst to have some understanding in order to complete his or her risk analysis and management repertoire. More importantly, as systems become larger and more complex, the aspects of safety, security, and disaster recovery concerns increasingly are simultaneously present and interact with one another. How one trades each other off can be extremely complex, and can have far-reaching consequences. Further, one must also be aware that although computer systems may be able to replicate the tasks of people in the name of increased safety or efficiency, they infrequently have any of the "common sense" of the people they replace.[5]

As we will shortly see, each topic is an elaborate subject in itself and deserves a book of its own. However, because space limits what can be reviewed, our aim will be to concentrate mainly on the aspects required to conduct a good risk analysis, rather than how to best design or implement a safe, secure, or disaster-proof system. We will only be able to provide an impression of what is required, which undoubtedly will mean some other important or favorite item will also be left out, for which we apologize. Our goal, by the end of the chapter, is to be able to recognize the primary sources of risk and the general approaches for identifying, evaluating, and managing them. The references provide a much more in-depth knowledge about the design and implementation issues, which a risk analyst should become very familiar with, if he or she is not already, before conducting any serious analysis and management exercise. Keeping Dr. Lao's three lessons in mind, we begin first with an examination of software safety issues.

5.1 Software Safety

A question which quickly jumps to mind when examining the issue of software safety is why is it considered different from "normal" software risk considerations? Shouldn't safety be considered as a risk in all software systems? The obvious answer is yes, and we will examine later the potential penalties for a business which does not consider software safety as an important issue, but as we have mentioned earlier, the immediate magnitude and severity of a consequential risk which can be traced to the software in these situations is unequal to most risks the analyst will face. Let's try to explain what we mean through an example.

When a company's payroll system goes down, there is very little danger of incurring a "loss of life, limb, or property." A payroll system can be off-line for as many as three days without major disruption within, or to, the business. Inconvenient yes, but the business will most likely continue on. Manual methods of writing checks can still be done, albeit more slowly and less efficiently. Compare this to the Gripen aircraft, where the incorrect operation of the flight control software affects the aircraft in milliseconds, causing it to become literally uncontrollable. Manual overrides are impossible to set quickly enough, and wouldn't work anyway (a human cannot adjust the aircraft's flight attitude with enough accuracy for it to achieve stable flight). Thus, the *severity* and *magnitude* of the risk's consequence are important characteristics of safety situations.

Notice several other important dissimilarities between the nature of these two software systems. In the Gripen, the application computer software is part of what is called an embedded system; i.e., a system in which a computer is part of a greater system. Embedded computer systems usually perform critical elements of the overall system's operational control functions, most often in real time. When a flaw occurs, it can *directly* impact the overall *system's* behavior. Compare this to the payroll system's software, which is usually a stand-alone application and doesn't (typically) negatively affect the computer system in which it runs when it has an execution flaw. In fact, it is very difficult to consider safety issues involving software without considering the system in which it is used. Furthermore, if the Gripen had crashed into a city, the possible harm done to others could have been catastrophic. A payroll system doesn't affect the lives of those outside its nearby area of use. Thus, another characteristic one must consider with software safety is the *degree of control* the software influences in its operating environment; i.e., the operational boundaries affected when a flaw occurs.

Another aspect of safety situations is the *immediacy* of the consequence. The immediacy of the risk consequence is important because, in safety situations, the amount of reaction and notification time can change an unsafe situation into a safe one. In the Gripen, the pilot has virtually no response time when the flight computer exhibits a critical error, whereas in other types of systems, an error might allow for other alternatives to be selected to avert the impact of the error. Again, in the payroll system, checks can still be written in a manual manner, if need be. Thus, we can list the *amount of time for risk management* to occur as yet another important characteristic of safety situations.

In the comparisons above, we have concentrated predominantly on the operational aspects of software safety; i.e., what happens when the computer software, as part of the operational control of a system, does not work correctly. While computers are increasingly being embedded into systems which have direct influence over critical elements of a system's operational control, they are also being used increasingly in the design of systems which have no computers associated with them whatsoever. These nonoperational uses of software must also be accounted for as situations where safety considerations come into play. The resulting systems which are created using software might be unsafe in their operation as a result. These second-order effects are particularly worrisome as they are hard to prevent a priori.

For example, in his book *To Engineer Is Human*, Henry Petroski relates the work of the Electric Power Institute, which has been testing the ability of structural analysis computer software to predict the behavior of large transmission towers.[6] A full-sized tower was constructed in Texas where the actual structure could be subjected to controlled loads, and the resultant responses recorded. The computer predictions of the structural behavior of the tower were only within 60% of the actual measured value 95% of the time. The designers using the software, however, expect (and thought they were getting) an accuracy of within 20% of the actual measured value 95% of the time.

To say the least, the engineers were surprised and dismayed when informed of the inaccuracy of the computer model. The differences between the modeled system and the real system shown in this example are not unique, but are often unknown or overlooked by designers who place a tremendous faith in the numbers their CAD/CAM systems generate. This same faith is often shown by software engineers who often assume that their software support systems work perfectly, or that a successful static compilation equates to a successful execution. As Petroski notes, it is failures, not successes, which should lead the way to future success. Designs, however, which are created with computers have little experience of failure, let alone success. However, they are seen as helping do things that man cannot, and thus their weaknesses are overlooked. This faith has led designers to create structures having potential hazards that, all too often, are only beautiful hypotheses slain later by an ugly fact, which becomes clear when the design fails. Thus, we can add *indirect impacts* of nonoperational software on system behavior as another important characteristic of safety situations.

One may have noticed we have concentrated on the software aspects of safety, and have excluded the computer hardware aspects. These too, are part of the domain covered by the subject of software safety, although we will not concentrate too much of our effort in this direction. But to give an example of its importance, consider that in two studies, nearly 10% of all software errors and 35% of all software failures identified were later found as really being hardware related, such as a transient fault causing the corruption of data.[7,8] The Air Force data presented in Figure 3.24 seems also to bear this out. In fact, at the same level of development, hardware appears likely to fail three times as often as software, with hardware-related software errors also occurring nearly three times as often as software-alone errors. Overlooking the *hardware consequences* when contemplating software safety is dangerous and careless.

So one can see, there are a number of characteristics which indicate when we should consider the issue of safety in designing or developing all types of systems. These include the severity and magnitude of the risk's consequence, the operational boundaries affected when a flaw occurs, the immediacy of the consequence, the amount of time required for risk management to occur, the indirect impacts of nonoperational software on system behavior, and the reliability of the hardware. But to understand software safety, we really need to reverse fields a little bit and examine more closely what is meant and is implicated by the term *safety* itself.

5.1.1   What is safety?

Defining safety, like defining risk, is not altogether an easy chore. It is akin to trying to wade into a swamp without getting either dirty or wet. When we considered risk in Chapter 1, we stated it to be an event, action, thing, etc.:

1. Having a loss associated with it
2. Where uncertainty or chance was involved
3. Some choice was also involved

Each of these elements is a necessary but not individually sufficient condition for a risk to exist.

Safety, on the other hand, can be defined as the freedom from exposure to danger, or the exemption from hurt, injury, or loss.[9] In other words, if we can eliminate condition 1, one can be considered to be in a safe state.

One must be careful not to jump to conclusions, however, such as the ultimate in safety is the state where one is not exposed to risk. For if we keep condition 1 above, but eliminate either condition 2 or 3, we will not be exposed to a risk, but we will still be in an unsafe state (recall that this combination makes the situation, and its consequences, certain). Thus, if a risk is present, we can consider ourselves in an unsafe state, but the converse does not necessarily hold true. For this book, we will assume that risk situations exist, but we will keep in mind the implications of certainty situations on safety.

The above definition of safety, when risk exists, is intuitively an unappealing and, ultimately, not a practical one. The binary nature of a situation either being in a safe or unsafe state doesn't fit into the characteristics of safety situations we encountered earlier. In these, the *degree* or *amount* of hurt, injury, or loss came into consideration, and the loss incurred was aimed more at property than strictly pecuniary. The typical use of the term safety implies that it is more of a variable and, therefore, subjective attribute than strictly a binary metric. One cannot ever be completely free from all unsafe situations, and furthermore, not all "unsafe" conditions are equal, which one can presume by the hierarchical use of words hurt, injury, or loss in the definition. The current trend in software engineering seems to be to view safety as a quality of the software, which again makes its variability within a specific context an important characteristic.[10] But in so doing, we must assent also to the fact that this means safety is a subjective measure, which implies in turn that a level of safety may be acceptable to one person, but not to another. This makes risk, and safety, probability and judgmen, intertwined and inseparable. And once we concur in that, then we get into the great debate swirling around risk analysis and management, which become especially vehement when it includes issues of safety.

There are two major philosophic schools of thought concerning risk analysis, quantitative and qualitative, which are often at odds with one another.[11-14] The quantitative school believes that probabilities are primarily reflections of the *actual* frequency of events, thus are "objective," and can be used for predictions of future events. Members adhering to this philosophy hold that, "the real value of probabilistic risk analysis is in understanding the system and its vulnerabilities," and that given proper data, risk analysis can indicate when a project should continue, be changed, not be implemented, or be halted. There is a recognition of the limitations the quality of the input data imposes on the value of the analysis, but overall, the dependence on subjectiveness is, wherever possible, minimized.

The qualitative school does not play the "numbers game." Members of this philosophic school tend to believe that the assignment of probabilities primarily reflects the *assignee's* belief or confidence that an event will occur, and does not reflect the actual frequency of events. As one strong proponent explained, "statistics don't count for anything... they have no place in engineering anywhere." Risk is minimized and contained not by statistical test programs, but by paying particular attention to the details involved within a system's design. Quantitative risk analysis is seen at best as measuring the relative difficulty of a project, but it should not be seriously used as a basis for whether to implement or cancel a project.

The debate is often very much one of personal philosophy, reviving the arguments once seen in physics between the applicability and usefulness of classical mechanics vs. statistical mechanics. Many feel uncomfortable with a view of life controlled by probabilities. And it is not hard to understand why. A major encyclopedia article on the subject of probability theory has a *caveat emptor* warning, much like a consumer protection label for unsafe goods: "The reader should be warned that the philosophy of probability is highly controversial and thus the views expressed in this article would be rejected by many competent theorists."[15] Probability theory is strong in practice, but weak philosophically.

When probability theory is carried to the extreme, it can resemble the story of the young analyst and the general who were arguing about how World War III is going to come out. The general, exasperated, says to the kid, who has all kinds of advanced degrees, "Well *!**! it, we'll just have to start the war and see how it turns out." The analyst says in response, "That would be totally invalid. You'd only get one run out of the experiment."[16] On the other hand, when one is dealt a bridge hand of 13 cards, the probability of being dealt that particular hand is less than one in 600 billion (600,000,000,000). It would be absurd, however, for one to be dealt a hand, examine it carefully, calculate that the probability was less than 1 in 600 billion, and then conclude that he or she must not have been dealt that very hand because it is so very improbable.[17]

Furthermore, if carried to an extreme, one can get into trouble rapidly by worshiping calculations, as the U.S. military did in Vietnam, where everything was quantified, and anything that was not was thrown on the garbage heap. Among the things that were discarded, however, were precisely those things that make war what it is: man against man, not machine against machine.[18]

Given the above, it is not hard to understand why, when considering multimillion dollar software projects which do not involve the potential for losing human lives, the arguments over which philosophic school of risk analysis is "appropriate" become extremely heated, and when human life becomes a concern, the arguments become outright obdurate. This is because now one is dealing with what is an acceptable degree of safety, and no one likes having that decision made for or taken away from them. As we stated in the preface, this book leans towards the quantitative side, acknowledging the caveats on the validity of, and limitations implicit in, the data used to compute the probabilities. But we also accept William Rowe's tenet that subjective perception of risk or safety has to be the basis of their acceptance, regardless of the objective or quantified evaluation.[19] In the next chapter, we will see how these two schools of thought influence a person's view of risk taking.

Therefore, regardless of whether one believes probabilities are fundamentally subjective or objective, one is still left with a problem: how to deal with the topic of acceptability of the degree of safety evaluated. Framed another way, how much reliance should be placed on safety-critical computer systems involved in either the operation or design of C^3I, nuclear power plants, space vehicles, etc., or how safe is safe enough?

To adequately answer "how safe is safe enough," one must struggle to define the concept of "acceptability," for as we have just pointed out, in situations involving safety, it becomes a very personal choice. Consider, for example, the concept of the safety and acceptability of a risk as used by Lowrance.[20] A thing is safe if it is judged to be acceptable. Acceptability, however, can be used to mean such different things as: (1) a conscious decision, perhaps based upon some balancing of good and bad, or progress and risk; (2) a decision implying a comparison, possibly subjective, with threats from other causes, these latter being "acceptable" in relation to one of the senses provided here, or perhaps just historically and possibly unconsciously; or (3) the passive but substantive fact that nothing has to or can be done to eliminate or curtail the risk being deemed "acceptable."

The discussion becomes even more complicated when we include perceived risks as well as real risks. These perceived risks change both for the individual as well as for society in general. Since we base our understanding of "how safe" on subjective perception, safety judgments too must take into account the perception of safety risks as well. This is often difficult for design engineers and risk analysts to rationally contend with, and is a constant source of frustration. For instance, it is very difficult to understand why people who are comfortable driving on the Washington, D.C. beltway in rush hour on a rainy morning are afraid of flying in clear weather. The chances of being involved in a serious mishap are much less in taking a plane trip than in driving on the beltway. Local automobile insurance companies, in fact, can predict with a remarkable degree of accuracy the number of accidents its policy holders will have driving the beltway, and there are many more deaths and injuries due to serious accidents on it per year than caused by U.S. air disasters. However, the *perception* of safety to the average driver when taking a plane trip is much less, and a primary reason is the feeling of the lack of control of the risk one is accepting.[21]

It is easy to say, in these circumstances, that people must be rational, and possess realistic expectations of safety. Even though evaluations of safety are assumed to be based upon rational man (see note 34 in Chapter 1), the amount of control, or the lack of it, will be the primary driver in the perception of the acceptability of risk by those potentially affected in a safety situation, *regardless* of the reality. As we will see later in the section on software safety techniques, perception also influences engineers in the type of evaluation techniques one uses in an analysis.

Acceptance of a safety risk is not only influenced by the degree of risk, but whether there were any feasible methods to avert it if the consequences were to occur. There are basically two approaches to answering this question.[22] In the first approach, one can "simply" compare the direct gains to the direct losses involved in accepting a safety risk or not accepting it. The analysis in this case is basically rational and economic. If the balance is negative, there is no motivation for proceeding, unless the balance is redressed. On the other hand, a favorable balance will provide incentives for taking a risky alternative. The decision is basically boolean—either yes or no, with no marginally "grey" areas to consider.

The second approach is noneconomic in its approach to making a decision about safety. It involves the comparison of indirect gains to indirect losses. With this method, the "unquantifiable" aspects associated with a risk must be taken into account. Environmental impact studies are a prime example of this approach. Factors other than those which are purely economic are involved, and must be considered in the balance of the risk against its consequence. One factor that might be considered is the difficulty and cost in providing levels to achieve certain benefits,[23,24] as illustrated by the curve in Figure 5.1. Shown are the relative costs of achieving different levels of the effectiveness of safety risk aversion techniques which one might want to be considered as input. The leftmost point is where no safety risk aversion is done at all. This in essence means there is no money spent on safety management, and the risk consequences are accepted, depending on the course of nature or the vagaries of fate.

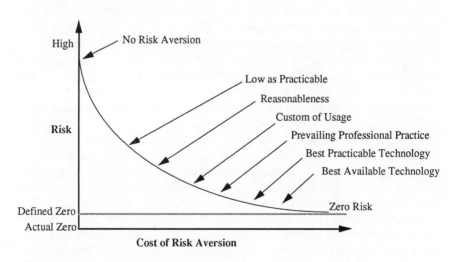

Figure 5.1 Risk vs. Technology Available to Avert Risk

The second point of effectiveness is termed as low as practicable. Its exact position is a subjective one, but it has to do with the generally accepted belief of what can and cannot be done to reduce a risk. In other words, it is the area where the resources spent by society to avert a risk is the same spent on averting a similar risk. Drinking alcohol was once considered a major health risk and was banned in the United States, but this turned out to be impracticable. Now its sales are regulated, as are its advertisements. The health risk is now assumed by the general public in both a personal and public manner (through tax dollars to pay for alcoholic rehabilitation).

The next five categories have increasing effectiveness, but also have increasing cost. They are: reasonableness, custom of usage, prevailing professional practice, best practicable technology, and best available technology. Reasonableness, custom of usage, and prevailing professional practice are the middle levels of risk aversion effectiveness. They are best understood in comparison to the last two categories of safety management effectiveness listed. Best practicable technology is where a safety risk can be reduced given "best industry practice," whereas the "best available technology" is the point where a technology for safety risk management has been demonstrated, but has not yet been applied on a wide-scale basis.

The last level is where there exists "zero risk" in the sense that a safety risk has been averted to the greatest possible extent. It is not, however, the actual zero risk point where the risk becomes a certainty. The risk is, however, no longer considered a safety risk. The zero risk point is based upon subjective judgment, but it can be considered the point where all parties would agree that no risk exists. It is also the point of prohibitive costs. The rule of thumb for most engineers is that the perfectly safe device will be too late, too heavy, or too expensive. During World War II, for example, the British had a saying that stated something to the effect that the third best system specified was the ideal one, since the second best was always too late, and the first never got built.

With indirect approaches to deciding what is an acceptable level of risk, there exist a number of different balancing points to be evaluated, instead of just two. Where the consequences of accepting a safety risk overwhelmingly favor the benefits over the cost, one says there is a favorable balance, and a decision on acceptability can be made with assurance. However, if the balance is only slightly in a positive direction, then one has what is termed a marginal balance. Now the decision may be in doubt. Likewise, if the costs generally outweigh benefits, then a marginally unfavorable balance exists, and again the decision may be in doubt. Where the costs far outweigh benefits, then there is an unacceptable balance. In Figure 5.2, we have illustrated the idea of a typical marginal balance that exists between the acceptable and unacceptable areas.

When one considers the acceptability of a safety risk, one must not only balance the decision with possible consequences, but with the cost effectiveness of risk reduction, and any reconciliations of inequities as a result of the decision. In other words, there must be a balance between what is feasible in the way of making a situation safe, and what is acceptable. The cost-effectiveness of reducing safety risk is an economic issue, with important underlying social overtones. In the United States, for instance, the concept of government is based upon the notion of rights, which is not always fully compatible with a strict cost/benefit approach to risk reduction.[25] Only if the decision under consideration is purely economic in nature can one apply the first decision approach to determining acceptability.

On the other hand, if the decision is based upon indirect gains and losses, then the decision making must reconcile the possible inequities that will result. There are elements to be considered that can shift the balancing point. For example, a safety risk, and whether its aversion is required, might be viewed differently from the perspectives of the sponsor, developer, and user, respectively. For instance, illustrated in Table 5.1 are just some of the considerations influencing safety judgments. Not to reduce a particular risk, the manifestation of which might be acceptable to the developer, might not be anywhere near acceptable to the user. This is especially true in the area of operational risks. As the report on the Challenger disaster said, "Safety criteria are designed to permit launch. They should not be allowed to force a launch."[26] Even when positive decisions are made, some group might suffer, or the

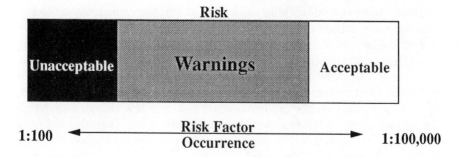

Figure 5.2 Unacceptability vs. Acceptability of Risk

TABLE 5.1 Considerations Influencing Safety Considerations

Risk assumed voluntary	Risk borne involuntarily
Effect immediate	Effect delayed
No alternatives available	Many alternatives available
Risk known with certainty	Risk not known
Exposure is an essential	Exposure is a luxury
Encountered occupationally	Encountered nonoccupationally
Common hazard	"Dread" hazard
Affects average people	Affects especially sensitive people
Will be used as intended	Likely to be misused
Consequences reversible	Consequences irreversible

benefits might not be evenly distributed. Equity of distribution of risks, benefits, and costs is ultimately a value judgment of fairness and social justice.

5.1.2 System/Software safety techniques

In this section, we plan to review some of the general techniques available for use in evaluating software safety situations or reducing safety concerns. However, to truly understand which safety analysis or containment method should be applied, it is necessary to understand somewhat more the root causes of safety problems in systems. We say systems, because our emphasis will be focused towards *system* safety. Software, as we indicated earlier, may only be a small, albeit very critical, part of an overall system, but it is the system context one must ultimately be concerned about. Before we proceed much further, we also need to increase our vocabulary.

Given these considerations examined so far, we have chosen for our purposes to use the following definition of safety developed by McKay.[27] A system is considered safe when "the probability that the system, including all hardware and software and human-machine subsystems, will provide appropriate protection against the effects of faults which, if not prevented or handled properly, could result in endangering lives, health, property, and/or environment." Notice a few things about this definition. First, it takes a system's perspective, and includes not only software, but hardware, human beings, and the greater social context in which they operate. This social context we will examine in the next chapter. However, an aspect of the system's perspective is the great challenge posed in building software systems by the human element, and how to ensure that human actions, either as operator inputs to the system, or as a response to specific information being processed and presented by the system to the human operator, do not cause unsafe conditions. The only way to handle all of the diverse elements which can impact the safety of a system is to integrate software, system, and the ultimate business or social reasons for the system being built in the first place.

Second, the definition talks about "appropriate protection" against the effects of faults. This is an important concept, as not only does one not need to have an absence of faults to have a safe system, but it acknowledges that it is unfeasible to eliminate all faults. However, this means one must proactively move to screen the system against faults. If there exists a means to contain the effects of a fault, then the system can still be considered safe, even in the presence of faults. The route to contain failure can either be fail-safe procedures, which are used to limit the amount of damage caused by a failure; fail-operational procedures, which provide full system functionality in the face of a failure; or fail-soft procedures, which provide a previously decided degraded functional performance in the face of a failure.[28]

Third, this definition makes it very clear that safety and reliability, while linked, are not equivalent, nor is reliability sufficient for obtaining safety. Reliability is concerned with the probability that a system or component performs its mission or task over a specific length of time. The concept of reliability *excludes* the consequences of failure and causes that happen to be external to the system or component. In other words, reliability is aimed at making a system free from failure, whereas safety is primarily concerned with limiting the effects of the failure to life and property of the environment when a failure occurs. Furthermore, a system can operate reliably, but still be unsafe. Increasing system reliability may increase safety, but sometimes the opposite can also occur.

Finally, the definition is very close to our concept of risk. The definition speaks of a choice, a chance, and a loss, which are the same component elements of risks, and thus we will be able to use the same types of techniques to identify, estimate and evaluate situations which involve safety. Safety, then, becomes a specific type of risk analysis and management problem, where the losses involve life, health, property, and/or the environment. However, it is important to again note that the management of safety will be different from the management of risk. The objective of risk management is *to make present risks lower*, while the objective of safety (risk) management is *to ensure that present risks do not increase.*

Now, for a few more definitions. When we spoke of a fault above, we were speaking of a "manifestation of an error, or an accidental condition which causes a functional unit to fail to perform its function."[29] A fault may cause a failure (i.e., the *termination* of the ability of a functional unit to perform its required function, or the inability of a system component to perform a required function within specified limits) and is usually caused as a result of an error (i.e., human action that results in an uncertain situation). Errors in software systems typically are a result of a user-originated error, for instance, the human operator follows procedures incorrectly, or from a developer-originated error; e.g., the developer writes incorrect program code.

Often, in the literature on safety, one sees the term *hazard* used instead of fault. They are not exactly the same, however. A hazard is an intrinsic property or condition that has the potential to cause an accident (i.e., a source of risk), whereas an accident is defined as an undesired consequence, often associated with an unwarranted transfer of energy due to the lack or failure of barriers and/or controls, inflicting losses to life, health, property, and/or environment. Nitroglycerin is a hazardous material, especially when shaken or exposed to heat. It possesses intrinsic properties which make this so. In our case, when considering a system context, software itself might be considered a hazard, since software itself might be considered to possess intrinsic properties which have the potential to cause an accident. For this book, however, we will not pursue this line of reasoning (except where the consequences of not considering safety are concerned) and will follow the definitions and thinking more traditionally found in the software literature.

Note, moreover, that a risk and a hazard, although close and often used interchangeably, are also not equivalent. A hazard represents only the potential for harm (i.e., consequences), whereas a risk also includes the choices involved and the likelihood of harm occurring. Looking at hazards by themselves, one does not know what threat they are representing, the chances of the threat becoming a reality, or how serious are the possible outcomes. Risk analysis provides the context in which hazards can be evaluated. In software systems, for example, safety critical software functions can directly or indirectly cause or allow a hazardous state to exist.[30] Safety critical software is thus defined as containing safety critical functions.

5.1.2.1 Why do systems fail? The objective of software safety is, then, to prevent accidents from occurring. This leads us back to our original question, why do systems fail? The answer, not too strangely, can again be traced directly back to the same fundamental reasons that risk itself exists: There is either a lack of knowledge, a lack of control, and/or a lack of time that comes into play. The source of the problem usually manifests itself when unusual, unexpected combination of events occur, and the system as designed is not able to cope. Recall from Chapter 2 the section on system theory. We stated that a system can be defined by elemental attributes called *state variables*. These state variables are used to define the set of possible values of the system (at some time **t**). The system, therefore, can be described by a *state vector*,

$$\mathbf{x} = \begin{vmatrix} x_1 \\ x_2 \\ x_3 \\ ... \\ ... \\ ... \\ x_n \end{vmatrix} \qquad (2.1)$$

such that, for each $\mathbf{x}_i$ (i =1..n) of the state vector, $\mathbf{x}$ represents one of the system states. The changes to the states over time form what is called the *state trajectory*. The totality of the space in which the trajectory may move is called the *state space of the system*. If $x_1(t)$ is the value of that state in the present time, and $x_1(t + s)$ the value of the variable at some future time, one can write a mapping of present state trajectory into the future state trajectory as follows:

$$\begin{vmatrix} x_1(t) \\ x_2(t) \\ x_3(t) \\ ... \\ ... \\ ... \\ x_n(t) \end{vmatrix} \begin{matrix} \rightarrow \\ \rightarrow \\ \rightarrow \\ . \\ . \\ . \\ \rightarrow \end{matrix} \begin{vmatrix} x_1(t + s) \\ x_2(t + s) \\ x_3(t + s) \\ ... \\ ... \\ ... \\ x_n(t + s) \end{vmatrix} \qquad (2.2)$$

When this mapping is as above, where a one-to-one mapping exists, one says the system is *deterministic*. However, when the state variables can map to a many-to-one or a one-to-many basis, then the system is said to be *indeterminate* or *probabilistic*. In systems where there are many different types of state variables, or they are not well defined, or the state trajectory has many complex mappings, one says that the system is poorly structured, or messy, resulting in boundaries that may be unclear or difficult to identify.

When designing or constructing systems, especially as they become more complex, one becomes less certain about the number of state variables that are involved or their transitions. Furthermore, in real systems, the mappings of the state transitions are more likely to be indeterminate or probabilistic. The result is that system interactions are likely to be unexpected and incomprehensible for certain periods of time, thus increasing the risk of system failure. Thus one should not be startled that complex systems fail, but be more surprised that they work at all. Given typical system characteristics (i.e., interactive complexity and tight coupling), multiple and unexpected interactions of individual system component failures are inevitable.[31] The more complex and tightly coupled the system, the more likely that a brittle system will be the result. This is an expression of an integral, intrinsic characteristic of these type of systems, and is not a statement of the frequency of failures that may occur. For example, we all die, which is an intrinsic characteristic of living, but we do it only once. The key idea is to understand that complex systems will fail—the trick is to try to design the system in such a way to contain the effects of the failure from becoming a safety concern.

5.1.2.2 Provision for safety. The question one must answer in the design of a system which might have an impact on safety is, as Alan Borning stated, to what extent are we able to state and codify our intentions so that all circumstances are covered?[32] This covers not only known intentions of the system which we were not able to articulate, but what we should have intended, if we had only known. Initially, one must try to understand the wider couplings that are involved in a system and its operating environment. Defining the proper system of interest is fundamental to accomplishing this. For example, for a very long time there was no relationship discerned between dams and their capability to cause earthquakes when sited near fault zones. Once this link was established, the suitability of siting dams in certain locations became a greater concern. Figure 5.3 furnishes once again some examples of systems which have varying degrees of interaction and coupling, measured by the numbers of levels and degree of interconnectiveness.[33] We have

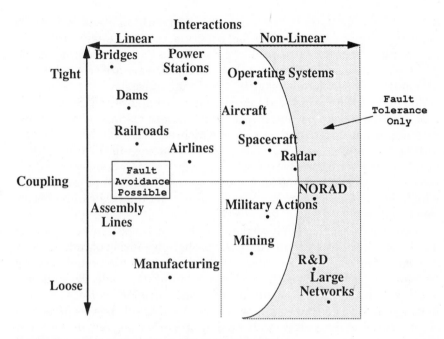

Figure 5.3 Types of Systems Interactions and Coupling

also illustrated where only fault tolerance, rather than fault avoidance, is possible to contain the effects of failure. Systems possessing high coupling and highly complex interactions are the ones which will more likely have failures associated with them. Systems of this type may also have a very strong negative effect on the ability of humans to maintain proper system operation in the presence of failures.[34] Three Mile Island, Chernobyl, and other nuclear power plant incidents are just some of the more noteworthy examples.

In computer systems, the system of interest involving safety concerns becomes a bit more confusing. There exist many subcomponents which have tight coupling and highly complex interactions. The operating system is one, as is the computer architecture itself. The binding of application to operating system to architecture is a prime example of a system with tight coupling and highly complex interactions. When embedded into larger systems, such as command and control systems, the probability for failure quickly approaches unity. For example, there are approximately 3.3 software errors per thousand in large software systems.[35] This should not be surprising, as you may recall, from Chapter

3, there are as many as 10^{20} unique end-to-end paths in a moderate-sized program.[36] Even assuming a perfect program, to execute each only once, assuming it took 1/1000 second, the sun would burn out before you get done. What is worse is that not all errors in software are created equal, as small errors do not necessarily have small effects.

The move towards reduced instruction set computers (RISC), UNIX-type operating systems, object-oriented database management systems and programming techniques, each of which are "less complex" (initially, at least) than what existed before, are all reactions to the difficulty of building large systems. By trying to simplify the interactions and reduce the couplings involved, the idea is that one can build computer systems which do not fail as often, or ones in which the failures can be better contained.

Again, the tactic is not to incorporate a change, in the name of reducing a risk, which will instead increase the probability of risk of catastrophic failure. Using computer architectures which are simpler in nature may decrease the complexity of the underlying application code, for instance, but this gain may have been purchased at the cost of not having the built-in safeguards to operate safely when a software fault has occurred. As Henneman and Rouse have indicated, if properly designed, as a system becomes more complex, it should become more resistant to the effects of system failures.[37] Failures should take longer to propagate through the system, thus allowing for more time to gain information and control, and to put in place proper failure containment schemes. The effects of any one failure on system performance therefore should be minimized due to the number of alternative paths through the system. The downside in complex systems is that finding failures becomes more difficult. A failure may not be recognized until it begins to overwhelm the safety mechanisms.

What this implies, of course, is that the most effective means to avoid accidents during a system's operation is by eliminating or reducing dangers during design and development of the system. Thus, it is essential to realize that a system must be designed with safety in mind from the beginning. However, this is not always that easily accomplished, as safety concerns often need to be considered. Consider the turret explosion aboard the battleship U.S.S. Iowa (BB-61). In this accident, a premature explosion occurred in the turret during a practice firing mission before the breach was properly closed. As a result, over 50 of the approximately 77 Navy seamen manning the turret were killed. The reason for the disaster is still being debated, but the reason why so many persons were killed was because of the need for manually operating the turret, specifically to avoid the use of electrical machinery that might create sparks and cause fires. Additionally, within the turret, there existed many interlocks and flame-tight skuttles to keep any fire which might occur in circumstances like this one from spreading to the rest of the ship. The interlocks worked properly and saved the ship, but it was at the sacrifice of the men inside the turret.

5.1.2.3 Analysis methods. In this book's companion, *Software Engineering Risk Analysis and Management*, we explored a number of methods for identifying, estimating, and evaluating risks. Since we view safety as a particular type of risk, these general methods can be used to help investigate where safety issues may be of significance. Rather than review these methods again, we feel that this section should concentrate on those methods which have been developed especially for safety risk analysis.

Before we begin, it is useful to remember that all risk or safety analysis techniques have three things in common. First, their primary purpose is to help ensure that the obvious is not overlooked. This is another way of saying that they help impose a disciplined framework from which to investigate a problem. A good analyst constantly looks for ways a system may fail, and does not dismiss events because the common knowledge says they "cannot possibly happen." Second, every technique tries to impose some stability into the evaluation process. Without this stability; i.e., a reference point or "ground zero," one cannot tell if one is actually improving safety, or determine the amount of improvement. And third, each technique or analysis method looks for the same risk, but from different angles of attack. Although it may seem redundant to do this, no single method can identify every risk, and from certain perspectives, a risk may not be observable. As we pointed out earlier, hardware errors often cause or are mistaken for software errors, and more than one technique will be necessary to discover these types of errors. It is wise to conduct two or three different types of analysis where safety is concerned.

As we have mentioned before, there are two schools of philosophic thought in performing risk analysis, and these two schools of thought impact the type of safety techniques utilized and, more importantly, how their evaluation results are regarded. Designing for safety can be thought of as the primary technique used by the qualitative school, with safety analysis as an important adjunct element. The quantitative philosophy also designs for safety, but views the quantitative techniques as primary drivers for safety. This distinction is important, because it influences the importance given to the analysis results. Those holding the design for safety view will tend to be "more positive" about their ability to be able to design safe and reliable systems, thus exhibiting a propensity for discounting analysis which provides "defective" or "nonsupportive" numbers. This group tends to take more risk. The opposite is true of the quantitative school, which tends to be more risk averse. The numbers derived from the quantitative analysis are held in higher regard and tend to influence the decisions about safety.

It is difficult to say which school is correct. This author believes that healthy skepticism is required in developing systems which have safety as a concern, and that both approaches are required. The NASA shuttle program, as well as almost all the previous NASA space flight programs, was a product of the "design for safety philosophy." However, analysis showed that there was a 1:21 to 1:909 probability of a catastrophic failure of a shuttle booster.[38,39] The lower end number was ignored as being unreasonable (we will examine in the next chapter why this belief was held). After the *Challenger* disaster, NASA adopted a more quantitative approach to its safety analysis. We will deal in the next chapter with the idea of risk taking and how the two philosophies influence thinking on, and taking action against, risk.

Good system safety analysis practice begins at system concept, and continues throughout the life cycle of the system design and on into its operation. And as one would think, there are standard analysis techniques available to help in each phase of a system's life. We will not try to delve into a great amount of detail on any one analysis, but will try to provide the purpose of the analysis, when it is used, its general procedure, the type of results of the analysis, the nature of the results, the information requirements, and its weakness or limitation. For specific details, one should consult any one of the references.[40-49]

5.1.2.3.1 Preliminary hazard analysis.
Preliminary Hazard Analysis (PHA) is usually the first safety analysis technique to be applied. It is an inductive technique performed anywhere from the system concept to the early design phase of a system. Its purpose is to search for, and identify, very early on the *hazards* which are present. The PHA thus gives the system engineers some time and guidance in what safety issues may affect the later design stages. The PHA is not meant to effect the control of the hazard, but to recognize all the implications of the hazard. It is most effective when applied to a system development where past history gives little or no forewarning of potential safety problems.

The input required for a PHA includes any available system design objectives, design specifications, equipment specifications, system energy sources, interface specifications, environmental data, operational concept documents, and governmental regulations concerning possible hazards. Any relevant historical data of like systems and their failures would also be of value. The output of the PHA is a list of hazards with recommendations for their possible containment or elimination, which may be used to develop system safety requirements, as well as general performance and design specifications. The hazards may be also classified according to their importance, such as shown in Table 5.2, thus marking the beginnings of a safety risk analysis.[50] The nature of the output of the PHA is necessarily qualitative, with its primary limitation being that unless a safety risk analysis is conducted, one cannot determine from the PHA alone the effects of different means to contain the hazard or prioritize the hazards or their containment procedures.

5.1.2.3.2 Fault hazard analysis. Fault Hazard Analysis (FHA), also sometimes referred to as a Subsystem Hazard Analysis (SSHA), is another inductive technique performed usually after the PHA occurs during the early system definition and design stages. It is meant to concentrate on smaller units of the system for the purpose of investigating hazards that may have come to light as the system becomes more defined. The FHA is also meant to examine certain high priority hazards identified in the PHA, as well as ones which the certainty of the hazard is not well understood. The FHA tries to answer in greater detail how an individual system component or module can fail, and what possibly can happen if it does fail.

The input to the FHA are the PHA, the refined system design, the component description and function, interface and dependency definitions between and among components, the failure modes of the component, and any environmental data of relevance including critical human inputs which might be subjected to error. The output is a qualitative assessment of what may occur when the component fails, what may inadvertently happen when a hazard is encountered, and recommendations for containing or eliminating the failure and *their* implications. The weakness of the FHA is that there is no guarantee of anticipating every interaction that occurs, nor is there a guarantee of being able to deal with marginally safe states.

TABLE 5.2 Hazard Classification Schemes

**System Safety Program Requirements
(Mil-STD-882B)**

Category I
Catastrophic: May cause death or system loss

Category II
Critical: May cause severe injury, severe occupational
illness, or major system damage

Category III
Marginal: May cause minor injury, minor occupational illness,
or minor system damage

Category IV
Negligible: Will not result in injury, occupational illness,
or system damage

NASA Handbook 5300.4 (ID-2)

Category 1
Loss of life or vehicle, or loss of life or injury to public

Category 1R
Redundant hardware element, failure of which could
cause loss of life or vehicle

Category 2
Loss of mission, including postlaunch abort or launch
delay sufficient to scrub mission

Category 1R
Redundant hardware element, failure of which could
cause loss of mission

Category 3
All others

Department of Energy 5481.1—Nuclear

High
Hazards with potential for major on-site or off-site
impacts to people or the environment

Moderate
Hazards that present considerable potential on-site impacts to people
or environment, but at most only minor off-site impacts

Low
Hazards that present minor on-site and negligible off-site
impacts to people or the environment

5.1.2.3.3 System hazard analysis. System Hazard Analysis (SHA) usually is performed after FHA as the design "hardens," and continues until the design is complete and accepted. The outcomes of the PHA and FHA are used as inputs to help determine where the system's design needs to be changed to accommodate safety concerns surfaced thus far. The SHA is a qualitative analysis which looks for common-cause problems, common-mode problems, and correlated failure analysis. The aim is to try to expose combinations of events or failures (independent or dependent), including the failure of safety devices, as well as degradation due to normal "wear and tear," that may cause problems later. Also, interfaces between subsystems, between the system and its operators, and the system and its environment are closely examined. The SHA is like the FHA except that it examines how system operations and failures can affect the safety of the system and its subsystems, whereas the FHA concentrates more on individual component failures. The SHA possesses the same weaknesses as those found in the FHA.

5.1.2.3.4 Operability hazard analysis. Operability Hazard Analysis (OHA), sometimes also called Operability and Support Hazard Analysis (OSHA) or Hazard and Operability Studies (HazOp), focuses on hazards that result from tasks, activities, or operational system functions that can occur. OHA's purpose is to identify hazard and operability problems which could compromise the system's ability to carry on correctly and in a safe manner. It is a generally qualitative set of analyses which occur during the late design phase when the system's design is very firm and/ or nearly complete (or when a redesign of the system has been planned). A systematic search for hazards is generated, examining the system's instrument diagrams and flow charts at critical junctions, for effects which might be deviations from the normal operating parameters. To be most effective, the OHA should be timed such that any hazards identified which have not been considered in the PHA, FHA, or SHA or changes that could result in the design because of the analysis can be effectively incorporated into the system's design and operation.

The input to the OHA are the complete set of detailed engineering documentation (plans, design drawings, procedures, etc.), including support facilities required, and description of how the system's instrumentation is suppose to work. The output of the OHA are possible deviations from the normal operating parameters, causes of these deviations, the consequences of the deviations, and possible containment strategies. The weakness of an OHA is twofold. First, if the design documentation is not complete, the analysis may be incomplete. Second, since the OHA is left until late in the design phase, if no time is left for correcting deviations, the OHA is only worthwhile for the next redesign.

5.1.2.3.5 Failure mode and effects analysis.

Failure Mode and Effects Analysis (FMEA), also called FMEA/CIL (critical items list) or FEMA/CA (critical analysis), is aimed at studying the potential failures, both hazardous and nonhazardous, that occur in order that their source can be eliminated. Used during design, implementation, and system operations, it identifies all of the ways a component of the system can fail, and each failure mode's effects on the system. By applying a criticality analysis, the potential seriousness of the failures can be ranked.

The FMEA/CA procedure proceeds basically as follows: the failure mode is identified, the effect of failure determined, the cause of the failure resolved, the probability of the occurrence of failure established, the severity of the failure rated, the possibility of detecting the error before it becomes a problem rated, the assignment of a risk priority number to the failure, and finally deciding what corrective action is required. The process is, as one can see, bottom-up in its approach. It is also qualitative in nature, except when the probabilities are assigned (if the probabilities can be accurately determined, that is). Required as input are the system design, equipment list, function descriptions, and operation concept documents. The weakness of the FMEA is that it is time consuming, is not good at identifying combinations of errors, or for identifying operational input errors.

5.1.2.3.6 Fault tree analysis.

Fault Tree Analysis (FTA) is really a top-down technique applied during the design and operational phases that is used in conducting some of the more general analyses above. The technique uses a deductive approach which emphasizes cause or sequence of events causing the failure of a system, in contrast to the PHA, which emphasizes the hazard itself and its effect. It uses as input the complete knowledge of the system's functions, its failure modes and their effects (this can be obtained from the FMEA). As a result of the FTA, a list of equipment and/or operator failures that can result in a specific malfunction, ranked qualitatively by importance, can be created. Additionally, hidden failure modes that result from subsystem interactions and combinations of malfunctions may be uncovered.

The FTA approach is graphical in nature, with a tree being used to diagram the logical connections, using boolean logic, between failure modes of a system. The top of the tree, or the *top event*, represents an undesirable event, such as equipment failure, human error, or function malfunction. The construction of the rest of the tree follows a systematic procedure which first identifies the general events; i.e., failure states, which, when logically combined, will result in the undesired top event. Then these secondary failure states will be investigated, and the failure states which are required to be combined to cause them will be identified and modeled. This process of determining the series-parallel relationships of the system which leads to the top event continues until all basic failure modes, or components of the fault tree, have been identified. If there exists probabilistic information concerning events, system components, and/or subsystems failure's available, then a quantitative analysis can be performed. Figures 5.4a and 5.4b illustrate some of the symbols used in a FTA and an application of it to a nuclear reactor.

By analyzing the tree in some detail, one can determine the set of events which cause the top event to be explicitly identified. The fault tree can then be used to demonstrate the effects of redesign or failure containment, such as trying to interrupt the chain of failures. In the latter case, the dual of the fault tree is used to find the model for preventing or containing the top event. This dual is ultimately the desired outcome of FTA.

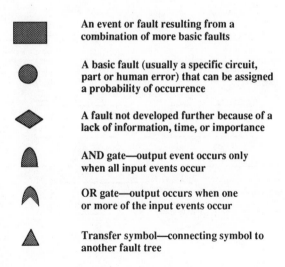

An event or fault resulting from a combination of more basic faults

A basic fault (usually a specific circuit, part or human error) that can be assigned a probability of occurrence

A fault not developed further because of a lack of information, time, or importance

AND gate—output event occurs only when all input events occur

OR gate—output occurs when one or more of the input events occur

Transfer symbol—connecting symbol to another fault tree

Figure 5.4a Basic Fault Tree Symbols

The weaknesses of FTA lies in two fundamental areas. The first is that a fault tree can become exceedingly complex, thus practically, the tree must be limited to one top event (it can represent a failure mode of more than one event, however) and one specific aspect of the system. Choosing the correct granularity of the fault tree model is important to its usefulness. Second, and just as important, one needs to be careful to consider the independence or mutual dependence of the events entering a particular boolean logic gate in order to ensure a correct selection of the probability method (conditional, joint, or mutually exclusive). An experienced computer hardware designer, because of a strong background in this type of analysis, would be an asset to the team performing the FTA.

5.1.2.3.7 Event tree analysis. Event Tree Analysis (ETA) or incident sequence analysis identifies potential accidents by means of "forward analysis" from an initiating event, such as equipment failure, human error, or function malfunction.[51] The event trees define the specific sequence of failures that is necessary for an accident to occur or, from an

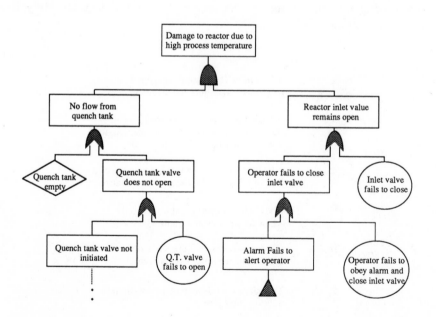

Figure 5.4b Partial Fault Tree

initiating event, the sequence of corrective responses to that event, as shown in Figure 5.5. The ETA differs from FTA in that the FTA uses deduction, or "reverse analysis," to trace from an undesired event back to its basic causes. The FTA defines the specific component failures necessary for a particular safety function or safety system to fail, for example. ETA, by use of a decision tree, can depict their initiating events, and system safety functions, to determine the successes and failures of the safety functions as a malfunction occurs and is propagated through the system. The ETA will depict the accident sequences and define the chronological relationships between initiating and subsequent events, and is especially well suited for analyzing events that can have varied outcomes. Accidents are ranked to determine the most important risks encountered.

ETA occurs usually during a system's design and operation phases, utilizing the knowledge of initiating events, the system's equipment functionality, and system's safety functions. The weaknesses of this mostly qualitative approach are that it is poor at handling partial failures or time delays, which can occur between an event initiation and the event actually occurring. We should note that if the event probabilities

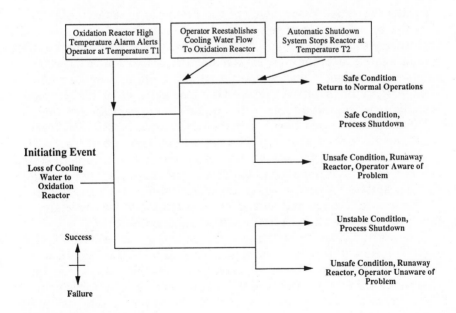

Figure 5.5 Sample Event Tree

are known, then the expected probability of sequences can be defined, however.

5.1.2.3.8 Human reliability analysis. The last analysis procedure we wish to describe is the Human Reliability Analysis (HRA). This mostly qualitative analysis, as the name implies, tries to identify the risks (rather than hazards) associated with human interaction with the system, either required or incidental. The analysis takes place during the design, implementation, and operational phases of the system's life.

The input to the analysis process includes all the system's operational procedures, layouts, functions, tasks, as well as human factors and psychological studies which have been conducted. Critical timing information, especially where human operators may need to react to manually impose system safety constraints, are especially needed. The output are lists of events, with priority rankings, where human interaction with the system contributes to significant risk. The weakness of the analysis again stems from not being able to account for all possible interactions except in trivial cases, as well as the typical lack of information about human reliability performance when interacting with the system in question.

5.1.2.3.9 Safety verification. One of the problems in safety analysis is that the techniques themselves can be so complicated that they are themselves sources of error.[52,53] Thus, some type of verification of the system's safety after the analysis is completed is still required. However, safety verification is different from what we encountered earlier in Chapter 3, in that safety verification is aimed at never letting an unsafe state be reached, but an incorrect, but safe, state is still allowable. In other words, one is not trying to demonstrate correctness. Verification must be able to show that either a fault cannot occur, cannot make the system reach an unsafe state, cannot steer a system into an unsafe state, or if it does occur, is not dangerous. This becomes clearer if one thinks of the four states of a system when considering safety and correctness. It is either in a correct and safe state, a correct and unsafe state, an incorrect and safe state, or an incorrect and unsafe state.[54]

There are many formal techniques for conducting software verification, such as formal proofs, and the reader can examine the references for further details. One of the most widely used techniques is to use fault tree backward analysis because the number of unsafe states is usually smaller than the number of incorrect states. However, current validation cannot guarantee that correct and safe states exist. Furthermore, imperfect execution environments are the norm, not the exception, thus making techniques like static code verification inadequate. Run-time errors are especially difficult to detect, although some work towards helping resolve this problem is underway at NASA. [55]

5.1.2.3.10 Safety improvements: How can software engineering help? As we have mentioned earlier, the easiest way to eliminate a risk is to design it out. Hazard prevention by designing them out is the cheapest and most effective means to improve safety. Another way, of course, is to perform hazard control such as to make the design "bullet or GI"-proof or firewalling. These are accomplished by building in safety factors or barriers which prevent the unsafe condition from spreading. These techniques try to compensate for any risks that might be encountered that were not thought about. In the worst case, the system may decide to shut itself down to avoid a catastrophe. In other cases, it may attempt to redirect the direction of the system, attempt triage (chose a safety objective which might have to be sacrificed), or attempt recovery.[56] An alternative way of stating it is to allow for the possibility of ignorance; i.e., a margin of error that allows for all the corollaries to Murphy's Law to take place. An example is found in commercial jet engine parts, where a life limit is set for each major aircraft component. The life limit is the time a part can be allowed to be used before it is replaced, whether or not it has worn out. The life limit varies depending on the part, but on certain parts, such as first stage engine fan disks (the part which is suspected to have caused the 1989 United Airlines Sioux City crash), it is set at one-third the theoretical calculations of actual life limits.[57]

In building systems which have safety critical software, the approach to including safety factors most often is seen in the shape of redundancy. This redundancy can take many forms. Often, such as that seen in Figure 5.6, it is seen in the form of hardware redundancy.[58] These same forms can be used and replicated in software, with one of the favorites called *N-version* programming. In this case, a number of versions of the same program specification are created separately by different programming teams to try to contain failures caused by poorly defined specifications. The outputs of the different versions are then compared and a "vote" is taken to determine which result is the "correct" one. The method of voting can be very complex, and is often based on sophisticated heuristics, since the agreed value may not be in fact "correct," but the consensus of the different versions.

The space shuttle uses a type of N-version programming. It has five computers, four of which are running the same program. (Note, the

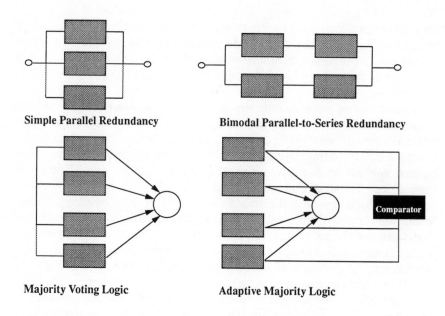

Simple Parallel Redundancy · · · Bimodal Parallel-to-Series Redundancy

Majority Voting Logic · · · Adaptive Majority Logic

Figure 5.6 Some Typical Examples of Hardware Redundancy

computers do not have room to hold all the programs required for a typical mission. Therefore, the astronauts have to load new programs for each phase of the mission from tapes. There may be more than five of these tapes in use during a mission.) If one computer is out of agreement, the mission can continue. If two computers are out of agreement, however, the mission has to be curtailed. The fifth computer serves as a safety back-up. It is physically separated from the other four, and has its cabling routed through different circuits as well. It has both the ascent and descent programs loaded, and it is meant to be used only to get the shuttle home in case of a major problem.

N-version programming can help reduce or eliminate errors caused by misinterpretations of the specifications, reduce the replication of identical programming errors, and overcome errors which might be present in the hardware which a certain code sequence might trigger, to name just a few. N-version redundancy is often coupled with hardware redundancy to try to maximize failure containment, and often to try to perform fault detection.

Certain N-version programming techniques have been shown to yield up to 7–10-fold improvement in software reliability.[59] One must not be lulled into thinking that by adding redundancy in the form of multiple versions, one does not have to worry about conducting safety analyses. It has been shown, for instance, that common error problems/common failure errors have been found in and up to 8 distinct versions of an N-version system.[60] This occurs because independently developed program versions can fail dependently.[61] To overcome this problem, in general, when performing N-version programming, one should strive for utilizing different (i.e., diverse) types of requirement and design methodologies for each of the individual versions. The greater the diversity, the more independent the versions are likely to be, and the more likely (with caveats) they will fail independently.[62]

Additionally, it is possible for a hardware fault to cause a software failure which can bypass many hardware safety mechanisms and negatively affect independent redundant processors.[63] Furthermore, even if no individual component fails, because of a problem that can exist when comparing finite precision numbers, an N-version system may not be able to reach consensus. Called the *Consistent Comparison Problem*, no general practical solution exists to overcoming it, or for predicting its probability of occurrence.[64] And as an added concern, this problem may cause failures that would not have occurred if N-version programming or other some similar non–fault-tolerant approach had been originally left out. Finally, N-version programming may increase reliability, but it may not be able to prevent an accident from occurring, since the approaches to increase reliability may not be compatible with those to reduce accidents (see note 58). Thus, one must be aware that adding in safety features may in fact lower it in some cases, and therefore safety trade-offs must be made explicit.

Applying software IV&V and quality control across the life cycle are the other favorite software engineering means of trying to increase safety. As we saw in Chapter 2, here one tries to eliminate unacceptably large flaws by minimizing deviations from an acceptable norm and by rejecting inferior workmanship. For situations involving software safety, and programs with not many resources to throw at it, the primary concentration of the IV&V and quality control efforts should be aimed at the software requirements, since these will influence system safety the most. Software requirements can be placed into criticality classes, as illustrated in Figure 5.7, which depicts the system requirements which will impact overall system safety the most.[65] The very critical and highly critical requirements are then investigated first, with any resources left over used to attack the less critical requirements. One then can assign safety priority factors to the requirements that, in contrast to software

Estimated Program
Source Lines Involved

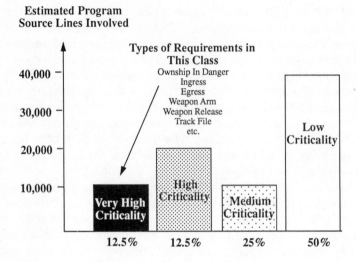

Figure 5.7 Example of Requirements Criticality Analysis for Naval Combat System

requirements, which show what the system will do, depict what the system must not do. A good rule of thumb is that when safety situations are expected, the requirements should minimize a system's complexity by separating safety critical functions and data, and judiciously limiting the critical actions placed in software. If this can be accomplished, then the verification of, and confidence in, the system's safety can more easily be gained.

The techniques above, especially fault tree analysis, have all been applied with some degree of success to software projects with safety requirements. Fault trees have the most experience behind them, and have been used for determination of safety requirements, detection of logic errors, detection of multiple failure sequences, detection of common-mode, detection of common-cause failures, detection of critical run-time areas, and selection of test data. The reader is encouraged to review the references for examples.

5.1.3 Cost of software safety

A question that arises, and which we touched upon a bit earlier, is what are the costs of conducting software safety? In the distribution of hazards to be faced and benefits to be gained, who will pay? Will those who benefit end up paying, or is the burden shifted to others? Resources spent on safety, after all, are resources that cannot be spent someplace else. There are no simple answers, and in the end, all are political, in the general sense of the word.

Thoreau, in *Walden*, wrote that "the cost of a thing is the amount of what I will call life which is required to be exchanged for it, immediately or in the long run." The severity of the hazard, or potential consequence of an accident, will ultimately determine the cost; i.e., the amount people are willing to pay, to attain safety. When safety is concerned, the equation becomes a bit fuzzy, as not all of the money spent is equal in every situation. Table 5.3 illustrates the *wide* range of the amounts of money spent on trying to save a human life in various situations.[66]

These costs are often calculated in the following manner.[67] Assume the following:

$$C_{SE} = \text{cost of safety effort}$$
$$C_M = \text{cost of loss per mishap}$$
$$M' = \text{mishap rate}$$
$$N = \text{number of periods or cycles}$$
$$M_{Total} = \text{number of mishaps}$$

TABLE 5.3 Cost of Saving a Life

Activity	Cost ($1985)	
Cervical cancer screening	75,000	
	10,000	(U.K)
Breast cancer screening	225,000	
	22,500	(U.K)
Mobile intensive care	110,000	
Liver transplant	150,000	
Mandatory seat belts	500	
Nuclear industry employee and public	75,000,000	
	45,000,000	(U.K)
Smoke alarms in houses	1,250,000	(U.K)
Prevention of collapse of high-rises	150,000,000	
Asbestos lung cancer (proposed)	30,000,000	
Toxic air:		
coke-oven emissions (proposed)	682,000,000	
benzene (proposed)	5,880,000,000	

The loss during the system's life cycle is:

$$C_{SE} = \text{based upon actuals } M_{Total}C_M,$$
$$\text{or, based upon a rate} = M'C_M N \qquad (5.1)$$

The loss rate during a specific period is:

$$(\text{Mishap rate}) \bullet (\text{Average loss per mishap}) = M'C_M \qquad (5.2)$$

The overall value to an organization of a safety program equals the cost of a safety program, or in other words, the cost of the mishap prevention effort and of the losses, or:

$$\text{Value over a period} = C_{SE} + M_{Total}C_M \qquad (5.3)$$

The increased cost of an additional safety effort can be justified only by decreasing the mishap number or rate of the mishaps occurring, their severity, or both. The product of these two factors must exceed any added cost to be economically justifiable. A comparison of the two efforts for the same system would show that the savings during the entire system life cycle is:

$$M_{Total1}C_{M1} - M_{Total2}C_{M2} + (C_{SE2} - C_{SE1}) \qquad (5.4)$$

Another way of calculating safety costs is through the concept of risk leveraging.[68] Risk leveraging reflects the cost-benefit considerations in prioritizing risk aversion tasks. Risk leveraging is computed as:

$$\frac{\text{Risk Exposure } {}_{[Before]} - \text{Risk Exposure } {}_{[After]}}{\text{Risk Aversion Cost}} \qquad (5.5)$$

where Risk Exposure = (Risk Probability) $\bullet$ (Loss of Utility). The loss of utility accounts for the "unquantifiables" to be given consideration.

The single greatest difficulty in computing the real cost of preventing a potential safety situation is that it is very much like trying to calculate how much should go into terrorism prevention. One cannot ever be certain, when an accident does not occur, whether it's the safety devices which are the reasons why, or whether the system was designed well enough that the safety devices were superfluous. There are no easy answers, although the penalties for ignoring software safety if an accident occurs can be very severe.

5.1.4 Penalties for ignoring system and software safety

In the section above, we spoke of the cost of making software safe. However, these costs do not include the addition legal, image, and reputation costs if, despite good intentions, or common practice, something goes wrong and an accident occurs. Recently, for example, a therapeutic radiation device was responsible for the deaths of at least three cancer patients and injuries to many others when a fundamental flaw in the software controlling the device occurred.[69] A primary cause was the lack of any type of formal safety analysis being conducted on the system's design and operation. When an operator tried to correct an erroneous command and reentered the information in the "edit" mode, the device dispensed a much higher radiation dosage than intended. Not only was this tragic, but given the technical reason for its occurrence, the accident seems avoidable. Because of accidents like the one above, the trend in the United States today is to use the judicial system to make manufacturers of products accountable for their products via damage awards to customers who are injured by using their products.[70] In this view, software itself is considered a hazard, and thus possesses intrinsic properties which can make a product unsafe. This is a different view from how software is typically seen within the computing world, but one which will be challenged very soon.

Before going much further, let me state very clearly that I am not a lawyer, and product liability law is not within my general expertise. But I can say without reservation that for owners of companies that either produce or sell software in any quantity, software must be viewed as a hazard and its targeting as a potential product liability concern will increasingly find its way onto the agendas of the executive board.

One obvious reason is that product liability is one of the most serious of all business liabilities. Over the past decades, states have generally abandoned the old interpretation that manufacturers were exempt from liability for defective products. It is increasingly common for courts to hold the manufacturer, and seller, almost totally responsible for injury or property damage due to an unsafe or defective product. Furthermore, the trend in liability cases is to now only show that there is some probability that the product could have caused the harm.[71] In other words, overt negligence during the design, development, or testing does not have to be proved.[72]

Companies can be penalized for not keeping proper records of product sales and distribution, of project failures, and of customer complaints.

Liability also extends to how the product is represented. Misrepresenting the character or quality of a product through advertising is a liable activity if it causes injury or property damage. Thus, the use of the term "computer control," which many companies advertise for purposes of making an added, beneficial selling point, either for performance, convenience, or safety reasons, can amplify the developer's and seller's liability. The potential penalties for not making software safe are becoming increasingly enormous, and as Kolb and Ross have stated, "The choice engineers, designers, and their employers no longer have is whether or not to pursue safety goals."[73]

Liability is not only having an impact in the United States. In Europe, for example, the European Economic Commission (EEC) is contemplating a regulation which states that no product will be able to be sold within the EEC without it being shown to be "safe," where safe means "presenting no unacceptable risk." Unfortunately, this concept hasn't yet been fully defined, and will likely only be done so in court. In some countries in the EEC, such as the United Kingdom, chief designers are already legally liable for damage and injury caused by design errors, including those found in software. The U.K. Ministry of Defense has gone so far as to consider proposing that on systems that use safety critical software, as defined by MoD-Std-0056, the application of formal methods and mathematical models as defined in MoD-Std-0055 will be required to show that a system is safe. Only software developers that can *prove* they do not have safety critical software will be exempt from the requirements in MoD-Std-0055.[74,75] Ignoring safety in products will ultimately mean not being able to sell commercial products or bidding on defense contracts in the United Kingdom.

The potential implications on the way software engineering will be performed in the future are enormous. As we saw in Chapter 2, risk acceptability often involves political, economic, and moral decisions that many consider in the software field to be outside the decision making realm of software engineers. Whether this is right or wrong—and I think it is wrong—the subject will most likely be taken out of the hands of the software engineer anyway, and placed instead into the hands of the courts. When that happens with regularity, the quality of the development process, the quality of the personnel used, the quality of the documentation kept, and the intent of the software and its use, all will come more into play in everyday business that develops or uses software.

Software is already being seen by some as a hazard, and companies may want to begin thinking about how they may reduce the amount of software or spread of software used in a system. Furthermore, since to prove that negligence was not the cause in a liability case, companies will have to document everything about the development process, which will probably increase the inherent costs of development and negatively impact productivity. This goes directly against the current trend in which one tries to increase productivity by reducing paperwork. Complete traceability will also be necessary, thus the software used to develop software may be liable as well. It may well happen that the individual software engineer may find him or herself legally liable for the safety of the code they produce. I believe it is only a matter of time before society will insist that the software profession will have to face up to its legal, as well as moral, obligations.

5.2 Software Security

If you were to mention the term "risk management" to most software practitioners, the first thing that would typically come to mind are not the risks associated with software engineering, but instead computer security. Computer security is currently in vogue, with hardly a week passing by without some sort of newspaper or magazine article written about hacking, computer viruses, or the like. The latest spate of articles circulating recently concerned the so-called "Friday-the-13th" virus, which never materialized, which was replaced a few weeks later with the "Halloween" virus, which also didn't materialize. One which did occur was an elaborate computer blackmail attempt, where thousands of people around the world were mailed a floppy disk which, after it was loaded, threatened to interrupt the computer's operations or erase its memory unless $378 was mailed to a fake address in Panama.[76]

The amount of news coverage being devoted to computer security has both its positive and negative points. On the plus side, the general recognition of the problem has been dramatically increased. It would be uncommon to find someone who owns or works with a computer not to be cognizant of viruses and the like (or at least recognize the term), and individual companies are placing more effort in trying to reduce their computer security problems. In 1988, the Computer Virus Industry Association reported that 70,000 cases of system infections had been confirmed, while others estimated that over 400,000 actually occurred, but were for the most part not reported.[77] As a result, some $750 million were spent in 1988 on computer security services and devices, or about .2% of the annual information technology expenditures.

On the minus side, the coverage has reached a point where it has often trivialized the underlying causes of computer security problems and their very real effects, much to the detriment of those trying to get computer security to be taken seriously. Many articles speak of how one needs to *just* encrypt all the code and data, or *just* monitor password entry attempts, or *just* keep the operating system source code from being accessed, or the loss of information is *not that* great, or cause *that much* harm, and so forth. Articles even appear to be making heros out of those who steal information or break into computer systems. Often these articles perpetuate the notion that hacking is a harmless game, and owners of computers which are hacked into deserve it anyway for being so careless. Important issues, such as how security problems can turn into safety risks, are overlooked. Luckily, it should not be long before the press finally grows weary of the issue and moves on to other things.

Companies may be more aware of the issues of computer security, but it does not mean that many are actually doing anything about it. In a 1988 *Wall Street Journal* survey, 65% of the firms surveyed stipulated that they were heavily dependent on their computers to conduct their business.[78] Furthermore, 20% declared that they were completely dependent on their computers. Unfortunately, almost all also stated that computer security measures were virtually nonexistent, which by implication means they are placing their faith in that old standby security countermeasure, *luck.*

The reason for not being too concerned about software security seems to lie in the delusion held by senior executives that their computer systems are reasonably well protected.[79] This leads to a corporation becoming complacent about security matters. The potential impact of this neglect can be staggering.[80] The FBI reported that the average bank robbery nets the robbers approximately $19,000, while those criminals engaged in traditional fraud nets $23,000. In comparison, the average reported computer theft was estimated to be about $625,000. We say average "reported" theft because many thefts are never revealed, since the company or companies involved do not wish to make it known how poor (i.e., how "unlucky") their computer security measures were. It is estimated that the total value of lost or stolen data across the United States is currently running as high as $3–5 billion per year, and in actuality, may be many times higher if you include the cost of lost intellectual property rights. With electronic data interchange (EDI), which allows different corporation computer systems to communicate to one another to order supplies, pay invoices, etc., becoming more widespread, the value of stolen information and real products can only climb higher.

Of course, not all of the data is lost by theft or fraudulent means. Many of the losses occur because of mishaps, such as power failures, operational errors, software errors, etc., occurring to or within the computer systems themselves. The National Institute of Science and Technology (the old National Bureau of Standards) reported that 65% of computer security losses are due to mistakes, errors and omissions, 13% are due to dishonest employees, and 6% are due to disgruntled employees.[81] Many authors group all such occurrences of failures as issues that fall under the computer security umbrella.[82–84] However, we prefer to separate accidental losses of data or accidental physical damage to computer hardware caused by natural disaster or the like, into the category of software disaster recovery concerns, which we will deal with explicitly in the next section. Accidental disclosure of data, or the malicious damage of physical computing assets, on the other hand, we still consider as a relevant security issue.

As we prefaced the section on software safety, the following discussion on computer security can only highlight the more general issues of this very complex and rapidly changing field, and should be viewed as only an introduction. Furthermore, the terms and definitions often vary in the literature, but we have tried whenever possible to use the most commonly accepted terminology. As a risk analyst, you are urged to consult the references, especially the three-volume set edited by Rein Turn, which contains a selection of papers spanning 10 years and shows the development and changes in the direction of computer security thinking.[85] With that as a short introduction, let's examine the issue of computer security in more detail.

5.2.1 What is security?

The definition of computer security is not an easy one to come to grips with. Traditionally, computer security was mostly concerned with the physical protection of the computing assets to prevent theft or damage to the hardware or information in the form of tapes, disks, printouts, etc., or to prevent accidental loss of computing services. Computer rooms were physically locked, and only authorized personnel were allowed within these mini-Fort Knoxes, although the "unwashed" could peer through the glass partitions at the blinking lights and mag-tape units whirling around.[86] This author recollects having to carry three types of computer control access cards, along with two more identification badges to show guards who signed you in and out, just to get into a part of the computing center. However, the inner sanctum atmosphere and glass enclosures, which are still hallmarks of most computing centers, were found not to be all that effective in protecting the *data* from unauthorized access, especially as more of the access to the data resided outside the glass walls.

It soon became apparent that physical protection of the main computing assets alone was not going to be sufficient. Although resource sharing of computer assets via time-sharing always posed somewhat of a security hazard, the problem became acute with the advent and widespread use of computer communication networks interconnecting with personal computers. The rapid change in technology, which allowed easier access to data, as well as permitting more data to become non–computer center resident, coupled with the change in computing culture, altered the path of thought concerning what constituted computing security. These two drivers, technology and cultural, are still being modified with unparalleled rapidity today, which makes any definition of computer security about as lasting as a flowering tulip in spring. This can be better understood by taking a short historical review.

5.2.1.1 Technology change. As we indicated, a major technology driver for computer security was the advent of resource-sharing systems which then-existing physical security measures could not adequately cover. The problem of security posed by these types of systems first whacked the U.S. Department of Defense in a major way in 1967, which immediately took, and still takes, the leading role in defining what is meant by secure computer systems.[87,88] Up until 1967, DoD computing was basically batch-oriented, with a negligible amount of remote job entry. The methods to safeguard information in those systems were essentially nothing more than extensions to the traditional manual methods used to safeguard classified documents.

However, during the period of 1964–1966, the U.S. government, especially DoD (which was, and still is, the largest single customer of computing equipment), was purchasing new computer systems which started to distribute computer resources among different devices and peripherals. Time-sharing, multiprogramming, on-line access, and multiprocessing were making an appearance and transforming the nature of the security problem. We take these architectural features as very common items today, but 25 years ago computing was very different. In batch, a system was devoted to running essentially one job, but with multiprogramming and multiprocessing, numerous jobs at different levels of classification could now be potentially executed simultaneously. People also didn't physically need to be in contact with the computer to write or submit jobs, either. The addition of these new features helped increase the efficiency and productivity of the computer systems, but allowed for many more entry points of unauthorized access.

For the next 10 years or so, computer security efforts were directed at trying to understand how to make these computer systems trusted. There was much learning to be done, and one of the more interesting episodes of the period was that every time someone thought they had implemented a secure system, someone else would come by and break into it. The U.S. government even had special "Tiger Teams," whose job it was to break into supposedly secure systems, especially those whose implementors were foolish enough to brag about their system's impenetrability. For the greater part, security efforts were directed at the individual components of the computer architecture, such as the operating system or database. Also, considerable effort was spent on cryptography, and for a long while this was thought to be the answer to the security problem, at least until it was shown that full security through cryptographic means was impractical, especially since it was easier to break cryptographic codes than was originally thought.

The 1970s was a period marked by great improvements in security understanding, but also suggested the first winds of change in the culture of computing. On the improvement side, academics and practitioners found that one could gain access into computer systems by a number of different ways other than the "correct" one, the favorite being through flaws, errors, or carelessness in the design of the systems themselves. This startled many people, especially the designers, because instead of just worrying about users breaking into the system, computer programs were being used to manipulate other programs to do things that the designer hadn't thought about or thought possible. It is easy today to suggest that no one should have been surprised, but again, remember the timeframe—getting a program to run was a major accomplishment. Getting it to run right and efficiently were added bonuses. Making it secure on top of everything else was unheard of. People were still arguing over whether programming was an art or a science, and discussions about the need for "go-to" statements could cause a brawl. The greatest problems encountered during this time revolved around trying to build security into multiuser, resource-sharing systems.[89] The attempts produced very large programs which, due to the nature of programming, contained many errors, which rendered them insecure. Moreover, while many exercises in getting into computers were harmless, there began to exist a base of users who saw it as a way to make some easy money. Computing was beginning to reach the general populace, and with it followed the normal distribution of criminal activity.

In the mid-1970s, the advent of the low cost microprocessor led soon afterwards to the personal computer, which took away the major barrier impeding access to a computer system. When personal computers were coupled with low cost access to networks, computing exploded in the 1980s. This explosion in use forced computing security to take an even bigger turn away from worrying only about physical computer assets. Whereas before, computer security was concerned with the problems of resource sharing and finding automated control methods to implement security, now one had to worry about communications security, which lent itself more to human control of the security problem. The definition of the boundary of the computing system, and the required security corridor around it, kept changing, not only in response to the technology advances, but because those successfully breaking into the system kept pushing it further outward. Instead of worrying primarily about computer security, one now had to worry about information protection.

This produced some profound changes in the way computer security was viewed by the late 1970s. For one, there emerged an effort to define what was meant by a secure, or trusted system, and the manner in which one could verify it. To be effective, the definition had to take into account the three aspects of computing; i.e., processing, storage, and transmission, and the security problem posed by the transition of data from one aspect to another, as shown in Figure 5.8. Furthermore, the definition of

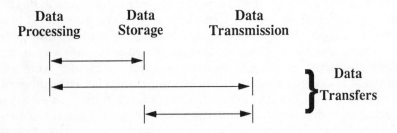

Figure 5.8 Areas of Security Risk in Computing

computer security had to also deal with these transitions in such a way as to allow for the three basic elements of information protection: confidentiality (i.e., allowing access only to the authorized person), integrity (i.e., ensuring that the data held is correct), and availability (i.e., being able to get at the data when you want it without "undue" difficulty). Additionally, the value of information had to be included in the equation, rather than just the value of the computing equipment itself. Moreover, the definition of security had to be made in such a way as to provide users with a metric with which to evaluate the degree of trust that could be placed into a computer system, as well as to provide guidance to those manufacturing or acquiring computer systems as to what security features to build into new or planned commercial products.

Given all the parameters above, the DoD in 1983 defined in a document entitled the *Trusted Computer Systems Criteria,* a concept of a trusted computing base (TCB), which is:

> the totality of protection mechanisms within a computer system—including the hardware, firmware, and software—the combination of which is responsible for enforcing a security policy. It creates a basic protection environment and provides additional user services required for a trusted computer system. The ability of a trusted computing base to correctly enforce a security policy depends *solely* (emphasis added) on the mechanisms within the TCB and on the correct input by system administrative personnel of parameters (e.g., a user's clearance) related to the security policy. [90]

A trusted computer system was then defined as, "a system that employs sufficient hardware and software integrity measures to allow its use for simultaneously accessing a range of sensitive or classified information."[91]

Since its publication, the *Trusted Computer Systems Criteria* has become a de facto standard in the United States for defining a trusted computing system. To help users and manufacturers evaluate the degree of trust, seven levels or criteria of trust have been defined, as shown in Table 5.4. These range from systems which have minimal security to those which have the highest level of trust that current technology can provide. The criteria are divided and ordered in an hierarchical manner into four major divisions, D, C, B, and A, with "A" being reserved for systems providing the most comprehensive security. Each major division provides a sizeable improvement in the overall confidence one can place in the system to protect sensitive information. Within a division are classes, which indicate less substantial gains in security over the previous class or division. Within each class, four major sets of criteria are addressed: security policy, accountability, assurance, and

TABLE 5.4 Trusted Computer Base Classifications

Class D
Minimal Protection

This class is reserved for those systems that have been evaluated but that fail to meet the requirements for a higher class.

Class C1
Discretionary Security Protection

A class C1 system nominally satisfies the discretionary security requirements by providing separation of users and data. It incorporates some form of credible controls capable of enforcing access limitations on an individual basis. The C1 environment is expected to be one of cooperating users processing data at the same level(s) of security.

Class C2
Controlled Access Protection

Systems in Class C2 enforce a more finely grained discretionary access control than those of C1, making users individually accountable for their actions.

Class B1
Labeled Security Protection

B1 systems require all the features of Class C2 systems. In addition, an informal statement of the security policy model, data labeling, and mandatory access control over named subjects and object must be present. The capability must exist for accurately labeling exported information.

Class B2
Structured Protection

Class B2 systems have a clearly defined and documented formal security model that requires discretionary and mandatory access control found in Class B1 systems, to be extended to all subjects and objects in the ADP system. In addition, covert channels must be addressed. The system must be carefully structured into protection-critical and non–protection-critical elements. The system is relatively resistant to penetration.

Class B3
Security Domain

Class B3 systems must satisfy the reference monitor requirements; i.e., that it mediate all accesses of subjects to objects, be tamperproof, and be small enough to be subjected to analysis and test. A security administrator is supported, audit mechanisms are expanded to signal security-relevant events, and system recovery procedures are required. The system is highly resistant to penetration.

Class A1
Verified Design

Class A1 systems are functionally equivalent to those in class B3, in that no additional architectural features or policy requirements are added. The distinguishing feature of systems in this class is the analysis derived from formal design specification and verification techniques.

documentation. The first three represent features necessary to satisfy broad security objectives, while documentation describes the type of written material in the form of user guides, manuals, and test and design documentation required by each class. These criteria are defined within the *Trusted Computer Systems Criteria* document itself.

Assurance of the correct and complete design and implementation for a system at a particular division and/or class is gained through testing of the security portion of the system in question. Systems representative of the higher B and A divisions derive their security attributes more from their design and implementation structure than from hardware components which have been added on to provide security. In other words, to achieve the higher levels of trustworthiness, security has to be designed in from the beginning, rather than added on later.

As a risk analyst, the criteria are a useful means to identifying and evaluating the security risks inherent within a system. Currently, most commercial systems can achieve a C1 or C2 rating without major difficulty, and certain operating systems have achieved a B2 level of trust. However, a B3 level operating system is not expected before 1991, and an A level system should not be expected any time soon after that.[92]

5.2.1.2 Cultural aspects of security. As we mentioned earlier, technology was a major driver for the changes in the perception of what constituted computer security, but one would be remiss to ignore the cultural aspects. The major driver from a cultural perspective on computer security has been the issue of privacy of computer data concerning individuals. The privacy issue has been one that has dogged computing since the early 1960s, and became a matter of high profile, public contention in 1965, when the federal government recommended that a Data Service Center be established.[93] This center was to establish a centralized database of all personal information collected by federal agencies for statistical purposes, and was ostensibly going to be used only for obtaining statistics in support of federal programs and decisions. However, the overwhelming negative reaction by the press, the Congress, the legal profession, and, most importantly, the public quashed that recommendation, especially after testimony by computer specialists showed how information could be accessed by unauthorized or unscrupulous persons.

As a result of the spotlight cast by the National Data Center's recommendation, and the use of extensive record keeping by nongovernment agencies such as credit bureaus, hospitals, banks, etc., the U.S. government passed a number of laws to help ensure an individual's right to privacy. Among these are: the *Fair Credit Reporting Act of 1971*, which bars credit agencies from sharing information with anyone but authorized customers; the *Privacy Act of 1974*, which bars federal agencies from letting information they collect for one purpose be used for a different purpose; the *Right to Financial Privacy Act of 1978*, which sets strict procedures when federal agencies want to rummage through customer records in banks; the *Counterfeit Access Device and Computer Fraud and Abuse Act of 1984*, which established as felonies the perpetration of financial fraud through the use of computers and the perpetration of malicious, unauthorized access (intentional unauthorized access or exceeding access authority were defined as misdemeanor crimes); the *Computer Fraud and Abuse Act of 1986*, which sets out expanded criminal penalties for gaining unauthorized entry into computer systems operated by federally insured institutions or those which operate interstate; the *Computer Security Act of 1987*, which requires the periodic training in computer security awareness and accepted computer security practices for all employees involved in management, use, or operation of a federal computer system within or under the supervision of a federal agency; the *Video Privacy Protection Act of 1988*, which prevents retailers from disclosing video rental records without the customer's consent or court order, and the *Computer Matching and Privacy Protection Act of 1988*, which regulates computer matching of federal data for verifying eligibility for federal programs or for recouping delinquent debts. Unfortunately, there are numerous loopholes in the protection statutes that allow most of the data to be shared legally anyway, so most of these laws provide only the most minimal protection.[94,95]

A sharp-eyed individual will notice a certain irony, and definite measure of American cultural sensibilities, expressed by the data which is not deemed private. Video rental records are explicitly protected by federal statute, but medical or insurance records are not. Someone stealing confidential medical information from a computer system, such as whether a person has tested positive for AIDS or had an abortion, can be theoretically prosecuted under the *Computer Fraud and Act*, but one should not hold out much hope of this actually happening, as only one person has ever been convicted under it.[96]

In the United Kingdom, there exist even fewer privacy laws when it comes to computerized data. In fact, up until recently, stealing any amount of data off computers was not considered a crime at all. Now it carries a maximum £2000 fine, which isn't a bad cost/benefit ratio, if one considers a recent case where thieves literally walked away with £500,000 of unique computer software along with the company's competitive edge, and handed it over to a competitor. Hacking, moreover, is still not considered a crime if data cannot be proved to have been stolen (reading it is not considered theft). And in a bit of perversion, the *Data Protection Act of 1984* defines penalties for *owners* of computer systems who fail to protect them adequately against "ill-intention," but it does not sanction penalties for those who have the ill-intentions!!

Unfortunately, governmental bodies tend to be reactive, not proactive, and thus lag far behind technological changes to society. Where computing is concerned, it is no different, if not a mite worse in that regard. Legislators tend to focus too much on the instrument of the crime; i.e., the computer, and not the assets which are taken; i.e., the knowledge contained within the computer. The computing industry hasn't helped matters much in regard to privacy, and in many ways security, either. The industry is fundamentally different from others in that the sharing of knowledge has always been a tenet of its philosophical foundations. One of the reasons for the rapid acceleration of computing has been the fact that knowledge has been shared so readily with anyone possessing an interest. For the longest time the problems associated with sharing were minimal, as (admittedly) the information was shared within an elite, away from the public scrutiny. The public, for its part, is very tolerant towards the computing industry because its members usually professed an ideal and often naive view of what would be done through computing (computers for the benefit of mankind, and that sort of thing). However, as computing has reached the general public, and its impact is becoming increasingly profound, the very openness of the industry has made data abuse more of an issue. Computers, by their very nature, allow massive negative impacts by individuals, much like altering a cold tablet's chemistry at the factory. The trend of open systems will test how one can balance the industry's and public's gains from the opportunities presented by openness vs. the possible problems caused by the facility to abuse the system.

5.2.2 Computer security vulnerability

Computer security has elements of both prevention of risk and lowering of risk, in contrast to the primary aim of software safety, which is the prevention of a risk causing harm if it should occur. To decide how to best implement computer security measures, one is required to understand the various ways information in a system can be accessed in an unauthorized manner. Figure 5.9 illustrates but a few of the ways unauthorized access to information can be made. When networks are involved in the transmission of data, there are many other ways to get data. Notice that one not only has to be concerned with attempts to destroy or steal data, but to make use of the information system in ways not intended. To aid in our understanding of a computer system's vulnerabilities, we will examine a number of the more common susceptibilities below.

One of the simplest and safest ways to gain access to unauthorized information is through a procedure called *data diddling*. This involves altering data either within a computer system, or before it enters the system, such as filing a false number of hours worked on time cards to a payroll system. Data diddling can be accomplished by anyone having access to the process of data manipulation, such as in its creation, recording, transportation, encoding, examination, checking, conversion,

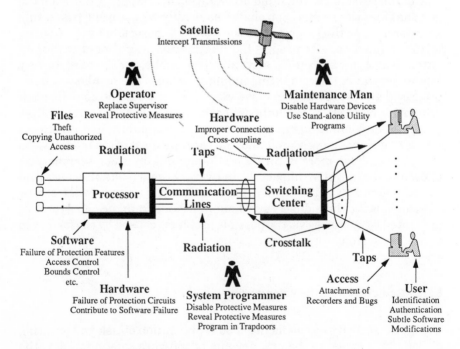

Figure 5.9 Typical Unauthorized Access

or transformation. If data can be accessed, it can be diddled with. Consistency checks on information is a way to reduce this type of threat.

While data diddling usually involves active participation of a user, there are threats that do not require any human intervention. A *Trojan horse* are computer instructions covertly hidden in a larger, authorized program that will, upon execution, make the computer perform unauthorized functions, while simultaneously allowing the program it is hidden within to perform normally. The Trojan horse is the most serious type of computer security threat because there are no practical methods for its prevention or detection. Trojan horses are often buried in large software applications or operating systems, where the sheer magnitude of the code makes its detection an impossibility. Done correctly (e.g., the extra code does not arouse suspicion by making the host program act abnormally, does not alter data, or from a cursory examination of the code it seems to perform an intended function for the program it inhabits), a Trojan horse can exist for a very long time without detection. However, once the breached program is purged, the threat is eliminated, although the longer-term security ramifications may linger. Trojan horses, for example, can be used to obtain passwords, system privileges, or other sensitive information by copying or diversion techniques. Stealing is especially hard to detect if the data is only copied, and not physically removed or altered in any manner. Trojan horses, because of their potency, are the favorite technique for those engaged in fraud and theft.

People who break into computers, being inventive and somewhat egotistical sorts, and therefore not enthused by the fact that a Trojan horse has a finite life, decided something should be added to extend their existence. Thus, *computer viruses* were conceived. Viruses are similar to Trojan horses, in that they inhabit a normal program, but unlike Trojan horses, a virus can attach itself to other programs, as well as replicate itself. Further, it can possibly change its initial function based upon information residing in the computer. Purging of the originally infected program is not an effective way of removing the virus, as one of its first tasks is to increase its survival probability by infecting other programs. Ninety percent of all users who purge their systems of a virus can expect to be reinfected within 90 days.[97] Viruses can remain dormant for months or even years before becoming active by coming "alive" when the computer's internal clock or calender reaches a certain time, or some other special set of occurrences or values are reached. This technique was learned from another extension of the Trojan horse, called *logic or time-bombs*, which do virtually the same thing.

Viruses can be passed by electronic mail, by being placed on a diskette for massive distribution, or, more commonly, by the illegal but common copying of a friend's "borrowed" disk that has been infected. Over 110 different viruses have been detected to date, and new strains are appearing almost weekly.[98] Seven were discovered in December 1989 alone. They have originated from all over the world, including Pakistan and Bulgaria. Viruses seem to be used primarily to destroy information, disrupt computer operations, or for publicity purposes, rather than for stealing information, since once installed, the originator has little direct control of its actions. One of the more insidious ones is the "123nhalf" virus, which wipes out half the rows and columns in files created by Version 3 of Lotus's 1-2-3 spreadsheet program. Viruses have also been constructed which are meant to attack virus-hunting programs. In fact, one supplier of an "antivirus" program decided to no longer upgrade its product to combat new viruses. The company felt that it would get into an endless battle of of response/counter-response.[99] It may not be long before coordinated viruses are developed that can, say, divert products of a certain type in an EDI system to another location and simultaneously block attempts to stop it.

An independent program that is like a virus, in that it has the ability not only to replicate itself, not require a host program, and also purposely move from computer system to computer system (as opposed to a hit or miss pollination approach) over networks, is called a computer *worm*.[100] Worms are particularly troublesome, as their goal in life is to eat up an infected computer's available memory by endless duplication of itself, thus slowing the operation of the system to a standstill. Worms are more easily detected than viruses, because they are fairly large (a virus may be as small as 1200 bytes, but worms may require over 3000 lines of high level code), do not require a host program, and do not attempt to disguise themselves. Even if they are not found immediately, they will, in time, become obvious because the system response time starts to suffer. Although usually not created for the purpose of destroying information as in the case of viruses, their removal presents a time-consuming and costly process.

Another computer system access technique is called using a *trap door*. A trap door is a piece of software in the operating system or application program that provides a path for a person to break into the operating system or application program reliably and without detection. Trap doors may be illicitly put into place by a developer, like Trojan horses, or by "accident," as in the case of leaving debugging programs in the program or operating system. Sometimes trap doors exist because of inadvertent design logic flaws in the operating system or application. Trap doors are not as much of a problem as Trojan horses, as usually one needs to have knowledge of the source code of the application or operating system to make use of them. This is not to say that it is impossible, but trap doors are much harder to exploit without this knowledge.

Superzapping is somewhat like a trap door, except that it is the use of a legitimate system maintenance tool or utility to gain access to unauthorized information. Because a computer system isn't perfect, it occasionally malfunctions in such a way that recovery and restart are only possible by accessing and modifying normally restricted areas of the system's internals. To accomplish a recovery and restart, most computer manufacturers provide the system programmer and/or the system administrator with the means to bypass all normal system controls. These programs, some of which can be purchased commercially, allow a person to logically connect to another's terminal, thus letting one view the screen and enter keyboard input to whatever process is executing. Unfortunately, these tools or utilities are the virtual keys to the kingdom, and in the wrong hands, can do tremendous damage. Usually only the system administrator or system programmer has authorization to use these programs, but they are often kept in program libraries which can make them vulnerable to theft.

Trojan horses, viruses, trap doors, and superzapping are deliberate attempts by individuals to gain access to information to which they have no authorized access. Sometimes information can accidentally leak by means of a *covert channel*. A channel is an information transfer path within a computer system. A covert channel is a channel that is not a normally used path for transferring information, and therefore is not conventionally protected by security controls. Covert channels abound in a computer system. They exist whereever information can be modified by one process or read by another, either directly or indirectly. Any of the paths that define the transitions shown in Figure 5.8 are potential covert channels.

Typically, covert channels are divided into two types: *covert storage channels* and *covert timing channels*.[101] Covert storage channels involve the direct or indirect writing of a storage location by one process and the direct or indirect reading of the storage location by another process. As an example, consider when one process writes to a disk that is shared by another process of a different authorization level. The second process may be able to read from the disk information it is not trusted to view. A covert timing channel is one in which one process signals information to another by modulating its own system resources, such as the CPU time, in such a way that this manipulation affects the real response time observed by the second process. Related, but not considered a covert timing channel security breach, is the *asynchronous attack*, which is an attack on the computer system rendered possible by the lagtime between a request that is checked for validity and the time that the request is executed.

The final program-related access approach we wish to discuss is the *salami technique*. This is to deliberately have an application program manipulate the information in such a way as to steal small amounts of information at a time which will most likely go unnoticed. For example, a program may be used to compute the amount of social security benefits for which an individual may be entitled. Say also that a fixed benefit is suppose to be divided equally among the recipients. It may turn out that a person is supposed to get a benefit of 125 dollars and 66.7 cents. The .7 is rounded off (usually down) to an even 125 dollars and 66 cents. However, that .7 cents, when summed up across thousands of individuals, adds up to a significant amount of money. Obviously, to make this technique effective, one must have access to many accounts, the perpetrator must not get greedy, and the same accounts should not be continuously tapped. Any type of financial accounting program is susceptible to this type of threat.

A couple of other techniques of interest include *piggybacking and impersonation, electronic eavesdropping, scavenging,* and *electronic picketing.* Piggybacking and impersonation are means to gain access to a controlled environment by hiding behind a legitimate access process. This may be accomplished either physically, by identifying yourself with forged or stolen documents as a person who has legitimate access, or electronically, through stolen passwords or hard or soft taps onto the communication lines.

Electronic eavesdropping of communication lines is a well-known threat which we will not delve into, but the reader can review the references for a more in-depth look at the various ways eavesdropping, such as wire-tapping, use of miniature microphones, inductive taps, microwave interception, etc. can be accomplished.[102,103]

Scavenging is obtaining information that may be resident in or on a computer system after a job has finished executing. One can physically scavenge, such as obtaining discarded listings, carbon paper, source documents, scratch disks and tapes, or electronically scavenge by searching buffers for improper erasure, or memory locations, and so forth.

Electronic picketing is fairly new and refers to the use (or abuse) of a computer system by authorized users to further a political aim or work grievance. This is not exactly a problem of stealing data or harming it, but is a security problem nevertheless. The picketers try to disrupt normal computer system's operations by various means, such as: trying to slow down the system by submitting massive amounts of compile or link and load jobs simultaneously; trying to tie up internal or external communication channels; or, in EDI systems, deliberately causing errors by data diddling on supply ordering forms. Electronic picketing is hard to stop, and already some signs of *electronic walkouts, electronic lockouts,* and *secondary picketing* via EDI systems are starting to appear.

Although not all-inclusive, the above examples illustrate the types of threats to computer system security that a risk analyst should at least be aware. Although we haven't mentioned it in any detail, it should also be obvious that the analyst must also consider the various human candidates that may pose a threat, such as trusted workers, family members, girl/boy friends, hackers, career criminals, and advocates of extreme positions, left or right. In the next sections, we examine some of the general approaches to recognizing where security risks exists.

5.2.3 Approaches to recognizing security risks—Security risk analysis and management

In the previous section, we discussed a number of different methods one can use to gain access to information in an unauthorized manner. In this section, we will to review some of the approaches a risk analyst can apply to help identify where information protection risks might occur. Our concentration will necessarily be more towards an examination of risk analysis approaches, rather than any in-depth examination of the methods for conducting risk management. Acceptable risk management, as we will see, has as much to do with the architecture of the computer system as with the security policies elaborated, and the various techniques to be used are too wide and varied to be covered adequately here.

In general, the philosophy espoused for conducting security risk analysis and management are divided into the same ones we have encountered before, but with a different set of terminology and a bit different flavor. In doing security risk analysis, the driving factor is the underlying level of security desired as defined by the company's and/or project's security policy. The policy defines, either implicitly or explicitly, the risk referent, in a similar fashion as the Risk Estimate of the Situation defines the overall objectives of a software development project. Without having this knowledge available, it is virtually impossible to perform a reasonable risk analysis or to determine the appropriate risk management approaches to be undertaken, because there is nothing to measure the risks against. This may be obvious, but the lack of defined security policies is more the norm than the exception. Not having a policy is a prime reason why the risks are not visible until it is too late. It is also why, when a security violation is detected, the answer by the installation manager to the question of whether it can happen again or in some other way is typically an agitated, "We don't know."

There are a number of different models of security risk analysis and management, so to aid us in seeing what is involved, we will look at two different models that were proposed 10 years apart to see how views on security have changed.

5.2.3.1 Campbell and Sands risk management model (RMM). The risk management model (RMM) proposed by Campbell and Sands in 1979 was one of the first to recognize the importance of information security, as opposed to computer security.[104] The RMM recognized that this meant that security had to be a corporate level function and responsibility, rather than a straight ADP function since, if the information contained in the computer systems were stolen or compromised, the owners of the data absorbed the losses, and not the ADP department. The ADP department, since it wouldn't sustain the true loss, would be inclined to accept the risk from a lack of computer security rather than divert its funding to counter ADP security weaknesses. This ADP perspective, which may be "reasonable" from their point of view, is still unfortunately very prevalent today, and explains why corporate computer security is weak across the board.

The Campbell and Sands model, illustrated as a tree in Figure 5.10, divided computer security risk management into eight steps: *value analysis, threat identification and analysis, vulnerability analysis, risk analysis, risk assessment, management decision, control implementation,* and *effective review. Value analysis* is meant to determine the relative value of the facility or its operation, as well as its components, for the purposes of evaluating its susceptibility to exploitation. The objective is to attempt to determine what part or process within the facility might be singled out for attack. Value analysis consists of three analytical

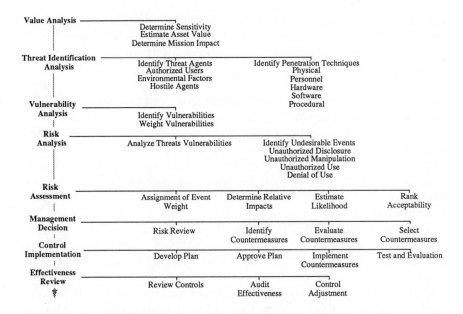

Figure 5.10 Campbell and Sands Security Risk Management Model

procedures designated: determination of information sensitivity, determination of the mission impact of loss of denial or support, and estimation of the asset value of the automated resources. Information sensitivity consists of a bottom-up approach, beginning with each application and extending to all computer and networking processing levels, to identify the types and amounts of sensitive data being held and processed. The determination of the impact of the loss of support analyzes what happens to each organizational mission if the computer system was partially or totally lost for varying periods of time. The estimation of the computer support asset value investigates the replacement or cost value of the fixed asset base of the physical computing facility, ADP equipment and supplies, software, and any other supporting assets.[105]

The next step in the RMM approach is the *identification and analysis of the threat*. Threats are categorized into three general categories: environmental factors, authorized users, and hostile agents. The threats can be subdivided into either actual threats (i.e., ones that have been documented) or perceived threats (i.e., ones for which there is no hard evidence). Once the threats are identified, then an analysis is made of the different penetration techniques that might be used. These techniques include both deliberate and unintentional approaches. The penetration techniques are then placed into one of five classes for analysis purposes: physical, personnel, hardware, software, or procedural.

The third step in the process is to complete a *vulnerability analysis*, which is to identify possible weaknesses existing in the defenses of the facility. To facilitate the vulnerability analysis, two substeps are instigated called vulnerability identification and vulnerability weighting. In the former, weaknesses or flaws in the design, implementation, or operation of the security controls are identified, and their relationships linked to a specified threat. In the latter, the vulnerabilities identified are placed into an arrayed order according to adjudged seriousness and potentiality for exploitation.

The fourth step in the RMM approach is the *risk analysis*. The purpose is to identify undesirable events through the analysis of the potential impacts of the threats and their possible exploitation of corresponding vulnerabilities previously identified. The risk analysis has two major substeps. The first is an analysis of threat vulnerabilities. This means that the various ways a threat can exploit a vulnerability are fully analyzed and documented. Then comes an identification of undesirable events; i.e., the potential unwanted occurrences resulting from the activity of a threat when exploiting a vulnerability, such as unauthorized disclosure of information, unauthorized manipulation of information, unauthorized use of information, or denial of service or use. These undesirable events and their relationship to a threat are logged and documented.

After the risk analysis is complete, a *risk assessment* is made. The primary objective of the risk assessment is to assess the severity of risks created by the combination of the threats, vulnerabilities, and their potential exploitation, as well as to weigh the likelihood of their occurrence. Risk assessment is a four-stage process, beginning with an assignment of an event weight, the determination of its relative impact, an estimate of its likelihood of occurrence, and, finally, a ranking of the event as either being an acceptable or unacceptable risk.

Once the risk assessment has been made, *management decisions* are required to determine how to proceed. First, a risk review of the assessments is made, to ensure the degrees of acceptability of the risks are within tolerable levels. Any type of risk coupling is also sought out. When complete, countermeasures are identified, which can be effectively used against the identified threats and vulnerabilities. Specific actions are recommended which will lessen or minimize their impact on system operation. Along with the identification of the countermeasures comes their evaluation to determine their true effectiveness, and their eventual selection as providing the best combination for the identified threats and vulnerabilities. This may mean deciding that certain information should not be kept on automated systems.

The seventh step is to *develop and execute a plan* to implement the countermeasures required. This means a plan must be developed, the necessary approval sought, the countermeasures actually implemented, and the countermeasures tested and evaluated.

The last step is an *effectiveness review*, which is a periodic review of the effectiveness of the security controls, and how any changes to the computer systems may have changed the vulnerabilities and/or threats. This is done by reviewing the security controls and any new ones added, auditing the effectiveness of the overall security controls and any new system facilities, and control adjustment where the security controls are finely tuned.

This security risk management model is very comprehensive and well thought out. RMM tries to avoid the precise quantification of risk impacts in terms of probabilities and monetary losses, such as the probability and cost to regenerate a lost database, preferring instead to be approximately right rather than exactly wrong. However, there are a few critiques that can be leveled at the model. First, the value of information held by the system is not really computed during the value analysis stage. Although the effects to the organization mission are identified, only the value of the information-processing technology itself is actually included. A magnetic tape might cost $100 to replace, but the actual value may be worth $100,000. For comprehensive evaluation, the cost in terms of a competitive edge, intellectual property rights, political embarrassment, etc. must be included. For example, in the U.S. Department of Defense, information is valued both by time and by loss value, which is related to the damage to national security (e.g., *grave damage, serious damage,* or just *damage*).

Second, RMM concerns itself more with prevention of security violations, and not their active detection or recovery from a security breach. Both of these aspects may be included in a countermeasure, but they are not explicitly identified in the RMM, and both are important to having a complete risk management approach.

Third, the model is aimed primarily at retrofitting security into an existing system, rather than as a design aid in building security into a system. The most effective security measures are those built in, not bolted on, and one must be aware that adding in security measures after the fact is not as effective. However, this particular weakness should not be seen as a major criticism, and the model is a good one to use from a risk analyst's perspective.

Finally, RMM takes a fairly long time and a great amount of effort to adequately implement. Again, this is not so much a fault of the model as a problem when dealing with a complex issue such as security. One concluding note. It is imperative that once a risk analysis model like the one above is created, at any level of detail, it not be circulated to too wide an audience. Simulating or modeling a computer are other methods used to find ways to gain unauthorized access, and with any comprehensive risk analysis, one is explicitly documenting a system's weaknesses.

5.2.3.2 Central Computer and Telecommunications Agency Risk Analysis and Management Methodology (CRAMM).

The government of the United Kingdom has developed via its Central Computer and Telecommunications Agency (CCTA) a partially automated risk analysis and management methodology called CRAMM.[106] Officially released in 1987, CRAMM is the approved preferred methodology for identifying justified security countermeasures for the protection of computer systems processing unclassified but sensitive data.

CRAMM has two distinct phases, as shown in Figure 5.11. The risk analysis phase consists of identification and valuation of physical assets and data assets, identification and determination of the levels of accidental and deliberate threats, the identification of the vulnerabilities of the identified assets which might be exploited by the identified threats, and an assessment of the risk indicated by the vulnerabilities, assets, and threat combination. These three factors are used to calculate the levels of risk to the information and computing assets. Risk management

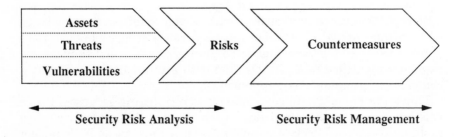

Figure 5.11 CRAMM Security Analysis and Management Model

involves the reduction of vulnerability by the use of countermeasures. These countermeasures may reduce the risk of a threat occurring, reduce the impact of such an occurrence, detect an occurrence, or facilitate recovery from an occurrence.

As we mentioned, the risk analysis phase consists of four parts. The first part identifies a system's physical and data assets to determine the impact if exploited, in terms of disclosure, modification, unavailability, and destruction. Exploitation covers both deliberate and accidental means. CRAMM helps determine precisely the nature and the boundary of the system under review by providing detailed advice in the form of a structured questionnaire. The questionnaire enables the risk analyst to establish the selection of qualitative data asset values, for the four possible impacts of disclosure, modification, unavailability, and destruction by deliberate and accidental means. The selection is aided by detailed guidance for valuation of data relating to issues of political embarrassment, commercial confidentiality, personal privacy, personal safety, and financial and legal implications. Guidance on valuation of physical assets according to either replacement or reconstruction costs are also included.

The second and third parts of the analysis phase are used to identify and assess the likelihood of deliberate or accidental incidents interfering with the computer system, as well as assessing the vulnerability of the system to an identified threat. CRAMM recognizes that a system consists of several kinds of assets, not all of which are subject to the same level of threat or degree of vulnerability. Therefore, a split of the system is performed to form groups of assets which can be considered together. Next, 22 generic types of threats are used as a basis to assess the qualitative threat and vulnerability for each relevant asset group, this time using pairs of structured questionnaires. The output of the assessment is a determination, either at a low, medium, or high level, of the vulnerability and threat.

In part four of the risk analysis, a risk assessment is conducted. For each asset group, the combination of the asset values and assessments of the vulnerabilities and threats are used to calculate security requirements or risk numbers on a scale of one to five (one being the baseline), for each of the four impact areas (disclosure, modification, unavailability, and destruction). These numbers are then used as the basis upon which to make a decision about the security requirements of the system under examination.

Once the risk analysis phase is complete, risk management begins, which consists of the selection of the appropriate countermeasure. The countermeasures are drawn from a continually updated library containing over 750 different countermeasures and matched against the security requirement identified during the assessment process above. The countermeasures are grouped by the security aspect (e.g., hardware, communications, personnel), as well as by type (e.g., reduction, detection, or recovery from the risk). If the system being investigated already has countermeasures, these are added in at this time (this helps evaluate the effectiveness of the current security measures taken, avoids prejudging their effectiveness, and shows where the security gaps exist in a more visible fashion). A comparison is then made to determine which countermeasures need to be added, and which existing ones are not justified. The cost of each countermeasure identified is listed, along with a specification of the actual or likely equipment required. CRAMM allows various "what-if" scenarios to be executed to determine the best selection of countermeasures for the money available. As with RMM, a periodic review is also part of the risk management process.

RMM is slightly more comprehensive than CRAMM in that it emphasizes the "what next" after the risk analysis is completed; i.e., the risk management phase dealing with plans and reviews. This is important, as having formal security plans in place may be the only way to collect on insurance if a major security problem such as fraud occurs. CRAMM, on the other hand, concentrates much more than RMM on the issues involving the value of information, recovery and detection from security violations, and is better suited than RMM for designing computer security into computer installations. The automated nature of CRAMM is a big plus in this regard. CRAMM is currently being integrated into the U.K. government's software engineering design methodology SSADM. This should help increase the inherent security of computer applications, and of the system design in general.

5.2.4 Approaches to safeguarding information—Designing security in

We haven't spent much time discussing how to design security into a computer system, since it is beyond the general scope of this book. However, as many as 80% of corporate computers are inherently unprotectable, and techniques such as CRAMM or RMM can only help make it more difficult, but not impossible, for someone to break into a system.[107] Effective security measures usually cannot be retrofitted in, thus to get a truly secure system, one must design it in from the beginning. As with safety, prevention is the best and overall cheapest way to enhance security. A risk analyst would be remiss if he or she did not investigate the areas where research is currently centered in trying to design security into a computer system, as it will indicate where system vulnerabilities presently exist.

Ignoring the aspects of the physical security of computing assets, designing security into a computer installation seems to primarily focus on three elements: the security within the computing assets themselves, the application program, and the telecommunication network. The focus of security within the computing assets concerns all aspects of the computer system excluding the network and application program. This means the hardware, operating system, the database, and the data itself. The emphasis in hardware security seems to concern the aspects of trying to provide better reliability through fault tolerance computing. By reducing the possibility of the system going down in the face of errors, or to recover from errors more quickly, security is indirectly enhanced.

Operating systems have been the preeminent center of attention in trying to enhance security since almost the beginning. The reason is fairly obvious, as operating systems control the allocation of computing resources, and therefore are the prime targets for an attack. Research in operating system security continues to emphasize the implementation of a security model. The model is an abstraction of a set of security policies, which in general, when implemented, must be impossible to bypass, must be tamperproof, and must be shown to be properly implemented.[108] There are a number of different models, the most famous being the Bell and LaPadula model, although there is significant disagreement among researchers about the robustness and approach of the model.[109,110]

Database security research also has been focusing on security models, although typically as a subset of operating security models. Most operating security models treat databases as another application program, although this view is being challenged as not acceptable in some quarters. An active area of research in database security is the encryption of data resident in a database as a means to make theft of data useless to an unauthorized user. However, current commercially available encryption techniques are fairly easy to overcome.[111]

On the application program side, historically there has been very little effort in trying to build in security from the start. Software engineering methods and techniques have primarily stayed away from the security (and safety) issues altogether. However, as we mentioned in the CRAMM section, efforts are now beginning to be made in defining integrated approaches to developing applications with security explicitly in mind.[112,113] Figure 5.12 shows one such attempt.

Network security efforts are currently divided into two schools of thought. One sees a network as the same as a computer, and the identical standards and models of security should be applied, while the other views a network as consisting of a set of computers and a communication network which require different standards and models.[114] The former perspective can be described as a more theoretical approach, while the latter is a more practical one. Currently, network security lends itself more to human control than automated control, and thus network security research has been focusing on providing automated security.[115] This has been in the form of network management techniques, which manage network resources, provide continuous surveillance of each network element, provide problem determination and isolation, aid in restoration of network services, and track and report possible security problems.

As one can quickly detect, the common theme among all the efforts to design security into the system is that a layered organization is the best approach. No single design element, whether it be the operating system, application program, or network, will alone be able to provide the level of security required. Further, information protection must take place both inside and outside the computer. A security policy is only as good as its implementation by the people involved, as they will always be the weakest link.

5.3   Software Operational/Disaster Recovery Risks

In this final section, we wish to explore the software risks associated with operational problems including disasters; i.e., an event which can cause a significant disruption in information service provision for a long enough period of time to negatively affect the operations of the organization.[116] As mentioned, these are sometimes included in the category of security risks, but since these are typically more accidental in nature, and are often overlooked in the glamour of the more interesting fraud and abuse issues, we felt that it was more appropriate to accommodate a separate review. Moreover, as it turns out, around 80% of the losses attributed to a computer system can be directly attributed to causes not directly related to security violations.[117] In one study, illustrated in Figure 5.13, out of 296 reported computer failures (i.e., the

Conceptual Analysis	Systems Design & Application Development			Testing & Integration	Operations & Evolution	
Pre-Analysis &Buy-Dev. Options	Security Planning	Security Analysis & Design	Organize & Train	Implementation & Operation	Surveillance & Control	
Security Strategy Review	Risk Management Review			Security Training	Security Test & Evaluation Review	Systems Software Security

Figure 5.12 Integrated Security Approach

system was knocked out), only 19 were found to be caused by security-related troubles.[118] Figure 5.14 shows which industries tend to be the most susceptible to software disasters.

When a computer system goes down, the impact can be massive. The cost of an unavailable computer system can run over $6 million an hour in lost sales to an airline. Figure 5.15 shows, for example, the results of an inquiry conducted to determine the average cost per hour of lost computer services to a business.[119] While the number of businesses

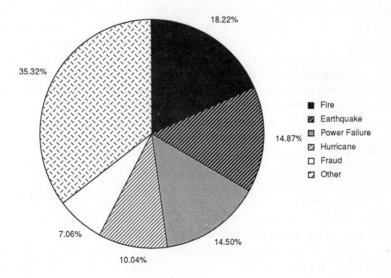

Figure 5.13 Causes of Computer Outages

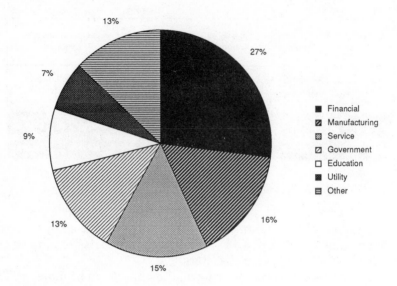

13%

27%

7%

9%

13%

16%

15%

■ Financial
▨ Manufacturing
▥ Service
▨ Government
□ Education
■ Utility
▤ Other

Figure 5.14 Industries Most Affected by Computer Outages

which lose over a million dollars an hour is surprising, what is especially interesting is the number of companies who do not know how much a lost hour costs them in lost business revenue. The AT&T network failure recounted in Chapter 1 has given many companies the answer the hard way. The cost of not knowing can be very high, as shown by a U.K. insurance company. It calculated that an organization's operations will be halved within 5 days of a major computer disaster, and that 90% of those companies hit by such a disaster go out of business within 5 years.[120] These findings correlate well with another study conducted by the Graduate School of Business Administration of the University of Minnesota, which found that essential company functions could only last 4 or 5 days after a data processing disaster, and that 93% of the companies without survival plans in place did not last 5 years. Most went out of business, in fact, in less than 18 months.[121]

One may ask, why isn't more contingency planning done, especially given the tremendous amount of damage to a business that a computing operational event or disaster can cause? We encountered most of the reasons in the security section, and we see them repeated here again: Most company executives think their computing installations are disaster-proof, and therefore, they do not feel any urgent need. They are not aware of the real magnitude of the problem until it hits them, by which time it is too late to recover. Therefore, the executives do not consider that

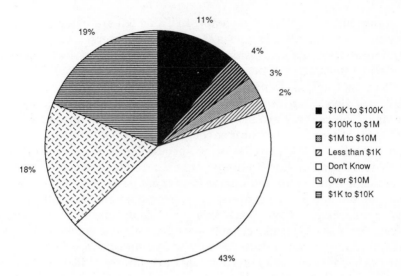

Figure 5.15 Cost of Lost Network Service Per Hour

finding the resources required to putting together disaster recovery plans, or to obtain back-up systems, or even to do back-ups, are high priority items on their agendas. This mindset was highlighted by a survey in the United Kingdom which revealed that 25% of MVS sites were skipping back-ups due to overloaded workloads.[122]

5.3.1 Planning for a software disaster—Risk analysis and management

Planning for a software disaster uses the same type of risk analysis and management techniques that we have utilized previously. We need to identify the risks, estimate the magnitude of the risk, evaluate the risk, and then manage the risk by either accepting it or averting it in some manner. Risk management approaches should include aspects of disaster prevention, but the main emphasis will be on recovery from the effects of the disaster, rather than prevention or detection, for the obvious reasons.

To begin our risk identification, one may wish to see if a security risk analysis like some of the ones described in the previous section exists. These analyses will be useful starting places to determine in general what risks are faced, and will later help in evaluating the cost involved in a computer installation disaster. In Table 5.5 are listed some of the various risks included as causes of software disasters. Each of these, as a minimum, should be considered. Another source of risks to consult is Federal Information Processing Standards Publication 31 (FIPS 31), written by the U.S. Department of Commerce and published in June 1974, entitled *Computer Security in ADP*. This document outlines which areas of the country are susceptible to natural disasters, and how to anticipate them. Local insurance companies can also provide data on the susceptibility of the installation to specific kinds of natural disasters such as flooding or storm damage. One must note that not only risks to computing equipment and information must be considered, but also to the personnel operating or using the equipment. Not all software disasters are caused by catastrophes. The major causes for loss of service which are most typically encountered are network component or line failure (25%), power failure (23%), application software failure (16%), hardware failures (14%), system software failure (14%), and human errors (8%).[123]

After the risks have been identified, they should be categorized in the usual way by whether they are known, predictable, or unpredictable. It would also prove useful for risk management if they were also categorized

TABLE 5.5 Types of Disasters

Natural Disasters
Floods
Winter Storms
Tornadoes
Hurricanes
Earthquakes

Man-made Disasters
Fires
Accidents
Burst Pipes
Thefts
Willful Destruction
Sabotage
Bomb Threats
Plane Crashes
Building Collapse

Political Disasters
Riots and Civil Disturbances
War
Strikes

by whether they are caused by a lack of information, a lack of control, or a lack of time.

After the risks are identified, their likelihood and severity need to be ascertained. The first step is to choose a measurement scale which best matches the accuracy and precision required for the estimate and later evaluation. Since most of the information will be qualitative in nature, we will usually use some type of ordinal scale. Any quantitative information will require a cardinal scale, although it is usually the case that a qualitative assessment will be good enough. The likelihood estimates of the risks associated with natural disasters will often be the easiest to find, while the likelihood of a terrorist activity will likely entail speculation for most organizations.

Once the risks are estimated, then they can be evaluated. To accomplish this, one needs to determine the criteria against which a risk consequence will be judged to be acceptable across the computer installation's expected life. The criteria should be able to be related to the success criteria that were determined during the risk estimate of the situation phase. The criteria for success and risk referent can be developed from the value of information kept by the facility, as it relates to the organizational missions the installation provides support for, and what happens if the installation is completely disrupted. Again, if a security analysis has already been completed, a good part of this analysis should already have been accomplished. A final input into the referent will be whether the reduction of service, manual procedures, or the complete withdrawal of service is deemed to be an acceptable response to a disaster.

The referents for what is deemed acceptable levels of disaster prevention, detection, and recovery should be influenced by the combination of financial losses, legal responsibilities, and business service operations. The financial losses can be computed by using worst-case scenarios, such as what happens if the computing service is lost for an hour, 4 hours, 8 hours, 24 hours, 1 day, 3 days, etc., up to 3 months. Accounting for the lost business revenue, as well as the cost of replacement of equipment, moving to new facilities, etc., also needs to be factored in. Insurance coverage should also be checked at this time to see what is, and isn't, covered.

Legal losses can be somewhat more difficult to determine. Management has a legal responsibility to safeguard its employees, its corporate resources, and its vital documents. Not doing so leaves one open to prosecution under the *Foreign Corrupt Practices Act of 1977*.[124] Consultation with other groups, such as labor relations, fire departments, police departments, etc. should form part of the legal evaluation process.

The retention of vital records is one area which is also often overlooked in a disaster situation and is part of this process. Table 5.6 represents some of the typical times records must legally be kept by a corporation.[125]

TABLE 5.6 Record Retention Periods Required by Government Regulation

Type of Record	Retention Period (years)
Accounting and Fiscal	
Accounts Payable Invoices	3
Checks, Payroll	2
Checks Voucher	3
Earnings Register	3
General Ledger	Permanent
Labor Cost Records	3
Payroll Registries	3
Manufacturing	
Bills and Material	3
Engineering and Specs. Records	20
Stock Issuing Records	3
Personnel	
Accident Reports and Claims	30
Changes and Terminations	5
Injury Frequency Records	Permanent
Job Ratings	2
Purchasing and Procurement	
Bids and Awards	3
Purchase Orders and Regulations	3
Security	
Employee Clearance Records	5
Visitor Records	2
Taxation	
Annuity and Other Plans	Permanent
Dividend Register	Permanent
Employe Taxes	4
Excise Reports	4
Inventory Reports	Permanent
Depreciation Schedules	Permanent
Transportation	
Bills of Lading	2
Freight Bills	3
Freight Claims	2

Business service interruption evaluation requires one not only to question the immediate financial and/or legal losses, but also the more intangible losses that may occur. These may include the loss of client goodwill, the loss of public image, and/or the loss of confidence in the overall health of the company. Companies using EDI services are especially susceptible to these types of losses because of the customer expectation of immediate response to requests, not to mention the inherent dependency on computing EDI requires.

During the evaluation process, one must examine the issues of prevention, detection, and recovery. The effectiveness of disaster prevention and detection will reside most often with higher management through the implementation of corporate policy making, although many of the natural disaster-type risks are out of anyone's control. For the greater part, recovery methods will be the only practical approach available for dealing with a computing disaster.

Depicted in Figure 5.16 are a number of recovery mechanisms available which require evaluation for suitability.[126] As can be seen, recovery services vary in their relative cost and in recovery time. *Hot standby service* is an internally located, fully equipped, duplicate computer room, which has an up-to-the-minute database maintained by database shadowing of the operational system. *Database shadowing* is the

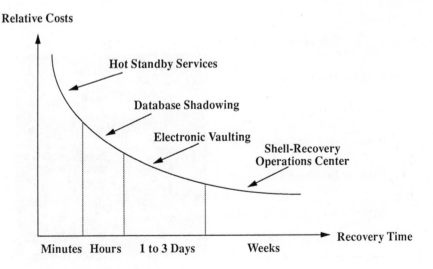

Figure 5.16 Typical Recovery Cost Trade-offs

capability to capture critical database updates on a transaction-by-transaction basis. This allows recovery to be done in a matter of minutes, although considerations of the risk of having co-located sites must be considered if natural disasters such as earthquakes or hurricanes are a major threat. A less costly version of hot standby is called a *hot site,* where the database shadowing lags behind the actual database by a few minutes. Operations can resume as soon as the database is reloaded and communications are restarted. In certain government agencies, such as HUD, by using hot standby, critical applications can be back on line within 4 hours.[127]

If one wants to trade time for cost, then one can eliminate the complete hot standby and perform *electronic vaulting*. This is the use of another site off premises connected via a communications line to the operational computer site. The database is shadowed, although it may not represent an up-to-the-minute log. By further trading time for cost, one can set up a *remote operational center*. This is a mobile, fully equipped computer installation that can be trucked to the site of a disaster.

Cold sites or *shells* again trade time for cost. Cold sites are computer installations which are ready (i.e., all the necessary power, air, cooling, etc. are installed) to take computer equipment as soon as it can be delivered. Modifications often occur at a cold site to make sure long delivery time items are already installed. The cold site can either be on the premises or be located remotely.

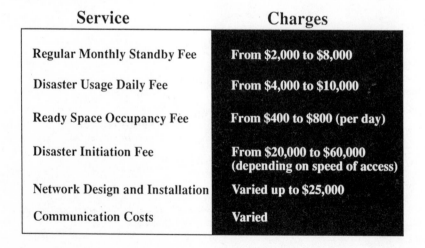

Service	Charges
Regular Monthly Standby Fee	From $2,000 to $8,000
Disaster Usage Daily Fee	From $4,000 to $10,000
Ready Space Occupancy Fee	From $400 to $800 (per day)
Disaster Initiation Fee	From $20,000 to $60,000 (depending on speed of access)
Network Design and Installation	Varied up to $25,000
Communication Costs	Varied

Figure 5.17 Typical Disaster Recovery Costs

All the services mentioned above can either be provided by the company itself, or through use of third parties, such as commercial service bureaus or equipped recovery operation centers, who specialize in disaster recovery. These services range from providing remote back-up and recovery services on a "first come, first served" basis, all the way to an "as needed" guaranteed basis. Care must be taken in using third parties to ensure that their operating configuration matches exactly to the one the operational site uses, or there could be trouble. The typical prices for these services are shown in Figure 5.17. As a general rule, some 75% of disaster recovery costs are spent on accommodation and equipment issues, especially communication links.[128]

One may also want to consider what happens if the back-up service is itself unavailable, or goes down, when a disaster occurs. Although beyond the immediate attention of this book, there has been some work directed towards addressing this problem.[129]

At this point in time, one should be able to answer the following:

- Have the significant software disaster risks been identified?
- How do these risks potentially impact the missions and objectives of the organization?
- Do these disaster risks contribute greatly to the potential financial, legal, or business operational costs of the company if they occur?
- Can these disaster risks be averted or handled in some way?

If any of these questions can be answered yes, then disaster risk management is conducted. Management will need to decide which is the most acceptable solution for the cost. After a decision has been made, a recovery plan needs to be created to implement the management decision. Tests of the recovery procedures are needed to also ensure the plan meets the recovery objectives. Later, monitoring should take place with periodic checks being conducted to ensure the recovery system is sufficient to meet any changes in the current computing requirements. Time to recovery is the most significant parameter to be rechecked, as it will be the prime driver in any cost equation.

Each company will have to decide for itself how worthwhile it is providing for a contingency against the effects of a software disaster, but with business dependency on computers only increasing, the cost/benefit ratio will get better. As with computing itself, disaster recovery planning will soon not be a cost decision, but a competitive decision. If your system goes down, then your customers will turn towards those companies whose systems did not. The "computer is down" will not be an acceptable excuse in the 1990s.

5.4 Summary

We started this chapter with a short story concerning three lessons: "exactitude is a virtue," "one cannot expect partial credit for failure," and "one must learn from one's past mistakes." Hopefully by now, one can perceive how these apply to the subjects of software safety, security, and disaster recovery, especially if one does not pay sufficient attention to what may happen when something goes wrong, as it surely will to every computing system ever built or likely to be built. The design and implementation of sound, safe, secure and disaster-tolerant systems is an extremely complex affair, which will only grow more so with time, with higher risks attendant to them. A few have tried to attack the problems in all three areas of risk simultaneously, but there is still much more work to be done before the different objectives of each type of risk, and the different approaches required, will be merged into a coherent theory.[130-133]

A question that will be asked more and more in the future by the public will be, "Why use systems which are dependant upon computers if they can wrought so much havoc?" The reasons which we in the profession currently give, such as computers provide advantages, in terms of cost, speed, and flexibility that older methods, such as human or analog control, do not have, will not be sufficient. We could also claim that over $750 million was spent on computing security in the United States in 1988. But keep in mind that this only represents .2% of the U.S. yearly spending on computing. Unless we take a more visible leadership position in trying to control the effects of the computers when they fail, and not try to hide behind the old argument that it is not in our domain, we will be faced with very unpleasant restrictions and legal responsibilities. The public already is starting to feel that computer systems are like the weather and beyond their control. It is our duty not to make them feel that way. Otherwise, we in the industry may find that courts will decide what the software requirements are or, worse, should have been.

Questions

1 How do you define safety in your everyday life? What are the characteristics which decide for you whether a situation is safe or not? How do these characteristics compare to your co-workers or classmates? How do you define software safety? Give an example which compares the various characteristics of a situation in which safety is, and is not, involved.

2 How is software safety like, or different from, software risk? Why? Answer by stating the differences in software safety risk management from typical software engineering risk management where safety is not a concern.

3 Does your philosophy concerning risk analysis lean more towards a quantitative approach, or qualitative, or neither, or both? Explain why, giving two examples where your approach is better than the other. Also give two examples where the other approach is better. Determine if the reasons are inherent in the approaches themselves, or for other reasons, such as political or social.

4 In a software system controlling an airplane, or a nuclear refinery, or a coal-burning plant, or your car's engine performance, how safe is safe enough? Compare the concept of safety in each case. Whose responsibility is it to ensure safety? The person writing the requirements? The designer? The tester? The purchaser and/or user?

5 The British had a saying in World War II to the effect that the third best system specified was the ideal one, since the second best was always too late, and the first never got built. Do you think this is true today? Do you think it is the right approach? How about when it concerns systems such as those listed in the preceding question?

6 What is the difference between a risk and a hazard? Is software a risk, or is it a hazard? In all cases? When, if ever, does it make a difference? Why?

7 Murphy's law states if someone can do it wrong, he or she will. What implications does this saying hold for software safety? For what other reasons do software systems fail? How can they be made not to fail?

8 One may be tempted to argue that one just needs to build a high quality, reliable system to get a safe system. Unfortunately, building such a system does not necessarily mean it is always a safe system. Explain why by explaining the differences between quality and reliability, quality and safety, as well as safety and quality.

9 What is a PHA? How is it different from a risk analysis? Compare and contrast FHA, SHA, OHA, and FMEA.

10 In Chapter 1, we described the glitch that caused the AT&T network to become disrupted. Investigate some of the references and describe which types of safety analyses might be applicable. Do you think a possible problem was viewing the system as a reliability system, rather than as an accident system? (Refer to note 58.)

11 Take a section of code from a program you have written, say of 50 lines or so in length, and consider it as a section of safety critical software. Now define a top event which represents some type of undesirable event, say a human input error, which could cause a malfunction in the program. Perform a Fault Tree Analysis on the section of code, identifying all possible system malfunctions which could have occurred due to the top event. Do you think an Event Tree Analysis would have worked better on finding possible safety problems? Postulate some solutions to overcoming any safety problems uncovered.

12 What are the penalties for ignoring software safety for companies and individuals? Do you think that liability for software designs should rest with the chief designer as they do in the United Kingdom?

13 Describe software security. Do you believe it is a general problem, or something that is only a real concern to the military?

14 Take the mainframe installation used at your college, university, or office, and describe the various ways to gain access to information within it. Is it easy or difficult to gain unauthorized access? Are there security countermeasures set up to discourage access? What would happen if the system under study were to go down for an hour? A day? A week? Three weeks?

15 How do the technological and cultural aspects of computing affect the way people view software security and software safety? Which is the driver today? What will be the driver in the 1990s?

16 How private are your records kept by the government, banks, hospitals, credit bureaus, and so forth? Do you think you can get unlimited and unhampered access to them? Do you think others can? Have you ever tried to get access to your own records at a credit service? If not, try to and report on your success or failure.

17 Why is EDI so susceptible to security problems such as Trojan horses, data diddling, electronic picketing, and so forth? Which are the ones to worry about the most? What can be done to strengthen EDI systems from these types of attacks?

18 Obtain a copy of the *Trusted Computer Systems Criteria* from a local library or defense contractor (it is unclassified). Also obtain a reprint of the Campbell and Sands paper on their risk management model. Again, taking a computer installation you are familiar with, do a full analysis of the installation, especially concentrating on the countermeasures aspect. Rate the installation's level of security against the level of security described in the TCSC. You may want to do this as a class/group project.

19 Report the findings above to the site manager and system administrator for reaction. What was it? Have they conducted a previous security audit?

20 What is a software disaster? Should it be considered a security issue, or something distinct?

21 Again, turning to your local computing center, how much would an hour's downtime cost? Is there a way of finding out? If not, why not?

22 Does there exist a disaster recovery plan at the installation? If so, what does it consist of? What types of recovery mechanisms are available?

23 In performing perfective maintenance, there is a high probability of introducing new errors into the system, thus frequently leading to consequences that were not expected and counterintuitive. Discuss the safety, security, and operational recovery implications of evolving a system.

24 Alan Boring, in a February 1987 *Communications of the ACM* article entitled, "Computer System Reliability and Nuclear War," states that the concept of reliability extends beyond merely keeping a system running and invades the realm of system intention or even what we should have intended—if we had only known. Respond to the question he then poses: To what extent are we able to state or codify our intentions in computer systems so that all circumstances are covered?

25 Russell J. Abbott, in a March 1990 *ACM Computing Surveys* article entitled "Resourceful Systems for Fault Tolerance, Reliability, and Safety," states that a resourceful system is one which is able to determine whether it has achieved its objectives or, if not, to develop and carry out alternative plans. Review Abbott's article and see if his description of resourceful systems and how they can be constructed will resolve Borning's concern expressed in Question 24.

References

1. "Flight Tests of Gripen To Resume This Year," *Aviation Week & Space Technology*, 26 June, 1989.

2. The Internet/Arpanet system is a collection of approximately 1200 networks and 85,000 host computers. The worm program invaded approximately 6200 computers, or about 7% of the system. For more details, see the "Special Section on the Internet Worm" in *Communications of the ACM*, Vol. 32, No. 6, June 1989, and Sheldon Richman, "Common Sense Helps in Virus Battle" in *The Washington Times*, December 20, 1989.

3. John E. Hopcroft and Dean B. Kraft, "Toward Better Computer Science," *IEEE Spectrum*, December 1987.

4. Peter G. Neumann, "SEN Risk Index, 1976 to Date," *ACM Software Engineering Notes*, Vol. 14 No. 1, January 1989.

5. Byran Kocher, "Everything Old Is New Again," *Communications of the ACM*, Vol. 33, No. 3, March 1990.

6. Henry Petroski, *To Engineer Is Human*, St. Martin's Press, New York, 1982.

7. Ravishankar K. Iyer and Paola Verlardi, "Hardware-Related Software Errors: Measurement and Analysis," *IEEE Transactions on Software Engineering*, Vol. SE-11, No. 2, February 1985.

8. Robert L. Glass, "Software vs. Hardware Errors," *IEEE Computer*, Vol. 23, No. 12, December 1980.

9. *Webster's Third International Dictionary*, G. & C. Merrian Co., Chicago, IL, 1976.

10. Nancy G. Leveson, "Safety as a Software Quality," *IEEE Software*, May 1989.

11. "Special Report: Designing and Operating a Minimum-Risk System," *IEEE* Spectrum, Vol. 26, No. 6, June 1989.

12. Paul B. Thompson, "Risk Objectivism and Risk Subjectivism: When Are Risks *Real?*" *Risk: Issues in Health & Safety*, Vol.1, No. 1, Winter 1990. This article provides a thorough coverage of the current debate swirling in risk analysis circles over the subjective and objective schools of thought.
    To be clear about my personal perspective, when I state, for example, that a software project has a 40% chance of success at its initiation, I do not view it as an absolute measure, but rather a relative one. The number is based upon what one would expect to happen in aggregate; i.e., across all projects given the same set of circumstances. The 40% may indicate a very low risk situation, for one must remind oneself that only about 40-60% of all projects across all industries *ever* succeed (refer back to note 20 of Chapter 1). Remember, a 100% chance of success can only be shown *after* the project is finished.
    Risks, as we keep saying, are only that—risks, not eventualities. If you accept a risk, and the risk occurs, it's the penalty you must be willing to pay. However, if taking a different path leads only to a 20% chance of success, then one has to weigh which of the two alternatives to take carefully. Again, the biggest obstacle one is confronted with is that it is not known whether a 40% chance of success at the beginning of a software project is good enough to make the decision to proceed. Given the lack of data from other projects to compare an analytical result with, well, one has a right to be a bit skeptical of the results of quantitative analysis, but *not* the analysis itself. At the end of the day, numbers cannot substitute for good engineers nor for good managers. Gut engineering based upon experience and *common sense* will always be the final arbitrator.

13. Special Issue on Reliability, *IEEE Spectrum*, Vol. 18, No. 10, October 1981.

14. Kai N. Lee, "Assessing Danger," *Science*, Vol. 193, 9 July, 1976.

15. Jeremy Campbell, *Grammatical Man*, Simon and Schuster, New York, 1982.

16. Thomas B. Allen, *War Games*, Berkley Books, New York, 1987.

17. John Paulos, *Innumeracy: Mathematical Illiteracy and Its Consequences,* Hill and Wang, New York, 1988.

18. Martin van Creveld, *Technology and War: From 2000 B.C. to the Present, The Free Press*, New York, 1989. For instance, one should not attempt with quantitative analysis to assign probabilities to mistakes, lousy plans, or of the selection of wrong courses of action.

19. William D. Rowe, *An Anatomy of Risk*, Robert E. Krieger Publishing Co., Malabar, FL, 1988. It should be clear that "real risks" are the object of natural science inquiry, whereas perceived risks are the object of social science inquiry. We will deal primarily with the second.

20. William W. Lowrance, *Of Acceptable Risk: Science and the Determination of Safety*, William Kaufman, Inc., Los Altos, CA, 1976.

21. William D. Rowe, *An Anatomy of Risk*, Robert E. Krieger Publishing Co., Malabar, FL, 1988.

22. Ibid.

23. Nicholas Rescher, *Risk*, University Press of America, Lanham, MD, 1983. Rescher states these as eliminable and ineliminable risks. Eliminable risks are those which, for a price, can be rendered risk-free. Ineliminable risks are those that one can never get to this state, either because the risk is "irremovable" or the cost is "impractical."

24. William D. Rowe, *An Anatomy of Risk*, Robert E. Krieger Publishing Co., Malabar, FL, 1988.

25. M. Granger Morgan, "Choosing and Managing Technology-Induced Risk," *IEEE Spectrum*, Vol. 18, No. 12, December 1981.

26. "Post-Challenger Evaluation of Space Shuttle Risk Assessment and Management," National Academy Press, January 1988.

27. Charles W. McKay, "Lifecycle Support for Computer Systems and Software Safety in the Target and Integration Environments of the Space Station Program," SERC presentation to NASA, 15 June, 1987.

28. Nancy G. Leveson, "Software Safety," *ACM Computing Surveys*, Vol. 18, No. 2, June 1986.

29. *IEEE Glossary of Software Engineering Terminology*, ANSI/IEEE Std 729-1983.

30. Nancy G. Leveson, "Software Safety," *ACM Computing Surveys*, Vol. 18, No. 2, June 1986.

31. Charles Perrow, *Normal Accidents: Living with High-Risk Technologies*, Basic Books, New York, 1984.

32. Alan Borning, "Computer System Reliability and Nuclear War," *Communications of the ACM*, Vol. 30, No. 2, February 1987.

33. Charles Perrow, *Normal Accidents: Living with High-Risk Technologies*, Basic Books, 1984.

34. R. L. Henneman and W. B. Rouse, "On Measuring the Complexity of Monitoring and Controlling Large-Scale Systems," *IEEE Transactions on Systems, Man, and Cybernetics*, Vol. SMC-16, No. 2, March/April 1986.

35. Ware Myers, "Can Software for the Strategic Defense Initiative Ever Be Error-Free?" *IEEE Computer*, Vol. 19, No. 11, November 1986. The trouble with quoting this type of number is that one does not know if it is good or bad. For hardware reliability, the basis for a statistical model is in the physical behavior of the hardware. But for

software, it is in the nature of the usage of the software by its users. Any particular user will start off with different initial conditions and different inputs. For fixed initial conditions, the software will behave exactly the same for all users whenever they use it. However, small errors, when they occur, do not necessarily have small effects. When counting software errors, is an array that is [0:99] that should be [1:100] a single error, or many? How about if there were 75 places that the array was used? And what if only 20 were found in testing? Further, to eliminate the error, one could change the boundary conditions or change each individual time the error was detected. To truly have a safe system, it must be extensively used. For more discussion of these issues, see P. A. Currit et al., "Certifying the Reliability of Software," *IEEE Transactions on Software Engineering*, Vol. SE-12, No. 1, January 1986, and David Parna's letter to the editor in *IEEE Computer*, Vol. 20, No. 2, February 1987.

36. Special Issue on Reliability, *IEEE Spectrum*, Vol. 18, No. 10, October 1981.

37. R. L. Henneman and W. B. Rouse, "On Measuring the Complexity of Monitoring and Controlling Large-Scale Systems," *IEEE Transactions on Systems, Man, and Cybernetics*, Vol. SMC-16, No. 2, March/April 1986.

38. "Post-Challenger Evaluation of Space Shuttle Risk Assessment and Management," National Academy Press, January 1988.

39. "Shuttle 51-L Loss: Officials Disagree on Data Assessing Shuttle Reliability," *Aviation Week & Space Technology*, 17 February, 1986.

40. "Designing and Operating A Minimum-Risk System," *IEEE Spectrum* (special report), Vol. 26, No. 6, June 1989.

41. Abraham Kandel and Eitan Avni, *Engineering Risk and Hazard Assessment,* Vols. I & II, CRC Press, Boca Raton, FL, 1988.

42. Aviva Brechner, "An Overview of Formal Methods of Risk Assessment," *IEEE Electro*, 1988.

43. Howard Abbott, *Safer by Design: The Management of Product Design Risks Under Strict Liability*, The Design Council, London, 1987.

44. Nancy G. Leveson, "Software Safety," *ACM Computing Surveys*, Vol. 18, No. 2, June 1986.

45. Michael O. Fryer, "Risk Assessment of Computer Controlled Systems," *IEEE Transactions on Software Engineering*, Vol. SE-11, No. 1, January 1985.

46. Ernst E. Frankel, *Systems Reliability and Risk Analysis*, Martinus Nijhoff Publishers, Boston, MA, 1984.

47. Harold E. Roland and Brian Moriarty, *System Safety Engineering and Management*, John Wiley & Sons, Inc., New York, 1983.

48. Nancy G. Leveson and Peter R. Harvey, "Analyzing Software Safety," *IEEE Transactions on Software Engineering*, Vol. SE-9, No. 5, September 1983.

49. "Reliability," *IEEE Spectrum* (special issue), Vol. 18, No. 10, October 1981.

50. Nancy G. Leveson, "Software Safety," *ACM Computing Surveys*, Vol. 18, No. 2, June 1986.

51. John Cohrssen and Vincent Covello, *Risk Analysis: A Guide to Principles and Methods for Analyzing Health and Environmental Risks*, NTIS, Springfield, VA, 1989.

52. Nancy G. Leveson, "Software Safety," *ACM Computing Surveys*, Vol. 18, No. 2, June 1986.

53. Nancy G. Leveson and Peter R. Harvey, "Analyzing Software Safety," *IEEE Transactions on Software Engineering*, Vol. SE-9, No. 5, September 1983.

54. Ibid.

55. Charles W. McKay, "Lifecycle Support for 'Computer Systems and Software Safety' in the Target and Integration Environments of the Space Station Program," SERC presentation to NASA, 15 June, 1987.

56. Jack Goldberg, "Some Principles and Techniques for Designing Safe Systems," *ACM Software Engineering Notes*, Vol. 12, No. 3, July 1987.

57. "Investigators Find Reconstructed Tail of DC-10 Riddled with Damage," *Aviation Week & Space Technology*, 7 August, 1989.

58. Eric J. Lerner, "Reliable Systems: Design and Tests," *IEEE Spectrum*, Vol. 18, No. 10, 1981. One must be careful not to apply redundancy in a haphazard fashion. One needs to understand whether one is dealing with a *reliability system* or an *accident system*. A reliability system is concerned with the probability of a system functioning successfully. An accident system is where one can arrange a set of events in such a way that the successful function of the system results in an undesired event. Sneak circuit analysis (i.e., searching for an unwanted circuit closure when other, desired circuits, are closed) is often conducted in an accident system.
   In some cases accident systems and reliability systems will be complementary, and sometimes they will not. For example, components linked in a series are undesirable for reliability systems, but are desirable for accident systems. Similarly, parallel components are desirable for reliability systems, but not for accident systems. Parallel-series systems are desirable for both. For more detail on these types of systems, refer to Harold E. Roland and Brian Moriarty, *System Safety Engineering and Management*, John Wiley & Sons, Inc., New York, 1983.

59. Nancy Leveson, "A Scary Tale—Sperry Avionics Module Testing Bites the Dust?" *ACM Software Engineering Notes*, Vol. 12, No. 3, April 1987.

60. Ibid.

61. D. E. Eckhardt and L. D. Lee, "A Theoretical Basis for the Analysis of Multiversion Software Subject to Coincident Errors," *IEEE Transactions on Software Engineering*, Vol. SE-11, No. 12, December 1985.

62. Bev Littlewood and Douglas Miller, "Conceptual Modeling of Coincident Failures in Multiversion Software," *IEEE Transactions on Software Engineering*, Vol. SE-15, No. 12, December 1989. It should be noted that another study by Brilliant, Knight, and Leveson, seemed to show that forcing diversity may not be as effective as first thought. They discovered that correlated failures in N-version systems seem to be a product of logically related faults, implying that separate developments may not prevent different implementation groups from making the same mistake. Furthermore, input domain–related faults may cause correlated failures, implying that correlated failures may occur even if implementors use entirely different algorithms and make different mistakes. For details, see Susan Brilliant et al., "Analysis of Faults in an N-

Version Experiment," *IEEE Transactions of Software Engineering*, Vol. 16, No. 2, February 1990.

63. W. B. Noble, "Developing Safe Software For Critical Airborne Applications," *Proceedings of IEEE 6th Digital Avionics Systems Conference*, December 1984.

64. S. Brilliant et al., "The Consistent Comparison Problem in N-Version Software," *IEEE Transactions on Software Engineering*, Vol. 15, No. 11, November 1989.

65. J. W. Mersky, "The Role of Verification and Validation in Risk Management," *NSIA Conference on Software Risk Management*, 30 September, 1987.

66. Abraham Kandel and Eitan Avni, *Engineering Risk and Hazard Assessment*, Vol. I, CRC Press, Boca Raton, FL, 1988.

67. William Hammer, *Handbook of System and Product Safety*, Prentice-Hall, Inc., Englewood Cliffs, NJ, 1972.

68. Barry Boehm, *Software Risk Management Tutorial*, TRW-ACM Seminar, April 1988.

69. Peter G. Neumann, "Risks: Cumulative Index of Software Engineering Notes—Illustrative Risks to the Public," *ACM Software Engineering Notes*, Vol. 14, No. 1, January 1989.

70. Walter Olson (ed.), *New Directions in Liability Law*, The Academy of Political Science, New York, 1988. In the United States, almost 15% of the price of a machine tool is accounted for by the manufacturer's product-liability insurance. Further, over the past 10 years, insurance costs have risen 500% and some 36% of manufacturers have stopped making some products due to product liability.

71. Ibid.

72. Madhav N. Sinha and Walter O. Wilborn, *The Management of Quality Assurance*, John Wiley & Sons, Inc., New York, 1985.

73. John Kolb and Steven S. Ross, *Product Safety and Liability*, McGraw-Hill, Inc., New York, 1978.

74. Gary Anthes, "U.S. Software Experts Track British Standards," *Federal Computer Weekly*, 18 September, 1989.

75. "Software Safety Focus of New British Standard," *IEEE Software*, May 1989.

76. Gervase Webb, "City Computer Blackmail Plot," *Evening Standard*, 13 December, 1989. On 1 February 1990 a person was arrested in connection with the scheme. The person had mailed out over 26,000 infected disks, and planned to mail out 2 million more. For more information, see "26,000 Trojan Horses Deployed in Computer Extortion Scheme," *The Washington Times*, 13 April 1990.

77. Sheldon Richman, "Common Sense Helps in Virus Battle," *The Washington Times*, 20 December, 1989.

78. *Wall Street Journal*, editorial, June 1988.

79. "How Safe Is Your System?" *Director*, July 1988.

80. "Taking the Byte Out of Crime," *Business Week*, 1 August, 1988.

81. Terrance Ireland, "Security Issues for C³I," *NSIA Conference on Software Technology Explosion in C³I*, 26 October, 1989.

82. Tricia Saddington (ed.), *Security For Small Computer Systems—An ECC Security Project*, Elsevier, Oxford, England, 1988.

83. Morrie Gasser, *Building a Secure Computer System*, Van Nostrand Reinhold, New York, 1988.

84. *Automatic Data Processing (ADP) Security—Policy, Procedures and Responsibilities*, AF Regulation 300-8, 15 May, 1983.

85. Rein Turn (ed.), *Advances in Computer Security*, Vols. 1, 2 and 3, Artech House, Inc., Dedham, MA, 1981, 1984, and 1988, respectively.

86. We had one system administrator, who, when told visitors were coming, would load up a diagnostic test program which would make all the front panel lights blink, printers spew out paper, and tape units wind and rewind the tapes. This made the computing center look incredibly active, and suitably impressed the visitors looking in from the other side of the glass.

87. Willis H. Ware (ed.), *Security Controls for Computer Systems*, Rand Corporation, 1 January, 1970, reissued October 1979.

88. There is a group, led by the Information Systems Security Association (ISSA), which is starting to take an important role in non–defense oriented security, but the U.S. DoD is still the primary driver on what constitutes a secure computing environment.

89. Rein Turn (ed.), *Preface in Advances in Computer Security*, Vol. 1, Artech House, Inc., Dedham, MA, 1981.

90. *Department of Defense Trusted Computer System Evaluation Criteria*, DoD-STD-5200.28, DoD Washington, D.C., 1985.

91. Ibid.

92. Terrance Ireland, "Security Issues for C³I," *NSIA Conference on Software Technology Explosion in C³I*, 26 October, 1989.

93. R. Turn and W. H. Ware, "Privacy and Security Issues in Information Systems," *IEEE Transactions on Computers*, Vol. C-25, No. 12, December 1976.

94. "Is Nothing Private?" *Business Week*, 4 September, 1989.

95. *Information Security Monitor*, IBC Technical Services Ltd., London, Vol. 3, No. 12, November 1988.

96. "U.S. Judge Rules Computer "Worm" Case To Be Tried," *The Washington Post*, 5 November, 1989. The first and only person to be indicted and convicted is the graduate student who allegedly created the famous Internet Worm in November of 1988, which ended up in over 6000 computer systems. He received a fine and a suspended sentence.

97. David Stang, "PC Viruses: The Desktop Epidemic," *The Washington Post*, 14 January, 1990.

98. Ibid.

99. "1stAid Abandons Virus Defense," *MACWORLD*, April 1990.

100. "Special Section on the Internet Worm," *Communications of the ACM*, Vol. 32, No. 6, June 1989.

101. *Department of Defense Trusted Computer System Evaluation Criteria*, DoD-STD-5200.28, DoD Washington, D.C., 1985.

102. "Thwarting the Information Thieves," *IEEE Spectrum*, Vol. 22, No. 7, July 1985.

103. Glenn Young, "Hidden Troubles Plague Leaky Networks," *Telecommunications Products Plus Technology*, June 1985.

104. R. P. Campbell and G. A. Sands, "A Modular Approach to Computer Security Risk Assessment," *AFIPS Conference Proceedings*, Vol. 48, NCC, 1979.

105. This type of analysis is in general useful, as it can explicitly show how much a company depends on and spends on information technology. It can also show what needs to be improved in the organization to gain the competitive edge, as explained in Chapter 2.

106. *CRAMM—The CCTA Risk Analysis and Management Methodology*, CCTA, London, 1988.

107. "How Safe Is Your System?" *Director*, July 1988.

108. Morrie Gasser, *Building A Secure Computer System*, Van Nostrand Reinhold, New York, 1988.

109. D. Bell and L. LaPadula, *Secure Computer Systems: Mathematical Foundations and Model*, The MITRE Corporation, Bedford, MA, 1973.

110. Joshua D. Guttman, "Workshop Explores Diverse Views of Computer Security," *IEEE Computer*, Vol. 22, No. 8, August 1989.

111. Peter Stephenson, "Micro Security Products," *Government Computer News*, 7 November, 1988.

112. Tricia Saddington (ed.), *Security for Small Computer Systems—An ECC Security Project*, Elsevier, Oxford, England, 1988.

113. Frederick G. Tompkins and Russell Rice, "Integrating Security Activities into Software Development Life Cycle and The Software Quality Assurance Process," *Computers & Security*, Vol. 5, No. 3, September 1986.

114. S. Walker et al., "Introduction to Network Security Evaluation," *7th Security Conference*, DoD/NBS, September 1984.

115. Glenn Young, "Hidden Troubles Plague Leaky Networks," *Telecommunications Products Plus Technology*, June 1985.

116. *Disaster Recovery: Contingency Planning and Program Evaluation*, QED Information Sciences, Inc., Wellesley, MA, 1985.

117. Terrance Ireland, "Security Issues for C³I," *NSIA Conference on Software Technology Explosion in C³I*, 26 October, 1989.

118. "Disasters Are High-Tech Nightmares," *USA TODAY*, 20 October, 1989.

119. Jack O'Neil, "What to Look for in a Network Monitoring and Control System," *Telecommunications Products Plus Technology*, August 1985.

120. Steven Mead, "Soft Landings for DP Disasters," *Software Management*, February 1989.

121. "COMPSEC '88," *Information Security Monitor*, Vol. 3, No. 12, November 1988.

122. Steven Mead, "Soft Landings for DP Disasters," *Software Management*, February 1989.

123. "*A Guide to Systems Reliability and Availability*," CCTA, London, 1988. One should notice from this list that many of the factors that can cause operational disruption are not totally within the control of the computing center, such as network component or line failure.

124. *Disaster Recovery: Contingency Planning and Program Evaluation*, QED Information Sciences, Inc., Wellesley, MA, 1985.

125. Ibid.

126. John Schladweiler, "The Strategic Value of Network Disaster Recovery Planning," *Network Management*, September 1989.

127. Vanessa Jo Grimm, "HUD Isn't Waiting for Disaster but Plans to Be Ready," *Government Computing News*, 18 September, 1989.

128. *Disaster Recovery: Contingency Planning and Program Evaluation*, QED Information Sciences, Inc., Wellesley, MA, 1985.

129. Yehuda Kahane et al., "Computer Backup Pools, Disaster Recovery, and Default Risk," *Communications of the ACM*, Vol. 31, No. 1, January 1988.

130. Charles McKay, "Some Notes on Risk Management," SERC/HTL Report, 16 June 1989.

131. Charles McKay, "Lifecycle Support For 'Computers and Software Safety' in the Target and Integration Environments of the Space Station Program," SERC/HTL Report, 15 June, 1987.

132. Peter G. Neumann, "On Hierarchical Design of Computer Systems for Critical Applications," *IEEE Transactions on Software Engineering*, Vol. SE-12, No. 9, September 1986.

133. Sarah Brocklehurst et al., "Recalibrating Software Reliability Models," *IEEE Transactions on Software Engineering*, Vol. SE-16, No. 4, April 1990. This article describes a technique for finding the most accurate reliability model for a given program.

The Perception and Politics of Risk: Risk Taking and Risk Organizations

"All the wise men were on one side, and all the fools were on the other ... And be damned, Sir, all the fools were right."

THE DUKE OF WELLINGTON

6.0   Introduction

In the previous chapters on risk analysis and management, we tended to treat risk in a precise, nonemotional, standoffish way. A risk was presented as something that could be described in a rational, hard-nosed, quantitative manner, and even if we were forced to use qualitative measures because the estimation criteria were soft or fuzzy, it did not matter that much. After all, we assumed the risk taker and/or risk analyst was a rational human being, not subject to biases or emotion, and thus could resolve conflict in a logical, unfeeling manner. Our understandings and perceptions of a risk and its potential consequences were assumed to be closely aligned to the "objective reality" of the situation.

However, in truth, the concept of risk revolves much more around subjective perception frequently infused with emotion than objective reality, with the consequence being that our model of the analysis process regularly breaks down. This is especially true, as we indicated in the previous chapter, in matters which include decisions that involve personal or public safety. In many current treatments of risk, all too frequently the how and the why of an individual or group's perception of risk is overlooked or understated. The influences are judged to be of only minor significance, or brushed away with words to the effect that the "analyst must take into account local conditions." Because these influences are hard to deal with, we eschew the issue by *assuming* that best judgment will be used. Few analysts try to delve into the question of what happens if, or when, this does not occur.

This lack of understanding of the importance of the human element involved in the perception of risk and its consequences is unfortunate, as it frequently sways individual judgments concerning risk identification, estimation, evaluation, and management in ways not easily predicted a priori. Further, when viewed with hindsight, the decisions do not make sense. For example, the "facts" used in a decision may only be apparent facts, assumed facts, reported facts, hoped-for facts, or half-true facts. The result, when the facts are found out not to be facts at all, is often called the "postdecision surprise factor," and is typified by the words, "What!!! I wouldn't have made that decision if I had known all the *real* facts!!!" We must note that sometimes it includes a bit more colorful language than that. Senior managers especially are not fond of surprises, and if they are not properly informed of any qualification to the accuracy of the information they were given from which to make a decision, there will be guaranteed trouble later on.

In this chapter, we intend to correct this ubiquitous oversight by investigating how the subjective perception of risk can slant the taking of risk or consider alternative courses of action derived during the process of risk analysis and management. We will examine such issues as:

- What influences and colors risk taking in an individual or group?
- How is risk perceived by an individual or group encountering different types of circumstances?
- What are the politics involved in risk decisions?
- How can the effects of subject perception be recognized, and possibly be avoided?
- How can an information technology risk management organization be created to deal explicitly with the problems of risk encountered within a business environment?
- Why do risk management organizations need to be treated on a par with, but differently from, others such as total quality management (TQM) and integrated resource management (IRM)?

Our ultimate goal is to attempt to make risk analysis less susceptible to subjective perception and more congruous with our original underlying assumption of objective reality. It must not be forgotten that at their root, software enterprises and the businesses they support are human enterprises, filled with risk. Put another way by Wallace Donham in a 1922 *Harvard Business Review*, "The executive must often gamble with his most important problems."

It is only through the understanding of our human frailties and strengths that we can ever hope to be able to deliver a system we want, when we want it. To do so, however, we must sometimes use the harsh spotlight of public review. Therefore, in trying to better understand the amount and the extent of the influence the perception of risk can have on decision making, we will begin by presenting three vignettes from different fields: politics, engineering, and aerospace. Each portrays the consequences that can occur when one underestimates or neglects the affects of the subjective perception of risk.

6.1 Three Stories of Risk Taking: Overlooking the Obvious, or How Believing Is Not Always Seeing

Below are three stories that involve risk taking and subjective perception. Within each of them one will find at least four recurring themes that we explore in depth later. One highlights how an individual's personal bias influences what is and is not considered a risk. Another centers not on the individual, but on the cultural view of risk. A third concerns the pervasiveness of subjective perception, regardless of whether one applies quantitative or qualitative approaches. The fourth involves how politics also distorts what actions one will take, and how much one is willing to risk, in certain situations. We will first start with a historical event, one which has dominated political thought and actions for the last 40 years.

6.1.1 Munich 1938

In September of 1938, the outbreak of a general European war appeared imminent. Reichskanzler Adolf Hitler had demanded that the Sudetenland region of Czechoslovakia be immediately ceded to Nazi Germany. On three occasions, British Prime Minister Neville

Chamberlain traveled to Munich to meet with Hitler, and finally, on September 30, Chamberlain and French Premier Edouard Daladier agreed to the majority of Hitler's demands. Arriving in England from this historic Munich Conference, Chamberlain waved to the press photographers a document which he triumphantly announced as guaranteeing "peace with honor. I believe it is peace for our time."

Unfortunately, things did not quite go as Chamberlain had led the British people to believe, for which he has been reviled ever since. For Hitler seized the rest of Czechoslovakia in March 1939, signed a nonaggression pact with the Soviet Union in August, and invaded Poland in September, which forced Britain and France to declare war on Germany. Chamberlain ended up with neither peace nor honor, for all his concessions. Chamberlain's appeasement at Munich has repeatedly been cited as a major reason for encouraging Hitler to make the political and military moves that he did, ending up with the deliberate provocation which led to war. The "lessons of Munich" have made such a lasting impression that over the past 45 years, they have often been invoked in the Western Alliance as *the* fundamental policy guidelines in its diplomatic risk assessment and approach to the Eastern and Asian Communist blocs since the end of the Second World War. *Si vis pacem, para bellum*: If you desire peace, prepare for war has been the Alliance's undeclared motto.

The Munich Conference and the events leading up to it have come under renewed study in recent years, yielding some useful insights which parallel situations and experiences the software and systems engineering risk analyst will confront. One such study has been performed by Robert Beck, entitled "Munich's Lesson's Reconsidered," which appeared in the Harvard University's Center for Science and International Affairs journal *International Security*.[1] Beck found that the studies of the events of the Munich Conference often swing between two schools of thought: One reaffirms that Chamberlain unnecessarily and wrongly appeased an aggressive Hitler, and acted as a wishful bumbler, while the other emphasizes the military, economic, bureaucratic, and political constraints Chamberlain operated under, reasoning that he had little other choice than to appease Hitler. Beck examines both proposals and concludes that a much more plausible explanation lies somewhere more towards the middle ground of both arguments.

Basically, Beck demonstrates that Chamberlain did operate under some very difficult constraints, but also was justly characterized as a naive individual who created many of these very same constraints. For example, in September 1938, it was true that the British populace did not want to go to war. The devastation of a whole generation in the First World War severely influenced the country's willingness, and especially the *political* will, to get involved in another continental war. This feeling of little stomach for war also extended across the whole of the British Empire, without whose support a war could not be successfully waged. The plight of the people in a remote section of Czechoslovakia was hard to sell as a *casus belli*.

Second, this general unwillingness to get involved extended to the United States, which had contributed much towards the final Allied victory in the First World War. After the breakdown of the Treaty of Versailles and the ravages of the Great Depression, America was determined to stay out of any potential European conflict. It also was not seen by Chamberlain's staff as a reliable source of material or men, if war were to come. The United States had let its armed forces diminish to such a token level that it was basically symbolic. It was useless as a fighting force. Other possible British allies such as France were not in much of a mood to get into a fight either, as they still viewed Britain as a potential economic, if not military, threat along with Germany. France likewise had let its military become hollow, depending instead on the Maginot line for its defense.

Third, British senior military advisors warned Chamberlain that Britain was strategically vulnerable to air attack, and could be knocked out of any war quickly by *Luftwaffe* bombers. Furthermore, the British Chiefs of Staff reported that "no pressure that we and our possible allies can bring to bear, either by sea, on land, or in the air, could prevent Germany from invading and over-running Bohemia and from inflicting a decisive defeat on the Czechoslovakian army."[2] British military forces were small, not very well equipped, and the rearmament process was not going well. The situation was so bad in the domestic armament's industry that the British army was actually dependent upon Germany *and* Czechoslovakia for many of their core armaments. These sources of supply obviously would not be available if war came, and it was felt it would take years before substitutes could be made by British industry. The conclusion reached by the military was that whatever happened, the British must not precipitate a war, for the most likely consequence was defeat.

Finally, Chamberlain himself was a very complex individual: naive, optimistic, easily swayed by public opinion, filled with a deep abhorrence of war, and possessing a sense of a personal mission to secure peace—all this while simultaneously harboring deep suspicions of German trustworthiness, and often thinking Hitler acted like a lunatic.

Unfortunately, the former considerations outweighed the latter. Chamberlain actually believed that he could exert influence over Hitler's actions. He felt that Hitler's rational side would dominate his more irrational, and dangerous, one. Moreover, Chamberlain felt that Hitler had only limited territorial aims, and for all his bombast, Chamberlain believed Hitler was telling the truth when he said that all Germany wanted was the Sudetenland. After all, Hitler was a politician like himself, and had to act a certain way in public. The Germany *public*, and the Sudetenland people themselves, Chamberlain thought, wanted the Sudetenland linked back to Germany, not Hitler himself. There would be no more demands made once Hitler and the German people were satisfied with gaining control of that part of Czechoslovakia. Of that, Chamberlain was utterly convinced.[3]

What is interesting is that upon closer examination, the situation was not so bleak as it initially appeared. The German armed forces were not nearly as strong or as well equipped as was believed. The British intelligence service at that time was fairly abysmal, and tended to estimate the German military strength as being higher than it really was for political purposes. The *Luftwaffe* did not nearly possess the required capability to strategically bomb the United Kingdom into submission from air bases inside Germany. At the time, the German military command wrote that they could not possibly support both an attack on Britain and simultaneously support its far reaching commitments elsewhere. Thus an attack was ruled out. The *Luftwaffe* was even stretched when it tried to do so 2 years later flying from bases inside of France.

Furthermore, although the British populace *did* oppose going to war, within a year it showed that it would, with vigor, if necessary. Chamberlain mistook the overall antiwar feelings as supporting his doctrine of concessions to Hitler. The polls taken during the spring and summer of 1938 indicated that Chamberlain's policy towards Hitler had only minority support among the British people. Further, this lack of majority support was discounted or deliberately suppressed by the press on the strong recommendations of the Chamberlain government. BBC broadcasts critical of Hitler were cancelled, antiappeasement newsreels cut or suppressed, and publications critically questioning the German claims to the Sudetenland revised.[4] When Chamberlain returned from Munich in September, the newspapers and newsreels bestowed an incredible amount of praise upon him, likening Chamberlain to a conquering Roman hero. Chamberlain manipulated and restricted the public debate of his policies, thus re-enforcing the solution that he wanted to believe as being correct. He violated one of politics' strongest maxims: You may lie to the people, but do not ever lie to yourself.

Moreover, Hitler was publicly denounced by many, such as Churchill, as being fanatical, as well as not being trustworthy. For example, Hitler had openly violated the World War I treaty stipulations against rearming; his philosophy about the sacrosanctity of the Fatherland, the superiority of the Aryan race, and the blatant racism against Jews and other minorities were documented in *Mein Kampf* as well as in public speeches; and the actions of his followers in carrying out his philosophy of murderous racism, notably during the October 1938 *Kristallnacht*, or Nazi Night of Terror, where 7,500 stores, 29 warehouses, 267 synagogues, and 171 houses were destroyed, 30,000 Jewish men arrested, 236 Jews were killed, and more than 600 permanently maimed, were well documented in the foreign press, such as the *New York Times*, which reported it as "a wave of destruction unparalleled in Germany since the Thirty Years' War." Even if each of these were not well read or suppressed in the popular press in Britain, Chamberlain was briefed on them by his staff.

But Chamberlain mirror-imaged Hitler with himself, giving Hitler personal qualities he in fact did not possess. This allowed Hitler at Munich to bluff in two ways: If Chamberlain had firmly said no to Hitler's annexation of Czechoslovakia, Hitler would have most likely acquiesced, at least for a time (he could not afford to risk a general war with Britain in September 1938 either), and if Chamberlain agreed to his demands, all the better, since it surely did not mark the negotiation limit at which British and French would fight.

However, Chamberlain's perceptions of these events were much different, and these perceptions influenced him much more than the reality of the situation. The fact that the risks and their consequences were overestimated was not seen, nor would they likely be seen because of the various selected biases involved: Chamberlain's optimistic personal views on Hitler and on the prospects of attaining peace; his own personal abhorrence of war; his criteria for success as a politician, which was to follow public opinion (even if it was wrong); to see other politicians being motivated in the same way as himself; and uncritical acceptance of military advice, especially the estimates of German military strength upon which a decision not to confront Hitler was strongly based. As Beck notes, the "worst-case" strategic military analysis of Nazi Germany, when combined with Neville Chamberlain's "best-case'" analysis of Adolf Hitler, proved to be a disastrous amalgam.[5]

6.1.2   Shuttle 51-L

From a risk analysis view, the events of Munich illustrate the problems of estimation error, how the bias of the analyst can affect how a risk is perceived and actions to mitigate it are hampered, how the culture of the organizational entities can keep one from adequately questioning the risk evaluations and risk management recommendations, and how popular opinion; i.e., the politics of risk, help spin the spider's silk, intertwining them all to form a tight and deadly web from which there is no escape. Popular support, one should note, cannot support a flawed policy for very long. This web does not only exist in situations such as the one described above, where, given the nature of politics and diplomacy, one expects to encounter it, but in situations which involve supposed technically dominated, objective decisions, where bias is an anathema.

One such set of events involved the accidental loss of the NASA National Space Transportation System (NSTS) vehicle 51-L, the *Challenger*. The *Challenger* disaster was the outcome of all the things that can go wrong when perceptions of risk are reinforced by internally set and externally abetted cultural biases. In Chapter 5, we spoke of the two different philosophies of risk analysis and management, quantitative and qualitative, which are often at odds with one another. Reviewing, the quantitative school of risk analysis believes that probabilities are primarily reflections of the *actual* frequency of events, thus are "objective" in nature, and can be used for predictions of future events. Members adhering to this philosophy hold that "the real value of probabilistic risk analysis is in understanding the system and its vulnerabilities," and that given proper data, risk analysis can indicate when a project should continue, be changed, not be implemented, or be halted. There is a recognition of the limitations the quality of the input data imposes on the value of the analysis, but overall, the dependence on subjectiveness is, wherever possible, minimized.

The qualitative school, on the other hand, does not play the "numbers game." Members of this philosophic school tend to believe that the assignment of probabilities primarily reflects the *assignee's* belief or confidence that an event will occur, and do not reflect the actual frequency of events. As one strong proponent explained, "statistics don't count for anything... they have no place in engineering anywhere." Risk is minimized and contained not by statistical test programs, but by paying particular attention to the details involved within a system's design. Quantitative risk analysis is seen at best as measuring the relative difficulty of a project, but it should not be seriously used as a basis for whether to implement or cancel a project.

NASA was, up until the time of the *Challenger*, a member of the second school.[6-8] NASA's philosophy was that risk was eliminated by improvements in reliability and quality. Reliability was designed in and defects tested out.[9,10] Part of the reason for this view was a straightforward engineering belief: Past experience had shown that design to be the most critical determinant of spacecraft performance. Although half the causes of component failure could not be determined (mainly due to being unable to recover the components), failures that could be uncovered showed 42% were due to design errors, 15% defective parts, 8% faulty workmanship, and 35% miscellaneous external causes. The record of success using the design philosophy approach was marked by ever-increasing success, as NASA went 0 for 4 in 1958 in successful launches to 8 for 14 in 1959, to 195 out of 246 in the 1960s, to 60 of 66 in the 1970s, and no failures from 1975 until the shuttle *Challenger* on January 28, 1986.

The nature of most of NASA's engineering also reinforced this view, as many of the systems were one-time only vehicles, or ones with limited life. It was thought that keeping statistical data would not prove useful, since old parts would not, or in most cases could not, be reused in the next generation system. Totally new designs would have to be used instead. Design experience; i.e., validation of the overall concept, was more important than quantitative tests.[11]

The other reason for NASA's philosophy was political. When the Apollo program was undertaken, it was a program of immense political significance. It was a symbol of American technology and pride in pursuit of the ideals of the "new frontier," representing an area of overt technological and political competition with the Soviet Union. If the competition could be won, it was felt by U.S. politicians, this could be exploited by translating it into strategic advantages in waging the Cold War by showing democracy's power over that of communism. This competition became even more consequential after the Kennedy assassination, since it was he who called for landing (U.S.) astronauts on the moon by 1970. Add in the factor that President Johnson had, as vice-president, been given the task of championing NASA, and could not politically afford to fail in realizing the late president's challenge, well, the pressure was very high to achieve the objective. Therefore, when a study was contracted to complete a full numerical probability risk assessment of the Apollo program, and later reported back that the chance of getting an astronaut on the moon and getting him safely back was less than 5%, the result by NASA officials was to "throw out that garbage;" i.e., the report, and suppress its findings. It was felt by NASA and others that the numbers and conclusions in the report could do irreparable harm, especially to the funding of the program. Thereafter, most quantitative assessment approaches were disbanded, and were to be officially avoided in the future.

As it turned out, astronauts were landed on the moon, and all came back safely. However, there were many near failures, although these were generally glossed over by NASA and the press. By the end of the program, NASA was seen as a model of reliability and quality engineering. More importantly, the culture of perceiving risk and managing it through the application of superior design was thoroughly ingrained in the organization. When the NSTS program was started, this philosophy naturally again took root. In fact, it took even deeper root because the amount of money for space exploration was much harder to come by as Congress and many others within the scientific community strongly criticized the program. Having a 75% contingency fund like on the Apollo program was not likely to occur. Furthermore, critics could not see the need for the NSTS in light of currently available boosters, and felt that any money spent by NASA could be put to more effective use. Thus, the internal NASA pressure to underestimate the risks and oversell the benefits involved became very substantial. It was difficult to check the estimates of risk and benefits objectively, since the NASA culture did not believe in risk estimation techniques which required statistical data, thus no data was ever kept. A classic catch 22, but one which kept the critics from prying too deep.

However, by law, estimates of the risks and benefits had to be made for cost justification purposes. As a result, engineering estimates were made ranging from 1 in 100 to 1 in 100,000 launches of an occurrence of a solid-fuel rocket booster (SRB) failure which could cause catastrophic loss of the NSTS vehicle. Interestingly, the working engineers supplied the lower figure, while management in their report to Congress used the upper. Both of these estimates were made even in light of the historical data which showed an SRB failure rate approaching between 1 in 34 using all previous launch data, or a better, but not significantly better, 1 in 59 launches if one instead used data which eliminated very early failures which happened during initial testing of the booster design. However, using management's numbers, a shuttle wasn't expected to suffer SRB failure for over 300 years of *daily* operation, whereas using the engineers' numbers, a catastrophic failure was almost a certainty given the planned number of launches![12] For *illustrative* purposes, in Figure 6.1 we have depicted how long one could expect to launch the NSTS before an explosion of an SRB occurred, if the NSTS was launched every 2 weeks, using different failure rates, and the failure rates were statistically invariable (i.e., design improvements or weaknesses are not introduced). In either case, the risk was either not acceptable or believable, except to Congress, which funded the program anyhow.[13] The safety board for NASA said for planning purposes a failure rate number of 1 in 1000 launches should be used, but management insisted that consideration of a 1 in 10,000 ratio was justified due to "unique improvements made in the design and manufacturing process" of the SRBs.[14]

The importance of these failure rate numbers should not be underestimated, since they represented the crucial basis for showing how the NSTS could be *the* cost-effective and safe way of launching earth orbit payloads. To accomplish that objective, the NSTS had to be able to replace all existing ways of launching payloads, thus had to be seen as

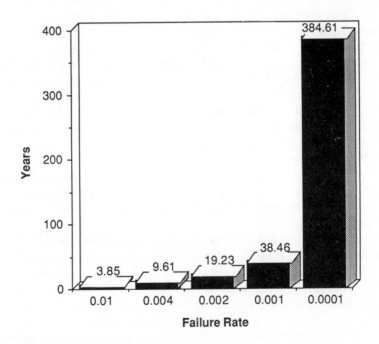

Figure 6.1 Estimated Years Before SRB Failure

being safe, routine, and cheap, rather than risky, infrequent, and expensive. NASA's efforts went so far as trying to make the NSTS appear as a space airliner, which implied that it would have the same reliability and safety as a plane (air travel is the least risky form of transportation next to walking). In effect, the NSTS would achieve reliability and safety by word association. Later, NSTS was touted as a space truck, again implying that it was a reliable, everyday vehicle. The public was led to believe, or surmised, especially when a teacher was allowed aboard the *Challenger*, that there were no dangers involved. Worse, NASA officials began to confuse their desires with reality. Even when the cost of the NSTS climbed to 20 times that of the original estimates, the alarm bells did not go off that something might be wrong with the initial assumptions.

Well, the rest, as they say, is history. An SRB failed on the twenty-fifth NSTS launch, killing the crew of the *Challenger*, and throwing the space program into a flat spin. Although the NSTS is flying again, confidence in NASA's ability, and to a degree its truthfulness, is low, and as a result, the next major program, the space station, is in jeopardy of never being able to attain adequate funding. NASA now applies quantitative risk analysis in conjunction with its quality design approach, and currently uses 1 failure in 78 launches as its official rate of failure of an SRB. This has moved the Office of Technology Assessment (not NASA) to advise Congress to build a fifth shuttle due to the likelihood of losing another shuttle within the next 10 years.[15] Further, whereas launches of satellites usually go relatively unnoticed, the launch of the nuclear-powered *Galileo / Jupiter* satellite on an NSTS mission brought protests and court suits to try to block it.[16] Additionally, the loss of shuttle 51-L left NASA's internal management shaken to the point where there has been a distinct change in attitude from before and after the shuttle explosion. One official remarked that he does not doubt, given the post-*Challenger* attitude, that if the same circumstances were encountered by *Apollo 11* (almost no fuel left, computer out, no immediately recognizable landing spot), it would have been ordered to abort instead of being allowed to attempt a lunar landing.[17]

One may rightfully ask, after reviewing all the data, how could such a thing like the events leading up to the loss of the *Challenger* occur? NASA obviously wasn't trying to kill the crew on purpose, so what went wrong? During the investigation into the explosion, engineers explained that they had been aware of the NSTS system's shortcomings, had solutions to most of them, and could have put solutions readily into affect under the suitable combination of political, economic, and management exigency. Unfortunately, the right combination of urgency was not present, and in fact, the reality and effects of this environment on the risks being undertaken had not been taken into account. A risk analysis must concern itself with what really happens, not what should happen.[18]

Thus, what we see occurring in the NSTS program was that, instead of having a selected perception of risk centered upon an individual's biases, the bias was built into the culture. A politic of risk was created. This institutionalized bias, coupled with the pressures of trying to create a system severely over budget in times of tight money, and under tremendous external criticism, lowered what was an acceptable level of risk. This confluence also predisposed how the level of risk was estimated and evaluated. Statements appear in NASA documents such as "the probability of a mission success is necessarily very close to 1.0"—did that mean that it is close to 1.0, or that it ought to be close to 1.0?[19] There is a big difference, yet no one seemed to have thought about the implications. Another example was how a safety factor was calculated. An O-ring that had eroded one-third the way through its radius was determined as having a safety factor of 3, even though it was designed *never* to have any erosion at all. As Dr. Richard Feynman, a member of the presidential commission investigating the explosion, pointed out, erosion was a clue indicating something was wrong, not something from which safety could be inferred.[20]

This misperception of the presence of high safety factors in turn lowered the threshold in which risk management was thought necessary, as well as how the risks were monitored.[21] As one NASA safety engineer stated, "basically you just have to have faith in the engineering," which most often leads to taking risks beyond that which can be safely assumed.[22] At its worse, it turns into the so-called titanic effect: The severity with which a system fails is in direct proportion to the intensity of the designer's belief that it cannot. Or, as the report on the *Challenger* disaster said, "Safety criteria are designed to permit launch. They should not be allowed to force a launch."

6.1.3 Commercial aviation in the 1990s

The final vignette we wish to share concerns the possible perceptions of safety the public will possess as it relates to flying commercial airliners in the 1990s. Unlike the previous two instances, the jury is still out here, although the public is currently very nervous about the risks that are being undertaken by the airlines and the government in the realm of commercial aviation. What actions the industry takes today in regard to these risks will influence the perception of risk to tomorrow's flying public.

In contrast to NASA, the airframe manufacturers, air carriers, and the FAA, which regulates them and air traffic control, belong to the quantitative school of risk analysis and management.[23] The FAA uses quantitative measures of acceptable risk, such as requiring any failures of flight-critical components to be "extremely improbable," which it defines as occurring less than once in every billion hours or events.[24] Other parts have lifetimes or cycles-times stipulated, meaning that they must be inspected and/or replaced after a certain number of hours in use or number of takeoffs and landings made. Parts are regularly inspected and tested, and statistics are kept on the failure rates of all critical components, as well as most noncritical parts as well. This approach is imposed by both FAA regulation and the manufacturers' maintenance guidelines. Manufacturers also regularly conduct full tear-down inspections in which the aircraft is literally pulled apart to see the effects of corrosion, how it is faring under the stress of landing and takeoff, and the like.

Aircraft parts, as well as the airframe in total, are usually designed as "gold-plated;" i.e., they are designed to be much more reliable than is minimally required. The use of fault tree analysis, statistical analysis, and common failure-mode effects analysis are just some of the ways the FAA regulations specify how components can be checked for reliability. The goal is not to design a plane that is perfect, since this is beyond what can ever be accomplished, but instead to design one which exhibits a random distribution of error. This situation would indicate that no inherent design flaw existed. The result of this quantitative approach has been the development of sophisticated aircraft carrying more passengers more miles and in more safety than ever before. Figure 6.2 shows the general decline in aircraft accident rates for different aircraft hull types over the last 30 years.[25]

The FAA, airlines, airframe manufacturers, and the flying public all accept that there is some risk to flying, but all agree that it should be minimal. The great debate that is now occurring in the aviation industry is what does minimal mean? Questions are being asked by industry observers, as well as by Congress, about whether flying has become in fact safer or whether it is more an illusion, and whether the current quantitative analysis approach to ensuring parts reliability has been good enough or will continue to be good enough in the future as new technology comes into the cockpit. Although the safety issue has been

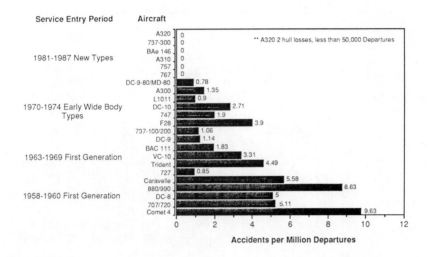

Service Entry Period   Aircraft

Figure 6.2 Hull Losses Per Million Departures

gaining momentum over the past 10 years, 1989 marked a critical pressure point in the debate by having more than three times as many fatal accidents involving large transports than the average of 3.69, and the highest rate since 1968. In 1989, there were 11 fatal accidents involving large commercial transports. Further, the overall number of accidents and fatalities have been climbing over the past 4 years after steadily showing a decline for the previous 10, as shown in Figures 6.3 and 6.4.[26] The trend in the average number of departures between passenger-fatal accidents has declined for the past 3 years, after climbing steadily throughout the 1970s and early 1980s. The trend in the average number of passenger hours between fatalities has remained flat for the last 3 years, after climbing steadily as well. These trends are making some people nervous that the 1989 increase was not a statistical aberration.

The reasons for the apparent increase in accidents are complex, requiring one to begin to trace back to events occurring nearly 10 years ago. First, there was the change in the airline industry itself, as a regulated industry became deregulated. The result was a rapid expansion in air carriers and a resulting increase in the volume of air traffic significantly beyond that which was predicted. This caught the industry by surprise and placed it in a bind. The competition introduced by

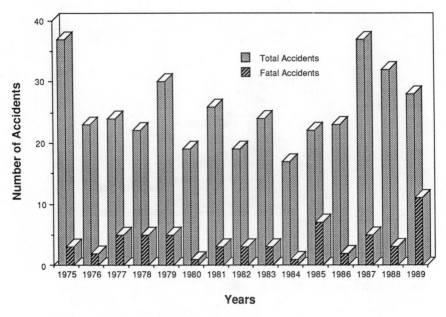

Figure 6.3 Safety Record of Large U.S. Transports

deregulation meant that in established air carriers, new planes could not be bought to replace old ones as quickly as before. With deregulation also came smaller profits and less predictability (i.e., more risk) in the cash flow. Newly created airlines could not afford modern planes either, and thus had to turn to used aircraft to put together a competitive fleet. This resulted in all airlines flying aircraft beyond their original design limits, which was, for most aircraft then in service, thought to be around 80,000 hours or 20 years of expected service life on average. This still can be seen in Figure 6.5, which illustrates the number of Boeing 727, 737, and 747 airplanes currently, and projected to be, exceeding 20 years in service today and over the next few years.[27] Boeing itself thought that 250 to 300 of its aircraft would have been retired by 1988, yet only 60 have indeed been retired.

Now, most aircraft engineers will argue that there is not an inherent finite life to an aircraft, that *if* you are willing to spent the money on maintenance, an aircraft can be flown for 50 years, as is the case today with the DC-3. It is in fact the economic issue, rather than the safety concern, they argue, that makes airlines modernize their fleet. Maintenance for older planes is costly because of the inability to obtain parts, and the fuel charges incurred by using older fuel-inefficient

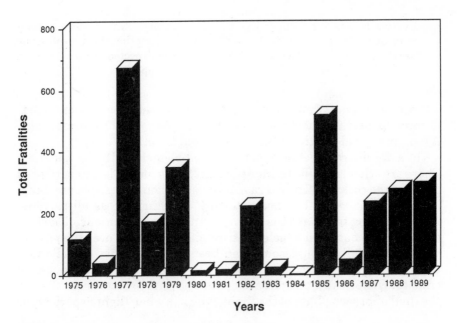

Figure 6.4 Fatalities Involving Large U.S. Transports

engines is also much higher. On the face of it, this seems to be true, but studies indicate that the relative cost of operating a used aircraft is similar in fact to that of a more modern one. A comparison of an old DC-9-30 and a new MD-82 showed that the differential in costs per available seat-mile was less than .1¢.[28] What this means is that older aircraft will be around for a longer time than even it is thought today. This is not bad per se, but deregulation has meant that many airlines, because of the cost pressures, are only meeting the minimum FAA standards concerning safety inspections.[29] On older aircraft, as the engineers said above, you have to be willing to spend the money on maintenance. If you are not, the situation becomes dangerous.

Fleet aging becomes even more of a concern because, to be honest, no one really understands whether modern aircraft can truly "last forever." The data is just not there, but the belief by designers and maintainers is. Or better, it was. That changed on April 28, 1988. On that day, the top half of a forward passenger compartment of a Boeing 737-200 tore off in flight. This event shook the entire industry, not because there was an accident, but *because no one thought it was possible.* After the incident, the general manager of Boeing said:

Everybody was dumbfounded that it could happen... There was a sudden realization in a lot of minds that we had been saying that the aircraft gives us warning, and that was not the case...We never expected to see a top come off an airplane. We just did not know it could happen.[30]

Since that time, there have been a number of other "unexpected" failures to aircraft components suspected to be caused by aircraft age. Again, many did not think they were possible, either.

The aging aircraft fleets are not the only problem caused by deregulation. There are other side effects. More aircraft flying means less experienced pilots in the cockpits. The average number of hours of experience found in the cockpit crews has been steadily declining across all carriers. Newer carriers tend have the least amount of crew experience. The lack of experience has been a factor in a number of crashes over the past 10 years. Especially troublesome has been the deficiency in following standard cockpit procedures, which has contributed to a number of crashes. Historically, aircraft accidents also tend to occur most often in the final approach phase of the flight, which is when flight experience is

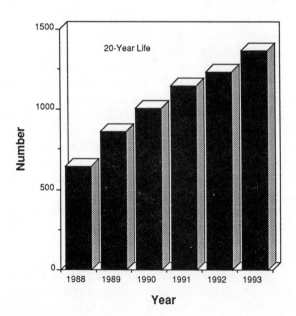

Figure 6.5 Estimated Number of 727, 737, and 747 Aircraft Exceeding Economic Design (Cumulative)

most needed. For reference, Figure 6.6 illustrates when accidents are most likely to occur.[31] Inexperience often leads one to take risks that a more experienced person would not. This is not only true in flying, but in life in general.

Also, airlines tend to schedule their flights for the premium flying hours of early morning and late afternoon, meaning more flights bunching up together. In one airport, the author counted 22 airplanes scheduled to take off between 7 and 7:05 pm, 13 of which were to depart exactly at 7 pm. If you are even the second plane of the 13 to leave the gate, you are already likely to be late in your arrival at your destination. This might mean trying to make up time in the air, or at the next city, skip some routine maintenance, or hurry the checklist in order to leave the gate this time on time. The cumulative effects can be hazardous.

This crush of traffic makes it hard to control, and the air traffic control (ATC) system is barely up to the responsibility. The effects of the

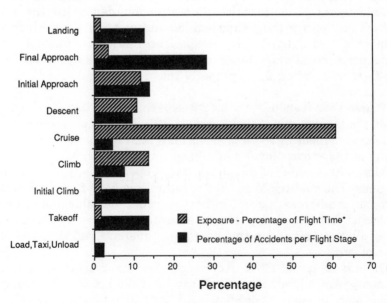

*Exposure percentage based upon average 1 hour flight duration

Figure 6.6 Aircraft Accident Occurrences

controller strike in 1981 where 11,000 controllers were fired are still apparent, as the number of controllers has not yet attained the levels they once were, nor does the work force possess the same level of experience. The GAO reports that the number of senior controllers is declining, and that in some control facilities over one-third of the controllers are eligible to retire within 4 years.[32] Additionally, the FAA has only recently embarked upon its modernization program of the ATC system at its 22,000 facilities to try to handle the increase in traffic and lack of controllers. Already there is some concern that it will not be up to the task, since it was designed for traffic projections that have already been superseded. As the program slips in schedule, estimates of how quickly the modernization program could be completed have been acknowledged by FAA officials as being overoptimistic.[33]

The air traffic congestion, the lack of experience in the ATC as well as with pilots, older aircraft, the pressures to do minimum maintenance, and the increase in the number of carriers all have impacts on safety. And we haven't even talked about effects of the disappearance and reappearance of carriers due to bankruptcies and takeovers, or the lack of experience in the work force of airframe manufacturers who are trying to build new airplanes to satisfy the tremendous demand, or the similar lack of experience in the ground maintenance crews, due to the increased number of aircraft flying. This inexperience has led to a number of fatal accidents, such as when cables to critical components were miswired at the factory, or when an improperly repaired rear pressure bulkhead collapsed.

If these are not enough, the safety issue that is starting to get a higher profile is the concept of fly-by-wire (FBW). FBW is of interest for the software engineering risk analyst as FBW is an approach which replaces many of the conventional mechanical controls, such as the stick and rudder, with a series of computers which operate many of the aircraft systems. The traditional method of controlling wing flaps and rudders through mechanical power, either hydraulic or cable-and-pulley, is replaced by a series of computer systems which evaluate and electronically relay pilot commands to the wing flaps, ailerons, rudders, and other control surfaces.

The advantage of FBW over mechanical approaches is of that of economy. An individual airplane can be made lighter, thus carrying either more passengers or allowing it to fly further. It is like getting a 10% savings in fuel burn. Additionally, it allows for the same flight deck and instrumentation, as well as the same flight characteristics, to be common among dissimilar airframes.

Presently, the European Airbus A320 is the most advanced, and most controversial, aircraft in the world. It is also an FBW aircraft. A major reason for its controversial nature is, as we observed in the section on software safety in Chapter 5, that there is no way to guarantee that software systems will work as envisioned. And so it is with the FBW computer controls in the A320. Although there has been disagreement on the issue, errors in the computer control software are thought to be likely contributing causes to three major A320 incidents, two resulting in crashes, which have occurred over the past 18 months.[34]

What is beyond doubt is that software errors in existing, less complicated, computer-dependant aircraft systems have been shown to be responsible for accidents and near accidents in other aircraft, and it can reasonably be assumed that some serious software errors will occur on the A320 (although the fact of their causing a crash cannot be directly inferred). Many safety experts also feel that the currently used international standard for airborne software systems, RTCA DO-178A, is woefully inadequate since it does not require formal verification of the safety of the software used to control FBW aircraft systems. The standard was developed before the full implications of FBW was understood, so there is a valid point.

Further, there is the problem of what happens when an event occurs on board an aircraft that the FBW programmers haven't thought about, such as occurred in 1983, when an Air Canada Boeing 767 ran out of fuel at 41,000 ft. over Red Lake, Ontario, due to a human error in calculating the fuel load required.[35] The programmers of the 767's flight control programs, needless to say, hadn't thought about the possibility that the 767 might turn into a 132-ton glider. The basic trouble with computer-controlled systems is that one wants them to work perfectly precisely at the time when they are likely to be severely overloaded.

One major trouble with FBW is that the public does not know the risks entailed. Another, which is worse, is that some in the aircraft industry tend to overlook or play down the inherent risks involved in FBW. All one has to do to see this is to peruse the advertisements touting the improved safety of FBW by the developers of such system. Examining the data, such as in Figure 6.2, does not show any marked improvement in FBW systems over mechanical systems. Segments of the industry look at FBW as a means to increase efficiency and lower cost, which they also infer and equate (incorrectly) as automatically conferring an increase in flight safety. Thus, FBW is not viewed as a source of safety risk. This is the identical cultural bias and selective perception we encountered previously in NASA.

Even the use of quantitative approaches to aircraft design does not guarantee that the more hazardous aspects of selective perception will disappear. Point of fact, quantitative approaches can increase the bias contained in subjective perception by making it *appear* that objective reality is being applied. In 1986, for instance, the airframe manufacturers bristled at the suggestion that an aging aircraft fleet could cause a safety problem. The inspections, statistical controls, etc., would surely indicate a problem, they claimed. But they didn't because the manufacturers were not looking for the problem in the right way. Their mindset was not tuned to being receptive to the risk anyway. In truth, at the time, one vice-president in charge of maintenance at one major carrier called the problem of aging aircraft a "myth," and contended that older aircraft were in general more reliable than newer aircraft.[36] Similarly, the new FAA ATC system will have millions of lines of Ada software code used to control the system. How safe will that system be? Given all the different causes of risk and their side effects, how much of a safety margin truly exists? As some airline observers have remarked, the question is not whether it is safe to fly, but is it as safe as it could be? Is the margin of safety eroding? The future of public confidence, and possibly of aviation, rests with the answers.

In each of the above stories, we encountered a number of examples of subjective perception vs. objective reality, and some of the consequences of mistaking one for the other. Our goal was not to malign good engineers, but to show how easily the subjective perception of risk can take hold without ever recognizing that it is there. Bias, existing either within an individual's mindset, an organizational body politic, or intrinsic within a culture, tends to blind one from recognizing a risk, and/or from applying the most applicable risk management approach. The acceptability of risk tends to get skewed as a result.

We also saw that there is nothing indigenous in either school of risk philosophy that automatically overcomes the problems of risk perception. Further, we discovered how the subjective perception of risk pervades risk taking and what constitutes the acceptability of risk, as well as what creates a politic of risk that is difficult to overcome. This latter point is important to remember, for it is the politics, in all of its various facets, that will ultimately guide what is considered a risk and its acceptability in every situation involving an organizational unit. In the following sections, we will attempt to delve deeper, demonstrating what factors influence the subjective perception of risk, how to recognize it, what can be done to overcome it, either by applying special techniques, the creation of risk organizations, or the application of a general risk philosophy to approaching a particular situation. Hopefully, when we are done, we can better approach the ideal and assumed use of objective reality instead of perceived reality in our risk analyses.

6.2 Whence Risk? The Elements of Subjective Perception

It is often hard to get a firm grasp of what we mean by the term "subjective nature of risk," especially as it relates to software engineering and the building of information technology systems. The simplest way of explaining it is by this simple analogy: A cow looks much different to a butcher than to a zoologist. Thus, when building information systems, the risks with which one is confronted appear much different at the business level than at the systems engineering level, or from the software engineering level. What may be perceived as a minor risk at the business level may in fact be a huge risk at the software engineering level, and vice versa. Without understanding from which perspective each group identifies a risk, or even which vocabulary is used to talk about a risk, the potential for building systems that are late, over budget, or do not meet the business's needs is greatly enhanced. And what's more, it matters very little whether a risk is "real" or not: The perception of risk will become the operating parameter. That is why it is imperative that as little bias as is *humanly* possible enters into our risk analyses.

In the next several subsections, we will investigate the different elements which motivate the subjective perception of risk. Note, also, that although we have chosen a particular division of topics, they are not independent of one another, but in fact are closely integrated. And one final, important reminder. In the pursuit of objective reality concerning a particular enterprise's risk, subjective perception does not only color the answers given to you by the engineers and managers as you interview them or read their papers, but it also can color your own thoughts, and your own analysis. Keep this in mind as you read over this section. It does little good to filter out everyone else's biases if yours remain.

6.2.1 Perceptions of risk

"One should expect that the expected can be prevented, but the unexpected should also have been expected," or so says Norman Augustine. He calls this the Law of the Amplification of Agony.[37] Augustine's advice is similar to that given to junior ministers when briefing the prime minister of England: Make sure you foresee all the unforeseeable problems in whatever proposal you are about to offer. These two operating principles are ones which information technology managers often have to deal with when trying to get funding for their programs. To help cope, when trying to implement these two ambiguous advisements, individuals resort to different and often biased strategies and behavior patterns. By turning to the work of cognitive psychologists, these stratagems can be identified by the risk analyst, which can aid immensely when trying to find out where the closet full of skeletons lay. Figure 6.7 lists some 27 different biases that can be encountered, some of which we will detail below.[38]

The first obstacle the analyst confronts in trying to discern these differing stratagems is that one person's risk is often another person's opportunity, and it is often difficult to sort out which is the appropriate perspective to base the analysis on. For example, the perspective involving a government information system development can take on any one of many, depending on the stakeholders involved. A perspective on a risk may be viewed from either the *process* of developing the system or from the *system* itself; from either the user or developer; or simultaneously from the sponsor, the user and the developer. Failure to recognize from which perspective the risks are viewed makes it very difficult to proceed sensibly. As a general rule, all stakeholder perspectives should be considered initially, and then reduced to an explicit, but finite, working set.

The second obstacle one is faced with when confronting subjective perception of a risk is the availability of information from which to make judgments about the risk.[39,40] It is very difficult to discover subjectiveness in a risk estimate, for example, if there is not enough information to do

Adjustment	Anchoring	Availability
Conservatism	Data Saturation	Self-Fulfilling Prophecies
Base Rate	Ease of Recall	Data Presentation Context
Expectations	Habit	Spurious Clues
Hindsight	Redundancy	Fundamental Attribution Error
Gambler's Fallacy	Fact-Value Confusion	Outcome Irrelevant Learning
Illusion of Control	Law of Small Numbers	Overconfidence
Reference Effect	Regression Effect	Wishful Thinking
Representativeness	Selective Perception	Order Effects

Figure 6.7 Biases and Filters that Affect Perception

an effective comparative analysis. In this book's companion, *Software Engineering Risk Analysis and Management*, we investigated the various sources of information that one can apply to identify risks, but the information gathered using these techniques rarely is of the magnitude, severity, or frequency necessary to compare risks.

Furthermore, when the information is eventually disseminated, individuals often misinterpret or misunderstand its meaning. This is termed *information availability bias* or the out-of-sight, out-of-mind phenomenon. Availability bias is related to the fact that if an event's occurrence is easily recalled (or sources of information are easily attainable), for instance, a plane crash caused by a terrorist bombing over Christmas, then an individual will tend to assign a higher magnitude or occurrence of loss to it. Information which is harder to access tends to slant the bias the other way. It has been demonstrated that individuals commonly *overestimate* the frequency of well-publicized events, while the frequency of less-publicized events is commonly *underestimated*.

Individuals, like Chamberlain in our earlier example, also tend to possess *selective* or *biased perception,* which creates another set of problems. In other words, anticipation of expected information will color one's thinking. Often, there is a threshold that needs to be met, and any information which is received that meets the individual's bias is kept, while any contrary information is automatically filtered out. This is also sometimes called *management bias* or *expert bias.* Management bias occurs when an individual views an uncertain parameter, say the cost of a software enterprise, as a goal, rather than as an uncertainty. It is typified by individuals wanting to reduce cost when a project appears to be exceeding estimates, rather than trying to discover whether the initial funding amount was correct. Expert bias occurs when the individual thinks they must be, or act like, an "expert," and therefore must be certain in their pronouncements. "Experts" are assumed not to be uncertain in their judgments, whatever the subject, thus leading to the problem of overconfidence. When the reference point or threshold is moved, one says that there is a *references effects* bias at work.

Another aspect of the selected perception phenomenon is that people tend to rely solely either on qualitative or quantitative information to the exclusion of the other. NASA during the pre-*Challenger* days and the airlines currently, exhibit this type of behavior. Related are the biases of *data presentation* and *base rate*. Data presentation bias is summarized information which may have a much greater impact than the same data in nonsummarized forms. Additionally, the manner in which it is summarized is important. Consider Figures 6.8a and 6.8b, which show the same American unemployment figures for 1987–1989, but using two different scales and presentation of axes.

Or consider the following: You and five of your companions have a choice of two escape routes from which to escape an avalanche.[41,42] One route will save two of you, whereas for the second route the probability is $1/_3$ that all six of you will make it, but there is a $2/_3$ probability that none of you will make it. Most people will chose the first option, as at least two of you will get out.

But consider this: If you take the first route, 4 of you will perish, but if you take the second route, the probability is $1/_3$ that none of you will die, but a $2/_3$ probability exists that all of you will. People confronted with this alternative will, in 5 out of 6 cases, choose the second route, reasoning that the first route will lead to 4 deaths, while the second has at least a $1/_3$ chance that everyone will get out. However, notice that these two examples are exactly the same. Changing of the measurement scale or changing the name of a risk parameter from a "sure loss" to "an insurance premium" also increases the bias found.

Base rate bias occurs when two events are compared using the number of occurrences of each event, but the overall rate of occurrence is omitted. This commonly happens when qualitative and quantitative data is intermixed. To overcome these biases, a single basis of assessment,

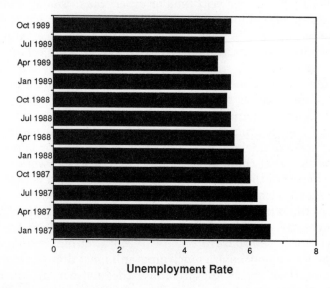

Figure 6.8a Data Presentation Bias—Wide Range

preferably quantitative, should be used in order that all evidence can be evaluated against a common scale.

Another aspect of the data presentation bias is in the use of the words chosen to describe a risk's likelihood, for example, especially when using a qualitative approach to summarizing the data. The words used to describe a risk are just too imprecise. Words such as:

- high
- probable
- not certain
- likely
- maybe
- little chance that
- we believe that
- improbable

- low
- expected
- doubtful
- quite certain
- unlikely
- hoped
- possible
- not unreasonable that

have different meanings to different people. This was shown graphically in a study conducted at the London School of Business.[43] When 250 executives were asked to rank 10 words or phrases similar to those listed

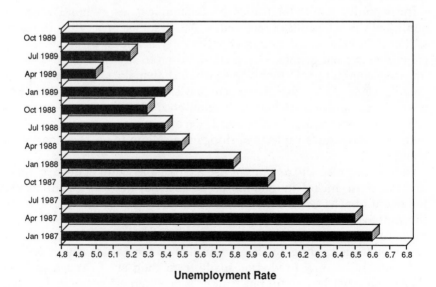

Figure 6.8b Data Presentation Bias—Narrow Range

above in decreasing order of certainty, only three people actually listed them in the same order. More interestingly, a study conducted a few months later had people changing their original ordering! NASA, for instance, applied the words "unlikely" to risks whose chances ranged from 1 in 250 to 1 in 20,000.[44] Not surprisingly, this problem of the inexact meaning of words has led to situations where decisions were made under false assumptions.

A number of other cognitive biases, not all of which are independent, should also be included when searching for indications of subjective perception at work.[45] As an example, individuals tend to believe they are more certain than they really are in any event. In other words, estimations of risk will tend to be either skewed in a positive direction (less risk) or a negative direction (more risk). Everyone believes that he or she holds a balanced view in matters of unemotional decisions, but this has been proved not to hold in practice.

Individuals also commonly demonstrate an inability to revise accurately and consistently initial estimates in the light of new information. This is called *conservatism* bias. People tend to hold on for a long period of time to their initial impressions. This is especially true when new risks are identified. Since they are rarely quantifiable when first identified, they will take on qualities that may have high degrees of bias (positive or negative) attached, which can prove to be difficult to dispel later.

Individuals seem to be insensitive to sample sizes, reliability, or the quality of the information received, which is sometimes called the *Law of Small Numbers*. The notion of probability is not an intuitive way of thinking for most people. This goes as far as to say that most people's intuitive combining of probabilities when they make the attempt is not usually compatible with the mathematics of probability, either. For example, recognition of whether the likelihood of a risk takes on a normal or Poisson distribution, or a combination of some other ones, is not high on most individual's ranking of things they claim to be knowledgeable about.

Individuals also will *anchor*, or use a particular point of departure, in making their initial judgments on situations, and revise all future judgments based upon that initial condition. This often occurs when there is too much information present. When this happens, the individual anchors to a particular point in the spectrum of information available, and adjusts according to that point. Thus, the initial condition can markedly affect any prediction made from then on. In cases such as these, one must be careful not to add "fudge factors" without thinking about their later side effects.

Individuals will often make predictions by a *simple matching rule*—the estimation of possible outcomes is the same as the intuitive impression of the distribution. This is illustrated by the old saying, "Give a man a hammer, and he will begin to look at the world as a collection of nails." The simple matching rule frequently occurs when *data saturation* is present, as the individual reaches a premature conclusion and ignores any further information that can appear. In other words, if an individual thinks that some technical risk is low, he or she will think that its contribution to cost risk is likewise low.

Individuals may have a desire for *self-fulfilling prophecies*. An individual only values information which supports a preconceived outcome. For example, a waiter gives bad service and a bad table to a scruffily dressed couple because he thinks they will tip poorly. When they do, it reinforces his view that scruffily dressed couples tip poorly. This particular bias is often seen in conjunction with *fact-value confusion bias, expectation bias,* and *fundamental attribution error bias.*

Fact-value confusion bias occurs when strongly held values are regarded and presented as facts. The result is often a form of wishful thinking, and is chronically encountered in software projects' get-well forecasts that are produced when the enterprise is in trouble. These forecasts are a problem in that they are self-reinforcing and are actually believed. Occasionally, this is also called the "inverse crying wolf syndrome."[46] Expectation bias occurs when the individual remembers information that supports previously held expectations and beliefs, and therefore attaches a higher level of validity to this information vs. some other which is counter to it. In situations where there is also data saturation, the individual will often use this preponderance of information to "prove" their point (there is so much information, any point can in fact be "proven"). Fundamental attribution error is when individuals blame failure on bad luck, but stress that any success was due to their inherent personal ability.

Other biases that may be encountered by the analyst include: the *gambler's fallacy* (assumption that an unexpected occurrence of a run enhances the probability of an event occurring); *habit* (application of a rule successfully in one situation, and then applying the same rule in a situation where it may not be as applicable); *hindsight* (the inability to ignore information from past occurrences of an event which may have no relevance to the current event); *illusion of control* (a good outcome occurs in spite of a poor decision, thus leading to a mistaken belief that more control is present than truly exists); *illusion of correlation* (mistaking two events as correlating, when in fact they do not; i.e., mistaking correlation for causation or coincidence); *order effects* (the order in which information is received affects how it is perceived); *overconfidence* (assuming the more data that is available, the more accurate the information); *redundancy* (assuming redundant information implies more reliability), and *spurious cues* (cues may only occur at infrequent intervals, but they are taken as occurring with more frequency than initially observed). There are of course phobias or fears that also are part of the bias mechanisms of individuals and groups, but we will leave these for another time.

The factors above have some rather significant implications to the conduct of the risk analysis process. For example, even in moderately complex enterprises, project plans are usually made up of events where a sequence or series of subevents must each occur before the project can be successfully completed. These chain-like events are termed *conjunctive events*. Any overestimation of the probability of the conjunctive events successfully completing can lead to unwarranted optimism that the overall project will also be completed. Unfortunately, this is exactly the tendency shown to manifest itself in individual decision making, and biases are reinforced by the tools most frequently used to perform project planning.

On the other hand, in risky situations, one must usually consider events where at least one of the subevents must occur. These are termed *disjunctive events*. This tree-like structuring of events is seen in complex systems, where the system can fail if any one of its critical elements fail. Even though the likelihood of failure in any one element may be small, the overall probability of failure may be high if many elements are involved. In other words, no single event may cause a failure, but the accumulation of error may. The AT&T failure discussed in Chapter 1 was a prime example of this. The switch that failed had software which meant to isolate errors and keep any one switch from bringing down the entire network. Unfortunately, when this software failed, the result caused havoc in other switches, causing them to go out of service even though there was nothing wrong. Individuals faced with the situation of disjunctive events often tend to underestimate or discount the effects of the overall distributional information. Again, using the most preferable technique for system construction; i.e., top-down design, reinforces this bias.

Because of the phenomenon above, assessors of risk tend to underestimate the overall probability of failure in complex systems, while simultaneously overestimating the probability of completing it on time. For example, in the evaluation of the space shuttle, quantitative risk analysis indicated that the probability of individual fuel leaks in the three auxiliary fuel units were low, but ignored the fact that there were so many places that leaks could occur that in fact 5 significant leaks had occurred during the first 24 missions.[47] On the ninth mission, almost 2 years before *Challenger*, escaping fuels self-ignited during shuttle reentry and exploded after the shuttle had landed. If the explosion had occurred before landing, the shuttle may have crashed. On a less somber note, this also helps explain why software development schedules are more often in reality underestimated, and software product quality overestimated, as they fit, respectively, in the conjunctive/disjunctive domains.[48]

Remember the two trends: those which are chain-like structures of conjunction can lead to overestimation, while tree-like structures of disjunction can lead to underestimation. Being aware of the various tendencies will help the risk analyst make more informed judgments (e.g., by recognizing a conjunctive event, an analyst will be aware of the likely presence of an inherent bias).

6.2.2 Risk perception framework

In the section above, we noticed a number of different biases that can filter the information received about a situation, and thus affect how one perceives a risk. In the information technology domain, the effects of these biases can be very subtle, but still highly influence the decisions made about specific risks. For example, system requirements rarely can be determined for more than 5 years in the future. The changes that occur to the technology, and their subsequent impacts on organizational practices, are much too rapid and uncertain to predict with any degree of certainty. However, the school of thought in many system development organizations is that *all* requirements of a system should be verified before the enterprise moves into the design stage. The fact that this is patently impossible does not deter them from trying, or from underestimating the efforts or time required. Nor does it stop them from trying to blame something, or someone, else for their problem.

The real culprit is that the development was modeled after an unacceptable, inappropriate, or poor model of system development. Unfortunately, the development team probably did not understand this, as they were just following what they understood to be good "software engineering practice." However, their knowledge was most likely based upon models of development that were more applicable 15 years earlier than to the activities they were currently involved in. Figure 6.9 illustrates this problem. The majority of system development organizations embarking on information technology enterprises are using a preponderance of 15-year-old (plus) technology, which has the effect of freezing how one goes about developing a system. This mindset creates an incorrect framework in which the developers, users, and sponsors evaluate the risks and benefits, as well as time and cost, involved. Even though enterprise after enterprise goes bust, or is over budget, or is late, it won't stop them from trying again to use the same framework. The fact that the model they are using is inherently wrong and encourages failure does not enter their mind because it is perceived as being correct. Thus, a tremendous amount of effort is spent on trying to fix symptoms of the problem instead of their causes by buying "productivity enhancement technology" such as CASE in hopes that overspending or lateness will be eliminated.

It should be clear that biases are not always, or even often, deliberate behavior, but are in fact the result of an individual's experience, past historical events, and the current operating environment. Why individuals act the way they do is a topic beyond the realm of this book, and the

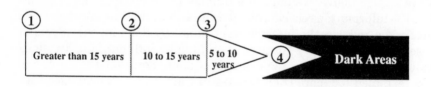

① **Edge-of-Knowledge:** Theoretical foundation and advancements in concepts, principles, or conceptual models.

② **State-of-the-Art:** Technology advancements signaled by at least three "production quality" mappings from conceptual to implementation models.

③ **State-of-the-Practice:** Utilization, where most "production applications" are today.

④ **Computing Museum:** Utilization, where too many of today's "production applications" should be, but are not.

Figure 6.9 States of Software Engineering (from Charles McKay)

interested reader should consult any one of the dozens of books on cognitive psychology, behavior theory, decision making, and motivational theory. Regardless of why, the biases listed above exist and occur, creating subconscious juggernauts which are required to be dealt with. Therefore, we are left with the question of what can be done by the risk analyst to either contain or minimize these biases, other than recognizing that they occur?

Two examples of techniques which help filter out biases are the *Delphi technique* and *probability encoding*. The Delphi technique is a structured way of applying a group consensus approach to eliminate individual bias.[49] The technique originated at the Rand Corporation as a means of predicting future consequences of then-current policy decisions. Basically, a group of experts are gathered and asked, by a group coordinator, their opinion about a topic, for example, an estimate of the likelihood of a specific risk and its possible consequences. Each expert writes down his or her opinion anonymously. They cannot discuss their opinions with any of the other experts, although they may ask the coordinator questions about the risk. In this way, detrimental face-to-face confrontation is avoided. The coordinator then prepares a summary of the experts' responses, circulates the summaries, and asks for another estimate. The previous estimates are then reconsidered in the light of this new data. The new estimate is prepared by the experts including the rationale for any new opinions they may have come to, or a defense of their previous one if they haven't changed. This goes on iteratively until a group consensus is reached or until the coordinator feels it is appropriate to stop (i.e., it is of questionable value to continue). During the entire process, the experts should not talk to one another.

The aim of the Delphi technique is to try to reach a group consensus and increase the accuracy of the estimate by surfacing and examining as many relevant issues as possible. The technique works if the participants do not hold too tightly to any individual bias, and/or if crucial information is not left out. Unfortunately, as we mentioned previously, experts often do not want to be seen as not being certain, even in anonymous circumstances. For these reasons, Rand has published a report that states the Delphi approach is of limited value.[50]

A similar but structurally different technique that can be used is called probability encoding.[51] Instead of a group getting together, as in the Delphi approach, a team of questioners conducts interviews with individuals concerning a particular subject. The subject selected is one for which a measurement is required in relation to some specific parameter. This is called a *variable*. The team has been trained to spot individual biases and to point them out to the interviewee, in hopes of overcoming their effects.

` Probability encoding consists of a seven-step process. These are: (1) motivation (identifying and understanding the individual's motivation and biases); (2) structuring (providing a definition of the variable to be assessed and identifying any assumptions about it); (3) conditioning (does the variable pass the "clairvoyance test;" i.e., could a clairvoyant give an unequivocal value to the variable?); (4) encoding (the quantification of the uncertainty of the individual's estimate of the variable's value); (5) verifying (does the individual really believe in the estimate?); (6) aggregation (making use of additional information from other individuals about the same variable to calibrate the results); and (7) discretizing (allowing an infinite number of possibilities to be reduced to a finite number). In specific circumstances, probability encoding is very good at overcoming individual or group estimation bias.

Another approach is to ascertain the certainty of the risk estimate and attempt to "buy" information about the risk itself. Typical techniques include building prototypes, doing simulations, performing surveys, conducting benchmark tests, or creating analytical models. However, before one starts spending money on buying information, one should investigate if it is worthwhile. How one can accomplish this is explained in detail in this book's companion, *Software Engineering Risk Analysis and Management*.

What really would be useful is a general framework from which one could consider the issue of subjective perception in risk as it relates to decision making. There are many frameworks around, such as the Rational Actor Model, the Satisficing/Bounded Rationality Model, the Incrementalism/"Muddling Through" Model, the Organizational Processes Model, and the Garbage Can Model. Rather than go through each of these in detail, the reader can refer to Andrew Sage's survey of these various models in his article, "Behavioral and Organizational Considerations in the Design of Information Systems and Processes for Planning and Decision Support."[52] Instead, we would like to review a more simple approach, and one we find particularly useful, to developing a framework. This framework is espoused by Theodore Taylor.[53]

In Taylor's view, one can say that a risk has two elements to it: its truth and one's perception of its truth. One can draw the logically different possibilities of how the two relate, as shown in the Venn diagrams depicted in Figure 6.10. The outer rectangle represents our universe of choice, and can be thought of as depicting the total set of decisions that can be made concerning a particular risk. An easier way to think about

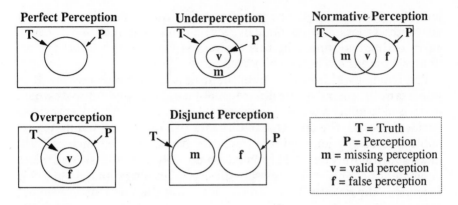

Figure 6.10 Truth vs. Perception

it may be to view it as the total of all technology that may have application to some projected information technology development. The circles within the rectangle denote subclasses within the universe of choice. The circle labeled "T" is used to enclose the domain of risk that is truly present, while circle "P" encloses the area where the domain of risk is perceived as being present. The interrelationships of these two subclasses can provide interesting perspectives on the risks that must be dealt with.

The five possible causes listed by Taylor run the spectrum from where the reality of risk equals its perception to that where the reality of risk has no intersection with the perceived risk. The more general cases lie in between these two extremes. The centermost case can be considered the "normative" case, in that it produces all the logical subclasses that are possible. Taylor labels these "v" for valid, representing the domain over which the real risk overlaps perceived risk; "m" for missing, which represents the domain wherein the perceived risk fails to account for the real risks; and "f" for false, which represents the extent to which the perceived risks are, in actuality, false.

One can take this framework to model and develop a process in which to investigate the subjective perception of risk as opposed to its objective reality, as shown in Figure 6.11. By applying techniques like the ones mentioned above, one can explicitly begin to depict how much certainty and uncertainty exists in a risk, as well as how much the perception of the risk itself influences the estimates of certainty. This framework is very good at forcing an individual or group to explain why their identification, estimates, or evaluations of risk *might be incorrect*, which is a method that has been found by psychologists to reduce confidence in early estimates, which in turn increases confidence in the overall analysis once the reasons are sorted out.[54]

The framework, however, must be used with some discretion. It is important to remember the different sources of bias and filtering which exist, and to apply a wide-ranging set of techniques to try to get them to surface. Second, the objective reality of a risk does not often match its subjective perception, and it is the latter "reality" with which the risk analyst ultimately deals. The effectiveness of the overall risk analysis is dependent not only on how closely these two "realities" match, but how to manage the risk itself. The process is not a static one. Third, one must be careful when dealing with multiple risks, especially those which are coupled to one another. One may change the reality of one risk by managing another. The feedback situation can be severe. And finally, the only way to get the subjective risk to be equal to the objective risk is through careful calibration and measurement. If you are analyzing a new software enterprise of some level of complexity, it is highly likely that you are closer to realizing the last case in Figure 6.10 than the first.

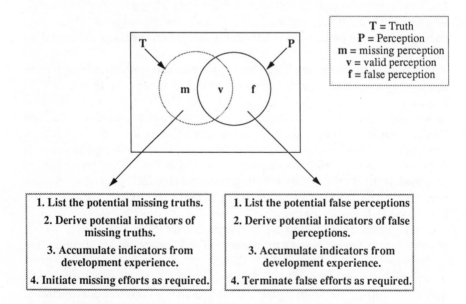

Figure 6.11 Taylor's Framework to Aid in the Identification of Truth and Perception

So far, we have examined the perception of risk from the angles of the biases which influence an individual, and from a framework which can be applied to remove some of those biases. Now we wish to shift angles again and investigate the influences involved in actually taking a decision about a risk. The biases mentioned previously influence how a risk is seen; i.e., they influence the analysis process, but there are other factors which are at work when an individual actually decides to act upon a risk; i.e., they influence the risk management process.

6.2.3 Risk taking

June 24, 1975. A Pan Am DC-8 pilot radios the control tower at Kennedy International Airport that there is a severe windshear on the approach to Runway 22 Left, and recommends to the tower that the approach be changed to another runway.[55] The tower acknowledges the report, but does not do anything about it, as the wind shear does not register on the control tower instruments. A few minutes later, an Eastern L-1011 pilot executes a missed approach because the windshear cut his landing speed dangerously close to his stall speed one mile short of the runway. The Eastern pilot also reports the wind shear they encountered to the tower.

Less than 2 minutes later, another Eastern flight moves into position for a final approach. The captain of the flight has heard the L-1011 report of windshear, and remarked, "This is asinine." Another crew member says, "I wonder if they're covering for themselves?," indicating that he thought the previous crew had messed up and was making up excuses for the missed approach. Less than a minute later, the aircraft crashed as a result of severe windshear, killing 113 out of the 124 aboard.

What makes someone take a risk like the one above? Was it just bad luck, the personality of the pilot, the pressure to try to make a landing, company culture, training, or was it a combination of things? In the crash above, part of the problem was not recognizing the severity of windshear as a major risk. It wasn't until 1982, after a number of planes had crashed, that the causes of windshear were studied and understood. Even then, knowing that it was a higher risk than was thought previously was not sufficient because detection of windshear was not readily available. Furthermore, pilots thought (and were not firmly instructed otherwise) that they could fly through any degree of windshear, and were in fact being instructed how to cope with it whenever it was encountered. Unfortunately, it took another accident in 1985, which killed 137, to dispel that notion.

Risk taking by an individual is a complex subject, and we will only be able to examine some of its dimensions. The analyst is urged to refer to the references for more information, as risk taking is at the heart of the risk management process. After the evaluation process of risk analysis is completed, someone will have to make the decisions about whether the risks identified and their severity are within acceptable limits, or whether some containment strategy or replanning exercise is warranted. Much of this will depend on whether the person is *risk averse*, or as Lao-Tzu wrote, "Than self-restraint, there is nothing better," or *risk taking*, which was expressed in this way by the Marquis de Vauvenargues, "Activity makes more men's fortunes than cautiousness."

Before we go into the detailed meanings of risk-averse or risk-taking personalities, we need to review quickly the basic causes of risk. If you recollect from Chapter 1, there are three things that make up a risk: A potential loss had to exist, uncertainty or chance was involved, and some choice among alternatives was required. These three aspects are called *the magnitude of the potential loss, the chance of the potential loss,* and *the exposure to potential loss.* There are also three fundamental factors which cause a risk to occur: Either there is a lack of correct information concerning the situation, a lack of control over the events, or a lack of time to gain the proper information, control, and so forth. How an individual views each of these three factors as they relate to the three aspects of risk will affect his or her attitude towards being a risk taker. Each personality type, in fact, acts differently with regard to these components of risk.

Kenneth MacCrimmon and Donald Wehrung have studied the characteristics of managerial risk takers and risk averters in impressive detail in their classic book, *Taking Risks.*[56] Through their studies, they have been able to summarize, as shown in Table 6.1, some of the general components risk takers *accept* and risk averters *require.* As one can see, a risk taker accepts a higher exposure to risk by acting with less information and needing less control than a risk averter. Risk takers tend to look for the best-case scenario, while the risk averter focuses on the downside analysis, probabilities of loss are biased upwards, and overemphasis is placed upon the potential losses or the exposure to loss. Risk takers accept higher risks and accept higher losses in comparison to risk averters. Risk averters tend to devote a great amount of effort in trying to reduce risks, as well as in monitoring how the risky situation develops, while the risk taker is much less concerned with modifying the risk or in managing it later.

TABLE 6.1 Traits of Risk Takers and Risk Averters

Risk Components	Risk Averter Requires	Risk Taker Accepts
Magnitude of Potential Loss	Low maximum loss Low stakes, commitment Low variability in payoffs More info on losses More control over losses	High maximum loss High stakes, commitment Higher variability in payoffs Less info on losses Less control over losses
Chances of Potential Loss	Low chance of loss Familiar environment Few uncertain events More info on chances More control over uncertain events Low uncertainty	Higher chances of loss Unfamiliar environment Many uncertain events Less info on chances Less control over uncertain events Higher uncertainty
Exposure to Potential Loss	Low exposure Shared responsibility More information on exposure More control over exposure	Higher exposure Sole responsibility Less information on exposure Less control over exposure
Other Risk	Control by self Contingency plans Consensus Exit from risky situations	Control by others No contingency plans Conflict Participation in risky situations

We should note that there is such a thing as being risk neutral, which economists often define as on a fair bet (50-50 odds), no attention is paid to the degree of dispersion of the possible outcomes. In other words, if one is risk neutral, one will bet only if the odds are favorable, but will continue to be interested in betting if it yields a profit on average, even after a string of losses. When one is risk averse, one refuses a fair bet, and will bet only if the odds are very favorable. For our purposes, we will tend to ignore the risk-neutral individual.

A specific individual can be of one type or the other without exhibiting all the characteristics listed above. Further, individuals will vary in their willingness to take risk dependent on the situation. In other words, because an individual may be a risk taker in business does not mean they are also a risk taker in their personal life. We will return to MacCrimmon and Wehrung's study a bit later, as they have some interesting results which the risk analyst might find useful. However, we wish to digress for a moment and return to one of the subjects earlier encountered, namely bias and filtering.

Being a risk taker or risk averter depends, we said, on how one views the multiple components of risk. However, these components of risk are subject to the biases encountered earlier. A person's attention, perception, memory and thinking are all liable to distortion, filtering, or bias by emotion and motivation.[57] Norman Dixon has studied how these affect military commanders, and has modeled the way in which an individual perceives and acts towards his or her environment, as shown in Figure 6.12. The individual has two interlocking feedback loops: The solid line depicts an individual's interaction with the environment (perception leading to response); the dashed line represents an internal loop, that between need and satiation. The internal loop acts upon the external one. In other words, as needs arise, social or biologic, neurotic or

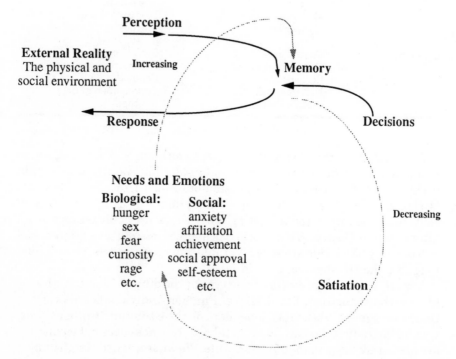

Figure 6.12 Influences on Individual's Perception of Reality

adaptive, they act upon the manner in which an individual perceives the external world, how he or she acts, and what is remembered.

Dixon, and others who study decision making, reminds us that all decisions entail some level of risk, and thus decision making inevitably will invoke some degree of fear.[58] The effects of needs upon an individual's perception become maximized when the needs are very intense and the external reality ambiguous or confused, such as in high pressure, risky situations. As the external stress increases, needs and emotions tend to dominate the individual's actions. Thus, decision makers often respond in predictable ways that render their judgments less than entirely rational: Common patterns include defensive avoidance (delaying decisions unduly), overreaction (making decisions impulsively in order to escape the anxious state), and hypervigilance (obsessively collecting more and more data instead of making a decision). Dixon, in his psychological study of senior military leaders, has stated that a number of these responses seem to appear with regularity in those officers who seem to be incompetent. He has listed a number of traits, as shown in Table 6.2, which are indications and predictors of incompetent military leaders. As the external pressure builds, these traits become more pronounced, and have caused unnecessary loss of life, as well as loss of battles and wars. The risk analyst might be advised to also look for these signs in software enterprises, as they are not confined only to senior military officers, and if encountered, will no doubt influence how a risk analysis, or the management of risk, will be received.

TABLE 6.2 Personality Traits of Incompetents

- An arrogant underestimation of the risks involved
- Equating work with sport or war
- An inability to profit from past experience
- A resistance to adopting and exploiting new or novel technology
- An aversion to gathering or using intelligence information
- Great physical bravery, but little moral courage
- An apparent imperviousness to human suffering, or its converse, an irrational and incapacitating state of compassion
- Passivity and indecisiveness
- A tendency to lay blame on others
- A love of the "frontal assault"
- A love of smartness, precision, and strict preservation of organizational hierarchy
- A high regard of tradition and other aspects of conservatism
- A lack of creativity, improvisation, inventiveness, and open-mindedness
- A tendency to disregard moderate risk tasks for ones so difficult that failure might seem excusable
- Procrastination

External pressures can be amplified or dampened by a number of factors, one of the more important being the culture of the organization within which the individual resides. Recall from Chapter 2, culture encompasses the values, rules, philosophies, heros, rites, and ceremonies of the organization or group in which one belongs. Also recollect there are four basic types of organizational cultures: tough guy/machismo; work hard/play hard; bet-your-company; and process type.

The tough guy/machismo organization is made up of individualists. The environment they perceive is one of big stakes, big risks, quick feedback, and make-or-break decisions. The organization focuses on speed, not endurance, and success is an all-or-nothing affair. People attracted to this type of firm are usually considered risk takers, and seem to exhibit risk taking in their personal and professional lives. Firms in construction, cosmetics, venture capital, investment banking and brokerage, advertising, and entertainment possess this type of culture.

The work hard/play hard culture is similar to the tough guy/machismo type, but instead of a few high risk ventures, the firm is faced with many low risk ones instead. Sales operations are examples of this type of culture. Firms in computer and office automation, automotive dealerships, door-to-door distributors, fast food franchises, and manufacturing production companies fit this type. Individuals who are members of this group also tend to lean towards being risk takers, but are not as strong in this personality as in the tough guy/machismo organization.

Opposite to the short-term operating styles above are companies which exhibit long-term cultures. The first type is the bet-your-company type. Firms with this culture are engaged in work that has extremely high risks, extremely high return, but very slow feedback on the success of the efforts. Survival takes stamina. Individuals in this type of organization are likely to be more risk averse, although they often perceive themselves as being risk takers. Organizations in aerospace, mining, nuclear power, petroleum, space, and the military exhibit this culture.

The last type of culture is called the process type. This culture operates in a low-risk environment, where feedback is basically nonexistent. Employees concentrate on how things are done, rather than on what things are done. Governmental organizations are a prime example, and are most often populated by risk-adverse individuals. Other process-type organizations include banks, insurance companies, utilities, and pharmaceutical companies.

The culture of the firm plays a significant part in how an individual perceives its environment, and what its expectations are from the environment in the way of risks. In tough guy/machismo-type firms, the senior management of a software system under development might not be too bothered or concerned with software engineering-type risks at all. Risks are to be taken, not avoided, and if the system works, fine, and if not, well, there is always a new project to work on. Large-scale developments would probably not be undertaken by these types of firms, because the feedback is not immediate, and the payoff is too far in the future. Thus, the size of the systems to be developed would be smaller, as would be the likelihood and magnitude of the risks involved. If the company tried to take on a larger job, or one that requires a different type of risk taking which is in conflict with its inherent culture, it would most likely fail. Such a case would be taking on high risk, high reward enterprises in organizations that only reward risk-aversion. This is one of the reasons why process-type organizations, especially governmental ones, fail in trying to develop information technology systems.[59]

Within an organization itself, the group in which an individual finds himself or herself will also structure the external pressure felt. The group often tends to accentuate the cultural pressures found within the organization. When a decision situation arises which is in conflict with the current cultural view, individuals can often be forced into, actively support, or unwittingly be seduced into reaffirming any extreme biases the culture itself possesses to support its view of the conflict. I. L. Janis terms this *group think*.[60] The symptoms of this process include:

- An illusion of invulnerability that becomes shared by most members of the group.
- Collective attempts to ignore or rationalize away items of information which might otherwise lead the group to reconsider shaky, but cherished assumptions.
- An unquestioned belief in the group's inherent morality, thus enabling members to overlook ethical consequences of their decisions.
- Stereotyping of competitors as either too deceitful for negotiation or too stupid and feeble to be a threat.
- A shared allusion of unanimity in a majority viewpoint, augmented by the false assumption that silence means consent.
- Self-appointed mind-guards to protect the group from adverse information that might shatter complacency about the effectiveness and morality of their decisions.

Group think has a greater tendency to occur in organizations in which the culture is strong, and where the individuals making up the group are homogeneous in background. Individual groups that are part of a homogeneous unit, such as accounting or information management, also may have a separate subculture within the overall culture. Group think can often arise when conflicts are between internal corporate groups, as well as from external conflict.

A less potent form of cultural inhibitions to risk taking which is often found in risk adverse organizations are called *judgmental gates*.[61] Organizations will sometimes set up exclusive hurdles over which specific parameters of the risk must pass before some decision on risk taking is made. These hurdles are not linear in character, but are weighted in some fashion. For example, consider the risk of making an investment and trying to attain an acceptable rate of return, as shown in Figure 6.13. Shown along the left axis is the frequency distribution of the actual return, and along the right axis the frequency distribution of the judgment about the return of a number of different potential investment projects. One can draw distribution patterns of the various

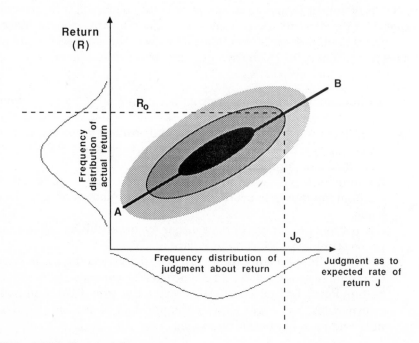

Figure 6.13 Judgmental Gates

average rate of returns, as shown, where the darker patterns representing the more common combinations of ratings and return. When a judgmental gate is used, the judgment criterion (J_0) will tend to be set to the right to increase the chance that the acceptable level of return (R_0) is met or exceeded, while ignoring the fact that a more ideal situation might exist towards the middle of the spread. However, as J_0 is moved to the right, fewer projects are allowed through the sieve, and as a result, many projects that would have exceeded the acceptable level of return, if funded, are turned down.

Local business cultures are themselves affected by national cultures. These add yet another ingredient to the perception of risk which needs to be considered. For instance, in the European view of management, *"mieux vaut ne rien faire que de decevoir,"* or "it is better to do nothing than to disappoint," is correct management behavior in risky situations.[62] The American view, however, is that doing something is better than doing nothing. The Europeans are not really advocating a policy of inaction, but often feel the need to let things sort themselves out, as Henri Queuille, the three-time president of France between 1948 and 1950, illustrated when he stated, "Any problem, however complex, can be solved by failing to take action." Europeans believe that one may miss opportunities by acting too quickly. That is why it is often perceived as a frustrating experience to work with Europeans if you are an American, and vice versa.

Before we finish this section, let's return once again to a micro-level view and the results of MacCrimmon and Wehrung's study on risk taking among management executives. Among their numerous findings, it turns out that the decision processes themselves which are typically used by managers in making their decisions are very simple ones.[63] Managers tend to focus in on only two or so attributes when making a risk decision, one of which is typically return on investment. Furthermore, managers tend to be more willing to take risks once in a risky situation than to enter a risky situation. This sometimes explains why software projects will quickly get out of control. A decision which has been found to be wrong which results in a higher risk will motivate a quicker decision than the same risk if it was encountered originally. Since it has a higher probability of not going right either, it may trigger a rapid succession of increasingly risky decisions. The result can be a project in complete chaos, or, as Alexis de Tocqueville remarked in a statement about the French Revolution, but which could equally be applied in these situations, "Men's minds were in a state of utter confusion; they knew neither what to hold on to, nor where to stop." Only after the situation is so bad, the morale so low, does the decision making stop. Reorganization or removing individuals is also a common way in which firms stop out-of-control decision making, although it often isn't clear if this is a proactive or reactive response.

Another finding was that the perception of needs/risks seems to depend on where one is positioned in the "food chain." Managers at the senior vice-presidential level and above are the greatest risk takers, and the most successful managers are risk takers. However, managers with the most seniority within a firm tend to be more risk averse than those with less seniority. This tendency becomes more pronounced in larger firms, as managers in larger firms are more risk averse than those in smaller firms. Furthermore, higher education does not inhibit risk taking, but age certainly does. Managers also seem to take more risks in their business decisions than in their personal lives, but also rate themselves as greater risk takers than they actually are.

We should mention one or two related findings from other reports. Managers also tend to gravitate towards supporting successful programs, rather than ones in trouble. Contrary to popular belief, managers spend their time on successes, and not on potential failures. However, this does not mean that risk-averse managers will lower the opportunity costs caused by failing programs by cutting losses early.[64] Faced with negative information about a project, managers have great difficulty in stopping it, frequently allowing it instead to limp along. It is not uncommon for an unsuccessful project to last as many as seven years before its final termination. Management, it seems, has much greater difficulty in stopping a project than embarking on one, and often take actions which will ensure its eventual failure.

It also appears that both managers and workers in the information technology business, specifically programmers, tend to have pervasively high levels of optimism, while designers seem to have a predisposition to overcommit.[65] It does not take too much imagination to visualize from where some of the problems in a software enterprise emanate, given the number of possibilities of volatile mixes of risk-taking and risk-averse personalities that occur across the various environments of interest. Again, organizations that have a common view of risk taking or risk aversion will likely operate effectively, while those which have internal conflicts can expect to have higher levels of friction because of the differences in the perception of risk.

6.2.4 Politics of risk

We have tried to indicate in the previous discussions that risk decisions are not made in a vacuum, but in fact are "abetted" by many parameters, such as individual biases and cultural factors. Another dimension one must consider is the political aspect. Political considerations are especially important in the affairs of risk, since almost everyone tries to *deny* their importance.[66]

The truth of the matter is that the politics of risk reach into every facet of risk analysis and management. It would be naive for the risk analyst to believe otherwise. Truth is often its first casualty. Consider, for example, the following statement from a leading proponent of the greenhouse theory, who was discussing about how scientists such as himself,

> ... need to get some broad-based support, to capture the public's imagination. That, of course, entails loads of media coverage. So we have to offer up scary scenarios, make simplified, dramatic statements, and make little mention of any doubts we must have ... Each of us has to decide what the right balance is between being effective and being honest.[67]

We may be tempted to dismiss that situation as only occurring in the larger public debates, and believe that our own engineering world, by nature of its "higher calling," is not subject to such manipulation, but as the NSTS debacle showed, this is not always true.

When we talk about the politics of risk, we are really speaking about the acceptability of risk as it relates to power. On a macro-scale, it is the acceptability of risk in the public's mind, such as the acceptability of technological risks where flying is the safest way of traveling, yet when a crash occurs, more people than ever are killed at once because we can fly so many more at a time. Or take the social risk presented by AIDS, the health risks presented by asbestos, cigarettes, pesticides, and so forth. On a micro-scale, it is whether the acceptability of a risk is such that trying to undertake a particular software enterprise will lead to a corporation's ability to compete, or will only accelerate its decline in the market.

The problem of politics becomes even greater when we try to define the acceptability of risk, which can mean to some that: (a) one must consider the risk and benefit together to determine acceptability; (b) one must set a firm level of risk which is acceptable, and any benefits which are present cannot be considered in making the risk more acceptable; and (c) no risk of any kind is acceptable. It should be obvious that how acceptability is defined has a tremendous impact on how a risk is perceived, and what must be done to manage it. But when acceptability is coupled with the qualities or dimensions of risk, as shown in Table 6.3, it can become very ambiguous.[68]

Politics is power, which can be broadly defined as man's influence over man, and the conflicts that arise over who shall have power over whom.[69] It has been a deep and self-conscious human concern of the last 5000 years, and pervades all of our actions to some degree. Politics is seen, exercised, and felt at all levels of human experience, affecting different types of actors including individuals, groups, and organizational entities, and involves the issues of power, authority, and leadership. The risk analyst can regard political power as the power employed in relation to collective associations. Collective acts require the cooperation and collaboration of more than one person and are a means by which the goals of the association are realized. The political process, then, becomes the process by which the association is constructed and operated, the objectives for action determined, and the resources required to sustain this action marshalled. Political power thus becomes defined in terms of the actors' effects on this process; i.e., the ability to act, the capacity to produce a result, and the strength to uphold the result over a period of time.

The analyst must be aware of which individuals exercise power, why, and their span of control in making decisions. In other words, who does what to whom with what effect? Otherwise, risks that exist may not be detected, or may be perceived from a vantage point that is incorrect.[70] A good analyst understands the behavioral relationships among the different participants in a software enterprise, and those who will be affected both directly and indirectly by them. It is useful to consider that individuals are usually value maximizers; i.e., they will always try to make the best possible situation for themselves.[71] The good analyst will seek to recognize the power relationships within an organization, the time it takes to influence behavior, the sequencing necessary to influence a behavior, the resistance that may be encountered, as well as the cost, the nature of the power exercised (is it direct or indirect), and the possibility of reciprocity where the behavior of the individual exercising power is in turn influenced by the person(s) attempted to be influenced.

TABLE 6.3 Dimensions of Risk *(Continued on Next Page)*

Dimension	Conditions associated with higher perceived risk	Conditions associated with lower perceived risk
Severity of Consequences	Large numbers of injuries or fatalities per event (e.g., airplane crashes)	Small numbers of injuries or fatalities per event (e.g., deaths from falls)
Probability of Occurrence	High probability of occurrence (e.g., heart and lung diseases in heavy smokers)	Low probability of of occurrence (e.g., rare diseases)
Catastrophic Potential	Fatalities or injuries grouped in time or space (e.g., large industrial explosions)	Fatalities or injuries distributed randomly in time or space (e.g., car accident deaths)
Reversibility	Irreversible consequences (e.g., AIDS)	Consequences appear reversible (e.g., TB)
Delayed Effects	Chronic effects that are delayed in time (e.g, cancer)	All effects immediately realized (e.g., burns)
Impact on Future Generations	Risks borne equally or more greatly by future generations (e.g., ozone depletion)	Risks borne primarily by current generations (e.g., sunbathing)
Impact on Children	Children specifically at risk (e.g., birth defects)	Risks threaten adults only (e.g., occupational risks)
Victim Identity	Identifiable victims (e.g., sailor lost at sea)	Statistical victims (e.g., highway fatality estimates)
Familiarity	Unfamiliar risks (e.g, ozone depletion)	Familiar risks (e.g., household accidents)
Understanding	Personal understanding lacking in mechanisms or processes involved (e.g., nuclear power plant accidents)	Personal understanding of mechanisms or processes involved (e.g., slipping on ice)
Scientific Uncertainty	Risks unclear or uncertain to scientists (e.g., risks about nuclear power)	Risk relatively well known to scientists (e.g., car accidents)

TABLE 6.3 (*Continued*) Dimensions of Risk

Dread	Risks evoke fear, terror, or anxiety (e.g., abandoned toxic chemicals)	Risks not dreaded (e.g., food poisoning)
Voluntariness	Involuntary exposures (e.g., air pollution)	Risks one's own choice (e.g., skydiving)
Controllability	Little personal control over risk (e.g., traveling on a commercial airliner)	Some personal control risk (e.g., driving an automobile)
Clarity of Benefits	Benefits from or need for activity generating risk questioned (e.g., nuclear power)	Clear benefits (e.g., traveling by car)
Equity	No direct benefits for those at risk from an activity (e.g., those living next to abandoned toxic waste site)	Seeming equitable distribution of risks and benefits (e.g., disease vaccinations)
Institutional Trust	Lack of trust in institutions responsible for management of risks (e.g., regulatory agencies with close ties to industry)	Responsible institutions well trusted (e.g., NIH risk management of recombinant DNA)

Software enterprises operate within organizations, and the risk analyst should try to recall that organizations can be regarded as structures which coordinate the behavior of individuals and groups. How power is concentrated as well as distributed to achieve the organization's goals will exert great influence on how an individual's risk is perceived. The power each group possesses and the influence it exerts on others is generally based upon five factors:[72]

- Coping with uncertainty
- Substitutability
- Workflow pervasiveness
- Immediacy
- Interdependence

Coping with uncertainty is an organization's ability to cope with confusion or chaos. An organization that can absorb or control uncertainty will have a high level of power. *Substitutability* is the ease in which an organizational structure can be replaced. If it can be easily supplanted, it will have low levels of power. *Workflow pervasiveness* means the extent to which an organization is connected to others. One with multiple connections should have a high level of power. *Immediacy* is the degree and speed of the impact an organizational structure would have on the rest of the structure, if it were to be removed. One with a high degree of immediacy would have a high degree of organizational power. Finally, *interdependence* is the degree to which other organizational structures are dependent on another one. One that is depended upon by many others should have a high degree of power.

Studies have reported that the factor with the greatest influence is coping, followed in order by immediacy, substitutability, pervasiveness, and interdependence.[73] The risk analyst needs to be aware that these factors are coupled with others which influence the control of a specific software enterprise development. For example, it has been shown that organizational arrangements shape the effectiveness of software practices.[74] This means that organizations with power can exert a strong influence on how software is developed within an organization. Furthermore, decisions made by both managers and individuals in an organization are significantly influenced by the organization's planning and control systems.[75] Organizations with power will also tend to dominate planning. Since most software enterprises are really made up of clusters of negotiations among various actors in the internal organization structure, as well as often among differing external organizational structures, again those which can exert power the greatest can influence the perception and acceptability of risks. Risks themselves also exist in how well these negotiations proceed, as risks may be "negotiated" away, increased, or in some other way changed under the guise of "requirements trade-offs," for instance. They also influence the perception of the risks identified, or the risks deemed as being acceptable.

The view on how to best develop or use information systems technology also depends on the level in the corporate structure where one sits.[76-78] For example, upper management perceives that productivity can be increased first by improved management techniques, then by better working environment and compensation, next by the education of the personnel, and finally by better automated methods. Middle management perceives productivity gains in the same order, but places more emphasis on education and automated methods. However, the developers see the order entirely different. They perceive that productivity can be increased by concentrating on automated methods first, then the working environment and compensation, next education, and finally management improvements.

It is beyond the scope of this book to investigate all the various aspects of politics as it relates to software development enterprises. However, the above provides a taste of why it is important, and because politics exists, it is a powerful force which affects the risk analyst in practice. British MP John Morley once said, "Politics is a field where the choice constantly lies between two blunders," and a third blunder for the risk analyst would be to ignore it.

6.3 Information Technology Risk Management Organization

In the previous section, we indicated that organizations are means to organize the behavior of individuals and groups. Thus, a means to better deal with the politics of risk is through the use of an organizational structure which can itself wield power. For example, in the last chapter we recognized that software system security had to be a corporate level function and responsibility, rather than a straight MIS/ADP function for reasons of politics. This was true because if the information contained in the computer systems were stolen or compromised, the owners of the data absorbed the losses, not the MIS/ADP department. The MIS/ADP department, since it wouldn't be the one sustaining the true loss, would be inclined to accept the risk from a lack of computer security rather than divert its own funding to counter MIS/ADP security weaknesses. This MIS/ADP perspective is "reasonable" from their point of view, as increasing security means there exists a decrease in their net resources, which means a lowering of the possibility of achieving their own goals and objectives, which in turn means a loss of power in being able to influence the organization, and so forth.

Not only is the example above illustrative of how a perspective on risk can change its relative importance, but *why* the analysis and management of an enterprise's *risk* in all its forms (meaning the combination of business risk, systems engineering risk, and software engineering risk) requires it to be performed within its own organizational structure. While the impact of information technology risks *and opportunities* cuts across all organizations, there exists no explicit internal constituency to manage it across the business. In other words, no single project or group "owns" an enterprise's risk and therefore is responsible for its aversion. This means it is often overlooked or ignored until it is too late.

Risk flows throughout an enterprise, being dampened by actions of one group and amplified by actions of another. Risk is a cross-management problem, and requires a cross-management; i.e., corporate, solution. Only an organizational structure which can gather information and coordinate all organizational activities for the greater good possesses the power to adequately manage risk.[79]

Some may be ready to protest immediately that precisely what is not required is another level of bureaucracy, especially a corporate one, and therefore, an information technology risk management organization is exactly what is not needed. Haven't a number of institutional structures already been set up to deal with information technology risk, such as tort and common law, insurances, voluntary and/or mandatory standards or regulations? Isn't risk management everyone's concern, and shouldn't it be attacked from that level?

I argue that the fact that risk management *is* everyone's concern is precisely why such an organization is needed to coordinate their activities. Support structures such as tort laws are reactive in nature, meaning that a company is forced to change its practice after being sued for damages. The worst kind of lawsuit is one where the suit could have been avoided, if senior management had known about the problem and an easy solution was available to correct it. Risk management may be every individual's responsibility, but there are many times that an individual cannot affect the risks that are created outside their own sphere of influence. Individuals often cannot obtain all the information they require, and thus will confine their search to only one closed boundary. MacCrimmon and Taylor stated it in another way when they warned that limiting information-seeking to only local searches is inappropriate for complex problems and is unlikely to succeed.[80] Resources to attack a risk often are multidisciplinary and, thus, cross multiple organizational boundaries.

Needless to say, failure to solve an important problem can be costly experience to an organization. But risk management has not yet been accepted within individual organizations, mostly because they do not understand the full business implications of risk. Those who have understood, and taken the time to establish true risk management organizations, have seen major benefits accrue. For example, one significant finding reported in a Boeing study was that those airlines with the best safety records had organizations and management committed to eliminating safety risks.[81]

One should not confuse information technology risk management with total quality management (TQM), or with integrated resource management (IRM) organizations, either.[82] Although complementary, they have their own places and missions within an organization. Similar in process, they are dissimilar in objective. To a risk manager, quality and reliability are risks, and TQM is a risk management approach for containing those risks. Correspondingly, having sufficient and appropriate resources to accomplish the job is also a risk, and IRM is a means to obtain and manage them.

Further, TQM assumes that the product or service whose process is being improved is at least implicitly desired by the customer. For government projects, this may be adequate, since the product is predefined. However, risk management makes no such assumption. In fact, part of its goal is to find out if a product or service is desired, and what impact does quality and reliability have on the customer's desires. It also attempts to understand what are the other risks (financial, technical, etc.) associated with producing such a product or service on the rest of the organization's objectives; i.e., what integrated resources are available. TQM and IRM are much more narrowly focused. Lower costs, higher quality systems, and greater product variety are like table stakes in poker: They are the price companies pay to get into the game.[83] How one calculates the risk of playing the cards one has in hand, and plays a particular card as a result, is what risk management is all about. With 65% of today's firms heavily dependent on their computers to do business, and 20% completely dependent, and with the history of wasted or ineffective development of information systems, it is a mistake not to have an organization devoted to managing information technology risk.

Risk acts as common vocabulary among diverse organizations. Risk is also a philosophy, a way of thinking, which changes one perspective on how to act. Organizations may not be able to understand the technical aspects of information technology, but they can understand if it increases or lowers their risks of meeting their business objectives. Further, the more upper management becomes aware of their own part in creating risks, and not only in alleviating them, the sooner the so-called "information technology crisis" will disappear. However, this can only be accomplished if the risks involved are made explicit. Only then can something be done about them.

The point is, it is important that *some* organization be responsible for predicting information technology risks confronted by a business in the future. This is strongly linked also to identifying what information technology can and cannot achieve for the organization. This means conducting and documenting the corporation's successes and failures with information technology. Only then might it really hope to move ahead. Only then can business opportunities be pointed out with increased certainty. Only then can one hope to identify how earlier actions concerning aversion of risk, and possibly having unintended consequences, can be avoided or exploited in the future. Thus, the risk management organization parallels that of the strategic planning organization. The latter charts the place where the company wants to be in the future, while the former tries to avert the obstacles which may prevent the company from reaching that goal.

To accomplish what we have outlined above, we modestly propose that the following information risk management organization be adopted in corporations, as shown in Figure 6.14.

Finally, the risk organization acts as an ombudsman between corporate organizations to surface risks before they become realities, and obtains and coordinates the necessary resources and management attention to avert them.

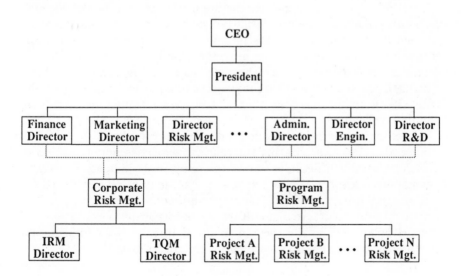

Figure 6.14 Possible Risk Management Organization

The strategy that the risk management organization can use to attain these objectives are many. However, they should as a minimum include:

- A risk management process by which business, system and software engineering, security, safety, and operational disaster recovery risks can be brought to levels or values that are acceptable to the final approval authority.
- Establishment of corporatewide levels of acceptable risk levels and/or success criteria.
- Institution of changes in organizational structure or operational methods to achieve such risk levels/success criteria.
- Establishment of a corporate-wide risk engineering methodology.
- Establishment of an information technology forensic engineering group tied to the TQM group to identify lessons learned in order that current and future IT risks can be managed.

An individual corporation may not be large enough to support a permanent organizational unit to accomplish all these functions and may wish to tailor them down to the circumstances. But in doing the tailoring, the overall functions stated above must be accomplished.

Tactically, these strategies can be implemented in different ways. A corporation may, for instance, decide to distribute actual risk management to each department which has to deal with the risks of information technology, either as a user or provider, instead of using a corporate organization. This avoids the resentment of having "corporate outsiders" who have no responsibility for the project coming in making suggestions which they are not responsible for, and then leaving. Risk analysts should be assigned to the project for its duration, otherwise there will likely be organized resistance to conducting risk analyses.

Special teams incorporating the relevant expertise may be set up to attack especially difficult, or important, enterprises instead of having a permanent staff. A crisis management team may also be required for projects that are out of control. Whatever approach is deemed best for the organizational structure and culture, some corporate coordination will always be needed as the people involved in managing information technology risk across an organization include at least the:

- Chief Executive Officer
- Chief Financial Officer
- Corporate Strategic Planner
- Marketing Director
- Corporate Legal Dept.
- Corporate Insurance Dept.
- External and Internal Auditors

- Operations Manager
- User Department Heads
- Corporate Security
- Sales Director
- Database Administrator
- Data Processing Manager
- Quality Assurance Dept.

Of course, the resources must be made available to the risk management organization, and it must also have senior management support. A risk ethic that is assumed and supported by the corporate hierarchy is the best way to make risk management happen.

A risk management organization, such as the one above, can only be justifiable when the risks faced by the corporation exceed the costs involved. There is no doubt that risk management costs money, and it is occasionally difficult to quantify. It is like the money spent on the prevention of terrorism: If it recedes, was it because of the money spent, or due to natural causes? Risk management is more like an insurance policy. You can pay some now, or you can pay a lot later.

What are some of the ways of making risk engineering succeed within a corporation?[84] To be successful, a company must first decide what, exactly, risk engineering can do for it. The company must see its relevance to the decisions that managers make, and this relevance must be carefully spelled out. For example, a single project in a large corporation may not mean very much if it fails, and thus why worry about it? Only when many projects are involved does the accumulation of failure impact the company.

Second, a whole range of risk engineering assessment techniques must be available, and there must be some common linkage between different specialties, such as finance and project development. It is important that all organizational views are supported, thus making general (and acceptable) definitions of success, as well as the acceptability of risk, critical.

Third, once the risk assessments are made, managers must trade off risks and returns in some structured way. Care must be taken to remind the managers that they still must exercise management judgment, that risk management models are not perfect, and not to blame the risk assessment techniques for the inherent difficulty in deciding risk/ benefits.

Monitoring of the risk results are a fourth requirement, with corporate level adjustments available, if the risks are not as predicted. The corporation should have a policy of contingency planning, and interest in helping projects in trouble, rather than ignoring them as they do now.

Finally, company problems and solution procedures must be brought into close alignment, or the risk organization will become ineffectual. One must realize that an approximate solution to an exact problem is better than an exact answer to an approximate problem. The right techniques for the right situation are required, as well as a firm understanding of the objectives of the project/business. The worse thing that can happen is to use a risk assessment technique which masks the real problems at hand.

In conclusion, by setting up a risk management organization, a company can assess the risk of their projects, separately and in the aggregate. This will then allow a company to maintain a portfolio of projects with different risks, thus allowing no single or small group of projects to undermine the company's current profitability or future survival.[85] Managers will be able to make more informed decisions, and ensure more successful outcomes.

6.4 Summary

"Oh well, if you don't make one mistake, you make another." This was the comment Lord Halifax made after it became clear that the Munich Conference had in fact been a dismal failure.[86] The question, of course, is how do you avoid making one mistake or another? The previous five chapters and the information in our first book on software engineering risk management are beginnings, but that all goes for naught if we cannot separate the real risks from the perceived risks in an information technology enterprise. If we in the industry cannot perceive that over-cost and late projects are symptoms of the disease, rather than its causes, we will continue to bang our collective heads against the wall, which will not only be frustrating, but cost a lot more money. Furthermore, we will unintentionally lead the public to assume that the risks involved with computer-controlled systems are minimal, when in fact they are not. How the public will react when it finds out how truly dependant and vulnerable we are to our computing technology is unknown, but it is likely to be detrimental to the industry at large, as the nuclear power industry found out.

In this chapter, we attempted to indicate the various sources of biases and information filters which can exist in a software enterprise, and some of the ways to recognize and dampen their effects. But remind yourself, these biases also affect you. Risk analysts are not magically immune. Consider, the following example. In 1974, an engineering problem was set up where seven reknowned engineers from academia and private industry were asked to predict the height at which a dirt embankment would collapse under its own weight. A span of estimates that would represent a reasonable margin of error was sought. Complex engineering studies as well as back-of-the-envelope analyses were conducted. The correct answer was found by a bulldozer piling dirt onto the embankment until it gave way. The result was that not only were all the answers wrong, but *none* of the *ranges* of estimates submitted included the right height.[87] Sometimes the hardest part of being a risk analyst is determining how to remove or minimize your own biases from affecting the results. There is no easy way, but the first step, as always, is to recognize that they are there.

Finally, it is easy to look at failed software projects and draw lessons from them. It is much harder to predict before they start what lessons one should apply. One lesson that is certain has been encapsulated by Dr. Feynman.[88] He wrote that, "For a successful technology to take place, reality must take place over public relations. Nature will not be fooled."

And so it is with risk analysis and management.

Questions

1 Epictetus wrote in *The Discourses of Epictetus*, circa A.D. 100, "It is for this reason, I suppose, that men put the processes of logic in the forefront, just as we put the testing of the measure before the measuring of the corn. And if we do not determine first what is the bushel and what is the scale, how shall we be able to measure or weigh anything?" How does this apply to the subjective perception of risk?

2 Review the three vignettes at the beginning of the story. Taking one of them, explain what steps could have been taken (or can be taken in the aviation case) to lessen the distance between the subjective perception of risk and the objective reality. Discuss how you would minimize the risks found in the four recurring themes that run through each.

3 Answer question 2, but this time, concentrate on the fly-by-wire issue. Refer back to Chapter 5 and discuss what safety techniques should be applied and why.

4 Increased air traffic will result in an increase in the number of accidents, even assuming a static hull loss rate. Discuss how and why the *perception* of air safety may degrade as 25 airplanes a year crash in the year 2005 as is now predicted. What can be done to change this perception?

5 Often, inexperienced engineers state solutions as requirements. Other than fuzzy thinking, what types of filtering and bias may be at play here?

6 Take a software project that you are familiar with. Give some examples of the types of perception bias you encountered. When errors were found, in say the requirements phase or design phase, were they of one particular type? How about in the other phases?

7 Again, using the software project from question 5 above, take two or three different errors you encountered and draw them using Venn diagrams as shown in Taylor's framework. Do you think that his framework would be useful in a real project? How would you improve it to make it more practical?

8 Whether software constitutes a risk or not often depends on one's attitude. As we saw, attitudes to risk come basically in two flavors. One was expressed by the great technologist, Herman Kahn, who wrote, "Risk taking is the essence of innovation." The other was articulated by Jackie Stewart, ex-world motorcar racing champion, "I don't like taking risks. I hate fear. I hate it, I really hate it." Kahn expresses the optimistic, let's press back the frontiers attitude, which almost all scientists and engineers take. Without innovation, society is stagnant. Only through failure can success be found.

Jackie Stewart, on the other hand, expresses a more circumspect view. Before the race, he constantly calculated the risks he was likely to encounter that day and tried to find ways to reduce them. He was an advocate for more race course safety, and by his own account, was not always the most popular man with racing officials because of it. He used to take his own anesthetist with him to races, figuring him to be the most valuable man around if there was a serious accident. While a surgeon might be able to repair him, the anesthetist would be needed to keep him alive to get to the surgeon. His was more a businessman's approach to taking risk.

Are you a risk taker or a risk averse person? How do you know? How do you think it affects how you plan and implement a software project?

9   Obtain a copy of Kenneth R. MacCrimmon and Donald A. Wehrung's book, *Taking Risks,* and apply the tests included to determine whether you are risk taking or risk averse. If a copy is unavailable, substitute Table 6.1.

10   It is often said that "public perception drives public policy." How does one overcome the pressures of culture, especially of group think? Has this ever affected you?

11   Words freeze ideas and often define our outlook on particular subjects like risk. Consider the wonderful ad for a certain high tech company which states that the handmaiden of every new technology is risk. There are no guidebooks to the new. Success or failure often hinges on instinct, and the willingness to invest in belief. Explain how the selection of these particular words influences the perception of risk of using new information technology. Give some examples.

12   Dr. Feynman throughout his career urged others to challenge themselves to overcome the problems of subjective perception, especially as it pertained to self-ego. He once related this short, poignant story to make his point, which I heard from a Cal-Tech professor:

Feynman really did not like getting the Nobel Prize for physics because of all the press and increased bureaucratic nonsense it caused. He said it never really came in handy except on the occasions when he had to sit in on physics seminars. Prior to getting his Nobel Prize, he would listen to the seminars which were really incomprehensible to him, but he didn't like to say so because everyone else just kept shaking their heads in agreement as the lecturer would make some point, and no one would ever ask any questions. Well, after he got the Nobel, he felt he could finally ask some questions. No one would think he was a dummy then. As it turned out, every one else had the same questions, but no one wanted to admit it, because everyone else was shaking their heads as if in agreement!!!

Explain how ego can affect the perception of risk, and its implications for risk analysis and risk management.

13   Information technology enterprises are really made up of clusters of negotiations: between individuals in units, between internal organizational units, between internal and external organizations. How are the politics of risk involved?

14   One area we did not talk about in the section on politics and risk was the theory of the Peter Principle, so named after the late Laurence Peters. According to this theory, in hierarchies every employee rises to his or her level of incompetence. This means that if you do your job to your supervisor's satisfaction, you will be promoted. If you perform adequately again, you will be promoted again. Eventually, you will be promoted to a job you cannot do, and there you will remain, as a meddlesome, obstructive incompetent. In time, Peters said, every post tends to be occupied by someone too incompetent to carry out its duties. How may the Peter Principle explain why many companies resist risk management, TQM, or IRM?

15 A Canadian psychologist has developed a controversial theory called risk homeostasis, which postulates that people tend to embrace a certain level of risk. He noticed that the mortality rates for accidental and violent deaths have remained oddly static throughout this century, despite all the advances in technology and safety standards. Thus, when something is made safer, somehow its new use tends to revert to the same level of risk. For example, a road with a particularly bad intersection which is made safer will have a falling accident rate there, but somewhere else along the road accidents will rise as a kind of compensating factor. Do you believe this to be coincidence? Do you think risk perception is at play; i.e., people will perceive the road as safer, and thus drive a little faster in areas they did not use too? Speculate on the implications for software systems undergoing safety analyses.

16 Consider the following headline from an article in the December 4, 1989, *Aviation Week & Space Technology:* "TQM Expected to Boost Productivity, Ensure Survival of U.S. Industry." Do you agree with the contention that TQM will ensure the survival of U.S. industry? Is it enough to ensure survival; i.e., is it a sufficient condition, or just a necessary one? Explain, specifically in the light of gaining competitive edges over other countries such as Japan, which has already applied TQM with vigor to its industry.

17 Do you believe that a risk management organization should exist as a separate entity within a business? Why or why not? What type of organizational resistance needs to be overcome to make such an organization successful?

18 In many fast-growing businesses, especially in the computing industry, their eventual downfall can often be traced to sloppiness due to their rapid growth, and second, to the ignorance of the impacts of their sloppiness due to arrogance gained by being so successful. How can a risk management organization help overcome these twin killers of fast-growing businesses?

19   In his excellent book, *Connections*, James Burke quotes a sociologist who wrote about the 1965 great New York power blackout, and the amazing fact that almost no one considered that the failure was anything more than momentary: "We can only conclude that it is too much to ask of us poor twentieth-century humans to think, to believe, to grasp the possibility that the system might fail ... we cannot grasp the simple and elementary fact that this technology can blow a fuse." The point being made is that because of our interdependence on technology, no man is an island. We can no longer really cope without it, and we must have faith that it will always work. What are the implications of this attitude to a user of information technology and his or her perception of the technological risks imposed, say to their livelihood, career, family?

20   In a recent aviation magazine, a designer of the "cockpit of the future" stated it would contain one man and one dog. The man is there to feed the dog. The dog is there to bite the man if he tries to touch anything. How do you feel about this? Does it make you uneasy? Why? Is it because you do not believe that the technology will become good enough on a plane to be completely computer controlled, or is there some deeper reason?

21   In a previous occupation, I was sent off to a training school which had two parts to it. One was on submarine sonar systems, and the other was on submarine combat systems. Both used identical computers. In the sonar part of the course, we learned about sonar principles and the sonar's operation. However, in the fire control part of the course, we learned all about the computer's operation, the software's design, and only later about fire control principles. Being involved with the implementation of both systems, and knowing that the software design was irrelevant to the operational user, I was rather intrigued by these two obviously different perspectives. Why do you think this happened? Can it be explained by the fact that sonar has been around for 50 years, and digital fire control systems for only 15? Does it show that one group was technology driven, and the other, market or application driven? What implications does the perception of a system have on its design, operation, or safety?

References

1.   Robert J. Beck, "Munich's Lesson's Reconsidered," *International Security*, Vol. 14, No. 2, Fall 1989. This excellent article goes into detail about the various studies undertaken in the examining of the events of Munich and its aftermath.

2.   Ibid.

3. To be fair, Chamberlain did repudiate the Munich document after Hitler seized the remainder of Czechoslovakia in March 1939, and in April 1939 he started the first peacetime conscription in British history. Unfortunately, war was to break out less than 5 months later, which did not allow much time for filling out a hollow military.

4. Robert J. Beck, "Munich's Lesson's Reconsidered," *International Security*, Vol. 14, No. 2, Fall 1989.

5. Ibid.

6. Many would contend NASA still is a member of the qualitative school today, even though official policy says differently. Cultural biases do not disappear by fiat.

7. Karl Esch, "How NASA Prepared to Cope with Disaster," *IEEE Spectrum*, Vol. 23, No. 3, March 1986.

8. Walter C. William, "Lessons from NASA," *IEEE Spectrum*, Vol. 18, No. 10, October 1981.

9. Trudy Bell and Karl Esch, "The Space Shuttle: A Case of Subjective Engineering," *IEEE Spectrum*, Vol. 26, No. 6, June 1989.

10. "Post-Challenger Evaluation of Space Shuttle Risk Assessment and Management," National Academy Press, Washington, DC, January 1988.

11. Of course, this type of environment is all the more reason why one should use quantitative approaches.

12. Richard P. Feynman, *"What Do You Care What Other People Think?,"* Bantam Books, New York, 1988. The late Dr. Feynman served as a member of the presidential inquiry into the *Challenger* explosion. His book provides a number of useful insights into how not to conduct risk analyses.

13. In congressional hearings held after the *Challenger* failure, it was reported that failure rates of the SRB were political footballs within NASA. Estimates of failure of 1 in 32 to 1 in 323 launches, as well as 1 in 21 and 1 in 909 launches were computed by the Air Force. However, these and other studies were not taken into serious consideration at the time by NASA. The Air Force, on the other hand, did, and insisted on keeping standard rocket boosters around just in case of a shuttle failure. The astronauts were never told of these risks, which upset them when they found out about it later, while many of the engineers who were familiar with the evaluations disagreed on their interpretation. For more details, see "Officials Disagree on Data Assessing Shuttle Reliability," *Aviation Week & Space Technology*, 17 February, 1986.

14. "How NASA Prepared to Cope With Disaster," *IEEE Spectrum*, Vol. 23, No. 3, March 1986.

15. Paul Mann, "Report Calls for Fifth Orbiter, Citing Probability Of Accident," *Aviation Week & Space Technology*, 7 August, 1989. In fact, based upon the data of 29 launches, the OTA reported there is a better than even chance of losing a shuttle within the next 12 missions (to help make a comparison, the current French Ariane rocket, based on a tried, older technology, has had one loss in 17 launches).

NASA seems to be afraid of going to Congress itself with these findings for fear of losing even more funding for the space station. Congress has a great habit, usually after the fact, of saying "Gee, if you were in trouble, you should have told us. We would have given you the money." In reality, as anyone who has been around government for more than 30 seconds knows, it won't. Congress will instead cancel the program. Thus, in government, one often finds a program which won't admit it has a problem, can't get the money to fix it even if it were honest and did admit there were problems, and, as always, it is the users who ultimately suffer.

16. Theresa Foley, "NASA Prepares for Protests over Nuclear System Launch on Shuttle in October," *Aviation Week & Space Technology*, 26 June, 1989.

17. *Wall Street Journal*, editorial, 24 July, 1989.

18. This yet another reason why risk analysts must use capabilities present, rather than intentions, during risk evaluation and especially risk management.

19. Richard P. Feynman, *"What Do You Care What Other People Think?"* Bantam Books, New York, 1988.

20. It's also bad engineering. One cannot infer a safety factor from a single statistical result.

21. This is contrary to how risk management should be run. Criteria should be increased with time towards ever more exacting standards. To do otherwise is to assume that because a risk did not occur once, it will not occur again. This fallacious argument is often used to justify the reduction in testing efforts of software programs after a number of previous programs have been tested successfully. It was used by some NASA officials to justify launching the NSTS again and again, even though safety problems were not corrected in the meantime. It is like playing Russian roulette. One miss implies another, when in fact they are independent events.

Further, NASA's two top critical safety rankings, 1 and 1R (1 means the loss of life or vehicle, while 1R means a redundant hardware element that could cause the loss of life or vehicle) were formally treated as being equal, even though the items in each category were substantially different in risk. This situation did not allow NASA to allocate its risk management resources effectively or recognize the differing consequences of the risks.

22. Trudy Bell and Karl Esch, "The Space Shuttle: A Case of Subjective Engineering," *IEEE Spectrum*, Vol. 26, No. 6, June 1989.

23. They also are big believers in the design in quality approach, but from a different perspective than NASA. The majority of new airplanes are built *bottom-up*. In other words, the properties and limitations of the materials used are well understood before building a component. In an engine, the turbine blades are experimentally tested to find out their limitations. These are then attached to a larger component and again tested for design deficiencies and limitations. This process continues until the full engine is tested out. By this time, the properties and limitations of the overall engine are fairly well understood. Any modifications that have to be made later have a good chance of being able to be put into place easily. NASA's approach to the NSTS engine design was *top-down*. It was designed and put together all at once with relatively little detailed analysis of the component's materials. When troubles started to arise, it became difficult to correct them. NASA's approach is a lot like how software systems

are built. See Richard P. Feynman, *"What Do You Care What Other People Think?,"* Bantam Books, New York, 1988, for more details about NASA's approach to designing the NSTS.

24. John Voelcker, "'Gold-Plated' Design," *IEEE Spectrum*, Vol. 23, No. 11, November 1986.

25. "Government, Industry Mount Major Effort to Characterize Aging Aircraft Issues," *Aviation Week & Space Technology*, 24 July, 1989.

26. James Ott, "10 Fatal Crashes Spark Call for New Safety Measures," *Aviation Week & Space Technology*, 24 July, 1989. Aviation experts like to point out that if a person was born on a commercial aircraft in 1980, and lived his or her whole life on a plane, one could expect to be 2600 years old before being involved in an accident, and would have a 29% chance of surviving. The accident rate per 100,000 takeoffs for 1989 was .328, down from .412 in 1988. However, the ratio of crashes involving deaths was .109, or 4 times the .027 ratio in 1988. The key question that many aviation experts are asking is not whether flying is safe, but rather, whether it is safe enough. Around the world in 1989, as a thought to ponder on, there were 35 major fatal airplane crashes involving jet and turboprop aircraft.

27. "Economics, Not Safety, Is Key Issue in Replacement of Older Transports," *Aviation Week & Space Technology*, 24 July, 1989.

28. "Old, New Aircraft Costs Are Similar," *Aviation Week & Space Technology*, 24 July, 1989.

29. One flight engineer told me that on one aircraft, there were so many tags on his instruments indicating maintenance was required, he thought it was Flag Day.

30. "Aging Aircraft Issue Presents Major Challenge to Industry," *Aviation Week & Space Technology*, 24 July, 1989. In the early 1950s, a similar event happened which also caught aircraft designers by surprise. This was when the British-built de Havilland Comet exploded in midair due to structural fatigue at many flight hours less than was thought required. Because of the Comet tragedy, metal fatigue in aircraft was reexamined and the present service lives of today's aircraft are many times that of the Comet. However, as with many things, the lessons of the past often have to be relearned.

31. James Ott, "10 Fatal Crashes Spark Call for New Safety Measures," *Aviation Week & Space Technology*, 24 July, 1989.

32. David Field, "Controllers Issue a Mayday," *The Washington Times*, 20 December, 1989.

33. Michael Mecham, "FAA Seeks $1-Billion Increase in 1991 to Fund Facilities, R&D Projects," *Aviation Week & Space Technology*, 18 December, 1989.

34. Jim Beatson, "Is America Ready to 'Fly by Wire'?" *The Washington Post*, 2 April, 1989. On June 26, 1988, an Airbus A320 crashed while on a demonstration flight at an airshow near Mulhouse, France. Three persons were killed. The crash occurred during clear weather. The pilot stated that the FBW computer delayed the airplane's response time and caused the crash. The French authorities rejected this and blamed the crash on pilot error.

On February 14, 1990, an Indian Airlines Airbus A320 crashed while landing at Bangalore, India, also during clear weather. Ninety-one passengers and crew died. The Indian government ordered the grounding of the aircraft until the cause of its crash could be determined. The French pilots' union called for the grounding of all Airbuses due to what they, and the French mechanics' union, termed inexplicable software errors in the FBW system. The head of the pilots' union was quoted as saying that, "Our pilots have found that the computer is not always in accord with the numbers given." The mechanics' union also claimed that the Indian airline did not have enough training to properly maintain the plane.

It is well known that trying to override the computer and attempt manual control in the Airbus requires five to six seconds, and if done during a critical time, this action can significantly increase the risk of an error. Indian aviation authorities speculate that this is what may have occurred. Shortly after the Indian Airlines crash, Northwest Airlines issued a pilots' bulletin advising of possible problems after a recent series of events related to suspected failures in the computer system. At least nine incidents involving computer malfunctions caused aborted takeoffs or emergency diversions to another airport. For more information, see David Field, "Machine at the Controls," *The Washington Times*, 15 February, 1990, "Airbus Pilot May Have Tried to Override Computer," *The Washington Times*, 16 February, 1990, and "Northwest Issues Alert After Airbus Problems," *The Washington Times*, 7 March 1990.

Airbus Industries, the manufacturer of Airbus, has belatedly responded to some of the concerns of the airlines operating the A300 series by proposing to install a series of safeguards to combat what they call "crew overconfidence" in the FBW computer system. Not surprisingly, they are blaming the crews, rather than the computer system itself, as the cause of the problems. This is exactly the point we were making in an earlier chapter when those responsible for the construction and operation of computer systems exclude the environment with which the system interacts. See "Airbus May Add to A320 Safeguards, Act to Counter Crew 'Overconfidence,'" *Aviation Week & Space Technology*, 30 April 1990.

35. David Hughes, "Human Factors Are Critical in Computer-Driven Systems," *Aviation Week & Space Technology*, 18 December, 1989.

36. "Keep Them Flying," *IEEE Spectrum*, Vol. 23, No. 11, November 1986.

37. Norman R. Augustine, *Augustine's Laws*, American Institute of Aeronautics and Astronautics, New York, 1983.

38. Andrew Sage, "Behavioral and Organizational Considerations in the Design of Information Systems and Processes for Planning and Decision Support," *IEEE Transactions on Systems, Man, and Cybernetics*, Vol. SMC-11, No. 9, September 1981.

39. Miley W. Merkhofer, "Quantifying Judgmental Uncertainty: Methodology, Experiences, and Insights," *IEEE Transactions on Man, Systems, and Cybernetics*, Vol. SMC-17, No. 5, September/October 1987.

40. Peter G. Moore, *The Business of Risk*, Cambridge University Press, Cambridge, England, 1983.

41. John Paulos, *Innumeracy: Mathematical Illiteracy and Its Consequences*, Hill and Wang, New York, 1988.

42. Nicholas Rescher, *Risk*, University of America Press, Latham, MD, 1983.

43. Peter G. Moore, *The Business of Risk*, Cambridge University Press, Cambridge, England, 1983.

44. Trudy Bell and Karl Esch, "The Space Shuttle: A Case of Subjective Engineering," *IEEE Spectrum*, Vol. 26, No. 6, June 1989.

45. Andrew Sage, "Behavioral and Organizational Considerations in the Design of Information Systems and Processes for Planning and Decision Support," *IEEE Transactions on Systems, Man, and Cybernetics*, Vol. SMC-11, No. 9, September 1981.

46. Norman R. Augustine, *Augustine's Laws*, American Institute of Aeronautics and Astronautics, New York, 1983. A more subtle example of fact-value confusion is when an individual believes there is a solution when there is none; i.e., an open-ended dilemma exists, rather than a closed-form problem. Tremendous amounts of time will be expended on finding "the" answer, rather than trying to manage the dilemma.

47. Trudy Bell and Karl Esch, "The Space Shuttle: A Case of Subjective Engineering," *IEEE Spectrum*, Vol. 26, No. 6, June 1989.

48. This also explains why large government projects usually only have two phases: The first is that it is too early to tell whether it is a success, and the second, it is to late to stop it regardless.

49. O. Helmer, *Social Technology*, Basic Books, New York, 1966.

50. Harold E. Roland and Brian Moriarty, *System Safety Engineering and Management*, John Wiley & Sons, Inc., New York 1983.

.51. Miley W. Merkhofer, "Quantifying Judgmental Uncertainty: Methodology, Experiences, and Insights," *IEEE Transactions on Man, Systems, and Cybernetics*, Vol. SMC-17, No. 5, September/October 1987.

52. Andrew Sage, "Behavioral and Organizational Considerations in the Design of Information Systems and Processes for Planning and Decision Support," *IEEE Transactions on Systems, Man, and Cybernetics*, Vol. SMC-11, No. 9, September 1981.

53. Theodore C. Taylor, "Perspectives on Some Problems of Concept Selection, Management and Complexity in Military System Development," *Naval War College Review*, Vol. XXXIV, No. 5/Sequence 287, September-October 1981.

54. "The Dangers of Overconfidence," *MIT Technology Review*, 12 July, 1989.

55. These facts were taken from the article, "The Menacing Microburst," *IEEE Spectrum*, Vol. 23, No. 11, November 1986.

56. Kenneth R. MacCrimmon and Donald A. Wehrung, *Taking Risks*, Free Press, New York, 1986. One should remember that each individual will make a choice that maximizes one's (perception of) gain. This is done through the three-step process of rationalization, evaluation, and maximization.

57. Norman F. Dixon, *On the Psychology of Military Incompetence*, Jonathan Cape Ltd., London, 1979.

58. Amitai Etzioni, "Humble Decision Making," *Harvard Business Review*, Vol. 89, No. 4, July/August 1989.

59. Francis A. McDonough, *An Evaluation of the Grand Design Approach to Developing Computer Based Application Systems*, Information Resources Management Services, U.S. General Services Administration, September 1988.

60. I. L. Janis, *Victims of Group Think*, Houghton Mifflin, Boston, MA, 1972.

61. Peter G. Moore, *The Business of Risk*, Cambridge University Press, Cambridge, England, 1983.

62. Jean-Louis Barsoux, "Management by Inactivity," *Director*, April 1989.

63. Izak Benbast and Ronald N. Taylor, "Behavioral Aspects of Information Processing for the Design of Management Information Systems," *IEEE Transactions on Systems, Man, and Cybernetics*, Vol. SMC-12, No. 4, July/August 1982.

64. Arthur Gerstenfeld, "A Study of Successful Projects, Unsuccessful Projects, and Projects in Progress in West Germany," *IEEE Transactions on Engineering Management*, Vol. EM-23, No. 3, August 1976. In this study, both successful and unsuccessful projects took about the same amount of time.

65. The dominant personality type in computing seems to be that of risk takers, rather than risk averters. This coupled with the pressures and overcommitment found on projects makes for a very unstable mixture. See, for instance, Fred Brooks, *The Mythical Man-Month*, Addison-Wesley Publishing Co., Reading, MA, 1975, and Harold Thimleby, "Delaying Commitment," *IEEE Software*, May 1988.

66. Amitai Etzioni, "Humble Decision Making," *Harvard Business Review*, Vol. 89, No. 4, July/August 1989.

67. Alston Chase, "Greenhouse Spoilers or Savants," *The Washington Times*, November 17, 1989. Some would argue that the person making such a statement is not truly a scientist, but has turned into a politician, and thus should be treated with the same level of respect.

68. John Cohrssen and Vincent Covello, *Risk Analysis: A Guide to Principles and Methods for Analyzing Health and Environmental Risks*, NTIS, Springfield, VA 1989.

69. We have drawn extensively in this section from the essay on "Political Power" in *Encyclopaedia Britannica*, Inc., Chicago, IL, Vol. 14, 1980.

70. It may also lead to having a perfectly sound analysis and set of recommendations that may not be accepted because they did not take into account the political power structure. Note, we are not attempting to pass judgment on whether the exercise of power is good or bad.

71. William Korbitz, *Modern Management of Water and Wastewater Utilities*, Garland Press, New York, 1981. Korbitz makes a distinction between factual and value content of decisions by individuals. The factual content of decisions are relatively nonnegotiable, whereas the value content would require technical and/or political trade-offs. Day-to-day operational issues are more factually oriented, since they are fairly repetitive, simpler, less risky or uncertain, and are based upon a sound base of information. Policy decisions, on the other hand, are more value oriented since they are less repetitive, span a longer length of time, and are more high risk since the base of information upon which they are made is uncertain.

72. H. Lucas, "Organizational Power and the Information Services Department," *Communications of the ACM*, Vol. 27, No. 1, January, 1984.

73. Ibid.

74. Walt Scacchi, "Managing Software Engineering Projects: A Social Analysis," *IEEE Transactions on Software Engineering*, Vol. SE-10, No. 1, January 1984.

75. T. Abel-Hamid and S. Madnick, "The Dynamics of Software Project Scheduling," *Communications of the ACM*, Vol. 26, No. 5, May 1983.

76. Barry Boehm, "Verifying and Validating Software Requirements and Design Specifications," *IEEE Computer*, Vol. 17, No. 1, January 1984.

77. Richard Fairley, *Software Engineering Concepts*, McGraw-Hill, Inc. New York, 1984.

78. Ware Myers, "The Need for Software Engineering," *IEEE Computer*, Vol. 11, No. 2, February 1978.

79. This, in fact, is the true job of the federal government. The federal government should do things that are not part of any natural constituency, but cut across many different ones.

80. K. R. MacCrimmon and R. N. Taylor, "Decision Making Problem Solving," M. D. Dunnette (ed.), *Handbook of Industrial and Organizational Psychology*, Rand McNally, Chicago, IL, 1976.

81. James Ott, "10 Fatal Crashes Spark Call for New Safety Measures," *Aviation Week & Space Technology*, 24 July, 1989.

82. IRM is usually defined as the orchestration of actions directed at maximizing the potential leverage from automation and optimization of information systems.

83. Richard B. Chase and David A. Garvin, "The Service Factory," *Harvard Business Review*, Vol. 89, No. 4, July/August 1989.

84. Eugene Carter, "What Are the Risks in Risk Analysis?" *Havard Business Review*, July-August 1972.

85. F. Warren McFarlan, "Portfolio Approach to Information Systems," *Harvard Business Review*, January-February 1974.

86. Robert J. Beck, "Munich's Lesson's Reconsidered," *International Security*, Vol. 14, No. 2, Fall 1989.

87. "The Dangers of Overconfidence," *MIT Technology Review*, 12 July, 1989.

88. Richard P. Feynman, *"What Do You Care What Other People Think?"* Bantam Books, New York, 1988.

The Future Business of Risk

*"If you can meet with Triumph and Disaster
And treat those two impostors just the same-"*

RUDYARD KIPLING'S *If*

"Be wary then; best safety lies in fear."

Hamlet (I,iii,43)

*"Perfection must be reached by degrees;
she requires the slow hand of time."*

VOLTAIRE

*"Man cannot know so far the connection of causes and events
as that he may venture to do wrong in order to do right."*

DR. JOHNSON RASSELAS *(ca. 1759)*

*"Man is a far more advanced species than the crocodile,
but all the same he would be ill-advised to
rely on this while swimming in the Ganges."*

HUGH SETON-WATSON

*"Wisdom is the right use of knowledge. To know is not to be wise.
Many men know a great deal, and are all the greater fools for it.
There is no fool so great a fool as a knowing fool.
But to know how to use knowledge is to have wisdom."*

SPURGEON

*"Pulling up a plant and examining its roots is not
the best way of predicting its future growth."*

CHARETTE

7.0 Introduction

Dr. Richard Feynman, the Nobel Prize winner, used to tell a delightful little story about why he found physics so interesting. He said that trying to understand physics was like trying to understand chess when you didn't know the rules and could only see part of the chess board. You try to infer the rules from what you can see and the movement of the pieces that come into view. After observing the play for a while, you may conclude you now comprehend it, and thus begin busily writing down the rules as you think you understand them, when, oops, in pops a piece you have never seen before, say a knight, and it acts much differently from the others you have been observing. After another period of time passes, you figure out that the pieces you have been observing have only limited characteristics, and are only pawns. Out goes your old theory, which had everything possessing the characteristics of pawns, and now you postulate everything acts like pawns and knights. Just when you thought you were getting comfortable with that concept, into view comes a bishop. And the process is repeated anew. Each fresh observation brings with it some additional information, and totally a different perspective on reality.

Risk analysis and management are very much like Feynman's chess analogy. Throughout this book, and the one preceding it, we have explored ways of challenging our notions about software development by confronting the conventional wisdom concerning the causes of software engineering failure. We have discussed a paradigm where it is the basic undercapitalization and underperformance of development resources, not the lack of software engineering or computing technology, that are the primary causes of these failures. We have demonstrated that the foundations of software development failure are manifested in risks which can be found, created, and exacerbated at any point in the development life cycle, starting from the initial business decision made to acquire, use, or develop a software system, through its systems engineering, down to the software engineering process model, methodology, and automation that are used in the system's implementation.

We have established that the longer these risks remained ignored, unnoticed, or unmanaged, the more they diminished the chances of a project's success. We have demonstrated that much of software development failure is caused by the mismanagement of these risks, most often by not recognizing that they exist, or ignoring them when they were recognized. We also showed that not all the risks that were identified can or should be avoided, but they all should be assessed, and explicit controls should be applied in proportion to each risk identified. Ultimately, risk analysis and management can only be based upon context, decisions, decision processes, and their interfaces to other decision processes, for any existing project within a model of a *business enterprise*; i.e., *an undertaking that is difficult, complicated, and has a strong element of risk.*

We have also shown that risk management is closely linked to the various elements involved in a business's strategic and tactical planning. The latter charts the place where the company wants to be in the future and the means to achieve that goal, while the former tries to avert the obstacles which may prevent the company from reaching that goal. Risk management implements and binds the various day-to-day tactics, such as bidding for a project, ensuring that current projects are successful, or evaluating the strengths and limitations of development processes and techniques, to the selected business strategy.

Finally, we have shown that software engineering risk analysis and management have limitations, and moreover, we have made them explicit. Risk management is not a panacea. One would be foolish to think that there is some silver bullet involved; i.e., that some risk technique will be able to guarantee that a project will succeed. There isn't any.[1] Risk management's true value lay not in generating risk evaluation numbers that can be tossed cavalierly around in meetings, but in helping promote the process of discovering where a software development might go wrong, and the means to minimize the consequences. Even with risk analysis and management, a software development may still ultimately fail, but it is always better to fight an enemy whose strength and disposition are known than to fight one that is invisible.

For the remainder of this chapter, we will first provide a cross-referenced review of the main ideas and issues covered in this book, and then take a quick glance at the future directions of risk management.

7.1   Risk Engineering Review

What we have tried to accomplish in this book is to show that when trying to effectively acquire, use, or develop information technology, one is faced with dilemmas to manage, not necessarily problems to solve. And a mechanism for successfully managing these dilemmas is through the application of risk management. What we intend to do in this section is provide a synopsis or quick-look review digest—crib notes, as it were—of the application strategies for the risk analysis and management that we discussed throughout the book. Like crib notes, we provide a specific question concerning an aspect of risk analysis and management, and then provide a general answer. These notes highlight *some* of the important aspects of risk analysis and management covered in the book, and are cross-referenced to the primary section or sections where more detailed information can be found. They can be used either to review the material, or as checklists to ensure that proper risk analysis and management procedures are being followed. However, they do not cover every section or every topic, and, like crib notes, are not meant to be used as a substitute for a thorough reading of the book.

We have also provided space to write down personal observations as well. Within this space, a software project manager may wish to write down pertinent questions to ask his project team leader about the risks to the project, or a senior manager may desire to do the same, but instead, to ask the software project manager what risks to the business he is taking on. The project manager may also want to ask his manager what risks he or she is saddling the project with as well. I would suggest that after each review section, questions exploring the why, where, when, who, how, and what-for's of the particular topic be generated for later consultation.

Recall that the objectives of software engineering risk analysis and management are meant to find the best available answers to the following questions:

- What are the risks to the business and the project?
- What is the probability of loss from them?
- How much are the losses likely to cost?
- What might the losses be if the worst happened?
- What alternatives are there?
- How can the losses be reduced or eliminated?
- Will the alternatives produce other risks?

How well one can get objective answers to these questions, and make rational decisions about the risks confronting a software project, and the risks that are undertaken by the business, will determine the ultimate success of the risk analysis and management process(es). For convenience, we will not review the definition of risk, as a complete set of notes dealing with the subject can be found in the Appendix.

7.2 Software Engineering Risk Analysis and Management Application and Strategy Overview

---

What are the major sources of software failure? [Section 1.1]

The three primary causes of risk are:

- Undercapitalization of resources, which concern the lack of sufficient resources being made available for a software development, acquisition, or a software system's application. It also includes the undercapitalization of ideas; i.e., not having a *raison d'être* for the information system.
- Underperformance of resources, which concern the inefficiency and ineffectiveness in resource application. When underperformance occurs, the parts making up the whole of a project's operation are worth more separately than when packaged together.
- Lack of recognition, consideration, or appreciation of the risks involved in the acquisition, development, or application of information systems.

Where are the sources of risks manifested? [Section 1.4]

- The sources of software development failure are manifested in risks which can be found, created, and exacerbated at any point in the development life cycle, starting from the initial business decision made to acquire, use, or develop a software system, through its systems engineering, down to the software engineering process model, methodology, and automation that are used in the system's implementation.

- Risks are also found in the application system to be acquired, developed, or applied, which might manifest themselves in safety, security, or operational/disaster recovery issues.

- Risks may also manifest themselves by the perception of risk itself taken by decision makers involved. Decision makers may hold particular biases which make objective reality and subjective perception unequal.

7.2.1 Business risks

What are some of the sources of information technology risks that manifest themselves in the business environment which may find their way to the software engineering environment?
[Sections 2.3.2 through 2.3.5]

The sources of risk an analyst must investigate include:

- The objectives of the company, why it uses information technology, what it expects to gain from information technology, and the resources it can apply toward the acquisition, development, or application of information technology.
- The industry sector(s) in which the business is involved, namely consumer, industrial, service, or government. This also means investigating the competitive components of the sectors which relate to information technology, and the prediction of future changes to the industry and information technology.
- The culture of the business, whether it is a tough guy/machismo, work hard/play hard, bet-your-company, or process type.
- The organization skills of the business in information technology.
- The organization structure of the business, whether it is matrix, participatory, or directive.

What are some ways business environment information technology risks that an analyst may find can be identified, estimated, and evaluated? [Sections 2.3.2.1, 2.3.3, 2.3.4, and 2.3.6]

Business environment information technology risks may be identified, estimated, and evaluated by:

- Evaluating the state of health and the inherent risks of the industry sector in which the business operates.
- Determining the business's most productive scale size, which measures the inherent productivity of a firm based upon its size and culture.

- Conducting evaluations such as TQM, Capability/Capacity Reviews, SEI Software Capability Assessment, Grey Beard Teams, Red Teams, Audit Teams, and percentage of win of bids.
- Evaluate the business's use of information technology via Porter's Value Chain analysis.
- Evaluate the business's use of information technology via Nolan's stage model.
- Evaluate the business's use of information technology via *Computerworld's* information technology ranking.

What are some of the ways a company can make information systems pay-off? [Sections 1.1 and 2.3.5.3]

Knowing why a particular information system is needed to support the business is the first order of business. All information systems should be able to be shown to either: lower a business's cost, increase its revenue volume, meet governmental regulations, protect market share, or diversify the business. A *reason* for supporting the business is mandatory before trying to buy, acquire, or use an information system.

Information systems pay off the most in return on investment when used to: (1) improve the quality of the finished product; (2) offer better customer service; or (3) enable management to do things that were not previously possible.

7.2.2 System engineering risks

What is systems engineering? [Section 2.4.1]

Systems engineering is a branch of management technology whose aim is to assist and support policy making and planning decisions which result in resource allocation or action. It is usually reserved for systems of large scale; i.e., when it involves interactions with many environments including technological, economic, legal, managerial, political, social, cultural, professional trade and intellectual, ethical and religious, military, and/or environmental. Systems engineering accomplishes its objectives by a structured approach to qualitative and quantitative formulation, analysis, and interpretation of the impact of policy and action alternatives upon the perspectives of the various parties affected by the system.

What are the two sources of systems engineering risk that an analyst must identify? [Sections 2.4.1.1 and 2.4.1.2]

The two sources of risk in systems engineering stem from:

- Policy objectives, which are defined as a definitive course of action(s), method of action(s), or doctrinal approach(es) selected from alternatives in the light of present conditions, to guide and usually determine present and future decisions.
- Engineering objectives. The engineering objectives concern the process of selecting and synthesizing the application of the appropriate scientific and technological knowledge in order to translate system requirements into a system design, and, subsequently, to produce the composite equipment, skills, and techniques and to demonstrate that they can be effectively employed as a coherent whole to achieve some stated goal or purpose.

What type of policy and/or engineering objective risks exist? [Sections 2.4.1.1, 2.4.1.2, and 2.4.2]

The primary risk in systems engineering is the overemphasis on political ideology over systems engineering, and pretending that it doesn't happen. This can be seen in the policy objectives of the Grand Design, Hardware First, and/or Software First. The masquerading of engineering objectives by political ideology is now so entrenched that for many information technology efforts, the cost of the effort is a function of what dollars are available, as opposed to being based upon a set of achievable and testable requirements driven by an organizational or operational need. It is rare to find an information technology project which can specify what is its bottom-line, break-even point.

The secondary source of risk is in the systems engineering/software engineering boundary. For small information technology programs, systems engineering is not a major concern. For larger programs, systems engineering is a must. This means one has to deal with a very complex ecosystem of risks, where the business risks and objectives are filtered before reaching the software engineering domain. If the filtering is not done properly, for instance, risks that should be resolved at the systems engineering level are instead having to be dealt with at an inappropriate software engineering level; risks that are created by the software engineering level are never debated, but should be at the appropriate business level; or risks that could be resolved by software engineering methods are preempted by system engineering decisions. The primary source of risk lies in the scaling-up process from small programs to large programs, and the fact that the process is not linear.

7.2.3 Software Engineering Risks

> What is software engineering? [Sections 2.5 and 3.1]

Software engineering is the definition, creation and application of:

1. A well-defined methodology that addresses a software life-cycle of planning, development, and evolution.
2. An established set of software artifacts that document each step of the life cycle and demonstrate traceability from step to step.
3. A set of predictable milestones that can be reviewed at regular intervals throughout the software life cycle.

> What are some of the sources of risk in software engineering?
> [Section 2.5]

- The sources of risk are manifested in the software engineering products and in the software engineering process.
- Product risk sources are related to the essence of the software and the domain knowledge required to build an application.
    - The essence risks are related to the irreducible attributes of software and can never be eliminated, only controlled within ever-changing limits. These attributes are complexity, changeability, conformity, and invisibility.

- – The domain knowledge risks concern the complexity of the application, the logical and physical architecture required to implement it, and so forth.
- • The process risk sources are related to the process models, methods, and automation used to develop the software product.

Where do some of the risks lie in the software engineering process models? [Sections 2.2.2.1, 3.1.1, 3.1.2, and 3.1.3]

- • The risks in process models, as well as in all software engineering methods and automation, lie in how well they avert the three underlying causes of risk: the lack of information, the lack of control, and the lack of time.
- • A minimum risk process model will possess good descriptive power, generality, and suitability to computerization. The less these attributes are present, the higher the risk a process model poses.
- • There are two primary process paradigms in use today: process-oriented and product-oriented. Product-oriented paradigms consider the system of interest of the development to be the software product itself, and the information it contains, whereas process-oriented paradigms concentrate on behavior; i.e., software is viewed as being intimately connected with wider environments of interest such as how it supports a set of business objectives. Product-oriented paradigms are currently predominant. Process-oriented process models pose less risk, however, than product-oriented models when one is required to link information technology use in a business to the software engineering context.
- • A specific process model's risk will be closely linked to the size of the system under development. The larger the system, the more critical it is for the business, and the greater the impact if the system fails. In order of increasing risk for developments having high business impact: spiral process models, operational/enactable models, rapid-prototyping models, design–driven models, waterfall models, and strict stage models. Note that all have risks in using them, and none map well to a model of the business enterprise.

Where do some of the risks lie in the software
engineering methods? [Sections 3.2 through 3.2.2]

- Software engineering methods are explicit prescriptions for achieving an activity or set of activities required by the software engineering process model used to develop a software application. Note the dual nature of software engineering methods: to help create an application, as well as to implement part of the process model. Thus, risks lie in how well a method can avert the causes of risk in attempting to meet both of these objectives.
- A process model will define the range and domain of the methods to be used within it. Methods may be localized to one phase of the process model; i.e., be phase dependent, or cross over many phases; i.e., be phase independent. Therefore, risks will flow into a method from the process model constraints placed upon it, as well as the methods will place constraint risks on the process model.
- When methods are interfaced or integrated together, they are said to form a methodology. Risks will be caused by how well the methods interface or integrate. Integrated methods tend to have less risk than interfaced methods.
- A minimum risk method will consist of five parts: viewpoint, domain, principles, media and guidance. It will possess three basic viewpoints: informational, functional, and behavioral. It will have an explicit domain of application, both in the process model, and in the application knowledge domain. It will possess seven basic principles or techniques: (1) modularity, (2) abstraction, (3) hiding, (4) localization, (5) uniformity, (6) completeness, and (7) confirmability. It will possess an appropriate level of media representation which is concise, correct, and readable. Finally, a minimum risk method will provide guidance as to what decisions are to be made, how to make them, and in what order they should be made.
- In general, all software engineering methods serve one purpose, and that is to reduce risk.

How do phase-independent methods avert risk?
[Sections 3.2.3.1 through 3.2.3.1.3.2]

- There are three broad categories of phase-independent methods: resource management, quality assurance (product assurance; configuration management; verification, validation and preventive testing), and reusability. Phase-independent methods are usually meant as risk aversion techniques, although resource management attempts to avert all three causes of risk, the others focus on the cause of risk related to the lack of control. If the methods are inherently not robust, or misapplied, then the effectiveness of each to avert risk is minimized.
- Resource management averts risk by planning for, controlling, and monitoring resource requirements for the development.
- Product assurance averts risks associated with a system which cannot: fulfill users' functional needs; be traced throughout the development process; meet the specification for performance; meet the agreed-upon price as expected; or meet the agreed-upon scheduled delivery date.
- Configuration management is concerned with identifying the configuration of a system at discrete points in time. It averts risk by the processes of identification, control, auditing, and status accounting.
- Verification and validation are concerned with how well the software product fulfills functional and performance requirements, and averts risks by evaluating the software product. The evaluation criteria used in the performance of verification and validation are completeness, ambiguity, feasibility, and testability.
- Preventative testing is concerned with minimizing the expected cost of software failure; i.e., how much damage can a software failure cause, and the likelihood of that failure. It averts risks by developing tests to be applied after the requirements, design, and implementation phases are completed, which stress the system against possible software failure.
- Reusability averts risk by trying to reuse a previously created artifact from another system development.

> How do phase-dependent methods avert risk?
> [Sections 3.2.3.1 through 3.2.3.2.4]

- Phase-dependent methods avert risk by primarily focusing on reducing the cause of risk associated with the lack of information.

Phase-dependent methods are generically divided into six types: requirements/specification, design, implementation, detection and demonstration testing, integration, and evolution.

- Requirements/specification methods describe what functionality was accorded to the software in a system and the reasons why. They also bind or obligate the software to meeting certain functional and nonfunctional objectives of the system requirements. Requirement/specification methods avert risk by the use of the principles of abstraction, decomposition, separation of concerns, and information hiding.

- Design methods, using the requirements/specifications as input, describe an abstraction, commonly called a design representation, which is a formal, coherent, and well-organized representation of how a computer program is supposed to accomplish the tasks allocated to software. Design methods avert risk through the use of abstraction, structuring, coupling, cohesion, information hiding, functional decomposition, data-flow design, data-structure design, and procedural design.

- Implementation concerns the production of a physical realization in a programming language of the design abstraction. The code produced in this phase should implement the design correctly and meet the resource, accuracy, and performance constraints defined in the specifications. Implementation methods avert the risks through the use of stepwise refinement, structured programming, program families, and object-oriented programming.

- Detection and demonstration testing involves the execution of the physical realization created to identify differences between expected and actual results (i.e., finding errors) and exercising the system to validate that it satisfies the specified requirements. Testing methods avert risk by path testing, branch testing, component testing, module testing, interface testing, white-box testing, and black-box testing.

- Integration concerns the merging of the separate components of the system into one single unit. Integration methods use incremental integration and big bang integration as avoidance approaches, with the former being preferred. Detection and demonstration testing are also used and applied to the fully integrated system.

- Although evolution is considered the last dependent phase, in reality, it is phase independent since all the phases of a development are potentially affected. The techniques used to avert risk in the evolution phase are the same ones used previously, but they are centered on resolving the risks associated with perfective maintenance, adaptive maintenance, and corrective maintenance.

- Every method has associated risks with its application. However, *not* using phase-independent or -dependent methods poses a higher risk in comparison with their use, and the level of risk increases with the size and complexity of the development. A cautionary note: If the methods used are not robust enough, even with their studious application, it may not be possible to mitigate the overall development risk to a level which is acceptable. The analyst should consult the individual sections for the risks associated with the methods used to avert risks in each phase.

7.2.4 Automation risks

What is software engineering automation? [Section 3.3]

Automation means to support a method which is an integral piece of the total process of a software enterprise through computer-aided mechanisms. The term automation is preferred to the other more commonly one used: "software tool." The term software tool implies a focus on a singularity of purpose; i.e., the automation only of a single method without the context of which it is a part. Tools alone do not build products. Methods are most effective in reducing risk if they form an integrated partnership with the underlying process model. Similarly, the automation of a single method that cannot interact with the other methods used in the process model is not only not very useful, but poses a risk in itself. The exacerbation of the risks in software engineering have typically been the result of applying software tools which tend to fail to support any standard development process, are too narrowly focused, or do not fit well with other methods, thus leaving information gaps between the process phase(s).

How are software engineering risks reduced
by automation? [Section 3.3.1]

Automation concentrates primarily on averting risks caused by the lack of time. Automation has the potential to reduce the labor needed to use the methods, and in many instances is the only realistic manner for applying many software engineering methods. The clerical aspect of most methods requires the keeping track of large amounts of information, and it is mentally and physically impossible to do so by hand on any enterprise of size. Because the clerical aspect of using methods is reduced through automation, there is often, but not always, a corresponding rise in productivity and a decrease in development cost and schedule.

The types of automation available to avert risks are: tool fragments, computer-aided software engineering (CASE) tools, CASE restructuring tools, CASE reengineering tools, CASE reverse engineering tools, Integrated Project/Programming Support Environments (IPSE), Software Engineering Environments (SEE), and Systems and Software Engineering Environments (S²EE).

What are the risks associated with using
automation? [Section 3.3.2]

There are six primary means of lowering the risks with software automation. First is to ensure that the automation being acquired or used is open. Second, any automation project should allow us to recapture our previous investments in software. Third, the automation should support the labor-intensive efforts within a process model. Fourth, the automation should support both the production of the software system, and the product itself. Fifth, the automation should support not only yesterday's investment, but also be able to support tomorrow's. Finally, the automation must be able to truly support multiple programs, or a range of business enterprises, and not just individual software projects.

7.2.5 Application risks

What is an application? [Sections 4.1 through 4.1.2]

An application consists of a process part, an architecture part, and a physical instantiation called an application realization (i.e., a system). Further, an application architecture consists of a conceptual structure and functional behavior (i.e., the process), which is distinct from its physical instantiation. The physical instantiation of an application architecture is technology dependent; i.e., an application architecture may be physically implemented in many different ways. An architecture, then, is the bridge used between the process defined within, and by, the application knowledge domain, and its physical realization. Neither the process, nor the physical realization, should be mistaken as the application architecture. They are each separate and distinct in their own right. Furthermore, an application architecture can be considered as the union of a logical software architecture and a logical hardware architecture, but *not* as the union of their physical realizations. The physical realization of an application architecture, which implements a knowledge domain's process, defines an application.

There is also a distinction between programs, applications, and application systems. Programs are made up of data structures and algorithms. Programs by themselves, therefore, are not considered applications. Programs, bound with their execution environments (i.e., execution/run-time support), together with the hardware in which they execute, we will consider as defining the application. Multiple applications, together with the hardware they execute on, we will state as defining an application system.

> How can applications architecture risks be identified, estimated, and evaluated? [Section 4.1.3 through 4.2.3]

Application architecture risks can be identified, estimated, and evaluated by evaluating the degree of decentralization among three critical attributes: the hardware architecture, the execution control, and the database organization. The amount of granularity in each of the three dimensions of decentralization will greatly influence the evaluation results.

The evaluation of risk inherent within application architectures requires one to first proceed from a technologically independent view, and then proceed to a technology-dependent one. For any application, there may be many technologically independent solutions. The final trade-offs in risk and benefit will come when the physical realization of these solutions occurs.

> What are some sources of risk associated with applications? [Section 4.3]

Sources of application risk include:

- The size and complexity of the algorithms required to implement the process defined by the application knowledge domain.
- Whether the application is time-critical/real-time.
- The robustness of the dynamic execution environment to support the application.
- The degree to which fault avoidance/fault tolerance is required.
- The degree to which human factors are involved.
- The *kansei* involved; i.e., the match of the application to the development process.

7.2.6 Software safety risks

> What is software safety? [Section 5.1.1]

Safety can be defined as the freedom from exposure to danger, or the exemption from hurt, injury, or loss. Safety ultimately depends on many factors, but an essential one is the subjective perception of safety held by those embracing a potentially unsafe situation.

> What are some of the attributes of software
> safety risks? [Section 5.1]

The attributes of software safety risks include the severity and magnitude of the risk's consequence, the operational boundaries affected when a software failure occurs, the immediacy of the consequence, the amount of time required for risk management to occur, the indirect impacts of nonoperational software on system behavior, and the reliability of the hardware.

> How are safety risks identified, estimated, evaluated?
> [Sections 5.1.1, 5.1.2.3, and the Appendix]

Safety is measured by both qualitative and quantitative means, each of which can also be translated into noneconomic and economic approaches. Noneconomic approaches compare indirect gains to indirect losses, while economic approaches relate direct gains to direct losses. Both approaches balance the cost against the benefit to be gained by accepting a safety risk.

Safety risk analyses use preliminary hazard analysis, fault hazard analysis, system hazard analysis, operability hazard analysis, failure mode and effects analysis, fault tree analysis, event tree analysis, human reliability analysis, and safety verification techniques.

How can software safety risks be averted? [Section 5.1.2.3.10]

Software safety risks can be averted by a number of means. These include:

- Firewalling
- Triage
- Redundancy such as N-version programming

Severe legal and financial penalties can be incurred if a software system is not safe. It is increasingly common for courts to hold the manufacturer and seller almost totally responsible for injury or property damage due to an unsafe or defective product. Furthermore, the trend in liability cases is to now only show that there is some probability that the product could have caused the harm. In other words, overt negligence during the design, development, or testing does not have to be proved.

7.2.7 Security risks

What is software security? [Section 5.2. and 5.2.1]

Computer security concerns the physical protection of the computing assets to prevent theft, damage, or unauthorized access to the hardware, information in the form of tapes, disks, printouts, etc., or to prevent accidental loss of computing services. Computing assets encompass all business data, including intangibles such as intellectual property.

> What are some of the ways computer security can
> be broken? [Section 5.2.2]

Security risks can come in many forms. These include data diddling, Trojan horses, computer viruses, worms, trap doors, superzapping, covert channels, salami accessing, piggybacking, impersonation, electronic eaves dropping, scavenging, and electronic picketing.

> What can be done to avert security risks? [Section 5.2.3]

Typically, a security analysis that is similar to a traditional risk analysis is conducted. These usually involve multiple steps such as information value analysis, security threat identification and analysis, information vulnerability analysis, security risk analysis, security risk assessment, management decision, countermeasure implementation, and review. The basic analysis tries to uncover all the information an organization has of value, identify the potential risks that could endanger that information, identify countermeasures to avert the risks, decide on which countermeasures can be afforded, and monitor their success over time. The weakest link in all security measures will be the human element.

7.2.8 Operational/Disaster risks

> What are operational/disaster recovery risks? [Section 5.3]

Operational/disaster recovery risks are events which can cause a significant disruption in information service provision for a long enough period of time to negatively affect the operations of the organization.

> What can be done to avert operational/disaster
> recovery risks? [Section 5.3.1]

The basic technique for averting operational/disaster recovery risks is to provide for a contingency system. There are a number of different types of contingency systems available, depending on the time requirement to get the system operational. In terms of highest price and quickest speed of recovery they are: hot standby services, database shadowing, hot sites, electronic vaulting, remote operational centers, and cold sites or shells.

7.2.9 Perception of risk

> What are some of the biases that can affect one's
> perception of risk? [Section 6.2]

There are more than 20 biases or filters that can affect risk perception. These include: information availability bias, over/underestimation bias, selected perception bias, expert bias, reference effects, data presentation bias, base rate bias, conservatism bias, Law of Small Numbers bias, anchoring, simple matching rule, data saturation, fact-value confusion bias, expectation bias, fundamental attribution error bias, gambler's fallacy, habit, hindsight bias, illusion of control, order effects, overconfidence, redundancy, spurious clues bias, and group think.

> Can risk perception bias or filtering be averted?
> [Sections 6.2.2 through 6.2.4]

To avert filtering and/or bias effects is quite difficult, but not impossible. Techniques such as the Delphi technique, probability encoding, and Taylor's method have been developed as ways to explicitly recognize and deal with the problems associated with bias, with some limited success. However, there are many factors which reinforce biases. Organizational cultures, where one sits in an organization, politics, the state of the immediate working environment, the individual's personality, all combine to affect the perception of risk. Thus, there are no foolproof methods for overcoming bias.

What differentiates a risk taker from a risk averter? [Section 6.2.3]

A risk taker accepts a higher exposure to risk by acting with less information and needing less control than a risk averter. Risk takers tend to look for the best-case scenario, while the risk averter focuses on the downside analysis, probabilities of loss are biased upwards, and overemphasis is placed upon the potential losses or the exposure to loss. Risk takers accept higher risks and accept higher losses in comparison to risk averters. Risk averters tend to devote a great amount of effort in trying to reduce risks, as well as in monitoring how the risky situation develops, while the risk taker is much less concerned with modifying the risks or in managing them later.

What are the goals of a risk management
organization? [Section 6.3]

* The primary objectives of the organization are very clear-cut: It must avert any risk which can be decisive in its current or future information technology enterprises, whether it be in its use, development, acquisition or sale.
* The secondary objective of the organization is to continuously evaluate the consequences of *success* and *failure* of the organization's information technology current and proposed enterprises to the overall business objectives.
* Third, it is to advise senior management on how it can direct the corporate resources to alleviate the risks that have been identified, estimated, and evaluated as possibly interfering with the overall business objectives.
* Fourth, the risk organization is to explicitly demonstrate the link between the corporate business enterprise and the software engineering enterprise, and the risks that are created by, and pass between them.
* Fifth, it serves as a means to prioritize software projects in case cuts must be made due to corporate reorganization, budgetary problems, etc., or to help keep the mix of high-risk and low-risk projects balanced in times of corporate expansion.

> Who should be involved in managing risk across
> an organization? [Section 6.3]

The people who should be involved in managing information technology risk across an organization include at least the:

- Chief Executive Officer
- Chief Financial Officer
- Corporate Strategic Planner
- Marketing Director
- Corporate Legal Dept.
- Corporate Insurance Dept.
- External and Internal Auditors

- Operations Manager
- User Department Heads
- Corporate Security
- Sales Director
- Database Administrator
- Data Processing Manager
- Quality Assurance Dept.

7.3   The Future of Risk Engineering

The future direction of software engineering risk analysis and management is very dependent on two sets of pushes and pulls. The push is arising from new technology, in new ways of developing software, and also from improvements in which to manage the risk of software development. In the latter case, risk management techniques are just beginning to investigate the incorporation of artificial information techniques, possibility theory, and fuzzy logic. One of these may help overcome some of the mechanical and philosophical problems with applying quantitative risk evaluation, as well as improve the current qualitative approaches to risk analysis.

The pull which will affect software engineering and information technology risk management is springing forth from business necessity. The 1990s will be the decade of risk engineering, just as the 1970s was the decade of software engineering and the 1980s the decade of total quality management. To understand why, consider Figure 7.1 for a moment.[2] This illustrates the history, and projected future, of desktop computing, but it can also be used as a general chart illustrating the trend in businesses' application of computing and information technology as a whole. Most companies are in the second or third phases, but many are poised to move into the fourth phase. To get there will require a business-driven perspective, rather than a technology-driven one, where a strategic approach, rather than a purely tactical one, is applied to information technology. It will also necessitate changes in organizational structures to make effective and efficient use of information technology.

Although the opportunities provided by a company being in the fourth phase can be tremendous, the risk will likewise be very high. These risks are both internally and externally derived. The internal sources of risk will be found in the amount of overhead within the business's enterprise process itself; i.e., the planning process, the day-to-day tactical decisions, the success or failure of current projects underway, and so forth. The external risks are those not so easily seen, but easily felt. The competition worldwide is growing faster than ever before. No industry sector, no industry niche is immune. In 1992, for example, every company in Europe will face competition from organizations in countries that never before *ever in their history* competed in their market place. The United States will face the same problem, not only from increased competition from Asian and Western European firms, but potentially from newly formed Eastern European firms as well. A company's action will be more and more influenced by risk, and will need to be risk management driven. If it cannot manage its risks adequately, the company will become risk driven, where the risks of doing business will coerce the company into taking decisions it does not want to make. This is a position that no company wants to end up in.

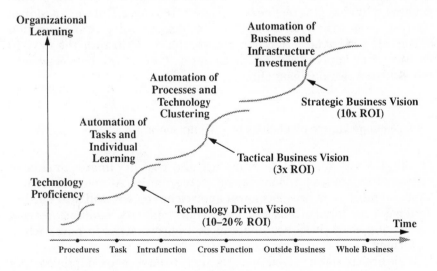

Figure 7.1 Organization Information Technology Learning and Utilization Pattern

Neither of these internal nor external risks are new, as they have been faced by businesses since the concept of a trade began to take root. However, the risks to businesses are much higher today than at almost any point in history. There are fewer new markets with more competitors, but fewer resources available. Further, as a company moves into the fourth stage shown in Figure 7.1, more risks will need to be managed than ever before to gain the same amount of opportunities. Each investment of capital carries with it higher risk.

Our old models of business and the processes used to create and sustain a business are decaying and can no longer sustain the weight of change. Recall the earlier statement by Russ Ackoff:

> Increases in the rate of change of technology have decreased the effectiveness of experience as a teacher. It is too slow. Trial and error require more time than is currently available between changes that require a response. The lag between stimulus and response brought about by reliance on experience permits crises to develop to a point where we are forced to respond to them with very little relevant knowledge. An increasing portion of society's responses are made out of desperation, not out of deliberation.[3]

Many businesses are duplicating this course in their own responses to the increases in competition.

We cannot control or direct the risks that arise from the pushes generated by changing business and societal changes. But we can control our responses to them. In the next two sections, we will give an indication of some of the changes that can be expected to occur over the next 10 years as they apply to risk management and which will help cope with the ever-complex business climate.

7.3.1 Changes to the mechanics of risk engineering

The first areas we wish to probe are the possible improvements in software risk analysis and management mechanics. Although there will likely be no change in the general approach; i.e., one will still need to perform risk identification, risk estimation, risk evaluation, risk monitoring, etc., there are likely to be improvements in how each is performed.

In the area of risk analysis, what is likely to be seen are improvements in the quality of information required to identify and estimate the magnitude and severity of risks, thus leading to more relevant and better quality data on why software projects succeed or fail. This will likely come through improved forensic software engineering. A new organization which will help improve forensic software engineering is called the Systems Engineering Risk Management (SERiM™) Institute. The Institute has been formed for investigate the risks involved for businesses who develop, acquire, or sell information technology.[4]

The Institute believes that to build systems effectively necessitates knowing what design decisions are required. But in building information technology systems, this isn't always possible, as the system to be built is new, and little previous design data exists. Thus, one needs to understand the risks in order to make intelligent decisions in the absence of concrete information.

Therefore, a part of the Institute's mission is the systematic collection and evaluation of historical data on information technology projects, which can then be used to guide businesses to make intelligent, rather than ad hoc, decisions concerning information technology risks. Another purpose of the Institute is to evaluate current information technology such as in telecommunications, computing, and systems/software engineering, for the risks they present to businesses attempting to apply them. A third purpose of the Institute is to improve the process of risk management, through better business enterprise models, better links between strategic planning, risk management, quality management, information resource management, as well as through improvement in the risk analysis and management techniques themselves.

There are a number of other centers and institutes that have been created to examine risk analysis and management. At the University of Houston at Clear Lake City, the High Technology Laboratory and Software Engineering Research Center led by Dr. Charles McKay is actively engaged in discovering ways to reduce the problems of safety risk on large scale software-intensive projects such as NASA's space station program. George Washington University has set up a Reliability and Risk Management Institute to concentrate on, as the name implies, reliability issues. The U.S. Congress has studied DoD software development, and concluded that no new technology is going to make software less costly, on time, etc. The only choice is to manage information technology risks better.[5] Thus, Congress has directed the Software Engineering Institute at Carnegie-Mellon to transfer technology about risk management to DoD projects. The American Society for Macro-Engineering, the Large Scale Programs Institute, Le Center International de Recherche et Formation en Gestion des Grand Projects in Canada, and the Major Projects Association at Templeton College England all study risk as it applies to major projects in various industries.

Improvements in software engineering risk management techniques will be seen primarily in the development of more and better risk monitoring and aversion techniques that are specifically tailored to information technology. Aversion strategies such as risk reduction, risk transference, and risk protection have not been adequately explored as they apply to information technology projects. Pecuniary aversion strategies have, but only in the sense that more money is thrown at a project after it is late and over cost. A comprehensive theory of contingency planning as it applies to information technology projects has, as of yet, not been formulated.

In the area of improvements in risk analysis techniques, the application of artificial intelligence techniques, possibility theory, and fuzzy logic are likely. In the artificial intelligence area, the application of heuristic rules, expert systems, and knowledge-based systems will come more into play, especially in the evaluation of risk. For instance, ITABHI Corporation's CYNIC™ Risk Engineering Framework Methodology, currently a paper-based approach, is being reconstructed using an expert system approach.[6]

The CYNIC™ Framework Methodology, illustrated in Figure 7.2, provides a comprehensive and systemic approach to conducting information technology risk analysis and management across the business, systems engineering, and software engineering domains. As an overview, CYNIC™ is driven by a set of risk engineering guidelines and standards which describe how a risk analysis should be conducted (i.e., the techniques to be used, the information required, historical data from which to compare analysis results, etc.) and provides the means to solicit the required analysis information from the organization/program/ project under study. During the risk analysis, both quantitative and qualitative approaches are utilized, with the results compared to a historical database. Results that do not match are further analyzed to determine the cause. When the risk analysis phase is complete, a range of risk management aversion strategies are analyzed to help find the "optimal" one for the circumstances. When the initial analysis and management phases are complete, information from them is then placed into a local database to provide the rationale for the risk management decisions taken, and for comparison purposes to later risk management requirements.

Using an expert system as a base for CYNIC™ will allow for a more complete analysis capability, especially in the discovery of risk

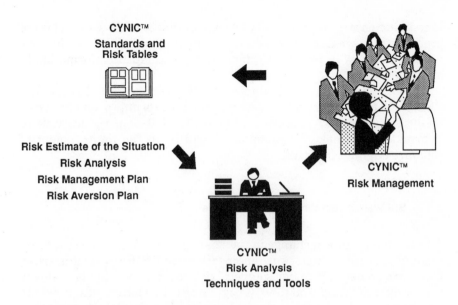

CYNIC™
Standards and
Risk Tables

Risk Estimate of the Situation
Risk Analysis
Risk Management Plan
Risk Aversion Plan

CYNIC™
Risk Management

CYNIC™
Risk Analysis
Techniques and Tools

Figure 7.2 CYNIC™ Framework Methodology

compounding and coupling issues, which is extremely difficult to perform today. Also, the expert system will allow for more complete analysis of the historical database for information concerning projects of similar size and complexity. Today, this is still done by hand.

Closely coupled with the use of artificial intelligence is the application of fuzzy logic and possibility theory.[7-14] Fuzzy logic is a kind of logic using graded or qualified statements rather than statements which are strictly true or false. It is used in situations where one cannot precisely define the situation by strict logic because the words describing the situation are imprecise. This occurs frequently when trying to perform risk evaluation. For instance, what does it mean to say something is a *low* risk? How does one quantify the concept of "low" such that it means something that can be measured accurately? Fuzzy logic provides a way of translating the concepts such as low, high, likely, unlikely, etc., into a form that can be usable by a quantitative evaluation techniques.

Possibility theory is a specific branch of the theory of fuzzy sets, motivated by the requirement for a systematic method for dealing with lexical elasticity and other forms of uncertainty which are not probabilistic in nature. It deals with the possible, rather than the probable values of a variable, with its possibility being a matter of degree. Possibility theory is complementary to probability theory, in that it addresses a class of problems in the management of uncertainty that probability theory does not, such as how to combine evidence under incomplete information in expert systems.

The combination of artificial intelligence, fuzzy logic, and possibility theory will possibly provide the most fertile areas of improvement in risk analysis mechanics. The other area which will help reduce risk in information technology developments will be in the improvement of software engineering itself.

7.3.2 Software engineering risk directions

Another major area of change in risk management that can be expected in the next decade is in software engineering itself. Software engineering, if you remember, is a major source of risk to a business. This is slowly becoming recognized, and there is beginning to be a backlash against the overpromises of software engineering as well as the risks it creates to building software. Many are beginning to express more vocally that software engineering is not a true engineering discipline, and that pretending that it is may be endangering public safety.[15,16] This backlash effect should be a healthy one because it will force software engineering and its various processes, methods, and automation to be measured against what every other past technology has been measured against: business risk.

New technologies have traditionally been applied to reduce some business risk. If its application instead increases the risk, one doesn't use it. This is just common sense. Unfortunately, in the computer field, we have been so busy inventing new technology, we haven't given a great deal of thought to whether it helps a business get its job done with less risk than before. The computer industry has always assumed that it did, which is not a little bit arrogant, especially given the opinion of the market as shown by the number of computer companies that fail every year.

The lack of information, control, or time, if you will recall, are the root causes of risk. Therefore, software engineering as a whole will have to be more concerned in the future with reducing business uncertainty, increasing its control of its environment, or increasing its time to make decisions, if it is going to be effective. Part of the changes required will be to identify explicitly the limitations and risks of using a particular software engineering method or tool, as well as whether it increases quality or productivity.

A major force in software engineering that will emerge in the next decade will be the move toward process-oriented process models and away from product-oriented models. The major impetus to change will come from a number of directions. First is the recognition that current process models must reflect and be part of a larger business enterprise model. Computing supports business needs, not the other way around.

Second, the further integration of telecommunications and computing will see information systems that are magnitudes larger than any experiences possessed by the authors of the current process models. As Ackoff said earlier, their experience as represented by current models will be irrelevant to the new development situations likely to be faced in the 1990s.

Third, technology advances, especially in object systems, which changes the focus of development to that of decisions and therefore risk. Object systems focus on context (i.e, relates to...), services (i.e., provided by, affected by,...), resources (i.e., provided by, affected by,...), constraints (i.e., on services, etc.), and faults/error conditions. Objects are encapsulations of decisions about development, and risk management will be required to aid in making the correct decisions.

Fourth, the continual embrace of the TQM philosophy will serve to highlight the problems of product-oriented process models, the lack of consideration of decisions and risk, and so forth. To do TQM well, and to apply its relevant elements such as quality loss functions effectively, requires investigating the risks inherent in a process and trying to find the means to correct them. Businesses will be forced to develop corporate enterprise models just to stay competitive.

And fifth, the final recognition and acceptance that current process models are only poor linear approximations of the nonlinear system dynamics which really occur in project developments, and as such, increase the instability in developments. This last idea, the idea of nonlinear software engineering process models, has been around for a long time, but has never been able to enter the mainstream of software engineering thinking. The closest current models have come to acknowledging their importance is to put in adaptive control loops between phases in some of the current process models. This thinking is beginning to change, and the adoption of nonlinear process models will mark a major revolutionary advancement in the way we build and manage software-intensive systems.

7.3.2.1 A generalized nonlinear risk conceptual model. Current process models can all trace their parentage to the stage models of the 1950s, and more closely to the waterfall model developed in the 1960s. However, if you reread Chapter 3 on process models, one can see that each new model was created to overcome a limitation of its predecessor. The previous model decayed, as it were. Recall the quote of Robin Hogarth we encountered earlier and keep this in mind for a little while: "Generalizations decay. At one time a conclusion describes the existing situation well, at a later time it accounts for rather little variance, and ultimately it is only valid as history."[17] The generalization that current software process models are based upon a reductionist view that software development could be assembled and disassembled into pieces, in other words, broken down into a life cycle consisting of a series of steps in some linear fashion. Software development was assumed to be scientific, therefore, repeatable.

For the small systems being built (in actuality, programs), this model of the development process and the assumptions upon which it was founded were adequate. But as the program size increased, and larger *systems* began to be built, the early models were no longer able to cope. The dynamics of the project that now had to be taken into account included those involving group activities, with all of its resulting messiness. These activities just did not match the earlier assumptions about how a software development took place. Thus, the earlier models of how software development was thought to occur were patched, just as programs are patched when a bug is found. Iteration among phases of the software life cycle was introduced, as were the concepts of phase-independent activities such as configuration management.

However, as system sizes grew increasingly larger, the dynamics of their development became even more complex, and the process models were patched even more. Instead of rethinking the problem and developing new models, we have ended up with process models which act just like programs that have been patched once too often.[18] This is a common complaint expressed by developers, who are often frustrated with the fact that current models of how software development should occur do not meet the reality of development.[19] We are now in the unenviable position of having process models which have been patched so often, they can no longer support the development of current systems, let alone those that the industry faces in the future. They violate the primary rule of process models: stability.

Before we go on, let's talk a little about the difference between linear and nonlinear systems. A linear system with constant coefficients can be described by a set of equations:

$$x(k + 1) = \mathbf{A}x(k) + \mathbf{B}u(k) \qquad (7.1)$$

in discrete time, and, in continuous time,

$$x(\mathbf{t}) = \mathbf{A}x(\mathbf{t}) + \mathbf{B}u(\mathbf{t}) \qquad (7.2)$$

For those not mathematically minded, basically a linear system is one which is capable of being represented on a graph as a straight line. Thus, a primary feature of a linear system is that any change in the input to the system does not make the system unstable. Thus, small differences in input to a linear system show small changes in output. In electronics, this is often described by the fact that the output signal in an electronic reproduction system reproduces the input signal faithfully. Thus, in a linear system, when beginning from different starting points, the same end point is reached.

In nonlinear systems, however, different starting points can lead to different end points, and where one starts can make the system become unstable. This situation is caused because feedback or iteration in the system is allowed. Playing the game, as it were, changes the rules. This can be seen by the fact that small differences in input can incur major changes in the output. In electronics, this is often described by the fact that the output signal in an electronic reproduction system does not reproduce the input signal faithfully. We have all encountered this, such as when a speaker using a microphone picks up his or her own voice from the speakers. Consider, for example, a typical nonlinear equation:

$$X_{n+1} = \mathbf{B}X_n(1 - X_n) \qquad (7.3)$$

What this equation says is that the next state of the system depends on the current state plus some change to the current state times some coefficient. If the variable $\mathbf{B}$ represented birthrate, then the equation could be used to model what occurs to a population in a closed environment. If the birthrate is too high, then the population will grow to a certain point until the food gives out, when the population will crash from starvation. Then, what is left of the population will increase again and die out in a periodic cycle. At certain birthrates, the population dies out completely, while at others, it reaches a stability point. If we let **B** represent the changes in requirements from one system increment to another and kept the resources stable, we would see the same cycles taking hold.

In software developments, however, requirements do not increase at a consistent level, nor are they all the same, nor do resources available for development remain constant. Thus, the nonlinearity of a system development is much more complex than Equation 7.3 implies. Small changes can have major impacts on the development. This is often seen when a very experienced person leaves, or a new requirement is added, or a single program error brings down the whole system.

The point is, software developments today are nonlinear in nature. In fact, they always were (most natural systems are nonlinear), and they always were known to be. However, the original process models did not account for the nonlinearity because their authors did not have to at the time. Linear approximations of the nonlinear nature of software development was, as it is said, close enough for government work. As long as the approximations were within 5–10%, there was no use trying to model the complexity of the development. The expense and effort were not worth it. But today, the process model's approximation errors are so great, we need desperately to go that next step and model the process as it actually exists. The simple iteration loops of the current models, such as the rapid prototype model or design-driven model, do not provide enough fidelity of representation to be of much worth in a large-scale system development. Although they are better approximations than the early waterfall models, their generalizations upon which their approximations rest are also decaying with time.

A better conceptual model might be, instead of looking at a software development as a series of linear steps as shown in Figure 3.2, to look at it as a nonlinear system consisting of a set of concentric circles, as shown in a simplified version in Figure 7.3. The innermost circle represents "the system," i.e., a product that is considered finished at some time **t**. We will say that this represents the equilibrium point of system development.

In an ideal development, one would start in the requirements phase and spiral down in a path towards the equilibrium point, as illustrated in Figure 7.4. Where we are at any point in time in the development process is represented by the start time, $x(t - s)$, plus some elapsed time. In a perfect development, the spiral would possess the shortest possible path from requirements phase to the equilibrium point. In real developments, the path may not be so direct, as it may be necessary to

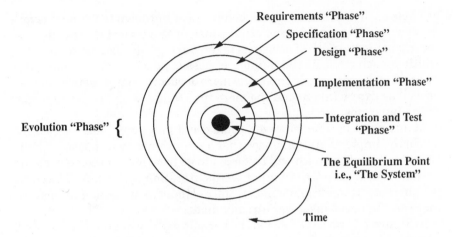

Requirements "Phase"

Specification "Phase"

Design "Phase"

Implementation "Phase"

Integration and Test "Phase"

Evolution "Phase" {

The Equilibrium Point i.e., "The System"

Time

Figure 7.3 Simplified Nonlinear Process Model (top view)

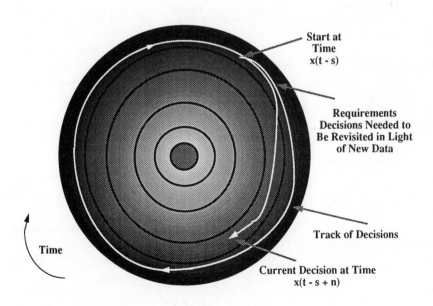

Start at Time x(t - s)

Requirements Decisions Needed to Be Revisited in Light of New Data

Track of Decisions

Time

Current Decision at Time x(t - s + n)

Figure 7.4 Decision Paths Mapped onto Simplified Nonlinear Process Model (top view)

go circle each phase many times before spiraling down to the next level, as shown in Figure 7.5. One could consider the trajectory traveled as representing the path of decisions taken during a development, and the width of each circle as the number of possible decision points possible. The wider the concentric circle, the more decisions that need to be made, as well as can be taken, and the more time (and energy) required to get to the innermost circle.

At any point in time, however, some event may occur, such as finding out in the implementation phase that a requirement was missed. Then, the direction of the path will be forced to go back out and come back in, as shown in Figure 7.6. In other words, iteration and feedback occurs, which causes the development to retrace some of its steps, and reconsider many of the decisions it has already made.

In Figure 7.7, we have labeled the various paths which can be followed as unstable, marginally stable, and asymptotically stable. The unstable path represents a major event that has occurred, the magnitude of which throws the development into instability. This often happens when an

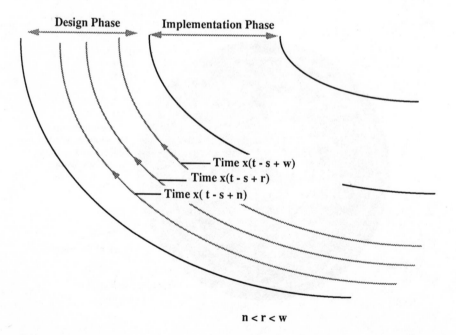

Design Phase   Implementation Phase

Time x(t - s + w)
Time x(t - s + r)
Time x(t - s + n)

n < r < w

Figure 7.5 Decision Path at Various Times, Mapped onto Simplified Nonlinear Process Model (enlarged, top view)

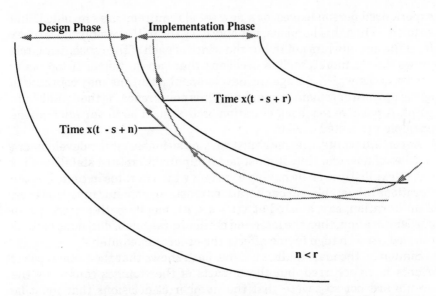

Figure 7.6 Decision Path at Varying Times, Mapped onto Simplified Nonlinear Process Model (enlarged, top view)

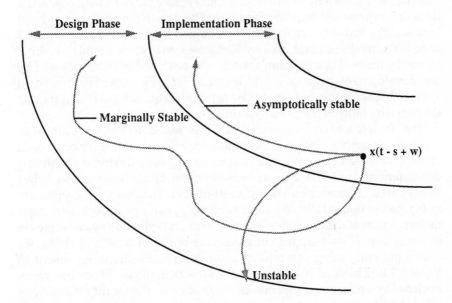

Figure 7.7 Various Types of Decision Paths Mapped onto Simplified Nonlinear Process Model (enlarged, top view)

experienced person leaves, or a new set of requirements are added, and so forth. When this happens, not only does the path possibly move away from the equilibrium point, but the width of each of the concentric circle grows due to more possible decisions that can be taken. If too many events occur which change the development path, one may continue to spiral upward or remain in one phase, thus never reaching the equilibrium point. A positive feedback situation occurs, such as in our microphone example presented earlier.

At certain points, the instability may be so high that the development reaches chaos, and thus it must be terminated to return stability. This can be explicitly seen by having a system which iterates in time. For the iterations to be stable, earlier iterations must be completed first. However, if an iteration, say, started at $x(t - s + n)$, has its path crossed by an earlier iteration, then the later and earlier iterations of decisions become coupled. Any change in one affects the other immediately.

Similarly, the marginally unstable path shows that the same types of events have occurred, but the impacts of the changes caused by the events are not so severe that the number of decisions that must be reexamined pushes the development in a backwards direction (i.e., must revisit old decisions). Minor events which do not make the development unstable are shown by the asymptotically stable path. In both cases, the iteration represents negative feedback; i.e., a path to regain control and increase the stability in the development process. If we were to represent time in the model, and rotate it by 90 degrees, so that we would be looking across it, instead of at it from the top, the path of decisions followed by the development process would begin to look like that illustrated in Figure 7.8, where one starts at the top (i.e., requirements) and travels down to the bottom (i.e., the system).

Now, for a few extra complications. First, we have shown the model as a set of concentric circles. As we have mentioned, the interior of each circle represents the decisions that must be made during a phase of a development. However, in a real development, there is not one path, but many paths of decisions all being made at once. In other words, there are many paths being followed simultaneously, each path representing a different part of the development organization trying to answer some set of questions. If we mapped these various paths in time and space, we would get something resembling a torus for each phase, as shown in Figure 7.9. Think of it as a sort of an electron cloud. Since the space enclosed by a phase enclosed marks (theoretically) the totality of decisions needed to be made to get a set of answers, we would hope that each

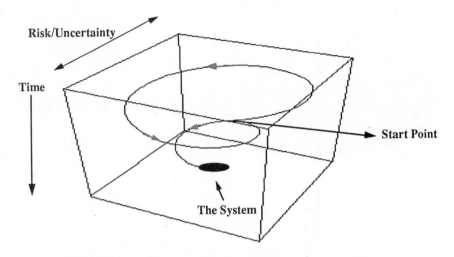

Figure 7.8 Tracing of a Single Decision Path in Time

successor phase would have a smaller torus defined for it, as is depicted. This is similar to the idea expressed by Alan Davis in Chapter 3, which stated that system requirements bind only the solution space.

Reflecting on the diagrams for a little while, it should be clear that a system's development cannot be sliced into individual torus as shown in Figure 7.9. In reality, the personnel making decisions concerning a system's development operate in almost all the phases simultaneously. One cannot artificially say one is in a requirements phase, or design phase, and so forth. In order to answer requirements questions, for example, one is often forced into asking design questions. The answers to these, in turn, may lead one to ask some detailed implementation questions. One must follow the paths of decisions and answers, wherever they may lead.

What this means is that a system is nothing more than a set of decisions that are bounded, both by the hardware and software. Programs that are run expand the decision space possible for any realization, as shown in Figure 7.10. Figure 7.10, in fact, shows a development and a system in execution. A similar diagram can also be used to represent a development, and its evolution phase, as shown in Figure 7.11. Compare this to Figure 7.12, which represents a more typical software development. In Figure 7.12, the design and implementation phases have to expand

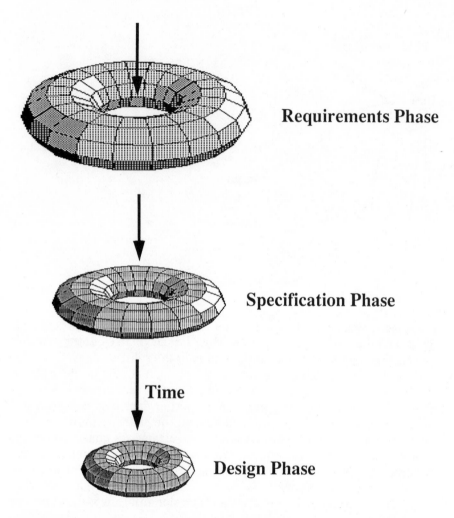

Requirements Phase

Specification Phase

Time

Design Phase

Figure 7.9 Phases of Nonlinear Process Model Separated in Time

the universe of discourse to answer questions that were not possible, or just weren't answerable during the requirements phase. One would like to bound the number of decisions made in time, as this shows an increase in the stability of the system.

Although doing mappings in time and space may seem a little complicated, there are a number of benefits for conducting risk management of using a nonlinear model of this type. For one, it can better represent what happens when major events occur during a

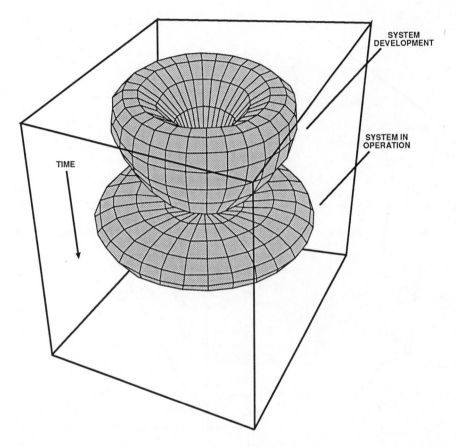

Figure 7.10 Nonlinear System Development and Operation

system's development. Every event, every change, every decision means a possible change in trajectory, and thus, more time and energy are required to reach the center. Too many changes, and one never completes the development.

Second, the path length or space encompassed by the various paths required are clearer ways of representing the amount of time that a development requires. To decrease the amount of time required, one either has to keep the path length to a minimum or increase the velocity of travel along the path. To accomplish this, either more energy is required (i.e., more capitalization) or less friction (i.e., fewer changes to the development, more performance from the resources, etc.).

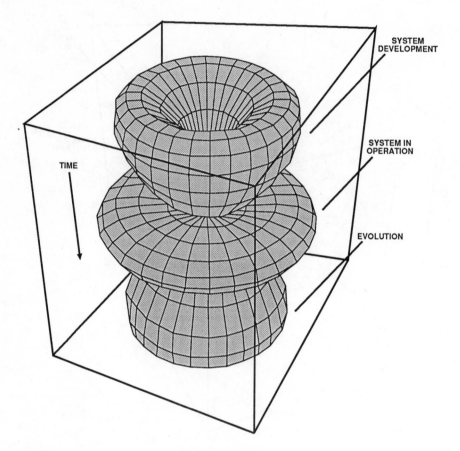

SYSTEM
DEVELOPMENT

SYSTEM IN
OPERATION

EVOLUTION

TIME

Figure 7.11 Nonlinear Development and Evolution

Third, this approach allows one to model a development as a set of decisions which evolve in time. This provides a close link to object-oriented means of development, and allows for the explicit recognition of both positive and negative feedback that occur during a development. Objects are, after all, nothing more than encapsulations of decisions in time.

Fourth, viewing a system's development in this manner can be theoretically modeled mathematically using dynamic models and nonlinear equations. For example, in an ideal system development, a Liapunov function should exist, thus indicating the best possible set of decision paths required. Currently, a more comprehensive theory of

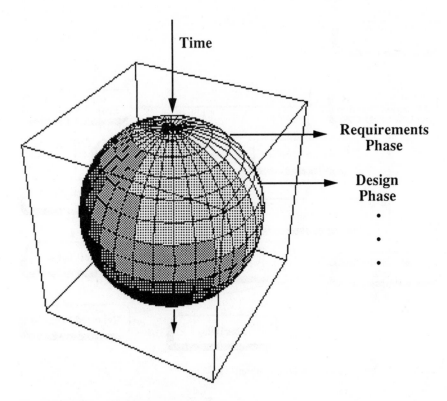

Figure 7.12 Typical Software Development

nonlinear software development is being formulated, which mathematically models a development using chaos theory.[20]

Some work has been done along the lines stated above in modeling software project management in a nonlinear fashion by Tarek Abel-Hamid and Stuart Madnick.[21] Their model, partially represented in Figure 7.13, takes a less graphical approach by showing the various decision states one can be in during a development. From their model, one can easily see the various feedback loops, both positive and negative, and their affects that can occur which we mentioned earlier. Notice that there is no solitary set path that one can follow, and that one can be in multiple decision states at the same time. Consider also how the outcome of one set of decisions affects another. Abel-Hamid and Madnick's work represents a major milestone in the development of process models, and should stimulate methods for alleviating some of the risks of using current process models that are no longer applicable.

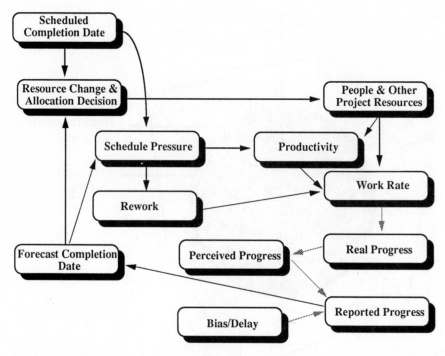

Figure 7.13 Dynamic Project Management

In conclusion, it is useful to recall that software development is a human activity, and it is only through an awareness of human strengths and frailties that we can hope to develop what we want, when we want it.[22] But to really do so means opening our minds to new ways of thinking which we may find uncomfortable.

References

1. Many in the computing industry keep looking for a software engineering silver bullet to solve all the problems involved in developing software. What they have forgotten is that computing itself was the silver bullet for many past business and scientific problems, and continues to be today. Furthermore, software was the silver bullet for computer (analog) hardware, allowing the spread and flexibility of computing technology that was limited previously.

2. Workstations & Networks, Nolan Norton Inc., 1989.

3.   Russ Ackoff, *Redesigning the Future*, John Wiley & Sons, New York, 1984.

4.   "The Center for Systems Engineering Risk Management," SERiM Institute, Fairfax, VA, 1990.

5.   "Bugs in the Program—Problems in Federal Government Computer Software Development and Regulation," Subcommittee on Investigations and Oversight of House Committee on Science, Space, and Technology, October 1989.

6.   "Reducing Your Business Risk via the CYNIC™ Risk Engineering Framework Methodology," ITABHI Corporation, Fairfax, VA, 1990.

7.   K. S. Leung and W. Lam, "Fuzzy Concepts in Expert Systems," *IEEE Computer*, Vol. 21, No. 9, September 1988. It should be pointed out here that many mathematicians are opposed to fuzzy logic, believing it not to have any firm mathematical foundation. But, as we encountered earlier, some do not think that probability theory is all that sound. It is beyond this book to get into these arguments. From an engineering perspective, if fuzzy logic can provide some heuristics for doing risk analysis better than what I can accomplish by not applying it, then I will opt for using it.

8.   Lofti A. Zadeh, "Fuzzy Logic," *IEEE Computer*, Vol. 21, No. 4, April 1988.

9.   Lofti A. Zadeh, "Making Computers Think Like People," *IEEE Spectrum*, Vol. 21, No. 8, August 1984.

10. Didier Dubois and Henri Prade, *Possibility Theory: An Approach to Computerized Processing of Uncertainty*, Plenum Press, New York, 1988.

11. Joseph F. Traub et al., *Information-Based Complexity*, Academic Press, New York, 1988.

12. Harry E. Stephanou and Andrew Sage, "Perspectives on Imperfect Information Processing," *IEEE Transactions on Systems, Man, and Cybernetics*, Vol. SMC-17, No.5, September/October 1987.

13. Alan R. Hooten, "An Exercise in Plausibility-Driven Design," *IEEE Computer*, Vol. 21, No. 7, July 1988.

14. Enrique H. Ruspini, "Possibility Theory Approaches for Advanced Information Systems," *IEEE Computer*, Vol. 15, No. 9, September 1982.

15. David Parnas, "Education for Computing Professionals," *IEEE Computer*, Vol. 23, No. 1, January 1990.

16. Robert L. Baber, "'Software Engineering' vs. Software *Engineering*," *IEEE Computer*, Vol. 22, No. 5, May 1989.

17. Robin M. Hogarth, "Generalization in Decision Research," *IEEE Transactions on Systems, Man, and Cybernetics*, Vol SMC-16, No. 3, May/June 1986.

18. David Parnas, "Education for Computing Professionals," *IEEE Computer*, Vol. 23, No. 1, January 1990.

19. Bill Curtis et al., "A Field Study of the Software Design Process for Large Systems," *Communications of the ACM*, Vol. 31, No. 11, November 1988.

20. Robert N. Charette, "Software Enterprise Engineering Risk Management Model," manuscript in preparation.

21. Tarek Abel-Hamid and Stuart E. Madnick, *Dynamics of Software Project Management*, Prentice-Hall, Englewood Cliffs, NJ, 1990.

22. Peter Salenieks, "Software Development: Advice by Analogy," *ACM Software Engineering Notes*, Vol. 14, No.1, January 1989.

Software Engineering Risk Analysis and Management Overview

The following excerpts from this book's companion, *Software Engineering Risk Analysis and Management*, cover the basic mechanics involved in software engineering risk analysis and management.

A.1 Risk Analysis and Management Overview

What is a risk?

Definition. For an event, action, thing, etc., to be considered a risk, there must be:

1. A loss associated with it

2. Uncertainty or chance involved

3. Some choice involved

The triplet, $< s_i, l_i, x_i >$, constitutes a particular risk, where s_i represents the scenarios of what can go wrong, l_i represents the generic likelihood of the scenarios happening, and x_i represents a measure of the consequences of the "ith" scenario. The set of all such triplets forms the totality of risk to the software development being performed. Thus, the definition:

$$\text{Risk} = \{< s_i, l_i, x_i >\}$$

becomes our formal definition of software engineering risk.

What is risk analysis?

The process of identification, estimation, and evaluation of risk is called risk analysis. Risk analysis is used to identify potential problem areas, quantify risks associated with these problems, and generate alternative choices of action that can be taken to reduce risk.

What is risk management?

The planned control of risk and monitoring the success of the control mechanisms is termed risk management. Risk management is involved with making a decision about the risk(s) after it has been analyzed. Four elemental tools are needed to effectively apply risk management. They are: (a) standards against which performance can be measured; (b) information to monitor actual performance; (c) authority to make required adjustments and corrections when they are needed; and (d) competence to implement the best solution from available alternatives.

What are the benefits of risk analysis and management?

- Better and more defined perceptions of risks, clarification of options, trade-offs, their effects on a project, and their interactions.

- Systemization of thought, thereby providing a consistent view of the problem situation.

- Confidence that all available information has been accounted for and that explicit identification of project assumptions has been made.

- Improved credibility of plans produced and communication of rationale for actions made, inside and outside the organization.

- Better contingency planning and a better selection of reactions to those risks that do occur.

- More flexible assessment of the appropriate mix of ways of dealing with risk impacts, allowing for less reactive management and more pro-active management.

- Better means to identify opportunities, and ways to take advantage of them.

- Feedback into the design and planning process in terms of ways of preventing or avoiding risks.

- Feed-forward into the construction and operation of projects in ways of mitigating the impacts of risks that do arise, in the form of responsible selection and contingency planning.

- Compatibility of decisions with project policies, goals, and objectives.

- Insight, knowledge, and confidence for better decision making, and overall reduction in project exposure to risk.

What are risk analysis and management not?

- Are not philosophers' stones.

- Do not solve problems in an engineering sense.

- Will not make the operating environment friendlier.

- Will not turn bad things into good ones.

- Will not provide hard, concrete data where there is none.

- Will not assure perceived risks are real ones.

- Will not assure a successful outcome every time.

- Are not blame analysis and management.

A.2 Risk analysis overview

When should a risk analysis be performed?

- Are significant amounts of software being developed for the system?

- Do software costs dominate the total system development cost?

- Will software contribute greatly to the operational and/or support costs of the system?

- Is software essential for the successful performance of the system's function?

- Does the software integrate or interface with a number of systems that must interoperate?

If any of the answers are yes, then risk analysis and management are recommended.

What are the tasks required in the performance of a risk analysis?

Task 1: Risk identification

Task 2: Risk estimation

Task 3: Risk evaluation

A.2.1 Risk identification

What is risk identification?

Risk identification is the comprehensive identification of potential risk items using a structured and consistent method; i.e., it tries to answer the question, "What can go wrong?" Risk identification, therefore, is the reduction in descriptive uncertainty of the situation under study.

> **What are the steps to performing risk identification?**

> **Step 1: Perform a risk estimate of the situation.**

- The basic goal of the software risk estimate of the citation is to clearly identify four elements of a project: its objectives, strategies, tactics, and means or assets to be used in accomplishing the objectives identified.

- Assure that objectives are measurable, and what constitutes their achievement; i.e., the project success criteria. Additionally, assure that there exist at least two alternative strategies and/or tactics for achieving the objectives, and identify the constraints that the resources place upon the objectives. Also identify any implicit project assumptions.

- Consider some of the following as possible project success criteria:

  - Maximize profit

  - Minimize cost

  - Minimize risk of loss

  - Maximize sales

  - Minimize cyclic fluctuations

  - Create a favorable image

  - Maximize quality of service

  - Maximize growth rate

  - Maximize employee satisfaction

  - Maximize firm's prestige

Step 2: Gather information to try to identify relevant risks.

Check the following sources of information:

- Traditional or folk knowledge

- Analogies to well-known cases

- Common-sense assessments

- Results of experiments or tests

- Reviews of inadvertent exposure

- Epidemiological surveys

Step 3: Categorize each risk.

- Categorize risks by whether they are:

    - Known
    - Predictable
    - Unpredictable, unidentifiable, unknown, or unobservable
  or
    - Direct or operational
    - Indirect or strategic
  or
    - Technical
    - Schedule
    - Cost
    - Operational
    - Support

- Categorize risks by whether they are caused by:

    - A lack of information
    - A lack of control
    - A lack of time

- After categorizing the risks in an appropriate manner, go on to the next step of risk analysis, risk estimation.

A.2.2 Risk estimation

What is risk estimation?

A risk estimate measures the chance of potential loss (i.e., the values of the risk variables identified during risk identification) and the exposure to potential loss (i.e., the consequences, or magnitude, of the risks identified). Overall, risk estimation is the reduction of measurement uncertainty.

What are the steps involved in risk estimation?

Step 1: Select a measurement scale.

- The values of the variables describing the system are determined. This requires determination of a measurement scale against which these values will be evaluated.

- Choose a measurement scale which best matches the accuracy and precision required for the estimate and later evaluation. The scale types available are:

    - Nominal (identity-taxonomy) scale
    - Ordinal (order-risk) scale
    - Cardinal (interval) scale
    - Ratio (zero reference) scale

Step 2: Match the source of estimation information to the selected measurement scale.

Risk estimation information will either be narrative, qualitative, or quantitative in nature. Narrative information requires a nominal or ordinal scale. Qualitative information requires an ordinal scale. Quantitative information requires a cardinal or ratio scale.

Step 3: Evaluate the biases of the persons or techniques involved in making a risk estimation.

- The lack of availability of information from which to make judgments limits the accuracy of the risk estimates. As information is disseminated, individuals often misinterpret or misunderstand its meaning. This is termed "information availability bias."

• A number of other possible estimation biases bear watching:

  – Selective perception
  – Anchoring
  – Expert bias
  – Sample-size insensitivity
  – Sample matching
  – Revision bias

• Be especially aware of biases and their impacts on conjunctive and disjunctive events.

Step 4: Reduce the uncertainty of the risk estimates.

• The uncertainty in a risk estimate can be reduced by a number of techniques. However, these techniques are limited by the process to which the risk belongs: behavioral, natural, or random.

• Select the proper uncertainty reduction technique. The techniques available include:

  – Delphi
  – Probability encoding
  – Buying information using prototypes, simulations, etc.

Step 4a: Determine the value of the reducing uncertainty.

In conjunction with Step 4, one should determine how worthwhile the reduction risk uncertainty is. The use of expected value calculations can be made to determine:

  – The expected value of possessing perfect knowledge
  – The expected value of buying sample information
  – The expected value of possessing imperfect information
  – The expected net value of buying sample information

Step 4b: Determine the value and utility of the information.

- In conjunction with Steps 4 and 4a, one should determine the value and/or utility of the information being sought for a risk estimate. Depending on the utility of the information being sought, a risk and its estimate may be accepted more easily than another, thus reducing the need for buying information.

- When the estimation of risk is completed, move on to risk evaluation.

A.2.3 Risk evaluation

What is risk evaluation?

Risk evaluation is the process whereby the responses to the risks are anticipated. Insight is sought into the consequences of the various possible decisions confronting the decision maker, with the general acceptability of individually projected consequences to a decision postulated.

What are the steps involved in risk evaluation?

Step 1: Determine the risk evaluation criteria.

Determine the criteria against which a risk consequence will be judged to be acceptable for different points in a project's life. The criteria should be related to the success criteria that were determined during the risk estimate of the situation phase.

Step 2: Determine the level of risk.

- Risk referents against which risks can be evaluated are required. These referents are stated as a probability of failure, or conversely, probability of success level for each individual risk, as well as for the system as a whole. A value should be agreed upon whereby a project should not continue, may continue, or may continue but with prejudice.

- The system risk referent may be an aggregation of the individual risks, or may be instead one or more risks that are prioritized as causing the most harm to the project.

- Care should be taken to identify any risk coupling or compounding that may occur.

- Apply evaluation techniques to determine the level of risk. These techniques include soft and hard approaches.

- Soft approaches to risk evaluation include:

    - Downside analysis
    - Risk prioritization
    - Top-10 risk evaluation
    - Table-driven evaluation

- Hard approaches to risk evaluation include:

    - Expected value calculation
    - Isorisk contour maps
    - Decision trees
    - PERT evaluation
    - Queueing models
    - Work breakdown evaluation
    - Putnam cost evaluation
    - COCOMO evaluation

Step 3: Compare risk to the risk referents.

- Compare the evaluated risk against its risk referent that was determined earlier. There are three possible outcomes:

    - Acceptable (the evaluated risk is less than the referent)
    - Impossible (the evaluated risk is much greater the referent)
    - Infeasible (the evaluated risk is greater than, but almost equal to the referent)

- If the system risk is evaluated as acceptable, then proceed to evaluate individual risks.

- If the system risk is evaluated as impossible, then determine whether the project should continue. If a determination is made that it should, then a project replanning effort to avert the identified risks must be made. Whatever course of action is selected, the risk analysis process should be repeated, because both replanning and risk aversion change the likely risks encountered.

- If the system risk is judged as infeasible, then determine whether the project should continue. If a determination is made that it should, then either replan the project to avert the risks, or continue with the plan as is, but with risk aversion strategies applied. Replanning is generally the recommended course of action. However, further evaluation of selected risks may prove valuable, and only minor replanning may be necessary. Risk aversion strategies are also highly recommended, and may prove more feasible in some cases than replanning.

- After the systemwide evaluation, the evaluation of individual risks should be completed and judged against the same evaluation criteria. The evaluation results should be used to determine risk aversion strategies.

A.3 Risk management overview

> When should risk management be performed?

- Have significant software risks been identified?

- Do these risks potentially impact the objectives of the project?

- Will these risks contribute greatly to the operational and/or support costs of the system?

- Can these risks be averted?

If any of these questions can be answered yes, then risk management is recommended.

> ## What are the tasks required to perform risk management?

Task 1: Risk planning

Task 2: Risk control

Task 3: Risk monitoring

A.3.1 Risk planning

> ## What is risk planning?

Risk planning is concerned with two issues: first, whether the strategy to be undertaken to carry out risk management itself is feasible and correct; and second, whether the tactics and means available to implement that strategy are in keeping with the overall objectives of the project.

> ## What are the steps involved in planning?

> ### Step 1: Determine the feasibility of risk control and/or monitoring.

If the system risk referent was not exceeded during evaluation, then risk control may not be required at this immediate time. If the project was only just infeasible, or barely feasible/acceptable, then risk control is required. However, risk monitoring is required in either instance.

> ### Step 2: Determine new risk referents for the project's risks.

The level of acceptable risk, both on a system level and at an individual risk level, will change in time, as the project proceeds along its way. Some effort should be applied to make the original system and individual risk referents more stringent with the passage of time to judge future aversion progress against them.

> ### Step 3: Determine the appropriate management approach.

- The level of acceptability of a risk and the cost to achieve that level of acceptability must be considered. In economic approaches, one compares the direct gains to direct losses that are involved in accepting a risk or not. In noneconomic approaches, one requires the comparison of indirect gains to indirect losses.

- Consideration of the difficulty and cost in performing risk aversion to achieve a certain benefit might also be warranted. Aversion of risk to levels of reasonableness, low as practicable, etc., should be investigated.

Step 4: Apply the cardinal rules of risk management.

- Four cardinal rules of risk management must be applied when making decisions:

  First, do no harm.

  "Adde parvum parvo magnus acerus erit."

  Never intentions, always capability.

  No management commitment, no risk management.

- Three rules should be applied in order, and in conjunction with the three principles of risk decision making. They are, in order of precedence:

  1. Dismissal of extremely remote possibilities

  2. Avoidance of catastrophes, insofar as possible

  3. Maximization of the expected values

A.3.2 Risk control

What is risk control?

Risk control involves the development and evaluation of the feasibility of the implementation of the plan's control mechanisms for the aversion strategies. It establishes control over any contingency that was placed into reserve.

What are the steps involved in risk control?

Step 1: Determine strategies for risk aversion.

Three basic classes of strategies can be used to avert risk. One can either change the consequences of a risk, change its likelihood, or change its magnitude. For any or all of these classes, there are a number of specific risk aversion strategies available. These include:

- Reduction strategies
- Protection strategies
- Transference strategies
- Pecuniary strategies

Step 2: Determine tactics for risk aversion.

Specific tactics for risk aversion are based primarily upon the process of software engineering; i.e., process models, methods, and automation. Selection of the proper tactic is dependent upon the specific aversion strategy required.

Step 3: Create a plan for risk management.

Develop a Risk Management Plan (RMP), a Risk Aversion Plan (RAP), and an updated RES. The RMP, RAP, and RES serve to detail the risk aversion strategies, tactics, and means to be used during risk control and monitoring. These plans are used as input to the risk management decision process.

A.3.3 Risk monitoring

What is risk monitoring?

Risk monitoring occurs after the decisions concerning aversion strategy and tactics have been implemented in order to (a) check if the consequences of the decision were the same as envisioned; (b) identify opportunities for refinement of the risk aversion plan; and (c) help provide feedback for future decisions about how to control new risks or current risks that are not responding to risk aversion, or whose nature has changed with time.

What are the steps involved in risk monitoring?

Step 1: Select the proper monitoring technique.

Risk monitoring techniques are basically of two types: those that monitor the process of software engineering and those that monitor the products of software engineering. Various techniques are available for each, some of which can be found in:

- IEEE Project P982 Software Reliability Measures
- AFSCP 800-14 Software Quality Indicators
- AFSCP 800-43 Software Management Indicators
- Reviews
- Walkthroughs
- Inspections
- Risk charting

Step 2: Apply the monitoring technique.

Periodic application of risk monitoring is required to judge progress in averting the currently known risks, and to surface any unobservable risks. Results of the monitoring effort should be used to determine the effectiveness of the risk aversion strategies, and the original accuracy and effectiveness of the risk analysis process. If the accuracy or effectiveness is found to be suspect, then senior management needs to be informed immediately, and a determination must be made as to whether a new risk analysis is required.

Index

For more information on risk analysis and management, consider:

Software Engineering Risk Analysis and Management
by Robert N. Charette

Software Engineering Risk Analysis and Management is the first book to set forth the principles and techniques of risk analysis and control as it applies to the software engineering field. Written for the practitioner or manager of software developments, as well as students in computer science and engineering, this book provides the framework from which software engineering risk analysis and management can be conducted in a *realistic* and *practical* fashion. *Software Engineering Risk Analysis and Management* provides:

- A discussion of the potential costs of using software in today's business environment.
- A description of the field of risk analysis and management, its history, and its basic principles and techniques.
- An in-depth examination of the mechanics of the risk analysis process, covering risk identification, estimation, and evaluation with practical advice given to their application.
- An in-depth examination of the mechanics of the risk management process, covering risk control, aversion, and monitoring.
- A systematic approach to applying risk analysis and management in software engineering developments.

Authoritative and pragmatic, *Software Engineering Risk Analysis and Management* is essential to anyone faced with trying to lower their exposure to risk faced in the development of software projects.

To obtain a free brochure on how to manage your information technology risks through the application of the risk engineering approaches discussed in this book, contact the author at the ITABHI Corporation, 9840 Main Street / Suite 201, Fairfax, VA 22031, 1-800-MGT-RSK1. The ITABHI Corporation specializes in risk engineering consulting and training for organizations developing, acquiring, or bidding on information technology projects in the United States, Europe, and Australia.

For information about *Software Engineering Risk Analysis and Management* and other McGraw-Hill books, call 1-800-2-MCGRAW in the United States; in other countries call the nearest McGraw-Hill office.